THE POLITICS OF THE PRESIDENCY

THE POLITICS OF THE PRESIDENCY

SIXTH EDITION

JOSEPH A. PIKA
University of Delaware

JOHN ANTHONY MALTESE
University of Georgia

A DIVISION OF CONGRESSIONAL QUARTERLY INC.
WASHINGTON, D.C.

CQ Press
1255 22nd Street, N.W., Suite 400
Washington, D.C. 20037

Phone, 202-729-1900
Toll-free, 1-866-4CQ-PRESS (1-866-427-7737)

www.cqpress.com

♾ The paper used in this publication exceeds the requirements of the
American National Standard for Information Sciences—Permanence
of Paper for Printed Library Materials, ANSI Z39.48-1992.

Cover design by Auburn Associates, Inc.

Printed and bound in the United States of America

07   06   05   04   03   5   4   3   2   1

LIBRARY OF CONGRESS CATALOGING-IN-PUBLICATION DATA

Pika, Joseph August
    The politics of the presidency / Joseph A. Pika, John Anthony
Maltese.—6th ed.
        p. cm.
Includes bibliographical references and index.
    ISBN 1-56802-858-X (alk. paper)
    1. Presidents—United States—Textbooks.   I. Maltese, John Anthony.
II. Title.
JK516 .P53 2004
352.23'0973—dc22

                                                    2003024085

TO MARY AND ANNA

CONTENTS

TABLES AND FIGURES

TABLES

FIGURES

PREFACE

AFTER MORE THAN TWO CENTURIES of change and development, the presidency stands not only as the nation's preeminent public office but also as its most problematic. Because presidents today are far more important for peace and prosperity than were their nineteenth-century counterparts, ensuring the selection of qualified candidates and enhancing the winner's effectiveness in office are major concerns of specialists and citizens alike. In the post–World War II period, however, few presidents have left office with a record of unqualified success. In fact, academic and media observers have labeled most presidents since Lyndon Johnson as "failures," although reputations sometimes improve with the passage of time.

Johnson enjoyed unparalleled success in getting his Great Society legislative program through Congress, but he could not extricate himself or the country from the Vietnam War. Richard Nixon managed to bring the war to an end and initiate new relationships with the Soviet Union and China, but Watergate cost him the confidence of the country. Gerald Ford and Jimmy Carter failed to convince voters that they could exercise effective leadership. Like Johnson, Ronald Reagan convinced Congress to approve his program of economic reforms, but the budgetary consequences of those policies and his mishandling of the Iran-contra affair tarnished his reputation—a tarnish that is receding as time goes by. George H. W. Bush and Bill Clinton were threatened by the same difficulties that beset Ford and Carter—a perception of ineffectiveness. Clinton also came to be viewed as possessing a severely flawed character, committing errors in his personal life that prompted an unsuccessful effort to have him removed from office. George W. Bush runs the risk of becoming the latest in a string of perceived failures when voters have the opportunity to evaluate his performance in the 2004 election. Like his predecessors, Bush is met with criticism of his performance at home and abroad. In particular, critics emphasize how Bush propelled the nation into war in Iraq, steered an uncertain rebuilding effort, and failed to create jobs. Given the inflated expectations of performance held by the public and political elites, it is reasonable to wonder if any president can be considered a success, but these executives also contributed to widespread disappointment through their own actions.

Our focus in *The Politics of the Presidency* is on how presidents govern—in the country and in Washington. The book views the presidency as essentially a political office; that is, the chief executive must govern more through skilled political leadership than through the assertion of constitutional prerogatives. We examine how effectiveness in office varies with the character, personality, and political style of the incumbent. Major developments in society, the U.S. political system, and the international arena also affect how well or how poorly a president does in office. By examining this full range of influences, *The Politics of the Presidency* provides a comprehensive treatment of the nation's most important political office.

Part I begins with an analysis of the origins and development of the presidency as well as an examination of the changing conceptions of the office. It then explores the president's relations with the public in electoral politics and in the process of governing. Next, it examines the kinds of people who have become president and the interactions between them and the office. Part II analyzes the president's relations with other government elites—members of Congress, the bureaucracy, and the judiciary. In Part III the focus shifts to how presidents formulate and implement domestic, economic, and national security policies. The book concludes with an analysis of how George W. Bush has handled five challenges commonly confronted by wartime presidents both at home and abroad.

This edition includes extensive discussions of George W. Bush's first three years in office—from the historic 2000 presidential election through the early stages of the 2004 presidential election. From the impeachment of Bill Clinton, to the first electoral college misfire in more than a century, to the terrorist attacks of 9/11 and the ensuing wars in Afghanistan and Iraq, we have chronicled the twists and turns of the past decade while incorporating findings from a wide range of scholarship. At the same time we have sought to retain a strong appreciation for historical development, starting with a discussion of the constitutional foundations.

We wish to thank Philip Mundo and Thomas Langston as well as three reviewers—Richard Conley, University of Florida; Laura Olson, Clemson University; and Daniel Tichenor, Rutgers University—for their helpful comments on the previous edition and on drafts of revised chapters. Their reflections helped our own thinking, even if we did not always follow their advice.

We are grateful to Brenda Carter, Charisse Kiino, Joan Gossett, and Rita Matyi of CQ Press for their encouragement and contributions to this edition. Jarelle Stein improved the book with her fine copyediting. We also appreciate the research assistance provided by Mark Cutrona, Julia Kohen, Josh Templet, and Brian Beedenbender, as well as the clipping services contributed by Frank Langr. John Maltese accepts primary responsibility for chapters 1, 3, 7, and 8, while Joseph Pika does so for chapters 2, 4–6, 9, and 10. Chapter 11 is a shared responsibility.

1 THE CHANGING PRESIDENCY

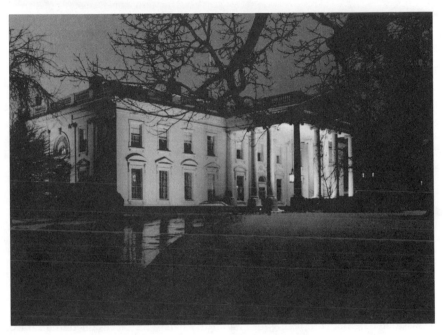

The White House—nerve center of the executive branch and home of its chief.

F OR MOST AMERICANS THE PRESIDENT is the focal point of public life. Almost every day, they see the president on television newscasts interpreting current events, meeting with foreign dignitaries, proposing policy, or grappling with national problems. This person appears to be in charge, and such recurrent images of an engaged leader are reassuring. But the reality of the presidency rests on a very different truth: presidents are seldom in command and usually must negotiate with others to achieve their goals. It is only by exercising adroit political skill in winning public and elite support and knowing how to use it that a president can succeed in office. For more than three decades this lesson has dominated scholarly accounts of the presidency, but it has not always been fully appreciated by either the public or the presidents themselves.

The Scope of Presidential Power

In some respects, presidents in the last half of the twentieth century were stronger than ever before. Presidents at the beginning of the century had embraced new, expansive views of presidential power that by midcentury were accepted as normal. They used the power of the "bully pulpit" to shape public opinion. With the advent of radio and television, they became the leading voice in government. Congress added to the power of presidents by requiring them to submit annual federal budgets for congressional approval—an action that made presidents policy leaders in a way they had never been before. Staff support for presidents increased dramatically. And by leading the United States to victory in two world wars and playing for high stakes in the cold war, presidents took center stage on the world scene.

And yet, since World War II, we have witnessed a string of "failed" or otherwise abbreviated presidencies. Of the ten presidents serving from 1945 through the end of the twentieth century, only three (Dwight D. Eisenhower, Ronald Reagan, and Bill Clinton) served out two full terms of office. Despite a strong rally of public support when they were thrust into the presidency, Harry S. Truman and Lyndon Baines Johnson left office repudiated by their own parties after they involved the country in controversial military conflicts abroad. Both could have run for another term, but neither chose to do so. John F. Kennedy was assassinated before completing his first term. Richard Nixon resigned in disgrace two years after his landslide reelection. Nixon's vice president, Gerald R. Ford, failed to win the presidency in his own right after completing Nixon's term, and Jimmy Carter lost his reelection bid after seeing his public approval ratings plummet to a record low of 21 percent in the face of the Iranian hostage crisis and runaway inflation. George H. W. Bush, whose approval rating skyrocketed to 89 percent during the Persian Gulf War, lost reelection the next year when faced with an economic recession and criticism of his domestic agenda. Even Ronald Reagan and Bill Clinton were distracted by scandal in their second terms. Reagan faced congressional investigations and an independent counsel probe into the Iran-contra affair (leading to guilty pleas and convictions of a number of administration officials). Clinton also faced an independent counsel probe and became the first president since Andrew Johnson in 1868 to be impeached by the House of Representatives (like Johnson, Clinton was ultimately acquitted by the Senate). Moreover, both Reagan and Clinton were constrained in their second terms by a Congress controlled by the opposition party.

Like such recent presidents as Kennedy, Nixon, and Clinton, George W. Bush entered office, in January 2001, with less than 50 percent of the popular vote. But unlike any president since Benjamin Harrison in 1888, Bush also came in *second* in the popular vote to his Democratic rival, Al Gore.[1] Bush won the electoral college vote only after the U.S. Supreme Court refused to allow a manual recount of the bitterly contested votes in Florida.[2] In Congress, the newly elected president found himself with only a slim majority of fellow Republicans in the House of Representatives and a Senate evenly divided between Democrats and Republicans for the first time since 1883. As a result of the questions about the legitimacy of his electoral victory and the closely divided Congress, some observers predicted that Bush, like his immediate predecessors, would face an uphill battle as president. Although the terrorist attacks of September 11, 2001, galvanized Bush's leadership position, the bumpy road encountered by many recent presidents reminds us that presidential power is not a fixed commodity. Formal powers mean little if presidents cannot convince others to follow their lead. As Richard Neustadt so succinctly put it: "Presidential power is the power to persuade."[3]

Dramatic changes in presidential fortunes are not new to American politics, nor are "failed" presidencies. Indeed, for a variety of reasons, only about 20 percent of all our presidents have served out two full terms. The very fact that they are the focal point of public life exposes presidents to intense scrutiny and allows them, as Stephen Skowronek puts it, to become "the lightning rod of national politics."[4] Through both success and failure, though, one might think that constitutional provisions would serve as a constant source of presidential power. As the following sections demonstrate, however, those provisions not only were a source of great debate at the Constitutional Convention but also have been subject to widely different interpretations by presidents and others ever since then. Quite simply, both the scope of presidential power and the conceptions of the office have changed dramatically over the years.

Inventing the Presidency

Those who invented the presidency in 1787 did not expect the office to become the nation's central political institution. In fact, Article II of the Constitution, which deals with the executive branch, is known for its brevity and lack of clarity, particularly in comparison with the carefully detailed description of the legislative branch in Article I. But within the presidency's vague constitutional description lay the seeds of a far more powerful position, one that has grown through elaboration of its explicit, *enumerated* powers as well as interpretation of its *implied* and *inherent* powers. Moreover, through the years Congress and the public have caused the range of responsibilities associated with the presidency to expand, particularly in response to changes in society and America's position in the world. What has developed over two centuries is the office that now stands at the center of American government and American politics.

The office of the presidency gained stature and a set of precedents from its initial occupant, George Washington. During the nineteenth century, however, the office languished, so much so, in fact, that Lord Bryce, the British chronicler of American government, felt compelled to explain in 1890 that because of the

This is James Hoban's original architectural drawing of the White House from 1792. Like the building itself, the office of the presidency has changed over time.

institution's weaknesses, great men do not become president. Government during this period centered on Congress and political parties (an American invention the Founders did not anticipate). A few presidents—most notably Thomas Jefferson, Andrew Jackson, and Abraham Lincoln—seemed to foreshadow strong presidents of the future, but most receded quickly from history. How, then, did the presidency come to assume its exalted position? The answer is complex and involves a variety of factors. At one level, the original design of the office—its structure, mode of selection, and powers—continues to exercise important influence on its operation today. The office has changed over time, however, partly in response to the influence of its occupants, partly in response to changing expectations in Congress and by the public, and partly in response to internal dynamics of institutional development.

Constitutional Design

In the wake of the events leading to the American Revolution, the colonists disparaged anything that resembled a monarch. Thomas Paine's enormously influential pamphlet, *Common Sense*, published in January 1776, sharply dismissed the institution of monarchy, calling it "the most prosperous invention the Devil ever set on foot for the promotion of idolatry."[5] Paine went on to call for a new government that had no executive. Some 120,000 copies of *Common Sense* were sold in just the three months following its publication.[6] The pamphlet's rallying cry against monarchy and executive power had hit a nerve.

In the weeks leading up to the Declaration of Independence, the Continental Congress urged the colonies to adopt new constitutions in anticipation of statehood. The resulting state constitutions that were drafted in 1776 and 1777 "systematically emasculated the power of the governors."[7] Pennsylvania's constitution, drafted by Benjamin Franklin, went the furthest. It provided for a unicameral legislature but no chief executive at all. Those states that did create chief executives made them subordinate to the legislature. Most governors served one-year terms, were elected by the legislature, and had little or no appointment or veto powers.[8] Even where governors were not chosen by the legislature (such as in Massachusetts), their powers were checked by a privy council.[9] New York stood out as the exception to this practice of weak governors and strong legislatures.[10]

As a result, most state legislatures became all-powerful. This led to something of a backlash against strong legislatures by other participants and observers of the political process. For example, after serving as governor of Virginia for two years, Thomas Jefferson strongly criticized the concentration of power in the Virginia legislature. Although the Virginia constitution explicitly called for the separation of the three branches, the executive and judicial branches were so dependent upon the legislative branch that their powers had been eviscerated. Mindful of the fear of executive power, Jefferson nonetheless wrote that his experience with the Virginia legislature had convinced him that "173 despots would surely be as oppressive as one."[11] If an unchecked executive could lead to tyranny, so too could an unchecked legislature. These experiences would inform the delegates to the Constitutional Convention in 1787 and make them more willing to accept a strong executive than they would have been immediately after the Revolution.

Experience with the Articles of Confederation also would inform the delegates. The Articles were a compact among the thirteen states that the Continental Congress had endorsed in 1777 and that all of the states had finally ratified by 1781. The Articles of Confederation not only avoided the creation of anything resembling a president but also failed even to create an independent executive branch. Over time, this omission proved problematic. Attempts to administer laws through ad hoc committees, councils, or conventions proved unsuccessful, and Congress found it necessary to create several permanent departments in 1781 (including treasury, foreign affairs, and war). Although Congress appointed eminent men such as Robert Livingston, John Jay, and Robert Morris to head them, the departments nonetheless remained mere appendages of the legislature.[12] Since the Articles of Confederation did not create a federal judiciary either, the resulting government revolved around a single legislative body. In the zeal to ward off monarchy, the principle of separation of powers had been ignored. However, because the states had not delegated much power to the national government under the new scheme, the Confederation Congress remained impotent. Indeed, the national government had so little power to control the states that the confederation seemed to be but a "cobweb."[13] Congress did not even have the authority to regulate commerce among the states. This led to a dire economic situation in which states fought with each other for economic advantage. Protective tariffs and trade barriers became routine weapons used by one state against another. Trade was further complicated by the fact that states had different currencies. Some states went so far as to pass legislation canceling their debts. With no federal judiciary to turn to, those affected by such legislation sometimes had no legal recourse. The resulting chaos was so great that it became a driving force for the Constitutional Convention.

Riots and mob actions in various states, culminating in Shays's Rebellion in Massachusetts, also signaled the need for change. Shays's Rebellion—an uprising in 1786–1787 by more than 2,000 farmers who faced foreclosures because of high property taxes and economic depression—underscored the chaos. Massachusetts had to rely on a volunteer army to stop the rebellion because the Confederation Congress was powerless to act. This failure of the Confederation Congress highlighted the need for a strong national government to maintain public order and prompted several states to vote to send delegates to the proposed Constitutional Convention. Even more significantly, it helped to legitimize the idea of a strong *executive*. As Forrest McDonald has written: "Shays' Rebellion stimulated many Americans, especially in New England, to talk openly of monarchy as a safer guardian of liberty and property than republican institutions could be, particularly in a country as large as the United States."[14]

As a result of these various experiences and events, delegates to the Constitutional Convention came to Philadelphia agreed that the power of the national government had to be increased, though they disagreed over *how* to increase it and how *much* to increase it. Virtually all agreed that the new constitution should impose some form of separation of powers with a distinct executive branch at the national level. But delegates disagreed fundamentally about what that executive branch should look like and just how strong it should be. Despite that disagreement, it is striking that in the eleven years since the Declaration of Independence, support for an executive (and even support for a *strong* executive) had increased dramatically because of recent experiences at both the state and the national levels. In short, the delegates brought with them to the task of designing an executive office two conflicting attitudes: a healthy skepticism for executive power and a new appreciation of its necessity.

Initial Convention Debates. James Madison, the thirty-six-year-old Virginian commonly credited as the chief architect of the Constitution, was the first delegate to arrive in Philadelphia. He was convinced that the national government had to be dramatically refashioned, especially to increase its power over the states, but he had given little thought to the issue of executive power. In a letter he wrote to George Washington two weeks before arriving in Philadelphia, Madison admitted that "a national Executive must . . . be provided" but confessed, "I have scarcely ventured as yet to form my own opinion either of the manner in which it ought to be constituted or of the authorities with which it ought to be cloathed."[15]

The "Virginia Plan"—written mostly by Madison but introduced on the first working day of the convention by fellow Virginian Edmund Randolph—

reflected this uncertainty. The plan called for an executive of unspecified size and tenure, selected by the legislature, and with unclear powers.[16] Indeed, the executive did not appear to be a matter of high importance to Randolph. His opening speech on May 29, 1787, included a lengthy analysis of the defects of the Articles of Confederation, but he failed to include the lack of an executive as one of them.[17]

When the convention began its executive branch deliberations on June 1, Randolph revealed his preference for a weak executive by arguing strongly for a plural executive. More than a quarter of the delegates agreed.[18] Although we now take a single president for granted, the question of whether there should be a singular or plural executive (one president or multiple presidents) was an open question for the delegates. Benjamin Franklin, for one, had long argued for a plural executive.[19] When Franklin's fellow delegate from Pennsylvania, James Wilson, moved that the executive should be singular, a "lengthy embarrassed silence ensued."[20] Franklin broke the silence by encouraging the delegates to express their views on the matter. The debate that followed was the first of many between advocates of a strong executive and those of a weak one.

Roger Sherman, a delegate from Connecticut, took the most extreme position on a weak executive. He saw no need to give the executive an explicit grant of power in the Constitution. As far as Sherman was concerned, the executive should be completely subservient to the legislature. Not only should the executive be "nothing more than an institution for carrying the will of the Legislature into effect," but the executive should "be appointed by and accountable to the Legislature only."[21] Rather than using the Constitution to settle whether the executive should be singular or plural, Sherman argued that Congress should be able to change the size of the office at will. Wilson's motion for a singular executive—a first step toward creating a strong one—eventually won on June 4. But Sherman's suggestion for legislative appointment—something that Wilson and other proponents of a strong executive vigorously opposed—had won on June 2. On yet another issue, presidential veto power, the delegates steered a middle course. After voting for a single executive, the delegates gave the executive a qualified veto power, subject to an override by a two-thirds vote of the legislature.

This, however, proved to be just the beginning of the debate over the position. On June 15, William Paterson introduced the "New Jersey Plan," which proposed simply amending the existing Articles of Confederation rather than replacing them with a new constitution. The plan reintroduced the idea of a plural executive and embraced the idea that the executive should be elected by Congress for a single term.[22] Although the primary motivation of the New Jersey Plan was to protect the power of small states (the Virginia Plan apportioned representation in the national legislature according to population; the New Jersey Plan called for equal representation regardless of size), it is clear that those favoring the New Jersey Plan preferred a weak executive.

Since the first debates on executive power in early June, Gouverneur Morris, a delegate from Pennsylvania, had joined the convention. Morris, who had spent most of his life in New York, became—along with James Wilson—one of the most influential proponents of a strong executive. He stood out because of his appearance—he had a wooden leg as a result of a carriage accident and a crippled arm as a result of a scalding as a child—but, as Richard J. Ellis has noted, "it was his rapier wit, infectious humor, and brilliant mind that set him apart and drew others."[23] On July 17, he began his offensive. Attempting to free the executive from its dependence on the legislature, Morris called for popular election by freeholders. Sherman vigorously objected, and Morris's motion was quickly defeated by a resounding margin. But the battle lines were drawn, and the debate over presidential selection was far from over.

Heated and sometimes confused debate over presidential selection continued for the next week, but when the delegates finished their debate on July 26, the plan for an executive that had been agreed upon in early June remained unchanged: legislative appointment of a single executive for one unrenewable seven-year term. Thereupon, the delegates turned their resolutions over to a five-member Committee of Detail chaired by James Wilson. Its task was to take the resolutions passed by the Committee of the Whole and turn them into a draft of the Constitution.

Committee Work and Final Action. One of the most notable contributions of the Committee of Detail was its decision to employ the word *president* to identify what the delegates had simply referred to as "the Executive." The word *governor*—suggested by John Rutledge of South Carolina—was rejected by the committee because of the negative connotations associated with the royal governors who had ruled the colonies. The committee chose *president* because it was an innocuous term. Derived from the Latin word *praesidere* ("to sit in front of or at the head of" and "to defend"), president had historically been used to denote passive guardianship rather than strong executive power. The presiding officer of Congress under the Articles of Confederation was called its president. George Washington, who performed a mostly ceremonial function at the Constitutional Convention, served as its president.[24] Arguably, this choice of a term helped to sugarcoat executive power and make it more palatable.

In its draft of the Constitution, the Committee of Detail followed the convention's wishes and gave the president relatively little power. But the fact that it gave the president a specific constitutional grant of power at all was significant. The alternative would have been to follow Sherman's suggestion and allow Congress to dictate presidential powers. The Committee of Detail followed the convention's recommendation for a single executive elected by Congress to one unrenewable term, subject to impeachment, and with a qualified veto power. The draft also gave the president the power to appoint executive officers, to grant pardons, and to receive ambassadors. But many powers traditionally associated with the prerogative of the executive—such as raising armies, making war, making treaties, appointing ambassadors, and coining money—were all withheld from the president and given to the legislative branch.[25]

George Washington presides over the signing of the Constitution by members of the Constitutional Convention in Philadelphia on September 17, 1787. This depiction of the event was painted by Howard Chandler Christy and hangs in the U.S. Capitol.

Convention debate resumed on August 6. When the delegates took up the article dealing with the president, it was obvious that they remained dissatisfied. But there seemed to be no agreement on how to improve things. When convention debate ended on August 31, the president remained largely unchanged. At that point, the convention sent unresolved issues to the Committee on Postponed Matters. The committee, chaired by David Brearly of New Jersey, consisted of one member from each state (including, significantly, Gouverneur Morris). It was in that committee that the final constitutional vision of the president took shape.

One of the most significant accomplishments of the Committee on Postponed Matters was its cobbling together of a compromise plan for presidential selection. This had been a major focus of debate throughout the convention. Various proposals had been introduced either for popular election of the president or selection by some sort of electoral college. But the delegates had always reverted back to selection by Congress. The Committee on Postponed Matters revisited this issue and offered a novel twist on an earlier suggestion that had been made by James Wilson. The committee proposed that a president—and a *vice president* (the first time this position had been recommended)—be chosen by an electoral college consisting of electors from each of the states. Each state would be free to choose its electors (equaling that state's combined number of senators and representatives in the U.S. Congress) as its state legislature saw fit. Electors would meet and vote in their respective states. Each elector would have two votes, only one of which could be cast for a candidate from that elector's state. When the votes from all states' electors were counted, the candidate with the most votes would be elected president and the runner-up would be elected vice president. If no candidate received a majority in the electoral college, the Senate would choose from among the five candidates who had received the most electoral votes. (Later the convention changed this provision so that the House of Representatives, with each state delegation having an equal vote, would decide the outcome in such cases.)

The committee's proposed electoral college seemed to resolve the problems that had stymied previous debate on presidential selection. First, it placated both large and small states. Basing the number of electors on the combined number of a state's senators and representatives served as a compromise between equal and proportional allocation of electors. Large states could support the plan with the hope that they would dominate the electoral college. At the same time, small states were placated by the fact that each elector could cast only one vote for a home-state candidate. Small states were further assured that if the election were thrown to Congress, each state would have an equal vote (this was true under both the committee's plan for Senate selection and the eventual constitutional provision for House selection). Second, the compromise plan satisfied proponents of an independent president and proponents of congressional selection of the president. Proponents of congressional selection argued that a presidential candidate would seldom get a majority of votes in the electoral college. Thus they believed that Congress would ultimately choose the president most of the time anyway, with the electoral college acting simply as a nominating convention. Advocates of an independent president, on the other hand, saw the electoral college as an explicit rejection of congressional selection. They discounted the argument that presidential candidates would seldom get a majority in the electoral college.[26] Even on those occasions when a candidate did not get a majority, Congress was limited in its choice to the five candidates with the most votes in the electoral college.[27] Clearly this limited Congress more than the original plan, in which congressional choice was unrestricted. Finally, the proposal for both a president and a vice president resolved concerns about succession if presidents did not complete their terms.

In addition to its plan for an electoral college, the Committee on Postponed Matters made a few other significant decisions. It shortened the president's term from seven to four years and made the president eligible for reelection to an unlimited number of terms. In addition—of great import to advocates of a strong executive—it gave the president a number of executive powers that the delegates had previously given to the Senate, including expanded appointment power and the power to make treaties. The resulting language was again a compromise. The president could *nominate* ambassadors and other public ministers, Supreme Court justices, and all other officers whose appointments were not otherwise provided for. Actual *appointment* would come only with the "advice and consent" of the Senate. And though the president could make treaties, they could be ratified only by a two-thirds vote of the Senate.[28]

The convention as a whole spent several days in early September scrutinizing the proposals of the Committee on Postponed Matters. The only major change came on September 6, when the convention gave the House of Representatives the power to choose the president if no candidate received a majority in the electoral college. The change was the result of fear among the delegates that the Senate was becoming too powerful. When voting for president, each state delegation in the House would have one vote. This guaranteed that each state would have an equal vote (a counterbalance to the electoral college itself, which gave large states an advantage).

On September 8, the delegates created a five-member Committee of Style, chaired by Gouverneur Morris, to write a final draft of the Constitution. This committee was responsible for the opening words of Article II of the Constitution: "The executive Power shall be vested in a President of the United States of America." As we shall see, the ambiguity of this sentence continues to be the subject of debate, and it stood in marked contrast to the opening words of Article I, which seemed to explicitly limit Congress's powers to those listed in the Constitution: "All legislative powers *herein granted* shall be vested in a Congress of the United States." Ironically, the opening of Article II, the meaning of which has been debated so often in subsequent years, was accepted by the whole of the Constitutional Convention without any debate over its specific language.[29] Thus the end result of the constitutional language regarding the presidency was compromise, although it was a compromise that ultimately favored the strong executive model more than the weak one (see Table 1-1). Credit for this usually goes to a small group of delegates (chief among them, James Wilson and Gouverneur Morris) who used their strategic positions within the convention's working committees to further their goal of a strong executive.

Interpreting the Constitutional Language

The ambivalence over executive power exhibited by the convention has become a permanent feature of American political culture. Like the delegates in 1787, Americans have had to confront the trade-off between tyranny and effectiveness—the one to be feared and the other to be prized. The antifederalists, who opposed ratification of the Constitution, frequently pointed to the risks inherent in a national executive, a post that some considered even more threatening than its British counterpart. As George Mason, a delegate from Virginia who ultimately refused to sign the Constitution, had argued: "We are not indeed

Table 1-1   Models of Executive Considered by the Constitutional Convention

Elements of executive	Weak-executive model	Strong-executive model	Decision by convention
Relation to Congress	To put into effect will of Congress	Powers independent of Congress	Powers independent of Congress but with checks and balances
Number of executives	Plural or single individual checked by council	Single individual with no council or only advisory one	Single individual with Senate advisory on some matters
Method of choosing	By Congress	By means other than congressional selection	Electoral college
Tenure	Limited term; not renewable	No limitation	Unlimited
Method of removal	By Congress during term of office	Only for definite, enumerated reasons after impeachment and conviction by judicial body or Congress	For treason, bribery, high crimes and misdemeanors, by impeachment by majority of House and conviction by two-thirds of Senate
Scope and source of powers	Limited powers delegated by Congress	Broad powers from Constitution, not subject to congressional interference	Broad powers delegated by Constitution
Appointment and foreign policy and war-making powers	None—province of Congress	Would appoint judicial and diplomatic officials and participate in foreign policy and war-making powers, including making of treaties	Appoints executive and judicial officials with consent of Senate; shares foreign policy and war-making powers with Congress; Senate must approve treaties negotiated by president
Veto	None	Veto over legislation passed by Congress, exercised alone or with judiciary	Qualified veto, may be overridden by two-thirds vote of House and Senate

Source: Joseph E. Kallenbach, *The American Chief Executive: The Presidency and the Governorship* (New York: Harper and Row, 1966), chap. 2.

constituting a British monarchy, but a more dangerous monarchy, an elective one."[30] But others, such as Alexander Hamilton, saw the newly created presidency as essential to effective government, the source of energy, dispatch, and responsibility in the conduct of domestic and foreign affairs.[31]

This ambivalence has been reflected over the years in differing interpretations of constitutional language concerning presidential power. As we have seen,

Article II of the Constitution opens with the words "The executive Power shall be vested in a President of the United States of America." The language drafted by Morris and the Committee of Style has proven to be, as presidential scholar Charles C. Thach Jr. put it in the 1920s, the "joker" in the game of presidential power.[32] Constitutional language limits both legislative and judicial power. Article I limits legislative powers to those "herein granted." Article III uses the phrase "the judicial power shall extend to," followed by an enumeration of those powers, which suggests the same sort of limitation of power as the one contained in Article I. But Article II contains no such limit. Whether this was intentional or not is unclear since the full convention never even debated the language. However, Thach points to letters that Morris wrote in which he admitted how much impact small, seemingly inconsequential changes of phraseology could have on the meaning of constitutional clauses. Although Morris did not refer explicitly to presidential power in these letters, his advocacy of a strong executive is well known, and Thach suspects that Morris embraced the language of Article II with "full realization of its possibilities."[33] By failing to limit executive power to those "herein granted," Article II suggests that the scope of presidential power is not confined to those powers enumerated in the Constitution. Carried to its extreme, this view gives the president unlimited powers. The ambiguity of the first sentence of Article II has led to three widely divergent theories of presidential power: the constitutional theory, the stewardship theory, and the prerogative theory.

Proponents of the *constitutional theory,* such as William Howard Taft, argue that presidential power is strictly limited. According to the constitutional theory, presidents have only those powers that are either enumerated in the Constitution or granted by Congress under its constitutional powers. As Taft put it in his book *Our Chief Magistrate and His Powers:*

The true view of the Executive function is, as I conceive it, that the President can exercise no power which cannot fairly and reasonably be traced to some specific grant of power or justly implied and included within such grant as proper and necessary to its exercise. Such specific grant must be either in the Federal Constitution or in an act of Congress passed in pursuance thereof. There is no undefined residuum of power that he can exercise because it seems to him to be in the public interest. . . . [Presidential power] must be justified and vindicated by affirmative constitutional or statutory provision, or it does not exist.[34]

In contrast, the *stewardship theory* holds that the president can do anything not explicitly *forbidden* by the Constitution or by laws passed by Congress under its constitutional powers. Theodore Roosevelt embraced this view as president and explained it in his *Autobiography:*

My view was that every Executive officer and above all every Executive officer in high position was a steward of the people bound actively and affirmatively to do all he could for the people. . . . I declined to adopt [the] view that what was imperatively necessary for the Nation could not be done by the President, unless he could find some specific authorization to do it. My belief was that it was not only his right but his duty to do anything that the needs of the Nation demanded unless such action was forbidden by the Constitution or by the laws. Under this interpretation of executive power I did and caused to be done many things not previously done by the President and the heads of the departments. I did not usurp power but I did greatly broaden the use of executive power. In other words, I acted for the common well being of all our people whenever and in whatever measure was necessary, unless prevented by direct constitutional or legislative prohibition.[35]

Taft, who had served as Roosevelt's secretary of war but later ran against him for president, took direct issue with the stewardship theory in his book:

My judgment is that the [stewardship theory], ascribing an undefined residuum of power to the President, is an unsafe doctrine and that it might lead under emergencies to results of an arbitrary character, doing irremediable injustice to private right. The mainspring of such a view is that the Executive is charged with responsibility for the welfare of all the people in a general way, that he is to play the part of a Universal Providence and set all things right, and that anything that in his judgment will help the people he ought to do, unless he is expressly forbidden not to do it. The wide field of action that this would give the Executive one can hardly limit.[36]

The *prerogative theory* is the most expansive of these three theories of presidential power. John Locke defined the concept of prerogative power in his *Second Treatise of Government* as the power "to act according to discretion for the public good, without the prescription of the law, *and sometimes even against it.*"[37] Thus the prerogative theory not only allows presidents to do anything that they are *not* forbidden to do but allows them to do things that *are* explicitly forbidden when in the national interest. Abraham Lincoln exercised such prerogative power at the outset of the Civil War. During the almost twelve weeks from the outbreak of hostilities at Fort Sumter, South Carolina, on April 12, 1861, to the convening of Congress in a special session on July 4, Lincoln stretched the executive's emergency powers further than ever before. This period has been described as a time of "constitutional dictatorship."[38] Lincoln unilaterally authorized a series of drastic actions: He called up the militia and volunteers, blockaded Southern ports, expanded the army and navy beyond the limits set by statute, pledged the credit of the United States without congressional authority to do so, closed the mails to "treasonous" correspondence, arrested persons suspected of disloyalty, and suspended the writ of habeas corpus in areas around the nation's capital. Admitting that most of these matters lay within the jurisdiction of Congress rather than the president, Lincoln asserted that they were done because of popular demand and public necessity and with the trust "that Congress would readily ratify them." But he deliberately chose not to call the national legislature into special session until he was ready to do so, and then he presented it with faits accomplis.

Although Lincoln's presidency was most dramatic in those early days of hostilities, he continued to exercise firm control over the war during the entire time he was in the White House. He controlled the mails and newspapers, confiscated property of people suspected of impeding the conduct of the war, and even tried civilians in military courts in areas where the regular courts were operating. To justify such actions, he appealed to military necessity, asserting that the Constitution's Commander-in-Chief Clause (requiring command of the armed forces) and its Take-Care Clause (that the laws be faithfully executed) combined to create a "war power" for the president that was virtually unlimited. Lincoln's success in defending that position is demonstrated by the fact that neither Congress nor the courts placed any significant limits on his actions.

A century later, Richard Nixon pointed to Lincoln's actions in an attempt to justify illegal covert actions he had taken as president. In fact, Nixon went so far as to claim that if a president chooses to do something illegal because he believes it to be in the national interest, it is—by definition—no longer illegal. As he explained in a televised interview with David Frost in 1977:

When the President does it, that means that it is not illegal. . . . If the President, for example, approves something because of the national security, or in this case because of a threat to internal peace and order of significant magnitude, then the President's decision in that instance is one that enables those who carry it out, to carry it out without violating the law. Otherwise they're in an impossible position.[39]

In short, the ambiguity of the opening sentence of Article II, Section 1, has allowed individual presidents to expand significantly the power of the office. As constitutional scholar Edward S. Corwin wrote in 1957, "Taken by and large, the history of the presidency is a history of aggrandizement."[40] By the 1970s, Arthur Schlesinger Jr. had coined the phrase "the imperial presidency" to describe the current conception of the office.[41]

Presidents have also relied on ambiguities in their specifically enumerated powers, in Sections 2 and 3 of Article II, to further that aggrandizement. Together, the enumerated powers have created at least five presidential roles that have evolved and expanded over time.

Commander in Chief. This role is specifically enumerated in Article II, Section 2 ("The President shall be Commander in Chief of the Army and Navy of the United States, and of the Militia of the several states, when called into the actual Service of the United States"). But did this language merely confer a title on the president or imply wide-ranging powers in times of emergency? Lincoln, of course, believed the latter. From this germ of constitutional power has grown the enormous control that modern presidents exercise over a permanent military establishment and its deployment. The Constitution stipulates that the legislative and executive branches share the war power, but the pressure of events and the presidency's institutional advantages in taking decisive action have led Congress to give greater discretion to the executive. Nor was this delegation of power completely unexpected. Recognizing the need to repel attacks when Congress was not in session, the Constitutional Convention altered language describing the role of Congress in armed hostilities from "make" war to "declare" war (Article I, Section 8, Paragraph 11), thereby expanding the president's realm of discretionary action.[42] Over time, presidents have invoked the Commander-in-Chief Clause to justify military expenditures without congressional authorization, emergency powers to suppress rebellion, the internment of American citizens of Japanese descent during World War II, and the seizure of domestic steel mills during the undeclared armed conflict in Korea in the 1950s.[43] Moreover, presidents have initiated the use of force far more frequently than they have awaited congressional authorization.

Chief Administrator. This role for the president is more implicit than explicit as set forth in the Constitution. It rests on the Executive Power Clause (Article II, Section 1, Paragraph 1) as well as passages dealing with the right to require opinions from the heads of government departments (Article II, Section 2, Paragraph 1) and the power to make personnel appointments subject to whatever approval Congress may require (Article II, Section 2, Paragraph 2). As the national government has grown, so too has the significance of these powers, but Congress has jealously guarded its own appointment and oversight powers, thereby denying the president anything approximating a monopoly of administrative power.

Chief Diplomat. When combined with the president's expanded war power, constitutional primacy in the conduct of foreign affairs establishes the office's claim to being the government's principal agent in the world, if not its "sole organ." Presidents are not only authorized to make treaties "by and with the Advice and Consent of the Senate" but also empowered to nominate ambassadors, subject to Senate approval (Article II, Section 2, Paragraph 2) and to receive diplomatic emissaries from abroad (Article II, Section 3). Presidents have varied in how closely they have collaborated with the Senate in making treaties, most waiting until after negotiations have been concluded before allowing any Senate participation. More significant, the conduct of foreign affairs has come to rely on executive agreements between heads of state in place of treaties. These agreements are not subject to Senate approval.[44]

Chief Legislator. A nascent constitutional role that stressed negative leadership (the veto) rather than positive leadership, this feature of the job did not fully develop until the twentieth century. Today the president's power to provide leadership for Congress rests primarily on the ability to shape the legislative agenda. Now considered a task for all presidents to fulfill, it stems from language in Article II, Section 3, that obliges the president to give "the Congress Information of the State of the Union" and to recommend such other measures for its consideration as deemed "necessary and expedient." Presidents now routinely develop extensive legislative agendas and present them to Congress and the nation at the beginning of each year. Moreover, the development of an activist national government has led presidents, their aides, and cabinet secretaries to submit detailed proposals for legislative consideration rather than await congressional reaction to their ideas.

Chief Magistrate. Perhaps the least clearly recognized area of presidential activity, but one that was important to the Founders' conception of executive power, was the general charge that "he shall take Care that the Laws be faithfully executed" (Article II, Section 3). Eighteenth-century conceptions of executive power did not draw sharp distinctions with judicial power: each type of official interpreted and applied the laws in the process of enforcing them. In addition, relations between these two branches of the new government were less distant during the 1790s than they are today.[45] Now presidents play a complementary role to that of the courts in the enforcement of federal laws; the executive branch helps by apprehending criminals and exercising responsibility for prosecution.

Although these presidential responsibilities are enumerated in the Constitution, what is most striking about them is their ambiguity. As a consequence, their effect on behavior—*what* presidents should do and *how* presidents should behave—is limited. Multiplicity provides presidents with the opportunity to select among a range of activities, and ambiguity gives them maximum flexibility in deciding how to go about the job. The constitutional job description is permissive rather than confining, providing presidents with great freedom in deciding how to invest energy but leaving them open to criticism for failing to fulfill tasks of lesser interest.

Expansion of the Presidency

Students of the presidency commonly divide the office's development into two major periods: traditional and modern. In the traditional era, presidential power was relatively limited, and Congress was the primary policymaker. The modern era, on the other hand, is typified by presidential dominance in the policymaking process and a significant expansion of the president's powers and resources. The presidency of Franklin D. Roosevelt was the turning point into the modern era. Political scientist Fred I. Greenstein argues that the modern presidency is distinguished by four features: (1) the president is expected to develop a legislative program and to persuade Congress to enact it; (2) presidents regularly engage in direct policymaking through actions not requiring congressional approval; (3) the presidential office has become an extensive bureaucracy designed to enable presidents to undertake points 1 and 2; and (4) presidents have come to symbolize the nation and to personify its government to such an extent that the public holds them primarily responsible for its condition and closely monitors their performance through intensive media coverage.[46]

A number of factors have contributed to this expansion of the American presidency. Several individual presidents, culminating in FDR, helped to precipitate the change. In addition, changes in the presidency have been established by Congress through statute, as a result of presidential actions that later became customary practices, and through institutional development. We will examine each of these factors in turn.

Expansion by Individual Presidents

Several early presidents—including George Washington, Thomas Jefferson, Andrew Jackson, and Abraham Lincoln—are often credited with providing their successors with an institutional legacy that left the office more powerful than before.[47] Although this is true to a certain extent, it is three twentieth-century presidents who are largely responsible for expanding presidential power and creating the modern presidency: Theodore Roosevelt, Woodrow Wilson, and, of course, FDR.

Theodore Roosevelt. As president, Theodore Roosevelt helped to spur the emergence of the United States as a world power. Concerned over the rise of Japan as a threat to American interests in the Pacific, Roosevelt sought and obtained a major role in negotiating the Portsmouth treaty, which terminated the Russo–Japanese War of 1905. Closer to home he intervened in the affairs of neighbors to the south when he considered it vital to the national interests of the United States, sending troops to the Dominican Republic and Cuba. Even more blatant was Roosevelt's role in fomenting the rebellion of Panama against Colombia so that the United States could acquire rights to build a canal. An avowed nationalist with the desire to expand U.S. influence in international affairs, Roosevelt ordered the navy to sail around the world as a symbolic demonstration of American military might. The image of mighty U.S. naval ships sailing off the shores of other countries would serve as a potent reminder to those nations that the United States was now a major world power. When Congress balked at the expense, he countered that there were sufficient funds to get the navy halfway there; if the lawmakers wanted the fleet back home, they would have to provide the money for the return trip.

Roosevelt also responded vigorously to the rapid industrialization of American life. He had charges pressed against corporations that violated antitrust laws, and he pushed legislation through Congress that gave the Interstate Commerce Commission power to reduce railroad rates. When coal mine operators in Colorado refused to agree to arbitration of a dispute with their workers, Roosevelt threatened to have troops seize the mines and administer them as a receiver for the government. He was the first American chief executive to intervene in a labor dispute who did *not* take management's side. Roosevelt also championed major reclamation and conservation projects as well as meat inspection and pure food and drug laws.

Perhaps most important, Roosevelt did much to popularize the presidency after three decades of lackluster leaders. (Of the eight men who served between Lincoln and Roosevelt, only Grover Cleveland is considered at all significant.) A dynamic personality, an attractive family, and love of the public spotlight enabled Roosevelt "to put the presidency on the front page of every newspaper in America."[48] Considering himself the "steward of the people" and seeing the office as a "bully pulpit" from which the incumbent should set the tone of American life, Roosevelt was the first president to provide meeting rooms for members of the press and to hold informal news conferences to link the presidency with the people. His style of leadership depended upon extensive use of popular rhetoric, a distinctive reinterpretation of statesmanship that ushered in the era of the "rhetorical presidency."[49] In keeping with his stewardship theory of presidential power, Roosevelt was also the first president to rely on broad discretionary authority in peacetime as well as in crisis.[50]

Woodrow Wilson. Although Theodore Roosevelt laid the groundwork for use of popular appeals during his presidency (1901–1909), it was Wilson (1913–1921) who linked inspirational rhetoric to a broad program of action in an effort to address domestic and foreign affairs in much the same way as a British prime minister. Jeffrey Tulis has argued that this effort rested on a systematic, ambitious reinterpretation of the president's role in the constitutional order.[51] A skilled public speaker, Wilson was the first president since John Adams to go before Congress in person to give his State of the Union message, a practice we now take for granted.[52] Like Jefferson, he was a powerful party chief who worked through congressional leaders and the Democratic caucus to influence legislation. He also did not hesitate to take his case to the people, casting himself as the interpreter as well as the representative of their interests.

During his first term in office, Wilson pushed through a vast program of economic reform that lowered tariffs, raised taxes on the wealthy, created a central banking system, regulated unfair trade practices, provided low-interest loans to farmers, and established an eight-hour day for railroad employees. When the United States became involved in World War I during his second term, Wilson went to Congress and obtained authority to control the economic as well as the military aspects of the war (rather than prosecuting it through unilateral executive action). This grant gave him the power to allocate food and fuel, to license trade with the enemy, to censor the mail, to regulate the foreign language press of the country, and to operate railroads, water transportation systems, and telegraph and telephone facilities. At the end of the war, he made a triumphant trip to Europe, where he assumed the leading role in the writing of the Versailles peace treaty.

Wilson also provided a lesson in how *not* to work with Congress: his adamant refusal to accept any reservations proposed by the Senate for the League of Nations Covenant of the Treaty of Versailles would ensure that the United States would not participate. Wilson's archenemy, Sen. Henry Cabot Lodge, R-Mass., calculated that the president's intransigence and personal hatred of him would be so intense that the president would reject all compromises proposed to the treaty. Lodge was right: Wilson, spurning the advice of his wife and of close friends such as Col. Edward House, avowed it "better a thousand times to go down fighting than to dip your colors to dishonorable compromise." A trip to win popular support for the league ended in a physical breakdown (Wilson suffered a stroke) and failure. As a result, the country whose leader proposed the League of Nations ended up not belonging to the organization at all.

Franklin D. Roosevelt. Confronted by enormous domestic and international crises, Franklin Roosevelt began a program of action and innovation unmatched by any chief executive in our history. In most respects, his service is now used as a yardstick against which the performance of his successors is measured.[53] When Roosevelt came into office in March 1933, business failures were legion, 12 million people were unemployed, banks all over the country were closed or doing business under restrictions, and Americans had lost confidence in their leaders as well as in themselves. Counseling the nation in his inaugural address—the first of four—that "the only thing we have to fear is fear itself," the new chief executive swung into action: a four-day bank holiday was declared, and an emergency banking bill was prepared within a day's time. During Roosevelt's first hundred days in office, the nation witnessed a social and economic revolution in the form of his New Deal. Congress adopted a series of far-reaching government programs insuring bank deposits; providing crop payments for farmers; establishing codes of fair competition for industry; granting labor the right to organize; providing relief and jobs for the unemployed; and creating the Tennessee Valley Authority, a government corporation, to develop that region. With these measures and others such as Social Security, public housing, and unemployment compensation, Roosevelt established the concept of the "positive state" in America—a government that has the obligation to take the lead in providing for the welfare of all the people.

Internationally, Roosevelt extended diplomatic recognition to the Soviet Union, embarked on the Good Neighbor policy toward South America, and pushed through the Reciprocal Trade Program, which lowered tariffs with other nations. In his second term, FDR began the slow and difficult task of preparing the nation for its eventual entry into World War II: he funneled aid to the Allies; traded fifty "over-age" destroyers to Britain for naval and air bases in the British West Indies, Argentia (Newfoundland), and Bermuda; and obtained passage of the nation's first peacetime draft. After Pearl Harbor, in his own words, "Dr. New Deal" became "Dr. Win-the-War." He took over economic control of the war effort granted him by Congress and established the victorious strategy of concentrating on defeating Germany before Japan. While hostilities were still going on, he took the lead in setting up the United Nations. Unfortunately, he died before he could see the organization established in 1945.

Roosevelt was an innovator whose actions reshaped the presidential office. He was not only an effective legislative leader but also a skilled administrator responsible for a thorough reorganization of the executive branch, including the creation of the Executive Office of the President. *(See chapter 6.)* Even more important, FDR was probably the most effective molder of public opinion the nation has ever known. He pioneered the use of "fireside chats" over radio to explain his actions to the people. In addition, he raised the presidential press conference to new heights as a tool of public persuasion. As a man who could take idealistic goals, reduce them to manageable and practical programs, and then sell them to Congress and the American people, Roosevelt has no peer.

Expansion through Statute

Congress is another major source of change in the presidency. Legislators have mandated activities that earlier presidents exercised on a discretionary basis or have formally delegated responsibility for activities that traditionally resided with Congress. One of the contemporary presidency's major responsibilities— serving as the nation's economic manager—is suggested nowhere in the Constitution.[54] Congress foisted this power on the president. In 1921, Congress passed the Budget and Accounting Act as part of an effort to increase the fiscal responsibility and efficiency of government. The act created the Bureau of the Budget as a part of the Treasury Department and required the president to use the expert advice of the bureau to propose annual fiscal policy to the government. Quite simply, the legislation compelled the president to take an active role in domestic policy formulation. As James Sundquist has written:

Before 1921, a president did not have to have a program for the whole of the government, and none did; after that date he was compelled by the Budget and Accounting Act to present a program for every department and every bureau, and to do it annually. Before 1921, a president did not have to propose a fiscal policy for the government, and many did not; after 1921, every chief executive had to have a fiscal policy, every year. That made the president a leader, a policy and program initiator, and a manager, whether he wished to be or not.[55]

There were, of course, strong presidents who exerted policy leadership before 1921, but nothing had compelled presidents to act. Likewise, it is wrong to assume that the Budget and Accounting Act automatically produced strong presidents. The first three presidents affected by the act—Warren Harding, Calvin Coolidge, and Herbert Hoover—dutifully submitted proposals to Congress but seldom exerted strong leadership to secure enactment.[56] That changed during the presidency of Franklin Roosevelt, who used the crisis of the Great Depression as a rallying cry for policy enactment.

Over time, Congress further expanded presidential power. It created the Executive Office of the President in 1939 as a source of expert advice to help presidents in the formulation of policy. Congress also added to the president's economic responsibilities by passing the Employment Act of 1946. As Sundquist explains, the act "compels the president to maintain a continuous surveillance of the nation's economy, to report on the state of its health at least annually, and if there are signs of pathology—inflation, recession, stagnation—to recommend corrective action."[57] Despite giving the president new tasks to fulfill, Congress did not surrender its traditional right to alter presidential proposals, thereby ensuring that tax rates and spending proposals would remain a mainstay of partisan politics as well as legislative-executive relations. (The politics of economic policymaking are examined in detail in chapter 9.)

Congress has taken comparable action in other areas as well. In 1947, Congress charged the president with the task of coordinating national security policy— foreign policy, intelligence collection and evaluation, and defense policy—through the creation of the National Security Council (NSC). Harry Truman resisted the newly created NSC as an intrusion on his powers and was slow to use it. In fact, no president can be *required* to use such a structure, but the more conflictive setting of the cold war saw one president after another establish administrative machinery designed to achieve the same goal of coordination of American foreign policy. *(See chapter 10.)* Thus we find that Congress may encourage presidents to provide leadership in areas wholly absent from the original constitutional design or encourage executives to devise new ways to exercise their traditional responsibilities.

Expansion through Custom and Practice

Across a wide range of presidential activities, "action based on usage may acquire legitimacy."[58] Nowhere in the Constitution did it say that presidents would serve as leaders of their party, but that task has been associated with the office since Thomas Jefferson first established his dominance of the Democratic-Republicans' congressional caucus. Enormous variation may be found in how presidents have pursued such activities and in how successful they have been. Some, like Jefferson, have had a close relationship with their party, while other executives have been virtually abandoned by their partisan allies (Rutherford B. Hayes). At other times, presidents have sought, and seemed to derive, greater influence by appearing to serve "above" party (Eisenhower). If the political parties continue to weaken or have difficulty reasserting themselves as structures vital to democracy, this informal part of the president's job description could disappear.

A second example of precedent and custom can be found in Theodore Roosevelt's attempt to mediate a labor-management dispute. Earlier presidents had intervened on the side of company owners, but Roosevelt put his prestige on the line when he sought to resolve the anthracite coal strike of 1902, a struggle that had paralyzed a vital industry. Other presidents followed suit: Wilson intervened in eight major disputes, Harding in two, FDR in eleven, and Truman in three.[59] The response of one president to emergency conditions had become an accepted precedent for his successors, if they wished to pursue it.

Institutional Sources of Change

Finally, it needs to be recognized that the modern presidency is no longer a one-person job—a reality that may have significant consequences for the office's evolution. Although designed to be unitary rather than plural, the modern presidency has become a working collectivity in order to dispatch the many responsibilities placed at the president's door. This shift toward what has been called the "institutional presidency"—a twentieth-century phenomenon—is partly a result of changing customs and practice, but it is also something that was furthered by statute. During Franklin Roosevelt's first term, the average number of full-time White House staffers was 47. By Richard Nixon's second term some thirty-five years later, that number had grown to well over 500.

Congress spurred along this increase in staff by creating the Executive Office of the President (EOP) in 1939 and then passing subsequent legislation to create additional staff units within that structure (such as the Council of Economic Advisers and the National Security Council). At the same time, presidents unilaterally created their own specialized staff units within the White House itself. These include the Congressional Liaison Office (to help secure congressional passage of presidential initiatives), the Office of Communications (to help communicate the president's agenda to the American people and to coordinate the flow of information from the many departments and agencies within the Executive Branch), and the Office of Public Liaison (to maintain support from interest groups). By some counts, the president's full-time executive staff under Nixon (including presidential advisers in the Executive Office of the President) grew to more than 5,000. During FDR's first term, comparable executive staff (including groundskeepers and the White House police force) numbered only 103.[60]

Presidential Culture

Understanding the presidency's institutional development provides an important perspective on roles played by the office, but one also needs to address a less concrete question: What does the presidency *mean* to Americans? The final section of this chapter focuses on the development of the office's emotional and psychological significance.

Despite the Framers' ambivalence toward executive power, the office of president quickly acquired mythic dimensions when it was filled by the country's first true hero. George Washington, argues Seymour Martin Lipset, supplied the virtues of a charismatic leader who serves as "symbol of the new nation, its hero who embodies in his person its values and aspirations. But more than merely symbolizing the new nation, he legitimizes the state, the new secular government, by endowing it with his 'gift of grace,'" the near magical qualities such leaders supposedly possess.[61] A cult of personality grew up around Washington so that well into the nineteenth century citizens displayed his likeness in their homes, named their children after him, and paid him endless tributes.

In the process of contributing stability and identity to the new nation, Washington also endowed the presidential office with a special meaning that has become part of our collective heritage. Bruce Buchanan refers to this as *presidential culture*, "widely held meanings of the presidency, derived from selected episodes in the history of the institution and transmitted from one generation to the next by political socialization."[62] Buchanan explains that families, teachers, and the media sustain this view of the presidency as an office with the ability to deliver the nation from danger as a result of its occupants' greatness. Somehow, it is widely believed, the institution "has the potential to make extraordinary events happen" and the incumbent "should be able to realize that potential."[63] Occupants of the position, then, are expected to live up to these levels of performance and are roundly criticized when they fall short.

Why have such unrealistic expectations taken hold? One reason is that we have glorified the memories of past presidents. The "great" presidents, particularly those who took decisive action and bold initiatives, and even some of the "not so great" are treated as folk heroes and enshrined in a national mythology—figures whose births we celebrate, whose virtues we are urged to emulate, whose achievements we memorialize, and whose sex lives continue to interest us long after their deaths. Schoolchildren throughout America are regaled with stories of Washington and Lincoln every February while looking at bulletin boards featuring their silhouettes. Every summer, thousands of vacationers make the pilgrimage to visit shrines located along the Potomac in Washington, D.C., or scattered throughout the nation in presidential libraries and museums. Historical and popular glorification, however, does not constitute the full story. The presidency has always been important in American civic life, but it may have assumed even greater proportions in the modern era, assisted by new technologies and resting on new conceptions of the office.

A number of political scientists have pointed to the importance of the presidency in meeting the emotional and psychological needs of the populace. In particular, it is argued that citizens have expressive needs for confidence, security, reassurance, and pride in citizenship.[64] In the view of Murray Edelman, citizens suffer from a "general sense of anxiety about the comprehensive function played in human affairs by chance, ignorance, and inability to comprehend, plan, and take responsibility for remote and complicated contingencies." The natural response is to seek emotional comfort through attachment to reassuring symbols, "and what symbol can be more reassuring than the incumbent of a high position who knows what to do and is willing to act, especially when others are bewildered and alone?"[65] We know that American children develop a highly idealized image of presidents that emphasizes both their power and their benevolence, a source of reassurance that may be transferred from childhood to adulthood.

Fred Greenstein suggests additional psychological needs that are met through the presidency. Citizens seeking to sort through the complexity of political life turn to presidents for cognitive assistance. Presidents personify the government and make it possible to become engaged by what would otherwise be an impersonal abstraction. By following the president's activities, citizens may also experience a sort of vicarious participation in public affairs, giving them a sense of power and control that ordinarily would be unavailable. As a symbol of stability, predictability, and national unity, the president soothes fears and enables us to proceed with our daily lives.[66]

Symbols, in fact, are central to the character of the presidential office, which has become particularly "potent as a symbol of the public welfare, built-in benevolence, and competence to lead."[67] Barbara Hinckley points out that "symbols evoke ideas the society wants to believe are true. . . . [They] can substitute for something that does not exist otherwise."[68] In fact, Hinckley argues that because the Constitution failed to clarify the presidency's nature and responsibilities, symbols have become enormously significant: "The office is undefined; thus presidents become what people want them to be."[69] And the people want them to be many things. The list of desirable personal attributes is impressive, as Ray Price, an aide to Richard Nixon during the 1968 presidential campaign, pointed out in a memo to the staff:

People identify with a President in a way they do with no other public figure. Potential presidents are measured against an ideal that's a combination of leading man, God, father, hero, pope, king, with maybe just a touch of the avenging Furies thrown in. They want him to be larger than life, a living legend, and yet quintessentially human; someone to be held up to their children as a model; someone to be cherished by themselves as a revered member of the family, in somewhat the same way in which peasant families pray to the icon in the corner. Reverence goes where power is.[70]

The problem for candidates (and incumbents) is how to project an image that matches these public expectations. Theodore Lowi has argued that "the expectations of the masses have grown faster than the capacity of presidential government to meet them."[71] According to Lowi, modern presidents resort to illusions to cover failures and seek quick fixes for their flagging public support in foreign adventures. As we shall see in chapter 3, advances in the means of communication have increased the ability of presidents to do this. Such behavior—portrayed by Lowi as rooted in the presidential institution, not in individual presidents' personalities—is ultimately self-defeating because it does nothing more than further inflate expectations and ensure public disappointment. This may help to explain the string of failed presidencies described at the outset of this chapter.

Conclusion: The Changeable, Political Presidency

There can be little doubt that today's presidency is a far cry from the office designed by the Constitutional Convention. Responsibilities have grown enormously as have means to fulfill them. So have the mythic dimensions of the office. Unlike the office that was launched in 1789, today's presidency is firmly rooted in the national consciousness as the consequence of childhood socialization and a secular mythology whose idealized images are magnified with the passage of time. There is no way to determine whether the office of president means more to Americans today than it did two centuries ago in terms of the emotional and psychological needs it meets, but certainly it occupies a more central—some observers would argue excessive—place in the public consciousness.

The contemporary presidency is not a static construct, however. As this overview of institutional development demonstrates, Americans' perceptions of the office and what they want from it can and will change over time. This has been true even over the past thirty years. All too often, observers of the presidency treat temporary conditions as if they were permanent—mistaking a snapshot for a portrait.

To summarize, the presidency is variable for several reasons. First, in no other public office do the personality, character, and political style of the incumbent make as much difference as they do in the presidency. As an institution, the presidency exhibits important continuities across administrations, but the entry of each new occupant has an undeniably pervasive effect on the position's operation. The presidency is also heavily influenced by changes outside the office and throughout the U.S. political system—whether in the formal political structure (Congress, the executive branch, the courts), in the informal political institutions (political parties and interest groups), in society at large, in the mass media, or in conditions surrounding substantive issues, particularly national security and the economy. Because of their extensive responsibilities, presidents must contend with all of these influences. Furthermore, although the Constitution and historical precedents give structure to the office, the powers of the presidency are so vague that incumbents have tremendous latitude to shape the office to their particular desires.

The presidency is not only highly *changeable* but also essentially *political.* Although on occasion, especially in times of crisis, presidents rule by asserting their constitutional prerogatives, they usually are forced to govern by political maneuvering—by trying to convince and persuade the many participants in the political process. This is a very complex task. Not only must they perform on the public stage of mass politics, but they must also master the intricacies of elite politics, a game played among skilled insiders. In the following chapters, we first examine "public politics" (chapters 2, 3, and 4) and then turn to the skills that presidents bring to relations with other public elites (chapters 5, 6, and 7). These separate dimensions are linked in discussions of major policy areas (chapters 8, 9, and 10).

NOTES

1. In fact, Gore won the popular vote by a margin of some 539,947 votes. This is almost five times the size of John Kennedy's 1960 popular vote margin of 114,673 votes over Richard Nixon and almost 30,000 votes more than Nixon's 1968 margin of 510,645 votes over Hubert Humphrey. In addition to Bush and Harrison, John Quincy Adams in 1824 and Rutherford B. Hayes in 1876 won the presidency without winning the most popular votes.

2. *Bush v. Gore,* 121 S.Ct. 525 (2000).

3. Richard E. Neustadt, *Presidential Power: The Politics of Leadership* (New York: Wiley, 1960), 26.

4. Stephen Skowronek, *The Politics Presidents Make: Leadership from John Adams to George Bush* (Cambridge: Harvard University Press, 1993), 20.

5. Quoted in Forrest McDonald, *The American Presidency: An Intellectual History* (Lawrence: University Press of Kansas, 1994), 127.

6. McDonald, *The American Presidency,* 126.

7. Richard J. Ellis, ed., *Founding the American Presidency* (Lanham, Md.: Rowman and Littlefield, 1999), 1.

8. McDonald, *The American Presidency,* 132–133.

9. Richard M. Pious, *The American Presidency* (New York: Basic Books, 1979), 23.

10. Sidney M. Milkis and Michael Nelson, *The American Presidency: Origins and Development, 1776–1993,* 2d ed. (Washington, D.C.: CQ Press, 1994), 5. One of the drafters of the New York state constitution, Gouverneur Morris, later played an

important role in the creation of presidential power at the 1787 Constitutional Convention.

11. Thomas Jefferson, *Notes on the State of Virginia,* quoted in Ellis, *Founding the American Presidency,* 4.

12. Charles C. Thach Jr., *The Creation of the Presidency, 1775–1789: A Study in Constitutional History* (Baltimore: Johns Hopkins University Press, 1923), chap. 3.

13. Pious, *The American Presidency,* 22.

14. McDonald, *The American Presidency,* 151.

15. Quoted in Ellis, *Founding the American Presidency,* 6.

16. Milkis and Nelson, *The American Presidency,* 2d ed., 13–14.

17. McDonald, *The American Presidency,* 163.

18. Ibid.,164.

19. Ellis, *Founding the American Presidency,* 31–32.

20. McDonald, *The American Presidency,* 164; see also Max Farrand, ed., *The Records of the Federal Convention of 1787* (New Haven: Yale University Press, 1911), 1:65.

21. Farrand, *Records,* 1:65.

22. Ibid., 1:244.

23. Ellis, *Founding the American Presidency,* 13.

24. This paragraph is based on McDonald, *The American Presidency,* 157.

25. Ibid., 171.

26. Ellis, *Founding the American Presidency,* 112–113.

27. We use the term *Congress* loosely here. As we have pointed out, the original recommendation of the Committee on Postponed Matters called for the *Senate* alone to choose from among the top five presidential candidates. As finally ratified, the Constitution called for the *House* alone to choose from the top five candidates. After the ratification of the Twelfth Amendment in 1804, the Constitution called for the House to choose from among the top *three* presidential candidates.

28. This account of the Committee on Postponed Matters is drawn largely from McDonald, *The American Presidency,* 176–178; see also Milkis and Nelson, *The American Presidency,* 2d ed., 21–22.

29. Edward S. Corwin, *The President: Office and Powers,* 4th ed. (New York: New York University Press, 1957), 12.

30. Quoted in Michael Nelson, ed., *Guide to the Presidency,* 2d ed. (Washington, D.C.: CQ Press, 1996), 30. Although this sort of hostility toward a strong executive was common among antifederalists, Herbert J. Storing has pointed out that there are greater differences of opinion among them than one might expect. Although some antifederalists continued to argue for a plural executive or an executive council, many agreed that a unitary executive was necessary. Storing points out that among antifederalists there was even "a fair amount of sympathy for a strong (even, under some circumstances, a hereditary) executive to resist the aristocratic tendencies of the legislature; and some of the Anti-Federalists objected that the President would be too weak to stand up to the Senate and would become a mere tool of aristocratic domination." Herbert J. Storing, ed., *The Complete Anti-Federalist,* Vol. 1 (Chicago: University of Chicago Press, 1981), 49.

31. Alexander Hamilton, *Federalist* No. 70.

32. Thach, *The Creation of the Presidency,* 138.

33. Ibid., 139.

34. William Howard Taft, *Our Chief Magistrate and His Powers* (New York: Columbia University Press, 1916), 139–140.

35. Theodore Roosevelt, *Autobiography* (New York: Macmillan, 1913), 388–389.

36. Taft, *Our Chief Magistrate,* 144–145.

37. Quoted in Corwin, *The President,* 4th ed., 8 (emphasis added).

38. Clinton Rossiter, *Constitutional Dictatorship* (Princeton: Princeton University Press, 1948).

39. Interview with Richard Nixon by David Frost, televised May 19, 1977; quoted in Craig Ducat, *Constitutional Interpretation*, 7th ed. (Belmont, Calif.: West, 2000), 206.

40. Corwin, *The President*, 4th ed., 30.

41. Arthur M. Schlesinger Jr., *The Imperial Presidency*, 2d ed. (Boston: Houghton Mifflin, 1989).

42. McDonald, *The American Presidency*, 173–174.

43. Louis Fisher, *Constitutional Conflicts between Congress and the President*, 3d ed. (Lawrence: University Press of Kansas, 1991), chap. 9.

44. Ibid., chap. 8.

45. Robert Scigliano, "The Presidency and the Judiciary," in *The Presidency and the Political System*, 3d ed., ed. Michael Nelson (Washington, D.C.: CQ Press, 1990), 473–476.

46. Fred Greenstein, "Change and Continuity in the Modern Presidency," in *The New American Political System*, ed. Anthony King (Washington, D.C.: American Enterprise Institute, 1978), 45–46.

47. See, for example, Corwin, *The President*, 4th ed., chap. 1.

48. Clinton Rossiter, *The American Presidency*, rev. ed. (New York: Harcourt, Brace, 1960), 102.

49. Jeffrey K. Tulis, *The Rhetorical Presidency* (Princeton: Princeton University Press, 1987), chap. 4.

50. Milkis and Nelson, *The American Presidency*, 2d ed., 208.

51. Tulis, *The Rhetorical Presidency*, chap. 5. Also see Jeffrey K. Tulis, "The Two Constitutional Presidencies," in *The Presidency and the Political System*, 6th ed., ed. Michael Nelson (Washington, D.C.: CQ Press, 2000).

52. Thomas Jefferson had discontinued the practice as an undesirable indication of monarchist tendencies.

53. William E. Leuchtenberg, *In the Shadow of FDR: From Harry Truman to Ronald Reagan*, rev. ed. (Ithaca: Cornell University Press, 1985).

54. James L. Sundquist uses the term *economic stabilizer*, and earlier Clinton Rossiter had used the term *Manager of Prosperity*. See Sundquist, *The Decline and Resurgence of Congress* (Washington, D.C.: Brookings, 1981), chap. 4.

55. Ibid., 39.

56. Ibid., 33.

57. Ibid., 66–67.

58. Fisher, *Constitutional Conflicts*, 24.

59. Corwin, *The President*, 4th ed., 175–177.

60. Gary King and Lyn Ragsdale, eds., *The Elusive Executive: Discovering Statistical Patterns in the Presidency* (Washington, D.C.: CQ Press, 1988), Table 4-1, 205. The precise size of presidential staff, though, is hard to calculate. For a discussion of this and an overview of the debates over how to count presidential staff, see John Hart, *The Presidential Branch: From Washington to Clinton*, 2d ed. (Chatham, N.J.: Chatham House, 1995), 43–45, 112–125.

61. Seymour Martin Lipset, *The First New Nation: The United States in Historical and Comparative Perspective* (New York: Norton, 1979), 18.

62. Bruce Buchanan, *The Citizen's Presidency: Standards of Choice and Judgment* (Washington, D.C.: CQ Press, 1987), 25.

63. Ibid., 28.

64. See especially Murray Edelman, *The Symbolic Uses of Politics* (Urbana: University of Illinois Press, 1964); and Fred I. Greenstein, "What the President Means to Americans: Presidential 'Choice' between Elections," in *Choosing the President*, ed. James David Barber (Englewood Cliffs, N.J.: Prentice Hall, 1974).

65. Edelman, *The Symbolic Uses of Politics*, 76–77.

66. Greenstein, "What the President Means to Americans," 142–147. It should be noted that in this essay Greenstein de-emphasized the likelihood that children

socialized to a positive feeling about the president as an authority figure would extend this reliance on an "unconscious symbolic surrogate of childhood authority figures" into adulthood.

67. Murray Edelman, "The Politics of Persuasion," in *Choosing the President,* 172.

68. Barbara Hinckley, *The Symbolic Presidency: How Presidents Portray Themselves* (New York: Routledge, 1990), 5.

69. Ibid., 8.

70. As cited in Michael Novak, *Choosing Our King: Powerful Symbols in Presidential Politics* (New York: Macmillan, 1974), 44.

71. Theodore J. Lowi, *The Personal President: Power Invested, Promise Unfulfilled* (Ithaca: Cornell University Press, 1985), xii.

SUGGESTED READINGS

Corwin, Edward S. *The President: Office and Powers, 1789–1984,* 5th ed. New York: New York University Press, 1984.

Ellis, Richard J., ed. *Founding the American Presidency.* Lanham, Md.: Rowman and Littlefield, 1999.

Farrand, Max, ed. *The Records of the Federal Convention of 1787.* New Haven: Yale University Press, 1911.

Lowi, Theodore J. *The Personal President: Power Invested, Promise Unfulfilled.* Ithaca: Cornell University Press, 1985.

McDonald, Forrest. *The American Presidency: An Intellectual History.* Lawrence: University Press of Kansas, 1994.

Milkis, Sidney M., and Michael Nelson. *The American Presidency: Origins and Development, 1776–1998,* 3d ed. Washington, D.C.: CQ Press, 1999.

Nelson, Michael, ed. *The Presidency and the Political System,* 7th ed. Washington, D.C.: CQ Press, 2003.

Neustadt, Richard E. *Presidential Power: The Politics of Leadership.* New York: Wiley, 1960.

Skowronek, Stephen. *The Politics Presidents Make: Leadership from John Adams to George Bush.* Cambridge: Harvard University Press, 1993.

2 ELECTION POLITICS

Before the era of air travel, presidential candidates traveled by car and train. Franklin D. Roosevelt is shown here waving to a crowd during the 1932 campaign that resulted in his dramatic victory and the subsequent introduction of the New Deal.

T HE FOCAL POINT OF AMERICAN political life is the presidential election. More citizens participate in this process than in any other aspect of civic life, and their choices have enormous significance for the nation and, indeed, for the world. Historians use presidential terms to break history into four-year blocks of time, and policymaking at the federal level follows the same rhythm. The election also serves as a unifying event, a collective celebration of democracy coming at the conclusion of an elaborate pageant replete with familiar rituals, colorful characters and plot lines that capture attention despite their repetition every four years.

Today's selection process bears little resemblance to what the Founders outlined in the original Constitution. Most of the changes have been extraconstitutional; that is, they have resulted from the evolution of political parties, coverage by the media, and citizen expectations rather than constitutional amendments. There has been almost constant tinkering with the rules governing presidential elections, with the movement consistently toward greater democratization. Even before the confusion that surrounded the outcome of the 2000 election, most dissatisfaction with the process centered on the remnants of indirect democracy that persist, particularly the national party conventions and the electoral college. The most recent election gave new life to the debate about election rules as the nation waited thirty-six days for the final results in Florida. George W. Bush secured a national victory after winning Florida's electoral votes by a margin of merely 537 votes out of nearly 6 million ballots. During the prolonged period of uncertainty that followed election day, Americans relearned the arcane workings of the electoral college and discovered the fallibility of voting methods and tally rules.

At the conclusion of this chapter, we review recommendations for reform intended to improve system performance and provide for a greater degree of direct democracy. To appreciate the current selection process and suggestions for reform, it is necessary to gain an understanding of the major transformations in the nomination and general election phases of the process.

Evolution of the Selection Process

In 1789 and 1792, electing a president was simple. Each member of the electoral college cast two votes, one of which had to be for a person outside the elector's state. Both times George Washington was elected by unanimous votes.[1] Both times John Adams received the second highest number of votes to become the vice president. In 1789, the process took only three months: there was no campaign, electors were chosen on the first Wednesday of January, they met in their respective states to vote on the first Wednesday in February, and the votes were counted on April 6. In 1792, the procedure took even less time. The contrast with today's process could not be sharper: candidates now launch nomination campaigns up to two years before the general election, spending millions of dollars in pursuit of the office, and everyone expects a winner to be declared on election night.

Consensus support for Washington ensured smooth operation of the selection procedure during the first two elections: there was widespread confidence that the nation's wartime hero would govern in the interest of all the people. The erosion of consensus triggered the development of a separate nomination procedure. Policy differences in Congress created the basis for an important institution not mentioned in the Constitution—the political party. By the early 1790s, the

Federalist Party had formed around the economic policies of Secretary of the Treasury Alexander Hamilton, and his supporters in Congress backed his programs.[2] Resigning as secretary of state in 1793, Thomas Jefferson joined James Madison, then serving in the House of Representatives, as a critic of Hamilton's policies, and they formed the rival Republican Party, which came to be known as the Democratic-Republican Party.[3] By the mid-1790s, cohesive pro- and anti-administration blocs had formed in Congress, and congressional candidates were labeled either Democratic-Republicans or Federalists.[4]

Political parties had an almost immediate impact on the electoral college. Electors became party loyalists, whose discipline was apparent in 1800, when Jefferson, the Democratic-Republicans' candidate for president, and Aaron Burr, the party's candidate for vice president, tied in the electoral college vote. Loyal to their party, the electors had cast their ballots for both candidates, but the Constitution had no provision for counting the ballots separately for president and vice president. Jefferson and Burr each received seventy-three votes to President Adams's sixty-five. The election was decided in the House of Representatives, where Jefferson won after thirty-six ballots. Hamilton broke the tie by throwing his support behind Jefferson, his longtime rival. Party loyalty, with infrequent exceptions, has prevailed in electoral college balloting ever since. (The Twelfth Amendment to the Constitution, ratified in 1804, provided for separate presidential and vice presidential balloting.)[5]

The rise of parties also fundamentally altered presidential selection by creating a separate nomination stage: the parties had to devise a method for choosing their nominees. Influence over presidential selection shifted from the local notables who had served as electors to party elites. In 1796, the Federalists' leaders chose their candidate, John Adams, and the Democratic-Republicans relied on their party members in Congress, the *congressional caucus*, to nominate Jefferson. Four years later, the congressional caucus became the nominating mechanism for both parties, a practice that continued until 1824, when the system broke down.

The congressional caucus allowed members of Congress, already assembled in the nation's capital and facing minimal transportation problems, to select a nominee. Because legislators were familiar with potential presidential candidates from all parts of the new country, they were the logical agents for choosing candidates for an office with a nationwide constituency. Caucuses provided a peer review of candidates' credentials, with one group of politicians assessing a fellow politician's skills, abilities, and political appeal. But the congressional caucus had serious flaws. It violated the constitutional principle of separation of powers by giving members of the legislative body a routine role in choosing the president rather than an emergency role, assumed only in the event of an electoral college deadlock. The caucus also could not represent areas in which the party had lost the previous congressional election, a problem quickly encountered by the Federalists, whose support was drastically declining. Moreover, interested and informed citizens who participated in grassroots party activities, especially campaigns, had no means to participate in congressional caucus deliberations.

By September 2003, ten candidates were seeking the 2004 Democratic presidential nomination, on stage here before a debate (from left to right): Sen. John Kerry, Mass.; Sen. Bob Graham, Fla.; Sen. Joseph Lieberman, Conn.; retired general Wesley Clark; Rep. Dennis Kucinich, Ohio; Sen. John Edwards, N.C.; former Vermont governor Howard Dean; Rev. Al Sharpton; former Illinois senator Carol Moseley Braun; and Rep. Richard Gephardt, Mo.

The 1824 election brought an end to nomination by congressional caucus. First, the Democratic-Republicans in Congress insisted on nominating Secretary of the Treasury William Crawford, who had suffered a debilitating stroke. Then, in the general election, Andrew Jackson, nominated by the Tennessee legislature, won more popular votes and more electoral votes than any other candidate but failed to achieve a majority in the electoral college. The election had to be decided by the House, where John Quincy Adams emerged victorious after he agreed to make Henry Clay, another of the five contestants, secretary of state in return for his support. These shenanigans permanently discredited King Caucus, as its critics called it. Favorite sons nominated by state legislatures and state conventions dominated the 1828 campaign, but this method proved too decentralized to select a national official. A device was needed that would represent party elements throughout the country and at the same time facilitate the nomination of a candidate.

National Party Conventions

What developed was the *party nominating convention,* an assembly made truly national by including delegates from all the states. Rail transportation made such meetings feasible, and the expanding citizen participation in presidential elections made the change necessary. Influence over selection of the party nominee therefore shifted to state and local party leaders, particularly those able to commit large blocs of delegate votes to a candidate.

Two minor parties with no appreciable representation in Congress, the Anti-Masons and the National Republicans, led the way with conventions in 1831.[6] To rally support in 1832, the Democrats, under President Andrew Jackson (elected in 1828), also held a convention. Major political parties have nominated their presidential and vice presidential candidates by holding national conventions ever since. National committees composed of state party leaders call the presidential nominating conventions into session to choose nominees and to adopt a platform of common policy positions.[7] Delegates are selected by states and allocated primarily on the basis of population.

Although today's conventions in some ways resemble those of 170 years ago, the nomination process has undergone drastic revision, especially since 1968, when Democrats introduced reforms that diminished the importance of conventions. Just as influence over selection of the party nominee shifted from Congress to party leaders, it has moved within the party from a small group of organization professionals to a broad base of activists and voters. The origins of this shift can be traced to the development of presidential primary elections early in the twentieth century (Florida passed the first primary election law in 1901).

Under the system that operated from roughly 1850 to 1950, party leaders from the largest states could bargain over presidential nominations. Most influential were those who controlled large blocs of delegates and would throw their support behind a candidate for the right price. These power brokers—hence the term *brokered conventions*—might seek a program commitment in the platform, a place in the president's cabinet, or other forms of federal patronage in return for support. To be successful, candidates had to curry favor with party and elected officials before and during the national convention. An effective campaign manager might tour the country selling the candidate's virtues and securing delegate commitments prior to the convention, but about half the conventions began with no sense of the likely outcome. Protracted bargaining and negotiation among powerful state and local party leaders were often the result. In 1924, for instance, the Democrats needed 103 ballots cast over seventeen days to nominate John W. Davis, an effort that must have seemed pointless later when he attracted only 29 percent of the popular vote. Nevertheless, the convention was a deliberative body that reached decisions on common policy positions as well as on nominees. Providing a way to accommodate the demands of major elements within the party established the base for a nationwide campaign.

In this respect, modern conventions are quite different. Not since 1952, when the Democrats needed three ballots to nominate Gov. Adlai Stevenson of Illinois for president, has it taken more than one ballot to determine either party's nominee.[8] Raucous floor battles over procedures and delegate credentials have given way to a stream of symbols and speakers whose appearances are carefully choreographed to appeal to a prime-time television audience. Today, modern conventions serve as ratifying assemblies for a popular choice rather than deliberative bodies, and candidates with popular appeal have the advantage over those whose appeal is primarily with party leaders.

Although much of the convention's business is still conducted in backroom meetings, the most important business—choosing the presidential nominee— already has been decided through the grueling process used to select convention delegates. Compared with their forerunners, modern conventions conduct their business in a routine fashion, adhere to enforceable national party standards for delegate selection and demographic representation, and are more heavily influenced by rank-and-file party supporters than by party leaders.[9] These changes appeared gradually through a process often fraught with conflict that centered on the rules governing delegate selection.

Recent Reform of the Selection Process

The pace of change accelerated when the Democratic Party adopted internal reforms following its loss of the presidency in 1968. In addition to the actions already noted, rules adopted by a variety of actors—100 state political parties and fifty legislatures, the national political parties, and Congress—reformed the process. Sometimes individuals turned to the courts to interpret provisions of these regulations and reconcile conflicts. In addition, the rules were adjusted so drastically and so often that, particularly in the Democratic Party, candidates and their supporters found it difficult to keep up.

Reform has been especially pervasive in the nomination process. Following their tumultuous convention in 1968, when Vietnam War protesters clashed with police in the streets of Chicago, the Democrats adopted a set of guidelines that reduced the influence of party leaders, encouraged participation by rank-and-file Democrats, and expanded convention representation of previously underrepresented groups, particularly women and African Americans. The result was a pronounced shift of influence within the party from *party professionals* toward *amateurs,* a term encompassing citizens who become engaged in the presidential contest because of a short-term concern such as an attractive candidate (candidate enthusiasts) or an especially important issue (issue enthusiasts).

States, seeking to conform to the party's new guidelines on participation, adopted the primary as the preferred means of selecting convention delegates. Primaries allow a party's registered voters—and in some states independents—to express a presidential preference that is translated into convention delegates. In most states, voters cast ballots for specific presidential candidates, but in some places only delegate names appear on the ballot. In sharp contrast is the party caucus, an alternate means of selecting delegates. The caucus is a local meeting of registered party voters that often involves speeches and discussion about the candidates' merits. A caucus is more social, public, and time-consuming (often requiring two hours to complete) than a primary, in which voters make choices in the voting booth. Ultimately, the caucus also produces delegates to the national convention, but it usually requires multiple stages. For example, delegates from the local caucuses go to a county convention that selects delegates to a state convention that selects the national delegates. In 1968, only seventeen states chose delegates through primaries, the remainder using caucuses dominated by party leaders; in 2000, forty-one states and the District of Columbia held primaries, and even the remaining caucuses provided for far greater participation.[10] Because of these changes, nominations are more apt to reflect the voters' immediate concerns, winners are known well before the convention, and the influence of party leaders has declined.

Abandoning the convention's traditional deliberative role, some observers argue, has come at a heavy cost. By transferring power to amateurs and by sacrificing the peer review exercised by professionals, many Democrats, in particular, fear they have been weakened organizationally and chosen less capable nominees, such as those who lost throughout most of the 1970s and 1980s. Moreover, the changes have enhanced the importance of the media. By operating as the principal source of information about the candidates and by emphasizing the "horse race"—who is ahead—the media have become enormously influential during the delegate selection process. So not everyone has been satisfied with the general movement toward a more democratized selection process, as evidenced by several counterreforms that appeared during the 1980s.

The Contemporary Selection Process

Now that the historical context has been set and some of the current concerns about the nomination process have been previewed, the discussion focuses on how the contemporary selection process operates. Despite the seemingly perpetual flux that characterizes presidential elections, it is possible to identify four stages in the process: (1) defining the pool of eligible candidates; (2) nominating the parties' candidates at the national conventions following delegate selection in the primaries and caucuses; (3) waging the general election campaign, culminating in election day; and (4) validating results through the electoral college.

No two presidential election cycles are identical, but the customary time line is relatively predictable (see Figure 2-1). Potential candidates maneuver for position during the one or two years preceding the election. Selection of convention delegates begins in January and February of the election year, with conventions typically scheduled first for the out party (the one seeking the White House): in 2004, July 26–29 in Boston for the Democrats, and August 30–September 2 in New York for the Republicans. Traditionally, the general election campaign begins on Labor Day and runs until election day, the first Tuesday following the first Monday in November, but modern campaigns really begin once the identity of major party nominees becomes clear, generally in March and April. Unlike in 2000, voters usually know the winner on election night, and the mid-December balloting by electors in their state capitals is automatic. Finally, the electors' ballots are officially tabulated the first week in January during a joint session of the U.S. Congress, presided over by the incumbent vice president. The duly elected president is inaugurated on January 20, a date set in the Twentieth Amendment.

Figure 2-1   The 2004 Presidential Contest Time Line

2003
  Stage 1
  Defining the pool
  of eligible candidates		

2004	**Jan.**	Federal matching funds provided to qualified candidates (1/2/04) District of Columbia non-binding primary (1/13/04) Iowa, first caucus (1/19/04) New Hampshire, first primary (1/27/04)

Stage 2
  Nomination
  (delegate selection,
  caucus-conventions,
  and primaries)
	Feb.
	Mar.
	Apr.
	May
	June
		Super Tuesday (2/3/04)
		Mega Tuesday (3/2/04)
		
		Last primaries (6/18/04)

Party conventions	**July** **Aug.**	Democratic convention, Boston (7/26–7/29/04) Republican convention, New York City (8/30–9/2/04)
Stage 3 General election campaign	**Sept.** **Oct.** **Nov.**	Labor Day (9/6/04) Election day (11/2/04)

Stage 4
  Validation in electoral college
	Dec.	Electoral college balloting,
		  state capitals (12/13/04)

2005	**Jan.**	Electoral college results, joint session
		  of Congress (1/6/05)
		  Inauguration day (1/20/05)

Defining the Pool of Eligibles

Who is eligible to serve as president? The formal rules relating to qualifications are minimal and have been remarkably stable over time. Individuals need to meet only three requirements, set forth in Article 2, Section 1, of the Constitution. One must be a "natural-born" citizen, at least thirty-five years of age, and a resident of the United States for fourteen years or longer.[11] In 2000, approximately 125 million Americans met these constitutional requirements, but the pool of plausible candidates is far smaller.[12]

The informal requirements for the presidency are less easily satisfied. People who entertain presidential ambitions must have what is generally called *political availability,* that is, the political experiences and personal characteristics that make them attractive to political activists and to the general voting public. Potential candidates accumulate these credentials through personal and career decisions made long before the election year. However, there is no explicit checklist of qualifications for the presidency. The closest one can come to determining what particular political experiences and personal characteristics put an individual in line for a nomination is by looking at past candidates. Even this approach poses some difficulties because the attitudes of political leaders and the public change over time.

Political Experience of Candidates

Who is nominated to run for president? Overwhelmingly, the answer is people with experience in one of a few civilian, elective, political offices. Nominees' backgrounds have changed very little since the last half of the nineteenth century.[13] Since 1932, with only two exceptions, nominees have been drawn from one of four positions: the presidency, the vice presidency, a state governorship, or a U.S. Senate seat. *(See Appendix B.)* Candidates with other backgrounds are seldom successful. For example, in 2000, five aspirants who lacked experience in elected office unsuccessfully sought the Republican nomination. In 1992, H. Ross Perot, a billionaire businessman, sought election without a party nomination and did so again in 1996 as nominee of the Reform Party.

Presidents and Vice Presidents. Since 1932, the party controlling the presidency has turned to the presidency or vice presidency for candidates, while the out party has turned primarily to governors and then to the Senate. In only one of the eighteen elections from 1932 to 2000 has the name of an incumbent president or vice president not been on the ballot, and the same pattern is likely to hold for 2004. Thirteen times, the incumbent president was renominated, and in four of the five instances when the incumbent president was either prohibited by the Twenty-second Amendment from running again (Dwight Eisenhower in 1960, Ronald Reagan in 1988, and Bill Clinton in 2000) or declined to do so (Harry S. Truman in 1952 and Lyndon Baines Johnson in 1968), the incumbent vice president won his party's nomination. The exception occurred in 1952, when Truman chose not to run for reelection, and Adlai Stevenson became the nominee rather than the vice president, seventy-five-year-old Alben Barkley.

There are no guarantees that an incumbent president will win the party's nomination, but it is enormously difficult for the party in power to remove these leaders from the national ticket. Incumbents have considerable advantages when it comes to winning the nomination, as demonstrated by Gerald Ford in 1976, Jimmy Carter in 1980, and George Bush in 1992. Party leaders are reluctant to admit they made a mistake four years earlier; incumbents can direct federal programs toward politically important areas or make politically useful executive branch appointments; and presidents enjoy far greater media exposure than others seeking the nomination. As a result, even unpopular presidents tend to be renominated. The Republicans chose Ford despite an energy crisis and slow economy; the Democrats renominated Carter when both inflation and unemployment were high, Americans were being held hostage in Iran, and Soviet troops occupied Afghanistan; and Bush was renominated in 1992 despite a weakening economy and charges that he broke a campaign pledge not to raise taxes. With no evidence of a challenge within his own party, George W. Bush expects renomination in 2004.

Incumbent vice presidents are more likely to win their party's nomination today than in the past.[14] Recent presidential candidates have chosen running mates who are arguably more capable than their predecessors, which makes these individuals more viable prospects for the presidency. Moreover, presidents now assign their vice presidents meaningful responsibilities, including political party activities (especially campaigning in off-year elections), liaison assignments with social groups, and diplomatic missions abroad. As the position's visibility and significance have increased, so have the political chances of its occupants improved.[15]

If it was an asset in securing the party's nomination, the vice presidency seemed a liability in winning the general election until George Bush's victory in 1988 broke a 152-year-old tradition of losing campaigns. Richard Nixon and Hubert Humphrey lost as incumbent vice presidents in 1960 and 1968, and Al Gore suffered a similar fate in 2000, despite winning a popular vote plurality.

Senators and Governors. From 1932 through 2000, the party out of power nominated ten governors, four senators, two former vice presidents, one general (Eisenhower), and one businessman (Wendell Willkie). (See Table 2-1.) Both major parties have looked to governors as promising candidates, except for the period from 1960 to 1972, when Sens. John Kennedy (D-1960), Barry Goldwater (R-1964), and George McGovern (D-1972), as well as former vice president Nixon (R-1968), won the nomination. Governorships later regained prominence with the nomination of former governors Carter (D-1976) and Reagan (R-1980) as well as sitting governors Michael Dukakis (D-1988), Bill Clinton (D-1992), and George W. Bush (R-2000). Only twice in the past seven elections did the party out of power not turn to a governor: former vice president Walter Mondale was the Democratic nominee in 1984, and Senate majority leader Robert Dole was the Republican nominee in 1996.

It is possible to argue that these patterns understate the importance of the Senate as a recruiting ground for president. Certainly, many senators have sought their parties' presidential nomination since the early 1950s. Senators share the political and media spotlight focused on the capital, enjoy the opportunity to address major public problems and develop a record in foreign affairs, and usually can pursue the presidency without giving up their legislative seat. Nonetheless, only twice in American history have senators been elected directly to the White House (Warren Harding in 1920 and Kennedy in 1960).[16]

Instead of serving as a steppingstone to the presidency, the Senate has often been one to the vice presidency, which then gave its occupants the inside track either to assume the presidency through succession or to win nomination on their own. This role of the Senate can be seen in the careers of Vice Presidents Truman, Nixon, Johnson, Humphrey, Mondale, Quayle, and Gore, who served as senators immediately before assuming their executive posts. (Interestingly, Gerald Ford, who succeeded to the presidency when Nixon resigned in 1974, had moved into the vice presidency from the House of Representatives. Dick Cheney, who was elected vice president in 2000, had served in the House before becoming secretary of defense and then becoming a businessman.) Service in the

Table 2-1   Principal Experience of In- and Out-Party Candidates
Before Gaining Nomination, 1932–2000

Election year	In party	Out party
1932	President (R)	Governor (D)
1936	President (D)	Governor (R)
1940	President (D)	Businessman (R)
1944	President (D)	Governor (R)
1948	President (D)	Governor (R)
1952	Governor (D)	General/educator (R)
1956	President (R)	Governor (former) (D)
1960	Vice president (R)	Senator (D)
1964	President (D)	Senator (R)
1968	Vice president (D)	Vice president (former) (R)
1972	President (R)	Senator (D)
1976	President (R)	Governor (former) (D)
1980	President (D)	Governor (former) (R)
1984	President (R)	Vice president (former) (D)
1988	Vice president (R)	Governor (D)
1992	President (R)	Governor (D)
1996	President (D)	Senator (R)
2000	Vice president (D)	Governor (R)

Senate, therefore, has been an important source of experience for presidents since 1932, but almost all have needed seasoning in the vice presidency.

Historically, governors seeking the presidency confronted major obstacles. It was difficult for them to gain national publicity unless they served in states with large cities that functioned as national media centers. Nor did governors have responsibilities of consequence in foreign affairs; instead, they were more closely tied to their home states, particularly when the state legislature was in session, than were senators. Laws often imposed term limits or governors were defeated for reelection because of public disappointment at their failure to solve major domestic problems without increasing taxes. Becoming sufficiently well known to be a viable presidential candidate was a major task.

Today, governors seem to have a competitive advantage over senators. Two of the last five presidents—Clinton and George W. Bush—moved directly into the Oval Office from a governor's mansion. Two others—Carter and Reagan—were former governors who were free to devote themselves full time to the demanding task of winning the nomination, an opportunity not available to the senators who sought the presidency in those years. Governors can claim valuable executive experience in managing large-scale public enterprises and thousands of state government employees in contrast to a senator's essentially legislative duties and direction of a small personal staff. Moreover, the public's concern with foreign affairs declined after 1976 and was replaced by anxiety over the domestic economy, taxes, the budget, education, and health care. This shift in public attitudes was especially evident in 1992 and 2000, when Clinton and George W. Bush benefited from the cold war's reduced prominence during their successful election campaigns. With the terrorist attacks of September 11, 2001, public concerns once again shifted to national security, and one might expect Senators to once again gain precedence over governors in the nomination contest.

Among those who announced campaigns for the 2004 Democratic presidential nomination by mid-2003, senators outnumbered governors five to one. Four sitting Democratic senators—John Kerry, Mass.; John Edwards, N.C.; Joseph Lieberman, Conn.; and Bob Graham, Fla.—had announced their candidacies, as had former senator Carol Moseley Braun, Ill. Howard Dean, former governor of Vermont, was the sole candidate with executive experience. In addition to these candidates, three others launched campaigns in the first half of the year: Reps. Richard Gephardt, Mo., and Dennis Kucinich, Ohio, were joined by Reverend Al Sharpton, a minister and civil rights activist. Retired general Wesley Clark, who had served from 1997 to 2000 as NATO Supreme Allied Commander and led Operation Allied Forces in Kosovo, entered th race late: on September 17,2003.

Personal Characteristics of Candidates

Although millions meet the formal requirements for president, far fewer meet the informal criteria that have guided past choices. Most constraining have been the limits imposed by social conventions on gender and race. So far only males of European heritage have been nominated for president by either of the two major parties, although several women and African Americans have waged national campaigns since 1972, and former representative Geraldine Ferraro of New York was the Democrats' 1984 nominee for vice president. Presidential aspirants also have had to pass other "tests" based on personal characteristics, although these informal requirements have undergone change in the past four decades.[17]

Until 1960, it seemed that candidates had to meet unspoken demographic and religious requirements: that they hail from English ethnic stock and practice a Protestant religion. The successful candidacy of John Kennedy, a Roman Catholic, in 1960, challenged the traditional preference for Protestants. (Alfred Smith, also a Catholic, was nominated by the Democrats in 1928 but lost the general election.) Today, little is made of the fact when Catholics pursue the nomination. The Republican senator Barry Goldwater was the first nominee from a partly Jewish background, and Sen. Joseph Lieberman, an Orthodox Jew, joined the Democratic ticket in 2000. Other recent candidates have come from Irish, Norwegian, and Greek heritage, suggesting that the traditional preference for English stock has weakened.

Representing an idealized version of home and family life also seemed essential to winning nomination. These criteria have undergone modest change. Nelson Rockefeller's divorce in 1963 from his wife of more than thirty years and his rapid remarriage virtually ensured the failure of his efforts to win the Republican nomination in 1964 and 1968. The marital status of several later candidates was an issue as well, but then in 1980, Reagan became the first president to have divorced and remarried.

Public attitudes about other moral and ethical questions have become important. Gary Hart's widely reported extramarital affair ended his presidential hopes for 1988, even though he began the campaign as the clear front-runner. Bill Clinton's alleged extramarital relationships and drug use also became issues in 1992. However, allegations of prior drug use and an admission of alcohol abuse did not damage George W. Bush in 2000. Although traditional moral and ethical tests regarding divorce may have changed, it is not clear which standards will continue to receive media attention and elicit public response, particularly in an era when religion and political activism seem to mix more readily than in the past.

Thus several of the informal qualifications applied to the presidency have altered with the passage of time, probably in response to changes in the nomination process itself as well as broader currents in U.S. society. One observer suggests that the proliferation of presidential primaries "provides a forum in which prejudices can be addressed openly."[18] The vice presidential nomination offers a way to confront traditional social views indirectly, as was the case with Ferraro and Lieberman. We might expect something similar to happen with an African American candidate in the near future.

The development of a more common culture and the nationalization of American life in general, brought about by modern communication and transportation, have reduced the importance of parochial concerns—the candidates' religious, ethnic, or geographic background—and increased the emphasis on their experience in the national political arena and their association with national issues. Moreover, as other groups that are still socially or politically disadvantaged—African Americans, women, and immigrants from Asia, Latin America, and eastern and southern Europe—begin to occupy governorships and seats in the U.S. Senate, they will enhance their chances of becoming serious candidates for the presidency.[19]

Competing for the Nomination

Once the pool of eligible candidates is established, the selection process begins. This phase has two major components: choosing delegates to the two parties' national conventions and selecting the nominees at the conventions. By far the more complicated of these steps, the selection of delegates has been the principal focus of party reform efforts since 1968. Prior to the conventions, candidates crisscross the country to win delegates, who then attend the convention to select the party's nominee.

The first primary of 2004 will be held in New Hampshire on January 27, eight days after the Iowa caucuses. Delegate selection will extend into June, when a limited number of states and the District of Columbia will hold primaries, the last of the party contests to choose delegates.[20] Through this complex process, the Republicans will choose about 2,522 delegates, and the Democrats 4,351.[21] Consistent with post-1968 reforms, most delegates will be chosen through primaries.

Millions of Americans participate in primaries: in 2000, for example, 14.66 million voted in Democratic primary elections, and another 20.71 million in Republican primaries.[22] Caucus participation is less easily calculated, but in 1996 nearly 200,000 attended seven Republican caucuses.[23]

In truth, the nomination contest begins much earlier than January of the election year. For example, in pursuing the 1988 nomination, former Delaware governor Pierre "Pete" DuPont officially declared his candidacy in September 1986; thirteen others followed suit in 1987, nine before the Fourth of July. By starting their campaigns early, candidates hope to amass the financial backing, attract the media attention, and generate the popular support necessary to ensure eventual victory. On May 30, 2002, former governor Howard Dean became the first candidate to indicate he would seek the 2004 nomination. Perhaps the key event in setting the field, however, occurred in mid-December 2002, when former vice president Al Gore shocked the political world by announcing he would not seek a rematch with President Bush. In the wake of Gore's announcement, eight more candidates quickly emerged, and President Bush announced his campaign for renomination on May 16, 2003.

The Nomination Campaign

The nomination campaign is a winnowing process in which each of the two major parties eliminates from the pool of potential candidates all but the one who will represent the party in the general election. As the political scientist Austin Ranney points out, the nomination phase of the campaign is more important than the election stage because "the parties' nominating processes eliminate far more presidential possibilities than do the voters' electing processes."[24] A nomination campaign is long, arduous, and relatively unstructured: aspirants typically do not know how many opponents they will face or who they will be; candidates start two or more years early and drop out along the way. Instead of a simultaneous nationwide campaign, the competition historically has taken place in weekly stages, with candidates hopscotching the nation in pursuit of votes, though that schedule has been changing. Planning and conducting such a campaign are enormously difficult tasks. Most first-time candidates must organize a nationwide political effort, a chore that dwarfs the campaign required to win a Senate seat or governorship in even the largest states.

Preliminary planning is essential, and presidential hopefuls spend considerable time before January of the election year laying the groundwork. Journalist Arthur Hadley called this period the "invisible primary," a testing ground for the would-be president to determine whether his or her candidacy is viable.[25] Candidates must assemble a staff to help raise money, develop campaign strategy, hone a message, and identify a larger group of people willing to do the advance work necessary to organize states for the primaries and caucuses. Visits are made to party organizations throughout the country, especially in pivotal early states such as Iowa and New Hampshire, to curry favor with activists. Competition often takes on the trappings of a full-fledged campaign, with candidates broadcasting television ads, engaging in debates, and seeking to finish well in prenomination popularity contests known as straw polls.

Because the media's coverage provides name recognition and potentially positive publicity, developing a favorable relationship with reporters and commentators is crucial. Those hopefuls the media ignores because they do not regard them as serious contenders find it almost impossible to become viable candidates. Adverse publicity can seriously damage a candidacy. Most candidates' campaigns are scuttled during the "invisible primary" stage.

Financing Nomination Campaigns

It is more important than ever that candidates for the nomination begin raising funds early. They can qualify to receive federal funds that match individual contributions of $250 or less if they can raise $100,000 in individual contributions, with at least $5,000 collected in twenty different states. By checking a box on their federal income tax forms, taxpayers authorize the government to set aside $3.00 of their tax payments for public financing of campaigns—a system introduced in the 1976 election. (Participation in this system has dropped from 25.5 percent of all tax returns in 1976 to only 11.8 percent in 2000, resulting in recurrent shortfalls.)[26] Candidates who accept public financing—and since 1976 only John Connally, Steve Forbes, Maurice Taylor, Orrin Hatch, and George W. Bush, all Republicans, have chosen not to do so—must also accept limitations on total expenditures and a cap on spending in individual states that is based on population. For 2000, the national expenditure ceiling for the prenomination campaign was $45.6 million, up from $37.1 million in 1996.[27] That figure was adjusted upward for inflation in 2004.

By providing partial funding of nomination campaigns, congressional reformers in the 1970s sought to establish a system of broad-based citizen contributions, replacing the financial support of a small number of "fat cats," who previously bankrolled candidates.[28] In 2000, ten candidates qualified for $57.74 million in matching funds, up from $55.95 million in 1996.[29] The federal government also provided $13.512 million to the Democratic and Republican Parties to finance their nominating conventions, but this constitutes a minor portion of the total cost.[30] The Federal Election Commission (FEC), a bipartisan body of six members nominated by the president and confirmed by the Senate, oversees the administration of these provisions.

Personal money played an unprecedented role in the prenomination stage of the 1996 campaign. Steve Forbes loaned his campaign $37.5 million, and Maurice Taylor spent $6.5 million of his own resources. Neither was ultimately successful, but Forbes dramatically influenced the Republican nomination process by outspending his rivals in several early contests. Because he received no public funds, Forbes was not subject to the state spending limits imposed on his competitors. He launched a $12.5 million media blitz during the last three months of 1995 that concentrated on Iowa, New Hampshire, and other early events. Even Bob Dole, who led all candidates in fund-raising, could not match such expenditures since he had to observe federal limits.[31] This experience partly shaped Bush's strategy in 2000. Anticipating that Forbes would pursue a similar tactic the second time around, Bush raised a record $94 million in private funds, double that of Forbes and McCain, his closest competitors, and therefore had to observe none of the spending limits associated with public funding.[32] For 2004, the Bush campaign planned to double that fund-raising effort, not to combat nonexistent Republican challengers but to gain an advantage against the Democratic nominee during the March to August period prior to the conventions.

In the postreform era, most candidates raise funds from a large number of individual contributors, often through direct mail solicitation.[33] In 2000, for the first time, contributions made through the Internet were important, especially for McCain and Bradley. In early 2003, former governor Dean was benefiting most from contributions made online. Public funds open the door for candidates who formerly could not afford to mount a nomination campaign because large contributors would not support them. However, while public funds have reduced financial disparities among candidates, their financial resources are still highly unequal, and the field's leading fund-raiser almost always wins the nomination.[34]

Superior financial resources enable candidates to compete in more of the early nomination contests, help them extend their fund-raising lead, make it possible to survive poor results (such as Bush's loss of New Hampshire in 2000), and make them stronger in later primaries. Failing to do well in early caucus and primary contests means more than losing delegates to opponents; it also means that contributions stop. Moreover, under the campaign finance law, federal matching funds must be cut off within thirty days if a candidate receives less than 10 percent of the votes in two consecutive primaries. Leading Republican candidates in 1995 worked aggressively to reach the target of $20 million in contributions by year's end, the consensus target among political consultants on what it would take to run a "serious" campaign.[35] Bush's record fund-raising in 2000 dramatically raised that threshold so that in planning for 2004, Democratic candidates were anticipating a $30 million threshold as Bush aimed for $200 million.[36]

Approaching the 2004 election, candidates confronted a remarkably uncertain campaign finance picture. In March 2002, Congress adopted, and President Bush signed into law, the Bipartisan Campaign Reform Act of 2002 (BCRA), the final product of multiyear reform efforts by Sens. John McCain, R-Ariz., and Russ Feingold, D-Wis., and Reps. Christopher Shays, R-Conn., and Martin Meehan, D-Mass. Most of the reforms focus on congressional elections, but many observers believe the changes may have exacerbated, rather than solved, problems in financing presidential elections. The Campaign Finance Institute convened a blue-ribbon task force in July 2002 on Financing Presidential Nominations.[37] Because the two major parties have frontloaded their nomination contests in the past few election cycles, candidates reached the spending limit and secured a majority of delegates early in the campaign, several months before the convention. Parties used soft money as a way to pay for the presumed nominee's campaign during this middle period, a practice made illegal by the BCRA, though the provisions confront a constitutional challenge, *McConnell et. al. v. The Federal Election Commission et. al.* The Supreme Court heard oral arguments in the case on September 8, 2003. The new law allows individuals to contribute more (increased to $2,000 from the previous $1,000)[38] but fails to increase the portion eligible for matching funds beyond the $250 limit in place since 1976.

The net result is a public funding and primary system that creates strong incentives for candidates not to take public funds. The new system will favor very wealthy candidates or ones who—like George W. Bush in 2000—can tap established networks of major donors during the "invisible primary" before Iowa and New Hampshire, raising enough money early to avoid public funding and sail through to the end. The calendar and funding system rules will also favor front-runners, making it hard for primary voters to give others a second look.[39]

Candidates must decide not only how to raise funds but also how to spend them. In the face of overall campaign spending limits as well as expenditure limits in each state, money must be carefully allocated. Because they want to win the first primaries and caucuses, candidates are inclined to spend heavily in the very early stage of the campaign, which can create problems in later competition. This was an especially pressing problem for Dole in 1996, when he nearly reached the spending limit by April, fully three months before the convention.

Dynamics of the Contest

Candidates who begin the election year as leaders in the public opinion polls frequently go on to win nomination. This pattern prevailed from 1936 through 1968, was interrupted in four Democratic contests between 1972 and 1992, but returned in the 1990s.[40] In the last two elections, early leaders won the nomination in both parties, Bill Clinton and Bob Dole in 1996, and Al Gore and George W. Bush in 2000. Leaders in the polls must guard against verbal slips, personal indiscretions, and the assumption that early popularity is permanent.

When deciding which contests they should emphasize in their nomination campaigns, candidates take into account the premium placed on competing in as many locations as funds will allow. This is especially true for Democrats, whose rules call for proportional allocation of delegates: as long as candidates achieve at least 15 percent of the vote, they are awarded a share of delegates proportional to the vote share.[41] The earliest contests, traditionally the Iowa caucuses and New Hampshire primary, attract most of the major contenders because they are the first tests of rank-and-file voter sentiment. Although the number of New Hampshire delegates is small, victory ensures immediate attention, as it did for Kennedy in 1960 and Carter in 1976. Pat Buchanan was the surprise winner in 1996, with a slim 1 percent victory margin over Dole, and McCain defeated George W. Bush in 2000 by the relatively wide margin of 48.5 to 30.4 percent. As was the case for McCain, the relatively small New Hampshire electorate enables candidates with more modest financial resources to conduct labor-intensive campaigns.

A new twist in the 1988 campaign was the large number of primaries held on Tuesday, March 8—a day consequently known as Super Tuesday. Twenty states selected delegates, sixteen through primaries and four through caucuses. In 1992, only eleven states participated in Super Tuesday, but the Democratic designers accomplished their goal of boosting the chances of a moderate candidate when Clinton won all six of the southern primaries and two caucuses, while Paul Tsongas, his principal rival, claimed victories in just two primaries and one caucus. George Bush, who swept all sixteen of the 1988 Super Tuesday primaries, repeated this success in March 1992. Likewise, Dole won all seven Super Tuesday primaries in 1996.

The competitive situation was more complex in 2000. Super Tuesday was March 14, when the focus was on southern contests, but March 7 was an even bigger prize—variously dubbed "Titanic" and "Mega" Tuesday by the media— when eleven states, including California and New York, held both Republican and Democratic primaries and five additional states held Democratic primaries. (Many states had moved their contests forward in the calendar, producing a *front-loaded* schedule.) More than one-quarter of the Republican convention delegates and more than one-third of the Democratic delegates were chosen on this single day.[42] The front-runner, Al Gore, defeated Bradley in all primary contests on both days, clinching the nomination by mid-March. In 2000, the real showdown between Bush and McCain occurred in South Carolina, nearly three weeks after the New Hampshire primary but before the March contests. Both Republican candidates targeted the state as crucial, and the campaign turned negative. Bush emerged with a 53 to 42 percent victory. Although McCain scored several later victories, Bush won the larger contests on Titanic Tuesday, prompting McCain to withdraw from the race even before Super Tuesday, resulting in a clean sweep for Bush in the southern primaries.

Primaries held later in the election calendar once played an important role in nomination contests. Until 1996, California scheduled its primary on the final day of delegate selection, giving Golden State voters the chance to determine a party's nominee, as with Goldwater in 1964 and McGovern in 1972. With the early selection of a nominee in 1996, new Republican rules were adopted that encouraged states to schedule their primaries later in 2000 by providing them with bonus delegates.[43] But the schedule was only slightly less front-loaded in 2000, and the contests were concluded earlier than ever—March 9, when both McCain and Bradley, the number-two candidate in each party, discontinued their campaigns.

As the 2004 primary calendar began to emerge, a similar competitive schedule seemed certain. The two parties set a "window" for delegate selection that ran from February 3 to June 8. Two exceptions were Iowa and New Hampshire, where candidates engage in "retail" politics, meeting with voters on a more personal basis than is possible in larger states, where candidates must rely on media advertising in practicing "wholesale" politics. The Iowa caucuses were scheduled for January 19 and the New Hampshire primary for January 27. Scheduling questions lingered, however; after the District of Columbia scheduled its nonbinding primary for January 13 to dramatize the demand for statehood, New Hampshire decided not to move its event earlier but could still decide otherwise. Unlike 2000, when Democrats had nearly five weeks of inaction after New Hampshire, the party scheduled a number of critical events for February, including important primaries in Arizona, Delaware, Missouri, South Carolina, Virginia, and Wisconsin, as well as caucuses in Michigan, New Mexico, and Washington. As in other years, states positioned themselves as early in the process as possible, and more states than ever wanted their contests before March 2, when California, New York, and Texas, among others, would hold their primaries.[44]

State caucuses operate in the shadow of the primaries, although they remain important for candidates able to mobilize an intensely motivated group of supporters who can exert greater influence than in a primary. The Iowa caucus, long the initial delegate selection contest, has diminished in importance as a launching pad for presidential contenders. McCain sidestepped Iowa altogether in 2000 to focus on New Hampshire. When primaries do not produce a clear victor, candidates devote more attention to delegates chosen in caucus-convention states, as in the 1976 Republican contest and the 1984 Democratic race, but the role of caucuses has been steadily declining.

Media Influence and Campaign Consultants

The media play an enormous role in the nomination campaign. "For most of us, the combination of media coverage and media advertising *is* the campaign; few voters see the candidates in person or involve themselves directly in campaign events."[45] As the nomination process has grown in complexity, the influence of the media also has grown. Candidates who must campaign in a score of states within two weeks, as they did in 1992, 1996, and 2000, necessarily rely on the media to communicate with large numbers of potential voters. Televised advertisements, network- and station-sponsored debates, and prime-time news coverage are critical to candidates' efforts. Even talk-show appearances became an important communication link in the 1990s.

The media tend to focus on the game aspects of the preelection-year maneuvering and the early contests. As candidates begin to emerge, journalists concentrate on the race for financial contributions, the reputations of professionals enlisted to work on a campaign, and speculations about the candidates' relative chances of success based on polls and nonbinding straw votes in various states. Once the delegate selection contests begin, the media focus on political tactics, strategy, and competitive position more than on the candidates' messages and issue stands, particularly in coverage of Iowa, New Hampshire, and the compressed schedule of contests in March. In general, the media use a winner-take-all principle that, regardless of how narrow the victory or the number of popular votes involved, gives virtually all the publicity to the victorious candidate. In the 1976 Iowa caucuses, for example, Carter was declared the "clear winner" and described as leading the pack of contenders even though he received only about 14,000 votes, 28 percent of the 50,000 cast; he actually trailed the "uncommitted" group.[46] Gore defeated Bradley in the 2000 New Hampshire primary by a mere 49.7 to 45.6 percent, but Bradley's narrow loss was a less important story than Gore's victory.[47] A surprise showing by a runner-up, however, may garner the most attention: after winning a mere 16 percent of the votes to finish an unexpected second in the Iowa caucuses in 1984, Hart got as much publicity as Mondale, who captured three times as many votes.[48]

As the fate of presidential candidates has passed from a small group of party professionals to rank-and-file voters, media-based appeals have grown in importance. Voter attitudes evolve during the course of the nomination contest, in large part because of the media's influence. The media help determine who the viable candidates are, label the "winners" and "losers," and influence the results of future contests as voters, as well as contributors, gravitate toward the winners and desert the losers. Public opinion polls reflecting voters' presidential preferences are a fixture of media coverage. Favorable polls impress media representatives as well as political activists and many rank-and-file voters, leading to more victories for the poll leaders in both nonprimary and primary contests. The result of this reinforcement process is that by the time the delegates gather for their party's national convention, one candidate usually has enough delegates to receive the nomination.[49]

The National Convention

No part of the selection process has undergone more dramatic change than the nominating conventions. Long the province of party leaders, today's conventions are largely media extravaganzas choreographed to project images designed to reawaken party loyalty, appeal to contemporary public concerns, and project the most desirable aspects of the newly anointed presidential ticket. In short, the convention is important for two reasons. First, whatever may have happened during the long search for delegates, the actual nomination occurs at the convention. Second, a well-run convention can boost a candidate's chances in the general election.

Nominating the Ticket

Since the early 1950s, conventions have offered little drama about the choice of the presidential nominee. In the twenty-eight conventions held by the two major parties from 1948 through 2000, only two nominees—Thomas Dewey in 1948 and Adlai Stevenson in 1952—failed to win a majority of the convention votes on the first ballot. In all other cases, victory has gone to the candidate who arrived at the convention with the largest number of pledged delegates. Nonetheless, there is an air of excitement that still surrounds the traditional balloting.

Selecting the vice presidential nominee is the convention's final chore and the only chance to create any suspense. Although in theory the delegates make the choice, it has been a matter of political custom since 1940 to allow presidential nominees to pick their own running mates after conferring with leaders whose judgment they trust. Parties traditionally attempt to balance the ticket—that is, broaden its appeal by selecting a person who differs in helpful ways from the presidential nominee. George Bush's links to the eastern establishment and moderate wings of the Republican Party complemented the conservative, western Reagan in 1980. Ferraro balanced the 1984 Democratic ticket geographically and in other ways: the first woman to serve as a major party candidate in a presidential contest, she was also the first Italian American.

In 1988, Dan Quayle brought generational balance to the ticket, and he was enthusiastically supported by the party's conservative wing. But the media raised questions about Quayle's ability to perform as president should the need arise, his service in the National Guard during the Vietnam War, and his modest academic performance. Quayle remained on the Republican ticket in 1992 despite speculation about his replacement. Clinton violated political tradition by selecting Al Gore, a fellow southerner and baby boomer, but the choice was well received by the party faithful and probably helped Clinton erode Republican support in this crucial region. For the 1996 election, Dole chose Jack Kemp, a one-time presidential candidate who was highly popular with Republican activists. In 2000, George W. Bush asked Dick Cheney to join the ticket. Although a fellow western conservative, Cheney brought extensive Washington and White House experience to offset Bush's inexperience. In what the media described as a "bold" move, Gore added Joseph Lieberman to the ticket, thus breaking a long-existent barrier to having a practicing Jew on a national ticket. Lieberman's early criticism of Clinton's personal conduct also helped Gore to further distance himself from the incumbent president.

The final night of the convention is devoted to acceptance speeches. The presidential nominee tries to make peace with former competitors and to reunite party factions that have confronted one another during the long campaign and the hectic days of the convention. Major party figures usually come to the stage and pledge their support.

Conducting Party Business

Parties continue the writing and adopting of a convention platform, although participants acknowledge that winning presidential candidates may disavow planks with which they disagree. Because delegates, party leaders, and major groups affiliated with the party have strong feelings about some issues, the platform provides an opportunity to resolve differences and find a politically palatable position.[50] Civil rights and the Vietnam War once prompted major disagreements within the Democratic Party; civil rights, foreign policy, and abortion have been major bones of contention among Republicans.

Despite intraparty differences, conventions provide strong incentives for compromise, to bring back to the fold a disgruntled segment of the party that might otherwise offer only lukewarm support during the fall election or launch a third-party effort. To avoid such damage, almost every presidential candidate decides to provide major rivals and their supporters with concessions in the platform and a prime-time speaking opportunity during the convention. Occasionally, this tactic can backfire. At the Republican convention in 1992, Pat Buchanan was given an opportunity to address a national audience, but his address proved so controversial that the invitation was not extended four years later.

National nominating conventions have become so predictable that network television coverage was dramatically reduced in 1996 and 2000. To obtain the traditional "gavel to gavel" coverage that ushered in the television age, viewers had to follow proceedings on cable networks such as CNN or on the Internet, where more than fifty outlets had a presence at the conventions. Parties may have become so adept at scripting these quadrennial gatherings that their very existence is jeopardized.[51]

The General Election

With nominees selected, the nation moves into the general election period. Candidates must develop new political appeals for this stage, primarily a one-on-one contest between the nominees of the two major parties (although a strong independent candidate such as Ross Perot in 1992 and 1996 may also run). The campaign's audience increases greatly: more than twice as many people vote in the general election as participate in the nomination process. Candidates and staff must decide how they can win the support of these new voters as well as appeal to people who identify with the other party and partisans who backed losing candidates for the nomination. A further complication is time: this nationwide phase of the presidential contest is compressed into ten weeks, traditionally running from Labor Day to election day.

The general election phase differs from the nomination phase for two reasons: the way the electoral college works and the distinctive provisions of the campaign finance laws. Compared with changes effected in the nomination stage, the constitutional requirements surrounding the president's election have been remarkably stable over time, but campaign finance laws have undergone significant change since 1972. Both the college and the laws are critical considerations in how the campaign is waged.

The Electoral College

To understand how candidates plan and carry out their general election strategies, it is necessary to keep in mind the ultimate goal: winning a majority of electoral college votes (those cast by state electors). At first, electoral votes were determined by congressional districts. The winner of a popular vote plurality in each district would receive the associated electoral vote, with the statewide winner of the popular vote getting the two electoral votes representing senators. However, legislatures soon began to adopt the "unit" or "general-ticket" rule, whereby all the state's electoral votes went to the candidate who received the plurality of the statewide popular vote. This rule benefited the state's majority party and maximized the state's influence in the election by permitting it to throw all its electoral votes to one candidate. By 1836, the unit system had replaced the district plan. Since then, two states have returned to the old plan: Maine in 1969, and Nebraska in 1992.

The final product is a strange method for choosing a chief executive. Although most Americans view the system as a popular election, it is not. When voters mark their ballots, the vote actually determines which slate of electors pledged to support the party's presidential candidate will vote. In a few states, electors' names appear on the ballot with or without the candidate's name. The electors are party loyalists, chosen in primaries, at conventions, or by state committees. In mid-December, the electors associated with the winning candidate meet in their state capitals to cast ballots. (Twenty-seven states and the District of Columbia attempt by law to bind the electors to vote for the winner of the popular vote, but there is some question whether such laws are constitutional.)[52] The electoral votes are transmitted to Washington, D.C., and counted in early January. Next, the presiding officer of the Senate—the incumbent vice president—announces the outcome before a joint session of Congress. If, as usually happens, one candidate receives an absolute majority of the electoral votes, currently 270, the vice president officially declares that candidate president. Because the winner of the popular vote usually wins in the electoral college as well, we call this final stage of the selection process the "validation" of the popular vote outcome. For candidates who win without a popular vote plurality, as George W. Bush did in 2000, the electoral college may validate a victory but not necessarily provide legitimacy.

Financing the General Election

The financial resources needed to mount a nationwide campaign are significantly greater than those required to win the nomination. For the general election, complete public financing is provided to nominees of the major parties; any party that won 25 percent or more of the popular vote in the last presidential election is considered a major party. In the 2000 presidential election, the federal government gave each major party candidate $67.56 million, up from $61.8 million in 1996, and that figure will be adjusted for inflation in 2004.[53] Candidates of minor parties, those that won between 5 percent and 25 percent of the vote in the previous election, receive partial public financing and can raise private funds up to the major party limit. Candidates whose parties are just getting started or did not win at least 5 percent of the vote in the previous election receive no help, a major disadvantage. Ross Perot sought no federal funds in 1992 but spent an estimated $63 million of his own money to mount a major campaign effort. In 1996, however, he accepted $29 million in federal funds and was limited to using only $50,000 of his own money in the general election. As the official Reform Party nominee in 2000, Pat Buchanan received $12.6 million as a result of Perot's 8.4 percent share of the vote in 1996. But the party will be ineligible for public funding in 2004 after Buchanan's poor showing of 0.43 percent. Candidates of parties that won less than 5 percent of the vote in the previous election can be partially reimbursed after the current election if they receive at least 5 percent of that vote. Ralph Nader of the Green Party came closest to this goal with a 2.7 percent share of the national vote in 2000, achieved with $3.3 million in private contributions.

Campaign expenditures other than those from public funding may be paid by two sources. Until adoption of the BCRA in 2002, there had been no limit on *independent campaign expenditures,* which are made by individuals or political committees that advocate the defeat or election of a presidential candidate but are not made in conjunction with a candidate's campaign. The new law prohibits corporations and labor unions from spending treasury funds on candidate-specific ads close to an election.[54] In addition, BCRA placed new limits on fund-raising and spending by state and local party organizations. Until 1996, party organizations raised funds, commonly called *soft money,* that had largely been used for grassroots activities such as distributing campaign buttons, stickers, and yard signs; registering voters; and transporting voters to the polls. Spending from these sources has varied: between 1988 and 1992, independent expenditures declined from $10.1 million to about $4 million, while soft money expenditures remained steady at $42.5 million.[55] However, in 1996, the Democratic and Republican Parties enormously expanded their use of soft money to fund *issue advocacy* campaigns, media advertisements that do not expressly support or oppose a candidate but ostensibly educate the public about an issue or a candidate's position on an issue. The Democratic National Committee launched an aggressive series of such ads in mid-1995, designed to help Clinton even before the nomination contests began. When Dole ran short of money in late spring 1996, the Republican National Committee stepped in with a similar campaign to help their expected standard-bearer. The two parties spent a combined total of more than $65 million in these efforts. In 2000, these activities grew even larger: the national parties spent more for television advertising in the presidential election than did the candidates.[56] Most of these efforts were targeted on a short list of key "battleground states," including California, Michigan, Missouri, Ohio, Pennsylvania, and Tennessee. In Florida, the key to Bush's victory, pro-Bush expenditures exceeded those for Gore by about $4 million. In 2000, independent expenditures by political groups favored Gore by a margin of seven to one, with Planned Parenthood leading the way.[57] The BCRA "prohibits federal candidates and officeholders, and groups they control, from raising, directing or spending soft money" and will presumably bring to a halt the activities triggered by Clinton's aggressive fund-raising in 1995–1996.[58]

Until recently, the system of public financing introduced in the 1976 election was viewed as a success: major party candidates no longer depended on wealthy contributors and other private sources to finance their campaigns; expenditures of the two major party candidates were limited and equalized, an advantage for

Democrats who were historically outspent by their opponents.[59] The 1996 and 2000 experiences with soft money have called into question the adequacy of current regulations and their future for both presidential and congressional elections. These concerns gave rise to the BiPartisan Campaign Reform Act of 2002.

Targeting the Campaign

As in the nomination process, candidates must decide which states will be the focus of their efforts in the fall campaign. The most important consideration is the electoral college: a candidate must win a majority—270—of the 538 electoral votes.[60] This fact places a premium on carrying the states with the most electoral votes (see Figure 2-2). In 2000, by winning the eleven largest states—California, New York, Texas, Florida, Pennsylvania, Illinois, Ohio, Michigan, New Jersey, North Carolina, and Georgia or Virginia—a candidate could win the presidency while losing the other states and the District of Columbia. Naturally, candidates from both major parties concentrate their personal visits and spending on the most populous states.

Another element affecting candidates' decisions on where to campaign is the chance of winning a particular state. Are the party's candidates generally successful there, or do the results swing back and forth from one election to the next? Distinctly one-party states are likely to be slighted by the major party candidates as a waste of time. Swing states with large populations naturally draw a good deal of attention.

In formulating campaign strategy, therefore, candidates and their advisers start with the electoral map as modified by calculations of probable success. The electoral college creates fifty-one separate presidential contests—fifty states plus the District of Columbia—primarily following the winner-take-all principle, the goal of which is a popular vote victory in each, no matter how small the margin. The winner in a large state benefits from the unit or general-ticket system by getting all the state's electoral votes. In 2000, Bush won Florida by a margin of 537 votes of the 5.94 million legitimate ballots cast.[61] Nonetheless, he won all 25 of the state's electoral votes, giving him a one-vote margin of victory in the electoral college, 271–266.[62] Bush's victory in Florida was not finalized until a controversial 5–4 U.S. Supreme Court decision that reversed the Florida Supreme Court's order for a statewide recount, which led to Gore's final concession on December 13. Gore first conceded on election night after early returns showed him trailing in Florida, but he reversed field a few hours later when totals changed. It took more than a month to resolve the Florida outcome as the nation followed the confusing process of recounts and court maneuvers. *(See the discussion in chapter 7.)*

Electoral votes have been reapportioned for the 2004 presidential election, reflecting the results of the 2000 census and adjusted representation in the House of Representatives. New York and Pennsylvania each lost two House seats. Connecticut, Illinois, Indiana, Michigan, Mississippi, Ohio, Oklahoma, and Wisconsin each lost one. The biggest gainers were Arizona, Florida, Georgia, and

Figure 2-2   State Size by Number of Electoral Votes, 2004

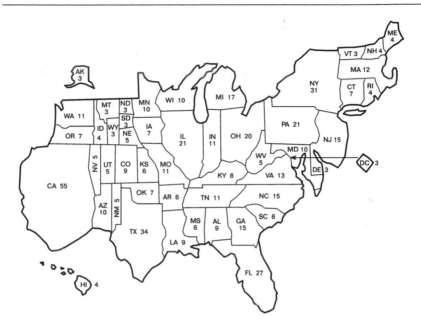

Source: For more information on shifting state electoral vote totals over time see http://uselectionatlas.org/INFORMATION/information.php.

Texas, with two seats each, while California, Colorado, Nevada, and North Carolina each gained one seat.[63]

The regions that have been important in recent presidential contests are the Middle Atlantic states of New Jersey, New York, and Pennsylvania and the Midwest states of Illinois, Michigan, Missouri, and Ohio. These seven industrial states controlled 143 electoral votes in the 1992–2000 elections and also tended to be highly competitive, which means that campaign efforts there have been very important in deciding which candidate prevailed. Because these states are so consistently the focus of campaign efforts, analysts refer to them as the "battleground" states. Although they will have seven fewer electoral votes over the next decade, they will probably remain critical.

In formulating a strategy likely to produce victory, Democratic candidates have recently confronted a difficult strategic problem, most of it due to the historic realignment of the South in presidential politics. For many decades following the Civil War, southern voters were a bastion of solid Democratic support and critical to their candidates' success. Until 1992, no Democrat had ever won the White House without carrying a majority of southern states, but southern voters had not supported the party's nominee since 1976, when they helped to elect Jimmy Carter. Carter was the first southern presidential nominee (other than

Lyndon Johnson, who had succeeded to the office) since before the Civil War. Southern support evaporated in 1980, when only Georgia supported its favorite son. No southern state voted for the Democratic ticket in 1984 or 1988. The Solid South was a Republican stronghold until Clinton cut into Bush's support in 1992 by winning four states: Arkansas, Georgia, Louisiana, and Tennessee. But unlike Carter, Clinton would have won in the electoral college in both 1992 and 1996 without the southern support. In 1992, Clinton amassed 370 electoral votes by winning thirty-two states, each state that had voted for Dukakis in 1988 as well as all but one of the twelve where the previous Democratic nominee had won at least 45 percent of the vote.[64] Clinton totaled 379 electoral votes in 1996, winning twenty-nine of the same states and adding two longtime Republican strongholds—Arizona and Florida.

The tables were turned in 2000. George W. Bush won the entire South, including Gore's home state of Tennessee and Clinton's of Arkansas. All together, eleven states switched columns from 1996, including West Virginia, a Democratic stronghold, Florida, and New Hampshire. In the latter two states, it can be argued that votes cast for Ralph Nader cost Gore the election. Nader's vote came predominantly from liberal Democrats. With his strength in the Northeast, in the upper Midwest, and on the West Coast, Gore could have won the election with either the Granite State's four votes or Florida's twenty-five. But Bush supporters can also argue that votes for Patrick Buchanan, the Reform Party candidate, may have denied Bush victories in New Mexico and Wisconsin and their sixteen electoral votes.[65] *(For 2000 election results, see Appendix A.)*

Appealing for Public Support

Presidential campaigns spend millions of dollars and untold hours pursuing two goals: motivating people to vote and winning their support for a particular candidate. Several factors other than campaign appeals determine who votes and how they vote. Voters' choices depend on their long-term political predispositions, such as party loyalties and social group affiliations, and their reactions to short-term forces, such as the particular candidates and issues involved in specific elections. Candidates and their campaign professionals try to design appeals that activate these influences, attract support, and counter perceived weaknesses.

Because the audience is larger and the time is shorter during the general election period than during the nomination period, candidates use their resources primarily for mass-media appeals. Advertising expenditures have risen accordingly, with campaigns spending half their public funding on radio and television messages. Since 1952, television has been the chief source of campaign information for most Americans. In addition, polls indicate that people are more inclined to believe what they see on television than what they read in the newspapers or hear on the radio. Increasingly, however, advertising is targeted on selected markets in key electoral college states rather than being national in scope, a pattern especially apparent in 2000.

Long-Term Influences. Students of elections have categorized influences on voter decisions as either long-term or short-term. Long-term influences include partisanship and group membership, while the short-term ones include issues, candidate image, and campaign incidents.

Partisan loyalty, although still important for a large part of the public, has become less significant as a determinant of election outcomes. Conditions have changed considerably since researchers studying presidential elections in the 1950s concluded that the single most important determinant of voting was the voter's *party identification.*[66] This general psychological attachment, shaped by family and social groups, tended to intensify with age. For the average person looking for guidance on how to vote amid the complexities of personalities, issues, and events of the 1950s, the party label of the candidates was the most important reference point. Partisanship was also fairly constant: about 45 percent of Americans in 1952 and 1956 said they thought of themselves as Democrats, and about 28 percent viewed themselves as Republicans, for a combined total of nearly three-fourths of the electorate. When asked to classify themselves further as "strong" or "weak" partisans, both Republicans and Democrats tended to divide equally between those two categories. Independents in 1952 and 1956 averaged about 23 percent of the electorate.

In the mid- to late 1960s, however, partisan affiliation in the United States began to change (see Table 2-2). Beginning with the 1968 election, the number of independents started to increase, primarily at the expense of the Democrats; by 1972, independents constituted one-third of the electorate. Even voters who stayed with the Democrats were more inclined than formerly to say they were weak, rather than strong, party members. This trend progressed one step further in 1988, when some polls found that independents outnumbered Democrats. Since 1968, more people also identify themselves as independents than as Republicans. The rise in the number of independents has occurred primarily among younger people, particularly those who entered the electorate in 1964 or later. Voters who have come of age since that time are much more likely to be political independents than voters of earlier political generations, a development that has been linked to the influence of Vietnam and Watergate.

Total partisanship—the combined percentage of citizens declaring themselves Democrats or Republicans—fell to its lowest level between 1972 and 1976, rebounded slightly in the 1980s, and sank again to that level in 1992, with another modest uptick in 1996. (Republicans had scored modest gains of roughly 5 to 10 percent after 1980, gains that offset Democratic losses of the same size. Republican identification rose during the period of their startling success in winning control of Congress in 1994, but then receded to previous levels.) Although the trend away from party affiliation seems to have stopped, the parties have been unable to lure the public back. The percentage of independents has remained strong for nearly three decades. For the 2000 election, Democrats composed 34 percent of the electorate and Republicans 24 percent, with independents at 40 percent. But 15 percent of independents leaned Democratic and

Table 2-2   Party Identification, 1952–2000 (Percent)

Party	1952	1956	1960	1964	1968	1972	1976	1980	1984	1988	1992	1994	1996	1998	2000
Strong Democratic	22	21	20	27	20	15	15	18	17	17	18	15	18	19	19
Weak Democratic	25	23	25	25	25	26	25	23	20	18	18	19	19	18	15
Total	47	44	45	52	45	41	40	41	37	35	36	34	37	37	34
Strong Republican	14	15	16	11	10	10	9	9	12	14	11	16	12	10	12
Weak Republican	14	14	14	14	15	13	14	14	15	14	14	15	15	16	12
Total	27	29	30	25	25	23	23	23	25	28	25	31	27	26	24
Independent	23	23	23	23	30	34	37	34	34	36	38	35	35	36	40

Source: Data drawn from The National Election Studies, Center for Political Studies at the University of Michigan's Institute for Social Research; *The NES Guide to Public Opinion and Electoral Behavior*, Table 2a.1, www.umich.edu/~nes/nesguide/toptable/tab2a_1.htm.

Note: Responses to the question: "Generally speaking, do you usually think of yourself as a Republican, a Democrat, an Independent, or what?"

13 percent leaned Republican.[67] Because partisanship remains an important factor for so many voters, campaigns seek support from their own identifiers by activating traditional loyalties, yet they also attempt to lure identifiers of the other party by blurring traditional themes, a tightrope act that can confuse the general public.

Social group membership is another potentially important influence on voting that candidates try to tap. Patterns of group support established during the New Deal have persisted during succeeding decades, although with decreasing vibrancy. In the 1940s, Democrats received most of their support from southerners, union members, Catholics, and people with limited education, lower incomes, and a working-class background. Northerners, whites, Protestants, and people with more education, higher incomes, and a professional or business background supported Republican candidates. Table 2-3, which is based on Gallup polls, shows the support of various groups on the eve of presidential elections from 1952 through 2000. The support of many groups for their traditional party's candidates declined over that period. The most significant drop for the Democrats came in the southern white vote: in 1988, only one in three white votes went to Dukakis, and only 26 percent of white males supported the Democrat.[68] The only group that significantly increased its support for its traditional party candidate over this period was nonwhites, whose support for Democrats strengthened between 1964 and 1988 but then returned to the 1952 level.[69] In the 2000 election, both election-eve polls and exit polls showed that the racial and gender gaps were especially large. Bush won 53 percent among men but only 43 percent among women, compared with Gore's 42 and 54 percent, respectively. African American support for Bush (8 percent) was among the lowest for any Republican presidential candidate since 1960, and Gore won about two-thirds of the Hispanic vote, although Bush's share was 10 percent higher than that of the 1996 Republican candidate.[70]

Table 2-3 also shows that group preferences can vary greatly from election to election. In 1964, when the very conservative Barry Goldwater was the Republican standard-bearer, all of these groups, including those that typically support the GOP, supported the Democratic candidate, Lyndon Johnson. In 1972, the opposite occurred; when the very liberal George McGovern ran on the Democratic ticket, all the groups that usually sympathize with that party, except for nonwhites, voted for Republican Richard Nixon. In 1992, Bush's support declined from 1988 levels in virtually every category, but the decline was especially marked among men, the college-educated, and baby boomers, the voters between thirty and forty-nine. Dole rebounded among men and the college-educated but not enough for victory in 1996, whereas George W. Bush's victory in 2000 was built on solid support among men, an overwhelming lead among southerners, and substantial improvement among older voters from 1996.

The weakening of party loyalties means candidates must target many groups. Organized labor, far from a monolithic entity, has been seriously divided in recent elections, and both camps have openly courted ethnic groups. Moreover, new groups have emerged as critical factors: women, fundamentalist Christians, young voters, and Hispanics have attracted particular attention. But because many American voters have lost their partisan anchor, short-term influences — such as candidates, issues, events—and presidential performance are now more important to them.

Short-Term Influences. Voters look for many qualities in a president. During the 1984 campaign, for example, the Michigan Center for Political Studies found that Reagan was favored over Mondale on leadership (commands respect, inspires) and integrity (decent, moral), and Mondale was preferred on competence (hard-working, intelligent) and empathy (compassionate).[71]

In a 1988 election day poll, voters concerned with experience and competence overwhelmingly supported Bush, while those who wanted a more caring president and one more likely to introduce change disproportionately supported Dukakis. Those who saw Dukakis as too liberal predictably supported Bush, but those worried about dirty campaigns leaned toward Dukakis.[72] In a 1992 exit poll that asked voters what qualities mattered most in deciding how they voted, more than one-third cited the ability to bring about change, with Clinton winning 67 percent of those votes. He also led among voters concerned about which candidate had the best plan for the nation, cared about people, and had the best vice presidential candidate. Bush led among voters concerned with experience, trustworthiness, and good judgment in a crisis.[73]

In 1996, Dole won 84 percent of those mentioning honesty and trustworthiness (20 percent of respondents), but Clinton won 72–89 percent of those who mentioned caring, having a vision for the future, and being in touch with the 1990s—more than one-third of the voters.[74] In 2000, honesty was the trait

Table 2-3   Group Voting Patterns in Presidential Elections, Selected Years (Percent)

Group	1952 Stevenson	1952 (R) Eisenhower	1960 Kennedy	1960 (R) Nixon	1964 Johnson	1964 (R) Goldwater	1968 Humphrey	1968 (R) Nixon	1968 Wallace	1972 McGovern	1972 (R) Nixon
Sex											
male	47	53	52	48	60	40	41	43	16	37	63
female	42	58	49	51	62	38	45	43	12	38	62
Race											
white	43	57	49	51	59	41	38	47	15	32	68
nonwhite	79	21	68	32	94	6	85	12	3	87	13
Education											
college	34	66	39	61	52	48	37	54	9	37	63
high school	45	55	52	48	62	38	42	43	15	34	66
grade school	52	48	55	45	66	34	52	33	15	49	51
Occupation											
professional, business	36	64	42	58	54	46	34	56	10	31	69
white collar	40	60	48	52	57	43	41	47	12	36	64
manual	55	45	60	40	71	29	50	35	15	43	57
Age											
under 30	51	49	54	45	64	36	47	38	15	48	52
30–49	47	53	54	46	63	37	44	41	15	33	67
50 and older	39	61	46	54	59	41	41	47	12	36	64
Religion											
Protestant	37	63	38	62	55	45	35	49	16	30	70
Catholic	56	44	78	22	76	24	59	33	8	48	52
Region											
East	45	55	53	47	68	32	50	43	7	42	58
Midwest	42	58	48	52	61	39	44	47	9	40	60
South	51	49	51	49	52	48	31	36	33	29	71
West	42	58	49	51	60	40	44	49	7	41	59
Members of labor union families	61	39	65	35	73	27	56	29	15	46	54
National	45	55	50	50	61	39	43	43	14	38	62

Sources: Excerpted from *Gallup Report,* November 1988, 6, 7; *The Gallup Poll Monthly,* November 1992, 9; 1996 data provided by Gallup Organization from poll conducted November 3 to November 4, 1996; 2000 data released Nov. 6, 2000, and posted on Web site, www. gallup.com.

Note: NA = Not available.

Table 2-3 (Continued)

1976		1980			1988		1992			1996			2000		
(R)		(R)				(R)	(R)				(R)			(R)	
Carter	Ford	Carter	Reagan	Anderson	Dukakis	Bush, G.	Bush, G.	Clinton	Perot	Clinton	Dole	Perot	Gore	Bush, G.W.	Nader
53	45	38	53	7	44	56	37	39	19	45	39	11	38	53	5
48	51	44	49	6	48	52	36	48	10	53	34	6	48	43	4
46	52	36	56	7	41	59	40	40	15	44	41	9	39	52	4
85	15	86	10	2	82	18	12	76	4	78	9	4	78	12	4
42	55	35	53	10	42	58	39	43	14	44	44	6	42	49	5
54	46	43	51	5	46	54	37	45	12	52	30	11	46	44	4
58	41	54	42	3	55	45	35	43	15	NA	NA	NA	NA	NA	NA
42	56	33	55	10	NA	NA	NA	NA	NA	NA	—	—	NA	NA	NA
50	48	40	51	9	NA	NA	NA	NA	NA	NA	—	—	NA	NA	NA
58	41	48	46	5	NA	NA	NA	NA	NA	NA	—	—	NA	NA	NA
53	45	47	41	11	37	63	44	38	14	54	27	13	43	45	9
48	49	38	52	8	45	55	35	43	17	49	36	10	41	50	5
52	48	41	54	4	49	51	37	46	11	48	39	6	46	46	3
46	53	39	54	6	42	58	NA	NA	NA	NA	—	—	NA	NA	NA
57	42	46	47	6	51	49	NA	NA	NA	NA	—	—	45	45	5
51	47	43	47	9	51	49	33	47	15	59	26	9	52	38	6
48	50	41	51	7	47	53	35	45	13	47	39	8	43	47	4
54	45	44	52	3	40	60	42	40	13	45	39	9	36	56	3
46	51	35	54	9	46	54	36	43	15	48	38	8	43	47	6
63	36	50	43	5	63	37	NA	NA	NA	NA	—	—	NA	—	—
50	48	41	51	7	46	54	37	44	14	49	36	9	43	47	5

mentioned most by voters (24 percent), and 80 percent of those who mentioned it voted for George W. Bush, also perceived as the stronger leader and more likeable. Gore was regarded as more experienced, better able to deal with complexity, and more caring about people.[75]

Because the public focuses so much attention in a presidential campaign on the candidates themselves, the personality and character the aspirants project are particularly important. Each campaign organization strives to create a composite image of its candidate's most attractive features. To do this sometimes means transforming liabilities into assets: age becomes mature judgment (Eisenhower); youth and inexperience become vigor (Kennedy). Alternatively, a candidate can direct attention to the opponent's personal liabilities, a move that has proved beneficial even though some voters see such an effort as dirty campaigning and beneath the dignity of the office.

The 1988 and 1992 campaigns provide good examples of how candidates try to shape each other's image. Bush succeeded in creating a negative portrait of Dukakis in 1988. Dukakis enjoyed a largely favorable image before the summer conventions, but Bush's pollsters discovered it was based on very little information.[76] Interviews conducted with small groups of Democrats who had supported Reagan in 1980 and 1984 shaped the Bush campaign's charges that the Democratic nominee was sympathetic to criminals, weak on defense, opposed to saying the pledge of allegiance in school, and a liberal who favored high taxes and big government.[77] Bush launched a similar effort against Clinton in 1992. First he tried to picture Clinton as the failed governor of a crime-filled state with environmental problems and as an unpatriotic antiwar activist. Then Bush focused on the issues of trust and taxes in the final weeks of the election. But these negative tactics proved less successful against Clinton than they had against Dukakis for at least two reasons. Since 1988, observers have demanded more supporting evidence for campaign charges. Furthermore, unlike Dukakis, Clinton met all negative charges with broadcast rebuttals and attacks of his own that focused on Bush's role in the Iran-contra incident, his administration's pro-Iraq actions prior to the Persian Gulf War, and his violation of 1988 campaign promises.[78]

Issues are the other major short-term influence on voting behavior. University of Michigan researchers in the 1950s suggested that issues influence a voter's choice only if three conditions are present: the voter is aware that an issue or a number of issues exist, issues are of some personal concern to the voter, and the voter perceives that one party represents his or her position better than the other party does.[79] When the three conditions were applied to U.S. voters in the 1952 and 1956 presidential elections, researchers found that these criteria existed for relatively few voters. About one-third of the respondents were unaware of *any* of the sixteen principal issues about which they were questioned. Even the two-thirds who were aware of one or more issues frequently had no personal concern about them. Finally, many of those who were aware and concerned about issues were unable to perceive differences between the two parties' positions. The analysts concluded that issues *potentially* determined the choice of, at the most, only one-third of the electorate. (The proportion who *actually* voted as they did because of issues could have been, and probably was, even less.)

Studies of political attitudes in the 1960s and 1970s demonstrate a change: the number and types of issues of which voters were aware increased.[80] Voters during the Eisenhower years had exhibited some interest in traditional domestic matters, such as welfare and labor-management relationships, and in a few foreign policy issues, such as the threat of communism and the danger of the atomic bomb. Beginning with the 1964 election, however, voters' interests broadened to include concerns such as civil rights and the Vietnam War. The war in particular remained an important consideration in the 1968 and 1972 contests and was joined by new matters, such as crime, disorder, and juvenile delinquency— sometimes referred to collectively along with race problems as "social issues." Naturally, the issues that are salient vary from election to election. For example, the economy and jobs led the list in 2000, followed by education, social security, taxes, world affairs, health care, and prescription drugs.[81] Voters were able to perceive significant issue differences between Bush and Gore, but neither candidate was consistently favored.[82]

Incumbency. Incumbency may be viewed as a candidate characteristic that involves issues as well. Service in the job provides experience no one else can claim. Incumbency also provides concrete advantages: an incumbent already has national campaign experience (true for all incumbents except Gerald Ford), can obtain media coverage more easily, and has considerable discretion in allocating benefits. As noted earlier, incumbency has been especially important since World War II because of the pattern of recruitment. Until the elder Bush's victory in 1988, incumbency seemed to provide advantages solely to presidents and not to incumbent vice presidents. Gore's loss in 2000 reestablished the historical pattern.

Of the five incumbent presidents who ran for reelection between 1976 and 1996, only Reagan and Clinton succeeded, and of the past four incumbent vice presidents who sought the presidency, only Bush was elected. The defeats of Ford, Carter, and Bush demonstrate the disadvantages of incumbency, particularly if service in the presidency coincides with negative economic developments such as a recession and high inflation or an unresolved foreign crisis for which a president is blamed, even if erroneously. Experience in the job, then, is not a political plus if a sitting president's record is considered weak or national conditions seem to have deteriorated under the incumbent's stewardship. The president may be held accountable by voters who cast their ballots *retrospectively* rather than *prospectively;* in other words, these voters evaluate an administration's past performance rather than try to predict future performance.

Retrospective voting has been suggested as the major explanation for Carter's defeat in 1980 and Bush's in 1992. To illustrate the problem, one can contrast what many perceived as Carter's failure to resolve the hostage crisis in Iran with the respect many believed the nation enjoyed after Reagan's first term. Bush's foreign policy success in the Persian Gulf War made his apparent inaction in dealing with the slowing economy all the more vivid. In the 1996 election, Clinton benefited from the conditions of peace and prosperity during his first term, but this record was not transferred to his chosen successor. Al Gore failed to highlight these accomplishments during the campaign as he tried to distance himself from Clinton to avoid association with the president's questionable personal conduct. In doing so, he also distanced himself from the administration's achievements.[83] As the 2004 election unfolds, both George W. Bush's performance at home with the economy and abroad in the war against terrorism will be criticized by the Democratic challengers.

Presidential Debates. Voters have the opportunity to assess the issue positions and personal characteristics of presidential and vice presidential contenders during nationally televised debates. Debates, first staged in 1960, have been held each election year since 1976; they quickly became the most important and most widely watched campaign events. Candidates recognize the danger of making a mistake or committing an embarrassing gaffe on live television, a particular danger for incumbents. Ford misspoke in 1976 when he suggested that countries of Eastern Europe were not under Soviet domination; Reagan appeared to be confused and out of touch during his first debate with Mondale in 1984 but rallied in the second encounter. Challengers try to demonstrate their knowledge of issues and their presidential bearing to a nationwide audience. Kennedy in 1960, Reagan in 1980, and George W. Bush in 2000 seem to have benefited the most from debating a more experienced opponent, in part because they exceeded performance expectations and dispelled negative impressions. Most candidates prepare carefully prior to the meeting and follow a conservative game plan of reemphasizing themes already made prominent during the campaign. As a result, the exchanges often seem wooden rather than extemporaneous, an impression heightened by the cautious rules approved by the respective camps. Bush surprised many by holding his own in 2000, while Gore appeared both overaggressive and given to exaggerating his own accomplishments. The heightened postdebate media attention was especially critical of Gore. Bush, on the other hand, met a credibility threshold that was more important than scoring on debating points. At the outset of the debates, Gore had led in the polls by a few percentage points, but by the end Bush held a narrow advantage.

In 1992, the first three-way presidential debates included Ross Perot, who met the two party nominees in three different formats: questions posed by the traditional panel of journalists, by citizens at a town meeting, and by a single moderator. The formats allowed for greater interaction and extemporaneous exchange among the contestants rather than triggering the patented responses that had characterized so many past meetings. Perot did not get the same chance in 1996, nor did Pat Buchanan or Ralph Nader in 2000. The Commission on Presidential Debates, a joint venture sponsored by the Democratic and Republican Parties, concluded that these candidates could not win the election and so excluded them.

The first televised presidential debate, watched by an estimated sixty-six million viewers, took place on September 26, 1960, between Republican vice president Richard Nixon and Democratic senator John F. Kennedy. Howard K. Smith acted as the moderator.

Single vice presidential debates were held in 1988, 1992, 1996, and 2000. Dan Quayle's performance was the focus of the first two encounters. Much younger than Lloyd Bentsen, his 1988 opponent, Quayle was repeatedly asked what he would do if forced to assume the duties of president. When Quayle compared himself to former president John F. Kennedy, Bentsen pounced with withering directness: "Senator, I served with Jack Kennedy. I knew Jack Kennedy. Jack Kennedy was a friend of mine. Senator, you're no Jack Kennedy." Quayle never recovered.[84] In 1992, Quayle debated Al Gore, the Democrat, and James Stockdale, Perot's running mate, who watched as his younger opponents struggled to dominate one another. Gore's encounter with Jack Kemp in 1996 previewed some of the problems he would experience in 2000. Gore was so focused on the campaign message that he appeared even more wooden than usual. The Cheney-Lieberman debate in 2000 was a more cordial and mature exchange than the presidential series, suggesting to some viewers that the vice-presidential candidates should have been leading the tickets.

Televised debates enable even the least engaged citizen to develop an impression of the major party contenders. However, candidates have become more adept at staging, and the public may now expect more than just a polite exchange of policy challenges as candidates try to display assertiveness, empathy, humor, or "character."

Election Day

One of the ironies of presidential elections since 1960 is that, although more citizens have acquired the right to vote, a smaller proportion have exercised that right. As Table 2-4 indicates, the estimated number of people of voting age has more than doubled since 1932. After reaching a peak in 1960, however, the percentage of people who voted declined in the next five presidential elections. Despite a modest increase in 1984, only 50.1 percent went to the polls in 1988. This pattern was unexpectedly reversed in 1992, when 55.2 percent went to the polls.[85] The resurgence proved short-lived, however; only 49.1 percent showed up in 1996, the lowest turnout since 1924. There was an uptick in 2000 to 51.3 percent, a modest gain in view of the tight race but at least movement in the desired direction.[86]

The decline in voter participation runs counter to most theories of why people do not vote. Laws pertaining to registration and voting, said to prevent citizens from going to the polls, have been eased in most states. Federal laws made it much easier for a person to register and to vote for president in 1996 than in 1960. A person's lack of education is often put forward as a reason for not voting, but the level of education of U.S. citizens rose as participation declined. Lack of political information is yet another frequently cited explanation, but more Americans than ever are aware of the candidates and their views on public issues, thanks to media coverage and the debates. Finally, close political races are supposed to stimulate people to get out and vote because they think their ballot will make a difference in the outcome. Pollsters predicted that the 1964 and 1972 elections would be landslides and that the 1968, 1976, and 1980 elections would be close contests, but a smaller percentage of people voted in 1968 than in 1964, and participation also declined in 1976 and 1980 despite close contests. In 1984, there was a slight (0.5 percent) increase in participation, even though the outcome was hardly in doubt, while participation declined in 1988, a closer contest. From early in 1996, polls showed Clinton comfortably ahead, and many reports suggested voters expected the eventual outcome.

Why did voting decline in recent years, surge in 1992, decline again in 1996, and recover in 2000? Paul Abramson, John Aldrich, and David Rohde link the long-term decline to the erosion in political party identification and to lower political efficacy—the belief that citizens can influence what government does.[87] But these authors note that neither party identification nor political efficacy changed significantly in 1992 and 1996. There is evidence that Ross Perot's presence contributed to the 1992 turnout increase; 14 percent of Perot voters (which translates into nearly 3 million voters, a substantial portion of the increased turnout) indicated in exit polls that they would not have voted if the Texan had not been on the ballot. Neither major party made a concerted effort in 1992 to register new voters, although there were some nonpartisan turnout efforts,

Table 2-4   Participation of General Public in Presidential Elections, 1932–2000

Year	Estimated population of voting age (in millions)	Number of votes cast (in millions)	Number of votes as percentage of population of voting age
1932	75.8	39.7	52.4
1936	80.2	45.6	56.0
1940	84.7	49.9	58.9
1944	85.7	48.0	56.0
1948	95.6	48.8	51.1
1952	99.9	61.6	61.6
1956	104.5	62.0	59.3
1960	109.7	68.8	62.8
1964	114.1	70.6	61.9
1968	120.3	73.2	60.9
1972[a]	140.8	77.6	55.1
1976[a]	152.3	81.6	53.6
1980[a]	164.6	86.5	52.6
1984[a]	174.5	92.7	53.1
1988[a]	182.8	91.6	50.1
1992[a]	189.0	104.4	55.2
1996[a]	196.5	96.5	49.1
2000[a]	205.8	105.4	51.2

Sources: U.S. Bureau of the Census, *Current Population Reports*, Series P-25, No. 1085 (Washington, D.C.: U.S. Government Printing Office, 1994). 1996 and 2000 data from Federal Election Commission Web site, www.fec.gov, and U.S. Census Bureau Web site, www. census.gov.

[a]Elections in which persons eighteen to twenty years old were eligible to vote in all states.

including MTV's "Rock the Vote" feature aimed at young voters, the group with the lowest turnout rates. By 1996, the "Motor Voter" bill, which requires states to provide voter registration opportunities through driver's license agencies, among other public offices, had increased registration, and Democrats made a concerted effort to register newly naturalized citizens. Thus we cannot be certain what caused the changes. It is important to note, however, that even the 1992 turnout was still well below that for 1960 and that neither of the long-term causes of the voting decline noted above has been reversed.[88]

Validation

Translating the popular vote into the official outcome is the final stage of the selection process, in which the electoral college produces the true winner. Until 2000, it had been more than a century since the constitutionally prescribed process failed to do so or produced a winner who was not also the "people's choice," though we had been dangerously close to such an electoral college *misfire* on a number of occasions.

Despite the separation of the presidential and the vice presidential balloting in 1804, three possible ways for a misfire to occur remain. First, the electoral college does not ensure that the candidate who receives the most popular votes wins the presidency: John Quincy Adams in 1824, Rutherford B. Hayes in 1876, and Benjamin Harrison in 1888 became president even though they finished second in total popular vote to their respective political opponents. The same thing happened in 2000, when Gore won a national plurality of 543,895 votes but lost in the electoral college.[89] This had nearly happened in 1976, when Ford would have won if some 9,000 voters in Hawaii and Ohio had cast different ballots.

Second, candidates may fail to win an electoral college majority, thereby throwing selection into the House of Representatives. This situation occurred in 1800, 1824, and 1876. In 1948, Harry S. Truman defeated Thomas Dewey by more than 2 million popular votes, but if some 12,000 people in California and Ohio had voted for Dewey instead, the House would have determined the election. The same thing could have happened in 1960, 1968, and 2000 with the shift of a few thousand votes in close states.

The 1968 election illustrates a third danger of the electoral college system: an elector need not cast his or her ballot for the candidate who wins the plurality of votes in the elector's state. This problem of the *faithless elector* occurred eight times in the twentieth century, most recently in 2000, when a D.C. elector abstained. In 1988, an elector from West Virginia cast her vote for Bentsen as president rather than Dukakis. It is not particularly dangerous when isolated electors refuse to follow the result of their states' popular votes, but widespread desertion would be another matter.[90]

The electoral college as it operates today violates some major tenets of political equality that are central to our contemporary understanding of democracy. Each person's vote does not count equally: one's influence on the outcome depends on the situation in one's state. For the many Americans who support a losing candidate, it is as though they had not voted at all because under the general-ticket system all the electoral votes of a state go to the candidate with a plurality of its popular votes. Thus although Perot received 19,741,048 votes, 18.9 percent of the total cast nationally in 1992, he won no electoral votes because he finished first in no states nor in any of the House districts in Maine and Nebraska. Citizens who live in populous, politically competitive states have a premium placed on their votes because they are in a position to affect how large blocs of electoral votes are cast. Similarly, permitting the House, voting by states, to select the president is not consistent with the "one person, one vote" principle that has become a central tenet of American democracy.[91]

Proposals to reform the electoral college system attempt to remove the possibility of system failures and uphold a more modern understanding of democracy. They range from the rather modest suggestion of prohibiting faithless electors— votes would be cast automatically—to scrapping the present system and moving to a direct popular election. Intermediate suggestions would nationalize the congressional district plan used in Maine and Nebraska, divide electoral votes proportionally between (or among) the contenders, or provide the popular vote winner with a hundred bonus votes, enough to ensure his or her victory in the electoral college. No proposal is foolproof, and most must develop guards against new problems. Moreover, any change requires passage of a constitutional amendment, problematic because national legislators will calculate how the new system would affect their states' influence on the outcome (or their own chances to pursue the office) and vote accordingly.

Is the electoral college a constitutional anachronism that should no longer be preserved? In the aftermath of the 2000 election, attention once again focused on this eighteenth-century process, with many people stressing its inadequacies and others praising its genius. On December 7, 2000, Rep. Eliot Engel, D-N.Y., proposed two constitutional amendments to change the electoral college by requiring that electors be allocated either proportionally to the popular vote in each state or to the vote winner in each congressional district. These were just the latest in a long line of proposals; in fact, "there have been more proposals for Constitutional amendments on changing the Electoral College than on any other subject," more than 700 throughout U.S. history.[92] Defenders of the current system note that the most serious misfires occurred during periods of intense political divisiveness (for example, 1824 and 1876), when alternative selection systems would have been just as severely tested. Several of the close calls in the twentieth century, such as those in 1948 and 1968, occurred when political parties were suffering serious internal divisions. An examination of the historical conditions surrounding the misfires shows that only 1888 and 2000 offer clear examples of a popular-vote winner who lost the general election.[93] If popular vote rules had been in place in 2000, the chaos would have been even more widespread since the results would have been challenged in many states with close outcomes, not just in Florida. A national recount would have been far more complex than state-by-state challenges.

Defenders of the present system argue that it actually has been remarkably successful in producing peaceful resolutions even in tumultuous years. Its virtues include the requirement that candidates not only receive significant popular support but also have support sufficiently distributed geographically to enable the winner to govern. George W. Bush, for example, won thirty states in 2000, including eleven that had voted for Clinton in 1996. Even more significant, because of Bush's strength in the South and the West, "[h]ad the 2000 presidential election been conducted using the new numbers [from the 2000 census] rather than the numbers based on the 1990 census Texas Governor George W. Bush would have defeated Vice President Al Gore by a more comfortable 278–260 margin."[94] Ethnic minority groups, it is argued, receive special leverage under the present system because they are concentrated in states with large electoral vote totals and receive attention because their support might make the difference between winning all the electoral votes or none. Finally, there is concern that a system of direct election would encourage the development of minor parties based on regional or ideological interests that might organize in hopes of denying any candidate a majority or winning plurality and thereby force a runoff. Two-party stability, it is suggested, would be threatened.[95]

Analysts differ over the wisdom of retaining the present electoral system; even the recent brush with electoral crisis did not produce a uniform response. Maintaining government legitimacy is a shared concern. Historically, successful candidates unable to secure a popular vote majority gained legitimacy through an electoral college majority. This happened twice to Bill Clinton and now to George W. Bush, though Clinton at least won the popular vote plurality. Defenders of the electoral college believe legitimacy is achieved through continuity with the past while reformers believe it is achieved through enhancing popular control and avoiding controversy like that surrounding Bush's victory.

Transitions to Governing

For the individual and election team that prevail in this long, grueling process, victory requires a change in focus. Successful candidates suddenly realize that winning is the means to an end, not an end in itself. Making that transition is sometimes difficult. It involves putting together a team of political executives to staff the new administration as well as establishing a list of program and policy priorities. Much of this is accomplished during the transition, the period between election and inauguration. Many other tasks are tackled during the administration's first six months. Governing, however, offers a new set of problems. Frequently, the techniques that proved successful during the election are simply transferred to those challenges, but such methods are seldom sufficient to ensure success. In the modern presidency, governing involves some of the same activities as getting elected, but the two are far from identical, a lesson some incumbents are slow to learn.

The burning question for everyone is how effective will the president be in leading the nation. Presidents vary along a wide range of dimensions—abilities, interests, personality—even as the office exhibits certain commonalities over time. In chapter 4, we turn to the problem of understanding the ways a president's personal characteristics influence performance in office, and subsequent chapters focus on presidents' political success. First, however, we examine their relationship with the public between elections, a relationship that has grown increasingly important in modern times. In chapter 11, we offer a case study of George W. Bush's performance as president.

NOTES

1. Besides George Washington, James Monroe is the only candidate to approach this distinction; he won all but one electoral college vote in 1820. Michael Nelson ed., *Guide to the Presidency*, 2d ed., vol. 2 (Washington, D.C.: Congressional Quarterly, 1996), 1638.

2. William Chambers, *Political Parties in a New Nation: The American Experience, 1776–1809* (New York: Oxford University Press, 1963), chap. 2.

3. Jefferson's Republican Party actually served as the basis for the Democratic Party. The Democratic-Republican Party was officially designated the Democratic Party in 1840. Paul David, Ralph Goldman, and Richard Bain, *The Politics of National Party Conventions* (New York: Vintage, 1964), chap. 3.

4. Joseph Charles, *The Origins of the American Party System* (New York: Harper Torch, 1956), 83–94.

5. Other constitutional amendments dealing with presidential selection have expanded participation (Amendments 15, 19, 24, 26), set the term of office (20, 22), or sought to cope with death or disability (20, 25).

6. David, Goldman, and Bain, *National Party Conventions*, 50. The National Republican Party was soon to give way to the Whigs, with many Whig supporters joining the Republican Party when it was formed in the 1850s (57–59).

7. Ibid., 61.

8. First-ballot convention decisions have been surprisingly prevalent. Through 2000, the two major parties selected their candidates on the first ballot at fifty-five of eighty-one conventions. Many of the multiballot conventions were held from 1840 to 1888, when sixteen of the twenty-two went past the first ballot. What distinguishes the post-1952 era is that *none* of the twenty-four conventions went past one ballot.

9. Richard C. Bain and Judith H. Parris, *Convention Decisions and Voting Records*, 2d ed. (Washington, D.C.: Brookings, 1973), 1–6.

10. Thirty-nine states and the District of Columbia held primaries for both parties and eight states held caucuses for both. Michigan and South Carolina held caucuses for the Democrats and a primary for the Republicans, while Virginia held a Republican primary and a Democratic caucus.

11. Naturalized citizens (such as California governor Arnold Schwarzenegger, who was born in Austria) do not meet this requirement. There is some question whether persons born abroad of American citizens (one such is George Romney, former governor of Michigan and 1968 presidential contender, who was born of American parents in France) are also legally barred from the presidency.

12. Estimated by the author based on data from the U.S. Census Bureau. See especially Bureau of the Census, *The Foreign-Born Population in the United States* (Washington, D.C., March 2000), Figure 4.

13. John Aldrich, "Methods and Actors: The Relationship of Processes to Candidates," in *Presidential Selection*, ed. Alexander Heard and Michael Nelson (Durham: Duke University Press, 1987).

14. Before Richard Nixon's selection in 1960, the last incumbent vice president to be nominated was Martin Van Buren in 1836.

15. Joseph A. Pika, "Bush, Quayle, and the New Vice Presidency," in *The Presidency and the Political System*, 3d ed., ed. Michael Nelson (Washington, D.C.: CQ Press, 1990). Also see Joseph A. Pika, "The Vice Presidency: New Opportunities, Old Constraints," in *The Presidency and the Political System*, 6th ed., ed. Michael Nelson (Washington, D.C.: CQ Press, 2000).

16. Ronald D. Elving, "The Senators' Lane to the Presidency," *Congressional Quarterly Weekly Report*, May 20, 1989, 1218.

17. For a statement of informal expectations from three decades ago, see Sidney Hyman, "Nine Tests for the Presidential Hopeful," *New York Times*, January 4, 1959, Sec. 5, 1–11.

18. Michael Nelson, "Who Vies for President?" in *Presidential Selection*, 144.

19. For example, Jesse Jackson finished third behind Walter Mondale and Gary Hart for the 1984 Democratic nomination and second for the 1988 nomination. Jackson was again mentioned prominently in 1995 as a possible nominee, as was Colin Powell, another African American.

20. In 2000, Republicans held forty-two primaries and the Democrats thirty-nine.

21. At the time of writing, the Democrats' delegate total was set but the Republican total was still unsettled, and thus the total was calculated by the authors based on party guidelines.

22. Federal Election Commission Web site, www.fec.gov.

23. Harold W. Stanley, "The Nominations: Republican Doldrums, Democratic Revival," in *The Elections of 1996*, ed. Michael Nelson (Washington, D.C.: CQ Press, 1997), 22.

24. Austin Ranney, "Changing the Rules of the Nominating Game," in *Choosing the President*, ed. James David Barber (Englewood Cliffs, N.J.: Prentice Hall, 1974), 71.

25. Arthur Hadley, *The Invisible Primary* (Englewood Cliffs, N.J.: Prentice Hall, 1976). For a valuable update see Emmett H. Buell Jr., "The Invisible Primary," in *In Pursuit of the White House*, ed. William G. Mayer (Chatham, N.J.: Chatham House, 1996).

26. Congressional Research Service, "The Presidential Campaign Election Fund and Tax Checkoff: Background and Current Issues," March 2000, included as Table 1 in Anthony Corrado and John Green, "The Current Presidential Finance System: What Are the Issues?" The Campaign Finance Institute Task Force on Financing Presidential Nominations, 2003, www.cfinst.org/presidential/pdf/Green_Corrado_atHearings.pdf.

27. Anthony Corrado, "Financing the 2000 Elections," in *The Election of 2000*, ed. Gerald M. Pomper (Chatham, N.J.: Chatham House, 2001), 98.

28. Normally about 30 percent of the prenomination funding comes from public sources. Individuals are limited to contributions of $2,000 to a presidential candidate for each election, up from the previous $1,000 limit (the nomination and general election are considered separate contests), $5,000 to a political action committee (a group that contributes to more than one candidate), $20,000 to the national committee of a political party, and a total contribution of no more than $25,000 a year. Presidential candidates are free to spend an unlimited amount of their own and their immediate family's money on their campaigns, but if they accept public financing, their contributions to their own campaigns are limited to $50,000 per election.

29. This constituted only 17 percent of the prenomination funding, largely the product of efforts by George W. Bush and Steve Forbes to operate free of spending limits. Corrado, "Financing the 2000 Elections," 97.

30. Conventions are heavily subsidized by "soft money" contributions from corporations and individuals as well as by money from the cities hosting the event. On the 2000 public financing see, *FEC Record*, 26:4 (Washington, D.C., April 2000), 10. To finance the 2004 Republican convention in New York City, the host committee promised to raise $64 million in addition to $27 million contributed by the city to cover police, fire, emergency services, and insurance costs. By mid-June 2003, $60 million had been pledged by corporations and individuals. Randal C. Archibold, "G.O.P. Quick to Get Big Donors to Cover Cost of Convention," *The New York Times*, June 19, 2003, A1.

31. Anthony Corrado, "Financing the 1996 Elections," in *The Election of 1996*, ed. Gerald M. Pomper (Chatham, N.J.: Chatham House, 1997).

32. Corrado, "Financing the 2000 Elections," 98.

33. Not all individual contributions are small, and it is legal for political action committees to help finance nomination campaigns, but their contributions are not matched by federal funds as in the case of individuals. For example, in 1988, Vice President Bush received $1,000 contributions (the maximum) from 16,500 individuals in 1988 for a total of $16.5 million. Cumulatively, PACs contributed $3.114 million during the 1988 prenomination campaign, but that sum represented only 1.4 percent of total funding. Herbert E. Alexander and Monica Bauer, *Financing the 1988 Election* (Boulder: Westview, 1991), 23, 25.

34. It is not clear, however, whether the additional financial resources produce victory or whether contributors simply choose to give their money to the leading candidate.

35. Richard Berke, "In G.O.P. Presidential Field, a Race to Raise Money Is On," *New York Times*, February 2, 1995, 1.

36. Thomas B. Edsall and Dan Balz, "Kerry Shaded by Edwards in Fundraising Reports Fuel Reassessment," *Washington Post*, April 3, 2003, A3.

37. See www.cfinst.org/presidential/071802.html.

38. President Bush's fund-raising efforts for 2004 drew a variety of criticism. See, for example, Editorial, "The $2000 Hot Dog," *Washington Post*, June 22, 2003.

39. From the text of July 18, 2002, press release announcing creation of the Task Force on Financing Presidential Nominations, www.cfinst.org/presidential/071802.html. For additional data on the nominating system, see Corrado and Green, "The Current Presidential Finance System."

40. The exceptions were George McGovern, who defeated front-runner Edmund Muskie in 1972; Jimmy Carter, who surpassed Hubert Humphrey in 1976; Michael Dukakis, who bested the early leader Gary Hart in 1988; and Bill Clinton, who came from far behind to win in 1992.

41. In 1984, the minimum was 20 percent, a rule that favored the front-runner, Walter Mondale. Complaints from the defeated candidates Jesse Jackson and Gary Hart resulted in lowering the qualifying level to 15 percent for the 1988 contest, and that rule was continued in 1992, 1996, and 2000. Most Republican contests have been conducted under "winner take all" rules, although some states use proportional rules for both parties.

42. Eric M. Appleman, Democracy in Action, www.gwu.edu/~action/frontload.html.

43. Alan Greenblatt and Rhodes Cook, "Nominating Process Rules Change," *Congressional Quarterly Weekly Report*, August 17, 1996, 2299. For the 2000 election, see Andrew E. Busch, "New Features of the 2000 Presidential Nominating Process: Republican Reforms, Front-Loading's Second Wind, and Early Voting," in *In Pursuit of the White House 2000*, ed. William G. Mayer (New York: Chatham House, 2001).

44. Another effort by Republicans to revise their rules for 2004 was defeated at the Philadelphia convention, ensuring that the nation would once again contend with a compressed, front-loaded schedule in 2004.

45. Marjorie Randon Hershey, "The Campaign and the Media," in *The Election of 2000*, 47.

46. C. Anthony Broh, *A Horse of a Different Color: Television's Treatment of Jesse Jackson's 1984 Presidential Campaign* (Washington, D.C.: Joint Center for Political Studies, 1987), 4.

47. For discusion of the primary contests in 2000 and election results, see William G. Mayer, "The Presidential Nominations," in *The Election of 2000*.

48. Broh, *A Horse of a Different Color*, 44.

49. Exceptions to this pattern can be found when two candidates end the preconvention period fairly even, which Ford and Reagan did in 1976, McGovern and Humphrey did in 1972, and Mondale and Hart did in 1984; in each case, however, the preconvention leader took the nomination.

50. Judith Parris, *The Convention Problem: Issues in Reform of Presidential Nominating Procedures* (Washington, D.C.: Brookings, 1972), 110.

51. Edwin Diamond, Gregg Geller, and Chris Whitley, "Air Wars: Conventions Go Cable," *National Journal*, August 31, 1996, 1859.

52. "No elector has ever been prosecuted for failing to vote as pledged." From U.S. Electoral College FAQ, www.archives.gov/federal_register/electoral_college/faq.html#wrongvote. For a list of the state laws, see U.S. National Archives and Records Administration, www.archives.gov/federal_register/electoral_college/laws_2000.html.

53. *FEC Record,* 26:4 (Washington, D.C., April 2000), 10. Nominees receiving full funding may accept other direct contributions only to meet legal and accounting fees. So George W. Bush's enormous fund-raising advantage during the prenomination phase in 1999–2000 could not be repeated for the general election phase.

54. See Fred Wertheimer, president of Democracy 21, "Opening Remarks," conference on the Bipartisan Campaign Reform Act, June 23, 2003; published as part of Democracy 21's *Capital Bits and Pieces,* vol. 3, no. 10, www.democracy21.org/index. asp?Type=B_PR&SEC={C052F433-38ED-467D-8F7B-E64DE8CBC314}&DE= {28959239-F3C1-4ED7-A887-D6C8B32C5896}.

55. Alexander and Bauer, *Financing the 1988 Election,* Table 2-1. Herbert Alexander and Anthony Corrado, *Financing the 1992 Election* (Boulder: Westview, 1995), chap. 5, Table 5-1; Federal Election Commission, *The Presidential Public Funding Program* (Washington, D.C., 1993), 31.

56. Corrado, "Financing the 2000 Elections," 107.

57. Ibid., 109.

58. Wertheimer, "Opening Remarks."

59. Although presidential candidates are free to refuse public funds, no major party nominee has done so in the general election, perhaps because the maximum contribution limitations have made raising money from individuals and groups more difficult. Candidates may also think the public favors the use of public, rather than private, funds.

60. The Twenty-third Amendment, ratified in 1961, gave the District of Columbia the right to participate in presidential elections. Previously, District residents were excluded. Their inclusion accounts for there being three more electoral votes (538) than the total number of senators and representatives (535).

61. For election results and a brief account of the events surrounding the Florida outcome, see Gerald M. Pomper, "The Presidential Election," in *The Election of 2000,* 125–135. For an in-depth journalistic account of the Florida situation, see *Deadlock: The Inside Story of America's Closest Election,* comp. Political Staff of the *Washington Post* (New York: Public Affairs, 2001).

62. One elector from the District of Columbia, Barbara Lett-Simmons, who should have cast her ballot for Albert Gore Jr. and Joseph I. Lieberman, instead cast a blank ballot as a means of protesting the lack of D.C. statehood and therefore representation in Congress. Thus the two-party total is not 538. A copy of the ballot can be viewed at the Electoral College Web site of the National Archives, www. archives.gov/federal_register/electoral_college/2000_certificates/vote_dc.html.

63. Reapportionment was complex following the 1990 census. Because of widespread criticism, the Census Bureau agreed to conduct a postcensus survey to determine the extent to which some population groups had been undercounted. The results of that study would have called for further changes in congressional representation. However, the secretary of commerce recommended following the initial census findings rather than the adjusted figures. A similar debate followed the 2000 census, and Utah filed suit to have its residents serving as missionaries abroad included in the count, which would give it the additional seat awarded to North Carolina. On June 20, 2002, the Supreme Court decided in favor of North Carolina in the case of *Utah v. Evans.*

64. Dukakis won electoral votes from the District of Columbia and ten states in 1988: Hawaii, Iowa, Massachusetts, Minnesota, New York, Oregon, Rhode Island, Washington, West Virginia, and Wisconsin. He won 45 percent or more of the vote in California, Colorado, Connecticut, Illinois, Maryland, Michigan, Missouri, Montana, New Mexico, Pennsylvania, South Dakota, and Vermont. Of these states, only South Dakota did not support Clinton in 1992. That year, Clinton won only four southern states plus Kentucky and trailed Bush in the region's popular vote as well.

65. Gore lost New Hampshire by 7,300 votes; Nader garnered 22,198 there. Nader also received 97,488 votes in Florida, thousands more than Gore needed for victory. Bush lost New Mexico by 366 votes; Buchanan received 1,392 there. In Wisconsin, Bush lost by 5,708, while Buchanan secured 11,471. See official 2000 election results at www.fec.gov/pubrec/2000presgeresults.htm.

66. Angus Campbell et al., *The American Voter*, abr. ed. (New York: Wiley, 1964).

67. Paul R. Abramson, John H. Aldrich, and David W. Rohde, *Change and Continuity in the 2000 and 2002 Elections* (Washington, D.C.: CQ Press, 2003), 171.

68. Gerald M. Pomper, "The Presidential Election," in *The Elections of 1988: Reports and Interpretations*, ed. Gerald M. Pomper (Chatham, N.J.: Chatham House, 1989), 136.

69. Offsetting gains in nonwhite voting, white fundamentalist Christians have gained significance in national politics. This group has become solidly Republican and in 1988 composed nearly as large a proportion of the voting population as blacks (9 percent versus 10 percent). See poll results reported in Gerald M. Pomper, "The Presidential Election," in *The Election of 1996: Reports and Interpretations*, ed. Gerald M. Pomper (Chatham, N.J.: Chatham House, 1997), 134.

70. Pomper, "The Presidential Election," in *The Election of 2000*, 137. The reported data are based on exit polls rather than the final Gallup survey. Also see the discussion in Abramson, Aldrich and Rohde, *Change and Continuity*, chap. 5.

71. J. Merrill Shanks and Warren Miller, "Policy Direction and Performance Evaluation: Complementary Explanations of the Reagan Elections" (paper delivered at the annual meeting of the American Political Science Association, New Orleans, August 29–September 1, 1985), 60, 69.

72. Pomper, "The Presidential Election," in *The Election of 1988*, 143. The results of this CNN/*Los Angeles Times* poll also can be found in *National Journal*, November 12, 1988, 2854.

73. Voter Research and Surveys exit polls as reported in Paul J. Quirk and Jon K. Dallager, "The Election: A 'New Democrat' and a New Kind of Presidential Campaign," in *The Elections of 1992*, ed. Michael Nelson (Washington, D.C.: CQ Press, 1993), 81.

74. Exit poll conducted by Voter News Service and reported in Michael Nelson, "The Election: Turbulence and Tranquility in Contemporary American Politics," in *The Elections of 1996*, ed. Nelson, 57.

75. Pomper, "The Presidential Election," in *The Election of 2000*, 146.

76. Marjorie Randon Hershey, "The Campaign and the Media," in *The Elections of 1988*, 78.

77. Ibid., 80–83; Paul J. Quirk, "The Election," in *The Elections of 1988*, 76.

78. Nelson, "The Election: Turbulence and Tranquility," 58. Marion R. Just, "Candidate Strategies and the Media Campaign," in *The Elections of 1988*, 91–96.

79. Campbell et al., *The American Voter*, chap. 7.

80. For 1960s data, see Gerald M. Pomper, *Voters' Choice: Varieties of American Electoral Behavior* (New York: Dodd, Mead, 1975), chap. 8. For 1970s data, see Norman Nie, Sidney Verba, and John Petrocik, *The Changing American Voter* (Cambridge: Harvard University Press, 1979), chap. 7.

81. Pomper, "The Presidential Election," in *The Election of 2000*, 146.

82. Abramson, Aldrich and Rohde, *Change and Continuity*, chaps. 6 and 7.

83. Pomper, "The Presidential Election," in *The Election of 2000*, 142.

84. See the transcript of this debate and others at www.pbs.org/newshour/debatingourdestiny.

85. The 1992 turnout represented an increase of about 13 million voters over the 1988 total. Twenty-three candidates shared the votes, although only four—Bush, Clinton, Perot, and the Libertarian Party candidate, Andre Marrou—were on ballots in all fifty states. Federal Election Commission, press release, January 14, 1993.

86. The FEC Web site reports 105.586 million votes were cast in the presidential election. The voting age population in 2000 was estimated by the Bureau of the Census at 205.815 million. U.S. Census Bureau, Public Information Office, press release, March 14, 2001, www.fec.gov/pages/2000turnout/reg&to00.htm.

87. Paul R. Abramson, John H. Aldrich, and David W. Rohde, *Change and Continuity in the 1980 Elections* (Washington, D.C.: CQ Press, 1982), chap. 4.

88. Paul R. Abramson, John H. Aldrich, and David W. Rohde, *Change and Continuity in the 1992 Elections* (Washington, D.C.: CQ Press, 1994), 120.

89. Official results can be found at www.fec.gov/pubrec/2000presgeresults.htm.

90. In 1960, 1968, 1972, 1976, and 1988, single electors in Oklahoma, North Carolina, Virginia, Washington, and West Virginia failed to cast their ballots for the candidate receiving the popular vote plurality in their states. For complete results of electoral college voting, see Nelson, *Guide to the Presidency,* 1634–1658; see 1634 for a list of faithless electors and the FEC Web site for the D.C. results in 2000.

91. Numerous efforts emerged in the wake of the 2000 election to stress the unfairness of the current system. To explore the over- and underrepresentation of citizens depending on state of residence, see www.thegreenpapers.com/Census00/FedRep.phtml?sort=Elec#Elec.

92. See www.archives.gov/federal_register/electoral_college/faq.html#tie.

93. William C. Kimberling, "Electing the President: The Genius of the Electoral College," *FEC Journal* (fall 1988): 16.

94. Sean Scully, *The Washington Times,* December 29, 2000, A12. Gore carried all but two of the states that lost House seats, and Bush won all of the states that stood to gain seats except California.

95. Ibid., 19–20.

SUGGESTED READINGS

Abramson, Paul R., John H. Aldrich, and David W. Rohde. *Change and Continuity in the 1980 Elections.* Washington, D.C.: CQ Press, 1982.

___. *Change and Continuity in the 1984 Elections.* Washington, D.C.: CQ Press, 1986.

___. *Change and Continuity in the 1988 Elections.* Washington, D.C.: CQ Press, 1990.

___. *Change and Continuity in the 1992 Elections.* Washington, D.C.: CQ Press, 1994.

___. *Change and Continuity in the 1992 Elections, Revised Edition.* Washington, D.C.: CQ Press, 1995.

___. *Change and Continuity in the 1996 Elections.* Washington, D.C.: CQ Press, 1998.

___. *Change and Continuity in the 1996 and 1998 Elections.* Washington, D.C.: CQ Press, 1999.

___. *Change and Continuity in the 2000 and 2002 Elections.* Washington, D.C.: CQ Press, 2003.

Alexander, Herbert E., and Anthony Corrado. *Financing the 1992 Election.* Boulder: Westview, 1995.

Bartels, Larry M. *Presidential Primaries and the Dynamics of Public Choice.* Princeton: Princeton University Press, 1988.

Campbell, Angus, Philip Converse, Warren Miller, and Donald Stokes. *The American Voter,* abr. ed. New York: Wiley, 1964.

Heard, Alexander, and Michael Nelson, eds. *Presidential Selection.* Durham: Duke University Press, 1987.

Mayer, William B., ed. *In Pursuit of the White House: How We Choose Our Presidential Nominees.* Chatham, N.J.: Chatham House, 1996.

___. *In Pursuit of the White House, 2000: How We Choose Our Presidential Nominees.* Chatham, N.J.: Chatham House, 1999.

Nelson, Michael, ed. *The Elections of 1996.* Washington, D.C.: CQ Press, 1997.

___. *The Elections of 2000.* Washington, D.C.: CQ Press, 2001.

Pomper, Gerald M., ed. *The Election of 1996: Reports and Interpretations.* Chatham, N.J.: Chatham House, 1997.

___. *The Election of 2000: Reports and Interpretations.* Chatham, N.J.: Chatham House, 2001.

Rose, Gary L., ed. *Controversial Issues in Presidential Selection.* 2d ed. Albany: State University of New York Press, 1994.

Shafer, Byron E. *Quiet Revolution: The Struggle for the Democratic Party and the Shaping of Post-Reform Politics.* New York: Russell Sage Foundation, 1983.

Wayne, Stephen J. *The Road to the White House 1996: The Politics of Presidential Elections.* New York: St. Martin's Press, 1997.

___. *The Road to the White House, 2000, The Post-Election Edition: The Politics of Presidential Elections.* Boston: Bedford, 2001.

3 PUBLIC POLITICS

Woodrow Wilson throws out the first ball on opening day of the baseball season in 1916.
Wilson helped to usher in the modern public presidency.

F OR MORE THAN A CENTURY, students of the presidency have
argued that the chief executive's continuing relationship with the
American public is a major factor in governing the nation. Writing in
1900, Henry Jones Ford concluded that only presidents can "define issues
in such a way that public opinion can pass upon them decisively."[1]
Woodrow Wilson, anticipating his own approach to the office, echoed
that sentiment: "His [the president's] is the only national voice in affairs.
Let him once win the admiration and confidence of the country and no

other single force can withstand him; no combination of forces will easily over-power him."[2]

As discussed in chapter 1, this preeminent position was strengthened during the last half of the twentieth century. In 1960, Richard Neustadt explained how the presidents' "public prestige" (their "standing with the public outside Wash-ington") influences the decisions of other government officials and nongovern-mental elites, such as members of Congress and the bureaucracy, state gover-nors, military commanders, party politicians, journalists, and foreign diplomats.[3] By the mid-1980s, Samuel Kernell argued that "going public"—issuing cam-paignlike appeals for citizen support—rather than the traditional strategy of bar-gaining with other elites—had become the key to presidential success in the modern era.[4] For the past few decades, the most powerful tool for going public has been television. Kernell and Matthew A. Baum suggested in 1999, however, that the rise of cable television has made such appeals more difficult: hundreds of channels of alternate programming mean that presidents are losing the cap-tive audiences they used to command when all three major networks preempted their regular schedules to carry presidential appearances.[5] No matter the means or the difficulty involved, presidents cannot afford to stop courting voters after the returns are in on Election Day; modern chief executives must woo the Amer-ican public between elections just as they do during elections.

Despite a president's best efforts, maintaining public support is often a diffi-cult task. Approval ratings can change quickly and can be influenced by the state of the economy and crises abroad—events that are sometimes unrelated to spe-cific presidential action. In the week after the terrorist attacks on the World Trade Center and the Pentagon, George W. Bush's ratings shot up 35 points. However, George H. W. Bush enjoyed a similarly high 89% approval rating during the Per-sian Gulf War, only to have it dwindle to 32%—largely because of a faltering economy. After defeating Bush in 1992, Bill Clinton failed to generate high lev-els of public support during his first three years as chief executive but left office in 2001 with the highest approval rating of any departing president since the advent of public opinion polls.[6] Even in the face of impeachment, Clinton had maintained high job approval ratings—a factor that some observers attributed to the strong economy, and one that may have aided his acquittal in the Senate.[7] Interestingly, Clinton's high approval ratings did not help his vice president, Al Gore, secure electoral victory in the 2000 presidential election. Indeed, political scientist Charles O. Jones has argued that Clinton's efforts to boost his own pop-ularity may actually have hurt Gore.[8]

This chapter begins with an analysis of enduring public attitudes toward the presidency and then considers the ways chief executives try to hold the support of the American people. This includes the use of public appeals, targeted com-munications to interest groups and party activists, and efforts to use the media to the president's advantage. We conclude the chapter by arguing that these tac-tics have helped to create a "permanent campaign" that is waged by presidents between elections.

Public Attitudes toward the Presidency

Citizens relate to the presidency on many levels. At the conscious level, people develop attitudes toward three major components of a political system: the political community of which they are a part; the regime, or formal and informal "rules of the game" followed in the constitutional system; and the authorities, or public officials who hold positions in the government structure.[9] If these attitudes are sufficiently strong and positive, the public may follow its leaders even if it does not like a particular incumbent or the policies that leader advocates.

The president, it can be argued, is the focus of public attitudes in each of these three areas. Like the British monarch, the U.S. chief executive is the symbol of the nation, a personification of government capable of inspiring feelings of loyalty and patriotism, particularly in times of crisis when the leader becomes the rallying point for national efforts. For example, Franklin D. Roosevelt's political friends and foes alike turned to him for leadership when the Japanese attacked Pearl Harbor in December 1941. The same support arose when Ronald Reagan decided to invade the Caribbean island of Grenada in 1983, when Bill Clinton directed that cruise missiles strike Iraq in 1993, and when George W. Bush launched a full-scale invasion of Iraq in 2003. Calls to support the president quickly drown out critical voices.

Because presidents are central figures in the constitutional system, they can benefit from upholding the accepted rules of the game or suffer from violating them. Many Americans felt that Richard Nixon violated his constitutional obligations as well as basic democratic values by placing himself above the law during the Watergate scandal; evidence indicated that he participated in a cover-up designed to hide the truth about an illegal break-in directed by White House aides. The Monica Lewinsky scandal, however, showed that many Americans seemed to make a distinction between the types of abuses of power that Nixon engaged in and Clinton's efforts to cover up a sexual affair with Lewinsky. Most viewed Clinton's affair as a private matter that had nothing to do with his job as president.[10]

Finally, presidents are major actors in the policy-making process; the positions they adopt elicit support or opposition, and their overall performance in office becomes the object of citizens' evaluations. Again, Clinton showed that Americans could make a distinction between job performance and personal approval. On leaving office in January 2001, a Gallup poll (taken before his controversial pardon of fugitive financier Marc Rich) showed a 65 percent job approval rating but only a 41 percent personal approval rating. An earlier, April 2000, Gallup poll was even more striking: 59 percent job approval but only 29 percent personal approval.

Fred Greenstein has suggested that presidents meet a variety of psychological needs of the citizenry. As a *cognitive aid*, the president can make government and politics comprehensible; by focusing on the president's activities, citizens simplify a distant and complex world. The president also provides an *outlet for feel-*

ings experienced by supporters and opponents, giving citizens the opportunity to develop and express emotions about politics. On the subconscious level, some citizens may seek *vicarious participation*, a desire to identify with a powerful political figure much as people do with fictional figures and entertainment personalities. Presidents symbolize *national unity* as well as *stability* and *predictability*, providing citizens with psychologically satisfying feelings that may meet fundamental needs for membership and reassurance. Finally, presidents serve as *lightning rods* within the political system, figures to blame for bad times and to credit for good times.[11] Because presidents play a central role in the nightly dramas communicated on television news—not to mention the round-the-clock cable news outlets such as CNN, Fox News, and MSNBC—their importance as objects of psychological feelings may be greater today than ever before.

Beyond basic beliefs and psychological needs, the public also has views about the day-to-day operation of the political system—in particular, the major issues of the day and the policies the government should follow in dealing with them. These views, generally assumed to be less stable and enduring than beliefs about the political culture, are often described as matters of "public opinion." A citizen's attitudes on policy issues and presidential performance depend on his or her identity with a particular group, such as a political party, and his or her social, economic, and geographic background. As the nation's leading political figure, the president is expected to develop and help put into effect controversial policies that are binding on the entire populace. People respond favorably or unfavorably to each chief executive's particular personality and political style and to the events that occur while a president is in office. People also assess presidents by the way they relate to particular groups—political parties as well as social (religious, ethnic, racial), economic (business, labor), and geographic divisions of the population.

Thus many diverse factors affect public opinion of the president. At times, people see the chief executive as the embodiment of the nation; on other occasions people link the president with a particular issue or policy they favor or oppose. After examining the symbolic importance accorded the presidency, we turn to political socialization and how people develop their attitudes toward the presidency. We then look more closely at public opinion polls.

Symbolic Dimensions of the Presidency

The Ronald Reagan Presidential Library opened on November 4, 1991, a day marked by speeches from five presidents (Nixon, Ford, Carter, Reagan, and Bush—the largest number of former and current chief executives alive at the same time since 1861) and appearances by six first ladies (starting with Lady Bird Johnson) as well as offspring of Franklin D. Roosevelt and John F. Kennedy. It was perhaps the largest assemblage of presidents and presidential families in history.[12] The library, located in Simi Valley, California, cost $60 million to construct and devotes 22,000 of its 153,000 square feet to exhibits commemorating the Reagan years. Every president since Herbert Hoover has had a library erected in his name to house the papers of his administration and his pre-presidential career, explain his record to the public, and define his legacy to the nation. President Clinton's will be in Little Rock, Arkansas, and is scheduled to open in the fall of 2004. It will contain nearly 80 million pages of documents, 9 million photographs, and 75,000 artifacts—more material than has been collected for any other presidential library. (For a National Archives Web site offering an overview of the presidential library system and links to each of the individual libraries, go to www.nara.gov/nara/president/address.html.) All presidential libraries combine commemoration with facilities for research. Most visitors choose only to view relics from a president's life, items drawn from childhood through retirement, and to reexperience personal memories and moments of drama through museum-like displays, many of which are interactive.

The presidential libraries, therefore, have a significance that extends beyond their ostensible purposes. In many respects, they can be viewed as shrines constructed to commemorate the lives and achievements of the most recent heroes in the nation's collective memory, a veritable presidential pantheon whose most sacred shrines, the Washington Monument and Lincoln Memorial, are located in Washington, D.C. Presidents stand at the center of what might be termed an "American mythology," a collection of stories and interpretations loosely linked to historical events but serving larger purposes in our collective experience: to celebrate basic values held in common, extol national virtues, and maintain unity in the face of enormous national diversity. In addition to the commemorative sites, Americans have created national holidays, public rituals, and icons, as well as a collection of stories, some of them apocryphal, which are passed on to our children. All attest to the presidency's symbolic importance.

Ceremony and pomp surround the presidency, another indication of the importance of the office in national life. A presidential inauguration resembles the coronation of a king, complete with the taking of an oath in the presence of notables and "the hailing by the multitudes."[13] Public appearances are accompanied by a display of the special presidential seal and the playing of "Hail to the Chief" as the president arrives. News conferences are conducted under a set of rules designed to communicate deference and respect as much as elicit hard news.

Particular occasions have been elevated to ritualistic status. The State of the Union message, for example, allows the president to outline an agenda for Congress and the nation. Woodrow Wilson resurrected this ceremony after more than a century of disuse; today it is an annual occasion for high drama and solemn pronouncements aimed as much at the prime-time television audience as the political elites in attendance. Members of Congress, the cabinet, and the diplomatic corps as well as distinguished visitors gather in the House chamber and chatter expectantly until the sergeant-at-arms solemnly announces the president's arrival, at which point the audience respectfully rises to its feet and applauds. Following a formal introduction from the Speaker of the House, there is another standing ovation. After the speech, a phalanx of congressional leaders accompanies the president as he leaves the hall, and members reach out along the way to shake hands or just to touch the presidential person.

These outward manifestations of respect, made part of recurrent governing rituals, indicate the near reverence accorded the position of president. Respect for the *presidency* as distinct from the *president,* the current officeholder, is deeply ingrained in American political culture. George Washington and his advisers gave the office dignity by enhancing its ceremonial functions and designing a set of "republican rituals," for which no direct precedents existed, based on their exclusive experience with monarchy.[14] But Washington's major contribution to the presidency was to imbue the office with nearly mythical stature. At one time, Washington's likeness was so widely displayed that it became a virtual icon, the picture of a venerated saint displayed by fervent believers in hopes of deriving blessings.[15] The hero worship lavished on Washington during his lifetime and the subsequent cult that developed in commemorating his service to the nation ensured that the presidency will always be associated with the nation's own sense of moral virtue and collective destiny.[16]

In the late nineteenth century, Washington's birthday became a day of national celebration second only to the Fourth of July. In many states, Abraham Lincoln's birthday, too, came to be celebrated as a holiday. Eventually, the two were combined into Presidents' Day. Every February, American schoolchildren are taught stories about these presidents whose youthful endeavors illustrate the fundamental virtues of truthfulness ("Father, I cannot tell a lie"), honesty (walking miles to return change), and hard work (wilderness surveyor and rail-splitter). In like ways, we celebrate the lives of Washington's successors, but we also expect them to live up to the heroic qualities of their predecessors.

Consistent with this symbolic role, the nation routinely turns to the president to perform a variety of ceremonial chores, many of them minor, such as lighting the national Christmas tree and issuing proclamations on the observance of special days. But Americans also call upon presidents to perform more important symbolic tasks, such as helping citizens deal with their collective grief when disaster strikes. For example, President Bush expressed the feelings of millions when he publicly mourned the thousands of deaths caused by the terrorist attacks on September 11, 2001, and when he memorialized the crew of the lost space shuttle *Columbia* in February 2003. Likewise, President Clinton provided solace and reassurance in the face of sudden, inexplicable death after the bombing of the federal building in Oklahoma City on April 19, 1995.

The presidency, more than any other aspect of political life, links Americans with both the past and the future. In focusing on the current White House occupant, citizens simultaneously derive a sense of fulfillment from past accomplishments and reassurance about the future. Presidents often help to evoke such feelings of continuity through symbolism. When President Clinton gave his farewell address on January 18, 2001, he was flanked by busts of Abraham Lincoln and Franklin D. Roosevelt. When George W. Bush took the oath of office two days later, he used the same 1767 Bible used in the inauguration ceremonies of

George Washington, Warren Harding, Dwight D. Eisenhower, Jimmy Carter, and his father, George Bush. As the newest chief executive gave his inaugural address, former presidents Carter, Bush, and Clinton sat behind him. (Gerald Ford, who had suffered a minor stroke the previous summer, did not attend.)

Barbara Hinckley has argued that presidents and their speechwriters are highly attuned to the public's expectations of a chief executive. In turn, the White House projects "a symbolic presentation of the presidential office" expressed through the chief executive's public actions and statements.[17] Her study (tracing the Truman through Reagan administrations) showed that, with remarkable consistency, the picture portrayed to the public emphasized several common themes: the president, the American people, and the nation were presented as indistinguishable from each other and as together carrying out most of the work of "government"; Congress, when mentioned, was usually dismissed rather than recognized as an equal branch of government; identifiable population groups were pictured as sharing in the larger purposes that unite the nation; political and electoral activity was far less prominent in presidential discourse than references to religious objects such as God and the Bible; presidents were presented as being without peers and enjoying a unique relationship with the public.[18]

As Hinckley suggested, there is always the possibility that the public might be able to reshape the presidency and its position in the constitutional order by altering expectations of the office and its occupants. After the Democrats' humiliating defeat in the 1994 midterm elections, for example, it looked as though Congress might be able to assert itself as a prime force through the Republicans' "Contract with America." Although House Speaker Newt Gingrich, R-Ga.—the chief architect of the contract and the leader of the "Republican revolution"—dominated the headlines during his first hundred days as Speaker, he quickly lost his momentum.[19] Then, in the famous budget battle of 1995–1996, President Clinton reasserted himself. Republicans called for sharp budget cuts that would affect major entitlement programs such as Medicaid, Medicare, and Social Security. Clinton called such cuts irresponsible and rallied the opposition to the Republican plan. Deadlock over the budget led to government shutdowns in November and in December of 1995 and in January 1996. The public blamed the Republicans for the shutdowns by a margin of two to one, and Clinton emerged victorious from the budget battle. One poll showed that Gingrich's approval rating had plummeted to 25 percent, while Clinton's had risen to 52 percent. Had Congress won instead, the stage might have been set for a more long-term shift in the balance of power between Congress and the president—one that might have undermined the president's symbolic position as the nation's leader.

Such a scenario, though, is very unlikely. Even if Congress had won, it is hard to imagine the presidency being displaced from its preeminent position—at least for long. Individual presidents may face periods of weakness and defeat, but the power of the presidency itself endures. As we have seen, enormous pressures for continuity have developed around the presidential office. Expectation of heroic performance and belief in the identity between presidents and the nation are attitudes deeply embedded in the political culture. Collectively, these beliefs about the presidency provide the incumbent with a remarkably durable base of popular support.

Developing Attitudes toward the Presidency

Not surprisingly, the president is the public official most likely to be correctly identified in surveys. Traditionally, presidents have also enjoyed general respect and admiration. In Gallup polls asking Americans to name the man, living any-where in the world, whom they most admire, the president of the United States has almost always been the first choice.[20] President Bush was the clear-cut win-ner in 2001 and 2002. Despite Whitewater and Monica Lewinsky, President Clinton had remained the most admired man in the world in every Gallup poll from 1993 through 2000 (although he tied with Pope John Paul II in 2000, a year when there was relatively little consensus among Americans about what man they most admired). First ladies usually top the list of most admired women. Hillary Clinton earned that distinction every year of her husband's pres-idency and even edged out first lady Laura Bush in 2002. (Laura Bush came in first in 2001.)[21]

Often, favorable attitudes are expressed toward the "generalized abstract" president rather than toward any specific incumbent.[22] The initial basis for these attitudes is formed in childhood through a process social scientists call "political socialization." Political scientist Paul Beck has argued that there are three condi-tions necessary for an "agent" of political socialization (such as an individual or an institution) to shape one's attitudes: exposure, communication, and receptiv-ity. In other words, one cannot be influenced unless one is exposed to that agent, actually receives communication from that agent, and is receptive to that agent's views. Parents are the most important agent of socialization for young children. School is another significant agent. As children get older, peers become more important in shaping attitudes.[23] So, too, do the media.

Early work on the development of childhood attitudes toward the president showed that children viewed the president as both powerful and benevolent.[24] In the *cognitive* (knowing) world of the young child, the president personified the government. Until they were teenagers, most children were not even aware that the president shared the running of government with Congress and the Supreme Court. In addition to children's awareness of the president's importance, studies also underscored the *affective* (emotional) dimension of children's attitudes toward the president. Thus they thought of the president as a "good" person who cares about people, wants to help them, and wants to "get things done."

There are several explanations for why young children developed these favorable attitudes about the president. Parents who viewed the president favor-ably might have passed on these views to their children; those who did not might have suppressed their unfavorable views for fear of undermining the child's respect for authority. Children's favorable attitudes toward other authority figures, such as teachers, might also have carried over into their respect for the president.[25] Yet another explanation for children's favorable views emphasized their vulnerability: they wanted to believe the president is a good person who will protect, rather than threaten, them.

Other research, however, found that not everyone experienced the same socialization. Poor children in Kentucky were found to be much less favorably disposed toward the president, regarding him as less honest, less hardworking, less caring, and less knowledgeable than had the urban middle-class children of previous studies.[26] Nearly a quarter of these children viewed the president as a malevolent, rather than a benevolent, leader. Moreover, after revelations of the Watergate scandal in the early 1970s, a study of middle-class children found that they were less likely to idealize the chief executive than were their earlier counterparts; nor did they assign the president as important a role in running the country or making the laws.[27] Within just a few months of President Nixon's resignation, however, these views began to moderate.[28] Indeed, evidence suggests that children are able to distinguish between the person temporarily occupying the office and the presidency itself. They therefore can respect the institution without respecting the incumbent, an attitude that can carry over into their adult years and provide a solid basis of support for the U.S. political system.

Political scientists have continued to study childhood socialization,[29] although recent studies have not tended to focus on the specific question of childhood attitudes toward the president. However, a CNN–Gallup poll of children ages eleven to seventeen conducted February 4–9, 1999, (during the impeachment trial of President Clinton), sheds interesting light on the question. The poll showed that children had a considerably lower opinion of the president than did adults surveyed at the same time. Although 65 percent of the adults approved of Clinton's handling of his job, only 42 percent of the children did. Even more striking, when the children were given a list and asked, "Please tell me whether each of the following are people you, personally, look up to as role models in your life," in last place was "The President" (at 34 percent), behind "Your parents" (94 percent), "Your teachers" (77 percent), "Your friends" (72 percent), "Sports stars" (65 percent), "Music, TV and movie stars" (61 percent), and "Other elected officials" (41 percent). When asked more specifically, 65 percent of the children stated that they did *not* look up to "The President." Only 26 percent of the children said that they would like to grow up to be president of the United States someday, and only 45 percent of adults said that they would like for their children to grow up to be president.

Tracking Public Opinion

Since 1938, the Gallup organization periodically has polled a cross section of Americans on whether they approve or disapprove of the way the president is handling the job. The emphasis of the question is on performance in office rather than personal qualities, a virtual "continuing monthly referendum" on how the president is handling the job.[30] (Up-to-date results of these polls can be accessed online at www.gallup.com.) In recent years, many other organizations have also conducted polls, including ones measuring presidential approval ratings. (These, too, can be accessed online by going to www.govspot.com and clicking on "Polls/Opinion.")

Independent pollsters are not the only ones keeping a finger on the pulse of public opinion: every president since Richard Nixon has retained his own paid polling consultants.[31] Earlier presidents, such as Franklin Roosevelt, had secretly sought polling data from unpaid, unofficial advisers.[32] White House pollsters go far beyond simple tracking of presidential approval. As political scientist Diane Heath has written, presidential pollsters "helped their administrations isolate constituencies by focusing on what linked individuals to the president and the administration's policies."[33] Thus the White House has highly specific polling data on everyone from homeowners to born-again Christians. At the height of the energy crisis in the 1970s, President Carter's pollsters even created polling categories based on the type of home heating used by the respondent.[34] By focusing on specific demographic groups and identifying issues that resonate with them, presidents are able to engage in highly targeted public appeals.

Presidents also use polling and focus groups to test language that they plan to use in speeches.[35] For example, the Reagan administration used focus groups in 1987 and 1988 to help plan the president's State of the Union address, his speech to Congress about the summit meeting with Soviet leader Mikhail Gorbachev, and his response to the Iran-contra affair. Using such focus groups helped the White House to fashion messages that were both appealing and believable.[36] Similarly, Bill Clinton made extensive use of polls and focus groups in formulating his agenda. Some observers have described the Clinton White House as driven by polls.[37] Molly Andolina and Clyde Wilcox have noted that President Clinton often frustrated opponents by his "ability to cut right or left, depending on prevailing sentiments." They point out that in his second term he adeptly embraced issues that enjoyed popular support so that even in the face of a Senate impeachment trial in February 1999, 69 percent of the respondents of a Pew Research Center survey liked Clinton's policies.[38] Thus despite the scandals and the impeachment, Clinton is the only president since polling began whose average Gallup job approval rating was higher for his last year in office (60 percent) than for his first (48.8 percent). No doubt the upward trajectory of Clinton's job approval ratings was also buoyed by a surging economy. This is an exception to the general rule that presidents deplete their public support as time goes by.

Paul Brace and Barbara Hinckley have called this depletion of public support a "decay curve."[39] This decay can be attributed to the deflation of unrealistically high expectations of performance, and the curve typically bottoms out near the thirtieth month of an initial term. Brace and Hinckley suggest that this decay normally occurs "irrespective of the economy, the president, or outside events." If a president is fortunate enough to be reelected, an uncertain prospect at best, the decline usually begins earlier and follows a steeper path. Beyond this cycle, though, Brace and Hinckley recognize that events that capture the public's attention may increase or diminish presidential support. In general, events that "dramatize conflict in the nation," even if the president has taken no action to trigger them, are likely to reduce support. Events that "unify the nation around its symbols" are likely to increase support. Thus President Bush's approval ratings soared after the September 11, 2001, terrorist attacks and spiked upward when the United States invaded Iraq in March 2003. Still, the decay curve was evident. Bush's Gallup approval rating dropped consistently from a high of 90 percent in September 2001 to 57 percent in the March 3–5, 2003, poll—a steady decay of about six points every three months.[40] It then jumped to 69 percent in a March 24–25, 2003, Gallup poll taken just after the start of the war in Iraq but fell back to 50 percent within six months.[41] Such events suggest that domestic or international events beyond the control of presidents may conspire to increase or decrease their public support, though some presidents may be responsible for their own good or bad fortune by taking actions that trigger positive or negative public responses.[42]

To the extent that presidents rely on public support for policy success, the decay curve suggests that they are well advised to "hit the ground running" and accomplish as much as they can as early as they can in their administrations.[43] Along with public support, other pieces of political "capital," such as a mandate from a strong electoral margin and congressional support, are also likely to be strongest at the outset of a president's term.[44] David Gergen, an adviser to Presidents Nixon, Ford, Reagan, and Clinton, recognized this early on. As a member of Reagan's transition team in 1980, he wrote a detailed memorandum comparing the first hundred days of every administration since that of Franklin Roosevelt. In it, he showed that the successful presidents were those who immediately established a clear and simple agenda and used their capital to achieve it.[45] Reagan followed Gergen's advice and framed his entire legislative agenda around just four major issues that the administration carefully promoted and implemented. In contrast, both Jimmy Carter and Bill Clinton—despite a Congress controlled by their own party—largely squandered their first years in office.

Like Reagan, George W. Bush charted a clear-cut legislative agenda for his first hundred days in office. For Bush, those days were especially important. He came to office without a clear electoral mandate (indeed, he lost the popular vote to Al Gore), without strong support in Congress (although enjoying a small Republican majority in the House, the Senate was evenly divided between Republicans and Democrats), and his initial Gallup job *dis*approval ratings were at 25 percent, the highest of any new president since polling began. His approval ratings were also bifurcated by a distinct partisan wedge, which political scientist Gary Jacobson identified as the largest for any newly elected president in polling history. According to Jacobson's analysis of the twenty-eight Gallup and CBS News/*New York Times* presidential approval polls of Bush taken before September 11, 2001, "Bush's approval ratings averaged 88 percent among self-identified Republicans but only 31 percent among Democrats. This 57-point difference marked Bush as an even more polarizing figure than the former record holder,

Bill Clinton (with an average partisan difference in approval of 52 points for the comparable period of his administration)."[46] Success at selling his legislative agenda—with a tax cut designed to please his Republican base and education reform designed to win bipartisan support—became a way for Bush to demonstrate his leadership ability, win broader public support, and build political capital. As discussed in chapters 5 and 11, however, Bush did not achieve legislative success on these issues during the first hundred days. He did secure passage of a tax cut on May 26, 2001, but that victory was overshadowed by the stunning defection of Sen. James M. Jeffords of Vermont from the Republican Party. Jeffords's decision to become an independent threw control of the Senate to the Democrats, threatened to derail the rest of the president's legislative agenda, and led to renewed criticism of Bush. The terrorist attacks of September 11, 2001, altered the political landscape and gave Bush a second chance to prove himself. His approval ratings skyrocketed from 51 to 90 percent—the highest presidential approval rating ever recorded by the Gallup Poll.[47] September 11 also temporarily minimized the partisan wedge. Support among Democrats rose more than 50 points almost overnight (from an average of 30 percent before September 11 to an average of 81 percent in the month following the terrorist attacks). Support from fellow Republicans rose from 89 to an amazing 98 percent in the same period.[48] That temporarily narrowed (17-point) differential returned to a gap averaging 54 points by November 2002.[49] Even the successful U.S. invasion of Iraq in the spring of 2003 did little to alter the partisan gap.[50]

Figure 3-1 shows results of the Gallup poll on presidential performance from Eisenhower through George W. Bush. An examination of the figure shows evidence of the decay curve for every president except Clinton. It is also clear that starting in the mid-1960s, it became common for presidential approval ratings to fall below 50 percent. Even incoming presidents have confronted lower ratings in recent years. Eisenhower and Johnson both had approval ratings of 78 percent when Gallup first gathered information about them as president, and Kennedy had an approval rating of 72 percent—even though he received only 49.7 percent of the popular vote in the 1960 election.[51] No president since Carter, however, has had an initial job approval rating of more than 58 percent (George W. Bush's was 57 percent). Until the second Bush (whose first-year average of 66.4 percent approval was skewed upward by the events of September 11), there had been a similar decline in average first-year ratings (from 69.9 percent for Eisenhower's first year to 48.8 percent for Clinton's). Some of this decline may have been attributable to cynicism borne of Vietnam, Watergate, Iran-contra, and Whitewater. In addition, television may have helped to demystify the presidency, and the decline may also have reflected a persistent trend toward tighter presidential elections (often coupled with a lack of enthusiasm for either candidate) and "divided government" (in which one party controls the White House and another controls Congress). Neither George W. Bush in 2000 nor Bill Clinton in 1992 or 1996 received 50 percent of the popular vote. Even Ronald Reagan's "landslide" in 1980 amounted to only 50.7 percent of the

Figure 3-1 Presidential Approval, 1953–2003

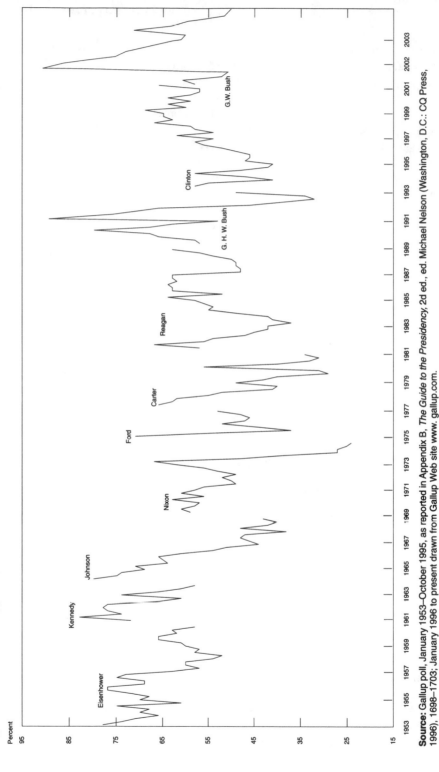

Source: Gallup poll, January 1953–October 1995, as reported in Appendix B, *The Guide to the Presidency*, 2d ed., ed. Michael Nelson (Washington, D.C.: CQ Press, 1996), 1698–1703; January 1996 to present drawn from Gallup Web site www. gallup.com.

Note: Question: "Do you approve or disapprove of the way _____ (last name of president) is handling his job as president?"

*The last Gallup poll for G. W. Bush was conducted on September 19–21, 2003.

popular vote (although he won 90.9 percent of the electoral vote). For whatever reason, Americans seem warier of new presidents than in times past—less willing to give them the benefit of the doubt and more apt to withhold support until they prove themselves.

Rallying Public Support

Presidents are not passive objects of public attitudes. Rather, presidents and their aides take the initiative in shaping public perceptions. Over time, the White House has developed several specialized staff units devoted to maintaining favorable public relations and for promoting its agenda on Capitol Hill, with interest groups, and with members of the president's own party.[52] In performing these tasks, aides take actions and fashion appeals designed to win the support of different kinds of audiences, including other elites, the public at large, and specific constituencies.

The Rise of the Public Presidency

We now take public appeals by the president for granted, but as noted in chapter 1, scholars such as Jeffrey Tulis contend that the rise of the "rhetorical" presidency is really a twentieth-century phenomenon.[53] Arguably, the now commonplace practice of presidents "going public" to build public support for specific legislative initiatives is one of the most significant changes of the modern presidency.[54] As presidents have embraced public appeals, the source of presidential power has expanded from narrowly defined constitutional underpinnings to a broader plebiscitary base.[55] (For an alternate view, see the recent revisionist account of political scientist Mel Laracey.)[56]

Tulis argues that presidents avoided the widespread use of public appeals in the nineteenth century because they adhered to a fundamentally different understanding of our political order than the one commonly held today. Their avoidance of public appeals reflected the Founders' distrust of "pure" or "direct" democracy. Although the Founders believed that public *consent* was a requirement of republican government, they nonetheless felt that the processes of government should be insulated from the whims of public *opinion*. Thus they attempted to instill "deliberation" in government through such things as indirect elections, separation of powers, and an independent executive. In such a system, public appeals by the president were proscribed because they were thought to "manifest demagoguery, impede deliberation, and subvert the routines of republican government."[57] Policy rhetoric by presidents—to the extent that it existed—was primarily written, and principally addressed, to Congress (as opposed to modern-day policy rhetoric, which is primarily spoken, and principally addressed, to the people). Thus it was *"public* (available to all) but not thereby *popular* (fashioned for all)."[58]

Presidents avoided "going public" (which is specifically designed to whip up public opinion) because it went against the existing interpretation of the constitutional order. That is not to say that other sorts of popular appeals were never made. Government-sponsored partisan newspapers flourished in the early part of our history and were clearly a means of generating public support—often by ridiculing the opposition with highly inflammatory articles.[59] *The Federalist Papers* themselves are another early example of public appeals. Indeed, Federalists made a point of befriending key printers, thus forming a network for the distribution of information favorable to the Federalist cause.[60] Once in power, Federalists were accused of thwarting the circulation of opposition papers through control of the post office.[61] Arguably, however, the authors of these early examples designed them primarily to build public consent for broadly based structures—partisan newspapers for emerging political parties, and *The Federalist Papers* for a new form of government—rather than as more direct tools for mobilizing public opinion for congressional passage of specific policy initiatives.[62] Securing legislation remained an elite process of bargaining.

Nineteenth-century presidents did not maintain total public silence. They made occasional speeches to the people and even made some tours around the country (called "swings around the circle"). But public speeches were not as important as public appearances on those tours. President Washington, for example, initiated a "grand tour" of two months' duration by visiting the South in 1791, a region where suspicions of central authority had run strong during the constitutional ratification campaign. Washington himself emphasized the importance of "seeing and being seen" on the tour, and though the president gave public remarks, Tulis emphasizes that they contained only "general articulations of republican sentiment, not even a clear enunciation of principle."[63]

Indeed, eighteenth- and nineteenth-century presidential speeches had an overall character very different from presidential speeches given today: they were largely ceremonial and usually devoid of policy content. They were also much less frequent. Tulis calculated that from George Washington through William McKinley presidents averaged thirteen public speeches a year—80 percent or more of them very brief "thank you" remarks. The first eleven presidents averaged three public speeches a year.[64] In comparison, Clinton averaged one public speech almost every other day during his first three years in office.[65] To underscore the very different nature of rhetorical "common law" that existed in the nineteenth century, Tulis points out that Andrew Johnson was the first president to engage in a full-scale popular appeal over the heads of Congress for the passage of legislation and that he had an article of impeachment brought against him for doing so.[66]

Tulis identifies Theodore Roosevelt and Woodrow Wilson as catalysts for the new rhetorical presidency. He cites Roosevelt's public campaign to win passage of the Hepburn Act (legislation that gave the Interstate Commerce Commission authority to regulate railroad shipping rates) as the first example of a president securing legislation with the help of going public.[67] Use of the "bully pulpit" dovetailed neatly with Roosevelt's broad "stewardship theory" of presidential power. *(See chapter 1.)* Like Roosevelt, Wilson believed that presidents had powers beyond those specifically enumerated in the Constitution, and he saw public opinion as an important source of that additional power.[68] Thus he expanded the use of rhetoric and used it in new ways. He was the first elected president to have engaged in a full-scale speaking tour as part of the general election campaign.[69] Once in office, Wilson changed the norms of presidential rhetoric. He was the one largely responsible for the shift to policy rhetoric primarily spoken and principally addressed to the people. When Wilson delivered his State of the Union report orally—the first president to do so since John Adams—he had clearly fashioned his message for the people even though he presented it to Congress. One of Wilson's most dramatic appeals for public support—his whistlestop train tour to promote the League of Nations—was cut short by the stroke he suffered in Colorado on September 26, 1919.

Presidential Appeals

Appeals for public support are now a routine part of presidential governance. Presidents use that support as a bargaining chip with Congress—a way to persuade (or coerce) it to follow their leads. George W. Bush embraced that strategy as soon as he entered the White House. He spent his first week in office promoting his proposed education reforms. He and others in his administration stayed "on message" so that what they said about education reform would be the major topic in the news. The White House spent subsequent weeks promoting other aspects of the president's agenda. Bush used his first address before Congress on February 27, 2001, to mobilize public support for his plans. He then followed up the address with speaking tours to promote the centerpiece of his agenda: a proposed $1.6 trillion tax cut. In just the two days following his address to Congress, Bush gave speeches touting his tax cut in Pennsylvania, Nebraska, Iowa, Arkansas, and Georgia. The explicit purpose of these speeches was to urge the American people to put pressure on Congress to pass the president's initiatives. When the House of Representatives approved the president's tax cut on March 8, Bush was still on the road—visiting states where Democratic senators who opposed the plan would be facing tight reelection battles in 2002. In Fargo, North Dakota, the president urged a cheering, flag-waving crowd to put pressure on their senators: "If you like what you hear today, maybe e-mail some of the good folks from the United States Senate from your state," Bush said. "If you like what you hear, why don't you just give 'em a call and write 'em a letter."[70]

Like Bush, President Clinton used his annual State of the Union addresses to build public support for his policies—and himself. His 1998 State of the Union came just one week after the Monica Lewinsky story broke. In the firestorm of media coverage that immediately followed the news of the Lewinsky affair, many media commentators predicted that Clinton would be forced to resign or would be impeached. Even Clinton's former communications director, George Stephanopoulos, predicted resignation or impeachment if the story proved to be true.[71] Initial public opinion polls showed a drop of 5 percentage points in

Clinton's job approval rating. Many advisers counseled him to postpone his State of the Union address or to use it as a forum for responding to the allegations and apologizing to the American people.[72] Instead, Clinton gave the address as planned and never mentioned the Lewinsky affair. Fifty-three million Americans watched him give one of the best speeches of his presidency. In it, he outlined his policy goals. Public reaction was overwhelmingly positive, and his Gallup approval rating surged to 67 percent (the highest of his presidency to date) and stayed high for the rest of his term. The speech arguably did much to save his presidency. He gave a State of the Union address at a similarly awkward time—and with equal success—during his Senate impeachment trial a year later. When weighing whether to convict Clinton, senators must have been mindful of his soaring job approval ratings (which, according to Gallup, had reached another new high of 73 percent just after the House voted to impeach).

In addition to major prime-time television speeches such as the State of the Union, presidents give many minor speeches to groups around the country. Presidents ration their major speeches out of fear that the tactic will lose effectiveness if overused. In the face of competition from rival cable channels, the major networks have even begun to refuse airtime to the president if they feel the speech is not important enough. Even when the networks do cover a speech, viewers with cable or satellite channels can easily tune the president out by choosing alternate programming.[73] Minor speeches allow the president to target appeals to specific constituencies. When given on the road, they can also generate considerable local media coverage. As can be seen in Figure 3-2, these speeches have increased dramatically in recent years.

Corresponding with this increase in "going public" is a similar increase in presidential travel (see Figure 3-3). This dramatic increase began under Reagan and reflects the "permanent campaign" for public support that presidents now wage while in office.[74] Even Clinton's inability to run for a third term did not deter him from campaign mode. George W. Bush followed suit. He crisscrossed the country to stump for his tax cut proposals in 2001 and 2003 and barnstormed for fellow Republicans before the 2002 midterm elections (visiting fifteen states in just the last five days before the election).[75] Although most presidential travel is domestic, modern presidents have significantly increased their foreign travel as well. Political scientist Richard Rose has dubbed this "going international." As Rose puts it, presidents can no longer do their jobs simply by staying in the United States. "Whereas Herbert Hoover spent only three days abroad in his term of office and Franklin Roosevelt spent only nine days abroad in his first term, Richard Nixon spent fifty-nine days abroad in his first four years in office, and Jimmy Carter fifty-six days."[76] George W. Bush spent sixty-five days abroad (a total of fifteen foreign trips to thirty-two nations) in just over two-and-a-half years in office.[77] Such trips highlight the president's role as head of state and can paint a picture of the president as diplomat and peacemaker. Nixon's dramatic trips to China and the Soviet Union in 1972 (an election year) were beamed back live to American television with newly developed satellite technology. Reagan's

Figure 3-2   Presidential Addresses, 1929–1995 (Yearly Averages for First Three Years of First Term)

Source: Samuel Kernell and Gary C. Jacobson, *The Logic of American Politics* (Washington, D.C.: CQ Press, 2000), 241.

Note: To eliminate public activities inspired by concerns of reelection rather than governing, only the first three years have been tabulated. For this reason, Gerald Ford's record of public activities during his two-and-one-half years of office has been ignored.

aIncludes television addresses only.

trips abroad provided many memorable television moments, including his emotional visit to the Normandy beaches of France (which became the backdrop for dramatic reelection ads in 1984).

Aside from foreign travel, "going international" has also come to include efforts by presidents to monitor and build public opinion abroad. Reagan was the first to do this in a systematic way.[78] The Reagan administration made a concerted effort to reach an international audience in 1981–1982 to deflect criticism of the president's decision to deploy nuclear weapons in Europe. This included an extensive public relations campaign in western Europe, including a speech by President Reagan transmitted live by satellite and timed to air in prime time on European television.[79] George W. Bush took going international to new heights. After the September 11 terrorist attacks he created the Coalition Information Center (CIC), an around-the-clock White House communications operation to build public support abroad for the war on terrorism (especially among Muslims in the Middle East). Its director, James Wilkinson, coordinated daily press briefings at CIC offices around the world (including Washington, London, Islamabad, and Kabul) and stressed the need to respond rapidly to breaking news everywhere. "It may be 3 o'clock in the morning in the United States," Wilkinson explained, "but somewhere in the world, a journalist is on deadline."[80] The never-ending news cycle created by globalization required a twenty-four-hour news operation at the White House. In January 2003, the White House expanded the CIC and turned it into a permanent Office of Global Communications

Figure 3-3   Days of Political Travel by Presidents, 1929–1995 (Yearly Averages for First Three Years of First Term)

Number of days

| | Hoover (1929–31) | Roosevelt (1933–35) | Truman (1945–47) | Eisenhower (1953–55) | Kennedy (1961–63) | Johnson (1965–67) | Nixon (1969–71) | Carter (1977–79) | Reagan (1981–83) | Bush (1989–91) | Clinton (1993–95) |

■ Foreign   ■ U.S.

Source: Samuel Kernell and Gary C. Jacobson, *The Logic of American Politics* (Washington, D.C.: CQ Press, 2000), 243.

Note: To eliminate public activities inspired by concerns of reelection rather than governing, only the first three years have been tabulated. For this reason, Gerald Ford's record of public activities during his two-and-one-half years of office has been ignored.

directed by Tucker Eskew. In the days leading up to the U.S. invasion of Iraq, the office issued a daily bulletin called "The Global Messenger" to counter Iraqi "propaganda" with "truthful, accurate and effective messages."[81]

Appeals by Surrogates

Presidential surrogates, ranging from the vice president and members of the cabinet to party officials and political consultants, also promote the president's agenda through speaking tours, satellite interviews with local media outlets, and nationwide television appearances on the Sunday morning talk shows and cable outlets such as CNN, MSNBC, and Fox News. Nixon was one of the first presidents to aggressively choreograph the use of these surrogates as part of a broader strategy of going public. He sought to build, as his chief of staff, H. R. Haldeman, put it, "a stable of television personalities from within the Administration."[82]

Nixon was also one of the first presidents to use late-night talk shows and other entertainment outlets to promote himself and his agenda. He appeared on the popular Jack Paar television talk show in 1963 to chat, play the piano, and help rebuild his image after his stinging loss to Pat Brown in the 1962 California gubernatorial race. He made a one-line ("sock it to me") cameo appearance on *Rowan and Martin's Laugh-In* during the 1968 presidential campaign. Once in the White House, Nixon hired a full-time staffer named Al Snyder (a former television executive from New York) to book television appearances for administration officials. Snyder sent Vice President Spiro Agnew on the *Tonight Show with Johnny Carson* and Attorney General John Mitchell on the *Dick Cavett Show* and even arranged for the White House communications director, Herb Klein, to cohost the Cavett show. Snyder also booked more traditional appearances on programs such as *Meet the Press* and arranged local media appearances by administration officials along with advising them where and how to get the best media exposure when they traveled around the country.[83] Another Nixon staffer, Virginia Savell, coordinated speaking tours by administration surrogates. In Nixon's first year in office, she arranged for surrogate speakers to crisscross the country promoting everything from Nixon's proposed family assistance plan to postal reform.[84]

Surrogates—be they traveling around the country on speaking tours or appearing on television—now follow a carefully scripted "line of the day" that is part of the broader message the administration is trying to convey at that point in time. Thus when George W. Bush focused on education reform during his first week in office, his surrogates followed suit. Education Secretary Roderick Paige made the rounds on the morning shows and cable news outlets, as did Vice President Dick Cheney and White House chief of staff Andrew Card. Republican members of Congress joined in, as did other proponents of education reform. In everything from public speeches to background interviews with reporters, administration surrogates stressed education reform. At the same time, the White House arranged for photo opportunities, such as that of the president reading to children at a local school.

The point of such activities is to convey a carefully orchestrated message that is reinforced by different people in a variety of contexts. Such coordination was clearly on display on December 19, 1998, the day the House of Representatives voted to impeach President Clinton. In a morning statement to reporters, White House press secretary Joe Lockhart three times decried "the politics of personal destruction." House minority leader Richard Gephardt repeated the line that morning in a speech on the floor of the House. So, too, did the president in his Rose Garden speech after the impeachment vote.

One advantage of surrogates is that they can be used to target very specific constituencies. Another way of targeting specific constituencies is through links with interest groups, as we will see in the next section.

Targeted Communications: Presidents and Interest Groups

Presidents have come to recognize the value of targeting appeals to organized interests and mobilizing interest groups to support presidential policy. Liaison with such groups is now an important part of governance. As Mark A. Peterson has written, "Working with (as well as working against) interest groups to piece together support among the public and in Congress played a large role in the [Clinton] administration's political and policy strategies."[85] People who organize to advocate a particular interest are highly attentive to public issues affecting their members. These groups also have ongoing links with Congress and the bureaucracy that provide them with policy-making influence. It is not surprising, therefore, that they are a prime target of presidential communication. For example, presidents give major public addresses on business to conventions of the National Association of Manufacturers or the Chamber of Commerce of the United States and on labor relations to meetings of the American Federation of Labor–Congress of Industrial Organizations (AFL-CIO). Chief executives also dispatch surrogates to meet with these groups and to promote the administration's programs. White House aides serve as a channel for private communications with group representatives and will sometimes arrange meetings with the president.

Interest groups want to hear about current matters of public policy, but they also want to be reassured that the president is sympathetic to the problems group members face. Not surprisingly, chief executives pay particular attention to the groups that helped them get elected. They hope to convert their electoral coalition into one that helps them govern as well. Democratic presidents typically have focused on labor unions and civil rights organizations; Republicans have concentrated on business and professional organizations. Presidents also know that as the leader of the nation, they are supposed to represent *all* the people, not just those who supported their election. Chief executives cannot afford to ignore prominent interest groups, even those politically opposed to them.

Presidents also have established channels for routine communication with particular groups through systematic White House liaison. Truman used David Niles, formerly on FDR's staff, as a liaison with blacks and Jews.[86] Eisenhower, who cultivated an image of being above politics, de-emphasized, but did not completely ignore, group relations, and the Kennedy and Johnson administrations designated White House staff members to work with Jews, Catholics, and other groups. Gradually, however, the range of group ties became more predictable. Presidents since Nixon have assigned aides to work with eight population groups: business, labor, Jews, consumers, blacks, women, Hispanics, and the elderly.[87] Most of these ties are pursued through the Office of Public Liaison, a White House staff unit first conceived and implemented in the Nixon administration (under the direction of Charles Colson) and officially consolidated and named an independent staff unit under Gerald Ford.[88] George W. Bush's liaison director, Tim Goeglein—himself an evangelical Christian—also targets Christian outreach.[89]

The Office of Public Liaison has been a part of each administration since Nixon's and has sometimes played an important role in promoting administration policies. People who serve in the liaison office articulate the demands of interest groups inside White House circles and rally the support of interest groups behind the president's programs. Despite this dual purpose, there is little doubt that the office exists primarily to further the president's wishes rather than those of interest groups; aides who reverse these priorities encounter difficulties.[90] The Bush administration, in particular, has earned a reputation for freezing out groups that question its policies. Often the tactic is employed against groups that would generally be viewed as supportive of the president as part of a White House effort to induce a unified Republican front.[91] The administration also learned from the mistakes of its predecessors. For example, one of President-elect Clinton's first public policy statements in 1992 was a commitment to change the government's policy on gays in the military. The move helped to convey the image that Clinton was a captive of the left wing of his party. After both the military and influential members of Congress opposed such changes, Clinton compounded his problems by retreating to a policy of "don't ask, don't tell," which angered gay groups at the same time that it made him appear weak. Similarly, Republicans appeared to be captive to the right wing of their party when they regained control of Congress in 1994, elevated Newt Gingrich to Speaker of the House, and declared their "Contract with America." In contrast, Bush carefully fashioned himself as a "compassionate conservative" and consciously distanced himself from some aspects of his party's right wing. Even after Republicans regained control of Congress in 2002, the White House reportedly cautioned social conservatives that their issues could not come first. Fearful of overreaching, the White House stressed its sympathy for their agenda but counseled restraint in implementing it.[92]

Targeted Communications: Presidents and Political Parties

Outreach to political parties is also an important part of the modern public presidency. Presidents since Harry Truman have assigned staff to serve as liaisons with their political parties.[93] As early as Richard Nixon, this staff was referred to as the Office of Political Affairs, although it did not become a freestanding entity listed in the *U.S. Government Organization Manual* until the Reagan administration.[94] As political scientist Kathryn Dunn Tenpas has noted, the precise functions of the office have changed a good deal from president to president, but there are at least three core functions. First, the office serves as a formal liaison to national, state, and local party organizations as well as to congressional campaign committees. Such a liaison is a two-way street. On the one hand, it allows the White House to monitor the actions of relevant political actors and receive input from them. On the other hand, it provides an opportunity for the White House to mobilize political support from these actors. Thus Harry S. Dent—head of Nixon's Office of Political Affairs—mobilized state Republican chairs to lobby U.S. senators from their states to vote for Nixon Supreme Court nominee Clement Haynsworth in 1969 and to orchestrate a grassroots letter-writing campaign on behalf of the nomination.[95] The office made similar efforts on behalf of George Bush's Supreme Court nominees, David Souter and Clarence Thomas, in 1990 and 1991. The office also uses such ties to promote the president's legislative agenda. This includes building support *for* presidential initiatives and mobilizing *opposition* to programs the president does not support. For example, the office may use pressure from party activists to help gain votes for cloture and help guard against veto overrides, and it may also apply grassroots pressure on members of Congress to vote against legislation. Creating a groundswell of grassroots opposition can also make it easier for the president to oppose certain policies. The first George Bush used the Office of Political Affairs very effectively to help stop campaign finance reform.[96]

Second, the office serves as liaison with major supporters of the president. This includes private citizens who have donated money to support the president's political activities. If such a supporter requests a signed photo from the president or a White House tour, the Office of Political Affairs arranges it. Some alleged that the Clinton administration went beyond this simple sort of constituent service and improperly used the office to raise funds and reward donors. A 1998 report by the House Committee on Government Reform and Oversight, chaired by Rep. Dan Burton, R-Ind., pointed to efforts by members of the Office of Political Affairs under Clinton to create a computerized White House database to identify potential donors. This was part of a broader effort to share information on White House databases with the Democratic National Committee. "This is the President's idea and it's a good one," Marsha Scott, a member of the office, wrote in a draft memorandum to White House chief of staff Mack McLarty in 1994. She wrote that the database would be used to "identify and contact key supporters in all fifty states" and would allow the White House to identify, by early 1995, "key financial and political folks in each state who can work with us."[97] Another memo, dated October 25, 1994, noted that the president wanted the database to correlate contributions from individuals and their invitations to, and attendance at, White House events.[98] In other words, the Office of Political Affairs used the list to reward donors with invitations to meet the president, attend White House functions, or sleep over in the Lincoln Bedroom.

Finally, the office engages in what Tenpas calls "electioneering." In part this includes planning early reelection strategies for presidents in their first terms. Tim Kraft engaged in such planning in the Carter administration before becoming Jimmy Carter's campaign manager for the 1980 election, just as Ed Rollins and Lee Atwater worked in the office during the first Reagan administration before moving over to the 1984 Reagan-Bush campaign headquarters.[99] Most recently, Ken Mehlman served as the director of George W. Bush's Office of Political Affairs before moving over to manage Bush's 2004 reelection campaign.[100] Often the office looks for ways to expand the president's electoral base in anticipation of a reelection bid. It was especially important for Clinton to expand his electoral base because he won the White House in 1992 with just 43 percent of the popular vote. George W. Bush—winning the White House with roughly 48 percent of the popular vote—was in a similar situation when he first took office in 2001. In addition to engineering reelection strategies, the office uses presidential resources to help elect members of Congress from the same political party as the president. During the 2002 midterm elections, Bush's eleven-person office scheduled campaign appearances by leading Republican celebrities, such as former New York mayor Rudolph Giuliani, to help regional candidates raise money and win votes.[101] Typically, the office arranges presidential appearances in the candidate's home state or congressional district, coordinates photo opportunities for the candidate at the White House, and maintains liaison with House and Senate campaign committees.

Presidents, of course, are eager to influence the outcome of midterm congressional elections (which fall midway between presidential elections). The president's party usually loses seats in midterm elections.[102] Nonetheless, the Democrats under Clinton in 1998 and the Republicans under Bush in 2002 bucked that trend. Normally, though, there are limits to what a president can accomplish, especially in elections for the House of Representatives. For one thing, the sheer number of contests (435 every two years) precludes participation in many of them. (Bush's efforts in the 2002 midterm elections have been called "unprecedented," with a record ninety campaign appearances, yet he still made personal campaign appearances for only twenty-three congressional candidates.)[103] For another, there is good evidence that the off-year House elections are primarily local, not national, events. Scholars who have examined off-year congressional elections report the same basic finding: how people vote has more to do with their evaluations of the congressional candidates than with their assessment of the president.[104] Moreover, incumbency is a valuable asset for congressional candidates; they benefit from previous campaign experience, close relationships with voters, greater knowledge of issues, and superior financial resources, which give them a considerable advantage over their opponents.[105] Presidents who attempt to campaign against sitting members of Congress therefore face almost insurmountable odds. Bush in 2002 was aided by the fact that there were few vulnerable House seats to defend and, most significant, that the redistricting after the 2000 census favored Republicans.[106] That, coupled with his record number of campaign appearances and his tireless fund-raising (the president attended 75 fund-raisers, taking in a record $144 million), led to a gain of six seats in the House.

Senatorial midterm elections usually offer a somewhat more encouraging opportunity for presidents who wish to influence results. Approximately one-third of the Senate's one hundred seats are at stake every two years, so the chief executive can concentrate on these contests in a way not possible for House races. Bush made campaign appearances for sixteen Republican Senate candidates in 2002, and the Republican Senatorial Campaign Committee launched an aggressive series of television ads attacking Democratic incumbents for failing to support homeland security.[107] That combination—together with high turnout among Republican voters—led to the Republicans' picking up two Senate seats (enough to shift control in the Senate to Republicans). Although sitting senators are in the same position as House members in being able to bring their names to the attention of constituents, incumbency is not as advantageous for a senator as it is for a House member. Senators represent an entire state rather than a small district, and the prestige associated with being a senator means races will be hard fought. Challengers are much more visible to the electorate than are those who run against House incumbents. Popular presidents, therefore, are better able to help candidates who challenge incumbent senators of the opposite party by increasing the challengers' visibility through public association. A good example of this was Bush's efforts on behalf of Republican candidate Saxbe Chamblis in Georgia, who went on to defeat incumbent Democratic senator Max Cleland in 2002.

Midterm election outcomes depend on the condition of the national economy and the president's standing in public opinion polls at the time of the elections.[108] Voting in these contests tends to be *negative;* that is, those who disapprove of the president's performance in office are more likely to cast their ballots in such elections than those who approve.[109] Gary Jacobson contends that the president's role in congressional elections is essentially indirect: the state of the economy and the president's ratings in the public opinion polls influence the caliber of candidates who run in congressional elections. If, for example, these are not favorable, the opposition party will be able to field an unusually large proportion of formidable challengers with well-financed campaigns, and the president's party in Congress may lose a considerable number of seats.[110] Democrats fared miserably in the 1994 midterm elections when Bill Clinton's Gallup approval ratings came near their lowest point—fluctuating between 39 percent on September 6 and 48 percent on October 22, 1994. On the other hand, Democrats fared unusually well in the 1998 midterm elections when Clinton's approval ratings remained consistently high, hovering near 66 percent despite the looming threat of impeachment. (See Table 3-1.) Bush's approval rating just before the 2002 elections was (at 63 percent) not quite as high as Clinton's in 1998, but it still tied with Ronald Reagan's 1986 rating "for second highest in any postwar midterm election."[111]

The President and the Media

Historically, the most important link between the president and the American public has been the press. In the early years of the Republic, the press was as partisan as it is in many European countries today. The partisan press reached its peak during the presidency of Andrew Jackson, when federal officeholders were expected to subscribe to the administration organ, the *Washington Globe,* which was financed primarily by revenues derived from the printing of official government notices.[112]

The partisan press began to decline during the presidency of Abraham Lincoln. The establishment of the Government Printing Office in 1860 destroyed the printing-contract patronage that had supported former administration organs.[113] The invention of the telegraph led to the formation of wire services, which provided standardized and politically neutral information to avoid antagonizing the diverse readerships of the various subscribing newspapers. Advertising provided newspapers with a secure financial base independent of the support of presidential administrations. By the end of the nineteenth century, "news about the White House was transmitted to the public by independent, nonpartisan news organizations," a factor that continues to affect relationships between the president and the press today.[114]

Table 3-1   Losses by President's Party in Midterm Elections, 1862–2002

Year	Party holding presidency	President's party: gain/loss of seats in House	President's party: gain/loss of seats in Senate
1862	R	−3	8
1866	R	−2	0
1870	R	−31	−4
1874	R	−96	−8
1878	R	−9	−6
1882	R	−33	3
1886	D	−12	3
1890	R	−85	0
1894	D	−116	−5
1898	R	−21	7
1902	R	9[a]	2
1906	R	−28	3
1910	R	−57	−10
1914	D	−59	5
1918	D	−19	−6
1922	R	−75	−8
1926	R	−10	−6
1930	R	−49	−8
1934	D	9	10
1938	D	−71	−6
1942	D	−55	−9
1946	D	−55	−12
1950	D	−29	−6
1954	R	−18	−1
1958	R	−47	−13
1962	D	−5	3
1966	D	−47	−4
1970	R	−12	2
1974	R	−48	−5
1978	D	−15	−3
1982	R	−26	1
1986	R	−5	−8
1990	R	−10	−1
1994	D	−55	−9
1998	D	4	0
2002	R	8	1

Source: Harold W. Stanley and Richard G. Niemi, *Vital Statistics on American Politics, 2003–2004* (Washington, D.C.: CQ Press), 2003.

Note: Each entry is the difference between the number of seats won by the president's party in that midterm election and the number of seats won by that party in the preceding general election. Because of changes in the overall number of seats in the Senate and House, in the number of seats won by third parties, and in the number of vacancies, a Republican loss is not always matched precisely by a Democratic gain, or vice versa.

[a]Although the Republicans gained nine seats in the 1902 elections, they actually lost ground to the Democrats, who gained twenty-five seats after the increase in the overall number of representatives after the 1900 census.

Not until 1896, though, did the White House become a regular beat for reporters. Not surprisingly, given their role in establishing the public presidency, both Woodrow Wilson and Theodore Roosevelt formalized innovative ties with those reporters in the early part of the twentieth century. Roosevelt began the practice of meeting with them (often during his late afternoon shave). In 1902 he had a pressroom built in the new West Wing of the White House and began having an aide, William Loeb, give daily press briefings. Wilson continued the practice of daily press briefings (conducted by Joseph Tumulty) and became the first president to hold regularly scheduled press conferences. He held his first in the East Room of the White House on March 15, 1913—just eleven days after his inauguration—for 125 reporters.[115]

In the twentieth century, several media took their place beside newspapers as important channels between the president and the people. Radio became a dominant force in communications in the 1920s, as did television in the 1950s. By the end of the century, cable and satellite technology had dramatically increased the number of potential sources of news and commentary, and the Internet had revolutionized the way people communicate and gather information. The emergence of broadcast technology, coupled with the array of "new media" (cable, satellite technology, and the Internet) by century's end, allowed presidents to communicate messages directly to the people rather than having their messages relayed (and interpreted) by journalists.

The Presidential Media

Today, an enormous variety of media cover the words and actions of the U.S. president. These media differ in the ways they deal with executive branch developments and in their target audiences. They also vary in importance to chief executives and their programs. Over the past fifty years, the way Americans get information has undergone a fundamental change. In 1959, 57 percent of the public claimed to get most of their news from newspapers and 51 percent from television (more than one response was allowed in the survey); only 19 percent claimed to get their news from television alone. By 1997 only 37 percent cited newspapers as a principal source, and 69 percent cited television; 47 percent claimed to get their news only from television.[116] A Gallup poll conducted March 29–30, 2003, found television to be the main source of information about the war with Iraq for 86 percent of the respondents (3 percent said newspapers were their main source, 6 percent said the radio, and 4 percent said the Internet).[117] This pattern developed with the spread of television ownership: only 9 percent of households had television sets in 1950, a figure that grew to 87 percent by 1960 and 98 percent by 1980.[118] As one would expect, White House attention to television coverage rose over the same period.

In addition, the White House must be attentive to the most influential media figures—a select group of columnists, elite reporters, anchors of the broadcast news, and executives of the media organizations. Indeed, there is substantial evidence that the stated views of news commentators and experts have a greater impact on citizens' policy preferences than the president's own comments.[119]

Syndicated columnists earn White House attention because they reach powerful audiences outside government, including business and labor leaders, lobbyists, and academics, as well as top officials in government—members of Congress, members of the bureaucracy, judges, governors, and mayors. These columnists influence views on the political feasibility of a president's proposed programs. They deal in matters of opinion rather than just factual developments affecting the presidency. "They are guaranteed space, they have no assigned topics, they are freed from the pressure of breaking news stories at deadline, and they have the opportunity to introduce their own perspectives into their stories."[120] George Will epitomizes this sort of columnist, and he appears regularly on television.

Television anchors such as Dan Rather, Peter Jennings, and Tom Brokaw are important to the president because of the size of the audiences they reach (until recently, more than 26 million people each weekday night)[121] and the respect they command. They are joined now, of course, by the twenty-four-hour cable news networks and their coterie of anchors and commentators. According to Gallup, the percentage of Americans who say they watch cable news networks daily is up from 23 percent in 1995 to 41 percent in 2002, while the percentage who say they watch network news daily is down from 62 percent in 1995 to 47 percent in 2002.[122] Because far more people watch television than read newspapers, the information the ordinary citizen receives about the presidency depends on what is included in the evening news and covered on outlets such as CNN and Fox News. At the same time, television coverage of the presidency has serious limitations: newscasts devote very little time to the most important stories (about seventy-five seconds on the average); emphasis is placed on events that are visually exciting; a focus on the president personalizes complex developments; and broadcasts usually lack in-depth reporting and analysis.[123] Sound bites of the president speaking on the evening network newscasts have shrunk from an average of forty-two seconds in 1968 to less than seven seconds in 1996.[124]

Cable provides some additional television outlets for presidents. C-SPAN carries many presidential speeches in their entirety, as well as White House press briefings. Cable news channels also offer a degree of expanded coverage, though actual news stories are similar in length to those on the evening newscasts. Most significantly, cable has given presidential surrogates many more venues to state their cases. When Fox and MSNBC joined the cable news lineup in 1996, they relied heavily on talk shows to fill their airtime. Such shows are cheap to produce and require limited resources. They are also popular with viewers—so much so that CNN followed suit and expanded the number of its talk shows in 2001.

Helping to shape both print and broadcast coverage are the bureau chiefs and other media executives who determine which stories are covered, how they are handled, which reporters will cover the White House, and who should be represented in "pools" that travel with the president to cover significant events. The White House press corps is also an important determinant of what will be reported and how it will be reported. These are the reporters assigned to the White House itself. They attend the daily press briefings, travel with the president, and have as their primary responsibilities the task of reporting what the president is doing. Some members of the press corps are especially influential.

This question-and-answer session on MTV is an example of candidate Bill Clinton using "narrowcasting" in the 1992 presidential election to transmit direct, targeted messages to young voters.

Reporters for the *New York Times* and the *Washington Post* are examples because of the readership of their papers—in addition to public officials and important people in the private sector, their readers are the other Washington reporters.[125] The *Times,* in particular, is known to influence network news decisions about which stories to cover.[126] Significant as well are the reporters for the wire services—Associated Press (AP) and United Press International (UPI)—because they provide coverage of the president for newspapers across the country. Collectively, the press corps frames most of what we read and see about the president.

Presidents pay a price for alienating the press corps, as Bill Clinton found out in the early days of his first term. One of the first decisions of his communications director, George Stephanopoulos, was to restrict the access of the press corps: he closed off the upstairs foyer in the West Wing, where he and the press secretary had their offices. For more than twenty years, members of the White House press corps had been free to wander that foyer in search of news. They could chat informally with communications officials or poke their heads into the press secretary's office to get a quick answer to a question. It was a clear symbol that reporters and officials were on an equal playing field. For Stephanopoulos, giving so many reporters access to such a cramped space might have seemed like a burden to him and his staff. But the decision to restrict access to the area infuriated the press corps. As reporter Ann Compton put it, the foyer had become a "no-fly zone" symbolizing the hierarchical relationship between reporters and officials.[127] In the new arrangement, reporters had to wait downstairs to be spoon-fed. Reporters felt the White House was not even making much of an effort to do that. Calls from downstairs were not returned in time for reporters to meet their deadlines, and some felt that when they were invited upstairs, they were not treated with respect.[128] As a consequence, President Clinton started out his presidency by losing the goodwill of the White House press corps. "Put it this way," said Karen Hosler, Washington correspondent for the *Baltimore Sun* and president of the White House Correspondents Association, "we're not going to cut them any breaks."[129]

One reason why Clinton and his aides felt they could get away with such treatment of the White House press corps was the rise of the new media.[130] Cable, satellite technology, and the Internet provided unparalleled opportunities for direct communication with the American people. In the 1992 presidential campaign, Clinton very effectively followed a strategy of "narrowcasting"— using media outlets such as MTV, the *Arsenio Hall Show, Phil Donahue,* and Don Imus's radio talk show to transmit direct, targeted messages to particular constituencies. Once Clinton was elected, he and his advisers planned to continue that strategy and expand their use of the new media to bypass the critical filter of the White House press corps. This included innovative use of the Internet and extensive use of cable outlets, talk radio, and local media. Sidney Blumenthal, who later joined the Clinton White House as a communication strategist, touted such possibilities for unmediated communication in an article in the *New Yorker.* There he wrote that the "Old Media," such as the White House press corps and the three network news shows, were "anachronistic" and were "no more likely to return than are the big bands."[131] By the time Clinton left office, swing dancing was the rage and the White House had learned to appreciate the old media. A 1998 Gallup poll showed that Americans continued to get most of their news from the old media and, even more important, *trusted* it more than the new media.[132] In the new environment, narrowcasting and circumvention of the White House press corps had its place. But that symbiotic relationship between the White House and the old media continued to exist, and that worked only if the White House courted the press corps and fed it information instead of snubbing it. In contrast, President George W. Bush and his aides carefully cultivated relations with the press corps, while at the same time taking advantage of narrowcasting and circumvention.[133] In an effort to target the 133 million Americans who surf the Internet, the Bush administration maintains a sophisticated Web site at www.whitehouse.gov, which includes streaming video of presidential speeches, the text of all presidential remarks, an archive of all the daily White House press briefings since Bush took office, photographs, pages in Spanish, a virtual tour of the White House—including a tour of the Press Room led by the press secretary (not to mention "Barney-Cam"—a tour from the perspective of the president's dog), and even a "kids only" page. The Web site averaged a million hits a day at the outset of the administration but had risen to nearly 14 million hits a day by the spring of 2003. A record 44 million hits occurred on September 11, 2001.[134]

We turn next to the two White House staff units that deal most directly with the press and communications planning: the Press Office and the Office of Communications.

The White House Press Office

Franklin Roosevelt officially created the White House Press Office in 1933. As we have seen, a routinized White House relationship with the press had been in place since Theodore Roosevelt directed William Loeb to provide daily briefings for reporters. Every president after TR assigned a member of his staff to deal with the press, with Herbert Hoover being the first to hire an aide for whom the press was the *sole* responsibility. That man, George Akerson, served from 1929 to 1931 and was the equivalent of a modern-day press secretary, although that post was not formally created until FDR came to office in 1933.

The Press Office maintains day-to-day contact with the reporters assigned to cover the White House. It is housed in the West Wing. The Press Room (where daily briefings take place) and space for reporters are located downstairs in an area that used to house a swimming pool. (President Nixon converted the area during his first term.) Junior staff has space next to the Press Room in what is called the Lower Press Office. Senior staff members, including the press secretary, have their offices upstairs. All together the Press Office consists of about twenty people, some of whom specialize in a certain issue area (such as foreign affairs). These include several deputy press secretaries as well as the junior staffers who write press releases and do other sorts of research. The most visible (and most senior) member of the Press Office is the press secretary.

The press secretary is the most important person in the executive branch for day-to-day contact with the presidential media. Typically holding two daily briefings, the press secretary provides routine information on executive branch appointments and resignations, on presidential actions and policies, and on the president's schedule—visits, meetings, and travel plans. By the end of an administration there may have been more than 2,000 such briefings. In addition, the press secretary holds private meetings with select reporters to provide background information to explain the president's actions on a particular problem or program.

Press secretaries try to balance serving the interests of three constituencies: the president, members of the White House staff, and members of the media.[135] The secretary can perform well only if granted continuous access to, and the confidence of, the president so journalists may assume that the news comes from the chief executive. If presidents try to be their own press secretaries, as may have been true of Lyndon Johnson, even a capable and influential person such as Bill Moyers will not succeed in managing the message.[136] When secretaries are excluded from White House decisions, as appeared to be the case with Clinton's first press secretary, Dee Dee Myers, their credibility suffers.

The modern era's press secretaries have varied in effectiveness. Among those considered successful are Stephen Early (for FDR), James Hagerty (for Eisenhower), Jody Powell (for Carter), and Mike McCurry (for Clinton). Some, such as Hagerty and Powell, benefited from the fact that their presidents kept them informed on virtually everything going on in the White House. But sometimes even well-informed press secretaries do not want to know everything. After leaving office, Mike McCurry admitted that he purposely stayed out of the loop so that he could truthfully respond that he did not know all the answers to the Monica Lewinsky affair.[137] On the other hand, Nixon's press secretary, Ron Ziegler, was so out of the loop that he, like Dee Dee Myers, lost credibility with reporters. This was true even before the Watergate affair when, after months of denying any White House involvement, Ziegler was forced to declare those denials "inoperative." Indeed, Nixon purposely diminished the importance of the press secretary when he became president. White House reporters considered Nixon's choice of Ziegler—who was only twenty-nine years old and had no background in journalism—a slap in the face.[138] Another secretary who never had a particularly good relationship with reporters was Larry Speakes, who became Reagan's press spokesman when James Brady was shot and incapacitated in the assassination attempt on the president. After leaving office, Speakes provoked cries of outrage when he admitted in his memoirs that he had manufactured presidential quotes during Reagan's Iceland summit meeting with Soviet leader Mikhail Gorbachev in November 1985. Fearing that Reagan was being upstaged, Speakes created a public relations solution to the problem, and the fabricated quotes were given prominent attention back home.[139]

The White House Office of Communications

Richard Nixon created the White House Office of Communications in 1969.[140] Its functions are quite different from those of the Press Office. As originally conceived, the Office of Communications had four primary goals: (1) long-range communications planning, (2) the coordination of news from all the many departments and agencies of the executive branch, (3) outreach to local media, and (4) oversight of presidential surrogates. Thus while the Press Office is largely *reactive* (responding to the questions and needs of the White House press corps), the Office of Communications is primarily *proactive* (responsible for setting the public agenda and making sure that all the players on the presidential team are adhering to that agenda). This includes setting the "line of the day" and choreographing presidential photo opportunities.

The precise jurisdiction of the Office of Communications has varied some from administration to administration. Outreach to local media, for example, has sometimes been subsumed by a subunit of the Press Office. In fact, the Press Office itself has sometimes been a subunit of the Office of Communications (and vice versa). For at least part of the administrations of former presidents Reagan, Bush, and Clinton, the Office of Communications became an umbrella term for a variety of offices that fell under the supervision of the communications director. At various times, this included the Press Office, as well as the Offices of Planning, Speechwriting, Advance, Public Liaison (outreach to interest groups), Media Affairs (outreach to local media), Political Affairs (outreach to members of the president's political party), and Public Affairs (liaison with public information officers throughout the executive branch).

For Nixon, a primary motivation in creating the office was to install a mechanism for bypassing the critical filter of the White House press corps. Outreach to local media, the coordination of surrogate speakers, and using venues such as television, radio, and mass mailings to communicate directly with the people were all a part of that effort. For presidents since Reagan, the emphasis has been on long-range communications planning (although tactics of circumvention are often part of that plan). As mentioned above, the Bush administration not only maintains the Office of Communications but also a new Office of Global Communications designed to reach a worldwide audience. Vice President Dick Cheney, who had considerable experience with communications planning as White House chief of staff for President Ford, has stressed that it is essential for the White House to manage presidential news. "That means that about half the time the White House press corps is going to be pissed off," Cheney admitted, "and that's all right. You're not there to please them. You're there to run an effective presidency. And to do that, you have to be disciplined in what you convey to the country. The most powerful tool you have is the ability to use the symbolic aspects of the presidency to promote your goals and objectives." That means the White House has to control the agenda. "You don't let the press set the agenda," Cheney emphasized. "They like to decide what's important and what isn't important. But if you let them do that, they're going to trash your presidency."[141] Responsibility for controlling the communications agenda rests with the Office of Communications and a variety of other communications advisers—some of whom are not officially members of the White House staff.

Such sharing of communications responsibilities is not unusual. For example, in his first term, President Reagan benefited greatly not only from the skill and experience of communications director David Gergen (who had also served in the Nixon and Ford administrations and came back as a communications adviser to President Clinton in 1993) but also from that of James A. Baker III and Michael Deaver, other members of the White House staff who carefully managed the president's media and public image. This team was especially adept at selecting the "line of the day" (often as part of a broader "theme of the week") and creating "photo opportunities" featuring the president to highlight it. As Donald Regan later wrote: "[Deaver] saw—designed—each presidential action as a

Photo-ops such as Bush's "tail-hook" landing on the USS Abraham Lincoln *in May 2003 are designed to convey specific images to the public. These images of the president in his "top gun" gear are intended to reinforce the message of a strong, courageous leader in control.*

one-minute or two-minute spot on the evening network news, or picture on page one of the *Washington Post* or the *New York Times,* and conceived every presidential appearance in terms of camera angles. . . . Every moment of every appearance was scheduled, every word was scripted, every place where Reagan was expected to stand was chalked with toe marks."[142] Reagan, the former Hollywood actor, followed the script masterfully. The administration of George W. Bush has also proved to be adept at staging photo opportunities, including his May 2003 "tail-hook" landing in an S-3B Viking Navy jet on the USS *Abraham Lincoln*. President Bush told reporters that he had actually flown the jet himself en route to the ship. Initially the White House said that the president had to take the jet because the ship was out of helicopter range. It turned out, though, that the ship was in easy helicopter range—only thirty miles off the coast of California, with cameras carefully positioned so as not to see the coastline.[143] Nonetheless, photographs of Bush in his "top gun" gear conveyed the image of a strong, courageous leader in control. (Such attempts at image making do not always work—just ask 1988 Democratic presidential nominee Michael Dukakis, who looked ridiculous when his aides arranged a photo op of him driving a tank.)

Presidential Press Conferences

Presidents, of course, cultivate their own ties with reporters—often through off-the-record sessions when traveling on *Air Force One* and during other informal gatherings. Presidential press conferences are one of the best-known avenues for interaction between presidents and reporters. Franklin Roosevelt perfected the art of the press conference. He held a total of 998 while president—an average of almost 7 a month. His were informal gatherings—usually held in his office—and there was strict control over how reporters could use material from the press conferences (as there had been since President Wilson first began the practice of regular press conferences in 1913). Nonetheless, FDR's system—as Samuel Kernell has pointed out—was one of "hard news, openly conveyed."[144]

The emergence of broadcast media and their desire to cover press conferences eroded the intimacy of these interactions between presidents and reporters. It also reduced the White House's dependence upon reporters to communicate the president's views to the public. Radio and television became ways to reach the masses directly. Indeed, press conferences came to be used more to meet the people than to meet the press when President Kennedy began the practice of televising them live in 1961. (Eisenhower had allowed filming, but the White House controlled which clips could be broadcast.) As President Nixon's chief of staff bluntly put it in a 1970 White House memo: "The President wants you to realize and emphasize to all appropriate members of your staff that a press conference is a TV operation and that the TV impression is really all that matters."[145] Nixon also began the practice of prime-time televised news conferences. Kennedy's were almost always held at either 11:00 A.M. or 4:00 P.M. Lyndon Johnson never held one after 4:50 P.M. Nixon changed that. He preferred 9:00 P.M. Back in the age when the networks preempted regularly scheduled programs to cover such conferences, that time guaranteed a large audience. It was also just late enough that it was difficult for the morning newspapers to dissect the president's performance. By the next evening's network news programs it was already "old" news. The first George Bush and Bill Clinton both held most of their press conferences during midday rather than prime-time evening hours. Although their sessions were less widely viewed (CNN was the principal source of coverage), the two presidents held press conferences quite frequently and therefore earned points with reporters for their accessibility. George W. Bush held few press conferences during his first two-and-a-half years in office. As of March 2003, he had held only eight solo press conferences (compared with thirty by Clinton and fifty-eight by the first Bush at that point in their first terms).[146] These included prime-time press conferences after the September 11, 2001, terrorist attacks and before the March 2003 invasion of Iraq. All three presidents supplemented press conferences with more informal exchanges with reporters. Presidents have more control over informal exchanges, since questioning can be stopped at any point.

Without the strict ground rules that earlier presidents had used to control what information reporters could use from press conferences, recent presidents facing live television coverage of their press conferences have sought other ways to minimize risks. Members of the president's staff have drawn up a list of questions likely to be asked by reporters, together with suggested answers and supporting information. Some presidents have held full-scale mock news conferences for practice. Reagan, for example, liked two-hour practices, dividing the time between foreign policy and domestic policy. Errors would be pointed out, and the president's performance critiqued by staff. On the day of the news conference, photos of the reporters expected to attend were fixed to their likely places on a seating chart, and difficult questions were reviewed.[147] The emphasis, in short, shifted to performance.

President Nixon liked to emphasize the appearance of risk he was taking in such performances. He likened himself to "the man in the arena" facing hostile adversaries when he confronted the press. To symbolize his lack of fear of these adversaries, he sometimes held press conferences with no podium to shield him from reporters. But, overall, presidents control the interchange at these conferences. At times, the White House limits questions to domestic policy or foreign policy, and presidents can always refuse to answer certain questions on the grounds that the subject matter is too sensitive for public discussion, a frequent response to foreign and military questions.

The success of a press conference depends on the skills of the president. President Eisenhower came across badly in them. He appeared to have trouble expressing himself clearly and grammatically and displayed meager knowledge about many vital issues of the day. Revisionist accounts have suggested that he may have used this as a tactic to avoid sensitive issues.[148] President Johnson also came across poorly in formal televised press conferences. On the other hand, FDR and Kennedy were masters of the press conference. Roosevelt had a keen sense of what was newsworthy and even suggested reporters' lead stories to them. He also prepared members of the press for actions he took on controversial problems by educating them initially with confidential background information; consequently, reporters tended to support his decisions because they understood his reasoning. Kennedy, who had served a brief stint as a newspaperman and enjoyed the company of reporters, used his press conferences to great advantage; his ability to field difficult questions impressed not only the members of the press but also the public. Clinton did not have the close relationship with reporters that Roosevelt and Kennedy enjoyed, but he also performed well in press conferences.

Most people who have studied or been involved in modern-day press conferences have concluded that they serve primarily the interests of the president rather than those of the media. As George Reedy, press secretary to Lyndon Johnson, has pointed out, a president rarely receives an unexpected question on an important issue in a conference, and should that happen, the president could respond with a witty or a noncommittal remark.[149] Michael Grossman and Martha Kumar summarize the president's advantage as follows: "The President decides when to hold a conference, how much notice reporters will be given, who will ask the questions, and what the answers will be."[150]

In managing their relationships with the media, presidents must take into account their particular strengths and weaknesses. Nicknamed the Great Communicator, Reagan benefited enormously from his previous professional experience in radio, films, and television. To take advantage of those skills, the president frequently addressed the nation on prime-time television and used a series of Saturday radio broadcasts to explain and justify his administration's policies. The administration also avoided, or restricted the use of, other media formats that President Reagan did not handle as well as prepared speeches, specifically those that required him to give spontaneous answers to questions. He did not participate in call-in shows and seldom invited reporters to the White House for informal, on-the-record question and answer sessions. Reagan seldom would answer impromptu questions from reporters at photo sessions, and he held fewer press conferences in eight years than President Carter did in four. Nationally televised speeches were Reagan's best vehicle for communicating his views to the American people.

Relations between the President and the Media: Conflict or Collusion?

It is common for presidents to view the press unfavorably. George Washington, whom journalists treated rather well, was inclined not to run for a second term because of what he considered a critical press.[151] Since then, virtually all presidents have expressed outrage, indignation, resentment, or consternation over their treatment in the media. In turn, members of the press have criticized the way presidents have handled media relations. Typically, chief executives are accused of "managing" the news and, as their terms in office progress, of becoming increasingly isolated from the media and the American people. Some, such as Lyndon Johnson and Richard Nixon, also were charged with deliberately lying to the media and the public. More recently, Bill Clinton was accused of lying about his relationship with Monica Lewinsky (prompting the famous debate about what the meaning of "is" is), and George W. Bush was accused of misleading the public when he included an unsubstantiated charge in his January 28, 2003, State of the Union address that "Saddam Hussein recently sought significant quantities of uranium from Africa." The charge raised the specter of Iraq as a nuclear threat, and was part of Bush's effort to convince Congress and the American people that war with Iraq was justified. Bush's own Secretary of State had already dismissed that particular claim as not credible, and CIA director George J. Tenet later admitted that those words "should never have been included in the text written for the president."[152]

There is little question that a built-in conflict exists between the president and the media. Chief executives want to suppress information they feel will endanger the nation's security or put their administrations in a bad light. Members of the media are eager for news, however sensitive it may be, and they have an interest in criticizing the president and the president's associates as a means of getting the public's attention—thereby creating a demand for the journalists' services. They have also had an increasing penchant for what might be called "attack journalism": stories focused on scandal.[153]

Despite the potential for conflict, there is a basis for cooperation between presidents and the press that ultimately produces a collusive relationship.[154] Quite simply, the two are mutually dependent: neither presidents nor the press can perform their jobs without the assistance of the other, and cooperation is, therefore, mutually beneficial. The president must be able to communicate with the public through the media, and the media must have the administration's cooperation if they are to cover the most important official in the national government and give the public an accurate assessment of presidential activities. Moreover, the White House offers a range of media services designed to seduce reporters into favorable coverage. The product is an *exchange relationship*, a set of negotiated terms for the interaction between the media and the president that favors the White House and disadvantages the public.[155] As David Broder has argued, "We have been drawn into a circle of working relationships and even friendships with the people we are supposed to cover. The distinction between press and government has tended to become erased."[156]

Grossman and Kumar have argued that the general relationship between the president and the media goes through certain predictable phases.[157] During the initial period of "alliance," both parties agree that the focus should be on the new administration's appointees and its proposed goals and policies—the presidency is "open"; reporters are likely "to have their phone calls answered, to be granted interviews, and to get information that has not been specifically restricted."[158] During the second phase, "competition," the president wants to concentrate on portraying members of his administration as part of a happy team, committed to common goals and policies, while the media focus on conflicts among personalities in the administration and controversies over policies.[159] Presidents restrict access to themselves and others in the administration and may even go on the attack against especially critical reporters or organizations. The final phase of presidential-media relationships is "detachment." Surrogates manage the news, and presidents appear only in favorable settings scheduled to coincide with major events. The media, in turn, engage in more investigative reporting and seek information from sources other than the White House.

The Clinton administration's relationship with the press did not seem to follow the typical phases identified by Grossman and Kumar. There was an unusually brief period of "alliance," relations becoming obviously strained within a matter of months. As we have seen, Clinton got off to a rocky start with the White House press corps by pointedly circumventing them and restricting their access. The period of "competition" set in early, and Clinton exacerbated it by offering outspoken criticism of the press on several occasions, including a bitter public exchange with Brit Hume of ABC News on June 12, 1993, and a first-year-ending interview with *Rolling Stone* magazine that blamed the media for giving a false impression of his administration.[160] Moreover, one study found that television news coverage provided, on balance, more negative than positive comments for all but one of the administration's first sixteen months in office. In fact, nearly three-quarters of all network reporters' assessments of Clinton were found to have been negative.[161] Administration spokespersons quickly latched on to the report as a way to explain why the president was getting no credit for the good economic conditions (Robert Lichter found that 60 percent of the network stories on the economy were negative),[162] and there was an upsurge in stories considering whether the press had been harsh in its treatment of the president. Although the precise content of coverage may be debated, it is clear that Clinton was the darling of neither establishment nor nonestablishment (such as talk radio) media.[163]

Many people in the executive branch help presidents deal with the media, but the media also have their share of resources. A large number of reporters cover the White House, many of whom have expertise in substantive areas such as law, science, welfare, and defense policy.[164] Nonetheless, members of the media may not use their skills to full advantage. Journalists covering the presidency generally lack confidence in dealing with the substance of policies and consequently focus their coverage on four areas in which they feel most comfortable: administration scandals, internal dissension, a public gaffe or tactical blunder, and the ebb and flow of electoral contests and public opinion polls.[165] The result is unintended collusion between the presidency and the media that keeps the public less, rather than more, informed about American government. This line of criticism, focused on journalistic norms and practices, goes beyond those who believe that particular presidents received less vigorous scrutiny than they deserved. For example, some observers have suggested that Reagan's vaunted "Teflon coating" (a term commonly used during his presidency to suggest that negative stories did not seem to stick to Reagan) was the product of poor journalism.[166]

The ever-increasing speed with which news is reported—and the emergence of a never-ending news cycle—has arguably made the media less careful in what they convey about the president and other political figures. In their haste to keep up with the opposition, news organizations often pick up and report breaking news stories without independent corroboration. As Bill Kovach and Tom Rosenstiel have written: "Information is moving so fast, news outlets are caught between trying to gather new information and playing catch-up with what others have delivered ahead of them. The result for any news organization is a set of flexible standards that are often bent beyond recognition as the organization relies on another's reportage."[167] The Internet, in particular, has altered the way news is reported. The traditional old media had served as a gatekeeper of what news was reported. With the Internet, however, virtually anyone can post a story. Thus the "Drudge Report" broke the Monica Lewinsky story on the Internet, and the Internet came to shape the way the media covered the story of the scandal.

Before the Monica Lewinsky story erupted in 1998, the major media outlets had an unwritten rule that they would not use Web sites to break a story.[168] That changed with the Lewinsky scandal. With news organizations struggling to stay ahead of the competition, Web sites became important. After the "Drudge Report," the first mainstream coverage of the Lewinsky scandal appeared on the

Washington Post Web site, followed by the *Newsweek* Web site. (*Newsweek* had been investigating the story for a year and had not previously published it because Kenneth Starr, the independent counsel investigating the president, had asked the magazine not to do so.)[169] In the ensuing drive to scoop the competition, errors were made. The *Dallas Morning Herald,* for example, posted an erroneous story on its Web site saying that a Secret Service agent was an eyewitness to a presidential tryst. The editors pulled the story, but not before other news outlets, such as ABC, had reported it.[170]

A study by the Committee of Concerned Journalists examined 1,565 statements and allegations contained in media reports of the Lewinsky scandal in the first six days after the story broke. It found that the press "routinely intermingled reporting with opinion and speculation—even on the front page."[171] Among the specific findings of the study:

- Four in ten statements (41 percent of the reportage) were not factual reporting at all— here is what happened—but were instead journalists offering analysis, opinion, speculation, or judgment.
- Forty percent of all reporting based on anonymous sourcing was from a single source.
- Only one statement in a hundred (1 percent of the reporting) was based on two or more named sources.[172]

Such situations prompted CNN senior analyst Jeff Greenfield to express concern about what he called an "echo effect": news organizations picking up and repeating without independent corroboration a story from a single source. He expressed concern that even unreliable stories gained credibility through the simple act of repetition in various news venues.[173] The constant chatter of talking heads on twenty-four-hour cable networks further exacerbated the echo effect. Another report by the Committee of Concerned Journalists suggested that these talking heads were responsible for the most blatant errors and distortions in the coverage of the Lewinsky scandal. For example, rumors of Clinton liaisons with other interns that would never have merited coverage by a responsible news organization were fair game on these talk shows.[174] This continues to be a cause of concern as talk shows proliferate. In 2001—facing falling ratings and stiff competition from Fox News and MSNBC—CNN, as noted above, expanded the number of its talk shows and decreased its coverage of hard news.[175]

Conclusion: The Permanent Campaign

The rise of the public presidency corresponds with the development of "the permanent campaign." Sidney Blumenthal popularized that phrase in a 1982 book of the same name (although the phrase had been used before—notably in a transition memo from adviser Pat Caddell to President-elect Jimmy Carter in 1976).[176] Blumenthal noted that the traditional distinction between *campaigning* and *governing* had broken down and that the resulting permanent campaign had remade government "into an instrument designed to sustain an elected official's popularity."[177] More recently, Hugh Heclo described the permanent campaign this way:

[P]ermanent campaign is shorthand for an emergent pattern of political management that the body politic did not plan, debate, or formally adopt. It is a work of inadvertence, something developed higgledy-piggledy since the middle of the twentieth-century. The permanent campaign comprises a complex mixture of politically sophisticated people, communication techniques, and organizations—profit and nonprofit alike. What ties the pieces together is the continuous and voracious quest for public approval.[178]

The presidency of Bill Clinton is a quintessential example of the permanent campaign in action.[179] Charles O. Jones noted that Clinton remained in full campaign mode even in his eighth year in office—unable because of the Twenty-second Amendment to the Constitution to run for a third term. "Here was a prime example of the campaigning style of governing, practiced by a virtuoso," Jones wrote.[180]

The White House staff units discussed in this chapter are important tools for waging that campaign. The problem with such tactics is that campaigning—by its very nature—is *adversarial,* while governing is—or at least should be—largely *collaborative.* As Heclo puts it, "campaigning is self-centered, and governing is group-centered."[181] When the permanent campaign becomes the predominant governing style, however, collaboration becomes difficult. Not surprisingly, recent years have seen a breakdown of the elite bargaining community that used to collaborate to produce policy. Samuel Kernell has noted that this bargaining community is neither as isolated from public pressure nor as tightly bound together by established norms of elite behavior as it used to be.[182] He contends that presidents used to promote their programs primarily by negotiating with other political elites in Congress and the executive branch, but today they more often choose to "go public" by circumventing those elites and appealing directly to the American people for support.[183] Presidents do this through the means we have discussed in this chapter: public speeches, public appearances, and political travel, coupled with targeted outreach using White House staff units such as the Office of Communications and the Office of Public Liaison.

Although these new developments undoubtedly have affected the presidency, the fact remains that there are limits to a president's ability to transform public opinion into public policy.[184] If presidents want to see their programs adopted and implemented, they must also use the powers and institutional arrangements of their office, and they must work with Congress, the executive branch, and the courts to accomplish their purpose. In chapter 4, we examine the personality traits and skills that presidents bring to this task.

NOTES

1. Henry Jones Ford, *The Rise and Growth of American Politics: A Sketch of Constitutional Development* (New York: Macmillan, 1900), 283.

2. Woodrow Wilson, *Constitutional Government in the United States* (1908; reprint, New York: Columbia University Press, 1961), 68.

3. Richard E. Neustadt, *Presidential Power: The Politics of Leadership* (New York: Wiley, 1960), 86–107.

4. Samuel Kernell, *Going Public: New Strategies of Presidential Leadership*, 3d ed. (Washington, D.C.: CQ Press, 1997).

5. Matthew A. Baum and Samuel Kernell, "Has Cable Ended the Golden Age of Presidential Television?" *American Political Science Review* 93 (March 1999): 99–114.

6. The numbers in this paragraph are based on Gallup polls. See Appendix B in Michael Nelson, ed., *Congressional Quarterly's Guide to the Presidency*, 2d ed. (Washington, D.C.: CQ Press, 1996), 1698–1703, for Gallup presidential approval ratings from 1949 to 1995. The latest Gallup polls can be found on the Web at http://www.gallup.com. Summaries of polls from a variety of polling organizations can be found at http://www.pollingreport.com. President Clinton's final Gallup job approval rating (based on nationwide surveys taken on January 5–7, 2001—before Clinton pardoned Marc Rich) was 65 percent. Other polls showed similar results: CNN/*Time* showed Clinton's job approval rating at 64 percent, CBS showed it at 68 percent, and NBC/*Wall Street Journal* showed it at 66 percent. Ronald Reagan came closest with his final Gallup job approval rating of 63 percent. For an account of Clinton's early low poll ratings, see George C. Edwards III, "Frustration and Folly: Bill Clinton and the Public Presidency," in *The Clinton Presidency: First Appraisals*, ed. Colin Campbell and Bert A. Rockman (Chatham, N.J.: Chatham House, 1996).

7. Molly W. Andolina and Clyde Wilcox, "Public Opinion: The Paradoxes of Clinton's Popularity," in *The Clinton Scandal and the Future of American Government*, ed. Mark J. Rozell and Clyde Wilcox (Washington, D.C.: Georgetown University Press, 2000), 171–194.

8. Charles O. Jones, "Preparing to Govern in 2001: Lessons from the Clinton Presidency," in *The Permanent Campaign and Its Future*, ed. Norman J. Ornstein and Thomas E. Mann (Washington, D.C.: American Enterprise Institute, 2000), 206–207.

9. David Easton, *A Systems Analysis of Political Life* (New York: Wiley, 1965), chaps. 10–13.

10. Andolina and Wilcox, "Public Opinion," 189. For example, a CBS/*New York Times* poll conducted September 22–23, 1998, showed that 65 percent of those surveyed felt the affair was a private matter (83 percent of Democrats thought it was a private matter, as opposed to 67 percent of independents, and 40 percent of Republicans). See also Robert J. Spitzer, "The Presidency: The Clinton Crisis and Its Consequences," in *The Clinton Scandal and the Future of American Government*, 3–4.

11. Fred I. Greenstein, "What the President Means to Americans: Presidential 'Choice' between Elections," in *Choosing the President*, ed. James David Barber (Englewood Cliffs, N.J.: Prentice Hall, 1974), 144–146.

12. *New York Times*, November 5, 1991.

13. Joseph E. Kallenbach, *The American Chief Executive: The Presidency and the Governorship* (New York: Harper and Row, 1966), 275.

14. Barry Schwartz, *George Washington: The Making of an American Symbol* (Ithaca: Cornell University Press, 1987), 58–63.

15. Schwartz's discussion of the various public portrayals of Washington and their iconography is especially valuable. It may be of interest to students to note which figures' portraits appear on the most widely circulated coins and currency of the time.

16. Schwartz, *George Washington*, esp. part 2.

17. Barbara Hinckley, *The Symbolic Presidency: How Presidents Portray Themselves* (New York: Routledge, 1990), 130.

18. Ibid., 131–133.

19. Colin Campbell, "Demotion? Has Clinton Turned the Bully Pulpit into a Lectern?" in *The Clinton Legacy,* ed. Colin Campbell and Bert A. Rockman (New York: Chatham House, 2000), 56.

20. Findings of the Survey Research Center at the University of Michigan in the mid-1960s indicated that of all the occupations in the United States, including "famous doctor," "president of a large corporation like General Motors," "bishop or other church official," "Supreme Court justice," and "senator," more than half the adults named the president as the most respected.

21. Tracy Connor, "Strange Bedfellows: Bush, Hil Top Most-Admired List," *New York Daily News,* December 29, 2002, 6.

22. Samuel Kernell, Peter Sperlich, and Aaron Wildavsky, "Public Support for Presidents," in *Perspectives on the Presidency,* ed. Aaron Wildavsky (Boston: Little, Brown, 1975), 148–181.

23. Paul Allen Beck, "The Role of Agents in Political Socialization," in *Handbook of Political Socialization: Theory and Research,* ed. Stanley Allen Renshon (New York: Free Press, 1977), 117–118.

24. Fred Greenstein, *Children and Politics* (New Haven: Yale University Press, 1965); Robert Hess and Judith Torney, *The Development of Political Attitudes in Children* (Chicago: Aldine, 1967); David Easton and Jack Dennis, *Children in the Political System: Origins of Political Legitimacy* (New York: McGraw-Hill, 1969).

25. Jerry L. Yeric and John R. Todd, *Public Opinion: The Visible Politics,* 3d ed. (Itasca, Ill.: Peacock, 1996), 54.

26. Dean Jaros, Herbert Hirsch, and Frederick J. Fleron Jr., "The Malevolent Leader: Political Socialization in an American Subculture," *American Political Science Review* (June 1968): 564–575.

27. Jack Dennis and Carol Webster, "Children's Images of the President in 1962 and 1974," *American Politics Quarterly* (October 1975): 398.

28. Christopher Arterton, "Watergate and Children's Attitudes towards Political Authority Revisited," *Political Science Quarterly* (fall 1975): 477–496. Cf. Christopher Arterton, "The Impact of Watergate on Children's Attitudes towards Political Authority," *Political Science Quarterly* (June 1974): 269–288.

29. For example, David O. Sears and Nicholas A. Valentino, "Politics Matters: Political Events as Catalysts for Preadult Socialization," *American Political Science Review* (March 1997): 45–65.

30. Paul Brace and Barbara Hinckley, *Follow the Leader: Opinion Polls and Modern Presidents* (New York: Basic Books, 1992), 19.

31. Diane J. Heath, "Presidential Polling and the Potential for Leadership," in *Presidential Power: Forging the Presidency for the Twenty-first Century,* ed. Robert Y. Shapiro, Martha Joynt Kumar, and Lawrence R. Jacobs (New York: Columbia University Press, 2000), 382.

32. Robert M. Eisinger, *The Evolution of Presidential Polling* (New York: Cambridge University Press, 2003), 3.

33. Heath, "Presidential Polling," 384.

34. Ibid., 387.

35. Ibid., 392.

36. John Anthony Maltese, *Spin Control: The White House Office of Communications and the Management of Presidential News,* 2d rev. ed. (Chapel Hill: University of North Carolina Press, 1994), 213–214.

37. Carl M. Cannon, "Hooked on Polls," *National Journal,* October 17, 1998, 2438 ff.

38. Andolina and Wilcox, "Public Opinion," 183.

39. Paul Brace and Barbara Hinckley, "Public Opinion Polls: The New Referendum," in *Understanding the Presidency,* ed. James P. Pfiffner and Roger H. Davidson

(New York: Longman, 1997), 125. See also Brace and Hinckley *Follow the Leader*. An earlier study that made a similar finding about the decay of presidential support was John Mueller, *War, Presidents, and Public Opinion* (New York: Wiley, 1973).

40. Jeffrey M. Jones, "Bush Approval Ratings One Year after the Peak," *Gallup Tuesday Briefing* (October 1, 2002), http://www.gallup.com (supplemented by approval ratings posted at http://www.gallup.com).

41. Gallup poll taken July 25–27, 2003.

42. Brace and Hinckley, *Follow the Leader*, 23–24, 32, 24.

43. James P. Pfiffner, *The Strategic Presidency: Hitting the Ground Running*, 2d ed., rev. (Lawrence: University Press of Kansas, 1996).

44. Paul C. Light, *The President's Agenda: Domestic Policy Choice from Kennedy to Clinton*, 3d ed. (Baltimore: Johns Hopkins University Press, 1999).

45. Maltese, *Spin Control*, 180.

46. Gary C. Jacobson, "The Bush Presidency and the American Electorate" (paper prepared for delivery at the conference on "The George W. Bush Presidency: An Early Assessment," Woodrow Wilson School, Princeton University, April 25–26, 2003 [draft of April 21, 2003]), 4 (available online at http://www.wws.princeton.edu/bushconf).

47. Jones, "Bush Approval Ratings."

48. Jacobson, "The Bush Presidency," 6–7.

49. Ibid., 13.

50. For example, a CBS News poll conducted April 26–27, 2003, showed a 49-point differential between Democrat and Republican approval ratings for Bush.

51. Johnson's first approval ratings came just after President Kennedy was assassinated in 1963. On taking office in January 1965, after being elected in his own right, Johnson's approval rating was 71 percent.

52. Bradley H. Patterson Jr., *The White House Staff: Inside the West Wing and Beyond* (Washington, D.C.: Brookings Institution Press, 2000). See also Charles E. Walcott and Karen M. Hult, *Governing the White House: From Hoover through LBJ* (Lawrence: University Press of Kansas, 1995), chaps. 3 and 10.

53. Jeffrey K. Tulis, *The Rhetorical Presidency* (Princeton: Princeton University Press, 1987).

54. Kernell, *Going Public*, chap. 2.

55. Jeffrey K. Tulis, "The Two Constitutional Presidencies," in *The Presidency and the Political System*, 6th ed., ed. Michael Nelson (Washington, D.C.: CQ Press, 2000), 115–116.

56. Mel Laracey, *Presidents and the People: The Partisan Story of Going Public* (College Station: Texas A&M University Press, 2002).

57. Tulis, *The Rhetorical Presidency*, 95.

58. Ibid., 46; see, generally, chaps. 1 and 2.

59. See, for example, Richard L. Rubin, *Press, Party, and Presidency* (New York: Norton, 1981); Culver H. Smith, *The Press, Politics, and Patronage* (Athens: University of Georgia Press, 1977).

60. Robert A. Rutland, *The Newsmongers* (New York: Dial Press, 1973), 58.

61. Frank Luther Mott, *American Journalism* (New York: Macmillan, 1941), 119–120.

62. Laracey, however, contends that every president from 1800 to 1860 "supported a newspaper that was regarded as at least the semiofficial voice of his administration" and argues that those newspapers are "the forgotten way of going public" for many nineteenth-century presidents—especially those from Andrew Jackson through Abraham Lincoln (1829–1865). From Ulysses S. Grant through the second administration of Grover Cleveland (1869–1897), however, Laracey admits that presidents did not engage in the tactic of going public. See Laracey, *Presidents and the People*, 8, 146.

63. Tulis, *The Rhetorical Presidency,* 69.

64. Based on Table 3-1 in Tulis, *The Rhetorical Presidency,* 64.

65. Samuel Kernell and Gary C. Jacobson, *The Logic of American Politics* (Washington, D.C.: CQ Press, 2000), 242.

66. Tulis, *The Rhetorical Presidency,* 91–93.

67. Ibid., 106.

68. James W. Caesar, *Presidential Selection: Theory and Development* (Princeton: Princeton University Press, 1979), 181–184.

69. Tulis, *The Rhetorical Presidency,* 182.

70. "Bush Tax Cuts Clear First Hurdle," *World News Tonight,* American Broadcasting Company (ABC), March 8, 2001.

71. George Stephanopoulos, *Good Morning America,* ABC, January 22, 1998, transcript no. 98012217-jl4. See also John Anthony Maltese, "The New Media and the Lure of the Clinton Scandal," in *The Clinton Scandal and the Future of American Government,* 198.

72. Kernell and Jacobson, *The Logic of American Politics,* 239.

73. Baum and Kernell, "Has Cable Ended the Golden Age?"

74. For a discussion of the permanent campaign and its impact on presidential governance, see Norman J. Ornstein and Thomas E. Mann, eds., *The Permanent Campaign and Its Future* (Washington, D.C.: American Enterprise Institute, 2000).

75. John C. Fortier and Norman J. Ornstein, "Congress and the Bush Presidency" (paper prepared for delivery at the conference on "The George W. Bush Presidency: An Early Assessment," Woodrow Wilson School, Princeton University, April 25–26, 2003 [draft of April 11, 2003]), 39 (available online at http://www.wws.princeton.edu/bushconf).

76. Richard Rose, *The Postmodern President,* 2d ed. (Chatham, N.J.: Chatham House, 1991), 38.

77. This information covers foreign travel through August 2003. It was provided by Mark Knoller of CBS News.

78. Maltese, *Spin Control,* 195.

79. Mark Hertsgaard, *On Bended Knee: The Press and the Reagan Presidency* (New York: Farrar Straus, 1988), 273.

80. Quoted in Johanna Neuman, "Response to Terror: Public Diplomacy Is Shaped in President's Ornate War Room," *Los Angeles Times,* December 22, 2001, A3. See also John Anthony Maltese, "The Presidency and the News Media," in *Media Power, Media Politics,* ed. Mark J. Rozell (New York: Rowman and Littlefield, 2003), 4–5.

81. Elaine Monaghan, "U.S. Set to Bombard Globe with Words," *The Times* (London), March 20, 2003, 4. The executive order of January 21, 2003, creating the office, as well as a White House fact sheet, "New White House Office Coordinates Global Communications," dated January 21, 2003, can be found at the White House Web site, http://www.whitehouse.gov.

82. Memo, H. R. Haldeman to Herb Klein, March 20, 1969, in "Memos/Herb Klein (March 1969)," Box 49, H. R. Haldeman Files, Nixon Presidential Materials Project. For a thorough discussion of the use of presidential surrogates from Nixon through Clinton, see Maltese, *Spin Control.*

83. Maltese, *Spin Control,* 34, 222.

84. Ibid., 35.

85. Mark A. Peterson, "Clinton and Organized Interests: Splitting Friends, Unifying Enemies," in *The Clinton Legacy,* 147.

86. Joseph A. Pika, "Interest Groups and the White House under Roosevelt and Truman," *Political Science Quarterly* (winter 1987–1988): 647–668.

87. Joseph A. Pika, "Interest Groups and the Executive: Presidential Intervention," in *Interest Group Politics,* ed. Allan J. Cigler and Burdett A. Loomis (Washington, D.C.: CQ

Press, 1983), 318. Also see Mark A. Peterson, "The Presidency and Organized Interests: White House Patterns of Interest Group Liaison," *American Political Science Review* (September 1992): 612–625; Joseph A. Pika, "Opening Doors for Kindred Souls: The White House Office of Public Liaison," in *Interest Group Politics*, 3d ed., ed. Allan J. Cigler and Burdett A. Loomis (Washington, D.C.: CQ Press, 1991); Martha Joynt Kumar and Michael Baruch Grossman, "Political Communications from the White House: The Interest Group Connection," *Presidential Studies Quarterly* (winter 1986): 92–101; Walcott and Hult, *Governing the White House*, chap. 6; and Bradley H. Patterson, *The Ring of Power: The White House Staff and Its Expanding Role in Government* (New York: Basic Books, 1988), chap. 14.

88. For a discussion of Colson and his tactics as Nixon's liaison with interest groups, see Maltese, *Spin Control*, 38, 82–84.

89. James Harding, "Preaching to the Converted," *Washington Post*, January 4, 2003, A1.

90. Kumar and Grossman, "Political Communications," 98.

91. Dana Milbank and Jim VandeHei, "Bush's Strong Arm Clubs Allies Too; Lawmakers, Activists Say Tactics for Enforcing Loyalty Are Tough and Sometimes Vindictive," *Washington Post*, March 21, 2003, A6.

92. Linda Feldmann, "How Far Bush Will Go on Conservative Agenda?" *Christian Science Monitor*, December 3, 2002, 3.

93. Patterson, *The Ring of Power*, 230.

94. Kathryn Dunn Tenpas, "Institutionalized Politics: The White House Office of Political Affairs," *Presidential Studies Quarterly* (spring 1996): 511.

95. John Anthony Maltese, *The Selling of Supreme Court Nominees* (Baltimore: Johns Hopkins University Press, 1995), 77.

96. Tenpas, "Institutionalized Politics," 514.

97. House Committee on Government Reform and Oversight, *Investigation of the Conversion of the $1.7 Million Centralized White House Computer System, Known as the White House Database, and Related Matters*, 105th Cong., 2d sess., 1998, H. Rept. 105 828, 43–44 (available online at http://www.house.gov/reform/neg).

98. Ibid., 44.

99. Tenpas, "Institutionalized Politics," 512.

100. Elisabeth Bumiller, "Preparing to Raise the Curtain on 2004," *New York Times*, June 23, 2003, A17.

101. Cynthia Kopkowski, "Politicians Hitch Bandwagon to Stars," *Atlanta Journal-Constitution*, July 20, 2002, 1A.

102. Losses by the president's party in midterm elections have been remarkably predictable. In the thirty-five midterm elections from 1862 through 1998, the president's party lost seats in the House of Representatives in thirty-two (1902, 1934, and 1998 are the exceptions) and in the Senate in twenty-one of the elections. Harold W. Stanley and Richard G. Niemi, *Vital Statistics on American Politics, 1999–2000*, 5th ed. (Washington, D.C.: CQ Press, 2000), Table 1-16, 48.

103. Fortier and Ornstein, "Congress and the Bush Presidency," 39.

104. Thomas Mann presents his findings on the 1974 elections in *Unsafe at Any Margin: Interpreting Congressional Elections* (Washington, D.C.: American Enterprise Institute, 1978), 92; Lyn Ragsdale presents her findings on the 1978 elections in "The Fiction of Congressional Elections as Presidential Events," *American Politics Quarterly* (October 1980): 375–398.

105. David Leuthold, *Electioneering in a Democracy: Campaigns for Congress* (New York: Wiley, 1968).

106. Jacobson, "The Bush Presidency and the American Electorate," 11–12. Indeed, Jacobson argues that redistricting is largely responsible for the Republican gains in 2002. Also see Gary C. Jacobson, "Terror, Terrain, and Turnout: Explaining the 2002 Midterm Elections," *Political Science Quarterly* (spring 2003): 1.

107. Fortier and Ornstein, "Congress and the Bush Presidency," 39–40.

108. Edward Tufte, "Determinants of the Outcomes of Midterm Congressional Elections," *American Political Science Review* (September 1975): 812–826.

109. Samuel Kernell, "Presidential Popularity and Negative Voting: An Alternative Explanation of the Midterm Decline of the Presidential Party," *American Political Science Review* (March 1977): 44–66.

110. Gary Jacobson, *The Politics of Congressional Elections* (Boston: Little, Brown, 1983),138 ff. Jacobson argues that the 2002 midterm elections are "entirely consistent" with such a model. He further adds: "Contrary to a great deal of postelection commentary, the results of the 2002 midterm congressional elections were neither surprising nor historically anomalous" (Jacobson, "Terror, Terrain, and Turnout," 1).

111. Jacobson, "Terror, Terrain, and Turnout," 3.

112. James Pollard, *The Presidents and the Press* (New York: Macmillan, 1947), chap. 1.

113. William Rivers, *The Opinion-Makers* (Boston: Beacon Press, 1967), 7.

114. Michael Baruch Grossman and Martha Joynt Kumar, *Portraying the President: The White House and the News Media* (Baltimore: Johns Hopkins University Press, 1981), 19.

115. Elmer E. Cornwell, *Presidential Leadership of Public Opinion* (Bloomington: Indiana University Press, 1965), 17; Stephen Hess, "Press Relations," in *Encyclopedia of the American Presidency,* ed. Leonard W. Levy and Louis Fisher (New York: Simon and Schuster, 1994), 1230.

116. *TV Dimensions 2000* (New York: Media Dynamics, 2000), 245.

117. "Poll Topics & Trends: Media Use and Evaluation," http://www.gallup.com.

118. Harold W. Stanley and Richard G. Niemi, *Vital Statistics on American Politics,* 5th ed. (Washington, D.C.: CQ Press, 1995), Table 2-1, 47.

119. Benjamin I. Page, Robert Y. Shapiro, and Glenn R. Dempsey, "What Moves Public Opinion?" *American Political Science Review* (March 1987): 23–43; and Donald L. Jordan, "Newspaper Effects on Policy Preferences," *Public Opinion Quarterly* (summer 1993): 191–204. Page, Shapiro, and Dempsey examined the impact of television reports, whereas Jordan concentrated on the effects of newspaper.

120. Grossman and Kumar, *Portraying the President,* 209–210.

121. Stanley and Niemi, *Vital Statistics on American Politics,* 5th ed., Table 2-2, 48–49.

122. Darren K. Carlson, "How Americans Get Their News," *Gallup Poll Tuesday Briefing,* December 31, 2002, http://www.gallup.com.

123. There are some notable exceptions to this rule. The *NewsHour with Jim Lehrer,* broadcast nightly by the Public Broadcasting Service (PBS), takes an hour to examine two or three topics in depth; ABC's *Nightline* looks at one topic for half an hour. PBS's *Washington Week in Review* uses major political reporters to analyze the significant news developments of the previous week; CNN provides continuing coverage as well as expanded focus on Washington, as on *Inside Politics.*

124. Baum and Kernell, "Has Cable Ended the Golden Age?" 99.

125. Stephen Hess, *The Washington Reporters* (Washington, D.C.: Brookings Institution Press, 1981), chap. 2; Leon Segal, *Reporters and Officials* (Lexington, Mass.: D. C. Heath, 1973), chap. 1.

126. Hess, *The Washington Reporters,* 31.

127. Quoted in Burt Solomon, "How a Leak-Loathing White House Is Putting the Press in Its Place," *National Journal,* February 13, 1993, 416.

128. Tom Rosenstiel, *The Beat Goes On: President Clinton's First Year with the Media* (New York: Twentieth Century Fund, 1994), 10.

129. Quoted in Leslie Kaufman, "The Young and the Relentless," *American Journalism Review* (March 1993): 30.

130. For a discussion of this, see Richard Davis and Diana Owen, *New Media and American Politics* (New York: Oxford University Press, 1998).

131. Sidney Blumenthal, "The Syndicated Presidency," *New Yorker,* April 5, 1993, 42.

132. Frank Newport and Lydia Saad, "A Matter of Trust," *American Journalism Review* (July-August 1998): 30.

133. For an early account of Vice President Cheney's role in circumventing the press corps, see Eric Schmitt, "Talk Show Debut Suggests Cheney Role," *New York Times,* January 29, 2001, A18.

134. Elisabeth Bumiller, "Bush Online: Smiles, Spin, and a Dog as Tour Guide," *New York Times,* May 19, 2003, A16.

135. Grossman and Kumar, *Portraying the President,* chap. 5.

136. M. L. Stein, *When Presidents Meet the Press* (New York: Messner, 1969), 166.

137. John F. Kennedy Jr., "Mike McCurry's About-Face," *George* (March 1999): 78.

138. Maltese, *Spin Control,* 24, 29.

139. Larry Speakes, *Speaking Out: Inside the Reagan White House* (New York: Scribner's, 1988), 136, 153.

140. For a full account of the office and its precursors, see Maltese, *Spin Control.*

141. Interview with John Anthony Maltese, March 10, 1989, Washington, D.C., quoted in Maltese, *Spin Control,* 2.

142. Donald T. Regan, *For the Record* (New York: Harcourt Brace Jovanovich, 1988), 248.

143. William Douglas, "Bush's 'Great Image,'" *Newsday,* May 2, 2003, A06; Dana Milbank, "Explanation for Bush's Carrier Landing Altered," *Washington Post,* May 7, 2003, A20; Elisabeth Bumiller, "Keepers of Bush Image Lift Stagecraft to New Heights," *New York Times,* May 16, 2003, 1.

144. Kernell, *Going Public,* 63.

145. Quoted in Maltese, *Spin Control,* 44.

146. Editorial, "Another Question, Mr. President?" *Washington Post,* March 9, 2003, B6.

147. Patterson, *The Ring of Power,* 174.

148. Fred I. Greenstein, *The Hidden-Hand Presidency: Eisenhower as Leader* (New York: Basic Books, 1982), 66–70.

149. George Reedy, *The Twilight of the Presidency* (New York: New American Library, 1970), 164.

150. Grossman and Kumar, *Portraying the President,* 244.

151. Pollard, *The Presidents and the Press,* 14.

152. David E. Sanger and James Risen, "C.I.A. Chief Takes Blame in Assertion on Iraqi Uranium," *New York Times,* July 12, 2003, A1; Christopher Marquis, "How Powerful Can 16 Words Be?" *New York Times,* July 20, 2003, sec. 4, 5.

153. Larry J. Sabato, *Feeding Frenzy: Attack Journalism and American Politics* (New York: Lanahan, 2000).

154. Grossman and Kumar, *Portraying the President,* chap. 1.

155. Michael Grossman and Francis Rourke, "The Media and the Presidency: An Exchange Analysis," *Political Science Quarterly* (fall 1976): 455–470. Also see Timothy E. Cook and Lyn Ragsdale, "The President and the Press: Negotiating Newsworthiness at the White House," in *The Presidency and the Political System,* 6th ed.

156. Quoted by Patterson in *The Ring of Power,* 170.

157. Grossman and Kumar, *Portraying the President,* chap. 11.

158. Ibid., 178.

159. This tendency first became apparent during the second year of the Reagan administration when reporters began to ask him more embarrassing questions (for instance, why he did not set an example by making more generous donations to private charities). They also appeared not to take seriously the president's statement that members of his administration were one big happy family.

160. Martha Joynt Kumar, "President Clinton Meets the Media: Communications Shaped by Predictable Patterns," in *The Clinton Presidency: Campaigning, Governing, and the Psychology of Leadership,* ed. Stanley A. Rehshon (Boulder: Westview, 1995), 167–171.

161. Study conducted by Robert Lichter of the Center for Media and Public Affairs as reported in Howard Kurtz, "The Bad News about Clinton," *Washington Post,* September 1, 1994, D1.

162. James Risen, "Clinton Gets Little Credit for Economic Turnaround," *Los Angeles Times,* September 5, 1994, A2.

163. Godfrey Sperling, " 'Clinton Bashing' and the Liberal Press," *Christian Science Monitor,* September 20, 1994, 19.

164. Stephen Hess showed that in 1978, 73 percent were college graduates and 33 percent had graduate degrees (*The Washington Reporters,* 83); Leo Rosten reported that in 1936, 51 percent were college graduates and 6 percent had an advanced academic degree; see *The Washington Correspondents* (New York: Harcourt, Brace, 1937), 159–160.

165. James Fallows, "The Presidency and the Press," in *The Presidency and the Political System,* 3d ed., ed. Michael Nelson (Washington, D.C.: CQ Press, 1990).

166. Hertsgaard, *On Bended Knee.*

167. Bill Kovach and Tom Rosenstiel, *Warp Speed: America in the Age of Mixed Media* (New York: Century Foundation Press, 1999), 51.

168. David Noack, "Clinton Sex Story Forces Print Media Changes," *Editor and Publisher,* January 31, 1998, 62. The remainder of this section is drawn from John Anthony Maltese, "The Presidency and the News Media," *Perspectives on Political Science* (spring 2001): 81–82.

169. Howard Kurtz, *Spin Cycle: How the White House and the Media Manipulate the News* (New York: Touchstone, 1998), 291.

170. Dan Trigoboff, "The 'Source' Heard 'Round the World,'" *Broadcasting and Cable,* February 2, 1998, 62.

171. Kovach and Rosenstiel, *Warp Speed,* 99 (the study is reproduced in Appendix 1 of their book).

172. Ibid.,100.

173. Trigoboff, "The 'Source' Heard 'Round the World,'" 62.

174. Alicia C. Shepard, "White Noise," *American Journalism Review* (January–February 1999): 20.

175. John Cook, "CNN's Free Fall," *Brill's Content* (April 2001): 1. Instead of hard news, the spring 2001 prime-time lineup on CNN consisted of the talk-show oriented programs *Wolf Blitzer Reports, The Point with Greta Van Susteren, Larry King Live,* and *The Spin Room.* Interspersed at 10:00 P.M. was a half-hour newscast anchored by Bill Hemmer.

176. Sidney Blumenthal, *The Permanent Campaign* (New York: Simon and Schuster, 1982); see also Ornstein and Mann, eds., *The Permanent Campaign and Its Future,* vii.

177. Blumenthal, *The Permanent Campaign,* 7.

178. Hugh Heclo, "Campaigning and Governing: A Conspectus," *The Permanent Campaign and Its Future,* 15.

179. George C. Edwards III, "Campaigning Is Not Governing: Bill Clinton's Rhetorical Presidency," in *The Clinton Legacy,* 33.

180. Jones, "Preparing to Govern in 2001," 185.

181. Heclo, "Campaigning and Governing," 11.

182. Kernell, *Going Public,* 23.

183. Ibid., 2.

184. Brandice Canes-Wrone, "The President's Legislative Influence from Public Appeals," *American Journal of Political Science* (April 2001): 313–329.

SUGGESTED READINGS

Brace, Paul, and Barbara Hinckley. *Follow the Leader: Opinion Polls and Modern Presidents*. New York: Basic Books, 1992.

Cornwell, Elmer E. *Presidential Leadership of Public Opinion*. Bloomington: Indiana University Press, 1965.

Edwards, George C., III. *The Public Presidency: The Pursuit of Popular Support*. New York: St. Martin's Press, 1983.

Eisinger, Robert M. *The Evolution of Presidential Polling*. New York: Cambridge University Press, 2003.

Grossman, Michael Baruch, and Martha Joynt Kumar. *Portraying the President: The White House and the News Media*. Baltimore: Johns Hopkins University Press, 1981.

Hinckley, Barbara. *The Symbolic Presidency: How Presidents Portray Themselves*. New York: Routledge, 1990.

Jacobson, Gary C. "Terror, Terrain, and Turnout: Explaining the 2002 Midterm Elections." *Political Science Quarterly* (spring 2003): 1.

Kernell, Samuel. *Going Public: New Strategies of Presidential Leadership*, 3d ed. Washington, D.C.: CQ Press, 1997.

Maltese, John Anthony. *Spin Control: The White House Office of Communications and the Management of Presidential News*, 2d ed., rev. Chapel Hill: University of North Carolina Press, 1994.

Ornstein, Norman J., and Thomas E. Mann, eds. *The Permanent Campaign and Its Future*. Washington, D.C.: American Enterprise Institute, 2000.

Patterson, Bradley H., Jr. *The White House Staff: Inside the West Wing and Beyond*. Washington, D.C.: Brookings Institution Press, 2000.

Shapiro, Robert Y., Martha Joynt Kumar, and Lawrence R. Jacobs, eds. *Presidential Power: Forging the Presidency for the Twenty-first Century*. New York: Columbia University Press, 2000.

Tulis, Jeffrey K. *The Rhetorical Presidency*. Princeton: Princeton University Press, 1987.

4 PRESIDENTIAL CHARACTER AND PERFORMANCE

In a dramatic moment intended to halt media reports and rumors, President Bill Clinton publicly denied in January 1998 having had a sexual relationship with "that woman," Monica Lewinsky, but was later forced to publicly apologize for lying about the relationship and to defend himself against impeachment charges.

PRESIDENT WILLIAM JEFFERSON CLINTON left office at noon on January 20, 2001, at the completion of a controversial eight-year roller-coaster ride on the national scene. A man of uncommon intellectual ability and verbal facility, Clinton left behind many lingering questions centered on his personal character and judgment. Retrospective evaluations of his legacy recognized the mixed nature of his performance as president, a record of "striking strengths [and] glaring failures."[1] Foremost among the latter was his relationship with former White House intern Monica Lewinsky. When word of the alleged affair swept the nation in January 1998, Clinton publicly denied having any sexual relationship with "that woman," a position he also took in providing a legal deposition in a civil suit for sexual harassment that had been filed against him by Paula Jones, a former Arkansas state employee. But after a sustained grand jury investigation into whether his testimony constituted perjury, Clinton grudgingly admitted the relationship had been "not appropriate" and "wrong" in a nationally televised speech on August 17, 1998. This brief, 10 P.M. address concluded a day in which the president had answered questions for four hours before Kenneth Starr, the independent counsel appointed to look into allegations of wrongdoing.[2] Ultimately the Republican House impeached Clinton on charges of perjury and obstruction of justice, but the Senate did not find him guilty, and he completed his term in office. *(See chapter 5.)*

Could we have predicted Clinton's performance in office? Did we know enough about his personal background and previous experience in elected office to have anticipated his record of dramatically alternating highs and lows? In what ways will George W. Bush's background, experience, and outlook affect his performance as a wartime president? The presidency invites such speculation because its occupants wield enormous power in a one-person office rather than as part of a collective institution. Moreover, during the last third of the twentieth century, enormous attention was devoted to the psychological makeup of chief executives. Many analysts attributed the conduct of the Vietnam War (1965–1973) and the Watergate scandal (in which White House aides covered up illegal activities committed to help the president get reelected) to the unique emotional needs of Presidents Lyndon Baines Johnson and Richard Nixon.[3]

In this chapter we look more closely at what kinds of people have served as president and how their personal qualities may have shaped their conduct. We are especially concerned with the backgrounds, skills, psychological traits, and management styles of presidents and how these factors influence their performances in office. We therefore examine the abilities and attitudes that presidents develop before entering office, ways in which their personalities affect how they do the job, and their habitual modes of working. We also look at the way presidents interact with their staffs, those assistants whose positions were created to extend presidents' personal capabilities. To conclude, we take a closer look at Bill Clinton to understand the factors that shaped his performance in office, and we offer a preliminary sketch of George W. Bush.

Determinants and Evaluations of Performance

For generations, historians and political scientists have argued about how important a leader's characteristics are for understanding and explaining events. Does one, for example, place great significance on the intelligence, stature, and wisdom of Abraham Lincoln in explaining the Union's ultimate victory? Or was victory the product of forces beyond Lincoln's control, such as the changing nature of modern warfare in an industrial age, which favored the North? Did America and the Soviet Union avert nuclear war during the Cuban missile crisis of 1962 because of the decision style adopted by John F. Kennedy? Or was the outcome the result of organizational routines for crisis management and other random occurrences perhaps not intended by either side during the confrontation? The larger questions, then, are, just how much importance should one ascribe to the president's personal characteristics, and are these elements powerful predictors of performance in office?

Specialists have not reached agreement on the importance of these factors, although there is widespread belief that it does indeed matter—and probably a great deal—who is president. As Fred Greenstein argues, "If some higher power had set out to design a democracy in which the individual on top mattered, the result might well resemble the American political system."[4] Every four years the nation devotes enormous effort and resources to selecting a leader, and this confidence in the difference an individual can make is revealed when citizens proudly explain that they "voted for the person, not the party." Public attention focuses on the presidency, with the mass media personalizing the solution to public problems and portraying presidents as the embodiment of the larger political process. Moreover, presidents and their media advisers encourage personalization when they highlight traits the public regards as desirable.

Not everyone agrees that presidents' individual characteristics are critical to understanding their accomplishments. The alternative is to stress the environment within which presidents operate as the truly significant determinant of outcomes. The most influential interpretation in this tradition is the work of Stephen Skowronek, whose analysis rests on comparison of presidents in decidedly different time frames. Thus Thomas Jefferson, Andrew Jackson, Lincoln, Franklin Roosevelt, and Ronald Reagan shared common "leadership tasks" associated with the decline and reconstruction of the links among societal interests and the political parties essential to a political order. Similarly, James Monroe, James K. Polk, Theodore Roosevelt, and Lyndon Johnson had more in common with each other—the position they inherited in relation to the dominant political order—than with their immediate predecessors and successors. Although the title of Skowronek's principal work—*The Politics Presidents Make*—emphasizes the role of leadership, the unfolding evolution of larger forces in American social and political life defines the tasks presidents confront and severely limits the possibilities they enjoy at the outset of their terms.[5]

Nonetheless, there is broad consensus among students of the presidency that each chief executive brings to the job a combination of attitudes, skills, strengths, and shortcomings that will influence his or her performance in office and may at times have an enduring effect on the nation's history. Disagreement still exists on the relative significance of these causal factors and exactly how they are related to job performance and policy outcomes. A number of analysts have suggested ways to conceptualize these issues; a modified, considerably simplified diagram based on two of the most prominent treatments is presented in Figure 4-1.

All presidents bring to the job enduring personality traits as well as attitudes and beliefs toward a wide range of political structures, institutions, and relationships. These personal characteristics and attitudes take shape within a distinctive social context—family situation, place in the community, educational experience, and so on. In addition, their adult professional experiences prior to entering office, particularly as those relate to role demands of the presidency, produce a personal style that may be more or less congruent with the demands of serving as chief executive. The presidential selection process filters out personal styles, skills, and competencies that are not role appropriate. Ultimately presidents may be more or less likely to produce successful outcomes as these individual traits interact with the situations the presidents confront. In concentrating on the importance of leaders' individual characteristics, one recognizes that presidents are in the position to have potentially decisive impacts on political events. Even if the environment, forces beyond the control of the individual leader, has a determinative effect on events, "environments are always mediated by the individuals on whom they act."[6]

Just as analysts disagree over the determinants of presidential behavior, so too do they disagree over how to evaluate a president's performance, although the general public and professional presidency watchers engage in evaluations all the time. Polls provide current, short-term assessments of public approval (discussed in chapter 3), and journalists constantly assess the administration's record in dealing with Congress or in addressing particular policy areas. Certain evaluation points have become institutionalized: the end of an administration's first hundred days in office (a carryover from Franklin Roosevelt's first term) always produces a spate of articles. Other evaluation points are at midterm and on departure from office.[7] In other words, the public, journalists, and academics are constantly engaged in *contemporary evaluation* of presidential performance.

Scholars and others use a variety of criteria. Bruce Buchanan has drawn broad distinctions between subjective and objective criteria. Judgments based on subjective grounds emphasize the "appearance and demeanor" of leadership, including success in projecting the image of integrity and charisma; the "moral desirability of a president's means or ends"; and the pragmatic test of self-interest—the extent to which the president contributed to a citizen's well-being. Objective criteria, on which professionals make their evaluations, focus on presidential skill in making things happen, especially short-term successes, or on the lasting results produced for the nation.[8] For example, in reflecting on the record of achievements by the Reagan administration, a number of works adopted the long view in assessing its legacy. As Bert Rockman put it, politicians can "leave greater or lesser footprints. Assessing the depth and durability of those marks is hazardous while the administration under evaluation is still in power. The real answers will come later—much later."[9]

Figure 4-1 Relationship of Background to Performance

Sources: Bert A. Rockman, *The Leadership Question* (New York: Praeger, 1984), 189; Fred I. Greenstein, *Personality and Politics* (New York: Norton, 1975), 27.

Bill Clinton's conduct has reawakened concern with "presidential character," a term with many contradictory meanings. James Pfiffner seeks to help the public address this murky area: How should Americans assess the personal failures of presidents when they lie about trivial or important matters, violate marriage vows, or intentionally seek to deceive the public?[10] Pfiffner reviews numerous instances of presidential untruths in terms of the teller's intent and the seriousness of the lie, a recognition that evaluation of this conduct depends heavily on context. Although "telling the truth . . . is an important ethical imperative for presidents," Pfiffner accepts the possibility of a "justified lie."[11] Thus lies to protect the national security, concerning trivial matters (for example, describing one's personal history or illustrating a point), or to prevent embarrassment and preserve political viability are less serious than those used to cover up important facts or deceive the public on policy matters. Pfiffner's discussion of Clinton's marital infidelity is placed in the context of Franklin Roosevelt, Dwight Eisenhower, John Kennedy, and Lyndon Johnson, other presidents known, or suspected, to have committed similar acts.[12]

Efforts to evaluate presidential performance and conduct are not new. Since 1948 scholars, primarily historians, have been asked on several occasions to "rate" American presidents. In essence they were to assess the "depth and durability" of presidential footprints and provide a *historical evaluation*. Table 4-1 shows the results of six of these efforts. Each poll was structured a bit differently and surveyed a different panel of "experts."[13] Yet one finds considerable consensus among participants on the top ten and the bottom ten, with the exception of Nixon, whose reputation has undergone a marked resurgence since his death in 1994. Because of the similar results across polls, Robert Murray and Tim Blessing concluded that historians "had in mind more than vague and uncritical generalities when they evaluated presidential performances."[14] Assessments of recent presidents are particularly susceptible to change with the passage of time. Note how Eisenhower moved from twentieth place in 1962 to ninth in both the *Chicago Tribune* poll in 1982 and the C-SPAN poll in 2000. Harry S. Truman's standing among professionals was already strong by 1962 and has remained so. Ronald Reagan's evaluation by historians has improved from below average to the borderline between average and above average.[15] The most recent survey included Bill Clinton, who finished in the middle of the pack at number twenty-one, just behind George H. W. Bush.

Table 4-1   Ratings of U.S. Presidents

Schlesinger poll (1948)	Schlesinger poll (1962)	Maranell-Dodder poll (1982)	*Chicago Tribune* poll (1982)	Murray-Blessing poll[a] (1982)	C-SPAN poll (2000)
Great	Great	Accomplishments of administration	Ten best presidents	Great	Overall leadership
1. Lincoln	1. Lincoln	1. Lincoln	1. Lincoln (best)	1. Lincoln	1. Lincoln
2. Washington	2. Washington	2. F. Roosevelt	2. Washington	2. F. Roosevelt	2. F. Roosevelt
3. F. Roosevelt	3. F. Roosevelt	3. Washington	3. F. Roosevelt	3. Washington	3. Washington
4. Wilson	4. Wilson	4. Jefferson	4. T. Roosevelt	4. Jefferson	4. T. Roosevelt
5. Jefferson	5. Jefferson	5. T. Roosevelt	5. Jefferson		5. Truman
6. Jackson		6. Truman	6. Wilson	Near great	6. Wilson
	Near great	7. Wilson	7. Jackson	5. T. Roosevelt	7. Jefferson
Near great	6. Jackson	8. Jackson	8. Truman	6. Wilson	8. Kennedy
7. T. Roosevelt	7. T. Roosevelt	9. L. Johnson	9. Eisenhower	7. Jackson	9. Eisenhower
8. Cleveland	8. Polk	10. Polk	10. Polk (10th best)	8. Truman	10. L. Johnson
9. J. Adams	Truman (tie)	11. J. Adams			11. Reagan
10. Polk	9. J. Adams	12. Kennedy	Ten worst presidents	Above average	12. Polk
	10. Cleveland	13. Monroe	1. Harding (worst)	9. J. Adams	13. Jackson
Average		14. Cleveland	2. Nixon	10. L. Johnson	14. Monroe
11. J. Q. Adams	Average	15. Madison	3. Buchanan	11. Eisenhower	15. McKinley
12. Monroe	11. Madison	16. Taft	4. Pierce	12. Polk	16. J. Adams
13. Hayes	12. J. Q. Adams	17. McKinley	5. Grant	13. Kennedy	17. Cleveland
14. Madison	13. Hayes	18. J. Q. Adams	6. Fillmore	14. Madison	18. Madison
15. Van Buren	14. McKinley	19. Hoover	7. A. Johnson	15. Monroe	19. J. Q. Adams
16. Taft	15. Taft	20. Eisenhower	8. Coolidge	16. J. Q. Adams	20. G.H.W. Bush
17. Arthur	16. Van Buren	21. A. Johnson	9. Tyler	17. Cleveland	21. Clinton
18. McKinley	17. Monroe	22. Van Buren	10. Carter (10th worst)		22. Carter
19. A. Johnson	18. Hoover	23. Arthur		Average	23. Ford
20. Hoover	19. B. Harrison	24. Hayes		18. McKinley	24. Taft
21. B. Harrison	20. Arthur	25. Tyler		19. Taft	25. Nixon
	Eisenhower (tie)	26. B. Harrison		20. Van Buren	26. Hayes
Below average	21. A. Johnson	27. Taylor		21. Hoover	27. Coolidge
22. Tyler		28. Buchanan		22. Hayes	28. Taylor
23. Coolidge	Below average	29. Fillmore		23. Arthur	29. Garfield
24. Fillmore	22. Taylor	30. Coolidge		24. Ford	30. Van Buren
25. Taylor	23. Tyler	31. Pierce		25. Carter	31. Harrison
26. Buchanan	24. Fillmore	32. Grant		26. B. Harrison	32. Arthur
27. Pierce	25. Coolidge	33. Harding			33. Grant
	26. Pierce			Below average	34. Hoover
Failure	27. Buchanan			27. Taylor	35. Fillmore
28. Grant				28. Reagan	36. Tyler
29. Harding	Failure			29. Tyler	37. W. H. Harrison
	28. Grant			30. Fillmore	38. Harding
	29. Harding			31. Coolidge	39. Pierce
				32. Pierce	40. A. Johnson
					41. Buchanan
				Failure	
				33. A. Johnson	
				34. Buchanan	
				35. Nixon	
				36. Grant	
				37. Harding	

Sources: Harold W. Stanley and Richard G. Niemi, *Vital Statistics on American Politics* 1999–2000 (Washington, D.C.: CQ Press, 2000), Table 6-2, 244–245; and C-SPAN Survey, February, 2000, www.americanpresidents.org/survey/historians/overall.asp.

Note: These ratings result from surveys of scholars and range in number from 49 to 846.

[a]The rating of President Reagan was obtained in a separate poll conducted in 1989.

In addition to analyzing 846 completed surveys, Murray and Blessing conducted sixty in-depth interviews with historians to determine their evaluative criteria. The most important personal trait contributing to presidential achievement, in the view of these participating historians, was decisiveness; intelligence, particularly the capacity for growth, and integrity were close behind.[16] Greatness, many seemed to feel, is achieved by those leaders able to exercise moral, inspirational leadership, who have "a capacity for creative innovation and an imagination that was fired by a clear vision of the future."[17] James MacGregor Burns's discussion of leadership emphasizes similar abilities as the source of "transformational" leadership, by which presidents appeal to the higher goals and motives of followers to achieve true change.[18] Fred Greenstein suggests that a president's job performance is shaped by six qualities: proficiency as a *public communicator; organizational capacity* to rally colleagues and structure activities; *political skill* insofar as it is linked to a *vision* of public policy; *cognitive style* in processing advice and information; and *emotional intelligence,* by which he means the ability to manage one's own emotions for constructive purposes.[19]

As Greenstein makes clear, it is now necessary to factor an additional consideration into assessing performance: modern presidents no longer govern alone. Since the 1930s they have been assisted by a large number of aides appointed to serve in the Executive Office of the President. Aides have the capacity to amplify a president's personal capabilities; mobilizing such efforts is a new dimension of the job just as public communications have taken on a much greater significance than they had prior to the twentieth century.

In examining the importance of individual characteristics, we turn first to a discussion of the backgrounds from which presidents have been drawn. As depicted in Figure 4-1, a president's life and occupational experiences are distant from the actual service in office and should therefore have only limited power to explain performance. Nonetheless, the patterns uncovered tell us something about leadership in America.

What Manner of Person?

Each president brings to the office a cumulation of life experiences derived from a position in American society and previous professional experience. The selection process, rather than producing a random sampling of Americans, favors some backgrounds over others. After reviewing the historical pattern for social background and education, scholars have found, not surprisingly, that presidents have disproportionately been drawn from traditionally dominant groups in American society. It is less clear, however, just what this has meant for performance in office.

Social Background

Although there is no single indicator of social status on which all Americans would agree, occupation is probably the most important criterion for social ranking in the United States.[20] Moreover, the occupation of a person's father provides a reasonably accurate picture of his or her class origins. By analyzing such origins, one can determine the extent to which presidents have achieved their positions of power as a result of their own abilities or thanks to the advantages of family background.[21] The presidency has long been cited as an example of how ability can enable individuals to overcome disadvantages and rise to power. But the reality of presidents' personal histories, argues Edward Pessen, contradicts "the log cabin myth" and demonstrates that "the political race here as elsewhere has usually been won by those who had the advantage of starting from a favorable position."[22] Pessen characterized the family background of each president through Reagan in terms of six basic groupings: upper-upper and lower-upper, upper-middle and lower-middle, upper-lower and lower-lower.[23] In making his evaluations, Pessen compared the presidents' family backgrounds with the economic and social conditions that existed at the time rather than using a permanent yardstick.

Five distinguished American families have produced ten presidents, more than one-fifth of the total. Included were John Adams and his son John Quincy Adams; James Madison and Zachary Taylor, who had grandparents in common; William Henry Harrison and his grandson Benjamin Harrison; cousins Theodore and Franklin Roosevelt; and George H. W. Bush, father of George W. Bush (unranked by Pessen). All five families meet Pessen's criteria for upper-class status as depicted in Table 4-2. It is also not uncommon for presidents to come from politically prominent families, also more often than not, upper-class. John Tyler was the son of a Virginia governor; William Howard Taft's father served as secretary of war, attorney general, and ambassador to Austria and Russia; and John Kennedy's father was the chairman of the Securities and Exchange Commission and ambassador to Great Britain. Franklin Pierce's father was governor of New Hampshire (though Pessen locates the family between the lower-upper and upper-middle classes). The father of George H. W. Bush and grandfather of George W. Bush accumulated a fortune working on Wall Street before being elected to the Senate from Connecticut.

Other chief executives from upper-class origins but whose fathers did not hold high political office include George Washington, Thomas Jefferson, James Monroe, James K. Polk, and Woodrow Wilson. Pessen ranks Chester Arthur as upper-middle class. There are also a number of presidents, including Pierce, Rutherford B. Hayes, Grover Cleveland, Warren G. Harding, Calvin Coolidge, and Truman, in a special bridge category between upper-class and middle-class origins. Altogether, Pessen considers sixteen presidents to be drawn from upper-class roots (the Bushes would make eighteen) and six more as bordering on this exclusive group—a total of twenty-four, more than half of all those who have served in the White House.

Ten presidents fall within Pessen's upper-middle category, leaving only seven who can be regarded as drawn from middle- or lower-class roots, and Bill Clinton would make an eighth. The presidents most socially disadvantaged include Andrew Johnson, whose father held a variety of jobs, including janitor and

Table 4-2   Pessen's Analysis of Presidential Social Class

Social Class	President
Upper-Upper	G. Washington, T. Jefferson, J. Madison, J. Q. Adams, W. H. Harrison, J. Tyler, Z. Taylor, B. Harrison, T. Roosevelt, W. H. Taft, F. D. Roosevelt, George H. W. Bush*, George W. Bush*
Middle-Upper	J. Polk, J. Kennedy
Lower-Upper	J. Adams, J. Monroe, W. Wilson
Lower-Upper/ Upper-Middle	F. Pierce, R. Hayes, G. Cleveland, W. Harding, C. Coolidge, H. Truman
Upper-Middle	A. Jackson, M. Van Buren, J. Buchanan, U.S. Grant, C. Arthur, W. McKinley, H. Hoover, L. Johnson, G. Ford, J. Carter
Middle	A. Lincoln, D. Eisenhower, R. Reagan, W. Clinton*
Lower-Middle	M. Fillmore, J. Garfield, R. Nixon
Upper-Lower	A. Johnson
Lower-Lower	None

Source: Edward Pessen, *The Log Cabin Myth: The Social Backgrounds of the Presidents* (New Haven: Yale University Press, 1984), 68.

*Presidents not rated by Pessen.

porter at an inn; Millard Fillmore, probably the only president truly born in a log cabin as the son of a dirt farmer; and James Garfield, whose father pulled the family into prosperity through manual labor as a canal worker in the Midwest. Despite the stories about Lincoln's modest background, his father owned more property and livestock at the time of Abraham's birth than did the majority of his neighbors, and his prominence continued to grow.

Three more recent presidents—Eisenhower, Nixon, and Reagan—were the sons of poor men who tried numerous jobs without much success. Eisenhower's father was a mechanic in a creamery for a time after an investment failed; Nixon's father was a streetcar conductor in Columbus, Ohio, before trying his luck as a painter, carpenter, glass worker, and sheep rancher; and Reagan's father worked on and off as an itinerant shoe salesman. Bill Clinton's father, a traveling salesman, died before his son was born, and Clinton's mother became a nurse anesthetist. His grandfather, with whom he lived until age four, was first the town iceman and later a neighborhood grocer, and his stepfather was a car salesman. The fathers of Lyndon Johnson, Gerald Ford, and Jimmy Carter met mixed success in business: Johnson's father traded in commodities and livestock; Ford's stepfather (the president was born Leslie King and adopted as Gerald R. Ford Jr.) operated a paint and lumber business; and Carter's father founded a successful peanut warehouse.

Although presidents have come from diverse backgrounds, those with upper-class origins have been the most prevalent, while most others were drawn from

Having Presidents Ford, Nixon, Bush, Reagan, and Carter together in 1991 for the dedication of the Reagan Presidential Library highlighted the distinctive attitudes, experiences, skills, and psychological dispositions that each occupant brings to the office of president.

prosperous and socially respected backgrounds. Even so, one can discern some changes over time. The first six chief executives came from socially, and in many cases politically, prominent families. Not wholly by coincidence, they served during the period when presidential candidates were nominated by congressional caucus. After both political parties adopted the national nominating convention in the early 1830s, candidates from less-privileged backgrounds also began to make it to the White House. Fillmore, Lincoln, Andrew Johnson, and Garfield—four presidents with humble origins—are concentrated in the period 1850–1880. Twentieth-century presidents were drawn from both upper-class (the two Roosevelts, Taft, Wilson, Kennedy, and George H. W. Bush) and modest family circumstances (Truman, Eisenhower, Nixon, Reagan, and Clinton). Though George W. Bush follows a pattern more typical of the nineteenth century—heir to an upper-class dynasty—there is no way to predict what the origins of other twenty-first century presidents will be.

Education

Education is often closely correlated with social class. Most U.S. presidents have been well educated. Only nine of the forty-two individuals (Cleveland served two, nonconsecutive terms, making George W. Bush the forty-third president) did not have any formal instruction at a college or university. Moreover, the trend has been toward chief executives with greater college training. Of the nineteen who have occupied the presidency in this century, only Truman did not attend an institution of higher learning.[24] The universities and colleges presidents attended are among the most highly regarded in the nation. Harvard University leads the list with five chief executives as alumni—the two Adamses, the two Roosevelts, and Kennedy (George W. Bush also has an M.B.A. from Harvard). Alma maters of other presidents include major private universities such as Princeton (Madison and Wilson), Yale (Taft and the two Bushes; Ford and Clinton also have Yale law degrees), Stanford (Herbert Hoover), Georgetown (Clinton), and a wide variety of prestigious smaller private colleges, such as Allegheny (William McKinley), Amherst (Coolidge), Bowdoin (Pierce), Dickinson (James Buchanan), Hampden-Sidney (W. H. Harrison), Kenyon (Hayes), Union (Arthur), and Williams (Garfield). Although less prevalent than private institutions, well-known public universities also figure among presidents' alma maters: Miami University of Ohio (Benjamin Harrison), the University of Michigan (Ford), the University of North Carolina (Polk), William and Mary (Jefferson, Monroe, and Tyler), and the two service academies, Annapolis (Carter) and West Point (Ulysses S. Grant and Eisenhower). Twentieth-century presidents hailing from families with more modest social standing attended less prestigious institutions: Johnson attended Southwest Texas State Teachers College; Nixon graduated from Whittier College in California before attending Duke University Law School; Reagan majored in economics and sociology at Eureka College in Illinois.

That so many presidents attended prestigious institutions of higher learning probably has less to do with innate abilities or career aspirations than with family status or a desire to improve their economic and social positions. An example is James Garfield, the son of a canal construction worker, who died when Garfield was two. Garfield managed, after a long struggle for education, to graduate from Williams College and become the principal of a church school before being admitted to the bar and eventually going into politics. More presidents attended private than public schools because private schools were established earlier, particularly in the northeastern states, such as New York and Massachusetts, which have produced ten presidents, and the midwestern states, such as Ohio, which has produced six. Several postwar presidents, including Eisenhower, Johnson, Ford, and Carter, attended public institutions, a trend that may become more pronounced. The selection of more presidents from states in which there are more public than private universities (such as the western states) would contribute to this trend. Although most citizens today would probably agree that a college education is essential if presidents are to understand the complex problems confronting the nation, no direct correlation between quality of institution or years of training and performance exists.

Career Experience

Although the family occupational backgrounds of the presidents are fairly broad, their own careers prior to and outside politics have been much less diverse. Twenty-five of the forty-two chief executives practiced law at some time. Other occupations include the military (W. H. Harrison, Taylor, Grant, and Eisenhower), education (Wilson and Lyndon Johnson), journalism (Harding and Kennedy), engineering (Hoover), and entertainment (Reagan). Washington and Madison were gentleman farmers. Carter combined farming with his family peanut business after giving up his career as a navy engineer to return to Georgia when his father died. George W. Bush was an oilman and managing general partner of a baseball team. Two presidents who pursued less prestigious careers before entering public life were Truman, who, in addition to trying his hand at farming, was a haberdasher and a railroad timekeeper, and Andrew Johnson, who was a tailor. It is not surprising that so many presidents were lawyers because that profession is closely linked with a political career. Law is a prestigious occupation, rewards skill in interpersonal negotiation and conciliation as well as verbal and argumentative facility, and enables its practitioners to return to private life more readily than is true of medicine or engineering, for example.[25] In recent years fewer chief executives have come from the law. Of the eleven presidents since World War II, only three—Nixon, Ford, and Clinton— were lawyers. As increasing numbers of people from nonlegal backgrounds— business and teaching, in particular—become senators and governors (the positions from which today's presidents often are recruited), still more presidents without legal training may occupy the White House.

Only three presidents, career military officers, had not held public office before becoming president. Taylor, Grant, and Eisenhower were thrust into the vortex of presidential politics because of heroic exploits in the Mexican War, Civil War, and World War II, respectively. As professional military men they had not even been involved in partisan activities. Taylor, elected as the Whig candidate in 1848, had never voted before in a presidential election and had no party affiliation.[26] Grant, the Republican Party candidate elected in 1868, had voted for James Buchanan, the Democratic standard-bearer in 1856, and had political views that have been described as "obscure."[27] Even more perplexing for party leaders was Eisenhower, the Republican Party candidate in 1952 and 1956, whom a number of liberal Democratic leaders had tried to draft for their party's nomination in 1948.[28]

For most U.S. chief executives, the road to the presidency involved a long apprenticeship in public office with careers usually begun at lower levels of the political system when they were in their twenties or thirties. Andrew Johnson and Coolidge began their public careers as city aldermen or councilmen. Others were first elected to county offices: John Adams was a highway surveyor; Truman a member of the county court, an administrative, not a judicial, position. Some presidents, including Jackson, Buchanan, Cleveland, McKinley, and Taft, ed public service as prosecuting or district attorneys; others, such as Hayes and Benjamin Harrison, served as city solicitors or attorneys. Clinton began his career in 1976 as Arkansas's attorney general. Several chief executives—Jefferson, Lincoln, and the two Roosevelts among them—began their public careers as state legislators.

The typical career pattern for these presidents was to move up the political ladder by winning offices representing progressively larger constituencies. Approximately two-thirds of the presidents served in either the House of Representatives or the Senate or both. Exceptions include Wilson, who spent most of his adult life as a professor of government and later as president of Princeton University; in 1910, at age fifty-four, he was elected governor of New Jersey, just two years before winning the presidency. Reagan was primarily a radio, movie, and television performer until his fifties, when he became active in national politics in Barry Goldwater's 1964 presidential campaign. In 1966 he was elected to the first of two terms as governor of California; in 1980 he was elected president. George W. Bush became governor of Texas in 1994 at age forty-seven and was reelected in 1998. Neither Taft nor Hoover held any elective office before being chosen president. Taft served as a judge at the county, state, and federal levels, and later became governor general of the Philippines and secretary of war. Hoover chaired the Commission for Relief in Belgium after World War I; oversaw prices, production, and distribution of food during World War I as U.S. food administrator; and later served as secretary of commerce under Harding and Coolidge.

Most presidents come to the White House from another high public office. *(See the discussion in chapter 2.)* Typical positions include the vice presidency, state governorships, Senate seats, and appointive executive office. From one era to the next, these offices have varied in the extent to which their occupants have been favored or disfavored in their pursuit of the presidency.

How is experience related to performance? Most observers assume experience can make a president more or less familiar with the problems confronting the nation as well as with the institutions and people who must collectively address these problems. Moreover, an earlier career in elective office may enable individuals to develop the skills necessary for exercising leadership—bargaining skills, facility in public speaking, and the capacity to persuade or inspire others. Candidates, therefore, usually argue that their particular blend of experience—whether in state, national, or nonpublic sectors—has made them best qualified for the position.

Background-Performance Links

How have scholars linked these biographical characteristics to presidential performance? Are there systematic patterns that would enable the public to predict which candidates will enjoy greatest success in office? Unfortunately, there are no simple answers.

Our review shows that most presidents achieved political success with a substantial boost from their family circumstances, advantages that included political and social standing as well as educational and professional opportunities unavailable to most of their fellow citizens. "The common characteristic [of presidents,] . . . for all their dissimilarities in other respects, has been the essential conservatism of their social, economic, and political beliefs. . . [A]ll of them were champions of the prevailing order," according to Pessen.[29] Because the selection process is not neutral toward social class, it seems likely that most presidential aspirants will sustain the status quo.

Two sociologists, E. Digby Baltzell and Howard G. Schneiderman, have more specifically sought to link class origin with performance in office. They correlate Pessen's analysis of class origins with a ranking of presidential performance based on the Murray-Blessing survey of American historians described earlier.[30] Their conclusion challenges some of the myths surrounding the presidency. "There has been . . . not only a high correlation between high social origins and getting to the presidency, as Pessen clearly has shown, [but] once elected to office, men of privileged origins have performed far better than those of lower social status."[31] Of the eight presidents ranked by historians as great or near great, five were from upper-class families (Washington, Jefferson, Theodore Roosevelt, Wilson, and Franklin Roosevelt), two from the upper-middle class (Jackson and Truman), and only one from the middle and lower classes (Lincoln, who is generally ranked number one). In contrast, no presidents drawn from the upper class are found among those regarded by historians as failures (Andrew Johnson, Buchanan, Grant, Harding, and Nixon). Overall, Baltzell and Schneiderman find that eleven of the fifteen upper-class presidents included in their study (73 percent) were judged to have performed above average in office, while only six of the twenty-one presidents drawn from below the upper class (29 percent) were comparably rated.[32] Although it does not provide a clear explanation for how background is translated into success, the Baltzell-Schneiderman analysis suggests that an upper-class background does make a difference: "Our best aristocratic traditions have stressed *doing* a better job rather than the prevalent, middle-class ideology which has always stressed *getting* a better job."[33]

Richard Neustadt is a forceful advocate of electing an experienced politician to the presidency. As he has argued since 1960, when the first edition of his influential book *Presidential Power and the Modern Presidents* appeared, "The Presidency is no place for amateurs."[34] This seemed an apt aphorism to capture the difficulties Eisenhower experienced in the presidency, although evaluations of his performance have risen over time. As articulated in some of Neustadt's later editions, experience enhances presidents' self-confidence, which in turn makes it easier for them to make the choices about power that are critical to success. Yet "the quality of experience" may count "more than the quantity," an admission Neustadt made after two highly experienced presidents, Lyndon Johnson and Richard Nixon, seemed to fail in office. Neustadt ultimately concluded that "the variety of experience is such that none of it can be applied predictively with confidence."[35] Bert Rockman reaches a similar conclusion after looking at the length and types of government experience in relation to performance. In comparing the government experience of the top ten and bottom ten presidents as ranked by an expert panel, the bottom ten actually had modestly *greater* government experience than the top ten (16.9 mean years versus 15.1) and more than twice as many years of congressional experience (7.6 mean years versus 3.7).[36] Experience, it appears, offers no guarantee of success.

We are left with fundamental uncertainties about how life experience may have a bearing on performance. In addition to social class and career experience, there has also been considerable interest in the psychological traits presidents bring to the office, the subject of the next section.

Psychological Characteristics of U.S. Presidents

In October 1972, just before voters were to choose between Richard Nixon and George McGovern, the political scientist James David Barber drew attention to the inherent shortcomings of evaluating a candidate's life experience when deciding how to vote. Barber made a prediction. The person who would win had grown up as part of a Republican family in a small town. He had excelled in school, studied piano, had a younger brother rowdier than himself, and had been elected president of his college class. Following military service during World War II, he had attended graduate school and followed an uncertain career path until gaining election to Congress in a contest marked by anticommunist appeals. After two terms in the House and service in the Senate, he was considered a member of his party's liberal wing and respected for hard work and independent thinking. The description fit both Nixon and McGovern. Despite the similarities in life experiences, few doubted that the two would make very different presidents.[37]

The similarity between the major party candidates in 1972 was uncanny even in light of the broadly similar backgrounds from which presidents are drawn. Yet no two people, regardless of how similar their life circumstances, will bring identical personalities to the office. They bring a set of distinctive psychological characteristics, features that may loom large under the intense pressures focused on the presidency. Psychological traits are more proximate to presidential behavior than life experiences, but that does not make them easier to study or evaluate. Fred Greenstein points out that psychologists view personality as a complex phenomenon, involving diverse factors such as how people adapt to the world by screening reality (cognition), how they express feelings (affect), and how they relate to others (identification).[38] These structures are likely to be deeply rooted, making it even more necessary to infer their existence rather than to observe them directly. Analysts, in short, introduce personality as a construct to account for the regularities in a person's behavior. For these reasons, examinations of psychological characteristics are more uncertain and subjective than examinations of professional experience and social backgrounds.

Despite these problems, political scientists and historians have used psychological concepts to help explain why political figures behave as they do, a field of study known as *psychobiography*. Several presidents, including Wilson, Lyndon Johnson, Nixon, Carter, and Clinton, have been the subjects of such biographies.[39] These studies tend to concentrate on the childhood experiences, particularly relationships with parents, and how such experiences shaped the presidents' self-perceptions, self-confidence or lack of it, and psychological needs.

Even with the upsurge in interest, analysts remain divided on how to conduct these studies and the theoretical framework within which they should be conducted. Two broad approaches can be adopted: single-subject case studies and multisubject case studies. The former seek to develop a comprehensive analysis of the full array of behaviors manifested by one person, with particular attention paid to explaining the origins of recurrent patterns. The latter also rely on close examination of biographical materials but seek to draw conclusions from similarities found among several actors' behavior.[40] An example of a single-subject case study is Alexander George and Juliette George's comprehensive work on Woodrow Wilson, which attempts to explain his strikingly complex and contradictory behavior. James David Barber's study *The Presidential Character* has identified similarities between Wilson's conduct and that of three other presidents—Hoover, Lyndon Johnson, and Nixon—so they may be treated as examples of a similar personality type.

Practitioners of these two styles of inquiry disagree on how analysis should proceed.[41] There are multiple, competing theories of personality and a lack of established rules on how such research should be conducted. Although the research remains controversial, it would be unrealistic to overlook the importance of personality in trying to understand the presidency because this office imposes fewer constraints on the occupant's behavior than does any other in American government. In other words, there is great opportunity for presidents to be themselves in performing day-to-day responsibilities.[42] Thus their emotional fitness for the job is enormously important.

Barber's Approach to Studying Personality

In 1972, Barber made another forecast, more famous than his election prediction, one that brought considerable attention to himself and the study of presidential personality. He predicted Nixon would be susceptible to the same "danger" Wilson, Hoover, and Johnson had been, namely, "adhering rigidly to a line of policy long after it had proved itself a failure."[43] Given the right set of circumstances, Nixon was likely to pursue a self-defeating plan of action even in the face of mounting evidence of its likely failure. The causes were rooted in his personality—his emotional needs—no less than they had been for the other three men. Nixon's conduct during Watergate, the extended investigations conducted by Congress during 1973 and 1974 into questionable campaign practices of the 1972 election, seemed to validate the prediction and the method on which it was based.

Was Barber's prediction lucky, or had he uncovered the secret of how to predict presidential performance based on systematic personality analysis? If so, the next step would be to make such insights available to voters before an election to produce more informed decisions.

Barber attempts to identify broad character patterns that will predict general patterns of presidential conduct in office. Central to his analysis are three personal characteristics—*character, world view,* and *style*—and two environmental conditions—*power situation* and *climate of expectations.* Together these elements determine the likelihood of presidential success. Character, the most important of Barber's analytic constructs, develops during childhood and is expressed in two analytic dimensions: energy and affect. Presidents may be active or passive in terms of the effort invested in their jobs; they also may be positive or negative about their positions. Both dimensions influence performance.

The resulting four-cell typology is presented in Figure 4-2, with the principal personality trait identified by Barber for each type. *Active-positives* evidence personal growth and adaptability; they enjoy their work and find it a challenge to use power productively as a means to pursue goals beneficial to others. Their success rests on a fundamental sense of self-confidence expressed in goal-oriented behavior. Yet they are flexible in their pursuit of goals and willing to change or abandon them rather than suffer a costly political defeat. In short, they are pragmatic politicians. Barber's active-positives include Franklin Roosevelt, Truman, Kennedy, Ford, Carter, George H. W. Bush, and Clinton.[44]

Active-negative presidents also invest a great deal of energy in being president, but unlike their active-positive counterparts, they do not appear to derive enjoyment from serving in the office. Rather than exercising political power for the benefit of the citizenry, active-negative chief executives seem to seek power for its own sake, exhibiting compulsiveness as if they are driven to pursue a political career instead of doing it for pleasure. This behavior arises from a poor self-image and lack of self-confidence, traits caused by painful childhood experiences; they seek power and domination over others as compensation for their own lack of self-esteem. In this pursuit, active-negatives may come to believe that the policies they favor are morally right, vital to the nation's interest, and impossible to compromise. They may pursue a course of action even if it obviously is not working, exhibiting a pattern of "rigidification" that can ultimately cause their own political failure. Thus they constitute a great danger to the nation. Barber classifies four twentieth-century presidents as active-negatives: Wilson, Hoover, Johnson, and Nixon.

Passive-positive presidents are not in politics to seek power either for the betterment of the American people or to compensate for their own sense of inadequacy. Rather, they choose politics because they are, in Barber's terms, "political lovers." They genuinely enjoy people and want to help them by doing small favors; in return, they feel they are wanted and loved. Barber suggests that passive-positive presidents have low self-esteem combined with a superficial optimism about life; they tend to let others set goals for them and find it difficult to make decisions. The danger they pose is one of drift, leaving the affairs of state undirected. Barber identifies three passive-positive chief executives: Taft, Harding, and Reagan.

Figure 4-2 Barber's Typology of Character

Affect

		Positive	Negative
Activity Level	Active	**Adaptive**: self-confident; power used as means to achieve beneficial results	**Compulsive**: power as a means to self-realization; "driven"; problem managing aggression
	Passive	**Compliant**: seek to be loved; easily manipulated; low self-esteem	**Withdrawn**: respond to sense of duty; avoid power; low self-esteem

Source: James David Barber, *The Presidential Character: Predicting Performance* in the White House, 4th ed. (Englewood Cliffs, N.J.: Prentice Hall, 1992).

Passive-negative presidents combine two characteristics one would *not* expect to find in the person who attains the nation's highest office: an unwillingness to invest much energy in that office and a lack of pleasure in serving. Such persons pursue public service because they believe it is something they *ought to do*. They have a fundamental sense of uselessness and compensate for it by dutifully agreeing to work on behalf of their fellow citizens. Exemplifying passive-negative chief executives are Coolidge and Eisenhower.

Barber examines two other personal factors that influence presidential behavior but play a smaller role in his analysis than character. *World view* consists of a president's "politically relevant beliefs, particularly his conceptions of social causality, human nature, and the central moral conflicts of the time."[45] Rather than dealing with specific policy issues, these attitudes are general in nature and therefore more likely to have wide applicability. Barber sees them as developed primarily during adolescence.

Style is the president's "habitual way of performing three political roles: rhetoric, personal relations, and homework."[46] Style focuses on how presidents typically work with words, people, and substantive problems. These patterns are developed largely during early adulthood, particularly in conjunction with the president's "first independent political success," which usually occurs in college or in a first elective or appointive office. *Character* colors both world view and style but does not determine them in any direct way.

Barber analyzed the life histories of presidents from Taft through George H. W. Bush, thereby covering all but three of the twentieth-century presidents (his discussion of Clinton was very preliminary). These analyses are summarized in Figure 4-3. Some of his classifications have been highly controversial, but after 1972 journalists sought out his views of each candidate during presidential elections, and he offered inauguration-eve predictions of how the new president would perform.

Views of Bill Clinton

Barber's analysis of Bill Clinton as an active-positive was only tentative.[47] Another analyst, Stanley A. Renshon, offered a "preliminary assessment" based

Figure 4-3 Barber's Characterization of Modern Presidents

Affect

	Positive	Negative
Active	Franklin Roosevelt Harry Truman John F. Kennedy Gerald R. Ford Jimmy Carter George H.W. Bush William J. Clinton George W. Bush*	Woodrow Wilson Herbert Hoover Lyndon Johnson Richard Nixon
Passive	William H. Taft Warren Harding Ronald Reagan George W. Bush*	Calvin Coolidge Dwight Eisenhower

Activity Level (row label on left)

Sources: James David Barber, *The Presidential Character: Predicting Performance in the White House*, 4th ed. (Englewood Cliffs, N.J. : Prentice-Hall, 1992). For Barber's views on Clinton, see the *News & Observer* (Raleigh, N.C.), January 17, 1993.

*Possible characterization (not evaluated by Barber).

on events of the presidential campaign and Clinton's first year in office, and those arguments have been expanded subsequently.[48] Renshon agreed that "on initial impression," Clinton would appear to be an active-positive. Throughout his academic and political career, Clinton was a prodigious worker, training himself in college to function on five hours of sleep and repeatedly reacting to setbacks with even higher levels of activity. Moreover, Clinton's efforts were dedicated to accomplishing purposes beyond simply advancing his own personal ambition.[49]

Renshon, however, noted that Clinton's frenetic activity is "closer to the driven investments of energy of active-negative Lyndon Johnson" than to the behavior of active-positives such as Kennedy and Truman.[50] Nor is it uniformly obvious that Clinton enjoyed the experience. Although Clinton apparently thrived on long days of interpersonal contact and campaigning, Renshon offers evidence of how intensely Clinton resents the limited appreciation he received in the press and from the public. This resentment was dramatically manifested by an outburst at the conclusion of an interview conducted by two journalists from *Rolling Stone* near the end of his first year in office. When asked about a young supporter who wanted to know what issues Clinton was "willing to stand up for and die on," the president exploded:

But that's the press's fault, too, damn it. I have fought more damn battles here for more things than any president has in twenty years, with the possible exception of Reagan's first budget, and not gotten one damn bit of credit from the knee-jerk liberal press, and I am sick and tired of it, and you can put that in the damn article.

I have fought and fought and fought and fought. I get up here every day, and I work till late at night on everything from national service to family leave to the budget to the crime bill and all this stuff, and you guys take it and you say, "Fine, go on to something else, what else can I hit him about?" So if you convince them I don't have any convictions, that's fine, but it's a damn lie. It's a lie. . . . I have fought my guts out for that guy, and if he doesn't know it, it's not all my fault. And you get no credit around here for fighting and bleeding.[51]

Linking this outburst to other features of the president's personality, Renshon suggested Clinton could be a hybrid type within Barber's framework, a border-line active-negative with a "strong need to be validated." Clinton, argued Renshon, had developed an idealized view of himself—his skills, his accomplishments, and his motives. "Most people wish to think well of themselves but Bill Clinton appears to have come to believe the *best* of himself and to have discounted evidence from his own behavior that all is not as he believes it to be." In this view, when Clinton's self-idealized image collides with criticism and refusal to acknowledge his accomplishments, anger and hurt emerge. Unlike active-negatives who use power to overcome low estimates of themselves, Renshon suggests "it is also possible that political leaders might well use power to validate high estimates of themselves," something Barber had not anticipated and Clinton might embody.[52] Fred Greenstein, writing toward the end of Clinton's presidency, agreed: "The ever-smiling, hyperactive Clinton has all of the outward signs of an active-positive character. Yet his actions, particularly his astonishing recklessness in the Monica Lewinsky affair, reveal him to be as emotionally deficient as any classically active-negative president."[53] Similarly, Renshon believes Clinton's behavior during the impeachment ordeal confirmed his original assessment of Clinton's recurrent behavior patterns: dislike of boundaries, nearly unbounded aspirations, proclivity to risk-taking, low impulse control, and reluctance to admit error.[54]

Greenstein's final assessment of Clinton as emotionally deficient (discussed earlier) was somewhat different from his initial one. In an earlier assessment, he had pointed out one quality of Clinton's that makes him unlike active-negatives: the "capacity (in spite of his thin-skinned tendencies) to admit his own failings" and make adjustments. Thus, unlike the compulsive tendency of Wilson, Hoover, Lyndon Johnson, and Nixon to pursue even self-destructive policies, Clinton appeared "incapable of sustained error."[55] Even early in Clinton's term, however, Greenstein had recognized that "much of what is puzzling about him [Clinton] stems from inner complexities that do not figure in Barber's (and perhaps any other) classification."[56] Indeed, Barber's effort to study presidential personality has attracted extensive commentary, examined in the next section.

Reactions to Barber

Because Barber's work was widely popularized in the press, it is important to assess its analytic quality. Academics have been especially critical, suggesting it suffers from the fundamental problem common to all studies in the field—

reductionism, paying "insufficient attention to the full range of possible psycho-logical and non-psychological determinants of behavior."[57] Insufficient attention is given to the impact of the environment on presidents, including the nature of the problems they confront, the political support they enjoy, and the constraints within which they operate.

Barber's classification of presidents also has been questioned. The behavior patterns associated with his character types fit some presidents grouped into the same cell better than others. For example, evidence on Eisenhower published after Barber completed his analysis suggests Ike was a more active president than was generally recognized when he was in office.[58] Hoover's reluctance to use extensive federal aid to restore the economy might better be understood as aris-ing from his worldview rather than unresolved emotional needs.[59] Another study, using markedly different methods, finds Reagan's personality to be most similar to those of Franklin Roosevelt and Kennedy, although Barber considered Reagan a passive-positive and the other two active-positives.[60] Barber acknowl-edges that no president fits any type perfectly, that each is a mixture of all four types.[61] Nonetheless, he argues, a dominant pattern can be identified.

Is Barber guilty of positing an ideal personality type that may also conceal a partisan bias? When Barber's study first appeared, all the active-positives were liberal Democrats. Republicans Ford and George H. W. Bush were subsequently added. What the approach may favor, however, is the heroic model of presiden-tial leadership, which assigns principal responsibility for solving national prob-lems to the White House. Barber recognizes that not all active-positives will be successful in office and may pose risks for the political system; their "hunger for and attention to results" may lead them to challenge structures and norms the public believes are better preserved than overturned.[62] Franklin Roosevelt's effort in 1937 to alter the structure of the Supreme Court by increasing its mem-bership to as many as fifteen posed a challenge to the tradition of checks and bal-ances and illustrates this possible danger.[63]

Can types other than active-positives achieve substantial success? Jeffrey Tulis argues that in Barber's terms Lincoln should be considered an active-nega-tive, but few would argue that his stewardship of the nation during the Civil War was unsuccessful.[64]

In sum, Barber's work does not represent a panacea to a nation searching for effective leaders. Like most social science, Barber's work is best thought of in terms of probabilities not certainties. In the long run, Barber aspires to present voters with the kind of information on candidate backgrounds and records that would improve the likelihood of informed electoral choices, but the kind of research necessary for personality analysis is difficult to undertake at any time and perhaps most difficult in the heat of an electoral contest. Journalists may be able to improve their coverage of candidates' records and identify behavior pat-terns of concern, but the chance of conducting a complete study of candidates' personalities in the midst of a campaign is negligible. Nor is it clear who in our society should be given such inordinate influence as to declare some personalities "fit" and others "unfit" for office. Therefore, the practical value of Barber's work remains a controversial and open question.[65]

Despite these criticisms of Barber, continuing to study the personalities of presidents and their emotional fitness for the position is of critical importance. Perhaps the most compelling justification comes from those who have experienced the power of presidential personalities firsthand. Clark Clifford, a longtime Washington power broker who served in the Truman and Johnson administrations, voiced the prevailing wisdom among government veterans: "The executive branch of our government is like a chameleon. To a startling degree it reflects the character and personality of the president."[66]

Management Styles of Modern Presidents

Presidents do not govern alone. Traditional presidents—those serving before Franklin Roosevelt—drew heavily on the assistance of cabinet secretaries and the bureaucracies they headed. Since Roosevelt, another source of advice and assistance has emerged to supplement more traditional sources. The modern presidency has become a collectivity of political and policy specialists whose expertise is placed at the president's disposal. To what extent do presidents use these institutional sources of assistance? How do they structure their advisory systems and make decisions? This section provides a brief discussion of the development of presidential staffing and the management styles presidents use with these assistants.

Just as important as attitudes drawn from life experiences, and skills developed in previous careers, is a president's aptitude for management. Aides have the potential to magnify presidents' skills, compensate for their shortcomings, and reduce the impact of dangerous personality traits.

The Development of Presidential Staffing

The presidential staff has grown substantially since Congress authorized its modern structure in 1939. Today the Executive Office of the President houses a wide range of expert staff units, including the well-known Office of Management and Budget, Council of Economic Advisers, and National Security Council (all discussed more fully in later chapters), as well as the lesser-known Office of U.S. Trade Representative and Office of Science and Technology Policy. Perhaps best known, and certainly most notorious in Washington circles, is the White House Office, a unit that has traditionally emphasized the president's personal and political concerns.

Like his predecessors, Franklin Roosevelt had a limited number of aides, many in clerical positions who were borrowed from other parts of the federal bureaucracy. Looking for a justification to expand these resources, in 1936 he appointed a blue-ribbon group of public administration professors, headed by Louis Brownlow, to study the modern president's management needs. The resulting structure, based on recommendations from that group but reorganized many times since, has always been viewed as a response to the Brownlow Commission's defining sentence: "The President needs help." As Roosevelt and others recognized, the president required additional "eyes and ears" as well as brains to help discharge the ever-growing list of responsibilities placed at the White House door. Presidential staffing, therefore, is an attempt to help presidents avoid "overload," the possibility that job demands will exceed the capacity of any individual, whose time and ability are finite. While the staff is a way to *amplify* the capabilities brought by one person to the presidency, it also may be seen as a structure that can *buffer* the direct impact of a president's personality on performance. Presidents have been given great latitude in their use of staff resources, a flexibility that ensures responsiveness to new problems and perceived needs.

Staff size, although a recurrent political issue, is difficult to monitor with precision. Best estimates place the size of today's Executive Office at approximately sixteen hundred employees.[67] Moreover, the percentage of positions at higher levels of policy-making responsibility appears to have increased substantially over the years.[68] Staff growth has been accompanied by a shift in influence, with one analyst going so far as to suggest that the new structure constitutes a "presidential branch" of government distinct from the larger executive branch.[69] Clearly, presidents can draw on a wide range of assistance outside and within the presidency.

Presidential Management Styles

Style is no doubt an overused term in describing characteristic patterns of presidential behavior, but a number of analysts have focused more narrowly on how presidents structure and use their advisory systems in making decisions. We term these behavior patterns a president's *management style*. Alexander George identifies three personality factors that determine that management style: the executive's habitual ways of dealing with information (acquiring, storing, retrieving, evaluating, and using it); the president's sense of competence in dealing personally with problems, which in turn determines the tasks delegated to others; and the president's orientation toward conflict, particularly the tolerance for competition and dissent among advisers.[70]

Because it reflects personality characteristics and distinctive traits, each president's management style is unique. However, most analysts agree that recent presidents have chosen to operate within one of three broad advisory structures (described by R. T. Johnson in the early 1970s), with multiple variations consistent with their management styles.[71] The *formalistic* pattern emphasizes clear division of labor among staff assistants, well-defined procedures, and a carefully controlled flow of information to the president, usually through a chief of staff, who tries to deflect problems not worthy of presidential attention. Truman, Eisenhower, and Nixon constructed and operated such systems, although differences in operation reflected the unique combination of needs and contributions each brought to the presidency. The *competitive* pattern, typified by Franklin

Roosevelt, encourages conflict among advisers and thrives on diversity of opinion, with the president reserving ultimate judgment to himself. Conflict is endemic to decision making within the American government, but Roosevelt encouraged even more of it. Under a *collegial* system, emphasis is on group problem solving, teamwork, and shared responsibility for outcomes, with the president participating in the process and choosing among identified options. Kennedy, particularly during the Cuban missile crisis, typified this style.

Johnson's three models are a starting point for describing how the systems work. Presidents may follow more than one pattern or construct hybrid combinations. Ford followed a collegial pattern in domestic policy but was more formalistic in foreign policy.[72] Carter's system has been described as a mixture of collegial and formalistic.[73] Reagan constructed a variant of the formalistic and collegial models during his first term, a system that drew considerable praise from many observers, particularly when its successor in the second term became less collegial and proved notably less successful.[74] Clinton's style, discussed later in the chapter, evolved from a highly undisciplined, sometimes collegial style to a somewhat more disciplined collegial pattern. George W. Bush seemed to adopt a formal style with considerable delegation from the outset. It is also important to note that the size of government, as well as the number and complexity of issues that confront modern presidencies, probably "forces every modern president to rely at least to some extent on formalistic procedures."[75]

In general, formalistic structures seem to place more modest demands on presidential time and knowledge. Delegating a larger range of tasks conserves time and may increase the probability that experts will deal with the problem. Because much of the work is processed in written form, the formal system is less appropriate for presidents who prefer to rely on group interaction, discussion, and even argument as part of the decision-making process. Competitive and collegial structures place heavier demands on the president, who not only must rely largely on his own substantive knowledge in making choices among competing alternatives but also must be able to monitor a policy-making process inherently political in nature. Advisers and the areas they represent push hard for the president to adopt their solutions, and the maneuvers used to gain an advantage are believed to be the keys to success. Unfortunately, winning such battles may come at the expense of good decisions.

In the modern era Democratic presidents, using Franklin Roosevelt as a model, often have adopted a different, more interactive advisory system, sometimes described as a "spokes-in-a-wheel" system, with the president at the center of several principal aides in and out of the White House. Such a system encourages dispute and argumentation. Republican presidents have mostly operated within a more highly structured system, in which the chief executive interacts with a single chief of staff or a limited number of advisers and relies more on systematic review processes. This approach is thought less susceptible to political maneuvering. George W. Bush seems to be following in this Republican tradition—relying most heavily on a small number of principal aides.

Each pattern has strengths and weaknesses, but unfortunately analysts disagree on the criteria to be used in evaluating the styles, and they even disagree on how the systems perform. There are no reliable measures of which systems produce decisions of higher quality or greater political responsiveness within reasonable spans of time.[76] Moreover, if the advisory systems ultimately reflect the kind of personality variables identified by Alexander George, it would be impossible to identify one as preferable because it might be inappropriate for the particular president asked to use it.

Multiple Advocacy: Learning a Decision Process

The best-known effort to prescribe a specific decision process for presidents to follow is Alexander George's system of *multiple advocacy.*[77] In essence, George has suggested that presidents should be able to learn a set of techniques to follow in managing advisers and making decisions. Although recognizing that a given president may find this style "uncongenial to his cognitive style and work habits," George believes the advantages would make it worthwhile for a president to consider. For example, Nixon found it painful to be the object of direct, face-to-face argument among his advisers, but he might have modified the system advocated by George to derive its benefits.[78]

George defines multiple advocacy as a *mixed* system that tries to ensure that presidents benefit from a wide review of policy options and hear a variety of viewpoints before making a final decision. It tries to build on the inevitable conflict among individual advisers and bureaucratic agencies by channeling that conflict in productive ways. The overall process must be structured so every relevant viewpoint receives a fair hearing. One of the major tasks, then, in operating such a system is monitoring the breadth of options being considered and the opportunities that advocates of such views have to be heard. To operate such a system, the president requires a full-time assistant, a "custodian-manager" who acts as an "honest broker" among the advisers pushing their positions on the president.

George's hope is that systematic review of options, one of the claimed benefits of a formalistic system, also can be achieved under multiple advocacy, with the added benefit of the open debate and discussion encouraged by competitive and collegial systems. The president should act as a magistrate—"one who listens to the arguments made, evaluates them, poses issues and asks questions, and finally judges which action to take either from among those articulated by advocates or as formulated independently by himself after hearing them."[79] Consistent with this role, presidents need to suppress the urge to announce their own preferences early in the process and ensure that they remain faithful to the premise on which the system rests, the guarantee of giving an equal hearing to all views.

Such a process can be time-consuming, and George recognizes that presidents would have to decide when it should be used. There may be times when they already know the policy they wish to pursue, and because constitutional responsibility in the American executive is unitary rather than collective, presidents can always exercise individual discretion. Paul Kowert raises another issue: "while some leaders thrive on diversity of opinion, others are immobilized by it," so "leaders must guard not only against too little advice, but also against too much."[80] If overwhelmed by information, a leader might withdraw from contentious issues and allow policy to drift into "deadlock," a plausible interpretation of Reagan's inaction in the face of growing budget deficits *(see the discussion in chapter 9)* and the exchanges of arms for hostages that lay at the heart of the Iran-contra incident *(see the discussion in chapter 10)*.[81]

Even George does not believe that use of a multiple advocacy system and the magistrate presidential style that accompanies it can ensure good decisions. Rather, he urges its adoption as a way to improve the quality of information made available to presidents and to prevent the bad decisions that result from faulty procedures.[82]

Understanding Presidents: The Cases of Bill Clinton and George W. Bush

Explaining presidential behavior and linking its determinants to performance is like putting together the pieces of a puzzle, but a puzzle whose final shape is uncertain. One way to illustrate how background, experience, personality, and management style shape behavior and performance is to take an in-depth look at individual cases. It is still too soon to provide a final evaluation of Bill Clinton's effectiveness in office, but we can trace major features of his life and explore ways in which these potentially affected his performance. The sketch of George W. Bush remains a work in progress but offers a starting point for thinking about these relationships.

Clinton and Bush offer strikingly contrasting personal portraits. Clinton's ambition to be president can be traced to his teenage years, and he systematically prepared to launch his political career at an early age. Bush was the classic "late-bloomer" and speaks openly of a life-changing event at forty. He did not enter politics until age forty-seven. Clinton was elected to office as a "new Democrat" seeking to move his party toward more moderate positions, but he encountered scathing criticism during his first year for being a vintage liberal. Bush ran as a "compassionate conservative" and a "different kind of Republican" but has been highly attentive to his conservative base. Although a product of the 1960s, an era known for its revolt against established power structures and social norms, Clinton, the first "baby boomer" president, has been consistently criticized for compromising with power centers, first in Arkansas and later in Washington. Bush, heir to one of the great political family traditions in American life, was always the iconoclast who challenged traditional authority but resisted the lure of 1960s-style rebellion. A booster of family values and a devout Baptist, Clinton confronted repeated charges of marital infidelity, culminating in the Lewinsky scandal. Bush is a born-again Christian who acknowledges an earlier problem with alcohol and making unspecified mistakes during his "irresponsible youth." Filled with nostalgic pride for his small-town roots, Clinton burned with ambition to succeed on larger stages. Bush claims small-town Texas as his adopted home despite the ready access he has always had to larger stages. Here are snapshots of their lives.

Clinton's Early Life

Bill Clinton entered life in the wake of tragedy. Shortly before the birth of William Jefferson Blythe III (Clinton's original name) in 1946, his natural father drowned in a roadside ditch following a car accident while driving from Chicago to Hope, Arkansas. The newly widowed Virginia Blythe, a wartime bride, completed her training as a nurse anesthetist in New Orleans, leaving her son with her parents for his first two years. Although his grandmother doted on Bill, her hot temper offset his grandfather's universal friendliness, traits later displayed by the adult Bill Clinton.

When Bill was four, his mother married Roger Clinton, a car dealer also known to deal in bootleg liquor who had been divorced by his first wife for abuse. The new family settled in Hot Springs, Arkansas, a resort town where gambling and prostitution were openly pursued. For the next twelve years, the future president lived in two very different worlds: a public world centered on school and church, in which he earned plaudits as a model citizen, and a private, turbulent world in which his stepfather had become an abusive alcoholic. The situation was stormy: after repeated episodes of abuse, Virginia divorced her second husband in 1962 (Bill provided testimony in the trial) only to remarry him three months later. During the interlude, Bill Blythe decided to change his last name to Clinton so that it would be the same as that of his younger half-brother, Roger Clinton.

Inevitably, this unhappy family life heavily influenced Bill Clinton's personality. As his most authoritative biographer, David Maraniss, argues, Clinton assumed the role of "family hero," one of the characteristic roles found among children of alcoholics. Not only does this child assume responsibility for protecting the family, but he may also serve as its redeemer to the outside world by winning awards and praise.[83] Clinton did both. He intervened in one instance to stop his stepfather from abusing his mother, and he tried to protect his half-brother. Through his high school successes, he brought glory to the family: he was fourth in his graduating class, junior class president, band major and all-state band member, and a delegate to Boys' State and Boys' Nation; as a Boys' Nation delegate, in a memorable moment captured on film, the sixteen-year-old shook the hand of John F. Kennedy. Other accounts note that children of alcoholics have an "exaggerated need to be agreeable."[84] Such children, sharing the concern of alcoholics that they are not worthy of being liked, decide personal accomplishments will make people like them.[85] It has also been suggested that "as a child of addiction," Clinton was predisposed to develop his own addiction, in this case a sexual one.[86]

Clinton went to Georgetown University's School of Foreign Service and succeeded in becoming a campus leader. "His political skills, his ability to think on his feet, to build coalitions and networks, were unrivaled on campus; but perhaps they were a bit too much, and he was too smooth," said Maraniss, resulting in a senior-year defeat for student president.[87] Clinton's lesson from the experience seemed to be played out later in life: work harder next time, talk to every possible voter, listen more carefully. Clinton assiduously built networks of acquaintances and potentially helpful contacts through an internship on Capitol Hill, work in political campaigns, and selection as a Rhodes Scholar. The latter delayed the onset of his own political career, exposing Clinton to a much wider world but posing the dilemma of how to avoid being drafted for military service in Vietnam. Like many other male college students of the Vietnam era, Clinton developed a strategy to avoid service. On returning from one year in Oxford, he arranged to enter the Reserve Officers Training Corps (ROTC) unit at the University of Arkansas, where he promised to enroll in the law school in the fall of 1969. This arrangement persuaded his draft board to cancel his induction, scheduled for late July. Instead of entering law school, however, Clinton returned to England and was saved by the new lottery system for selecting inductees—Clinton's high number was never called. These stratagems, plus a letter Clinton wrote to the University of Arkansas ROTC commander, formed the basis for charges that he dodged the draft.

When he returned to the United States in 1970, Clinton chose to enter the prestigious Yale University Law School. The school's lax attendance policies enabled him to gain valuable campaign experience in a Connecticut Senate campaign and in Texas as state coordinator for presidential candidate George McGovern in 1972. These campaigns widened his network of contacts to a new generation of political activists, heavily motivated by antiwar sentiments and the desire to reform the American political and economic systems. The other lasting effect from his time at Yale was a romance with Hillary Rodham, a no less brilliant and far more focused law school classmate.

Clinton's Prepresidential Political Career

Throughout college Clinton confided to friends his intention to pursue a political career in his home state. After serving for less than a year on the faculty of the University of Arkansas Law School, Clinton challenged the incumbent U.S. representative John Paul Hammerschmidt in what appeared to be a hopelessly one-sided contest. Instead, Clinton surprised the state's political establishment by running an aggressive, imaginative campaign, even though he lost by four thousand votes. As the campaign was coming to a close, Hillary Rodham left the House Judiciary Committee's Watergate investigation team, also joined the law school faculty, and became a major figure in Clinton's campaign. They married soon after. His unexpected competitiveness made another election contest inevitable, and in 1976 he easily won election as Arkansas's attorney general and served as Jimmy Carter's state campaign chairman at the same time.

Clinton's meteoric rise assumed an air of inevitability, and he won the governorship in 1978 with 63 percent of the vote, becoming the youngest U.S. governor in four decades.[88] Clinton's first two-year term as governor was not unlike his first two years as president. He pursued an overly ambitious, highly idealistic agenda of initiatives intended to reform Arkansas's education system and protect the environment from the timber industry. His young staff ruffled feathers in the Arkansas establishment and was unable to discipline Clinton's "loose, free-ranging management style," which included off-the-cuff comments to the press, an inability to adhere to a schedule, and excessive accessibility to any and all comers.[89] Successes were scarce, and the governor's ratings slipped; he narrowly won the 1980 primary against a weak opponent (Arkansas governors then served two-year terms) as voters protested newly raised automobile license fees and public safety crises triggered by protests of the Cuban refugees housed at Fort Chafee.

Clinton lost badly in the general election, the youngest defeated governor in American history. The experience was reportedly devastating, triggering months of soul-searching about what had gone wrong as Clinton unenthusiastically entered private law practice. He regained the governorship in 1982 and secured reelection in 1984, 1986, and 1990, after the term was lengthened to four years.

Clinton's return to power was eerily similar to later chapters in his political career. As he planned his return, Clinton turned to Dick Morris, a political consultant, the same adviser to whom Clinton turned in 1995 after the devastating Republican victories in the 1994 midterm elections. Then, as later, Morris urged Clinton to moderate his positions, to become more pragmatic and less idealistic. Another feature of that comeback is familiar. To regain public support, Clinton apologized to Arkansans for mistakes he had made as a young governor, essentially admitting that he had become "too big for his britches." A similar drama of apology and personal penance was played out in 1998–1999 as the Monica Lewinsky scandal produced his initial nonapologetic televised address to the nation in August, followed by gradually increasing statements of regret.

Clinton's governorship after 1982 was far different from his first term. Seasoned veterans replaced his youthful aides; the idealistic program of reforms was replaced with a more modest agenda of achievable reforms; compromises were struck with the state's most powerful economic interests.[90] Clinton pursued his most ambitious goal of restructuring public education by providing a major increase in funding while requiring that teachers pass a competency exam, something the education union, a onetime supporter of the governor, vigorously opposed. Again, there are remarkable similarities between Clinton's return to power and his record as president from 1994 onward.

Clinton's next career step was designed in Arkansas. He became chairman of the National Governors' Association in 1986, where he built networks and developed a new set of issue positions on job creation, welfare reform, and education for an expanded audience. He addressed the 1980, 1984, and 1988 Democratic National Conventions, delivering a long-winded nominating speech at the last. He had almost sought the 1988 nomination himself, agonizing for weeks over whether to run and then disappointing a gathering of friends who had come to Little Rock anticipating an announcement. Clinton's ambition collided with the reality of modern campaigns. He was reportedly dissuaded from announcing by a female aide who confronted him with a long list of women whose past relationships with him would be probed by the press.[91]

In the end, however, it proved only a temporary setback. In fall 1991 Clinton reversed a campaign promise to Arkansans that he would finish out his full term as governor and announced his candidacy for the presidency. As David Maraniss observes, Clinton had always performed well against the toughest competition: "In settings where he found himself among high-powered peers, whether with the Rhodes Scholars at Oxford or, much later, with the governors of other states, Clinton rose quickly to prominence, outpacing others with his ambition, affability, appetite for ideas and deal making."[92] He has always exuded supreme self-confidence in his skills and capacities, and throughout his life others had assured him of his presidential potential—his mother, his classmates, his fellow Rhodes scholars, his wife. The election, described in chapter 2, demonstrated his effectiveness as a campaigner and a political strategist.

Evaluating Clinton's Performance

The Clinton presidency is over, and we now know the end of the story. Many questions will never be answered. The most troubling are those surrounding his relationship with Monica Lewinsky, nicely summarized by Maraniss:

Why would someone who had achieved his lifelong dream needlessly jeopardize it? Why would an inherently cautious politician with an obvious need for public affirmation follow such a careless private path? . . . Why would someone with a deep distrust of his political enemies give them so much ammunition with which to attack? Why would someone with a near photographic memory, who could immediately recall a telephone number that he had not dialed in thirty years, seem so incapable of remembering and learning from history and his own mistakes?[93]

Speculation on these and related questions gripped the nation for fourteen months as the drama of the president and the intern unfolded. Clinton has been chastised for "a severe lack of self-discipline" and "defective impulse control,"[94] as well as "a self-delusion of invincibility" that fed his recklessness and could be traced to recurring traits in his character.[95]

Fascinating as these questions may be, we will never have definitive answers. The experience reaffirms, however, the importance of trying to avoid presidents who are "emotionally handicapped," as Fred Greenstein describes Johnson, Nixon, Carter, and Clinton. As he points out, "in the real world, human imperfection is inevitable, but some imperfections are more disabling than others."[96] Although Bill Clinton went to great lengths to show the nation he was effectively discharging his duties throughout the ordeal of his investigation and impeachment, there is the unavoidable suspicion that the nation's life and business were disrupted and that his own legacy would have been greater had he not had to devote endless hours to his legal defense.

Where can we draw more confident conclusions about Clinton's service as president? Clinton was the first president born after World War II, the first "to live in a relentless real-time media culture that magnified his every mistake," and the first elected president to be impeached.[97] He was a man of contradictions: "considerate and calculating, easygoing and ambitious, mediator and predator"; "sincere and deceptive at the same time"; "indecisive, too eager to please, and prone to deception" but also "indefatigable, intelligent, empathetic, and self-deprecating."[98] He projected "relentless optimism" and "great resilience" in the face of repeated setbacks inflicted on him by the media, his political opponents, and himself.[99] His political skills were prodigious, acknowledged even by some of his harshest critics, who recognized a "talent for language that is rare in politicians" and an "extraordinary gift for intimacy" revealed in his capacity to relate to people, to listen to their concerns, and to empathize with their problems.[100] Newt Gingrich, a longtime adversary, described Clinton as "'the best tactical politician, certainly of my lifetime.'"[101] Greenstein describes him as "political to the core," much like Franklin Roosevelt, Lyndon Johnson, and Richard Nixon.[102] There was, as well, near universal praise for his native intelligence and natural abilities as well as his energy.[103] Bert Rockman declared that Clinton is that "rare combination of a complex policy thinker and a sophisticated thinker about politics."[104] Perhaps it is precisely because of Clinton's prodigious talents that disappointment was widespread about his performance in office.

Some of Clinton's greatest problems seemed to flow from his most notable skills. Because of these virtuoso skills, people came to distrust his honesty and to question whether he held any strong beliefs. He was described as displaying a "chameleon-like quality," a "plastic political identity" that reflected the president's "habit of adapting to the people around him and trying to present to them the version of himself he thought each would most admire."[105] His verbal facility led some to suggest he suffered from an "almost pathological inability to tell the whole truth."[106] His reversals on policy were legendary, and his tendency to play word games heightened the impression of deception; instead of admitting to reporters during the 1992 presidential election campaign that he had smoked marijuana, for example, he denied having inhaled or having broken any laws. The central issue in the charges of perjury leveled at Clinton in the Lewinsky matter concerned his legalistic parsing of the phrase "sexual relations." Clinton maintained that the absence of intercourse meant that sexual relations had not occurred, despite the fact that he later acknowledged having had oral sex with the intern. Although an unusually gifted extemporaneous speaker, Clinton lacked verbal discipline. At first, Clinton found "it all too easy to deluge the public with details, and it appear[ed] to be difficult for him to transcend policy mechanics and convey the broad principles and values behind his programs . . . the antithesis of Ronald Reagan, who was notoriously innocent of policy specifics, but gifted at evoking larger themes."[107] His presentations of the 1998 and 1999 State of the Union messages, however, were extraordinary given the pressure-packed circumstances of speaking in the midst of a media frenzy over his relationship with Lewinsky and while the Senate was deliberating on impeachment.

Did Clinton offer the public, the press, and politicians a consistent policy vision? His harshest critics questioned whether he had any lasting principles that directed his activity: "Clinton means what he says when he says it, but tomorrow he will mean what he says when he says the opposite. He is the existential President, living with absolute sincerity in the passing moment."[108] Others suggested that policy reversals and waffling arose "partly because he cannot make up his own mind and partly because he wants to please the last group to have spoken to him"[109] or because his especially sophisticated mind enabled him to view policy matters from multiple angles.[110] A careful reading of his political history suggests that ideological consistency was never a hallmark of Clinton's political career, and he frequently abandoned allies when necessary. Clinton seems to believe in an activist government and, more than any other policy area, supported intervention in civil rights. Yet even that lifelong commitment was sorely tested in 1995 when he ordered a review of government-sponsored affirmative action programs (ultimately ordering few changes) and supported welfare reform before the 1996 election. His initiative to improve race relations, launched in 1997 and intended as a centerpiece of his second term, floundered on the national fascination with impeachment.[111]

Impatient activism and resilience were hallmarks of Clinton's service. Like Jimmy Carter, Clinton was accused of failing to set priorities among his many first-year initiatives, resulting in a serious overload of the congressional and public agendas. This overload is reminiscent of the problems encountered during his initial year as governor. As Clinton explained, "I'm the most impatient person on earth. If there is a legitimate criticism about me, it is that I have thrown myself against the wall this year. I've tried to do so many things that sometimes when I do things, no one notices."[112] That self-description, of course, puts the problem in its best light, the product of trying too hard and not getting sufficient credit. He has admitted to feeling "an urgent sense to do everything he could in life as quickly as possible" because of his father's death at the early age of twenty-eight.[113]

The capacity to bounce back from adversity was evident in the 1992 New Hampshire primary, when Clinton labeled himself the "Comeback Kid," a candidate who overcame damaging stories about marital infidelity, draft dodging, and marijuana use to finish a surprising second in the nation's most-watched primary. He demonstrated the same resilience following three major prepresidential crises[114] and twice during his presidency, after Democrats lost a congressional majority in November 1994 and during the extended inquiry that led to his impeachment in 1998. Crises triggered periods of introspection and self-correction, a capacity that helped him as president. Even when he was wrong he had the laudable ability "to admit his own failings" and make pragmatic adjustments.[115] Clinton seems to have learned about the job while serving as president; one would hope he also learned about himself.

George W. Bush's Life[116]

If Bill Clinton's lifetime challenge was to overcome the absence of a father, the challenge for George W. Bush was to escape his father's shadow. Born in Connecticut, where his father was completing college at Yale after returning from World War II, George W., as the family has always called him, adopted Texas as his home. Midland was the site of his childhood and his career in the oil industry, though he also spent time in Houston. (Far from being an isolated outpost, Midland has been described as "a rich man's town, a part of north Dallas or west Houston transplanted to the desert.")[117] Bush is the eldest of four sons and one daughter. His closest sibling died of leukemia at age four, an especially traumatic time for Bush (then seven) and his parents. In fact, this event has been portrayed as a critical moment in his life. Barbara Bush, his mother, slipped into an extended period of depression after her daughter's death. With his father often away on business, George W. took it on himself to keep her company and cheer her up, an effort leading to his habitual clowning and role as the family's "ebullient cutup." As a result of the close bond between Bush and his mother, family members suggest he possesses more of her "blunt outspokenness," "irreverence and readiness with a joke," and spontaneity than he does his father's "guarded, dignified" personality. [118]

There were two realities in Bush's childhood. On the one hand, he "grew up as the first son in a large, generationally extended family with wealth on all sides," enjoying the benefits of privilege (a New England summer home) and family ties hardly imaginable to most Americans.[119] On the other hand, descriptions of Bush's childhood in Midland sound like vintage Americana. Little League, picnics, and adventures with brothers and friends with Bush in the lead characterize the president's memories of those years. Bush attended public schools through seventh grade, spending one of those years in Houston, where he later attended an exclusive private school for two years. At that point his life took on a shadowlike quality, retracing the footsteps of his illustrious father. Bush entered his father's and grandfather's prep school alma mater, Phillips Exeter Academy in Andover, Massachusetts, to complete his high school years before moving on to Yale. He was an indifferent student at Andover, falling far short of his father, who had been senior class president and captain of the baseball team. George W. worked his way onto the baseball and basketball teams but was much more of a social leader, expressing opinions on everything (hence his nickname "Lip").[120] Although mediocre grades meant he was concerned about getting into Yale, where his grandfather and uncles also had attended, Bush entered as a legacy in 1964. Again, academics were not his major concern—he became president of his fraternity, known on campus as the "party fraternity," and like his father he was selected for membership in Skull and Bones, Yale's most elite secret society. Classmates recall Bush as fun loving, lacking pretense, and outspokenly supporting the Vietnam War in the face of overwhelming campus opinion but not a scholar.

Like Clinton who also graduated from college in 1968, Bush confronted the draft and pursued an avenue that kept him out of direct fire. This decision has become one of the more controversial features of his early life, with charges leveled that he received favorable treatment as the son of a member of Congress. Two weeks before his college graduation, the point at which his draft deferment would run out, Bush applied to the Texas Air National Guard and was immediately sworn in despite a waiting list. Some allege that strings were pulled; Bush argues that he wanted to follow in his father's footsteps and be a fighter pilot.[121] (The elder Bush was the youngest commissioned officer in the Navy during WWII and returned home with the Distinguished Flying Cross.) What followed were two years of training and a four-year commitment to part-time service. His unit was not sent overseas, and Bush completed his military obligation while working in a variety of jobs back home, none with much gusto, while he partied in Texas with considerable gusto.

In 1975 Bush graduated from Harvard Business School, where he is remembered for his iconoclastic behavior—pinching snuff, dressing shabbily, disdaining those aspiring to a career on Wall Street. After graduation he held several entry-level jobs in the Midland oil business. Bush and his family refer to these as his "nomadic" years, when he seemed to lack direction or purpose.

At age thirty-one Bush showed the first indication of political ambition. Over the years, he had worked in three of his father's campaigns and two Republican senatorial campaigns. When an unexpected retirement opened the House seat in West Texas, Bush, once again following in his father's footsteps, declared his candidacy and won the Republican nomination in a June 1978 runoff against a Reagan-backed conservative.[122] In the midst of the campaign, he married Laura Welch, a librarian who had known Bush in elementary school but had had no contact with him until a blind date put them together. His Republican adversary set the groundwork for the Democratic opponent, who charged Bush with being a privileged product of the eastern establishment and out of step with bedrock values of West Texas. Bush won 47 percent of the vote but lost the election. Reportedly, he concluded that his own political career would have to be delayed until his father was out of politics, a long wait since at that point George H. W. Bush was preparing to seek the Republican presidential nomination.

Perhaps in preparation for the day he could turn to a career in public service, the central feature of the family ethos of "making one's mark in the world,"[123] Bush looked to business as a way to create financial security, thus freeing himself to run for political office. Like his father, he entered the oil business in Midland, establishing a small independent oil drilling company. Bush no doubt benefited from his name and family contacts in winning the support of investors for such a high-risk venture. (It did not hurt to be the son of the U.S. vice president.) The business was not successful, limping along from year to year without any major finds and suffering from depressed oil prices. This was all part of a "nagging pattern that marked his life until past the age of forty: once again, he had followed his father's path but failed to achieve his father's success."[124] At a critical time when losses were mounting and his corporation millions in debt, the corporate assets were bought out, the debts assumed, and Bush was given stock and options of Harken Oil and Gas, a large Dallas firm whose board Bush joined. Again, the suggestion has been made that this success was not so much earned by Bush as the result of his name and special contacts. Even more controversial was Bush's sale of his entire stock holdings in the company in 1990, eight days before the announcement of major losses reduced the stock price by 25 percent. The Securities and Exchange Commission conducted an investigation into whether Bush had engaged in "insider trading," profiting from the privileged information available to a board member. No impropriety was found, although Bush's opponent in the 1994 Texas governor's race alleged otherwise.[125]

Bush's sudden turn in fortunes coincided with the turning point in his life: his foreswearing of alcohol on the morning after a boisterous fortieth birthday party in 1986 and his increasing spirituality on the heels of a 1985 conversation with the Reverend Billy Graham.[126] As the *Washington Post*'s close study of the president's life concludes, Bush was abusing alcohol though he was not an alcoholic—more a fraternity binge drinker than someone with an addiction. But alcohol had begun to cause problems for him, including a charge of DUI (driving under the influence) in Maine ten years earlier.[127] Bush sought to seize control of his life. "By doing so he would finally begin to close the gap between what was expected of him and what he had achieved."[128] Developing self-discipline was probably not an overnight conversion but involved foreswearing tobacco, establishing a vigorous exercise routine, and learning to harness his energy productively.[129]

His major independent success followed the 1988 presidential election, when George W. worked in the presidential campaign headquarters of his father, working closely with political consultant Lee Atwater and serving as principal liaison with evangelical Christian leaders and groups.[130] Bush put together an investment group that purchased the Texas Rangers baseball team and began the process of fashioning an identity distinctive from his father's. He served as the managing partner, the public face of the team. He handled public relations, built and maintained consensus among members of the management team he assembled, and used baseball as the way to become "a man of the people."[131] He oversaw the financing and planning for a new ballpark that ushered in an era of team success and greatly enhanced the value of the franchise. When the partnership sold its interest in 1998, Bush's original investment of $606,302 was worth more than $15 million.[132] By then, however, he had already reaped other benefits, riding his newfound identity to the Texas governorship.

Bush's Prepresidential Political Career

Although he unsuccessfully ran for Congress in 1978 and worked in numerous campaigns, Bush had never held elected or appointed public office until he became Texas's governor in 1995. He had considered running for the position in 1990 but ultimately agreed with advice from his mother and principal strategists that the time was not right, particularly with his commitment to the Rangers.[133] With his father's defeat in 1992, however, Bush was able to run for office with less fear of the criticisms he had encountered in the congressional campaign. Moreover, his success with the Rangers had established a separate persona for him as a Texas businessman.

His race against Ann Richards, the incumbent governor who had memorably parodied his father at the 1988 Democratic nominating convention, was remarkably similar to that against Al Gore six years later. Like Gore, Richards seemed intent on provoking Bush into an undisciplined verbal mistake. Bush never took the bait and remained tightly "on message" throughout the campaign, focused on the issues he chose to emphasize and sticking with broad themes rather than policy details. Richards had difficulty defending her record, and none of the rumors about Bush's wrongdoing in his youth or his questionable business dealings ever produced a major embarrassment. Bush won, 53 percent to 46 percent.

In 1998 Bush became the first Texas governor to be reelected to a four-year term (most governors had served for two years) when he defeated a weak opponent, 69 percent to 31 percent. The election was particularly noteworthy for the strong support Bush received from Hispanic voters and women, taken as an indication that he would run a strong national campaign if nominated for president. In fact, there had been open discussion about Bush's national ambitions during the campaign.[134] His presidential aspirations, however, were relatively recent. "Unlike almost any other serious presidential candidates in modern memory, no one who knew him [earlier in life] envisioned George W. Bush in the White House."[135] By one measure, Bush brings to the presidency "the scantiest record in public office of any modern President." But office-holding does not recognize his "two decades apprenticing as a kind of *de facto* political consultant,"[136] or the opportunity to be a participant-observer in his father's political career spanning nearly three decades. To focus on Bush's elected experience misses the full extent of his substantial "political" experience.

Bush as President

George W. Bush brings a diverse set of skills and experiences to the White House. On a personal level, he is gregarious, unpretentious, persistent, and highly adaptable. By all accounts, his interpersonal skills are outstanding. There is universal acknowledgment of how well he relates to a wide range of people, using humor and warmth as a way to make them comfortable, win their support, and mold coworkers into a team. This has been a central feature of his success in business and politics. No less than Bill Clinton, Bush has moved through life creating networks of contacts that have later played a key role in his financial and political success. He seems to elicit considerable personal loyalty. For example, his chief political adviser, Karl Rove, first joined him in the unsuccessful 1978 congressional race, and Bush's closest financial advisers are longtime friends and associates, such as Commerce Secretary Evans.[137] His humor prevents him from personalizing battles or taking himself too seriously; yet he is a determined competitor in politics no less than in sports.

By acknowledging some skeletons in his closet (particularly his partying as a youth) and by changing his behavior, Bush has shown a capacity for self-reflection and personal growth. (Of course, the changes were long-delayed.) In terms of Barber's typology, Bush appears best described as an active-positive. He exudes strong self-esteem, invests reasonably high levels of energy in discharging his duties, and seems to enjoy the position of president. He appears self-confident, and why not? After all, "how many Americans who at the age of forty were running a failing business and drinking too much turned their lives around so completely that within a dozen years they became not just a two-time governor of the nation's second-most populous state but also a serious contender for [and winner of] the White House?"[138]

Bush's pedigree connotes privilege—Andover, Yale, Harvard—yet his manner is decidedly populist. This could arise from discomfort with his own roots or the trappings of elitism, either conservative or liberal in origin.[139] He does not appear to agonize over decisions—if anything, he has a tendency to be impulsive, a potential weakness in the past, partially managed by his wife.[140] There is some evidence that he is likely to be impatient with policy details,[141] and critics question his intellectual ability. A fuller reading of his past would recognize that when engaged, he has considerable mental ability, demonstrated in his youth by mastering mountains of baseball statistics, in young adulthood by learning the intricacies of flying jet fighters, and later in overseeing the minutiae of his father's 1988 presidential campaign.[142] It would be fairer to say that he has not always applied that ability to its fullest. In that respect, Bush may resemble Reagan, an instinctive politician more comfortable with themes than specifics, somewhat incurious, and always ready to delegate. Bush brings a CEO style to the presidency similar to Reagan's but with important differences. Bush's style was honed during his period as managing partner of the Texas Rangers and reflects a stronger commitment to aggressive pursuit of clearly set goals. Bush's higher energy levels are also likely to make him less susceptible than Reagan to the danger of failing to monitor subordinates closely enough. Much like Reagan, Bush keeps the presidency in perspective; he enjoys the job but also enjoys his time away from it, an ability probably underrated by both journalists and academics.

Close your eyes, listen to speeches of George W. Bush and his father, and you will immediately note the similarities—the broken syntax, the occasionally labored delivery, the mangled vocabulary. Nonetheless, both men demonstrated they could rise to the occasion when it was important to perform well with a set speech, and George W. gained far more experience in working with the media and the public in the baseball business than his father did in his many government posts. Will George W. Bush possess the communication skills necessary for modern presidents to be successful? For much of his first year, Bush avoided the media, holding no prime-time press conferences until after 9/11 and relying on his White House staff to ensure that the administration's message structured media coverage. He relied on informal exchanges with the press and did not address the nation from the Oval Office until the night of September 11, 2001.[143] Once Bush found his voice, his direct, genuine delivery of speeches resonated effectively with most Americans, and he "became a compelling public presence" in delivering a series of forceful addresses following the terrorist attacks.[144] Will the content of his speeches provide more "vision" than was found in his father's? The knock on the elder Bush was the "vision thing," as he once dismissed it. Even after three years, George W.'s worldview is still a bit of a mystery, a montage of traditional conservative themes, laden with evangelical Christian overtones, and rejection of the liberal excesses found in the baby boom generation.[145] "Compassionate conservatism," Bush's own term for his philosophy, will ultimately be defined through his policy proposals and accomplishments. It is still unclear, however, whether Bush fully appreciates how presidents must teach the public and fashion a broad consensus behind national goals, a special challenge given Bush's significant policy departures.[146]

In two areas, economic and foreign policy, Bush's record has been far bolder than expected given the narrowness of his election victory and the absence of a mandate. With two large swipes of the tax-cutting knife, Bush reversed Clinton's legacy of reduced federal deficits and revealed himself to be a firm believer in supply-side economic theory. A slow economic recovery after the brief recession in 2001 led him to replace virtually his entire team of economic advisers; it fell to the new team to sell the second round of tax cuts as a jobs-and-growth plan, which will be heavily attacked during the president's 2004 reelection bid. The impact of these policies on the nation's long-term financial security is potentially enormous. *(See the discussion in chapter 9.)* In foreign affairs Bush "is leading a revolution" by reorienting the conduct and the substance of American foreign policy. Even before 9/11, the administration made clear its willingness to act through unilateral, rather than multilateral, strategies. After 9/11, by word and by deed the administration has asserted U.S. primacy in the world through a redefinition of national strategy and its aggressive use of force, particularly in Iraq where all major world powers except Britain opposed military action.[147] In contrast to economic policy, Bush has stuck with his foreign policy team even though their voices have often been discordant, with those of Defense Secretary Donald Rumsfeld and Secretary of State Colin Powell the loudest. Given the lack of consensus, it has fallen to the president to confidently steer a course intended to redefine America's place in the world. At this point, neither domestic nor foreign publics have accepted this new vision. *(See the discussion in chapter 10.)* At the time Bush assumed office, many observers wondered whether he had had enough political experience to be a successful president. As noted above, his political activity was far broader than the nearly six years he spent as Texas governor. His ground-up view of elections, gained through work in numerous campaigns, provides him with the confidence to make independent political judgments. It was less clear whether he had sufficient grasp of the broad range of policy issues that confront the president or the commitment to develop the knowledge base that he needs. Without experience of his own at the federal level, Bush chose notably experienced hands to help him, foremost Vice President Cheney, who has handled many challenging tasks: overseeing the transition, guiding the administration's legislative agenda through Congress, fashioning an energy strategy, and helping to revise the nation's defense doctrine. The competence and outlook of a president's team is especially important for a CEO-style executive, but Bush's performance suggests he has seldom, if ever, delegated the final say on administration policies. "Unlike Reagan, who often could not decide between his oft-feuding friends, or Clinton, who always saw every side to an argument, Bush quickly earned a reputation among his advisers for decisiveness,"[148] overruling public positions of Rumsfeld, Powell, and others during the early months of the administration. *(For more on the Bush team see chapter 6.)*

Conclusion: Seeking Presidential Success

Paul Quirk has posed a deceptively simple question: What does a president need to know? Quirk identifies a list of presidential competencies that could serve as the basis for making decisions about how best to allocate the president's time, energy, and talent as well as that of the White House staff and the innermost group of presidential advisers.[149] In Quirk's view, presidents require a minimal level of *substantive familiarity* so they can make intelligent choices among policy options. Moreover, presidents need a degree of *process sensibility* that reflects familiarity with how government decisions are made and carried out as well as with how such systems might best be designed. Finally, presidents need the capacity for *policy promotion,* the means to achieve their goals through bargains with other Washington elites and through appeals for broad public support. Every president brings a different mix of personal competencies to the job and needs to compensate for personal weaknesses or to complement strengths with the help of others. In Quirk's view, it is critical that each president have a well-designed strategy for how to succeed, what Quirk terms *strategic competence.* This strategy will involve decisions on how to allocate time, energy, and talent in relation to mastering substantive issues, delegating tasks, and establishing the prerequisites for successful delegation—for example, selecting personnel.[150]

How are these competencies developed? Implicitly, Quirk seems to suggest that experience in government at the federal level is a critical qualification for presidents. Without it, they have difficulty developing adequate levels of process sensibility and substantive familiarity. But Quirk's advice is directed more to presidents than to voters. Above all else, Quirk urges presidents to approach the office self-consciously, with an eye to developing a management strategy—know yourself and take the steps necessary for effectiveness. Only in this way can presidents hope to achieve some measure of success. It is not clear how readily presidents will accept such advice. Are they likely to recognize their own short-comings? One might expect that any newly elected president, imbued with ambition and flush with success, will proceed to the task of governing filled with self-confidence. Moreover, one might expect those presidents whose personalities drive them to pursue achievement will be least likely to undertake self-analysis.

In many respects, this chapter has explored a question similar to the one posed by Quirk: *What personal qualities make a successful president?* As we have seen, there are no simple answers. Competencies may be part of the solution, but so are temperament and attitudes. As this chapter demonstrates, we have little sense of how the qualities necessary for success are derived from family background, career experience, personality, and beliefs. This is true in no small measure because success is the product of these personal qualities interacting with the constraints and opportunities of situations. Despite this fundamental uncertainty, there remains a pervasive confidence that the president's personal qualities have the utmost effect on performance in office, and, therefore, the American people are likely to continue their search for men, and certainly one day women, with heroic qualities.

NOTES

1. Todd S. Purdum, "Striking Strengths, Glaring Failures," *New York Times*, December 24, 2000, A1.

2. For a detailed analysis of the speech on August 17, 1998, in light of Clinton's life, see David Maraniss, *The Clinton Enigma* (New York: Simon and Schuster, 1998). Jones's lawyers had been informed that secret tape recordings existed of telephone conversations between Monica Lewinsky and Linda Tripp that described the affair. The lawyers were then able to probe the relationship and elicit the president's denial. Lewinsky had been working in the White House during the fall of 1995. One evening, a flirtatious relationship with the president turned into a sexual encounter in the Oval Office suite, followed by nine others over the next eighteen months. Excruciating details of these encounters were provided in the report of Special Counsel Kenneth Starr to the U.S. House of Representatives in September 1998. This report formed the basis for Clinton's subsequent impeachment.

3. The most influential of these interpretations was offered by James David Barber, *The Presidential Character: Predicting Performance in the White House*, 4th ed. (Englewood Cliffs, N.J.: Prentice Hall, 1992).

4. Fred I. Greenstein, *The Presidential Difference: Leadership Style from FDR to Clinton* (New York: Free Press, 2000), 3.

5. Stephen Skowronek, *The Politics Presidents Make: Leadership from John Adams to George Bush* (Cambridge: Harvard University Press, 1993). For another work that deals with the importance of a president's environment, defined in a different way, see Bert A. Rockman, *The Leadership Question: The Presidency and the American System* (New York: Praeger, 1984).

6. Fred I. Greenstein, "Can Personality and Politics Be Studied Systematically?" *Political Psychology* 13, no. 1 (1992): 109. For a general discussion of studying personality and politics with special attention to the presidency, see Fred I. Greenstein, *Personality and Politics: Problems of Evidence, Inference, and Conceptualization*, 2d ed. (New York: Norton, 1975); and Rockman, *The Leadership Question*.

7. See, for example, Colin Campbell and Bert A. Rockman, eds., *The Clinton Legacy* (Chatham, N.J.: Chatham House, 2000).

8. Bruce Buchanan, *The Citizen's Presidency* (Washington, D.C.: CQ Press, 1987), 102–104. Buchanan proposes a set of "competent process standards" that are more susceptible to empirical verification (108–134).

9. Bert A. Rockman, "Conclusions: An Imprint but Not a Revolution," in *The Reagan Revolution?* ed. B. B. Kymlicka and Jean V. Matthews (Chicago: Dorsey, 1988), 205. Other works in this vein, important because of the significance attributed to the Reagan experience, include the following: Larry Berman, ed., *Looking Back on the Reagan Presidency* (Baltimore: Johns Hopkins University Press, 1990); Sidney Blumenthal and Thomas Byrne Edsall, eds., *The Reagan Legacy* (New York: Pantheon Books, 1988); Charles O. Jones, ed., *The Reagan Legacy: Promise and Performance* (Chatham, N.J.: Chatham House, 1988); and John L. Palmer, ed., *Perspectives on the Reagan Years* (Washington, D.C.: Urban Institute, 1986).

10. My thanks to Professor Pfiffner for sharing an advance copy of his book with me. Hence quotations are cited by chapter rather than by page. See James P. Pfiffner, *Character and the Modern Presidency* (Washington, D.C.: Brookings, 2001), chap. 1.

11. Ibid., chap. 2.

12. Ibid., chap. 4. Pfiffner's conclusion is that Clinton was reckless and irresponsible in his behavior and that he extended the effect of his lies by telling them to cabinet members and White House staff aides he knew would repeat the untruths. But the lies "did not constitute the same level of institutional threat to the polity that Watergate and Iran-Contra did." See chap. 6.

13. Arthur Schlesinger's initial effort polled fifty-five scholars, and his second included seventy-five, with historians constituting the greater part of each group. Gary Maranell and Richard Dodder included results from 571 historians, and the *Chicago Tribune* poll focused on forty-nine scholars who had studied individual presidents. The Murray-Blessing poll was based on 846 responses to a nineteen-page, 180-question survey sent to 1,997 Ph.D.-holding American historians with assistant professor rank (an additional 107 responses were returned late). Finally, the C-SPAN survey included 58 historians. For information on poll samples, see Henry J. Abraham, *Justices and Presidents* (New York: Oxford University Press, 1985), appendix B. For discussion of these efforts as well as their own, see Robert K. Murray and Tim H. Blessing, *Greatness in the White House: Rating the Presidents, Washington Through Ronald Reagan,* 2d updated ed. (University Park: Pennsylvania State University Press, 1994), chaps. 1 and 2. The ranking of Ronald Reagan was completed in 1988–1990 and is reported in this updated edition.

14. Murray and Blessing, *Greatness in the White House,* 24.

15. Tim H. Blessing and Anne A. Skleder, "Top Down: A General Overview of Present Research on Ronald Reagan's Doctrinal Presidency," in *Reassessing the Reagan Presidency,* ed. Richard S. Conley (Lanham, Md.: University Press of America, 2003), 30. The authors report the results of an unpublished poll about Reagan similar to the poll conducted in 1990.

16. Murray and Blessing, *Greatness in the White House,* 41–43, and appendix 8, 139. The personal traits conducive to success also were examined in terms of how they changed for different times. For the modern era, 1945 to the present, respondents ranked intelligence first and integrity second, with other qualities in declining order: sensitivity to popular demands, charisma, previous political experience, pleasing physical appearance, intense patriotism, and an aristocratic bearing.

17. Ibid., 63.

18. James MacGregor Burns, *Leadership* (New York: Harper and Row, 1977).

19. Greenstein, *Presidential Difference,* 5–6.

20. Donald Matthews, *The Social Background of Political Decision Makers* (New York: Random House, 1954), 23.

21. Edward Pessen, *The Log Cabin Myth: The Social Backgrounds of the Presidents* (New Haven: Yale University Press, 1984), 56–57.

22. Ibid., 171.

23. Ibid., 56–63. Pessen views a family's class as a combination of wealth and possessions, income and occupational prestige, lifestyle, status, influence, and power. He recognizes, moreover, that analysts' characterizations are subjective.

24. Truman attended night classes at the Kansas City Law School, but it was a proprietary institution not then affiliated with a university. It is now part of the Law School of the University of Missouri–Kansas City.

25. Max Weber, "Politics as a Vocation," in *Max Weber: Essays in Sociology,* ed. H. H. Gerth and C. W. Mills (New York: Oxford University Press, 1946), 85.

26. Hugh Montgomery-Massingberd, ed., *Burke's Presidential Families of the U.S.A.* (London: Burke's Peerage, 1975), 250.

27. Ibid., 320.

28. Robert Donovan, *Conflict and Crisis: The Presidency of Harry S Truman, 1945–48* (New York: Praeger, 1977), chap. 40. It should also be noted that military officers have demonstrated leadership skills and may be called on to develop substantial political skill while building careers or in dealing with foreign leaders. Eisenhower, for example, did both.

29. Pessen, *The Log Cabin Myth,* 171.

30. E. Digby Baltzell and Howard G. Schneiderman, "Social Class in the Oval Office," *Society* 26 (September/October 1988): 42–49. The ranking of presidential performance used in this study was conducted by Robert K. Murray and Tim H. Blessing and was first published in the *Journal of American History* 70 (December 1983): 535–555.

31. Baltzell and Schneiderman, "Social Class in the Oval Office," 47.

32. W. H. Harrison and Garfield were not rated because of the brief time they served in office.

33. Baltzell and Schneiderman, "Social Class in the Oval Office," 49.

34. Richard Neustadt, *Presidential Power and the Modern Presidents* (New York: Free Press, 1991), 151.

35. Ibid., 205.

36. Rockman, *Leadership Question,* 212. Rockman uses a performance ranking compiled by the *Chicago Tribune* in 1982.

37. We are indebted to Leonard P. Stark for this account and continuing stimulation on the subject of presidential personality. See his senior honors thesis, "Personality and Presidential Selection: Evaluating Character and Experience in the 1988 Election" (University of Delaware, 1991), 47–48. Barber's article was "The Question of Presidential Character," *Saturday Review,* September 23, 1972, 62–66.

38. Greenstein, *Personality and Politics,* 3.

39. Alexander L. George and Juliette George, *Woodrow Wilson and Colonel House: A Personality Study* (New York: John Day, 1956); Doris Kearns, *Lyndon Johnson and the American Dream* (New York: Harper and Row, 1976); Bruce Mazlish, *In Search of Nixon: A Psychohistorical Inquiry* (Baltimore: Pelican, 1973); Betty Glad, *Jimmy Carter: In Search of the Great White House* (New York: Norton, 1980); and Stanley A. Renshon, *High Hopes: The Clinton Presidency and the Politics of Ambition* (New York: NYU Press, 1996). For an excellent biography of Clinton that provides psychological insights but is not informed by psychological theory, see David Maraniss, *First in His Class: A Biography of Bill Clinton* (New York: Simon and Schuster, 1995).

40. For an extended discussion, see Greenstein's treatment of these issues in *Personality and Politics,* chaps. 3 and 4, as well as the introduction.

41. See, for example, Alexander L. George's discussion of Barber's book *Presidential Character* in George, "Assessing Presidential Character," *World Politics* 26 (Jan-

uary 1974): 234–282. This essay is reprinted with several related essays in *Presidential Personality and Performance*, Alexander L. George and Juliette George (Boulder: Westview, 1998), 145–197.

42. Although the call of conservatives during the Reagan years was "let Reagan be Reagan," Clinton's aides had begun the practice during his gubernatorial years of "protect[ing] Clinton from Clinton." See Maraniss, *Clinton Enigma*, 60.

43. Barber, *Presidential Character*, 34.

44. James David Barber, "Predicting Hope with Clinton at Helm," *News & Observer* (Raleigh, N.C.), January 17, 1993. Barber did not offer a preliminary evaluation of George W. Bush.

45. Barber, *Presidential Character*, 5.

46. Ibid.

47. Barber, "Predicting Hope."

48. Stanley A. Renshon, "A Preliminary Assessment of the Clinton Presidency: Character, Leadership, and Performance," *Political Psychology* 15, no. 2 (1994): 375–394. Also see a slightly revised version of the paper in *The Clinton Presidency: Campaigning, Governing, and the Psychology of Leadership*, ed. Stanley A. Renshon (Boulder: Westview, 1995), 57–87. Also see Renshon, *High Hopes*.

49. Maraniss, *First in His Class*.

50. Renshon, "Preliminary Assessment," 382.

51. Jann S. Wenner and William Greider, "The Rolling Stone Interview: President Clinton," *Rolling Stone*, December 9, 1993, 81.

52. Renshon, "Preliminary Assessment," 381, 380, 382.

53. Greenstein, *Presidential Difference*, 255.

54. Stanley A. Renshon, "After the Fall: The Clinton Presidency in Psychological Perspective," *Political Science Quarterly* 115, no. 1 (spring 2000): 41–65.

55. Fred I. Greenstein, "The Two Leadership Styles of William Jefferson Clinton," *Political Psychology* 15, no. 2 (1994): 357. Also see Greenstein's essay "Political Style and Political Leadership: The Case of Bill Clinton," in *Clinton Presidency: Campaigning, Governing, and the Psychology of Leadership*, 137–147.

56. Greenstein, "Two Leadership Styles," 358.

57. Greenstein, *Personality and Politics*, 19.

58. Fred I. Greenstein, *The Hidden-Hand Presidency* (New York: Basic Books, 1982). Barber, however, has responded that the new evidence confirms his original analysis even more fully. See Barber, *Presidential Character*, 522–525.

59. See George, "Assessing Presidential Character"; and Michael Nelson, "The Psychological Presidency," in *The Presidency and the Political System*, 4th ed., ed. Michael Nelson (Washington, D.C.: CQ Press, 1995).

60. Dean Keith Simonton, *Why Presidents Succeed: A Political Psychology of Leadership* (New Haven: Yale University Press, 1987), 151–152.

61. Barber, *Presidential Character*, 487.

62. Ibid., 298.

63. Ibid., 296–299.

64. Jeffrey Tulis, "On Presidential Character," in *The Presidency in the Constitutional Order*, ed. Jeffrey Tulis and Joseph M. Bessette (Baton Rouge: Louisiana State University Press, 1981), 283–313.

65. For another effort at guiding electoral choice, see Stanley A. Renshon, *The Psychological Assessment of Presidential Candidates* (New York: New York University Press, 1996).

66. Clark Clifford, "The Presidency as I Have Seen It," in *The Living Presidency*, ed. Emmet John Hughes (New York: Coward, McCann, and Geoghegan, 1973), 315, cited by Greenstein in *Presidential Difference*, 189.

67. Harold W. Stanley and Richard G. Niemi, *Vital Statistics on American Politics, 1999–2000* (Washington, D.C.: CQ Press, 2000), 250–251.

68. Joseph A. Pika, "Management Style and the Organizational Matrix: Studying White House Operations," *Administration and Society* 20, no. 1 (May 1988): 11.

69. John Hart, *The Presidential Branch: From Washington to Clinton* (Chatham, N.J.: Chatham House, 1995).

70. Alexander L. George, *Presidential Decisionmaking in Foreign Policy* (Boulder: Westview, 1980), 139–168.

71. See Richard Tanner Johnson, *Managing the White House* (New York: Harper and Row, 1974). Also see Johnson, "Presidential Style," in *Perspectives on the Presidency,* ed. Aaron Wildavsky (Boston: Little, Brown, 1975).

72. Roger Porter, "A Healing Presidency," in *Leadership in the Modern Presidency,* ed. Fred I. Greenstein (Cambridge: Harvard University Press, 1988), 218.

73. George, *Presidential Decisionmaking,* 159.

74. Colin Campbell, *Managing the Presidency: Carter, Reagan, and the Search for Executive Harmony* (Pittsburgh: University of Pittsburgh Press, 1986), 93–111; James Pfiffner, *The Strategic Presidency: Hitting the Ground Running* (Chicago: Dorsey, 1988), 30–37; and Buchanan, *Citizen's Presidency,* 124–133.

75. Alexander L. George and Eric Stern, "Presidential Management Styles and Models," in *Presidential Personality and Performance,* 263.

76. Pika, "Management Style," 9.

77. Alexander L. George, "The Case for Multiple Advocacy in Making Foreign Policy," *American Political Science Review* 66 (September 1972): 751–785. Also see George, *Presidential Decisionmaking,* chap. 11.

78. George, *Presidential Decisionmaking,* 203, 203–204.

79. Ibid., 201.

80. Paul A. Kowert, *Groupthink or Deadlock: When Do Leaders Learn from Their Advisers?* (Albany: State University of New York Press, 2002) 4, 23.

81. Ibid., chap. 6.

82. George, *Presidential Decisionmaking,* 204.

83. Maraniss, *First in His Class,* 38.

84. Greenstein, "Two Leadership Styles," 358.

85. Michael J. Kelly, "A Man Who Wants to Be Liked, and Is: William Jefferson Blythe Clinton," *New York Times,* November 4, 1992, A1.

86. Jerome D. Levin, *The Clinton Syndrome: The President and the Self-Destructive Nature of Sexual Addiction* (Rocklin, Calif.: Prima, 1998), 5.

87. Maraniss, *First in His Class,* 88.

88. Ibid., 357.

89. Ibid., 362.

90. Michael J. Kelly is highly critical of the last pattern, arguing that Clinton betrayed his populist roots and cozied up to the traditional centers of Arkansas power. See Kelly, "The President's Past," *New York Times Magazine,* July 31, 1994.

91. Maraniss, *Clinton Enigma,* 14.

92. Maraniss, *First in His Class,* 340.

93. Maraniss, *Clinton Enigma,* 42–43.

94. Greenstein, *Presidential Difference,* 174, 199.

95. Maraniss, *Clinton Enigma,* 43.

96. Greenstein, *Presidential Difference,* 200.

97. Purdum, "Striking Strengths," A1.

98. Maraniss, *First in His Class,* 124, 199, 355.

99. Purdum, "Striking Strengths," A13.

100. Kelly, "A Man Who Wants to Be Liked," A1; and Kelly, "President's Past," 25.

101. Quoted in Purdum, "Striking Strengths," A1.

102. Greenstein, *Presidential Difference,* 174.

103. Wenner and Greider, "Rolling Stone Interview," 40.

104. Bert A. Rockman, "Leadership Style and the Clinton Presidency," in *Clinton Presidency: First Appraisals*, ed. Colin Campbell and Bert A. Rockman (Chatham, N.J.: Chatham House, 1996), 9; and Maraniss, *First in His Class*, 347.

105. Kelly, "President's Past," 25; Campbell and Rockman, introduction to *Clinton Presidency: First Appraisals*, 169.

106. Kelly, "President's Past," 40.

107. Greenstein, "Two Leadership Styles," 356–357.

108. Kelly, "President's Past," 45.

109. Graham K. Wilson, "The Clinton Administration and Interest Groups," in *Clinton Presidency: First Appraisals*, 220.

110. Rockman, "Leadership Style," 355.

111. Jason DeParle and Steven A. Holmes, "A War on Poverty Subtly Linked to Race," *New York Times*, December 26, 2000, A1.

112. Wenner and Greider, "Rolling Stone Interview," 80.

113. Maraniss, *First in His Class*, 293, 349.

114. The three were the suicide of fellow Rhodes scholar Frank Aller, which came on the heels of Clinton's own personal torment over the Vietnam draft; his crushing defeat when he sought reelection after his first term as governor; and the arrest of Roger Clinton, his brother, for cocaine dealing. The latter episode produced an extensive round of counseling and the family's first open discussion of how it had been affected by his stepfather's alcoholism. During this period Clinton reportedly recognized how his own dislike of personal conflict and his desire to please were linked with his family experience. Ibid., 422.

115. Greenstein, "Two Leadership Styles," 357.

116. Two multipart series on the life and preparation of George W. Bush, originally published in the *Washington Post* in 1999 and 2000, provide the background for this sketch. Both can be found on the paper's Web site, www.washingtonpost.com/wp-dyn/politics/news/postseries. Separate installments are cited where appropriate.

117. Michael Barone, Grant Ujifusa, and Douglas Matthews, *The Almanac of American Politics 1980* (New York: E. P. Dutton, 1979), 867.

118. Lois Romano and George Lardner Jr., "Part 2: Tragedy Created Bush Mother-Son Bond," *Washington Post*, July 26, 1999, A1.

119. Hugh Heclo, "The Bush Political Ethos" (paper prepared for the conference on The George W. Bush Presidency: An Early Assessment, Princeton, April 25–26, 2003), 2.

120. Romano and Lardner, "Part 3: A So-So Student but a Campus Mover," *Washington Post*, July 27, 1999, A1.

121. Romano and Lardner, "Part 4: At Height of Vietnam, Bush Picks Guard," *Washington Post*, July 28, 1999, A1.

122. Romano and Lardner, "Part 5: Young Bush, A Political Natural, Revs Up," *Washington Post*, July 29, 1999, A1.

123. Hugh Heclo, "The Bush Political Ethos," 5.

124. Romano and Lardner, "Part 6: Bush Name Helps Fuel Oil Dealings," *Washington Post*, July 30, 1999, A1.

125. Ibid.

126. The reawakening of Bush's spirituality can also be traced to his participation in a weekly men's Bible study group organized in Midland. See Hanna Rosin, "Applying Personal Faith to Public Policy," *Washington Post*, July 24, 2000, A1.

127. This incident was revealed late in the 2000 campaign by a Fox-affiliate news reporter in Maine, temporarily throwing the Bush campaign off-balance. Bush admitted to having had too many beers at a local bar in Kennebunkport and to having been pulled over for driving erratically. He was fined $150 and had his driving

privileges suspended in Maine for thirty days, though they were not restored until 1978 because he was unable to attend a required rehabilitation program. Bush explained that he had not revealed the incident earlier because he sought to protect his daughters from learning of their father's dangerous behavior. See Dan Balz, "Bush Acknowledges 1976 DUI Arrest," *Washington Post,* November 3, 2000, A1; and Steven A. Kurkjian and David Armstrong, "Bush Downplayed Drinking: '78 Comments Got License Back," *Boston Globe,* November 4, 2000, A11.

128. Romano and Lardner, "Part 1: Bush's Life-Changing Year," *Washington Post,* July 25, 1999, A1. Bush has resolutely refused to answer reporters' questions on whether he engaged in illegal drug use. He has unequivocally declared his faithfulness to his wife but has not assumed a similar position on drug usage. Needless to say, this stance spurs media curiosity. For an extensive examination of this question and how it became an issue in the 2000 election, see Felicity Barringer, "When an Old Drug Question Becomes New News," *New York Times,* August 22, 1999.

129. Heclo, "The Bush Political Ethos," 18.

130. Hanna Rosin, "Applying Personal Faith," A1.

131. Dana Milbank, "Dispelling Doubts with the Rangers," *Washington Post,* July 25, 2000, A1.

132. Romano and Lardner, "Part 7: Bush's Move Up to the Majors," *Washington Post,* July 31, 1999, A1.

133. Ibid.

134. Exit polls showed Bush winning 46 percent of the Hispanic vote, an all-time high for a statewide Republican candidate. See R. G. Ratcliffe, "Election 98: Bush Leads Statewide GOP Blitz," *Houston Chronicle,* November 4, 1998, A1.

135. Romano and Lardner, "Part 1: Bush's Life-Changing Year," A1.

136. Heclo, "The Bush Political Ethos," 6–7.

137. Lois Romano, "A Fierce Loyalty Marks Bush's Inner Circle," *Washington Post,* July 26, 2000, A1. On Evans see Elisabeth Bumiller, "Texas Pals Are Still Sharing Adventures," *New York Times* May 26, 2003, www.nytimes.com/2003/05/26/national/26LETT.html.

138. Ivo H. Daalder and James M. Lindsay, "The Bush Revolution: The Remaking of America's Foreign Policy" (paper presented at the conference on The Bush Presidency: An Early Assessment, Princeton University, April 25–26, 2003), 7.

139. Hanna Rosin, "Bush's Resentment of 'Elites' Informs Bid," *Washington Post,* July 23, 2000, A1.

140. See the story of Bush's deciding to run for governor in Romano and Lardner, "Part 7: Bush's Move Up to the Majors," A1.

141. See the experience of Joseph Allbaugh, Bush's campaign manager in 1994, as reported in ibid.

142. Heclo, "The Bush Political Ethos," 19.

143. Fred I. Greenstein, "The Leadership Style of George W. Bush" (paper presented at the conference on The Bush Presidency: An Early Assessment, Princeton University, April 25–26, 2003), 12.

144. Ibid., 16.

145. For a thoughtful discussion of the generational and Christian influences on Bush's thinking, see the two articles by Hanna Rosin published in the *Washington Post* (cited in notes 126 and 139).

146. In their thoughtful evaluations of the Bush administration, both Greenstein and Heclo identify Bush's ability to fashion public and international support for the administration's policy visions as the principal unanswered question for this presidency. Greenstein, "The Leadership Style of George W. Bush," 25; Heclo, "The Bush Political Ethos," 25–26.

147. Daalder and Lindsay, "The Bush Revolution," 1.

148. Ibid., 21.

149. Paul Quirk, "Presidential Competence," in *The Presidency and the Political System*, 7th ed., ed. Michael Nelson (Washington, D.C.: CQ Press, 2003), 158–189; and Paul Quirk, "What Must a President Know?" *Transactional Society* 23 (January/February 1983).

150. Quirk, "Presidential Competence."

SUGGESTED READINGS

Barber, James David. *The Presidential Character.* 4th ed. Englewood Cliffs, N.J.: Prentice Hall, 1992.

George, Alexander L., and Juliette George. *Presidential Personality and Performance.* Boulder: Westview, 1998.

___. *Woodrow Wilson and Colonel House: A Personality Study.* New York: John Day, 1956.

Greenstein, Fred I. *Personality and Politics: Problems of Evidence, Inference, and Conceptualization.* New York: Norton, 1975.

___. *The Presidential Difference: Leadership Style from FDR to Clinton.* New York: Free Press, 2000.

Hargrove, Erwin. *Jimmy Carter as President: Leadership and the Politics of the Public Good.* Baton Rouge: Louisiana State University Press, 1988.

Kearns, Doris. *Lyndon Johnson and the American Dream.* New York: Harper and Row, 1976.

Maraniss, David. *First in His Class: The Biography of Bill Clinton.* New York: Simon and Schuster, 1995.

Mazlish, Bruce. *In Search of Nixon: A Psychohistorical Inquiry.* Baltimore: Pelican, 1973.

Pessen, Edward. *The Log Cabin Myth: The Social Backgrounds of the Presidents.* New Haven: Yale University Press, 1984.

Pfiffner, James P. *Character and the Modern Presidency.* Washington, D.C.: Brookings, 2001.

Renshon, Stanley A. *High Hopes: The Clinton Presidency and the Politics of Ambition.* New York: New York University Press, 1996.

Rockman, Bert A. *The Leadership Question: The Presidency and the American System.* New York: Praeger, 1984.

5 LEGISLATIVE POLITICS

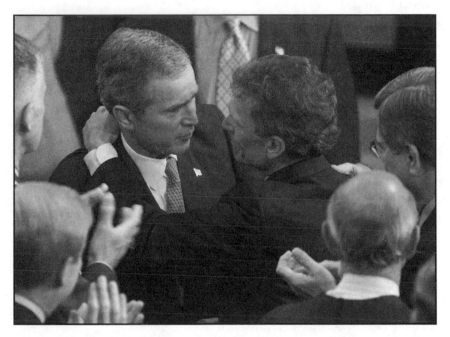

Following a presidential address to a joint session of Congress on September 20, 2001, the embrace between President Bush and Senate Majority Leader Thomas Daschle, D-S.D., symbolized the period of national unity and bipartisanship that followed the terrorist attacks of September 11.

THE NATION FREQUENTLY BECOMES FIXATED on relations between the president and Congress. The following three examples highlight the centrality of this institutional relationship. Twice during the winter of 1995–1996, the federal government shut down because Bill Clinton and the Republican-controlled Congress could not reach agreement on a new budget. No less dramatic was the winter of 1998–1999, when Clinton became only the second president in American history to be impeached by the House as well as the second to survive a Senate trial. On a different note, George W. Bush, signed a massive tax-cut bill into law on June 7, 2001, fulfilling a campaign pledge and reversing within a few short months one of Clinton's major legacies. This success cost him a Republican majority in the Senate, but Bush prevailed in the 2002 midterm elections and passed another tax-cut bill in 2003.

The Budget Battle, 1995–1996

The saga of the government shutdowns stretched over several months. On November 17, 1995, the Republican-controlled 104th Congress enacted a comprehensive reconciliation bill *(see chapter 9)* designed to produce a balanced budget in 2002. The bill would have reduced the growth of federal mandatory spending for several major programs (Medicare, Medicaid, and other welfare programs, and agriculture subsidies) as well as discretionary spending in education, job training, and environmental protection. The bill also would have cut taxes by $245 billion during the same period and transferred responsibility for caring for the poor to the states. In two votes, largely along party lines, the legislation passed the House 237–189 and the Senate 52–47.[1] President Clinton, while supporting the goal of a balanced budget, attacked the bill as unfair to the poor and the elderly. After he vetoed it, his negotiations with Republican leaders of Congress failed to produce a comprehensive agreement on how to balance the budget. Six of the thirteen major appropriations bills required to fund the government in fiscal 1996, which began on October 1, 1995, were not finalized. Moreover, congressional Republicans refused to raise and extend the limit on the national debt when the government's authority to borrow funds to meet its financial obligations lapsed in November.

At the heart of this confrontation was a philosophical disagreement over the future role of the federal government. Clinton proposed a ten-year plan to balance the budget (later reduced to seven) based on economic assumptions and data provided by the Office of Management and Budget (OMB). Republicans insisted on following a seven-year plan based on Congressional Budget Office information. The two sides differed over the size of tax and spending cuts. By mid-January 1996, they had moved toward each other's position and appeared ready to split the monetary differences. They could not, however, resolve the philosophical conflict over how to restructure Medicaid and Aid to Families with Dependent Children (AFDC).

As a result, two government shutdowns occurred: 800,000 federal employees were furloughed November 14–20 and 280,000 December 16–January 5. Although the Republican Congress had passed continuing resolutions temporarily extending funding to cover the agencies' operations, Clinton vetoed them because they had unacceptable budget conditions—ones seeking to reduce funding for the environment, education, Social Security, and Medicare. Eventually, temporary funding agreements ended the episodes (workers later collected back pay), but permanent appropriations were not finalized until April 1996.[2] In their struggle with Clinton, Republicans had used continuing resolutions and the debt limit extension bill as leverage to try to force his hand. They believed he would rather accept their terms than allow the government to shut down or default on obligations. To everyone's surprise given his earlier eagerness to compromise in legislative negotiations, Clinton proved resolute. Secretary of the Treasury Robert Rubin was able to use certain trust funds under his control to prevent default. Clinton's media campaign successfully painted the Republicans as extremists intent on damaging average citizens. The public placed more of the blame for the shutdowns on Congress than on the president.

The Impeachment Battle, 1998–1999

The high-stakes game of fiscal chicken played in 1995–1996 was an early battle on the rocky road of Clinton's relations with Congress; the stakes were raised considerably on December 19, 1998, when the House approved two articles of impeachment against William Jefferson Clinton. The House, by a 228–206 vote, accused him of lying under oath while giving testimony to a grand jury in August 1999 and, by a 221–212 vote, accused him of obstructing justice by hiding his improper relationship with a White House intern. (Two other articles of impeachment recommended by the House Judiciary Committee failed to be adopted by the full House.) These votes came at the end of a lengthy investigation by Independent Counsel Kenneth Starr. Originally named to investigate the president's possible involvement in a failed land development project in Arkansas (known as Whitewater), Starr expanded his investigation at several points to include other subjects of alleged wrongdoing.[3] The last was Clinton's testimony in connection with a civil suit brought against him by Paula Jones, a former state employee who charged him with making unwanted sexual advances in 1991, while governor of Arkansas. To document a pattern of sexual harassment with other state or federal employees, Jones's lawyers posed questions to the president about his relationship with former White House intern Monica Lewinsky. When Clinton denied the existence of that relationship in a court deposition and subsequently misrepresented it to the public and a grand jury, the ground was set for a constitutional confrontation.

Starr conducted a grand jury investigation throughout most of 1998. In the course of it he subpoenaed Clinton and deposed him by closed-circuit television on August 17, 1998, the first instance of such testimony by a sitting president. In September, the independent counsel filed a report with Congress (released to the public replete with salacious details) that formed the basis for the House Judiciary Committee's recommendation, in a straight party vote, that the House conduct an impeachment inquiry. Starr testified before the committee on two occasions in November, and Clinton responded to written questions. Throughout this period, the public's approval of the president remained surprisingly high and interest in the scandal surprisingly low. Observers suggested that the public had entered a period of "scandal fatigue" and wanted federal officials to return to business.[4] In addition, the public may have had greater tolerance of presidential misbehavior during a period of peace and prosperity. The White House may also have been successful in making the scandal appear to be nothing more than a question of sex and adultery, sources of concern but misdeeds falling far short of impeachable offenses. In fact, throughout this saga, the meaning of "high crimes and misdemeanors," the constitutional grounds for removing a president, remained a central question. Advocates of removal believed that undermining the "rule of law" enforced by the courts met that test; defenders of the president believed that personal misconduct did not constitute a threat to the republic.[5] "Clinton turned the struggle into a question of whether a president who was performing well should be removed for actions unconnected to his official duties."[6]

Following the December House vote, the Senate began the impeachment trial on January 7, 1999. There had been no proceedings of this kind since 1868, when Andrew Johnson avoided removal by a single vote. In the modern version, thirteen Republican members of the House served as managers and had three days to present their case; the president's legal team responded over three days. The managers were distressed that their fellow Republicans in the Senate seemed less committed to removal than they were. Majority Leader Trent Lott insisted on steering a path that would maintain the Senate's dignity, a strategy that reflected a realistic assessment of how difficult it would be to generate the two-thirds majority needed for removal when the Democrats held forty-five seats. A motion to dismiss the case, even though it failed by 44–56, revealed that the Democrats were relatively united: only one Democrat had crossed party lines rather than the dozen needed for conviction. Furthermore, when the House managers sought to conduct a very public trial with a long list of witnesses testifying to the president's immoral behavior, the Senate instead approved a short list of witnesses deposed in private, their videotaped testimony available only to Senate members.[7] In the end, neither article of impeachment received even a majority vote on February 12, when the Senate finally concluded its consideration. Article I failed by a 45–55 vote, with ten Republicans joining all Democrats in opposition. Article II failed as well by a vote of 50–50, with five Republicans joining all the Democrats. The president survived, but impeachment will always help define his place in history.

Clinton's relations with Congress had not always been stormy. During Clinton's first two years, the Democratic 103d Congress passed most of his legislative program, usually with little Republican support and some opposition from conservative Democrats. He relied on Republican support to pass two international trade bills opposed by organized labor and liberal House Democrats. Of the major bills he proposed during this period, only health care reform and welfare reform failed to be enacted. In contrast, the pattern of Clinton's legislative relations following the Republican takeover of Congress in 1994 is comparable to those of Richard Nixon, Gerald Ford, Ronald Reagan in his last two years in office, and George Bush. Like these predecessors who confronted an opposition-controlled Congress, Clinton was engaged in protracted conflict about the direction of public policy and institutional prerogatives—and ultimately for this president, his political survival.

Bush's 2001 and 2003 Tax-Cut Victories and Senate Setback

George W. Bush entered office with something no Republican president had enjoyed since 1955—a Republican majority in the House and the Senate. Despite repeated success in winning presidential elections and controlling the White House for two extended periods (1969–1977 and 1981–1993), the Republicans had not controlled both elected branches of government since the two years following Dwight D. Eisenhower's first electoral victory in 1952. But Bush's working majorities were small: nine votes in the House and only one in the evenly divided Senate, a vote to be cast by the vice president in the event of a tie.[8] Bush's hotly contested electoral victory was expected to produce a difficult working relationship with Democrats in Congress, and Bush made well-publicized efforts early on to consult with the opposition to promote bipartisanship and project a less confrontational tone. The media dubbed this effort the "charm offensive."[9] Ultimately, however, he put forward a relatively aggressive agenda that would rise or fall based largely on Republican unity. In short, he sought to "hit the ground running" with a focused legislative agenda that could be accomplished while his influence remained high.[10]

House Republicans were especially unified during the early months, adopting Bush's budget proposals and his $1.6 trillion tax-cut proposal with only modest changes. Senate Republicans proved less cooperative when two moderates refused to support the proposed budget because of the large tax cut, and Sen. John McCain of Arizona, Bush's opponent for the Republican nomination in 2000, continued to assert his independence.[11] Nonetheless, with the support of several moderate Democrats, Bush delivered on his primary legislative priority and his signature campaign promise of tax relief. The size of the cuts was close to the original proposal ($1.35 trillion) as were many of the details. Bush stressed the historic nature of the moment when he noted at the signing ceremony, "Tax relief does not happen often in Washington. . . . In fact, since World War II, it has happened only twice: President Kennedy's tax cut in the 60's and President Reagan's tax cuts in the 1980's."[12]

Many Republicans worried about the long-term consequences of this victory. Sen. James M. Jeffords, R-Vt., announced on May 24, just two days before the House and Senate approved the tax-cut bill, that he would become an independent and vote with the Democrats for organizational purposes. This meant Republicans would lose control of the Senate and Democrats would have an opportunity to define the agenda, block nominations, conduct investigations, and derail administration-sponsored legislation. Jeffords did give his word to Bush that he would not try to undermine the tax bill (he voted for it) and would not leave the party until June 5 or until the tax bill became law, whichever came later.

Why had Jeffords, just reelected to a third term, taken this drastic, though not unprecedented, step? Rumors and possible explanations swirled through

Washington. Some blamed the bullying tactics taken by the White House and Republican leaders to make Jeffords adhere to the party line in critical votes. It was also suggested that he had fought with the White House concerning large and small differences over education. The president had rejected Jeffords's insistence that more money be spent for special education, a program of particular concern to him as chair of the Health, Education, Labor, and Pensions Committee. It was also rumored that the White House had angered Jeffords by excluding him from a social function for the teacher of the year, a fellow Vermonter.[13] Jeffords mentioned neither of these in his public statement but pointed to the growing distance between the Republican Party's national agenda and his moderate Republicanism, which stressed the principles of "moderation, tolerance, and fiscal responsibility."[14] Bush, many argued, had placed such emphasis on maintaining support from the party's conservative wing that moderates felt their views on abortion, the environment, energy, judicial appointments, and missile defense were already being ignored and would not be respected in the future. During blunt discussions among Senate Republicans, the strategy of "governing from the right" was questioned by some and defended by others.[15]

Jeffords's defection was quickly forgotten after Republicans recaptured their Senate majority by picking up two seats in the 2002 elections, giving them a 51–49 margin of control. Bush, however, continued to face challenges as the Republicans' national party leader. During the media furor that followed apparently racist remarks by Trent Lott, R-La., at a retirement party for Strom Thurmond, R-S.C., Bush publicly chastised Lott and did nothing to intervene in his behalf. Lott resigned as Senate majority leader, and the president backed an alternative candidate, Dr. William Frist, R-Tenn., who was quickly installed. During another tax-cutting initiative in spring 2003, Bush had to intervene with squabbling Republicans to save his plan to stimulate the economy. House Republicans felt that Frist had surrendered to a small group of moderate Republicans who opposed a large tax cut, thereby undermining the president's original proposal for a $726 billion cut. House Republicans supported a $550 billion cut, but the Senate narrowly approved a cut of $350 billion, ultimately reduced to $320 billion when one Republican holdout made assistance to states the price of his support. Feelings ran high, and only after Bush, with the help of Vice President Cheney, brokered a compromise that accepted the Senate's dollar figure but embraced the specifics of the House version did a bill emerge and pass the Senate by a 51–50 margin, supplied by Cheney's tie-breaking vote.[16] In the end, "the president succeeded because of a set of tactics that involved remaining flexible in his goals, taking advantage of division among Democrats, campaigning vigorously in the states of crucial senators and knocking the heads of Congressional leaders who often seemed more interested in pride of authorship than in enactment of legislation."[17]

These incidents signaled the end of Bush's honeymoon period in relations with Congress and illustrate the complexity of legislative-executive relations.[18] *Intraparty* disputes can prove just as important as *interparty* ones, and presidents must worry about the strategic logic of their programs as well as the tactical nuances of working with individual legislators. Like his predecessors, Bush found that the skills and techniques of leadership that enabled him to capture his party's nomination and win the election do not always match those needed to sustain public and legislative support. Nomination and electoral politics require the ability to raise money, to build an organization composed of election professionals, to project an attractive and engaging image, and to sense the concerns of the public. But the politics of governing—legislating and administering—requires talents that can move a complex, cumbersome government to get things done. These talents include persuasion, personal and organizational leadership, and managerial skill.

The solutions to major national problems require congressional action, but Congress is seldom a fully cooperative partner with presidents. The stage is thus set for the kind of dramatic confrontations detailed above. This chapter begins by tracing the development of the chief executive's legislative role in the twentieth century and then presents an analysis of the constitutional relationship between the president and Congress. A discussion of the president's formal legislative powers and a description of presidential strategies to influence legislation follow. The chapter then analyzes what factors contribute to the success and failure of presidents in gaining their legislative goals.

Development of the President's Legislative Role

The Constitution, in Article 1, Section 8, grants Congress seventeen powers that cover a wide range of subjects—for example, levying and collecting taxes, borrowing money, and regulating foreign and interstate commerce—as well as the power to choose the means to execute the enumerated powers. Clearly, the Framers expected Congress, not the president, to have primary responsibility for formulating national policy and the president's legislative role to be minor. Until the twentieth century, most presidents limited their involvement in the congressional process. Even Thomas Jefferson and Abraham Lincoln, the two most inclined to lead Congress, encountered strong opposition, and their activism did not alter the pattern of congressional supremacy.[19]

Theodore Roosevelt and Woodrow Wilson greatly expanded the presidency's legislative role early in the twentieth century as the national government responded to the problems of industrialization and urbanization. Roosevelt worked closely with congressional leaders and sent several messages to Congress that defined a legislative program. He saw it as the duty of the president to "take a very active interest in getting the right kind of legislation."[20] Wilson, who as a political science professor had argued that strong presidential leadership of Congress was needed if the nation were to cope with its growing problems, took the lead in defining his program's goals, helped formulate bills, reinstated the practice abandoned by Jefferson of personally delivering the State of the Union message to Congress, used cabinet members to build congressional support for bills, and personally lobbied for some of his most important measures, such as the Federal Reserve Act and the Clayton Antitrust Act.[21] *(See the discussion in chapter 1.)*

Franklin D. Roosevelt undertook the next major expansion of the president's legislative role. Taking office in 1933, with the economy mired in the Great Depression, FDR called Congress into a special session; during a hundred-day period the president proposed, and Congress passed, legislation to meet the economic crisis. Together they overhauled the banking system, authorized a program of industrial self-government under the National Recovery Administration, buttressed farm income with the Agricultural Adjustment Act, regulated financial markets under the Truth in Securities Act, and created the Tennessee Valley Authority, a program of comprehensive development of one of the nation's most depressed areas. This period of unprecedented activity established the practice of assessing a new president's first one hundred days.

During the remainder of his first term, FDR continued to develop measures to promote soil conservation and restrict excess agricultural production; guarantee labor the right to organize and bargain collectively; and establish a system of social insurance to protect people against the loss of work due to economic slowdowns, physical disability, or old age. FDR established the expectation that the president would be actively involved at all stages of the legislative process by submitting a legislative program to Congress, working for its passage, and coordinating its implementation. Thus today's presidents behave much like FDR: they send Congress messages that analyze problems and outline proposed solutions, assign aides to monitor the bills and lobby for passage, ensure adherence to a common legislative program for the executive branch enforced through a central clearance process monitored by OMB,[22] and threaten to veto legislation that fails to meet presidential demands or that they regard as unwise or contrary to their purposes. Harry S. Truman and Dwight Eisenhower institutionalized the president's legislative role by creating structures and processes to assist in carrying it out on a systematic basis with help from the Bureau of the Budget (which became OMB) and the White House staff.[23]

By the mid-1960s, it appeared to some observers that the presidency now dominated the legislative process. In 1965, Samuel P. Huntington wrote, "[T]he congressional role in legislation has largely been reduced to delay and amendment." Such tasks as taking the initiative in formulating legislation, assigning legislative priorities, generating support for legislation, and determining final content had "shifted to the executive branch," which, in Huntington's view, had gained "at the expense of Congress."[24] Others argued that Congress remained vitally important to the process by constantly modifying and altering policy through appropriations, amendments, and renewals of statutory authorizations.[25]

Moreover, Congress and the president are not engaged in a zero-sum game in which the power of one necessarily decreases as the power of the other increases. Since 1933 Congress has increased its power by vastly expanding the subjects on which it has legislated. During this same time, presidents have also assumed greater responsibility as innovators of policy. In three brief periods of intense legislative activity—1933–1937, 1964–1965, and 1981—activist presidents (FDR, Lyndon Johnson, and Reagan) led responsive Congresses in the adoption of major changes in domestic policy. In the area of foreign policy, Congress responded to presidential leadership in establishing the role of the United States in world affairs during and immediately after World War II.

At times, Congress has responded to what was viewed as excessive presidential power. During the 1970s, for example, Congress expanded its control over the executive branch through increased use of the legislative veto *(see chapter 6)*, curbed presidential use of military force abroad with the War Powers Resolution *(see chapter 10)*, and strengthened its ability to determine federal spending by redesigning the congressional budget process *(see chapter 9)*.

All presidents since FDR, with the possible exception of Eisenhower, have aspired to lead Congress as a way to lead the nation. Some have succeeded temporarily; others have been totally unsuccessful. For example, in 1981, Reagan took command of bipartisan conservative congressional majorities, which passed his taxing and spending proposals and sharply altered the course domestic social and economic policy had followed since the 1930s.[26] But his period of dominance was short-lived; congressional critics of his policies regrouped in 1982, support among the Republicans sagged, and legislative concerns shifted as budget deficits soared to unprecedented levels. Reagan discovered, as had Roosevelt in 1937 and Johnson in 1966, that congressional approval of a president's program is not automatic. Congressional support must be cultivated and maintained and can rapidly disappear when conditions change. Reagan's immediate successor, George Bush, offered modest, rather than sweeping, initiatives, but he, too, could not develop sustained congressional support from a Democratic-controlled Congress. In contrast, congressional Democrats enacted much of Clinton's initial legislative agenda with only limited Republican help.[27] When Republicans won control of Congress in 1994, Clinton's agenda and strategies changed drastically, and the prolonged battles described earlier ensued.

Despite his much-publicized calls to reduce partisan conflict, George W. Bush initially advanced a notably conservative legislative agenda, reflecting Republican control of Congress. The dramatic party shift of Senator Jeffords forced the administration to reexamine its agenda and its tactics for winning congressional support. After the terrorist attacks of September 11, 2001, immeasurably strengthened his hand, Bush scored major successes on education reform, tax cuts, and foreign policy leadership. With the restoration of one-party government after the 2002 elections, he moved forward with his original agenda.

The Presidential-Congressional Relationship

Institutional competition between Congress and the presidency arises from the Constitution's separation of powers, but the Constitution also mandates a sharing of powers: joint action is required to authorize programs, appropriate money to pay for them, and levy taxes to provide the funds. Neither branch can achieve its goals or operate the government without the other. However, since 1970, presidential-congressional relations have been highly competitive because of heightened distrust between the branches and intensified party differences between presidents and members of Congress. Charles O. Jones describes the relationship as one in which "these separated institutions often *compete* for shared powers."[28]

Competition by Design: The Separation of Powers

James Madison's *Federalist* No. 51 makes it clear that the Framers had intended presidential-congressional conflict:

To what expedient . . . shall we finally resort, for maintaining in practice the necessary partition of power among the several departments, as laid down in the constitution? The only answer that can be given is . . . by so contriving the interior structure of the government as its several constituent parts may, by their mutual relations, be the means of keeping each other in their proper places. . . .

In order to lay a due foundation for that separate and distinct exercise of the different powers of the government, which to a certain extent is admitted on all hands to be essential to the preservation of liberty, it is evident that each department should have a will of its own. . . .

But the great security against a gradual concentration of the several powers in the same department consists in giving to those who administer each department the necessary constitutional means and personal motives to resist the encroachments of the others. . . . Ambition must be made to counteract ambition. The interests of the man must be connected with the constitutional rights of the place.[29]

The pattern of presidential-congressional relations has not been static. Some analysts point to a cyclical pattern of power aggrandizement by Congress or the presidency and a resurgence by the other that has operated from the Republic's beginning.[30] In the nineteenth century, the institutional surges and declines oscillated evenly within well-defined boundaries. However, U.S. economic, social, and technological transformations and emergence from international isolation during the twentieth century created conditions that called increasingly for executive, rather than legislative, decision making. The president can act more quickly, more decisively, and more consistently than Congress, which has difficulty ascertaining its institutional will and coherently pursuing its goals. Thus it can be argued that in the twentieth century, presidential surges have resulted in permanent expansions of executive power and presidential aggrandizements, such as Johnson's use of the war powers to involve the United States in the Vietnam War *(see chapter 10)* and Nixon's sweeping claims of executive privilege and his extensive impoundments of appropriated funds *(see chapter 6)*.

During the 1970s, Congress reasserted its constitutional authority in several areas and launched internal reforms, which continued throughout the 1980s and 1990s, that enhanced its legislative power.[31] Yet the nation found it needed presidential leadership to deal with difficult problems such as severe inflation, persistent budget deficits, economic interdependence, and international terrorism. Divided government prevailed throughout most of this period; congressional leaders provided a policy counterpoint to presidents from the other party. For example, Republicans followed their victory in the 1994 elections with a new collective assertiveness that threatened to undermine Clinton's leadership. Under the aggressive, ideologically conservative Speaker Newt Gingrich, House Republicans took action within the first hundred days of the new Congress on the ten priorities outlined in the *Contract with America,* an election manifesto most Republican candidates for the House had endorsed. Even this novel strategy to regain the legislative initiative did not restore congressional ascendancy as Senate Republicans pursued more moderate priorities and Clinton developed effective defensive tactics.[32]

The conflict between Congress and the presidency is not driven by partisan divisions alone. Even with a Congress controlled by his own party, George W. Bush has self-consciously sought to recover some of the ground his predecessors lost to assertive congresses in the years since Watergate. "The result has been the broadest expansion of White House power in decades: Bush has resisted sending documents or witnesses to Capitol Hill, imposed restrictions on access to the papers of former presidents and rapidly filled the confirmation pipeline with conservative candidates for judgeships."[33] Specifically, Vice President Cheney refused to submit information to the Government Accounting Office (GAO) when it sought documents on the energy task force he chaired; the administration refused to allow Director of Home Security Tom Ridge to testify before Congress to answer questions about the administration's antiterrorism strategy; and the administration invoked executive privilege—denying information to Congress to preserve the quality of advice the president receives—when it refused a House committee's request for documents related to a terminated Justice Department investigation.[34] Critics have been so concerned about decisions to delay declassifying documents from past administrations and making it easier to classify current information that they have concluded, "[T]his White House is obsessed with secrecy."[35] One legal expert wrote, "Bush wanted to not only revitalize executive privilege but also expand the scope of that power substantially."[36]

Conflicts from Constituency and Electoral Differences

In addition to institutional competition born of the separation of powers, conflict stems from the difference in the constituencies of the members of Congress and the president. The 535 congressional members represent constituencies that vary in geographic area, population, economic structure, and social composition. Every member depends for reelection on distinctive, constituency-based political forces, making all members necessarily narrow-minded in at least some policy orientations. Their claims to be acting in behalf of the national interest therefore must be judged in light of their constituency interests.

Congressional parties have the potential to overcome constituency-based fragmentation, but creating party unity is a struggle. Party leaders cannot command their members' votes, although the centralizing reforms of the 1980s and

1990s that were most evident in the House have given the Speaker limited power to speak on the chamber's behalf. The Senate majority leader remains heavily dependent on a stubbornly independent membership. Thus the national interest emerges in Congress through bargaining among members and blocs of members responsive to particular interests.

In contrast, presidents can point to the entire nation as their constituency and thus claim to speak authoritatively on behalf of the national interest or to act for various inarticulate and unorganized interests not adequately represented in Congress. Presidents can resist the demands of well-organized particular interests by posing as champions of the national interest, even though there may be times when they, too, respond to such pressures.

From 1946 to 1972, presidents took advantage of intraparty divisions to forge temporary majority coalitions to pass specific measures with bipartisan support. Congressional policymaking was deliberate, incremental, or piecemeal, and largely reactive to presidential leadership. Congress could not maintain consistency in its actions in different policy areas or cohesiveness within those areas. Speed, efficiency, consistency, and cohesiveness usually were lacking, except in a crisis.

After Nixon, however, presidents had less success in playing the national interest card, and party cohesion in Congress rose dramatically with a majority of one party confronting a majority of the other.[37] In part, this reflected the realignment of the South into a heavily Republican region so that the *conservative coalition,* the traditional alliance of Republicans with conservative southern Democrats, declined. It also reflected the growing capacity of party leaders to define a policy agenda with a distinctive ideological cast.

Changes in electoral politics also have widened the gap between presidents and Congress. Members of Congress are political entrepreneurs who routinely seek reelection through constituency-based electoral coalitions largely independent of party labels. Incumbents have been remarkably successful: since 1954, "an average of 93 percent of the House incumbents and 83 percent of the Senate incumbents who sought reelection were successful."[38] Members are nominated in direct primaries, their campaigns are financed heavily from nonparty sources, and they sustain electoral support through activities unrelated to party, such as providing service to constituents. Unlike parliamentary executives whose electoral success is directly linked to their party colleagues, presidents gain election on their own and seem to have less and less impact on the success of their copartisans in Congress. Presidential coattails—congressional seats won by candidates of the president's party because of strong public support—have nearly disappeared, and there are fewer seats in which the presidential victor's margin of victory exceeds that of the congressional candidates.[39] Both Bill Clinton and George W. Bush entered office with *negative coattails,* their parties losing seats in Congress as a result of the 1992 and 2000 elections. From 1956 to 1984, there was an increase in the number of constituencies supporting a presidential candidate of one party and electing members of Congress from the opposition, split-ticket voting, but that pattern has declined in the four most recent elections. This separation of presidential and congressional electoral coalitions means presidents can exert little leverage on members of their own parties by appealing to their shared electoral fates, and the potential to influence members of the opposition party has declined as well.

Divided Party Control of Government

Recent presidents have confronted a major strategic dilemma. Under the best of conditions, when a president's party controls both houses of Congress (since 1980, only two years for Clinton and two-and-one-half years for George W. Bush), party loyalty is a weak link. Even this connection is not available to a president faced with a Congress controlled by the opposition party. Since 1933, Democratic presidents have had to deal with an opposition Congress in 1947–1948 and 1995–2001, while Republican presidents have confronted full opposition control in all years except 1953–1954, 1981–1986, 2001–2002, and 2003–2005 (see Table 5-1).

Analysts differ sharply in their assessments of the consequences of divided partisan control. The critics of divided government argue that it renders unworkable the Constitution's already cumbersome and inefficient separation-of-powers structure.[40] Critics blame the large federal budget deficits of the late 1980s and 1990s on divided government, in which each branch has a stake in the failure of the other.[41] These critics also charge that divided government undermines electoral accountability because it is impossible for voters to hold either party responsible for policies adopted and results achieved since the last election.

Other researchers draw different conclusions. After a systematic empirical analysis of legislation and congressional investigations since World War II, David Mayhew concluded that it does not make "much difference whether party control of the American government happens to be unified or divided."[42] Morris Fiorina, acknowledging that divided government results in more "conflictual" presidential-congressional relations, asks whether its consequences are "necessarily bad."[43] Divided government may limit the potential for social gain through public policy, but it also limits potential loss through government action,[44] and divided government is the American electorate's way of establishing the coalition governments common in multiparty systems.[45] Divided government dominated presidential-congressional relations for most of the last quarter of the twentieth century and reemerged early in the twenty-first century.

Despite efforts to overcome internal fragmentation and fashion more coherent policy, Congress finds it difficult to compete with the relative decisiveness, cohesion, and consistency of the presidency as a national policy-making institution. Congress's oft-mentioned weaknesses—loosely structured congressional parties, party leaders with limited power, the absence of party discipline in congressional voting, the presence of strong committees and subcommittees, and the ambitions of individual members to enhance their reelection chances and to advance to higher office—may have been altered but the fundamental problems

Table 5-1   Partisan Control of the Presidency and Congress, 1933–2003

Dates	Presidency	Congress
1933–1946	Democratic	Democratic
1947–1948	Democratic	Republican
1949–1952	Democratic	Democratic
1953–1954	Republican	Republican
1955–1960	Republican	Democratic
1961–1968	Democratic	Democratic
1969–1976	Republican	Democratic
1977–1980	Democratic	Democratic
1981–1986	Republican	Senate-Rep. House-Dem.
1987–1992	Republican	Democratic
1993–1994	Democratic	Democratic
1995–2000	Democratic	Republican
2001 (through 6/6)	Republican	Republican
2001 (after 6/6)	Republican	Senate-Dem. House-Rep.
2003–	Republican	Republican

remain. The short-lived experiment with party government under Gingrich in 1995 is a case in point: many party members, worried about reelection, defied party leadership and moved to the center in 1996.

Even an internally fragmented Congress can be assertive, but its thrust is to negate or restrain, not direct, presidential action. At present, Congress values the function of "representation" over that of "lawmaking,"[46] which means it is responsive primarily to constituency interests and well-organized interest groups. It also means Congress is more comfortable with distributive policies and programs, which provide widespread benefits, than with redistributive policies, which change society's allocation of wealth and power. Ironically, presidents have assumed responsibility for exercising the lawmaking function that translates electoral mandates into policies with broad societal impact.

Patterns of Presidential-Congressional Policymaking

To make national policy, the president and Congress must resolve conflicts. Some analysts have identified patterns in this relationship, which vary according to issues, presidential leadership styles, and political context. Presidents tend to prevail in foreign and military policy and on those issues to which they attach high priority, such as Johnson's Great Society program.[47] Congress usually dominates on domestic policy, as it did in the 1970s, when it passed major legislation on the environment, consumer protection, and occupational safety; it also dominates on public works. Stalemate, in which differences prevent policy from moving forward, characterized much of the energy legislation proposed by presidents in the 1970s, as well as proposals for reducing the federal budget deficit in the 1980s and 1990s.

Occasionally, a proposal may be stalemated for years and then move rapidly to passage as conditions change or a new president takes office. For example, proposals for national health insurance had languished in Congress since first advanced by President Truman in 1946. The political climate turned favorable for liberal social legislation in 1964 and 1965, after JFK's assassination. Responding to Johnson's forceful leadership, Congress enacted legislation authorizing national health insurance for the elderly (Medicare). But progress at one point does not ensure later gains. An effort to establish national health care under the leadership of Bill and Hillary Clinton collapsed in 1993–1994, setting off a series of more limited proposals over the next decade to provide prescription drug coverage for senior citizens and revise Medicare.

Presidential ambition and leadership style can be important causes of conflict. An activist president committed to an extensive legislative program, such as FDR or Lyndon Johnson, normally tries to dominate Congress, whereas a less active president, such as Eisenhower, Ford, and the first President Bush, may be more inclined to cooperate with Congress or accept considerable congressional initiative in program development. The competitive setting affects how active a president will be. Presidents in the last two decades of the twentieth century confronted a significantly different strategic environment, one that curtailed their ambitions. Instead of seeking major legislative accomplishments of their own, they selectively facilitated pursuing items on the legislative agenda of the majority party, most often the opposition. Reagan, Bush, and Clinton were also forced to use veto threats more frequently than their predecessors to trigger negotiations.[48] Clinton, a moderate with an ambitious reform agenda, initially attempted to dominate Congress through the Democratic majority and its more liberal leaders, angering a small, but important, group of moderate and conservative Democrats.[49] After Republicans gained congressional majorities in 1995, Clinton portrayed their proposals as dangerously extreme but also established distance from liberal Democrats. This independence (called a strategy of "triangulation" as he positioned himself as the moderate force between liberal Democrats and conservative Republicans) enabled him to make alliances with any legislative group. For example, Clinton and congressional Republicans fashioned a major reform of national welfare policies in 1996 that angered many Democrats. Yet the latter rallied to his defense during the impeachment controversy.

George W. Bush entered office with a more ambitious legislative agenda than expected, given his narrow electoral victory. On some matters, most notably education reform, he sought common ground with Democrats, but on most issues (developing national energy and environmental policies, reforming Social Security, cutting taxes, reviewing national defense) he relied on support from conservative Republicans and a few conservative to moderate Democrats.[50] After Senator Jeffords's party switch, there were extensive discussions about how Bush's strategy would have to moderate.

Presidents have two sets of tools to accomplish legislative goals: (1) formal powers vested in the presidency by the Constitution and by statute, and (2) informal resources inherent in the office. Chief executives use formal and informal tools simultaneously. In the next two sections, each is examined separately.

The President's Formal Legislative Powers

Article II, Section 3, of the Constitution authorizes the president to call Congress into special session and requires that he "from time to time give to the Congress information of the state of the Union, and recommend to their consideration such measures as he shall judge necessary and expedient." Article I, Section 7, makes presidents direct participants in the legislative process by providing for their approval or disapproval (through the veto) of "every bill" and "every order, resolution, or vote to which the concurrence of the Senate and House may be necessary." These formal legislative powers are augmented by statutory delegations of authority to the president and to administrative agencies.

Messages to Congress and Agenda Setting

Although contemporary presidents have not gained much leverage by controlling congressional sessions, they have derived substantial power from their constitutional duty to report on the state of the nation and to recommend legislation. Since the Budget and Accounting Act of 1921 and the Employment Act of 1946, Congress has required that presidents annually submit messages explaining and justifying their budgets and reporting on the economy's condition. The State of the Union address and these fiscal messages enable presidents to set the congressional agenda by assessing the nation's problems and laying before Congress a comprehensive legislative program reflecting the president's goals and priorities. The messages are also efforts to enlist public opinion behind those priorities. (Chapter 8 examines the development of the president's domestic program.)

Individual members of Congress still introduce a multitude of bills independently of the president, but the chief executive is in a position to substantially influence, if not dominate, the congressional agenda. In a comprehensive review of how presidents helped set the congressional agenda from 1953–1996, George C. Edwards and Andrew Barrett drew important conclusions: (1) "The president can almost always place potentially significant legislation on the agenda of Congress"; (2) the president generates about one-third of "the total number of significant bills on the congressional agenda," ranging from a high of 68.6 percent under Kennedy in 1961–1963 to a low of 0 percent under Clinton in 1995–1996; (3) White House initiatives constitute a larger percentage of the congressional agenda under unified government than under divided government; and (4) "presidential initiatives are more likely than congressional initiatives to become law," with the success rate nearly twice as high under unified, rather than divided, government.[51]

Occasionally, Congress seeks to seize the full agenda-setting power. During the first Bush administration, the Democratic majority advanced proposals in areas the president did not address, such as civil rights and immigration. Even more dramatically, Speaker Newt Gingrich did much the same for Republicans following their 1994 victory, when Clinton's 1995 State of the Union address provided few specific legislative proposals and adopted a defensive posture toward the conservative agenda.[52] But these efforts to replace presidential leadership with a congressionally generated agenda proved difficult to sustain. Clinton reemerged as a legislative force in 1996 by taking advantage of the unpopularity of Republican tactics that closed the government and by adopting much of the Republicans' agenda.[53] Thus both recent efforts to wrest the agenda-making power from the president were short-lived.

The Veto Power

The Constitution establishes a major legislative role for presidents by requiring their approval of measures passed by Congress (Article 1, Section 7, Paragraph 2). Within ten days (Sundays excepted) after a bill or joint resolution is presented to the White House, the president must either (1) sign it into law; (2) disapprove or veto it and return it to the house of Congress in which it originated along with a message explaining this action; or (3) take no action on it, in which case it becomes law without the president's signature at the end of ten days. If Congress adjourns within that ten-day period and the president does not sign a measure awaiting action, then it does not become law and the president has exercised a "pocket veto." The president's action is final because adjournment prevents a measure from being returned to Congress for reconsideration and a possible override.

The veto is the president's ultimate legislative weapon; it carries the weight of two-thirds of the members of each house since that is what it takes to overturn a veto. In his classic treatise, *Congressional Government,* Woodrow Wilson noted the importance of the veto even when Congress dominated the national government: "For in the exercise of his power of veto, which is, of course, beyond all comparison, his most formidable prerogative, the President acts not as the executive but as a third branch of the legislature."[54] Andrew Jackson adopted a broad interpretation of the veto power, one giving him the right to reject legislation on the basis of its wisdom, merit, or equity as well as on constitutional grounds.[55] Presidents since 1933 have espoused this "tribunative" view of the veto and have used it often.

The data in Table 5-2 demonstrate a more extensive use of the veto by Roosevelt, Truman, and Eisenhower than by their successors. The data also show that from 1961 through 1995 Democratic presidents vetoed fewer bills than did the Republicans. Of course, Democrats controlled Congress throughout much of that time—the Senate from 1961 through 1980 and 1987 through 1994, and the House from 1961 through 1994. President Clinton exercised no vetoes during the 103d Congress, controlled by his own party, "the first time since the 32d Congress (1851–1852) and the administration of Millard Fillmore that an entire Congress served without prompting a presidential rejection."[56] George W.

Table 5-2   Presidential Vetoes of Bills, 1933–2003

President	Regular vetoes	Pocket vetoes	Total	Number of vetoes overridden	Percentage of vetoes overridden
FDR (1933–1945)	372	263	635	9	1.4
Truman (1945–1953)	180	70	250	12	4.8
Eisenhower (1953–1961)	73	108	181	2	1.1
Kennedy (1961–1963)	12	9	21	0	0.0
Johnson (1963–1969)	16	14	30	0	0.0
Nixon (1969–1974)	26	17	43	7	16.3
Ford (1974–1977)	48	18	66	12	18.2
Carter (1977–1981)	13	18	31	2	6.5
Reagan (1981–1989)	39	39	78	9	11.5
G. Bush (1989–1993)[a]	29	15	44	1	2.3
Clinton (1993–2001)	37	1	38	2	5.3
G. W. Bush (2001– [b]	0	0	0	0	NA

Source: www.clerkweb.house.giv/histhigh/congressional_History/vetoes.php, an authoritative compilation from the Congressional Research Service.

[a]President Bush attempted to pocket veto two bills during intrasession recess periods. Congress considered the two bills enacted into law because of the president's failure to return the legislation. The bills are not counted as pocket vetoes in this table.
[b]Through October 2003.

Bush accomplished the same feat with the 107th Congress. All of Clinton's thirty-seven vetoes occurred during the Republican-controlled Congresses of 1995–2000.

The veto power affects policy negatively and positively. It is negative by nature; once used, it signifies an impasse between the president and Congress, and prior policy is unchanged. Sometimes presidents find the veto the best means of emphatically communicating their intentions to Congress. Ford's sixty-six vetoes, for example, conveyed his social and economic policy preferences to a liberal Democratic Congress. The positive aspect of the veto lies in its use as a bargaining tool to "shape, alter, or deter legislation."[57] By threatening to exercise the veto presidents can define the limits of their willingness to compromise. They can state in advance what they will and will not accept, thereby reducing the likelihood of a showdown over a bill. Selective use of the threat to veto can be a means of avoiding, or of reconciling, greater conflict with Congress. For example, in 1989–1991, George Bush frequently threatened to veto bills as a way to "stimulate serious bargaining."[58] This was probably the goal of his son George W. Bush when he confronted a version of the "patients' bill of rights" passed by the Democratic-controlled Senate in June 2001. Part of a general effort he hoped to support, the bill had specific provisions he found unacceptable.

More generally, veto threats have become a major means for presidents to force opposition majorities to make policy concessions in the "high-intensity partisan environment" that has characterized Washington for the past two decades.[59] As the data in Table 5-3 illustrates, when confronted with Congresses controlled at least in part by an opposition majority, George H. W. Bush and

Table 5-3   Percentage of Major Measures Subject to Veto Threats in Selective Administrations

President	Congress (Years)	Veto Threats	Actual Vetoes
Nixon	91st (1969–70)	14%	5%
Reagan	97th (1981–82)	23	4
G. Bush	101st (1989–90)	52	9
Clinton	103rd (1993–94)	4	0
Clinton	104th (1995–96)	60	10
Clinton	105th (1997–98)	69	5

Source: Adapted from Barbara Sinclair, "Hostile Partners: The President, Congress, and Lawmaking in the Partisan 1990s," in *Polarized Politics: Congress and the President in a Partisan Era,* ed. Jon R. Bond and Richard Fleisher (Washington, D.C.: CQ Press, 2000), 145.

Clinton relied far more heavily on veto threats than had their predecessors Nixon and Reagan facing similar situations.

The President's Informal Legislative Influence

In 1960, Richard Neustadt startled students of the presidency when, in his now celebrated treatise *Presidential Power,* he asserted that the formal powers of the president amounted to little more than a clerkship. The Constitution, Neustadt argued, placed the president in a position of mostly providing services to other participants in national politics. "Presidential power," Neustadt declared, "is the power to persuade."[60] As the preceding examination of the president's formal legislative powers suggests, this is often the case in presidential relations with Congress. It is not enough for presidents to present a legislative program to Congress; they also must persuade congressional majorities to enact each statutory component of it. To do so, they employ mostly informal methods of influence. These tools can be used to exert indirect and direct pressure. Presidents may engage in bargaining, arm-twisting, and confrontation as general modes of working with Congress.

Indirect Influence

Presidents attempt to influence Congress indirectly through appeals to the public and by enlisting interest group support. A careful appeal, usually launched with a major public address, can generate pressure that causes Congress to act. Presidents are more likely to use popular appeals successfully in a crisis that appears to require congressional action. Success is less likely when public opinion is divided and substantial opposition to the president's position exists. In any case, presidents use such appeals selectively. Congress may object to the president's "going over its head" to the people too frequently. In doing so the president attacks, directly or by implication, the members' wisdom and motives.

George W. Bush used his first televised address to a joint session of Congress on February 27, 2001, to launch an aggressive, campaign-style strategy to win support for his major legislative proposals. The administration had already displayed impressive organization by focusing in successive weeks on education, religious faith-based charities, and tax cuts, critical elements of the Bush program. Moreover, it developed talking points for Republican members of Congress so the party message would be in harmony.[61] In the immediate aftermath of his speech (a striking contrast to Clinton's speeches in its brevity and emphasis on broad themes rather than policy specifics), Bush visited states where he had run well in 2000 and where key Democratic votes were located—Arkansas, Florida, Georgia, Iowa, Louisiana, Nebraska, North Dakota, Pennsylvania, and South Dakota. The president clearly wanted supporters attending the rallies to contact their Washington representatives. As Bush's spokesman explained, "Every day, in every way, whether it's at the White House or it's in travel, the president looks at how to get his plan across to the voters so voters can get their message to the Senators and congressmen."[62] The result of this carefully choreographed effort was the major tax-cut victory.

Marshaling the support of interest groups has become increasingly important to presidents. Since the mid-1960s, interest groups have grown in number and in the scope of their efforts to shape national policy. This growth stems in part from the declining role of parties as mechanisms for linking public opinion with public policy and in part from the increased participation of citizens in national policy politics. Interest groups facilitate this participation and take an active part in policymaking through informal alliances with congressional committees and administrative agencies.[63] Presidents find it helpful, if not necessary, to obtain interest group backing before moving on major legislation, and the national officers and federal relations directors of important groups often are consulted in the process of formulating such legislation. Clinton's failure to enlist the support of groups representing the pharmaceutical and insurance industries in his efforts at health care reform is widely credited with leading to the proposal's demise without even a vote. (Presidential liaison with interest groups is examined in chapters 3 and 8.)

Direct Influence

In their direct efforts to persuade Congress, presidents use two informal tools. They may grant or withhold services and amenities at their disposal as rewards for support or sanctions for lack of it, and they may become personally involved in the legislative process. Presidents vary greatly in their skills at exploiting these resources.

Favors. Bestowing or denying favors to members of Congress gives presidents a measure of leverage. Such favors may be given to an individual member or to important people in his or her constituency, or the favor may be of benefit to the constituency itself.[64] Favors given as rewards to congressional members include appointments with the president and other high-ranking officials; letters or telephone calls from the president expressing thanks for support; campaign assistance in the form of cash from the party's national committee, a presidential visit to the constituency, or a presidential endorsement; the opportunity to announce the award of federal grants to recipients in the constituency; invitations to be present at bill-signing ceremonies, to attend White House social functions, and to accompany the president on trips; and White House memorabilia such as pens and photographs. Favors for influential congressional constituents include appointments, appearances by administration officials at organization meetings, invitations to social functions, mailings on important occasions such as anniversaries, memorabilia, and VIP treatment such as White House mess privileges. To some extent, all members of Congress share in such benefits, but the president's supporters have readier access to them and feel more comfortable asking for them than do others.

The most important constituency-related rewards are jobs and projects. Congressional recommendations by members of the president's party greatly influence the selection of U.S. district court judges, U.S. attorneys, U.S. marshals, customs collectors for ports of entry, and a variety of lesser positions. Projects often regarded as rewards include military installations; research and administrative facilities; public works such as buildings, dams, and navigational improvements to rivers and harbors; government contracts with local firms; grants to local governments and educational institutions; and the deposit of federal funds in banks. Presidents cannot direct projects exclusively to their supporters, but they can exercise discretion whenever possible. As some federal activities are reduced in size, eliminated, or turned over to state governments, their potential for use as bargaining chips declines.

Involvement in the Legislative Process. Presidents can help themselves by becoming personally involved in the legislative process, but this requires knowledge and skill that are products of their political background, experience, and leadership style. To turn participation in the process to an advantage, a president should have knowledge of Congress and the Washington community, a sense of timing, a willingness to consult with congressional leaders and to give them notice in advance of major actions, sensitivity to the institutional prerogatives of Congress and to the personal and political needs of its members, and a balance between firmness and flexibility in resolving differences with Congress.

No president has ever possessed all of these skills. By most accounts, however, Lyndon Johnson exhibited more than any other modern president and made the most effective use of his involvement in the legislative process. He believed that constant, intense attention by presidents and their administrations was necessary to move their legislative programs through Congress.[65] His success in persuading Congress to enact the unfinished agenda of President Kennedy's New Frontier program and his own Great Society bills makes his approach to Congress a good example for study. It should be noted, however, that Johnson's legislative triumphs were aided in no small measure by contextual factors. In the aftermath of the Kennedy assassination, public support for the New Frontier measures was

President Lyndon B. Johnson included Dr. Martin Luther King, Jr. at the ceremony to commemorate the signing of the Voting Rights Act of 1965, one of the administration's major legislative accomplishments and a landmark of the civil rights movement.

high, and Johnson's landslide victory in the 1964 election also brought him large, liberal Democratic majorities in the House and the Senate.

Johnson grounded his legislative strategy in intimate knowledge of Congress as an institution and of its most influential members.[66] He knew whom to approach on specific issues and how to do so. Johnson also placed considerable emphasis on proper timing, waiting to send bills to Congress until the moment seemed right for the maximum support and least opposition. He sent bills singly, rather than in a package, so opposition would not develop automatically around several measures at once. In addition, he took care to consult with important senators and representatives in formulating legislation. Before sending a bill to Congress, the president and his top aides would hold a briefing for congressional leaders to explain its features. Cabinet secretaries were made responsible for the success of legislation in their areas, and the White House coordinated their efforts. Finally, when crucial votes were approaching on Capitol Hill, Johnson made intense personal appeals to the members whose votes served as cues for others and to members who were identified as uncommitted or wavering. Johnson sought to build congressional coalitions in support of his proposals. Through an analysis of head counts, used by Johnson's congressional liaison office to track

House members' positions on bills over time, Terry Sullivan found that the Johnson administration built coalitions not just by mobilizing friends, but even by "converting hard core opponents."[67]

When the Vietnam War changed the political context, Johnson's approach to congressional relations proved less effective. The president lost much of his touch with Congress as he became increasingly involved in foreign policy matters and as the momentum of the Great Society gave way to the unpopularity of the war. The loss of forty-eight Democratic seats in the House in the 1966 congressional elections also adversely affected Johnson's ability to push bills through Congress. Despite changes in the political environment, today's presidents might still benefit from emulating several features of Johnson's approach: gain detailed knowledge of Congress, respect its constitutional prerogatives, remain sensitive to its members' personal and constituency needs, and create the organizational and political capacity to build coalitions.

Despite making little effort to court Congress, Richard Nixon enjoyed modest legislative success early in his administration. His relations with Congress turned sour, however, when he challenged the Democratic majority by impounding, or refusing to spend, appropriated funds and by claiming substantial executive privilege under which administration officials refused to provide information to congressional committees. Like Johnson, Gerald Ford had intimate knowledge of Congress, and he worked to maintain good relations with its leaders. But as he confronted large, assertive Democratic majorities in both houses, his success was limited.

President Carter's inability to create a supportive climate in relations with the Hill is often cited as a reason for the limited success of some of his major legislative goals, such as welfare reform and a comprehensive energy conservation program. In contrast, President Reagan's congenial manner and relaxed style helped establish a generally positive, nonhostile attitude within Congress toward his legislative program, undoubtedly an important factor in the passage of tax-reform legislation in 1986. At critical points during the Ninety-ninth Congress, the tax bill seemed doomed, only to be resurrected as members responded to presidential appeals for what supporters termed an equitable tax system.[68]

A congenial climate with Congress may not always make a difference. The first President Bush, a former House member, maintained close contact with many of his one-time colleagues. But through the end of his third year, Bush had prevailed on fewer congressional roll calls than had his predecessors at similar points in their first terms.[69]

Although President Clinton lacked Washington experience, he had a close and cooperative relationship with the Democratic leadership during the 103d Congress (1993–1994).[70] His legislative achievements were substantial. In both 1993 and 1994, he won on 86.4 percent of the floor votes in Congress on which he took a position.[71] The list of major legislation enacted was impressive: his economic program, which included a major deficit reduction; family and medical leave legislation; reauthorization and revision of the Elementary and Secondary

Education Act; expansion of Head Start; motor-voter legislation; national service legislation; the Brady gun control bill; a comprehensive anticrime bill; the North American Free Trade Agreement (NAFTA); and legislation extending and expanding the General Agreement on Tariffs and Trade (GATT). Much of this list consists of Democratic initiatives that had been blocked during twelve consecutive years of Republican presidents.[72] Clinton failed, however, to secure passage of bills to reform health care and welfare, largely his own, rather than broadly shared, initiatives. Even though he was productive legislatively and attempted to address seriously the problems of declining middle-class incomes and economic dislocation stemming from changes in the U.S. economy and the globalization of markets, he received no political benefit from the voters in 1994.[73] Congenial relations with Congress were a distant memory by the time of the impeachment hearings, and Clinton's high first-year success rate on floor votes had hit a record low of 36.2 percent in 1995.[74] Clinton's experience demonstrates that presidential congeniality cannot compensate for philosophical differences, partisan divisions, and an assertive opposition.

Bush and Congress. George W. Bush, a Washington outsider without legislative experience, campaigned on a clear, limited agenda led by his promise to cut taxes and reform education, the issues most emphasized during his first year in office. Despite its controversial size and specific provisions, Bush secured passage of a $1.3 trillion, multiyear tax cut in May 2001, having relied on unified Republican support in the House and a few moderate Democrats in the narrowly divided (50–50) Senate. Education reform also seemed destined for early success based on a bipartisan coalition until the defection of Senator Jeffords, discussed earlier. With the Senate now controlled by the Democrats, action on education reform was delayed until the fall, and major provisions were modified to accommodate the new majority. By that time, the atmospherics in Congress had changed yet again. The terrorist attack of September 11, 2001, ushered in a nearly unprecedented era of "hyper bipartisanship," characterized by warm relations and regular meetings among all four party leaders and the president as well as near-unanimous votes on using force in Afghanistan, providing law enforcement officials with additional powers to combat terrorism (The Patriot Act), rebuilding New York City, and enhancing airport security.[75]

The love fest did not last long. Early in 2002, Bush and the Democrats locked horns over trade promotion authority, the new name for fast-track trade authority that allows presidents to negotiate trade agreements that will be moved through Congress quickly and without amendments. Bush ultimately won the battle in a dramatic 215–214 vote in the House.[76] The bigger battle, however, was over creation of a Department of Homeland Security, originally a Democratic proposal advanced in 2000 but embraced by the Bush administration in summer 2002. *(See chapter 6.)* This issue stood at the center of congressional politics during the lead-up to the midterm elections, with Senate Democrats insisting on a set of worker and union protections rejected by House Republicans and the president. When no final action could be taken, Bush made this the signature issue for the fall campaign when he launched an unprecedented effort in behalf of Republican candidates, contributing to victories that doubled the Republican advantage in the House (from 6 to 12 votes) and regained a Republican majority in the Senate. In the election aftermath, a lame duck session of Congress approved the Bush version of a Department of Homeland Security.

Despite the Republicans' renewed control of Congress, troubles lay ahead. A group of Republican Senators (including moderates Voinovich, Ohio; Snow, Maine; and Chafee, R.I.; as well as McCain, Ariz.) proved difficult votes for the majority to control and the minority Democrats exhibited greater unity than usual. The result was a major retreat on the administration's second tax-cut plan, reduced from $726 to $320 billion. Bush made every effort to win, mounting campaignlike efforts in the home states of reluctant Republicans and potentially vulnerable Democrats (Lincoln, Ark.; Nelson, Neb.), where he held rallies, generated media attention, and encouraged interest group activities. His efforts were ultimately unsuccessful. Nonetheless, Bush has demonstrated an astute strategic sense: he has adopted bold goals, compromised with Democrats when necessary (education reform and trade promotion authority), but generally relied on party unity in the House to strengthen his hand in negotiations with the more moderate Senate, where Democrats enjoy procedural opportunities to block action.[77] Despite the setback in not getting the tax reforms he had proposed, he declared victory and moved on.

Modes of Presidential-Congressional Relations

In their relations with Congress, presidents follow certain modes or patterns of behavior: bargaining, arm-twisting, and confrontation. Bargaining is the predominant mode, and occasionally the president bargains directly with members whose support is deemed essential to a bill's passage. In May 1981, for example, the Reagan administration agreed to revive a costly program to support the price of sugar in exchange for the votes of four Democratic representatives from Louisiana (where sugar is a key crop) on a comprehensive budget reduction bill.[78]

Presidents usually try to avoid such explicit bargains because they have limited resources for trading, and the desire among members for these resources is keen. Moreover, Congress is so large and its power so decentralized that presidents cannot bargain extensively over most bills. In some instances, the president may be unable or unwilling to bargain. Fortunately, rather than a quid pro quo exchange of favors for votes, much presidential-congressional bargaining is implicit, generalized trading in which tacit exchanges of support and favors occur.

If bargaining does not result in the approval of their proposals, presidents may resort to stronger methods, such as arm-twisting, which involves intense, even extraordinary, pressure and threats. In one sense, it is an intensified extension of bargaining, but it entails something more—a direct threat of punishment if the member's opposition continues. Among modern presidents, Johnson was perhaps the most frequent practitioner of arm-twisting. When gentler efforts failed, or when a once-supportive member opposed him on an important issue, Johnson resorted to tactics such as deliberate embarrassment, threats, and reprisals. In contrast, Eisenhower was most reluctant to pressure Congress. Arm-twisting is understandably an unpopular tactic and, if used often, creates resentment and hostility. Still, judicious demonstration that sustained opposition or desertion by normal supporters will exact costs strengthens a president's bargaining position.

Presidents unable to gain support through bargaining and arm-twisting may adopt a confrontational strategy. Confrontation might consist of appeals to the public, direct challenges to congressional authority, assertion of presidential prerogative, or similar tactics. Nixon confronted Congress often and more sharply than any other modern president. Disdaining the role of legislative coalition builder, he saw himself as deserving of congressional support by virtue of his election mandate and his constitutional position as chief executive. The most visible confrontation occurred between 1971 and 1973, when he challenged congressional spending decisions at variance with his budget proposals by impounding more than $30 billion that Congress had appropriated. Nixon also claimed Congress could not question thousands of executive branch officials or have access to routine documentary information.

A strategy of confrontation is unlikely to result in sustained congressional responsiveness to presidential initiatives. Congress has constitutional prerogatives and constituency bases of support that enable it to resist presidential domination. The imperatives for cooperation between the two branches are so great that most presidents try to avoid such confrontations, entering them only when the presidency's constitutional integrity is at issue.

To oversee this system of bargaining, negotiation, and occasional confrontation, Eisenhower established in the White House an Office of Legislative Affairs, staffed by knowledgeable specialists who lobbied legislators in behalf of the administration's program. Every administration since has maintained such a unit. Although some administrations have made subtle changes in assignments and techniques, the activities have become largely institutionalized, reflecting a clear set of expectations about how staffers will conduct the job. With such a staff in place, there is continuity in legislative-executive relations and a reduction in the variation resulting from presidents' individual abilities and skills.[79]

Explaining Presidents' Legislative Success

If all presidents approach Congress with the same formal powers and informal tools of influence and use well-established staff arrangements to oversee day-to-day relations, what accounts for their legislative successes or failures? Studies have identified at least six factors that affect presidents' ability to achieve their legislative goals: partisan and ideological support in Congress, popular support, style in dealing with Congress, the contexts in which they must operate, cyclical trends in presidential-congressional relations, and the content of their domestic program. It is not possible to assess the relative importance of each factor thoroughly, but all have come into play since 1933, when FDR inaugurated the modern legislative presidency. The first five factors will be examined here; the sixth, in chapter 8.

Congressional Support

Support in Congress depends heavily on the size and cohesiveness of a president's party strength there. George Edwards has shown that from 1961 through 1986, three Democratic and three Republican presidents consistently received strong support on roll call votes from their parties' congressional members.[80] John Kessel notes that presidents' partisans have recently provided higher levels of support: from 1953 through 1980, presidents received support 66 percent of the time from fellow partisans in the House and Senate; that level rose to 75 percent from 1981 through 1996.[81] Edwards and Jon Bond and Richard Fleisher have found, however, that support may vary by issue. Republican presidents receive stronger support overall on foreign policy legislation than on domestic policy issues, primarily because of increased backing from liberal Democrats on foreign issues.[82]

It is interesting to note that partisan support for presidents in Congress apparently owes little to the storied effect of presidential coattails. The ability of presidents to transfer their electoral appeal to congressional candidates of their parties declined steadily from 1948 to 1988.[83] Even in 1984, when Reagan won a landslide victory over the Democratic candidate, Walter Mondale, the measurable coattail effect was weak, though it was stronger than in 1980 and 1988.[84] Edwards attributes the decline to increased split-ticket voting, the reduced competitiveness of House seats, and the electoral success of incumbents since 1952.

Despite the shortening of coattails in presidential election years, some presidents have sought to improve their chances of success by campaigning for candidates from their own party during midterm elections. Such efforts are usually unsuccessful, but George W. Bush demonstrated that it can be done. (See chapter 3.) Bush sought to transfer his own relatively high public approval to Republican candidates by personalizing the election. By doing so, he could claim partial credit for bucking the historical trend in which members of the president's party lose seats in the midterm election, a trend violated over the past century only in 1934 and 1998.[85]

Because presidents cannot rely on full support from their own party members, they must build coalitions by obtaining support from some opposition members.[86] Coalition building is especially important when the opposition controls one or both houses—the situation for most presidents since 1969. Several factors other than party membership influence congressional voting decisions, including constituency pressures, state and regional loyalty, ideological orientations, and interest group influence.[87] On many occasions, presidents have received crucial support from the opposition. Eisenhower successfully sought Democratic votes on foreign policy matters; Republicans contributed sizable pluralities to the enact-ment of civil rights legislation in the 1960s; conservative Democrats, mainly from the South, often supported the domestic policy proposals of Nixon and Ford; con-servative Democrats in the House were essential to Reagan's 1981 legislative vic-tories; Clinton depended on Republican support for the passage of NAFTA and GATT; and George W. Bush received critical, though limited, support from Demo-crats on his tax-reduction and education-reform proposals.

Despite continuing instances when presidents assemble bipartisan coalitions to achieve legislative goals, there is evidence that over the past two decades the opportunity to build bipartisan coalitions has sharply declined. Internal congres-sional reforms and heightened unity among partisans in Congress have made the task of winning in Congress much more difficult.[88]

In summary, congressional support for the president is built primarily on fel-low partisans, but party affiliation by itself is seldom a sufficient basis for the enactment of the president's program. Constituency, regional, and ideological pressures reduce the number of partisan backers, and the president must try to attract support from opposition members on the basis of ideological orientations and constituency and regional interests. Thus a president's legislative success "is mainly a function of the partisan and ideological makeup of Congress."[89]

Popular Support

The prestige, or popular support, of presidents also affects congressional re-sponses to their policies. It has been widely observed that a popular president enjoys substantial leeway in dealing with Congress, and a president whose pop-ularity is low or falling is likely to encounter considerable resistance. Bond and Fleisher argue, however, that popular support is only marginally related to pres-idential success on congressional floor votes.[90] Similarly, Edwards finds that pub-lic approval is a background resource that provides presidents with leverage, but not control, over Congress.[91]

Although popularity is clearly, if marginally, related to congressional support for the president's legislative program and can be used as a tool of influence, it cannot be easily manipulated. There are factors, such as the erosion of popular support over time and the economy's condition, over which the president has no control.[92] Presidents can take advantage of their popularity when it is high to influence congressional opinion, as Johnson did in 1964 and 1965 and Reagan did in 1981 and, to a lesser extent, in 1985 and 1986 (his popularity then plum-meted because of the Iran-contra affair). George W. Bush sought to draw upon his strong approval ratings in this way in 2003 but had to retreat on the size and content of his tax-cut proposals and lost on the issue of oil drilling in Alaska's Arctic National Wildlife Refuge.

Presidential Style and Legislative Skills

The president's style in dealing with Congress has long been considered an important determinant of legislative success. Style encompasses the degree to which presidents are accessible to members; their interactions with, and sensitivity to, the members; and the extent of their involvement in the legislative process.[93]

Modern presidents have varied greatly in their accessibility. Johnson and Ford were usually available to members and leaders, whereas Nixon was remote and inaccessible most of the time. Kennedy and Reagan frequently sought contact through telephone calls. The senior George Bush maintained a wide range of congressional friends and acquaintances but was criticized for not consulting enough with influential party and committee leaders. During his first two years, Clinton was so accessible and made such efforts to cultivate personal relationships that his effectiveness may have been impaired.[94] That accessibility lessened when he was working with an assertive Republican majority and with Democrats who distanced themselves from a president they regarded as a political liability. George W. Bush met with a broad cross-section of representatives and senators during his first months in office (more than ninety members in his first week, including many Democrats)[95] as he tried to set a nonconfrontational tone in the nation's capital, and his relations with Democratic leaders improved markedly for several months after 9/11. Although accessibility on demand is not feasible because of the pressures on a president's time, it enhances congressional support if members know they can reach the president on matters of great importance to them. Accessibility to congressional leaders of both parties is particularly important if the president is to work effectively with Congress.

It is not clear how much interpersonal relations influence congressional support, but they are a distinctive part of a chief executive's style and affect the disposition of leaders and members toward the president. If nothing else, popularity with members of Congress can improve relations even when there are sharp differences over issues. If the president has strained personal relations, sustained congressional support will be difficult to achieve even when the president's party has a majority and many members share his goals.

Similarly, presidential involvement in the legislative process varies. Kennedy, Johnson, Ford, and Reagan maintained close interest in the course of legislation, and Johnson actively directed its progress on occasion. In contrast, Eisenhower, Nixon, and Carter were more detached. George H. W. Bush displayed a varied pattern of interest in the progress of legislation, ranging from detachment to active engagement during his four years, as during the 1991 budget negotiations. Clinton developed a reputation for making concessions so early in negotiations that he drew criticism for making it "too easy" for his opponents,[96] suggesting he was not an effective legislative tactician. George W. Bush appears to delegate most of these decisions to the experts in his administration, relying more heavily on his vice president's advice and assistance than did most of his predecessors. Unlike most vice presidents, Dick Cheney has an office on both the Senate and House sides of the Capitol building. Known briefly as the "fifty-first senator" because of his critical role in casting the tie-breaking vote before Republicans lost the Senate majority, Cheney attends weekly Republican policy meetings in the House and the Senate and regularly makes himself available to listen to congressional concerns. As Sen. Susan Collins, R-Maine, told the *New York Times*, "When I convey my views to the vice president, it's equivalent virtually to the president."[97] Cheney reportedly played a critical role in breaking the deadlock between House and Senate Republicans to gain passage of the 2003 tax reduction.[98]

Conventional wisdom holds that presidents' legislative skills are major determinants of congressional support for their programs, but empirical analyses provide little support for that argument. According to Edwards and others, presidential legislative skills are effective at the margins of congressional coalition building, not at the core.[99] Presenting a somewhat different argument, Mark Peterson states that presidents have some, but not unlimited, control over the timing, priorities, and size of their programs. By clearly establishing their priorities and adjusting their "ambitions to fit the opportunities of the day," he concludes, presidents can be perceived as successful leaders of Congress.[100] If nothing else, these analyses should caution observers against uncritical acceptance of personalized explanations of presidential success in Congress and encourage the search for other influences.

Contextual Factors

Most students of presidential-congressional relations agree that contextual factors over which the president has virtually no control—such as the structure of political institutions and processes, public opinion, the alignment of political and social forces, economic and social conditions, and long-term trends in the political system—are more important than legislative skills as determinants of congressional decisions. For example, the cultural context of American politics is a source of frustration for presidents attempting to influence Congress. Edwards posits that phenomena such as extremely high and often contradictory public expectations of presidential performance, individualism, and skepticism of authority are powerful constraints on presidential leadership.[101] Bond and Fleisher argue that Congress-centered variables, such as the partisan and ideological predispositions of members and leaders, determined by the outcome of the last election, are of greater importance than presidency-centered variables in explaining presidential influence in Congress.[102]

Taking a middle position, Peterson provides the most comprehensive and extensive analysis of contextual factors affecting presidential success in Congress. He identifies four contexts that shape congressional action on presidential programs: (1) the "pure context," which includes the "institutional properties" of Congress, political parties, and interest groups and over which the president has little influence and no control; (2) the "malleable context," which consists of "dynamic" political conditions resulting from electoral cycles and economic conditions and over which the president has "greater but unpredictable influence" and no control; (3) the "policy context"—a context the president can influence and to some extent control by making "strategic choices" in developing an agenda—which includes the consequence of various proposals for the political system, the relative importance of proposals for presidential policy goals, and the controversiality of proposals; and (4) the "individual context," which includes personal attributes, such as style and skills, and the choices the president makes concerning the organization of the presidency for the exercise of influence that distinguish the president and the administration.[103]

However one defines and classifies the contexts that affect the president's influence or success in Congress, it is important to recognize that they function to provide both constraints upon and opportunities for the exercise of presidential leadership. To a considerable extent, the president can do little to alter most of these contexts. What a president can do is take maximum advantage of the opportunities they present. In doing so, the chief executive can act as a facilitator who encourages change but not as a director who determines it.

Cyclical Trends

Long-term cyclical fluctuations in presidential and congressional power also appear to affect the fate of specific presidential programs. In 1933, FDR initiated a period of presidential ascendancy that lasted until Nixon and the Watergate scandal. During that time, Congress made extensive delegations of power to the president and to executive branch agencies, presidents assumed responsibility for legislative leadership, Congress acquiesced in presidential domination of foreign and military policy, and the public looked to the presidency more than to Congress to solve the nation's problems.[104] The president and Congress clashed often during that period, but the dominant trend was one of presidential aggrandizement. When conflict occurred, Congress usually took defensive stands against presidential assertiveness.

In 1973, Congress moved to reassert its constitutional prerogatives after being angered over the conduct of the war in Southeast Asia and President Nixon's assertion of budget impoundment powers and executive privilege. Seizing the opportunity afforded by Nixon's preoccupation with Watergate and the plunge in public support, Congress enacted the War Powers Resolution of 1973, the Budget and Impoundment Control Act of 1974, and the National Emergencies Act of 1976, major elements in a resurgence designed to restrain presidential power.[105] In 1974, the House Judiciary Committee approved three impeachment charges against Nixon, who resigned on August 9 before the House could act on them. His two immediate successors, Gerald Ford and Jimmy Carter, had to deal with a Congress intent on curbing presidential power and retaining the constitutional parity with the president it had at least partially regained. This period of congressional resurgence was marked by increased skepticism of claims for presidential prerogative, careful scrutiny of presidential proposals, demands for more extensive White House consultation with congressional leaders, and more exacting senatorial confirmation hearings on presidential appointments.

With Reagan, Congress was more willing to accept presidential policy leadership and less assertive in insisting on its institutional prerogatives. The presidential-congressional relationship did not, however, return to the one that prevailed under the "imperial presidency". *(See chapter 1.)*[106] Reagan's relationship with Congress bent, but did not break, in 1987, following Democratic successes in the 1986 congressional elections and public disenchantment with his detached leadership, which the Iran-contra affair revealed as resting on too much delegation of presidential authority.

Presidents Bush and Clinton had stormy relationships with Congress over the budget. In fall 1990, Bush became embroiled in a battle with members from both parties over the deficit in the 1991 budget. In October, a coalition of very liberal Democratic and very conservative Republican House members rejected a bipartisan plan negotiated by the administration and congressional leaders. Amid bitter exchanges within both parties, a compromise was reached. But even as that battle ended, a new one began, as most congressional Democrats and some Republicans sharply questioned Bush's handling of the Persian Gulf crisis and pressed him for a congressional vote of approval before initiating military action against Iraq. Although the administration insisted it had authority to initiate such action, Congress passed a resolution authorizing the use of U.S. forces to implement UN resolutions calling on Iraq to leave Kuwait or face economic sanctions and, if necessary, military action. Clinton's struggle was far more bitter and protracted. His battle with Congress over the 1996 budget escalated to new extremes with the two government shutdowns. The remainder of 1996 proved to be a temporary, election-year truce that provided new grist for postelection congressional investigations of Clinton-Gore fund-raising abuses. Conflict between the president and Congress escalated to new heights in 1998–1999 with the impeachment inquiry.

As noted above, George W. Bush's principal problem was with his party's moderates. Bush initially seemed intent on pursuing a more inclusive approach to working with Congress, one that would rest on cooperation with Democrats, but he increasingly relied on a strong conservative base in the House to achieve his goals. Republican moderates felt excluded, most dramatically illustrated by the Jeffords defection but also visible in problems with other Republican moderates over the 2003 tax proposals. In a closely balanced Congress, those in the middle may become objects for appeals from both sides and so wield decisive power, or they may be left out amid the ideological wrangling of extremes.

Conclusion

The experiences of recent presidents in their relations with Congress provide a few lessons. These presidents have found success far from automatic. It requires consultation before and during legislative consideration as well as a willingness to negotiate and bargain with Congress. Legislative proposals must be coordinated between the White House and the executive departments and agencies. More important, cooperation between the president and congressional leaders and between the institutional presidency and Congress is essential. The constitutional separation of powers does not allow the two branches to operate independently; rather, it requires that they exercise their shared powers jointly.[107]

The constitutional separation of powers requires cooperation but ensures conflict. The Framers sought to prevent tyranny by establishing a balance between executive and legislative power. But this relationship is continually in flux. First one branch has expanded its authority; then the other branch has reasserted its prerogatives, recaptured lost powers, and acquired new ones. The cycle of institutional aggrandizement, decline, and resurgence reflects certain strengths and weaknesses in the presidency and Congress and the respective abilities of the branches to respond to social forces, economic conditions, and political change.

The need for presidential-congressional cooperation is clear, but there are few ways of obtaining it other than through consultation involving persuasion and bargaining. Presidents cannot command congressional approval of their proposals any more than Congress can direct presidents in the exercise of their constitutional powers. The threat of government stalemate is always present, and more often than not policy is an unsatisfactory compromise of presidential and various congressional viewpoints.

As the United States moves through its third century of operation, the relationship between the president and Congress will be characterized—as it is today—by a degree of stability provided by the Constitution as well as by adaptations to social, economic, and political change.

NOTES

1. Alissa J. Rubin, "Congress Readies Budget Bill for President's Veto Pen," *Congressional Quarterly Weekly Report,* November 18, 1995, 3512.

2. Alfred Hill, "The Shutdowns and the Constitution," *Political Science Quarterly* (summer 2000): 274. Also see Peri E. Arnold, "Clinton and Institutionalized Presidency," in *The Postmodern Presidency,* ed. Steven E. Schier (Pittsburgh: University of Pittsburgh Press, 2000), 28–31.

3. Starr also investigated the firing of White House employees in the travel office ("Travelgate"), the potential abuse of FBI files by the Clinton White House ("Filegate"), and the suicide of White House counsel Vincent J. Foster.

4. Carl M. Cannon, "So Very, Very Tired," *National Journal,* February 6, 1999, 318–322.

5. "Mr. Ruff for the Defense," editorial, *New York Times,* January 20, 1999, A30.

6. Arnold, "Clinton and the Institutionalized Presidency," 31.

7. Evan Thomas, "Acquittal: The Inside Story," *Newsweek,* February 22, 1999, 24–31; Kirk Victor and Carl M. Cannon, "Promise and Peril," *National Journal,* January 23, 1999, 170–175.

8. The results of the 2000 congressional elections: House Republicans 221, House Democrats 212, independents 2, one voting with each party caucus; Senate Republicans 50, Senate Democrats 50. The Senate tie produced a Democratic-controlled Senate for three weeks while Vice President Gore voted with the Democrats, followed by Republican control after inauguration day, when Vice President Cheney voted with the Republicans.

9. Susan Crabtree, "Bush's Charm Offensive Suffers Slight Setback," *Roll Call*, February 5, 2001; Mark Lacey, "Bush to Attend Democratic Caucuses," *New York Times*, January 27, 2001, A11; David E. Sanger and Alison Mitchell, "Bush, the Conciliator, Meets with Democrats," *New York Times*, February 3, 2001, A10.

10. James P. Pfiffner, *The Strategic Presidency*, 2d ed. rev. (Lawrence: University Press of Kansas, 1996), ix. For a full discussion of the "cycle of decreasing influence" that underlies the need to "move it or lose it" at an administration's outset, see Paul C. Light, *The President's Agenda: Domestic Policy Choice from Kennedy to Reagan*, rev. ed. (Baltimore: Johns Hopkins University Press, 1991), 36–37.

11. Richard E. Cohen and David Baumann, "The GOP's Drive to Deliver," *National Journal*, May 12, 2001, 1402–1403. Ultimately, five Democrats supported the Bush budget plan, which included a large tax cut. The partisan conflict was intense, however, with Vice President Cheney casting two tie-breaking votes to keep the budget on track.

12. David E. Sanger, "President's Signature Turns Broad Tax Cut, and a Campaign Promise, into Law," *New York Times*, June 8, 2001, A18.

13. Frank Bruni and David E. Sanger, "Bush Defends His Stance Despite Stinging Defection," *New York Times*, May 25, 2001, A18; Katharine Q. Seelye and Adam Clymer, "Senate Republicans Step Out and Democrats Jump In," *New York Times*, May 25, 2001, A1.

14. Transcript of James M. Jeffords's announcement, *New York Times*, May 25, 2001, A18.

15. Richard L. Berke, "A Question of Governing from the Right," *New York Times*, May 25, 2001, A1.

16. Dana Milbank and Jim VandeHei, "Bush Retreat Eased Bill's Advance," *Washington Post*, May 23, 2003, A5; David E. Rosenbaum and David Firestone, "$318 Billion Deal Is Set in Congress for Cutting Taxes," *New York Times*, May 22, 2003, www.nytimes.com/2003/05/22/politics/22TAX.html.

17. David E. Rosenbaum, "A Tax Cut Without End," *New York Times*, May 23, 2003, www.nytimes.com/2003/05/23/national/23ASSE.html.

18. Others had suggested that the honeymoon ended when Bush initiated a hard-hitting campaign in early March 2001 to secure passage of the tax-cut proposal. Jeffrey Bell, "Keep Up the Tough Talk, Mr. Nice Guy," *Washington Post*, March 4, 2001, B1.

19. Stephen J. Wayne, *The Legislative Presidency* (New York: Harper and Row, 1978), 8–12.

20. Theodore Roosevelt, *Autobiography* (New York: Macmillan, 1913), 292.

21. Woodrow Wilson, *Constitutional Government in the United States* (1908; reprint, New York: Columbia University Press, 1961).

22. Richard E. Neustadt, "The Presidency and Legislation: The Growth of Central Clearance," *American Political Science Review* (September 1954): 641–670.

23. Richard E. Neustadt, "The Presidency and Legislation: Planning the President's Program," *American Political Science Review* (December 1955): 980–1018; Wayne, *The Legislative Presidency*; Larry Berman, *The Office of Management and Budget and the Presidency* (Princeton: Princeton University Press, 1979); Light, *The President's Agenda*.

24. Samuel P. Huntington, "Congressional Responses to the Twentieth Century," in *The Congress and America's Future*, ed. David B. Truman (Englewood Cliffs, N.J.: Prentice Hall, 1965), 23.

25. Ronald C. Moe and Steven C. Teel, "Congress as Policy-Maker: A Necessary Reappraisal," *Political Science Quarterly* (fall 1970): 443–470; John R. Johannes, *Policy Innovation in Congress* (Morristown, N.J.: General Learning Press, 1972); Gary Orfield, *Congressional Power: Congress and Social Change* (New York: Harcourt Brace Jovanovich, 1975).

26. In the Senate, the Republicans had a 53–47 majority. In the House, the 192 Republicans, who voted together on the major elements of President Reagan's economic legislation in a remarkable display of cohesion, were joined by a sizable bloc of conservative southern Democrats called the "Boll Weevils." In both chambers, Republicans and conservative Democrats maintained voting cohesion that enabled the majorities to enact the Reagan program.

27. For example, Clinton's budget proposals in 1993 passed by a single vote in both the House and the Senate without any support from Republicans. Barbara Sinclair, "Trying to Govern Positively in a Negative Era," in *The Clinton Presidency: First Appraisals*, ed. Colin Campbell and Bert A. Rockman (Chatham, N.J.: Chatham House, 1995), 121. Also see Barbara Sinclair, "The President as Legislative Leader," in *The Clinton Legacy*, ed. Colin Campbell and Bert A. Rockman (Chatham, N.J.: Chatham House, 2000), 72–83.

28. Charles O. Jones, *The Presidency in a Separated System* (Washington, D.C.: Brookings, 1994), 16.

29. Alexander Hamilton, John Jay, and James Madison, *The Federalist Papers* (New York: Modern Library, 1938), 335–337.

30. Lawrence C. Dodd, "Congress and the Quest for Power," in *Congress Reconsidered*, ed. Lawrence C. Dodd and Bruce I. Oppenheimer (New York: Praeger, 1977), 298–302.

31. James L. Sundquist, *The Decline and Resurgence of Congress* (Washington, D.C.: Brookings, 1981); Richard S. Conley, *The Presidency, Congress, and Divided Government: A Postwar Assessment* (College Station, Tex.: Texas A&M University Press, 2003), 20, 24–26.

32. David S. Cloud, "Republicans Pushing the Envelope with Confrontational Approach," *Congressional Quarterly Weekly Report*, August 5, 1995, 2331–2334.

33. Mike Allen, "Counsel to Assertive Presidency," *Washington Post*, May 19, 2003, A17.

34. Joel D. Aberbach, "The State of the Contemporary American Presidency: Or, Is Bush II Actually Ronald Reagan's Heir?" in *The George W. Bush Presidency: First Appraisals*, ed. Colin Campbell and Bert A. Rockman (Chatham, N.J.: Chatham House, 2003), chap. 11. My thanks to Professor Aberbach for providing me with a prepublication copy of his essay.

35. "Secrecy: The Bush Byword," editorial, *New York Times*, March 28, 2003, www.nytimes.com/2003/03/28/opinion/28FR13.html.

36. Mark J. Rozell, *Executive Privilege: Presidential Power, Secrecy, and Accountability*, 2d ed. rev. (Lawrence: University Press of Kansas, 2002), 147.

37. Conley, *The Presidency, Congress, and Divided Government*, 22.

38. Paul R. Abramson, John H. Aldrich, and David W. Rohde, *Change and Continuity in the 2000 and 2002 Elections* (Washington, D.C.: CQ Press, 2003), 199. For 2000, 97.8 percent of House incumbents and 78 percent of the Senate incumbents were successful.

39. Conley, *The Presidency, Congress, and Divided Government*, 14–19.

40. Among the leading critics of divided government are James L. Sundquist, "Needed: A Political Theory for the New Era of Coalition Government in the United States," *Political Science Quarterly* (winter 1988–1989): 613–635; Lloyd N. Cutler, "To Form a Government," *Foreign Affairs* 59 (fall 1980): 126–143; Cutler, "Now Is the Time for All Good Men," *William and Mary Law Review* 30 (fall 1989): 387–402; and Michael L. Mezey, *Congress, the President, and Public Policy* (Boulder: Westview, 1989).

41. Gary W. Cox and Samuel Kernell, "Conclusion," in *The Politics of Divided Government*, ed. Gary W. Cox and Samuel Kernell (Boulder: Westview, 1991), 242–243. Also see Matthew D. McCubbins, "Government on Lay-Away: Federal Spending and Deficits under Divided Party Control," in *Politics of Divided Government*, 113–153.

42. David R. Mayhew, *Divided We Govern: Party Control, Lawmaking, and Investigations, 1946–1990* (New Haven: Yale University Press, 1991), 198.

43. Morris Fiorina, *Divided Government,* 2d ed. (Boston: Allyn and Bacon, 1996), 107, 108.

44. Ibid., 110.

45. Ibid., chap. 7.

46. Roger H. Davidson and Walter J. Oleszek, *Congress and Its Members,* 8th ed. (Washington, D.C.: CQ Press, 2002), chap. 1.

47. The main components of the Great Society were the Economic Opportunity Act of 1964, which launched a "war on poverty"; the Civil Rights Act of 1964; the Voting Rights Act of 1965; the Elementary and Secondary Education Act of 1965; and the Medicare Act of 1965.

48. Conley, *The Presidency, Congress, and Divided Government,* 44–45.

49. This discussion follows Sinclair, "Trying to Govern Positively," 91–119.

50. Juliet Eilperin, "Bush to Woo Democratic Rank-and-File," *Washington Post,* January 22, 2001, A1.

51. George C. Edwards III and Andrew Barrett, "Presidential Agenda Setting in Congress," in *Polarized Politics: Congress and the President in a Partisan Era,* ed. Jon R. Bond and Richard Fleisher (Washington, D.C.: CQ Press, 2000), 120, 122, 127.

52. David S. Cloud, "Lack of New Proposals Reflects New Dynamic on the Hill," *Congressional Quarterly Weekly Report,* January 28, 1995, 259–260; Donna Cassata, "Swift Progress of 'Contract' Inspires Awe and Concern," *Congressional Quarterly Weekly Report,* April 1, 1995, 909–912.

53. Carroll J. Doherty, "Clinton's Big Comeback Shown in Vote Score," *Congressional Quarterly Weekly Report,* December 21, 1996, 3427–3428.

54. Woodrow Wilson, *Congressional Government* (1885; reprint, New York: Meridian, 1956), 53.

55. Joseph E. Kallenbach, *The American Chief Executive* (New York: Harper and Row, 1966), 354.

56. Mark A. Peterson, "The President and Congress," in *The Presidency and the Political System,* 6th ed., ed. Michael Nelson (Washington, D.C.: CQ Press, 2000), 476.

57. Robert J. Spitzer, *The Presidential Veto: Touchstone of the American Presidency* (Albany: State University of New York Press, 1988), 100–103.

58. Janet Hook, "Avalanche of Veto Threats Divides Bush, Congress," *Congressional Quarterly Weekly Report,* September 22, 1990, 2991. Hook cites an OMB spokeswoman as stating that the Bush administration had issued 120 veto threats since January 1989.

59. Barbara Sinclair, "Hostile Partners: The President, Congress, and Lawmaking in the Partisan 1990s," in *Polarized Politics,* 144. For a rational choice analysis of these interactions see Charles M. Cameron, *Veto Bargaining: Presidents and the Politics of Negative Power* (New York: Cambridge University Press, 2000).

60. Richard E. Neustadt, *Presidential Power: The Politics of Leadership* (New York: Wiley, 1960), 10.

61. Dave Boyer, "White House, GOP on Hill in Harmony," *Washington Times,* February 14, 2001, A1. On the speech, see Dan Balz, "President Begins His Toughest Sell," *Washington Post,* February 28, 2001, A1.

62. Ari Fleischer as quoted by Scott Shepard, Cox News Service, March 4, 2001. Also see Mike Allen, "It's Campaign 2001: President Hits the Trail to Pitch Tax, Education Plans," *Washington Post,* March 2, 2001, A6.

63. Theodore J. Lowi, *The End of Liberalism,* 2d ed. (New York: St. Martin's Press, 1979); Randall B. Ripley and Grace A. Franklin, *Congress, the Bureaucracy, and Public Policy,* 5th ed. (Pacific Grove, Calif.: Brooks/Cole, 1991).

64. Joseph A. Pika, "White House Office of Congressional Relations: A Longitudinal Analysis" (paper presented at the annual meeting of the Midwest Political Science Association, Chicago, April 20–22, 1978). See also the discussion in Kenneth E. Collier, *Between the Branches: The White House Office of Legislative Affairs* (Pittsburgh: University of Pittsburgh Press, 1997), 16–22, chap. 4.

65. Lyndon B. Johnson, *Vantage Point* (New York: Holt, Rinehart and Winston, 1971), 448; Doris Kearns, *Lyndon Johnson and the American Dream* (New York: Harper and Row, 1976), 226.

66. George C. Edwards III, *Presidential Influence in Congress* (San Francisco: Freeman, 1980), 117–120. For the origins of Johnson's knowledge of the Senate, see Robert A. Caro, *The Years of Lyndon Johnson: Master of the Senate* (New York: Knopf, 2002).

67. Terry Sullivan, "Headcounts, Expectations, and Presidential Coalitions in Congress," *American Journal of Political Science* (August 1988): 567. Elsewhere, Sullivan demonstrates that head counts are a valuable presidential tool for signaling congressional supporters and for obtaining information from them. "Explaining Why Presidents Count: Signaling and Information," *Journal of Politics* (August 1990): 939–962.

68. Jeffrey H. Birnbaum and Alan S. Murray, *Showdown at Gucci Gulch* (New York: Random House, 1987), 40–41, 94–95, 118, 169–171.

69. Chuck Alston, "Bush's High Public Standing Held Little Sway on Hill," *Congressional Quarterly Weekly Report,* December 28, 1991, 3751.

70. Sinclair, "Trying to Govern Positively," 96–100.

71. Steve Langdon, "Clinton's High Victory Rate Conceals Disappointments," *Congressional Quarterly Weekly Report,* December 31, 1994, 3619.

72. Conley, *The Presidency, Congress and Divided Government,* chap. 7.

73. Sinclair, "Trying to Govern Positively," 121.

74. Jon Healey, "Clinton Success Rate Declined to a Record Low in 1995," *Congressional Quarterly Weekly Report,* January 27, 1996, 193.

75. John C. Fortier and Norman J. Ornstein, "Congress and the Bush Presidency" (paper presented at the conference on "The Bush Presidency: An Early Assessment," Woodrow Wilson School, Princeton University, April 25–26, 2003), 24, 26.

76. Ibid., 34.

77. Ibid., 41.

78. Laurence L. Barrett, *Gambling with History* (Garden City, N.Y.: Doubleday, 1983), 334.

79. The most thorough study of this staff unit is by Kenneth Collier, *Between the Branches: The White House Office of Legislative Affairs* (Pittsburgh: University of Pittsburgh Press, 1997). Also see the discussion in John H. Kessel, *Presidents, the Presidency, and the Political Environment* (Washington, D.C.: CQ Press, 2001), 30–52.

80. George C. Edwards III, *At the Margins: Presidential Leadership of Congress* (New Haven: Yale University Press, 1989), chap. 3.

81. Kessel, *Presidents, the Presidency, and the Political Environment,* 26.

82. Edwards, *At the Margins,* 68–69; Jon R. Bond and Richard Fleisher, *The President in the Legislative Arena* (Chicago: University of Chicago Press, 1990), 171–175.

83. Gary C. Jacobson, *The Electoral Origins of Divided Government* (Boulder: Westview, 1990), 80–81.

84. Gary C. Jacobson, *The Politics of Congressional Elections,* 3d ed. (New York: HarperCollins, 1992), 161–162.

85. Fortier and Ornstein, "Congress and the Bush Presidency," 39–40. On midterm losses, see Abramson, Aldrich, and Rohde, *Change and Continuity in the 2000 and 2002 Elections,* 228.

86. Sullivan, "Headcounts, Expectations, and Presidential Coalitions in Congress," 573–582.

87. John W. Kingdon, *Congressmen's Voting Decisions* (New York: Harper and Row, 1981); Aage R. Clausen, *How Congressmen Decide* (New York: St. Martin's Press, 1973).

88. Conley, *The Presidency, Congress, and Divided Government*, 3–83.

89. Bond and Fleisher, *The President in the Legislative Arena*, 221.

90. Ibid., 182.

91. Edwards, *At the Margins*, 124–125.

92. John E. Mueller, *War, Presidents, and Public Opinion* (New York: Wiley, 1973).

93. Wayne, *The Legislative Presidency*, 166.

94. Elizabeth Drew, *On the Edge* (New York: Simon and Schuster, 1994), 54, 266.

95. Mark Lacey, "Bush to Attend Democratic Caucuses," *New York Times*, January 27, 2001, A11.

96. Drew, *On the Edge*, 266. For a more positive review of Clinton's personal effectiveness, see Pfiffner, *The Strategic Presidency*, 180.

97. Lizette Alvarez and Eric Schmitt, "Cheney Ever More Powerful as Crucial Link to Congress," *New York Times*, May 13, 2001, A1, A16.

98. David E. Rosenbaum and David Firestone, "$318 Billion Deal Is Set in Congress for Cutting Taxes," *New York Times*, May 22, 2003, www.nytimes.com/2003/05/22/politics/22TAX.html; David Firestone, "Congress Passes Tax Package, Sending It On to White House," *New York Times* May 23, 2003, www.nytimes.com/2003/05/23/politics/23CND-TAX.html; and Dana Milibank and Jim VandeHei, "Bush Retreat Eased Bill's Advance," *Washington Post*, May 23, 2003, A5.

99. Edwards, *At the Margins*, 211. Also see Bond and Fleisher, *The President in the Legislative Arena*, 219; Bert A. Rockman, *The Leadership Question: The Presidency and the American Political System* (New York: Praeger, 1984), 214.

100. Mark A. Peterson, *Legislating Together: The White House and Capitol Hill from Eisenhower to Reagan* (Cambridge: Harvard University Press, 1990), 267.

101. Edwards, *At the Margins*, 8–15.

102. Bond and Fleisher, *The President in the Legislative Arena*, 220–234.

103. Peterson, *Legislating Together*, 92–94, chaps. 4 and 5.

104. Arthur M. Schlesinger Jr., *The Imperial Presidency* (Boston: Houghton Mifflin, 1973).

105. Sundquist, *The Decline and Resurgence of Congress*.

106. In the second edition of *The Imperial Presidency* (Boston: Houghton Mifflin, 1989), Schlesinger maintains that Reagan moved two-thirds of the way toward restoring the imperial presidency. He met two of Schlesinger's "tests"—extensive presidential war making and heavy reliance on secrecy—but Reagan did not direct his powers against administration critics (451, 457).

107. This is the central theme of Peterson's *Legislating Together*, in which he advocates a "tandem institutions" perspective on presidential-congressional relations.

SUGGESTED READINGS

Bond, Jon R., and Richard Fleisher. *The President in the Legislative Arena*. Chicago: University of Chicago Press, 1990.

_____ eds. *Polarized Politics: Congress and the President in a Partisan Era*. Washington, D.C.: CQ Press, 2000.

Conley, Richard S. *The Presidency, Congress, and Divided Government*. College Station: Texas A&M University, 2003.

Cox, Gary W., and Samuel Kernell, eds. *The Politics of Divided Government*. Boulder: Westview, 1991.

Edwards, George C., III. *At the Margins: Presidential Leadership of Congress*. New Haven: Yale University Press, 1989.

Fiorina, Morris. *Divided Government*. 2d ed. Boston: Allyn and Bacon, 1996.

Fisher, Louis. *Constitutional Conflicts between Congress and the President*. 4th ed. Lawrence: University Press of Kansas, 1997.

Jones, Charles O. *The Presidency in a Separated System*. Washington, D.C.: Brookings Institution, 1994.

____. *Separate but Equal Branches: Congress and the Presidency*. 2d ed. Chatham, N.J.: Chatham House, 2000.

Mayhew, David R. *Divided We Govern: Party Control, Lawmaking, and Investigations, 1946–1990*. New Haven: Yale University Press, 1991.

Peterson, Mark A. *Legislating Together: The White House and Capitol Hill from Eisenhower to Reagan*. Cambridge: Harvard University Press, 1990.

Shull, Steven A., ed. *The Two Presidencies: A Quarter-Century Assessment*. Chicago: Nelson-Hall, 1991.

Spitzer, Robert J. *President and Congress: Executive Harmony at the Crossroads of American Government*. New York: McGraw-Hill, 1993.

____. *The Presidential Veto: Touchstone of the American Presidency*. Albany: State University of New York Press, 1988.

Sundquist, James L. *The Decline and Resurgence of Congress*. Washington, D.C.: Brookings, 1981.

Thurber, James A., ed. *Divided Democracy: Cooperation and Conflict between the President and Congress*. Washington, D.C.: CQ Press, 1991.

____, ed. *Rivals for Power: Presidential-Congressional Relations*. Washington, D.C.: CQ Press, 1996.

Wayne, Stephen J. *The Legislative Presidency*. New York: Harper and Row, 1978.

6 EXECUTIVE POLITICS

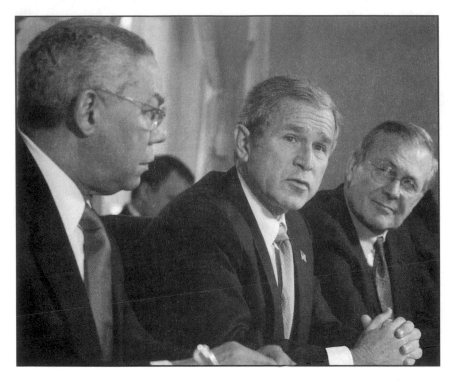

President Bush met frequently with members of his war cabinet following the terrorist attacks of September 11, 2001. Secretary of State Colin Powell and Secretary of Defense Donald Rumsfeld, shown in the White House Cabinet Room during one such November 2002 meeting, frequently disagreed on policy and courses of action.

A MERICANS COMMONLY THINK OF THE PRESIDENT as the "chief executive" of the federal government, held responsible for its many activities and responsibilities. If government fails to meet popular expectations, the president takes the blame. In the wake of 9/11, the president and his administration took responsibility for preventing another terrorist attack as well as for minimizing the consequences if one should occur. To accomplish this goal, President Bush proposed on June 6, 2002, and signed into law on November 25, 2002, legislation creating a Department of Homeland Security. As he declared, "We're taking historic action to defend the United States and protect our citizens from the dangers of a new era."[1] The mammoth new department (described by some as a "superagency") consolidated twenty-two agencies and units from other departments into a single entity expected to comprise 170,000 or more workers, making it the federal government's third largest department. This was the largest, single government reorganization in more than a half-century, since creation of the Department of Defense in 1947.

The department's primary mission is to (1) prevent terrorist attacks within the United States; (2) reduce the country's vulnerability to terrorism; and (3) minimize the damage, and assist in the recovery, from terrorist attacks that do occur within the nation's borders.[2] To accomplish these goals, the department has been organized into five directorates: Border and Transportation Security, Emergency Preparedness and Response, Information Analysis, Infrastructure Protection and Management, and Science and Technology.[3] Some units, including the Coast Guard and Secret Service, are not in a directorate (see Figure 6-1). Even with these changes, it was recognized that success would depend on extensive coordination with other federal agencies as well as with state and local officials, all of whom play important roles in securing the homeland.

Creation of a huge federal bureaucracy had not been the president's original solution. On October 8, 2001, he chose Pennsylvania governor Tom Ridge to serve as director of the Office of Homeland Security, a 100-person White House staff unit, and to oversee the Homeland Security Council, an interdepartmental coordinating committee designed to function much like the long-established National Security Council. Ridge, however, encountered resistance from his government colleagues when he proposed reorganizing their efforts, struggled to create new systems such as the color-coded alert system, and was drawn into protracted battles with Congress over its right to exercise oversight of his activities.[4] Congressional Democrats were especially critical of Bush's less than bold approach. By early May 2002, a bipartisan, bicameral proposal to create a Department of Homeland Security had emerged, and Sen. Joseph Lieberman, D-Conn., secured approval from the Government Affairs Committee (which he chaired) later in the month for creation of the department. Bush's sudden endorsement of creating a new department surprised most observers; by doing so, he regained the initiative on this high visibility issue. Although the turf battles proved long and bitter, Bush ultimately got most of what he sought, with numerous bureaucratic units moving into the new structure, some projected to prosper and others to suffer from the move: the Coast Guard (from Transportation), the Secret Service (from Treasury),[5] the Customs Service (from Treasury),[6] the Border Patrol (from Justice), the newly created Transportation Security Administration (federal airport baggage checkers, from Transportation),[7] the

Figure 6-1   Organizational Chart of the Department of Homeland Security, 2003

Source: www.dhs.gov

Federal Emergency Management Agency (independent agency),[8] Office of Domestic Preparedness (from Justice) and the National Domestic Preparedness Office (from the FBI), the Computer Security Division (from Commerce), and the National Communications System (from Defense).

Deciding which units should be housed in the new structure was probably the easy part; assembling a management team on short notice (see Table 6-1) and pulling all the pieces into a coherent whole presented a greater challenge. As public administration experts pointed out, it took nearly four decades for the military forces to work effectively in a single department; the Department of Transportation (created 1967) continues to founder from the fragmentation caused by multiple congressional committees favoring different modes of transportation; the Department of Energy, created in 1977 as a response to the oil

Creating the new Department of Homeland Security, headed by former Pennsylvania governor Tom Ridge, occasioned the largest reorganization of the federal government in more than a half-century.

crisis, also suffers from a fragmented congressional committee structure and deeply embedded organizational cultures difficult to mold into one.[9] Secretary Ridge's challenge is enormous. According to the White House, "88 congressional committees and subcommittees have jurisdiction over issues related to homeland security, and . . . that gives the Homeland Security Department a lot of congressional bosses to work with—and answer to—in its drive to make America safer."[10] This legislative cross-section included all senators and 95 percent of the House members in the 107th Congress. Similarly, the newly assembled pieces of the department brought with them established relationships with organized interests, who hoped to protect the access and services they enjoyed under the old arrangements, and a few newly organized interests as well.[11] To help the secretary tackle the task of creating a coherent department, the administration battled throughout the fall with the Democrat-controlled Senate and public workers' unions to "give the new agency's executives a free hand to reshuffle personnel and change the way employees are hired, paid, promoted and disciplined."[12] Ridge, then, confronted a nearly unprecedented task with nearly unprecedented powers.

Like Bush with his struggles to provide homeland security, most modern presidents have encountered difficulties in their efforts to direct the executive

Table 6-1   Leadership Team, Department of Homeland Security

Position	Experience
Secretary Tom Ridge	Governor of Pennsylvania 1995–2001
Deputy Secretary Vacant	
Under Secretary for Border & Transportation Security Asa Hutchinson	Congressman from Arkansas 1997–2001, Administrator of Drug Enforcement Administration, U.S. Attorney for Western District, Arkansas
Under Secretary for Emergency Preparedness & Response Michael Brown	Deputy Director and General Counsel Federal Emergency Management Agency, Head of Consequence Management, Working Group 2002, Chair of National Citizen Corps Council
Under Secretary for Information Analysis & Infrastructure Protection Frank Libutti	Deputy Commissioner of New York City Police Department Counter Terrorism, Special Assistant for Homeland Security, Department of Defense, Lieutenant General U.S. Marines
Under Secretary for Management Janet Hale	Assistant Secretary for Budget Technology and Finance, Department of Health and Human Services, Associate Administrator of Finance, House of Representatives, Associate Director for Economics and Government, Office of Management and Budget
Under Secretary for Science & Technology Dr. Charles E. McQueary	President of General Dynamics Corp., President of business units at AT&T and Lucent Technologies, Director, AT&T Bell Laboratories
Commandant U.S. Coast Guard Adm. Thomas H. Collins	Vice Commandant 2000–2002, Served in U.S. Coast Guard since 1968
Director, U.S. Secret Service W. Ralph Basham	Chief of Staff Transportation Security Administration, Director of Federal Law Enforcement Training Center, Served in U.S. Secret Service since 1970

Source: www.dhs.gov/dhspublic/display?theme=11 and associated links.

branch, whether it be working with existing entities or creating new ones. John F. Kennedy lamented the inertia of the State Department, and Ronald Reagan made his campaign attack on an overgrown federal bureaucracy one of his presidency's enduring themes. Recent presidents proposing to harness the potential of government to deliver much-needed services must overcome the cynical belief that bureaucracy is the problem, not the solution; thus Bill Clinton's proposal to solve the nation's health care problems fell victim to the charge that it would create a bloated federal bureaucracy. Richard Rose, who has studied the president as a manager, has remarked that the "president's title of chief executive is a misnomer; he can more accurately be described as a nonexecutive chief."[13] The essence of Rose's argument is that, even within the executive branch, presidential powers of command are limited and that a president's success as an administrator depends greatly on the ability to win the trust of others. Thus presidents confront an enormous challenge. The public both expects presidents to produce results and is unsure of government's role, not wanting it to become too intrusive.

This chapter examines the president's responsibilities as chief executive and the factors that affect administrative performance. It opens with a discussion of the president's executive role, its constitutional, legal, and administrative foundations. Then it explores the president's relationships with the executive branch and the cabinet. After establishing that the president's powers of command over the units of the executive branch are limited, the chapter analyzes the formal powers and managerial tools that modern presidents have available for discharging administrative duties.

The President as Executive

The president's executive role is grounded in ambiguous language in Article II of the Constitution: "the executive power" is vested in the president, who is directed to "take care that the laws be faithfully executed." The president may also "require the opinion, in writing, of the principal officer in each of the executive departments" and "grant reprieves and pardons." Modern presidents have tended to interpret these provisions broadly and have derived from them substantial additional powers. In addition to these constitutionally based powers, presidents have received extensive delegations of statutory authority from Congress.

Yet presidents confront a paradox. While they enjoy considerable formal legal powers and head a vast, complex military and civilian bureaucracy, their ability to direct that bureaucracy toward the achievement of the administration's policy objectives and program goals is actually limited. To understand that paradox, we must examine the constitutional relationship of the presidency to the legislative and judicial branches as well as the nature of the federal bureaucracy and the president's relationship to it.

In administration as in so many other areas, presidents require the cooperation of Congress since only Congress can authorize government programs, establish agencies to implement the programs, and appropriate funds to finance them.[14] However, presidents find that congressional cooperation may be difficult to obtain because presidents and members of Congress have different constituency and institutional perspectives regardless of party loyalties. There are also occasions when the exercise of presidential power must be acceptable to the judiciary. In short, presidential power is not self-executing, and it is subject to restraint.

Although the federal bureaucracy—which today comprises fifteen cabinet departments and scores of special agencies, with a total workforce of more than 4 million civilian and military employees—is called "the executive branch," it is really the creation of the legislative branch. When Congress establishes federal departments and agencies, its members are responding not only to presidential needs and requests, but also to demands and pressures from various constituency forces, interest groups, and the general public. As a result, the structure of the federal bureaucracy tends to reflect the political fragmentation and committee jurisdictions of Congress, which often leads, as with Homeland Security, to multiple committees overseeing the activities of the same department. Thus presidents do not look down upon subordinate administrative units from a position at the apex of a pyramid of authority but confront a complex and confusing array of departments and agencies with varying degrees of independence.

In addition, presidents deal with career civil servants who staff bureaucratic units and constitute a permanent federal government. These civil servants respond to demands from interest groups and to direction from congressional committees as well as to presidential leadership. Most modern presidents have entered office believing—or they soon become convinced—that they cannot take the support and loyalty of the bureaucracy for granted but must constantly strive to earn both.[15]

The president's task as the nation's chief executive is much more, therefore, than issuing commands or finding ways to bring a large complex bureaucracy under operational control. The president must secure congressional cooperation while suppressing the executive branch's natural tendencies toward conflict with the legislative branch and must give direction to the bureaucracy so that it will help accomplish the administration's goals. As the functions of the federal government expanded from the New Deal onward, the task of defining objectives and coordinating their achievement has grown increasingly difficult for presidents.

The President and the Executive Branch

Presidents need help in managing the federal bureaucracy. Originally, FDR expanded the White House staff and created other units in the Executive Office of the President for just this purpose—to help him define objectives, convert them into operating programs, allocate resources to the agencies administering the programs, and coordinate the implementation of programs within the federal government and among federal, state, and local governments. Political executives are also expected to assist the president: department secretaries and agency administrators appointed by the president outside the civil service are charged with directing the work of the career employees, coordinating the operations of their component bureaus, and developing and maintaining links with other federal departments and agencies and with state and local governments. Presidents quickly discover, however, that the reality of their relations with the federal bureaucracy bears little resemblance to the idealized vision that many hold.

Tension between the president, presidential agents, and the bureaucracy has been present in every modern administration. It exists, at least in part, because of what Hugh Heclo has identified as the distinction between "political leadership in the bureaucracy" and "bureaucratic power."[16] The direction and effectiveness of the political leadership presidents provide depend on their personalities, leadership styles, and values as well as on external events and conditions. In contrast, bureaucratic power is relatively permanent, not dependent on personalities and transitory factors. That power belongs to the career civil servants who compose the permanent government.

At least five general factors contribute to bureaucratic power and shape presidential-bureaucratic relations: the size, complexity, and dispersion of the executive branch; bureaucratic inertia and momentum; executive branch personnel; the legal position of the executive branch; and the susceptibility of executive branch units to external political influence. Major consequences of the interaction of these factors are presidential frustration and a pattern of policymaking often sharply at odds with the norm of democratic accountability; it is a system that obscures those responsible for a policy and a decision.

Size, Complexity, and Dispersion of the Executive Branch

The scope of federal government activities has exploded since 1933, tremendously increasing the number of agencies and the range of programs they administer. The federal budget for 2002 was $2.1 trillion, and there were more than 2.71 million civilian and 1.4 million active duty military employees. These employees oversee domestic programs that reach into every community in the nation and touch the lives of individuals from birth to death. Considerations of national security extend U.S. military and foreign policy activities around the world. Providing leadership and direction to the bureaucracy is difficult. It would be so even if the president could command prompt and unquestioning obedience.

The multiplicity of agencies and programs creates an additional obstacle to effective leadership. Overlapping jurisdictions lead in some cases to duplication of efforts and in others to contradictory efforts. Presidents must be coordinators. When they define goals for a policy area, they most often deal not with single administrative units but with many. Thus even after consolidating twenty-two administrative units into the Department of Homeland Security, the military services, FBI, and CIA remain outside units whose cooperation and coordination are critical to success.

The great size of the federal bureaucracy means its activities are widely dispersed. Presidents, their aides, and their principal political appointees are at the center of government. The people who operate programs, deliver services to individuals, and regulate the conduct of businesses and other organizations are at the periphery. These people, most of them civil servants, are there when a new president and staff take office and will be there after the political executives depart.

Bureaucratic Inertia and Momentum

Bureaucratic inertia means it is hard to get a new government activity started, and once it is under way, it is even more difficult to stop, or significantly redirect, it. In short, "bureaucracies at rest tend to stay at rest and bureaucracies in motion tend to stay in motion."[17] Much of this inflexibility arises because of organizational routines—prescribed operating procedures that have worked successfully in the past—or interest group efforts.

The momentum of ongoing programs especially frustrates presidents. Government commitments are reflected in public laws, the amount of money allocated for those activities in annual appropriations, and the number of civil service and military employees who carry out the activities. In 2002, mandatory expenditures constituted about 65 percent of the government's budget. The principal mandatory items included interest on the national debt; entitlement programs such as Social Security, Medicare, and Medicaid; federal retirement and veterans' benefits; and unemployment compensation. Even the remaining, discretionary portion of the budget is highly resistant to cuts because of support from groups benefiting from those expenditures. Presidents can influence the shape of the federal budget, but major changes usually require years to be implemented. From one year to the next, presidents tend to be limited to incremental changes.

Given their fixed terms of office and the usual scope of their objectives, presidents find the incremental adjustments possible through annual budgeting inadequate. For members of the permanent government, the time perspective is much different; they can afford to be patient. In the budget process, they fight to maintain their "base," which is their current appropriation, and to add as large an increment to it as possible.[18] Over time, small annual increases are transformed into large permanent gains. Bureaucratic momentum thus works to the advantage of the permanent government and acts as a constraint on presidents who attempt to counter it. President Reagan and his successors tried to overcome the effects of incremental budgeting by means of a top-down process that restricted total government spending and forced agencies and their supporters to accept cuts or limited growth.[19]

The large number of career federal employees pressures the president to maintain ongoing programs. Major reductions in personnel or redirection of their activities are economically and politically costly. People will oppose actions that threaten to deprive them of their jobs or that require them to move, undergo additional training, or reduce their sense of security and importance.

Most presidents can make only modest adjustments in the size and mission of the federal workforce. Clinton was somewhat more successful in this regard than other modern presidents, eventually eliminating more than 300,000 jobs at the end of seven years as part of the effort to "reinvent government" led by Vice President Al Gore.[20]

Bureaucratic Personnel

Presidents must depend on both political and career officials to operate the federal bureaucracy. Until 1883, when the Pendleton Act created the federal civil service, no distinction existed between the two groups. Presidents could theoretically appoint all members of the federal bureaucracy, a "spoils system" of tangible rewards for party members who had supported the election winner. With the creation and expansion of the civil service system, which opened government jobs to all citizens based on their qualifications, presidential control of government personnel declined, and the characteristics and roles of appointed and career officials became more distinctive, often hindering presidential direction of programs. George W. Bush argued that protecting the homeland was so critical that it required jettisoning some of the worker protections that had become part of the civil service system.

The political executives—those appointed by the president and charged with directing the careerists—are a weak substitute for the old patronage-based system and constitute what Hugh Heclo has called a "government of strangers."[21] Aside from cabinet officers, a few important subcabinet appointees, and the heads of major independent agencies, these political executives are largely unknown to the president and one another. Only loosely do they constitute a presidential team able to provide bureaucratic direction. "Although party is still the glue that seems to hold administrations together, this glue's consistency is much thinner than ever before and its holding power is greatly reduced."[22]

Cabinet selection involves the president directly in an attempt to build support for the administration by including representatives of various constituencies in the party and the country.[23] Although presidents sometimes appoint personal friends to especially important cabinet departments because of the close counseling relationship involved,[24] selection of other political executives is affected by multiple and often conflicting pressures: loyalty to the president, party membership, technical competence, the wishes of the cabinet member under whom the appointee will serve, and the demands of congressional members, interest groups, and state and local party leaders.

When done with care and planning, recruiting people to serve in an administration has the potential to be an instrument of control over policy, a tool of administrative management, and an important component of presidential relations with Congress, interest groups, and political parties. Consequently, it is a highly political process. Presidents since Eisenhower have used personnel staffs located in the White House to run the appointment process. The process is always chaotic at the start of a new administration because of the many positions to be filled, pressures for jobs from campaign workers and party members, and uncertainty about how to proceed. The number of inquiries from job seekers can be crushing, reaching nearly 1,500 a day in recent cases.[25] Eventually the search becomes fairly systematic.[26] Over time, centralization of appointment decisions in the Presidential Personnel Office has increased presidential control and bureaucratic responsiveness, but there have been costly consequences. As Thomas Weko points out, it permits job seekers, interest groups, members of Congress, and campaign contributors to press their claims directly on the White House staff, transferring into the White House conflicts once waged outside it, provoking conflict between the appointments staff and the administrative units, and diminishing the importance of program considerations.[27]

The process also depends on an active president who provides sustained support for the selection of appointees. Ronald Reagan excelled in this regard, whereas Richard Nixon's lack of interest contributed to his inability to establish effective control over the executive branch. The Reagan White House exercised tight control over recruitment, filling sensitive positions with loyal individuals committed to the president's ideology. Cabinet members could not conduct independent searches for subcabinet officials. Prospective appointees were screened for policy views, political and personal backgrounds, and if considered necessary, expertise. The Reagan administration took a long time to get its political executives in place (the next three administrations, Bush's, Clinton's, and Bush's, took even longer), but the result was tighter control over the executive branch and greater cohesion within it than other modern presidents have achieved.[28]

Bill Clinton's experience illustrates the difficulty presidents encounter. The Clinton personnel operation had almost 300 employees during the transition and more than 100 in the Presidential Personnel Office in March 1993. The operation's objective was creating a competent staff that also responded to the claims and demands of campaign workers and contributors and represented the diverse blocs, movements, and constituencies that had brought electoral victory. The operation's political success was reflected in the diversity of the appointees, recruited to reflect EGG, or "ethnicity, gender and geography."[29] However, the preoccupation with diversity, ethical concerns, and a series of botched nominations resulted in a slowed appointment pace that brought criticism from Congress, Democratic constituency groups, and the media.[30]

Because the outcome of the 2000 election long remained in question, George W. Bush's search for personnel got off to a late start. Even so, the administration was only a week behind Clinton's record in selecting the cabinet and was actually faster in naming the White House staff.[31] But there were other sources of delay. At the hundred-day mark, Bush was well behind Reagan and Clinton in getting appointees in place. With 488 top appointments to make, Bush had announced 177 candidates, but only 60 names had been submitted to the Senate and, of those, only 29 had been confirmed. This meant that "in nine of the fourteen cabinet departments, the secretary [was] the only senior policymaker who [had] been confirmed."[32] Candidates were delayed by the need to fill out extensive questionnaires, complete financial disclosure forms, and undergo background investigations. Other administrations have also encountered these hurdles, but with each new administration the delays have grown longer. Clay Johnson, Bush's chief talent scout, had hoped to get the full subcabinet in place by August 2001, accepting the inevitable delays of a laborious process.[33]

The political executives chosen are often amateurs in the precarious world of Washington politics, lacking the political knowledge and substantive skills needed to provide effective leadership. They quickly discover their dependence on top-level career executives and lower-ranking civil servants for the information and advice needed to serve the president effectively. That support is only obtained by paying a price, however, in the form of loyalty to the agency and support for its programs within the administration, before Congress, and with the public. Members of the president's team suddenly find themselves striking a balance between the often conflicting claims of the White House and the agencies they lead. In general, it takes twelve to eighteen months for political executives to master their jobs. Their average tenure, however, is only two years. The high turnover rates make it difficult to develop teamwork within departments and agencies. Cabinet secretaries are continually adapting to new assistants, and people on the same administrative level barely get to know one another. One result is that expectations and roles are in flux, and coordination and control problematic.

Political executives, who look upward to the president for support and direction and downward to the permanent government for support and services, are imperfect instruments for presidential control of the bureaucracy. They can best serve the president by winning the trust of the careerists, but to do so means maintaining a considerable degree of independence from the White House.

Conflicts between the White House and the career executives arise for understandable reasons. The relatively secure tenure of upper-level civil servants (as opposed to the expendability and shorter tenure of political executives) allows them to take a more gradual approach to resolving problems and to pursue their objectives obliquely and by indirection, generating less opposition. In contrast, political executives, urged on by the White House, tend to pursue their goals quite directly and to see virtue in conflict. In addition, a civil servant must remain politically neutral to remain a civil servant; hence he or she is cautious about becoming identified with a political party or appointee. Presidential appointees, many of whom are unfamiliar with bureaucratic ways, often mistake such caution for opposition or disloyalty. This viewpoint is reinforced by the high value career executives place on maintaining their relationships with clientele group representatives, congressional members and staff, and individuals outside the Washington community who are involved in, or knowledgeable about, their agencies' programs.

To correct perceived deficiencies in the career service and to increase presidential control over the higher civil service (those in GS-16 and higher positions), the Carter administration engineered the passage of the Civil Service

Reform Act (CSRA) of 1978. The CSRA established the Senior Executive Service (SES), a professional managerial corps of career civil servants whose members are eligible for financial bonuses. It also increased the ability of political executives to transfer career officials within and between agencies and to raise the number of noncareerists in the SES and lower positions.[34] Another provision of the CSRA replaced the three-person bipartisan Civil Service Commission with the single-headed Office of Personnel Management (OPM), which gave the president more control over the career service. Reagan's first director of the OPM, Donald J. Devine, aggressively implemented a partisan style of leadership.[35] Neither of Reagan's immediate successors, George Bush and Bill Clinton, used politicization of the career service as extensively as Reagan did to direct the executive branch.

Early in the twenty-first century, the Carter-era reforms have come under administration and congressional scrutiny. As Paul Light testified before the House Government Reform Committee, "we have now had twenty-five years to tinker, tweak, refine, adjust and retarget the reforms embedded in the 1978 Civil Service Reform Act," and some analysts now believe that those earlier changes "cannot work without comprehensive reform."[36] The administration of George W. Bush has challenged civil service practices in security-related departments (Homeland Security and Department of Defense) but has not yet proposed a set of systemwide civil service reforms.

Legal Arrangements

The ambiguous legal position of the executive branch is the fourth factor that affects a president's control over the bureaucracy. Although the Constitution charges presidents with responsibility for executing the laws, their legal position as chief executive is somewhat unclear because Congress has—with presidential approval—delegated authority to, and imposed duties directly on, various administrative officials. In some cases, such as independent regulatory commissions and the Federal Reserve Board, presidents have no formal power to direct agency actions or set agency policy. Their influence is based on budgetary and appointment powers and persuasive abilities. For cabinet members, heads of independent agencies, and other political executives with operating authority to whom Congress has directly delegated power, the situation is ambiguous. As chief executive the president, by virtue of the Constitution's "take care" clause, can command the decisions of subordinates. In doing so, however, the president risks confrontation with Congress and with the clientele groups and individuals affected by the administrative units involved. In addition, the Supreme Court long ago ruled that the president must not interfere with the performance of a "purely ministerial" duty that does not involve the exercise of discretion or judgment.[37] Nor may the president prevent the execution of the law by subordinates.

Congress has provided administrative officials with broad delegations of discretionary authority because legislation can seldom be drafted in sufficient detail to cover all contingencies. Legislators also have made vague and general grants of power because it is politically advantageous to shift difficult and potentially unpopular decisions to the bureaucracy. The Supreme Court has approved such delegations with the proviso that they be accompanied by clear statutory guidelines.[38] However, the Court's insistence on specific statutory standards has seldom been followed by Congress or by the lower courts.[39] The standards the Court uses have tended to be vague and unspecific, such as "just and reasonable rates," "excess profits," and "the public interest, convenience, and necessity." In spite of judicial review of the fairness of administrative procedures and judicial reference to the legislative history of statutes as found in congressional committee hearings, reports, and floor debates, administrative officials retain substantial discretionary authority that complicates the president's task of controlling the bureaucracy.

Susceptibility to External Influence

Weak political parties make the federal bureaucracy highly susceptible to forces outside individual departments, agencies, and bureaus. Parties do not provide administrative units with adequate political support, nor do they link programs with presidential policy goals. Thus presidential administrations lack internal policy cohesiveness, depending instead on the president's personal leadership to hold them together. In the face of external criticism and pressure, executive branch units frequently find little support within the administration. Demands on presidents are extensive, their energy and attention are not unlimited, and they tend to conserve their political resources for high-priority objectives.

If presidential support is lacking, the agency must look elsewhere for help in maintaining its authority, funding, and personnel. It turns to the public, especially to the individuals and groups affected by its programs, and it turns to Congress, particularly the committees or subcommittees with jurisdiction over its legislative authorizations and appropriations.

The regulations agencies promulgate and enforce, or the benefits and services they deliver, provide the basis for the development of enduring ties between them and their clientele groups. An agency without a well-organized clientele is in a precarious position. Clientele groups can publicize an agency's accomplishments and defend it against attack. In exchange, the agency administers its programs with a manifest concern for the clientele's interests. The agency consults with clientele group officials and with individual notables attentive to its activities. Such outsiders often participate in agency decision making through advisory councils and panels and informal personal contacts. Agencies seldom draft guidelines and regulations or award grants without extensive external participation and consultation. There is also a two-way flow of personnel between agencies and clientele organizations. These mutually beneficial relations are characteristic of most domestic policy areas in the federal government.

For example, the National Education Association (NEA) and several other education interest groups provide support and protection to the Department of Education in exchange for access and information. The NEA led the congressional effort to elevate the former U.S. Office of Education to departmental status in 1979 and the battle to prevent the abolition of the fledgling department during the Reagan administration. Department of Education political executives have found employment with the NEA and other education interest groups; on occasion, those lobbies have helped to recruit or have provided agency staffers.

Agencies also find it easy and convenient to develop strong ties to the congressional committees or subcommittees with which they deal. Congressional requests for consideration on appointments and grants, suggestions concerning program administration, and inquiries on behalf of constituents are quickly acknowledged. Congressional influence with the agencies strengthens the committee members in their constituencies.[40] Bureaucrats use their connections with committee members to effect changes in their statutory authority and gain favorable treatment during budget negotiations. Agencies may use their committee ties to obtain more funds than the president has recommended or to modify their activities in a way not fully in accord with presidential preferences.

Agencies are not, however, totally resistant to presidential directives; agencies and the president need each other to accomplish their goals. If the true test of presidential power is the president's power to persuade, one of the best measures of an agency's strength is the degree to which a president must "bargain with it in order to secure its cooperation."[41]

The President and the Cabinet

Most modern presidents have come to office announcing their intent to make more extensive use of the cabinet as a collective decision-making body than the previous incumbent did, pledges generally applauded by the media and academics. Yet, with the exception of Dwight Eisenhower, presidents have not used their cabinets as vehicles of collective leadership. As MaryAnne Borrelli summarizes, "cabinet government is a promise made by candidates, an ideal endorsed by presidents-elect, and a practice abandoned by presidents."[42]

This gap between expectation and experience suggests the public and most political leaders lack understanding of the cabinet. In point of fact, the Constitution places executive authority, ultimately, in the president alone. The notion of collective or collegial leadership—typically found among cabinet members in parliamentary systems, who share leadership responsibility—is incompatible with constitutional reality and inconsistent with American practice. The president is not first among equals; he is the person in charge. Cabinet members are presidential appointees, serving at the president's pleasure. There is no obligation to consult them as a group or to act according to their wishes. The cabinet has no formal constitutional or legal standing. It exists by custom, and presidents may use it as little or as much as they see fit. Clinton, for example, met with his entire cabinet only twice from the beginning of 1998 to May 1999.[43]

Yet the cabinet does have political significance. Members are the principal spokespersons for administration policy. They are also the top political executives expected to provide direction for those federal commitments deemed so important as to warrant cabinet-level status. Management tasks are perhaps becoming increasingly important to cabinet members as their service in the job has become longer. Whereas the average tenure of cabinet members in the Nixon administration was 1.73 years, the service of Clinton's cabinet members was 3.36 years by the middle of 1999, the culmination of a six-administration trend of lengthening service.[44] Finally, cabinet composition has great symbolic value as a means of representing major social, economic, and political constituencies in the administration's highest councils.[45] Newly elected presidents try to select cabinet members whose presence will unify those constituencies behind the new administration.

Political experience, group identification, and technical expertise are important criteria for selecting cabinet members. A study covering eight administrations found that on average, two-thirds of presidents' initial cabinet appointees since FDR have been "Washington outsiders" less familiar with their departments' program responsibilities and that presidents tend to appoint more experienced managers ("insiders") as replacements for their initial secretaries. Similarly, one finds the emphasis on group relations and "liaison" backgrounds early in administrations with the percentage of "generalists" increasing as the term progresses.[46]

Previous political and government experience were heavily emphasized in George W. Bush's initial cabinet appointments (see Table 6-2). Borrelli classifies five (33 percent) as insiders and ten as outsiders; seven came from "liaison" backgrounds and eight (53 percent) could be viewed as "generalists"; five had held significant roles in the presidential campaign, nine had previous executive branch experience, four were current or previous members of Congress, and seven had experience in state or local government.[47] There had been much speculation following the 2000 presidential election that Bush would nominate a number of Democrats to his cabinet as a way of recognizing the narrowness of his victory and broadening his base of support, but only Norman Mineta, secretary of transportation and a holdover from the Clinton cabinet, in which he served as secretary of commerce, enjoyed this distinction.

In general, presidents face constraints in selecting cabinet members. Appointees to head some departments, such as agriculture, generally must be acceptable to clientele groups. In choosing the secretaries of defense and of the Treasury, presidents may give special weight to the candidates' expertise and experience. Generalist administrators, however, often are named to head the Departments of Commerce, Health and Human Services, Housing and Urban Development, and Transportation.

Presidents often try to use the cabinet as a decision-making body early in their administrations, but most eventually abandon the effort and rely heavily on the White House staff instead.[48] They find that most cabinet members are concerned primarily with issues affecting their departments, and there is often competition between cabinet members for the president's attention. Cabinet meetings are unsatisfactory devices for focused, analytical discussion of major issues. At best

Table 6-2   George W. Bush's Initial Cabinet Appointees, by Criteria of Appointment

Position	Political Experience	Clientele or Ethnic Group Identification	Technical Expertise	Generalist	Pretenure Friendship
Inner Cabinet					
Defense Secretary					
Donald H. Rumsfeld	X		X		
Attorney General					
John Ashcroft	X			X	
Secretary of State					
Colin Powell		X		X	
Treasury Secretary					
Paul H. O'Neill			X		X
(replaced by John W. Snow 12/6/02)					
Outer Cabinet					
Agriculture Secretary					
Ann M. Veneman	X	X		X	X
Commerce Secretary					
Don Evans	X			X	X
Education Secretary					
Rod Paige	X	X	X		
Energy Secretary					
Spencer Abraham	X			X	
Health and Human Services Secretary					
Tommy G. Thompson	X			X	
Housing and Urban Development Secretary					
Mel Martinez	X	X			X
Interior Secretary					
Gale A. Norton	X	X	X		
Labor Secretary					
Elaine L. Chao	X	X		X	
Transportation Secretary					
Norman Y. Mineta	X	X	X		
Veterans Affairs Secretary					
Anthony J. Principi		X	X		
Cabinet-Level Positions					
EPA Administrator					
Christine Todd Whitman	X	X			X
(replaced by Michael Leavitt 8/11/03)					
OMB Director					
Mitchell Daniels Jr.		X	X		
(replaced by Josh Bolden 6/6/03)					
U.S. Trade Representative					
Robert B. Zoellick			X		X

Source: MaryAnne Borrelli, *The President's Cabinet: Gender, Power, and Representation* (Boulder: Lynne Rienner Publishers, 2002), chap. 2.

they can serve as forums for informal discussion of issues and problems and for the exchange of information. Presidents are the only source of cohesion and policy coordination. Individual cabinet members feel loyal to the president *and* to the permanent governments within their departments. These conflicting loyalties inhibit the development of an informal sense of unity and purpose, without which the cabinet cannot realize its potential as a formal advisory body and policy-making mechanism.[49]

There is a tendency in most administrations for one or two cabinet members to stand out and to develop close ties with the president. During Reagan's second term, Attorney General Edwin Meese III and Secretary of the Treasury James A. Baker III enjoyed considerable leeway in pursuing their own agendas without aggressive interference from the White House staff, provided they did not conflict with the president's ideological precepts.[50] Treasury Secretaries Lloyd Bentsen and Robert Rubin enjoyed independent stature in the Clinton administration because of their political and business experience, respectively.[51]

At the outset of George W. Bush's administration, observers were impressed with the influence of Vice President Dick Cheney, whose broad responsibilities and access provided him with more apparent clout than any of the cabinet members. This was especially pronounced after Bush publicly contradicted public positions of Secretary of State Colin L. Powell and Environmental Protection Agency Administrator Christine Todd Whitman during his first hundred days. After 9/11, Bush became a wartime president, a development that narrowed his circle of cabinet interactions.[52] *(See chapter 11.)* This has not been true only of Bush. There has been a tendency for modern presidents to develop close ties with the heads of the Departments of State, Defense, Treasury, and Justice. (There is every reason to expect Homeland Security to join this list.) Cronin refers to these as the "inner cabinet" departments because their activities and responsibilities are of the highest priority—civil rights, national security, the condition of the economy, and the administration of justice—and because they cut across the concerns of the public and all members of Congress. These matters tend to dominate the president's time and attention.[53]

The heads of the other departments constitute the "outer cabinet."[54] Their departments have more sharply focused activities and find themselves acting as advocates for clientele and congressional interests within the administration.[55] Frequently, those pressures conflict with the president's broader priorities. For a short time, the inner/outer distinction may have been changed in the wake of 9/11. As Stephen Hess suggests, "any department with important homeland security concerns instantly moved up a notch on the power ladder in Washington."[56] Nonetheless, Bush met daily with a "war cabinet" that consisted of Vice President Cheney, Chief of Staff Andrew Card, National Security Adviser Condoleeza Rice, Secretary of State Powell, Defense Secretary Rumsfeld, Treasury Secretary O'Neill, and CIA Director George Tenet. This team of inner cabinet members, several of their senior aides, and key White House assistants helped the president manage the immediate aftermath of the disaster and prepare the nation for a war on terrorism.[57]

Presidents generally look beyond the cabinet for policy advice. Since its creation in 1947, the National Security Council (NSC) and its staff have been used extensively by presidents for foreign and military policy matters *(see chapter 10)*. In economic policy areas, presidents work closely with the chair of the Council of Economic Advisers, the director of the Office of Management and Budget

(OMB), the secretary of the Treasury, and the chair of the Federal Reserve Board *(see chapter 9)*. In domestic policy areas, which involve primarily the outer cabinet departments, domestic policy staffs and OMB have provided assistance to the president in policy formulation *(see chapter 8)*, and cabinet committees, interagency committees, and policy councils have been employed to coordinate policymaking and implementation.

Cabinet committees, usually appointed on an ad hoc basis to handle specific problems, can focus quickly on them. Interagency committees, which operate mostly at the agency and subcabinet levels, may achieve a measure of coordination, but their work is often hampered by competition between agencies and by a lack of status and visibility.

Policy councils help presidents highlight particular problems. Nixon introduced a Domestic Council designed to perform many of the same services as the NSC, and Ford created an Economic Policy Board. Both units have appeared under various names in successor administrations. Reagan established seven cabinet councils in addition to the NSC to help move issues upward to the cabinet and then the president: commerce and trade, economic affairs, energy and natural resources, food and agriculture, human resources, legal policy, and management and administration. Over time, the system proved cumbersome, and for his second term, Reagan reduced the number of councils to two, the Economic Policy Council and the Domestic Policy Council. Despite the later streamlining, Reagan's cabinet council system is given high marks for "fostering the sense that policy development was a team operation between the cabinet officers and the White House."[58] President George H. W. Bush continued to utilize the Economic Policy Council and the Domestic Policy Council, but with apparently limited effectiveness due to squabbling and rivalries among his advisers.[59]

Clinton began his presidency with three policy staff units in the White House: the National Economic Council, the Domestic Policy Council, and the Office of Environmental Policy, headed by a presidential assistant or deputy assistant.[60] In addition, there were three high-level advisers on policy: Ira Magaziner, George Stephanopoulos, and first lady Hillary Rodham Clinton. The fragmentation of advice that this structure produced reflected Clinton's desire to be at the center of an informal, collegial policy-making process, which he ran like a continuous seminar.[61] With respect to selling and implementing his policy choices, however, Clinton preferred a more formal structure.[62]

George W. Bush retained the Domestic Policy Council and the National Economic Council as coordinating units at the outset of his administration and staffed each with trusted assistants.[63] But the administration also relied heavily on ad hoc task forces to work on particular policy problems. For example, Vice President Cheney headed the group that designed a national energy policy, and a second group was formed to review military preparedness. The principal Bush innovation in this area was creation of the Homeland Security Council, created on October 8, 2001, designed to coordinate efforts by the many government units that touched on homeland security; the president ultimately concluded that a department structure would be more effective.[64]

Presidential Control of the Bureaucracy

Although presidents face substantial obstacles in seeking to control policy-making and implementation, they do have resources for this effort. They have substantial powers granted by the Constitution, delegated by Congress, and derived from the nature of their office. The most important are the powers to appoint and remove subordinates, to issue executive orders, and to prepare the annual federal budget and regulate expenditures.

Appointment and Removal

The Constitution gives the president broad powers of appointment (Article II, Section 2, Paragraph 2), but it makes high-ranking officials subject to senatorial confirmation, and it authorizes Congress to vest the appointment of lower officials in the president, in department heads, or in the courts. Congress determines whether the Senate must confirm an appointment. The Senate can also narrow the president's discretion in making appointments by establishing detailed qualifications for various offices. Congress cannot, however, give itself the power to appoint executive officials.[65] Neither can it force the president to make an appointment to a vacant position.[66] The president's appointive powers also are constrained by political considerations and practices such as senatorial courtesy, whereby senators effectively have veto power over certain administrative and judicial appointments from their home states.

The Senate generally has given presidents considerable leeway in the appointment of top-level executives. But confirmation is not automatic, and the Senate has used rejections to express disapproval of specific individuals or practices.[67] Since Watergate (1972–1974), the Senate has tended to be more careful and procedurally consistent in examining nominees' backgrounds, qualifications, and relevant policy views. Enhanced vigilance has made the confirmation process "more tedious, time-consuming, and intrusive for the nominees," a situation exacerbated by interparty conflict.[68] For example, the Senate finally confirmed Richard C. Holbrooke as U.S. permanent representative to the United Nations in August 1999 after a fourteen-month odyssey that included two federal ethics investigations, four hearings conducted by the Senate Foreign Relations Committee, and "holds"—objections to a nominee that delay action—placed by several Republican senators in an effort to wrest concessions from the administration on unrelated matters. The prospect of such a tortuous and contentious process causes candidates to withdraw from consideration or decline invitations to serve.[69]

At the outset of his term, George W. Bush had about 1,200 full-time positions subject to Senate confirmation to fill,[70] and he confronted unusual hurdles in doing so. Already delayed by the 2000 election controversy, the new Senate was initially bogged down in a 50–50 stalemate, then experienced a change in the majority party from Republican to Democrat in June 2001, and finally experienced confusion after September 11. By early 2002, the Brookings Institution's Presidential Appointee Initiative announced that "the Bush administration is now the slowest in modern history to fill its top appointed positions."[71] During Bush's first year in office, it took an average of 181 days for nominees to be confirmed, up from Clinton's 174 days and Reagan's 142. Most of the blame for tardy action could be laid at the feet of Congress, but even twenty-three months into the administration, some positions still had not been filled, delays that could reflect heightened efforts to select candidates with compatible policy views.[72] Delays in staffing positions may make a difference. For example, in the case of the Securities and Exchange Commission, a five-member regulatory agency overseeing stock and bond trading, four seats remained vacant in the new administration while questionable accounting practices and corporate misdeeds rocked the investment community during 2002. Four nominees were confirmed on July 25, 2002; one nominee had waited seven months for a committee hearing.[73]

The Constitution also empowers the president to make appointments when the Senate is in recess. Such appointments must be confirmed by the end of the Senate's next session, but in the interim the appointee continues to serve. Senators often object to recess appointments to high-level positions because they feel inhibited from thoroughly examining people who have already begun their duties. Presidents now have fewer opportunities to make recess appointments, but President Clinton made extensive use of acting appointments after Republicans gained control of the Senate in 1995, and he encountered problems getting nominees approved. Temporary appointments became long running, a controversial exercise of this constitutional power. For example, the head of the Justice Department's Criminal Division served on an acting basis for two and a half years without even being nominated. Walter E. Dellinger III served as solicitor general—the federal government's lead lawyer before the Supreme Court—for more than fourteen months without ever having his name submitted for Senate approval because a major battle was expected.[74] George W. Bush made several controversial recess appointments, though they have attracted less public attention than his predecessor's.[75]

Complementing the appointment power, and fundamental to presidential control of the executive branch, is the removal power. Without the ability to remove subordinate officials on performance or policy grounds, the president cannot be held fully responsible for their actions or for a department's or agency's failure to achieve presidential objectives. The Constitution is silent, however, concerning the removal of executive officials other than through impeachment, a cumbersome process limited to instances of "bribery, treason, and other high crimes and misdemeanors."

Presidents have clashed with Congress over the removal power. The post–Civil War conflict between President Andrew Johnson and Congress over Reconstruction policy involved the removal power. In 1867, Congress brought impeachment proceedings against Johnson for violating the Tenure of Office Act, which it had passed over his veto. That statute authorized all persons appointed with the advice and consent of the Senate to continue to hold office until the president appointed, and the Senate confirmed, a successor. Johnson tried to remove Secretary of War Edwin Stanton without permission. Although Johnson survived the impeachment trial by one vote, the issue of the removal power remained unresolved. (Congress repealed the Tenure of Office Act in 1887.)

The Supreme Court dealt directly with the removal power in a decision involving a challenge to Woodrow Wilson's summary removal of a postmaster.[76] The Court invalidated an 1876 law that required senatorial consent for a post- master's removal. It held that the Constitution gave the president the removal power and Congress could not place restrictions on its exercise. Nine years later, however, the Court upheld the provisions of the Federal Trade Commission Act that limited the grounds for removal of its members.[77] The Court ruled that the president's unqualified power of removal is limited to "purely executive offices" and that Congress may prescribe conditions for the removal of officials perform- ing "quasi-legislative" and "quasi-judicial" functions. However, the Court has not clarified fully the meaning of these terms. A dramatic instance of the removal power occurred in August 1981, when Reagan fired 11,400 striking members of the Professional Air Traffic Controllers Organization. A U.S. court of appeals upheld the action, interpreting it as a discharge of the president's obligation to enforce a statute prohibiting strikes by federal employees.[78]

Executive Orders and Direct Action

Recent presidents have used executive orders and presidential memoranda to take dramatic action during their initial hours and days in office. Moments after delivering his first inaugural address, Reagan used a presidential memorandum to freeze federal hiring to support his contention that big government was the problem, not the solution; Clinton issued an executive order on ethics while still on Capitol Hill after delivering his first inaugural and then used high visibility presidential memoranda over the next several days to reverse the previous administration's prohibition on abortion counseling; George W. Bush issued three memoranda on his inauguration day, followed by several more in the next week to emphasize high-level policy priorities, including the redefinition of rela- tionships between faith-based programs and the government.[79] These examples illustrate a long-standing presidential practice: using a variety of unilateral instruments or direct administration to accomplish goals, including executive orders, directives, memoranda, proclamations, policy instructions, and interpre- tations of congressional intent.

Under a strict interpretation of separation of powers, presidents have no direct legislative authority. From the beginning, however, they have issued orders and directives on the basis of Article II. Most modern presidents have fol- lowed Theodore Roosevelt's "stewardship" theory of executive power (see chap- ter 1), which holds that Article II confers on them inherent power to take whatever actions they deem necessary in the national interest unless prohibited by the Constitution or by law. Executive orders have been a primary means of exercising this broad presidential prerogative power. "They are presidential edicts, legal instruments that create or modify laws, procedures, and policy by fiat," and have helped push "the boundaries of presidential power by taking advantage of gaps in constitutional and statutory language that allow them to fill power vacuums and gain control of emerging capabilities."[80]

Reliance on such strategies is especially prominent in crucial policy areas such as civil rights, economic stabilization, and national security,[81] or when conflict with Congress means action cannot be accomplished through legislation. In civil rights, Franklin Roosevelt established a Fair Employment Practices Commission in 1943 to prevent discriminatory hiring by government agencies and military suppliers. In 1948, Harry S. Truman ended segregation in the armed forces by executive order. In March 1961, John Kennedy issued a sweeping order creating the Equal Employment Opportunity Commission and giving it broad enforcement powers. Lyndon Johnson went further, requiring by executive order preferential hiring of minorities by government contractors.

FDR established broad precedents for the use of executive orders to achieve economic stability, and a number of his successors have followed suit. During World War II, he issued executive orders to establish the Office of Price Administration (OPA) and the Office of Economic Stabilization and to give them extensive powers over prices, wages, and profits. The OPA also rationed scarce consumer goods such as meat, butter, shoes, tires, and gasoline. As a basis for his actions, Roosevelt cited his responsibility to respond to the "unlimited emergency" created by the war. The Emergency Price Control Act of 1942 provided retroactive statutory endorsement for the establishment of the emergency agencies and the measures they implemented. In 1970, in the face of persistent inflation, Congress passed the Economic Stabilization Act, which authorized the president to issue orders that would control wages and prices, but with few criteria to guide these actions. On August 15, 1971, Nixon issued an executive order imposing a ninety-day freeze on nonagricultural wages and prices and establishing the Cost of Living Council to administer the controls. An October 15 order extended the controls and established additional machinery to aid in administering them.[82]

Presidents also have used executive orders and national security directives to guide foreign policy. In 1942, for example, FDR issued an executive order requiring the internment of all persons of Japanese ancestry living in the Pacific coastal states, 70,000 of them U.S. citizens. The Supreme Court upheld this massive deprivation of civil liberties on the basis of the commander-in-chief clause.[83]

President Carter made the heaviest use of executive orders among the past seven administrations; presidents since 1981 have used them less (see Table 6-3). President Bush issued more executive orders in the three months following 9/11 than he had in the previous eight months; several of them proved especially controversial (see chapter 11).[84]

Presidents have made extensive use of executive orders to accomplish a wide range of policy goals. Franklin Roosevelt issued one of the most controversial orders in 1942 when more than 110,000 Japanese Americans living on the West Coast were relocated to internment camps around the nation.

There is some disagreement over whether presidents confronted by a Congress controlled by the opposition party will make heavier use of executive orders. For example, year-to-year totals show that Clinton's use of executive orders actually declined rather than increased when he confronted a hostile Republican Congress after 1995, though he may still have used executive orders as a way to make progress on major policy initiatives.[85] In his exhaustive study of executive orders, Kenneth Mayer traces the pattern of their use from 1936 through 1995 and concludes that the issuance of orders "rises and falls in response to significant events."[86] The onset of war, for instance, triggers new administrative arrangements and regulations governing economic controls and wartime mobilization, just as peace requires their removal. The focus of executive orders has also changed over time. Orders dealing with executive branch administration, foreign affairs, and domestic policy increased during the period of 1936–1999.[87] Finally, Democrats make more use of executive orders than Republicans, more orders are issued at the end of a term and when the president's public support is low than under the opposite conditions, and more orders

Table 6-3   Executive Orders, 1969–1/21/2003

President/years in office	Total executive orders issued by administration	Executive orders per year
Richard Nixon (1969–1974)	346	62.9
Gerald R. Ford (1974–1977)	169	67.6
Jimmy Carter (1977–1981)	320	80.0
Ronald Reagan (1981–1989)	381	47.6
George Bush (1989–1993)	166	41.5
William J. Clinton (1993–2001)	364	45.5
George W. Bush (2001–1/21/2003)	110	55.0

Source: www.archives.gov/federal_register/executive_orders/disposition_tables.html.

are issued when the president's party is in the congressional majority, a counterintuitive finding.[88]

Phillip J. Cooper argues that the real question should be more about the content, than the quantity, of such actions and the reasons presidents use them. In particular, recent administrations use "presidential memoranda" alongside, and interchangeably with, executive orders; and Clinton is credited with issuing 536 presidential memoranda, many more than his predecessors.[89] Unlike executive orders, memoranda do not have to be published in the *Federal Register*, in which rules and orders appear, nor is there a procedure for developing them, thereby making them simpler to issue. Ultimately, the question will be whether Congress and others will accept such assertions of presidential prerogative. In fact, unilateral presidential action can be reversed. During the Korean War, the Supreme Court invalidated Truman's seizure of the steel industry on the grounds that he had not used the machinery established in the Taft-Hartley Act of 1947 to avert a strike.[90] More recently, we have the example of successor presidents reversing an action of their predecessors, as Clinton and the younger Bush did.[91]

From 1932 until 1983, Congress exerted a measure of control over executive lawmaking with the legislative veto. Provisions added to certain statutes gave Congress the power to review and reject executive orders or administrative regulations authorized by the legislation. The legislative veto took various forms. It allowed disapproval of regulations by concurrent resolution or by simple resolution of either house or by action of a committee of either house. In its most common form, the legislative veto required that the proposed action lie before Congress for a specified period—usually sixty or ninety days—during which either chamber could disapprove it. The president's reorganization authority, which Congress first authorized in 1939, carried such a procedure. Other major statutes that had a form of legislative veto include the War Powers Resolution of 1973, the Budget and Impoundment Control Act of 1974, the Federal Elections Campaign Act of 1974, and the National Emergencies Act of 1976. More than 250 statutes provided for some type of legislative veto before the Supreme Court declared it unconstitutional in 1983.

In *Immigration and Naturalization Service v. Chadha,* the Court held the one-house legislative veto provision of the Immigration and Nationality Act to an unconstitutional breach of the separation of powers.[92] The Court reasoned that the veto involved "the exercise of legislative power" without "bicameral passage followed by presentment to the President," that is, such actions were not subject to presidential concurrence or veto. Initial reaction to the decision was that it was not a definitive ruling and that somehow Congress would find a way statutorily to control executive branch lawmaking.[93] Although the Court threw out past practices, Congress has required agencies to obtain approval from the appropriations committees before taking specified actions and used informal agreements with agencies to achieve the same goal.[94]

Congress has also employed the joint resolution of approval before an executive action can be taken.[95] For example, the Reorganization Act Amendments of 1984 provide that a presidentially prepared reorganization plan submitted to Congress cannot take effect unless approved by a joint resolution within ninety days. This provision places the burden on the president rather than on Congress, and the president has only a specific number of days in which to act. In effect, the joint resolution of approval works like a one-house legislative veto: if either house refuses to approve an action, it cannot be taken. The major disadvantage of the device for Congress is that it requires much time, and extensive use of it would threaten the congressional agenda with legislative gridlock.

Presidents and Money

Presidents have substantial financial powers, delegated by Congress, which they use in their efforts to control the bureaucracy. The most important is the power to formulate the budget, which controls the amount of spending by federal departments and agencies. It also establishes the president's spending priorities, sets the timing of program initiatives, and distributes rewards to, and imposes sanctions on, executive branch units.[96] By controlling the total amount of the budget, the president can try to influence the economy's performance. *(See chapter 9.)*

Presidential use of the executive budget developed in the twentieth century. The enormous increase in expenditures during World War I, and the task of managing the sizable national debt that resulted, convinced Congress of the need for an executive budget. The Budget and Accounting Act of 1921 made the president responsible for compiling department and agency estimates and for submitting them annually to Congress in the form of a budget. The statute established the Bureau of the Budget (BOB), in the Treasury Department, to assist the president in assembling and revising the estimates. The statute barred departments and agencies from submitting their requests directly to Congress as they had done previously.

The initial emphasis in the development of the federal budget process was on control of expenditures and prevention of administrative abuses.[97] During the 1930s, the emphasis shifted from control to management. The budget was seen as a means of evaluating and improving administrative performance. The transfer of BOB in 1939 from the Treasury Department to the new Executive Office of the President symbolized the management orientation. BOB was to become the president's management arm. A decade later, the government adopted a performance budget organized by functions and activities rather than by line items representing objects of expenditure.

The most recent stage in the development of budgeting is its orientation toward planning. This emphasis attempts to link annual budgeting, geared to the appropriations process in Congress, to long-range planning of government objectives. The limited success of the planning orientation is reflected in the rapid arrival and departure of budgeting systems, such as the program planning budgeting system (PPBS) and zero-base budgeting (ZBB).[98] The budgeting process, as it had developed by the early 1970s, embodied all three orientations—control, management, and planning—but it was least effective as a planning device.

Because the annual budget process is inherently incremental and subject to restrictions and conditions imposed by Congress, the executive budget has only limited utility as an aid to presidential decision making. The budget cycle forces the president and Congress to act according to a timetable that stretches from twenty-two months before the start of the fiscal year (October 1) through the ensuing year. Congress and the bureaucracy are concerned primarily with how large an increase or decrease will be made in a department's or an agency's budget. From 1982 to 1997, huge federal deficits accompanied by strong public resistance to tax increases caused presidential and congressional budget decisions to be focused primarily on reducing spending. The emergence of a budget surplus in 1998 ushered in a debate between Republicans and Democrats over the need for tax cuts. Republicans finally won the struggle in 2001, when George W. Bush engineered a massive tax cut to be spread over eleven years, and then accelerated in the additional cuts of 2003. But when the threat of deficits emerged in mid-2001, questions again arose about the government's capacity to plan effectively, and several Democrats seeking the presidency in 2004 proposed that the tax cuts be rolled back. *(See chapter 9 for further details.)*

Congress makes its own budget decisions. It limits total spending through resolutions proposed by the budget committees in each house. Although the congressional budget total is usually fairly close to the president's, the priorities in the two budgets often differ sharply. Deficit politics constrained Bill Clinton when he attempted to use his first budget as a vehicle for policy change.[99] Although Congress narrowly (with no Republican support) accepted most of his five-year plan (1994–1998) to reduce the deficit by almost $500 billion, it embarrassed Clinton by rejecting a $16 billion package to stimulate the economy.[100] In 1995, the first Republican-controlled Congress in forty years ignored the administration's budget, which did not contain proposals for eventually eliminating the deficit, and adopted a budget resolution that projected a balanced budget in fiscal year 2002. Nearly two years of budget battles ensued, not resolved until a 1997 agreement was reached on how to balance the budget.[101] George W. Bush, in contrast, found a cooperative Congress controlled by his own party during the first half of 2001 and secured passage of his tax cut.

In addition to budgeting, presidents have certain discretionary spending powers that increase their leverage over the bureaucracy. They have substantial non-statutory authority, based on understandings with congressional appropriations committees, to transfer funds within an appropriation and from one program to another. The committees expect to be kept informed of such "reprogramming" actions.[102] Fund transfer authority is essential to sound financial management, but it can be abused to circumvent congressional decisions. In 1970, Nixon transferred funds to support an extensive unauthorized covert military operation in Cambodia. Nevertheless, Congress has given presidents and certain agencies the authority to spend substantial amounts of money on a confidential basis, the largest and most controversial being for intelligence activities.

Presidents also have exercised some measure of expenditure control through the practice of impounding or returning appropriated funds to the Treasury Department. Since George Washington, presidents have routinely impounded funds to achieve savings when actual expenditures fall short of appropriations.[103] They also have withheld funds when authorized or directed to do so by Congress for purposes such as establishing contingency reserves or imposing a ceiling on total expenditures. Presidents from FDR through Lyndon Johnson also impounded some of the funds Congress had added, over their objections, for various programs. Although such actions often drew congressional criticism, they did not lead to confrontation because they occurred infrequently and were generally focused on expenditures for specific programs or projects. Congress recognized that circumspect use of impoundments helped its members resist pressure for increased spending.[104]

Impoundment became a major constitutional issue during the Nixon administration. Sweeping impoundments in domestic program areas, especially agriculture, housing, and water pollution control, led to charges that the president arbitrarily and illegally had substituted his spending priorities for those of Congress. Nixon's impoundments differed from those of other presidents in several ways: they involved larger amounts; some were made in direct violation of explicit congressional instructions to spend the funds; some were designed to terminate entire programs rather than individual projects; and some were directed at appropriated funds that had not been included in the president's budget proposals. Moreover, Nixon claimed constitutional, rather than statutory, authority for impoundment[105] and used it as the primary weapon in a battle with Congress over domestic spending priorities. He did not bargain or negotiate but imposed his priorities by fiat.

Nixon's actions resulted in lawsuits to compel release of the funds; most were decided against the president on statutory grounds. Congress also passed the Budget and Impoundment Control Act of 1974. The Antideficiency Act of 1950 had limited the purposes of impoundments to establishing contingency reserves and the saving of money that otherwise would be wasted. The 1974 statute established procedures for congressional review by requiring the president to report all impoundments to Congress. Proposals to rescind appropriated funds, that is, to return them to the Treasury, must be approved by both houses within forty-five days. Either house can disapprove proposals to defer spending to the next fiscal year.

The Supreme Court's ruling invalidating the legislative veto affected congressional power to control impoundments. (Since the 1974 legislation called for approval of rescissions by both houses, *Chadha* did not invalidate that procedure.) The only way left for Congress to overturn a deferral of funds is by passing a bill or joint resolution. Because such a measure is subject to presidential veto, the president's deferral power is strengthened. Congress's most effective way of circumventing a possible veto is by attaching a rider canceling the deferral to an appropriation bill the president feels compelled to sign to keep the involved agencies operating. But riders are a cumbersome device. When Reagan began to defer sizable amounts ($5.4 billion for fiscal 1986) in his second term as a means of reducing spending on programs he opposed, Congress found itself without a viable means of controlling the deferrals.[106]

In 1996, Clinton was the beneficiary of the Republican Party's promise in its 1994 election manifesto, the Contract with America, to establish a line-item veto for the president's use in fighting the budget deficit, a power many governors enjoy. Clinton was the first, and probably last, president to enjoy this power. The Line-Item Veto Act authorized the president to cancel specific spending items or tax breaks rather than veto an entire appropriation bill only when the budget was in deficit. Ultimately, the Supreme Court invalidated this statute in 1998[107] but not before Clinton invoked the authority eighty-two times.

Presidential Management of the Bureaucracy

In addition to their formal powers, modern presidents have relied on managerial tools in their efforts to coordinate and direct executive branch operations. Three major tools—staffing, reorganization, and planning—have been employed with mixed results. This is not to argue that the public sector is inhospitable to modern management techniques, but to suggest that political forces significantly affect their use.[108]

Staffing

As discussed in chapters 1 and 4, the institutionalized presidency has grown steadily as presidents have used staff to direct the executive branch and fulfill their many roles. From the vantage point of the Oval Office it may sometimes seem that there are "people, people everywhere but none to do his will."[109] Although recent administrations have used presidential staffs and the cabinet in different ways, the long-term trend has been toward increasing reliance on a strong, sizable, centralized White House staff to protect the political interests of presidents, to act as their principal policy advisers, and to direct (as opposed to monitor and coordinate) the implementation of presidential priorities by the bureaucracy. Centralizing power in the White House may appear to have been a *linear* process, but Andrew Rudalevige effectively argues that centralization is *contingent* on the president's needs, the shifting environment, and estimates of the full range of available strategies for accomplishing presidential goals.[110]

Critics of this development argue that it has undercut the cabinet's advisory potential, narrowed the president's perspective on policy choices, and inhibited effective and responsive bureaucratic performance. Stephen Hess cautions that reliance on a centralized White House staff has been "self-defeating."[111] Experiences under Nixon and Reagan support this view. Yet Ford and Carter both tried a decentralized model of White House staffing and abandoned it in favor of hierarchical arrangements.

George Bush adopted the hierarchical model of organization from the outset. Former New Hampshire governor John Sununu served as White House chief of staff, functioning as the guardian of the president's political interests, serving as Bush's link to conservatives, and often appearing to set the administration's course on domestic social policy issues. In these roles, he was the target of considerable congressional and media criticism that ultimately made him a liability.[112]

The Clinton White House reflected the leadership style of a highly intelligent, energetic, enthusiastic, and enormously self-confident president who lacked self-discipline, assumed many personal responsibilities, had difficulty focusing his goals and managing his efforts, and was reluctant to delegate. Clinton entered office with no plan for organizing the White House and proceeded to staff it largely with consultants from his campaign and friends and political associates from Arkansas.[113] The staff lacked the Washington experience and political stature that might have prevented damaging early missteps such as the botched nominations of Zoë Baird and Kimba Wood to be attorney general, the conflict with Congress over ending discrimination against gays in the military, and the defeat of the economic stimulus bill.

Clinton's initial chief of staff, Thomas F. McLarty III, was replaced in June 1994 by Leon Panetta, the OMB director, who brought much-needed order. Panetta and his successors, Erskine Bowles and John Podesta, established control over the flow of communications and personal access to the president.[114] A greater degree of centralization and formal organization proved a necessity to counteract Clinton's lack of discipline. Clinton also demonstrated the ability to recognize his failings and take corrective action. White House staff personnel at the start of Clinton's second term were more pragmatic and less ideological and had more Washington experience than their first-term counterparts.[115]

George W. Bush has followed a modified version of the "spokes-in-a-wheel" White House structure so successful during Reagan's first term. In this model, a limited number of aides have access to a president who freely delegates responsibilities. Like Reagan, Bush had three principal aides. Andrew Card served as chief of staff, a position that has become so prevalent across both Republican and Democratic administrations as to warrant being described as "institutionalized." He was joined by Karl Rove, the political strategist, and Karen Hughes, the press and public relations adviser. Card had served as deputy chief of staff in the earlier

Bush administration. Rove and Hughes had been longtime aides to the younger Bush in Texas.[116]

Two other advisers have played a special role in the Bush administration. Vice President Cheney has been a looming presence, playing a central role even before the terrorist attacks of 9/11, the subsequent war in Afghanistan, and the intervention in Iraq, all of which further heightened his reputed influence. Cheney served as Ford's White House chief of staff and George H. W. Bush's secretary of defense during the Persian Gulf War. His previous White House experience no doubt contributed to creating a smoothly functioning staff system that drew high praise during its initial months. Cheney has been given some of the most challenging assignments in the administration, including relations with Congress, developing a national energy strategy, and being a full participant (some would say the major architect) of the administration's policies to counter terrorism and proliferation of weapons of mass destruction. He has been an effective spokesman for administration policy and has sometimes used his appearances to launch "trial balloons," policy ideas the administration wants to have broadly discussed without giving them the stature of a presidential pronouncement. This public role has also been played, at times, by Condoleeza Rice, a fellow veteran of the first Bush administration. Because of the prominence of international relations and conflict that emerged during Bush's first year in office, Rice has spent considerable time with the president and in brokering discussions between two of the most forceful members of the Bush cabinet, Secretaries Powell and Rumsfeld of State and Defense, respectively.

In striking contrast to Clinton, Bush emerged as a "disciplined delegator," who drew upon the services of his able aides from the outset.[117] Critics, however, raised the same questions as they had about Reagan and Eisenhower. When presidents delegate, "who's really in charge?" For critics, it seemed that Vice President Cheney was exercising more responsibility than his constitutional superior, an issue fueled by several health crises Cheney experienced during the administration's first months,[118] the president's absence from Washington on 9/11, and the vice president's prominence in policy-making circles.

Since the Reagan administration, the presidency has become increasingly centralized and politicized. Terry Moe defends these developments as an inescapable consequence of the extensive expectations that impinge upon the presidency.[119] A similar conclusion emerged from a 1986 symposium featuring eight former White House chiefs of staff (or their functional equivalents), who served presidents from Eisenhower through Carter. In their views, "the demands for activism and the requirements of self-reliance encourage presidents to look favorably upon the kinds of services provided by a rationalized White House run by a strong chief."[120] The Bush experience falls squarely in this pattern.

Reorganization

It has been almost an article of faith among political leaders and public administration theorists that executive reorganization can increase presidential power over the bureaucracy. Johnson, Nixon, and Carter believed the performance of the executive branch could be improved and the bureaucracy brought to heel through such changes. However, Johnson's efforts were nonconsequential, and Nixon's were interrupted by his resignation. By most accounts, the results of Carter's reorganization efforts—by far the most extensive—were modest.[121]

Organizational structure and administrative arrangements are significant because they reflect values and priorities and affect access to decision makers. The location and status of an administrative unit—as a department, an independent agency, or a component of a department—symbolize the importance of its goals and the interests it serves. Administrative arrangements also can contribute to or frustrate the achievement of accountability to Congress and the public. Reorganizing, however, does not necessarily result in increased operational efficiency, greater program effectiveness, or enhanced public accountability. There is no ideal form for a government agency or a consistent set of prescriptions for organizing the executive branch. One set of standard prescriptions tends to centralize authority; another tends to disperse it. The most profound consequences of organizational change are not in the "engineered realm of efficiency, simplicity, size, and cost of government"; rather, they lie in the areas of "political influence, policy emphasis, and communication of governmental intentions."[122] For example, the placement of the Occupational Safety and Health Administration in the Department of Labor rather than in the Department of Health, Education, and Welfare led to an initial focus of regulations on mechanical, rather than biological, hazards in the workplace. Experience has shown that although the rationale for reorganization is couched in the rhetoric of economy and efficiency, the crucial factors in decisions to reorganize are power, policy, and symbolic significance.

In 1939, Congress authorized presidents to propose executive reorganization plans that take effect after sixty days unless disapproved by both houses. When extending that authority in 1949, Congress allowed either house to disapprove such plans. Congress continued to renew the reorganization authority with little change until 1973, when it was allowed to lapse in the conflict with Nixon over his efforts to centralize control of the executive branch. In 1977, Carter requested and received renewal of the authority with provision for veto by either house. Neither Reagan, Bush, nor Clinton displayed any interest in using the reorganization power, while Bush's creation of the Department of Homeland Security has been his principal use of this power.

Carter's reorganization achievements exceeded those of his immediate predecessors and of his successors but fell far short of the thorough restructuring of the executive branch and reduction in the number of agencies he had promised. Congress passed legislation that established new cabinet Departments of Energy and of Education and allowed five reorganization plans to take effect. Carter and his staff were unprepared for the jurisdictional conflicts that accompanied congressional consideration of reorganization proposals.[123] The president also lacked a well-conceived, comprehensive, politically defensible strategy. The Carter experience indicates that reorganization has its uses, but they are more in the realm of policy and politics than management improvement.

The Clinton administration ignored reorganization in favor of the personnel reductions called for in Vice President Gore's *National Performance Review Report*, along with the report's recommendations to cut red tape, enhance customer satisfaction, empower employees, and eliminate unneeded functions. That report broke sharply with the administrative management paradigm that had dominated presidential efforts to manage the bureaucracy since the Brownlow Committee report of 1937. That philosophy, which the reports of the Hoover Commission (1949) and the Ash Council (1971) also embodied, "emphasized the need for democratic accountability of departmental and agency officers to the President and his central management agencies and through these institutions to the Congress."[124] In its stead, the Gore report embraced the entrepreneurial management paradigm popularized by David Osborne and Ted Gaebler in *Reinventing Government*.[125] They call for a "cultural and behavioral shift in the management of government" from a bureaucratic to an entrepreneurial government. In their view, public agencies are entrepreneurial organizations competing in a market environment in which success is determined by customer satisfaction. Clinton's reinvention effort evolved over time and in two later phases shifted attention to reducing government's cost and then to attacking complex problems, such as finding ways to create and maintain "safe communities," a highly complex issue for government to tackle.[126] Clinton's departure from administrative orthodoxy sparked extensive discussion among academics,[127] but in the short run, few conclusions can be drawn about his novel strategy.

George W. Bush made the Clinton strategy his own by adding a few distinctive features. He has sought to reduce government employment by ultimately making at least half of the federal jobs subject to competitive bidding from the private sector, and he sought to realize this goal by establishing numerical targets for outsourcing jobs—5 percent of commercial-like jobs in 2002 increasing to 15 percent by the end of fiscal 2003.[128]

Planning

Aaron Wildavsky defined planning as "current action to secure future consequences."[129] Foresight in anticipating problems and developing solutions is the essence of effective planning. A hallmark of successful corporate management has been long-range planning, but the federal government has not had a high degree of success here. Presidents have engaged in long-range planning with only limited success. As noted, attempts to combine annual budgeting with comprehensive planning through the program planning budgeting system and zero-base budgeting have not succeeded. Introduced throughout the government by Johnson in 1965, PPBS used cost-benefit calculations to choose between alternative programs and formulate long-range objectives. ZBB, a Carter project, compared the effects of alternative funding levels on long-term objectives within a single program. Both approaches entailed comprehensive attempts to relate spending decisions to long-range consequences. Each required extensive amounts of information and analyses that were never integrated with budget decisions. Thus bureau and agency officials did not find it worthwhile to take either process seriously. A fatal defect of PPBS and ZBB was neglect of the hard political choices involved in the budget process. Congress was not supportive of either device.

Nixon had introduced a similar technique that focused on goals, called management by objectives (MBO), to strengthen his oversight of the executive branch. He directed twenty-one departments and agencies to prepare rank-order lists of their principal objectives. After OMB reviewed the lists, the president approved objectives for each reporting unit. These presidential objectives then became the standard for monitoring the units' performances. MBO differed from the planning process of PPBS and ZBB in that it focused first on immediate objectives, then on intermediate objectives that could be achieved in a fiscal year, and finally on long-term goals.[130] Other than to continue multiyear budgeting introduced by Carter, Reagan demonstrated little interest in planning. He appeared to believe that domestic policy planning was socialistic and incompatible with a free market economy. George H. W. Bush, although neglecting domestic policy planning, was committed to, and actively involved in, foreign and defense policy planning. Generally, planning in these areas has been more successful than in domestic policy, and future presidents will always need to engage in national security planning. Clinton's proposals for reforming health care and the welfare system included planning that linked them to the five-year deficit reduction that was integral to the 1994 budget. But he exhibited little planning after the Republicans assumed control of Congress in 1995. Moving toward a balanced budget then became the overriding concern. In the administration's terminal years, creating a legacy was more important than planning.

With a heavy emphasis on pursuing legislative victories during its early months, the administration of George W. Bush did not show much attention to planning, with the notable exception of developing a coherent energy policy. Just two weeks into the new administration, Bush named Vice President Cheney to head a task force that released its recommendations on May 17, 2001, after meeting largely in secret. The administration's proposals primarily focused on ways to increase the supply of energy rather than conserve its use—encouraging oil and natural gas exploration, building electric transmission infrastructure, encouraging use of coal, and supporting nuclear power generation.[131] But the complex plan met enormous resistance in the face of electric outages in California, rising gas prices, and concerns about environmental protections. Questions arose about whether an "energy industry that put its financial backing solidly behind Bush's election has received a plan that offers support for every major form of energy production and distribution."[132] Even more difficult tasks of planning would lie ahead.

Conclusion

Can the president lead the executive branch? Many of the studies discussed here raise doubts.[133] Although presidents have substantial formal powers and managerial resources, they wrestle with the problem of controlling their own branch of government. Their capacity to direct its many departments and agencies in the implementation of presidential policies is limited by bureaucratic complexity and fragmentation, conflict between the presidency and the bureaucracy, external pressure and influence on the bureaucracy, and the extreme difficulty of establishing an effective management system within the government.

Important milestones in this effort can be found throughout the twentieth century. Roosevelt created the Executive Office of the President in 1939, providing his successors with a critical group of presidential loyalists and policy experts independent of bureaucratic pressures. Johnson's enthusiastic endorsement of the program planning budgeting system in 1966 started a series of experiments in using the budget as a planning instrument. Nixon's centralization of decisions in the White House is a strategy others have emulated. Carter established the potential as well as the limits of using reorganization as a management tool, and his sponsorship of the Civil Service Reform Act of 1978 created a new cadre of presidential allies in the civil service.

Ronald Reagan came closest to assembling these instruments of control into a coherent administrative strategy, a consensus that prevails even more than two decades after he assumed office.[134] Reagan's centralized control of appointments fashioned a relatively unified "team" by making ideological compatibility with his goals the principal criterion for selection. Reagan also used cabinet councils as a means to link the White House staff with the cabinet officials in directing policy efforts. Most important, he used the budget to enforce his spending priorities on departments and agencies. In the face of strong pressures to reduce spending, he reversed the traditional pattern of budget preparation from the bottom up, in which agencies attempt to protect their bases, and instituted top-down budgeting, with presidential and OMB decisions being determinative.[135] Finally, Reagan attempted to accomplish policy change administratively wherever possible. This involved establishing procedures for review of regulations by OMB, diminishing the intensity of regulatory enforcement, and reinterpreting agency functions and relations with clientele in accordance with the administration's ideology.[136]

Each president faces anew the challenges of asserting control. Reagan's successes did not extend to his successors, though they did provide guidance for future efforts. No doubt George W. Bush and his White House aides have been attentive students.

NOTES

1. John Mintz, "Homeland Agency Launched; Bush Signs Bill to Combine Federal Security Functions," *Washington Post*, November 26, 2002, A1.

2. See www.whitehouse.gov/deptofhomeland/bill/title1.html#101.

3. See www.dhs.gov/dhspublic/display?theme=13.

4. Ivo H. Daalder et. al., *Assessing the Department of Homeland Security*, Brookings, Washington, D.C., July 2002, www.brook.edu/dybdocroot/fp/projects/homeland/assessdhs.pdf. See especially 17–25 (numbered 1–9 in the document) for background on the emergence of the proposal.

5. Spencer S. Hsu, "A Public Coup for the Secret Service Agency May Gain Clout after a Move to Planned Homeland Security Department," *Washington Post,* August 14, 2002, A27.

6. Edward Walsh, "Changing Customs: Can Free Trade Flourish with Focus on Terrorism?" *Washington Post,* July 26, 2002, A31.

7. Sara Kehaulani Goo, "Fledgling TSA Offers Lessons: Lawmakers Urged Not to Ask Too Much of New Department," July 22, 2002, A13.

8. Walter Pincus, "FEMA's Influence May Be Cut under New Department," *Washington Post,* July 24, 2002, A17.

9. Sydney J. Freedberg Jr., Corine Hegland, and Margaret Kriz "Repeating the Past?" *National Journal,* June 14, 2002, www.nationaljournal.com/members/news/2002/06/0614nj2.htm.

10. Richard E. Cohen, Siobhan Gorman, and Sydney J. Freedberg Jr, "The Ultimate Turf War," *National Journal,* January 3, 2003, www.nationaljournal.com/members/news/2003/01/0103nj1.htm.

11. Siobhan Gorman, Sydney J. Freedberg Jr., and Peter H. Stone, "New Department, New Special Interests," *National Journal,* December 6, 2002, www.nationaljournal.com/members/news/2002/12/1206nj7.htm.

12. Christopher Lee and Stephen Barr, "New Agency, New Rules—and a Cost: Bush Gets Management Freedom, and a Measure of Mistrust among Workers," *Washington Post,* November 14, 2002, A31.

13. Richard Rose, "Government against Subgovernments: A European Perspective on Washington," in *Presidents and Prime Ministers,* ed. Richard Rose and Ezra N. Suleiman (Washington, D.C.: American Enterprise Institute, 1980), 339.

14. For a view that regards presidents as much more than passive participants in agency design, see David E. Lewis, *Presidents and the Politics of Agency Design* (Stanford: Stanford University Press, 2003).

15. James P. Pfiffner challenges this viewpoint and maintains that presidents tend to overestimate the opposition they will get from the bureaucracy. See Pfiffner, "Political Appointees and Career Executives: The Democracy-Bureaucracy Nexus in the Third Century," *Public Administration Review* (January–February 1987): 57–65.

16. Hugh Heclo, *A Government of Strangers* (Washington, D.C.: Brookings, 1977), 7.

17. Francis E. Rourke, *Bureaucracy, Politics, and Public Policy,* 3d ed. (Boston: Little, Brown, 1984), 32.

18. Aaron Wildavsky, *The New Politics of the Budgetary Process,* 2d ed. (New York: HarperCollins, 1992), 87–88.

19. David A. Stockman, *The Triumph of Politics: Why the Reagan Revolution Failed* (New York: Harper and Row, 1986).

20. Paul C. Light, *Thickening Government: Federal Hierarchy and the Diffusion of Accountability* (Washington, D.C.: Brookings, 1995), 32–33.

21. Heclo, *A Government of Strangers.*

22. G. Calvin MacKenzie, "Partisan Presidential Leadership: The President's Appointees," in *The Parties Respond: Changes in American Parties and Campaigns,* 4th ed., ed. L. Sandy Maisel (Boulder: Westview, 2002), 267.

23. Jeffrey E. Cohen, *The Politics of the U.S. Cabinet: Representation in the Executive Branch, 1789–1984* (Pittsburgh: University of Pittsburgh Press, 1988), chaps. 3, 4.

24. Thomas E. Cronin, *The State of the Presidency,* 2d ed. (Boston: Little, Brown, 1980), 282.

25. James P. Pfiffner, *The Strategic Presidency,* 2d ed. (Lawrence: University Press of Kansas, 1996), 57.

26. G. Calvin Mackenzie, *The Politics of Presidential Appointments* (New York: Free Press, 1981).

27. Thomas J. Weko, *The Politicizing Presidency: The White House Personnel Office, 1948–1994* (Lawrence: University Press of Kansas, 1995), 149–151, 157.

28. Richard P. Nathan, *The Administrative Presidency* (New York: Wiley, 1983), 74–76.

29. Joel D. Aberbach, "A Reinvented Government, or the Same Old Government?" in *The Clinton Legacy*, ed. Colin Campbell and Bert A. Rockman (New York: Chatham House Publishers, 2000), 120.

30. Weko, *The Politicizing Presidency*, 100–103.

31. John P. Burke, "The Bush Transition in Historical Context," *PS: Political Science & Politics* 35 (March 2002).

32. "At the 200-Day Mark, Presidential Appointments Process Again Bogs Down," Presidential Appointment Initiative, Brookings Institution, April 2001, www.appointee.brookings.org/news/100days_pressrelease.htm.

33. Clay Johnson interviewed by James A. Barnes, "Selecting the Players," *National Journal*, June 23, 2001, 1874–1876.

34. Mark W. Huddleston and William W. Boyer, *The Higher Civil Service in the United States: Quest for Reform* (Pittsburgh: University of Pittsburgh Press, 1996); Edie N. Goldenberg, "The Permanent Government in an Era of Retrenchment and Redirection," in *The Reagan Presidency and the Governing of America*, ed. Lester M. Salamon and Michael S. Lund (Washington, D.C.: Urban Institute Press, 1984), 381–404.

35. Chester A. Newland, "A Midterm Appraisal—The Reagan Presidency, Limited Government, and Political Administration," *Public Administration Review* (January–February 1983): 15–16.

36. Testimony of Paul C. Light before the Government Reform Committee, U.S. House of Representatives, May 6, 2003, 12, www.brookings.org/dybdocroot/gs/cps/20030505light.pdf.

37. *Kendall v. United States*, 37 U.S. (12 Pet.) 524 (1838).

38. *Panama Refining Co. v. Ryan*, 293 U.S. 338 (1934); *Schechter Poultry Co. v. United States*, 295 U.S. 495 (1935).

39. Louis Fisher, *Constitutional Conflicts between Congress and the President*, 3d ed. (Lawrence: University Press of Kansas, 1991), 98; Theodore J. Lowi, *The End of Liberalism*, 2d ed. (New York: Norton, 1979), chap. 5.

40. Morris P. Fiorina, *Congress: Keystone of the Washington Establishment*, 2d ed. (New Haven: Yale University Press, 1989).

41. Rourke, *Bureaucracy, Politics, and Public Policy*, 74.

42. MaryAnne Borrelli, *The President's Cabinet: Gender, Power, and Representation* (Boulder: Lynne Rienner Publishers, 2002), 15.

43. Carl M. Cannon, "The Old-Timers," *National Journal*, May 22, 1999, 1387.

44. Ibid., 1388. The average tenure of cabinet members for the past six administrations based on data from Shirley Ann Warshaw reported in *National Journal* was Nixon 1.73 years, Ford 2.04, Carter 2.47, Reagan 3.27, Bush 2.52, and Clinton 3.36.

45. Cohen, *The Politics of the U.S. Cabinet*, 173–176.

46. Borrelli, *The President's Cabinet*, 46–52. This pattern held true for seven of the eight administrations included in the study, with George H. W. Bush being the exception. Because Bush had been elected as a sitting vice president after eight years of Republican control, Borrelli suggests that Bush drew on his extensive network of experienced acquaintances and that the pool of outsiders was depleted. Borrelli's research covered administrations from Franklin D. Roosevelt through George W. Bush except for Truman, Kennedy, and Johnson. Also see Nelson W. Polsby, "Presidential Cabinet-Making Lessons for the Political System," *Political Science Quarterly* (spring 1978): 15–25.

47. Borrelli, 72–74.

48. Pfiffner, *The Strategic Presidency*, 41–42, 65–66; Stephen Hess, *Organizing the Presidency*, 2d ed. (Washington, D.C.: Brookings, 1988), 200; Shirley Anne Warshaw, *Powersharing: White House–Cabinet Relations in the Modern Presidency* (Albany: State University of New York Press, 1996), 228–233.

49. Richard F. Fenno Jr., *The President's Cabinet* (New York: Vintage Books, 1959), 132.

50. Ronald Brownstein and Dick Kirschten, "Cabinet Power," *National Journal*, June 28, 1986, 1582–1589.

51. James A. Barnes, "Like His Home-State Razorbacks . . . Clinton's Cabinet Plays to Win," *National Journal*, April 9, 1994, 852–853. Also see Warshaw, *Powersharing*, 198–227.

52. For discussions of pre-9/11management practices, see Lizette Alvarez and Eric Schmitt, "Cheney Ever More Powerful as Crucial Link to Congress," *New York Times*, May 13, 2001, A1. On the general operation of the administration, see John F. Harris and Dan Balz, "Conflicting Image of Bush Emerges," *Washington Post*, April 28, 2001, A1. Also see Alexis Simendinger, "Stepping into Power," *National Journal*, January 27, 2001, 246–248.

53. Cronin, *The State of the Presidency*, 270–272.

54. Ibid., 282–285.

55. Cohen, in *The Politics of the U.S. Cabinet*, finds a distinction between the older and the newer outer departments based on "the importance of interests in creating the department and on the complexity of its interest group environment" (144). The older departments—Agriculture, Commerce, Labor, and Interior—were created in response to demands from single interests that continue to provide them with some protection from presidential control. The newer departments tend to operate in "more complex interest group environments" that may result in "intradepartmental conflict among advocates of the competing interests" (138, 139).

56. Stephen Hess, *Organizing the Presidency*, 3d ed. (Washington: Brookings, 2002), 172.

57. Karen M. Hult, "The Bush White House in Comparative Perspective" (paper delivered at the conference on "The George W. Bush Presidency: An Early Assessment," Woodrow Wilson School, Princeton University, April 25–26, 2003), 20. For a detailed account of Bush's decision making in the aftermath of 9/11, see Bob Woodward, *Bush at War* (New York: Simon and Shuster, 2002).

58. Warshaw, *Powersharing*, 167.

59. Andrew Rosenthal, "Sununu's Out and Skinner Is In, but White House Troubles Persist," *New York Times*, February 11, 1992, Al, A13. Also see Burt Solomon, "Bush's Renovated Inner Circle Has a Bit of a Reaganesque Look," *National Journal*, February 8, 1992, 346–347.

60. John Hart, *The Presidential Branch: From Washington to Clinton*, 2d ed. (Chatham, N.J.: Chatham House, 1995), 91.

61. Margaret C. Hermann, "Advice and Advisers in the Clinton Presidency: The Impact of Leadership Style," in *The Clinton Presidency: Campaigning, Governing, and the Psychology of Leadership*, ed. Stanley A. Renshon (Boulder: Westview, 1995), 157.

62. Ibid., 159.

63. Margaret LaMontagne Spellings, who served as an adviser to Governor Bush in Texas, was named director of the Domestic Policy Council, and Lawrence Lindsey, a campaign adviser, became director of the National Economic Council. See *National Journal*, June 23, 2001, 1889, 1894. Lindsey was dismissed from his position in December 2002 and replaced by Stephen Friedman.

64. For a discussion of cabinet councils in the Bush administration, see Hult, "The Bush White House in Comparative Perspective," 14–26.

65. *Buckley v. Valeo,* 421 U.S. 1 (1976).

66. In 1973, President Nixon named Howard J. Phillips acting director of the Office of Economic Opportunity (OEO), an agency Nixon planned to dismantle. Phillips began to phase out its programs and withhold funds from it. Sen. Harrison A. Williams, D-N.J., took legal action to force Nixon either to submit Phillips's name to the Senate for confirmation or to stop dismantling the OEO. A U.S. court of appeals ruled that Phillips was illegally holding office and enjoined him from further actions. See James P. Pfiffner, *The President, the Budget, and Congress: Impoundment and the 1974 Budget Act* (Boulder: Westview, 1974), 116–117. Though the effort was thwarted, the decision did not settle the issue.

67. Three notable examples are the Senate's rejection of former senator John Tower, R-Texas, to be secretary of defense in 1989, its long delay in acting on the nomination of Dr. Henry Foster Jr. to be surgeon general of the United States, and its narrow support in 2001 for former senator John Ashcroft, R-Mo., to become attorney general. Tower had antagonized several of his former colleagues during his service in the chamber and was objectionable to many Democratic senators because of his hawkish views. Foster, a distinguished obstetrician and gynecologist, became a political football in the debate over abortion. The White House Personnel Office, in an inexplicable blunder, neglected to ask Foster if he had ever performed abortions until after the president announced the nomination on February 2, 1995. When Foster gave three different answers and explained them as due to a faulty memory, abortion opponents made the nomination a cause célèbre, and Sens. Robert Dole and Phil Gramm, both Republican presidential hopefuls, tried to outdo each other in their opposition to the nomination by threatening to keep it from coming to a vote in the Senate. The abortion issue then became entwined with Foster's credibility. Following confirmation hearings at which Foster performed very credibly, the Senate Labor and Human Resources Committee on May 24, 1995, approved the nomination by a 10–8 vote. A successful Republican filibuster prevented the nomination from coming to an up or down vote of the full Senate. John Ashcroft was a vehemently outspoken opponent of abortion whom Democrats suspected would not enforce the laws. After a surprisingly bitter debate, unusual in that senators seldom criticize one of their own, the full membership confirmed Ashcroft by a vote of 58–42.

68. Christopher J. Deering, "Damned if You Do and Damned if You Don't: The Senate's Role in the Appointment Process," in *The In-and-Outers,* ed. G. Calvin McKenzie (Baltimore: Johns Hopkins University Press, 1987), 119. Also see G. Calvin McKenzie, ed., *Innocent until Nominated* (Washington, D.C.: Brookings, 2001).

69. Anthony Lake withdrew from consideration as nominee to head the CIA in March 1997 after concluding that he would be subjected to endless delays and partisan criticism. Juliana Gruenwald, "Tenet Appears Likely to Win Confirmation as CIA Chief," *Congressional Quarterly Weekly Report,* March 22, 1997, 712–714. On the Holbrooke nomination, see Philip Shenon, "Holbrooke Nomination Passes One Hurdle but Faces Another," *New York Times,* July 1, 1999, A6; Philip Shenon, "Let's Slow Down on Holbrooke's Case, Lott Says," *New York Times,* July 23, 1999, A9; Eric Schmitt, "When Nomination Turns to Wrangling to Impasse," *New York Times,* July 28, 1999, A16; Miles A. Pomper, "Holbrooke Confirmed as U.N. Envoy," *CQ Weekly,* August 7, 1999, 1961–1962.

70. Committee on Governmental Affairs, United States Senate, *Policy and Supporting Positions* (Washington, D.C.: GPO, 2000), also known as the "plum book." For a fuller discussion, Bradley H. Patterson and James P. Pfiffner, "The White House Office of Presidential Personnel," *Presidential Studies Quarterly* 31 (September 2001): 420. Patterson and Pfiffner identify 1,125 full-time positions subject to confirmation, including 185 ambassadors, 94 district attorneys, 94 U.S. marshals, 15 in international organizations, and 4 in the legislative branch.

71. Press Release, Brookings Institution, March 1, 2002, www.appointee.brookings.edu/news/030102.htm.

72. On the hurdles confronted by candidates, see Paul C. Light, "Make It Easier to Say Yes," *Government Executive,* December 15, 2002, www.brookings.edu/views/op-ed/light/20021215.htm. On the attention devoted to nominees' records, see James A. Barnes, "White House: Bush's Insiders," *National Journal,* June 25, 2001.

73. Carole M. Plowfield, "Senate Failing to Perform Crucial Consent Role," *Roll Call,* July 29, 2002, www.brookings.edu/views/op-ed/fellows/20020729plowfield.htm.

74. Kirk Victor, "Executive Branch End Run," *National Journal,* May 16, 1998, 1112–1114. One of the most contentious cases focused on Bill Lann Lee, whose nomination as assistant attorney general for civil rights was bottled up in the Senate Judiciary Committee on three different occasions because of his allegedly liberal policy views, though a recorded vote was never taken for fear of antagonizing Asian American voters. Lee served in an "acting" capacity and was renominated by Clinton on two other occasions in an attempt to force Senate action. His service far exceeded the 120-day limit that Congress set for such appointments in the 1980s, but successive administrations have asserted great freedom in extending "acting" appointments indefinitely. On the Lee nomination, see Aberbach, "A Reinvented Government," 124–126; Richard L. Berke and Steven A. Holmes, "In Confirmation Delays, a New G.O.P. Strategy," *New York Times,* November 11, 1997, A14; John M. Broder, "While Congress Is Away, Clinton Plays with Idea of an End Run," *New York Times,* November 24, 1997, A12; Dan Carney, "Battle over Lee Could Escalate with Recess Appointment," *Congressional Quarterly Weekly Report,* November 29, 1997, 2955; David Byrd, "Affirmatively Acting," *National Journal,* March 6, 1999, 612–616.

75. Two included Otto J. Reich as assistant secretary of state for Western Hemisphere Affairs and Eugene Scalia as solicitor of the Labor Department, both of whom had voiced highly controversial policy positions in the past. See the discussion in Joel D. Aberbach, "The State of the Contemporary American Presidency: Or, Is Bush II Actually Ronald Reagan's Heir?" in *The George W. Bush Presidency: First Appraisals,* ed. Colin Campbell and Bert A. Rockman (Chatham, N.J.: Chatham House Publishers, 2003), chap. 11. My thanks to Professor Aberbach for providing me with a prepublication copy. Also Christopher Marquis, "Bush Bypasses Senate on 2 More Nominees," *New York Times,* January 12, 2002, www.nytimes.com.

76. *Myers v. United States,* 272 U.S. 52 (1926).

77. *Humphrey's Executor v. United States,* 295 U.S. 602 (1935).

78. Fisher, *Constitutional Conflicts,* 79.

79. Phillip J. Cooper, *By Order of the President: The Use and Abuse of Executive Direct Action* (Lawrence: University Press of Kansas, 2002), 15, 81–83. By April 4, 2001, Bush had revoked six of Clinton's executive orders. Hult, "The Bush White House in Comparative Perspective," 27 n. 77.

80. Kenneth R. Mayer, *With the Stroke of a Pen: Executive Orders and Presidential Power* (Princeton: Princeton University Press, 2001), 4.

81. For excellent discussions of presidential use of executive orders in the areas of information secrecy and intelligence organization as well as in civil rights, see Mayer, *With the Stroke of a Pen,* chaps. 5, 6.

82. *Amalgamated Meat Cutters v. Connally,* 337 F. Supp. 737 (1971).

83. *Hirabayashi v. United States,* 320 U.S. 581 (1943); *Korematsu v. United States,* 323 U.S. 214 (1944).

84. Hult, "The Bush White House in Comparative Perspective," 27.

85. For an interpretation that Clinton relied more heavily on such instruments after the Republicans controlled Congress, see Aberbach, "A Reinvented Government," 128; and Alexis Simendinger, "The Paper Wars," *National Journal,* July 25,

1998, 1732–1739. Some reports confuse distinctions among the different forms of unilateral presidential action rather than adhering to the definition of executive orders maintained by the National Archives and Records Administration.

86. Mayer, *With the Stroke of a Pen,* 70.

87. Ibid., Table 3.3, 82.

88. Ibid., 102.

89. Cooper, *By Order of the President,* 13, 90–91.

90. *Youngstown Sheet and Tube Co. v. Sawyer,* 343 U.S. 579 (1952).

91. Lawrence R. Jacobs and Robert Y. Shapiro, "Public Opinion in Clinton's First Year: Leadership and Responsiveness," in *The Clinton Presidency,* 201.

92. *Immigration and Naturalization Service v. Chadha,* 462 U.S. 919 (1983).

93. Joseph Cooper, "Postscript on the Congressional Veto," *Political Science Quarterly* (fall 1983): 427–430; Barbara Hinkson Craig, *The Legislative Veto: Congressional Control of Regulation* (Boulder: Westview, 1983), 139–150; Fisher, *Constitutional Conflicts,* 152.

94. Fisher, *Constitutional Conflicts,* 150–152.

95. Louis Fisher, "Judicial Misjudgments about the Lawmaking Process: The Legislative Veto Case," *Public Administration Review* (November–December 1985): 709–710.

96. Richard M. Pious, *The American Presidency* (New York: Basic Books, 1979), 256–257.

97. Allen Schick, "The Road to PPB: The States of Budget Reform," *Public Administration Review* (December 1966): 243–258.

98. Wildavsky, *The New Politics of the Budgetary Process,* 436–440.

99. Allen Schick, *The Federal Budget: Politics, Policy, Process* (Washington, D.C.: Brookings, 1995), 2–4.

100. Bob Woodward, *The Agenda: Inside the Clinton White House* (New York: Simon and Schuster, 1994).

101. Daniel J. Palazzo, *Done Deal? The Politics of the 1997 Budget Agreement* (Chatham, N.J.: Chatham House, 1999).

102. Louis Fisher, *Presidential Spending Power* (Princeton: Princeton University Press, 1979), chap. 4.

103. Ibid., 148.

104. Vivian Vale, "The Obligation to Spend: Presidential Impoundment of Congressional Appropriations," *Political Studies* (1977): 508–532.

105. Pfiffner, *The President, The Budget, and Congress,* 40–44.

106. Jonathan Rauch, "Power of the Purse," *National Journal,* May 24, 1986, 1261.

107. *William J. Clinton, President of the United States, et al., Appellants v. City of New York et al.* (1998). The case can be found at supct.law.cornell.edu/supct/html/ 97-1374. 25.html.

108. Peri Arnold concludes his authoritative study of "the managerial presidency" by observing that "no modern president has fully managed the executive branch." He further argues that the "managerial conception of the presidency is untenable" because it "places impossible obligations on presidents" and creates unrealistic "public expectations of presidential performance." Peri E. Arnold, *Making the Managerial Presidency: Comprehensive Reorganization Planning, 1905–1980* (Princeton: Princeton University Press, 1986), 361–362.

109. Andrew Rudalevige, *Managing the President's Program: Presidential Leadership and Legislative Policy Formulation* (Princeton: Princeton University Press, 2002), 7.

110. Ibid.

111. Hess, *Organizing the Presidency,* 230–231.

112. Jack W. Germond and Jules Witcover, "Bush Left with Little Room for Error," *National Journal,* December 22, 1990, 3104.

113. Fred I. Greenstein, "Political Style and Political Leadership: The Case of Bill Clinton," in *The Clinton Presidency,* 141, 142.

114. Burt Solomon, "Clinton's New Taskmaster Takes Charge," *National Journal,* August 6, 1994, 1872.

115. Todd S. Purdum, "The Ungreening of the White House Staff," *New York Times,* December 22, 1996, E10.

116. Karen Hughes returned to Texas in July 2002, setting up a potential vacuum that would need to be filled. For a discussion of the Bush staff system, see Hult, "The Bush White House in Comparative Perspective."

117. Alexis Simendinger, "Stepping into Power," *National Journal,* January 27, 2001, 247.

118. Stuart Rothenberg, "There's No Question about Who's in Charge at Bush's White House,"*Roll Call,* March 26, 2001, www.rollcall.com.

119. Terry M. Moe, "The Politicized Presidency," in *The New Direction in American Politics,* ed. John E. Chubb and Paul E. Peterson (Washington, D.C.: Brookings, 1985), 235–271.

120. Samuel Kernell, "The Creed and Reality of Modern White House Management," in *Chief of Staff: Twenty-Five Years of Managing the Presidency,* ed. Samuel Kernell and Samuel L. Popkin (Berkeley: University of California Press, 1986), 228.

121. John R. Dempsey, "Carter Reorganization: A Midterm Appraisal," *Public Administration Review* (January–February 1979): 74–78; Arnold, *Making the Managerial Presidency,* chap. 10.

122. Herbert Kaufman, "Reflections on Administrative Reorganization," in *Setting National Priorities: The 1978 Budget,* ed. Joseph A. Pechman (Washington, D.C.: Brookings, 1977), 403.

123. Dempsey, "Carter Reorganization," 75.

124. Ronald C. Moe, "The 'Reinventing Government' Exercise: Misinterpreting the Problem, Misjudging the Consequences," *Public Administration Review* (March–April 1994): 112.

125. David Osborne and Ted Gaebler, *Reinventing Government: How the Entrepreneurial Spirit Is Transforming the Public Sector from Schoolhouse to State House, City Hall to Pentagon* (Reading, Mass.: Addison-Wesley, 1992), 111.

126. Donald F. Kett, *Reinventing Government: A Fifth Year Report Card,* Center for Public Management Report 98-1 (Washington, D.C.: Brookings, September 1998).

127. In "The 'Reinventing Government' Exercise," Ronald Moe argues that Clinton's effort substitutes results for processes and amounts to abandonment of public law as the basis of political accountability (112). The political scientist James Q. Wilson doubts whether in the era of big government "political accountability can any longer be equated with presidential power." James Q. Wilson, "Reinventing Public Administration," *P.S.: Political Science and Politics* (December 1994): 671. The famed management consultant Peter Drucker called for a new theory that "asks what the proper functions of government might be and could be . . . [and] what results government should be held accountable for." Peter Drucker, "Really Reinventing Government," *Atlantic Monthly* (February 1995): 61.

128. Aberbach, " The State of the Contemporary American Presidency."

129. Aaron Wildavsky, *Speaking Truth to Power* (Boston: Little, Brown, 1979), 120.

130. Richard Rose, *Managing Presidential Objectives* (New York: Free Press, 1976), chap. 6.

131. Peter Behr, "Energy Plan to Fuel Long Fight; at Issue Is Environmental Cost of Plentiful, Cheaper Power," *Washington Post,* May 15, 2001, A9.

132. Peter Behr, "Bush Places His Bet on Energy Industry," *Washington Post,* May 18, 2001, E1.

133. See, for example, Arnold, *Making the Managerial Presidency;* Colin Campbell, *Managing the Presidency: Carter, Reagan, and the Search for Executive Harmony* (Pittsburgh: University of Pittsburgh Press, 1986); and Rose, *Managing Presidential Objectives.* Also see Walter Williams, *Mismanaging America: The Rise of the Anti-Analytic Presidency* (Lawrence: University Press of Kansas, 1990).

134. Nathan, *The Administrative Presidency.*

135. Allen Schick, "The Budget as an Instrument of Presidential Policy," in *The Reagan Presidency and the Governing of America,* 113.

136. Lester M. Salamon and Alan J. Abramson, "Governance: The Politics of Retrenchment," in *The Reagan Record,* ed. John L. Palmer and Isabell V. Sawhill (Cambridge, Mass.: Ballinger, 1984), 97; Joseph A. Pika and Norman C. Thomas, "The President as Institution Builder: The Reagan Case," *Governance* (October 1990): 444–447.

SUGGESTED READINGS

Arnold, Peri E. *Making the Managerial Presidency: Comprehensive Reorganization Planning, 1905–1980.* Princeton: Princeton University Press, 1986.

Borrelli, MaryAnne. *The President's Cabinet: Gender, Power, and Representation.* Boulder: Lynne Rienner Publishers, 2002.

Campbell, Colin. *Managing the Presidency: Carter, Reagan, and the Search for Executive Harmony.* Pittsburgh: University of Pittsburgh Press, 1986.

Cohen, Jeffrey E. *The Politics of the U.S. Cabinet: Representation in the Executive Branch, 1789–1984.* Pittsburgh: University of Pittsburgh Press, 1988.

Cooper, Phillip J. *By Order of the President: The Use and Abuse of Executive Direct Action.* Lawrence: University Press of Kansas, 2002.

Cronin, Thomas E. *The State of the Presidency.* 2d ed. Boston: Little, Brown, 1980.

Fisher, Louis. *Constitutional Conflicts between Congress and the President.* 3d ed., rev. Lawrence: University Press of Kansas, 1991.

Hart, John. *The Presidential Branch: From Washington to Clinton.* 2d ed. Chatham, N.J.: Chatham House, 1995.

Hess, Stephen. *Organizing the Presidency.* 3d ed. Washington, D.C.: Brookings, 2002.

Light, Paul C. *Thickening Government: Federal Hierarchy and the Diffusion of Accountability.* Washington, D.C.: Brookings, 1995.

Mayer, Kenneth R. *With the Stroke of a Pen: Executive Orders and Presidential Power.* Princeton: Princeton University Press, 2001.

Nathan, Richard P. *The Administrative Presidency.* New York: Wiley, 1983.

Pfiffner, James P. *The Managerial Presidency.* 2d ed. College Station: Texas A&M University Press, 1999.

___. *The Strategic Presidency.* 2d ed. Lawrence: University Press of Kansas, 1996.

Warshaw, Shirley Anne. *Powersharing: White House–Cabinet Relations in the Modern Presidency.* Albany: State University of New York Press, 1996.

Weko, Thomas J. *The Politicizing Presidency: The White House Personnel Office, 1948–1994.* Lawrence: University Press of Kansas, 1995.

7 JUDICIAL POLITICS

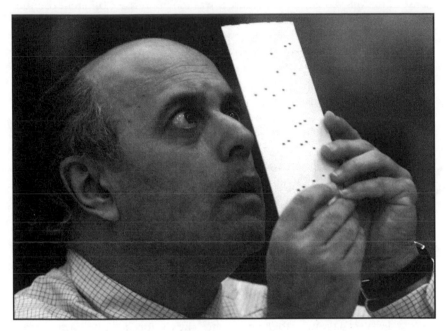

Controversy over how to count contested ballots in Florida led to court cases that culminated in Bush v. Gore. Canvassing board members, such as Judge Robert Rosenberg of Broward County, worked long and hard during their manual recount of those disputed ballots.

HIGH DRAMA GRIPPED THE NATION on December 12, 2000, when a 5–4 majority of the U.S. Supreme Court ruled that the manual recounts ordered by the Florida Supreme Court to determine the outcome of the contested presidential election between George W. Bush and Al Gore could not proceed. By calling a halt to the recounts, the Court effectively decided the outcome of the election: the original (and some said flawed) machine-tabulated results that gave Bush a razor-thin margin of victory would stand. The ruling precluded further challenges by Gore, who argued that the machines failed to count the ballots of many voters who had intended to vote for him.[1]

In all, seven of the Court's nine members agreed that Florida's "clear intent of the voter" standard governing manual recounts violated the equal protection clause of the U.S. Constitution because it was too imprecise.[2] Different counties could use different standards to determine voter intent, thereby leading to "arbitrary and disparate treatment" of members of the Florida electorate. In other words, identical ballots could lead to one person's vote being counted in one county but not in another (depending upon whether such things as a "hanging," a "dimpled," and a "pregnant" chad were thought to reveal the clear intent of the voter). The Court majority's per curiam decision—an unsigned opinion used either when the conclusion reached by the Court is so straightforward that no extended discussion is needed or (as in this case) when the Court is so fragmented that it can only reach agreement on the narrow result announced—held that this lack of a uniform standard for counting ballots did not provide "sufficient guarantees of equal treatment" and that the recount therefore violated the one-person, one-vote principle set forth by the Court in 1960s voting rights cases such as *Reynolds v. Sims* and *Gray v. Sanders*.[3]

Nonetheless, the seven members of the Court who joined the per curiam decision remained bitterly divided about whether such a violation could be overcome and whether a "safe harbor" deadline imposed by Congress in an 1887 law precluded recounts after that deadline (which happened to be the same day that the Supreme Court issued its ruling). The safe harbor deadline guarantees that a state's election results are binding on Congress if the state produces a conclusive result at least six days prior to the date when the electors are scheduled to meet (*U.S. Code*, vol. 3, sec. 5), which in 2000 was December 18.

Of the seven members of the Court who joined the per curiam decision, five voted to call a halt to the recounts. This five-person majority (William Rehnquist, Sandra Day O'Connor, Antonin Scalia, Anthony Kennedy, and Clarence Thomas—all of whom had been appointed by either Ronald Reagan or the first President George Bush) concluded that the safe harbor deadline was binding and that no recounts could take place after that date. As they put it, *U.S. Code*, vol. 3, sec. 5, "requires that any controversy or contest that is designed to lead to a conclusive selection of electors be completed by December 12."[4] According to these five, since it was already December 12, efforts to establish uniform standards that would not violate equal protection were fruitless because there would be no time to proceed with a recount. A slim 5–4 majority therefore ruled that recounts could not proceed and that the original machine counts already certified by the Florida secretary of state be considered official.

Bush v. Gore is a very complicated decision that produced four separate dissents: each dissenting judge (Stephen Breyer, Ruth Bader Ginsburg, David Souter, and John Paul Stevens) wrote one and was joined by one or more of the other three on various points within the dissents. Two of these dissents came from justices who had recognized a potential equal protection problem and actually joined part of the per curiam decision (Souter, appointed by President Bush, and Breyer, appointed by President Clinton). Souter and Breyer broke ranks with the other five justices who had joined the per curiam decision and dissented because they felt that the equal protection violation could be corrected by establishing a uniform standard for determining the clear intent of the voter and that recounts should then continue. Both Souter and Breyer insisted that the majority's emphasis on a rigid deadline for counting votes was misplaced. They dismissed, in Souter's dissent, the deadline issue as "not serious" because "no State is required to conform to sec. 5 if it cannot do that (for whatever reason); the sanction for failing to satisfy the conditions of sec. 5 is simply loss of what has been called its 'safe harbor.' And even that determination is to be made, if made anywhere, in the Congress."[5] Souter and Breyer therefore concluded that there "is no justification for denying the State the opportunity to try to count all the disputed ballots now." As Souter put it, "Unlike the majority, I see no warrant for this Court to assume that Florida could not possibly comply with this [equal protection] requirement before the date set for the meeting of electors, December 18."[6]

The remaining two members of the Court who had not joined the per curiam decision (Stevens, appointed by Gerald R. Ford, and Ginsburg, appointed by President Clinton) agreed with Souter and Breyer that the five-person majority had misinterpreted section 5 and thereby established an artificial deadline. Both agreed that the recounts should proceed. All four dissenters agreed that the Supreme Court should not have accepted the case for review.[7] As Justice Ginsburg wrote: "The extraordinary setting of this case has obscured the ordinary principle that dictates its proper resolution: Federal courts defer to state high courts' interpretations of their own state law. This principle reflects the core of federalism."[8]

Ginsburg and Stevens differed from the other two dissenters, however, by rejecting the view that the existing recount procedure violated equal protection. That is why neither Ginsburg nor Stevens joined the per curiam decision. As Ginsburg put it, "I cannot agree that the recount adopted by the Florida court, flawed as it may be, would yield a result any less fair or precise than the certification that preceded that recount."[9] Even Breyer, who had recognized a potential equal protection violation and joined the per curiam decision, admitted in his dissent (joined by Ginsburg and Stevens) that the majority's remedy "harms the very fairness interests the Court is attempting to protect."[10] Justice Stevens explained why: the majority's decision to stop the recount "effectively orders the disenfranchisement of an unknown number of voters whose ballots reveal their intent—and are therefore legal votes under state law—but were for some reason rejected by ballot-counting machines."[11]

E. Joshua Rosenkranz, president of the Brennan Center for Justice at New York University's School of Law, made a similar argument. He said that the majority never acknowledged that "the biggest disparity among Florida voters resulted from using different kinds of voting machines from one county to another. Voter

A casts his or her vote easily, simply and reliably, based on the latest optical scanning technology," he explained, "while his neighbor, Voter B, cast his or her vote on an archaic, dysfunctional, error-prone voting machine. By some estimates, Voter B's vote was up to 10 times as likely to be thrown out as Voter A's. What's more, the error-prone machines were more likely to be used in communities of color: just the sort of inequality *Baker v. Carr* was designed to fix."[12]

Indeed, Justice Stevens argued that if the majority really wanted to apply equal protection as rigidly as it seemed to claim, it should also call into question a wide range of other accepted practices, such as "Florida's decision to leave to each county the determination of what balloting system to employ" (since some ballots led to more "undercounts" than others).[13] The majority, however, claimed that its use of equal protection was confined only to this particular recount in this particular case.[14] As Rosenkranz put it, this caveat transformed the majority's "apparent love affair with political equality" into "just a one-night stand"[15]—an embrace of equal protection designed to achieve a political outcome that the majority favored.

Reasonable men and women can disagree about which of the positions articulated by the various justices in *Bush v. Gore* is correct. Nonetheless, a variety of factors led many people to repeat the argument that the Court's decision was driven more by politics than by legal reasoning. Most legal observers were surprised that the Supreme Court agreed to hear the case in the first place, since judicial restraint usually precludes review of this type of "political question"— especially before the issue has been exhausted in the political arena.

The 5–4 split in *Bush v. Gore* also helped to create the impression that the decision was politically motivated: the Court's more conservative members voted in the majority to stop the recount and the more liberal members dissented. The reasoning used by the justices reinforced the image of political motivation. Justices on both sides seemed to alter their positions to arrive at their results. Members of the majority who normally embraced states' rights and who usually deferred to state court interpretations of state law seemed all too eager to intervene. Dissenters, who were typically more critical of states' rights, now seemed converted to the cause.

Many commentators were particularly distressed by the majority's equal protection claim, arguing that it seemed to fly in the face of the Court's precedents. Even some of Bush's own lawyers thought it a weak argument when they first considered raising it.[16] As legal theorist Ronald Dworkin has written, the equal protection clause was designed to protect against discrimination: "it condemns not any difference in the way a state's law treats different citizens, but only certain distinctions that put some citizens, in advance, at a disadvantage against others." Dworkin went on to explain why the "clear intent of the voter" standard governing the recount did not violate equal protection:

Voters who indent a chad without punching it clean through run a risk that a vote they did not mean to make will be counted if they live in a county that uses a generous interpretation of the "clear intent" statute; or they run a risk that a vote they meant to make will be discarded if they live in a county that uses a less generous interpretation. But since neither of these risks is worse than the other—both threaten a citizen's power to make his or her vote count—the abstract standard discriminates against no one, and no question of equal protection is raised.[17]

In a stinging portion of his dissent in *Bush v. Gore,* Justice Stevens (joined by Ginsburg and Breyer) emphasized that the Court should not have agreed to hear the case and argued that its decision to do so had undermined its legitimacy. "It is confidence in the men and women who administer the judicial system that is the true backbone of the rule of law," he wrote. "Time will one day heal the wound to that confidence that will be inflicted by today's decision. One thing, however, is certain. Although we may never know with complete certainty the identity of the winner of this year's presidential election, the identity of the loser is perfectly clear. It is the Nation's confidence in the judge as an impartial guardian of the rule of law."[18]

Never before had the Supreme Court so directly determined the outcome of a presidential election through one of its rulings. Backlash against the Court was swift and harsh. Democrats chided the majority's ruling as a blatantly political, conservative activist decision. Thousands of angry letters poured into the Supreme Court. Several members of the Supreme Court bar (those eligible to argue cases before the Court) resigned in protest—a response court officials had not seen before. Reports claimed that the case had polarized law clerks for the justices: those for the more liberal justices were said to be "dismayed at the court's role in the case," while clerks for the more conservative justices viewed the majority's ruling as "one of integrity" and were angered by the criticism of the Court.[19] When Justices Kennedy and Thomas appeared before a congressional committee on March 29, 2001, Rep. Jose E. Serrano, D-N.Y., told them that his constituents—most of whom were black or Latino—were "angry, bitter, and disenchanted" by *Bush v. Gore.*[20] Kennedy and Thomas defended the ruling, as had Chief Justice William Rehnquist in a public speech on January 1, 2001.

One of the most novel responses to *Bush v. Gore* came from Yale law professor Bruce Ackerman, who suggested that the Senate should refuse to confirm any of the new President Bush's Supreme Court nominees because of the ruling. "In our democracy," he wrote,

there is one basic check on a runaway Court: presidential elections. And a majority of the justices have conspired to eliminate this check. The Supreme Court cannot be permitted to arrange for its own succession. To allow this president to serve as the Court's agent is a fundamental violation of separation of powers. It is one thing for unelected judges to exercise the sovereign power of judicial review; it's quite another for them to insulate themselves yet further from popular control. When sitting justices die or retire, the Senate should refuse to confirm any nominations offered up by President Bush.[21]

It is possible that George W. Bush will have the opportunity to appoint at least two or three justices to the Supreme Court, especially if he is reelected. As the

Court ended its 2002 term in June 2003, John Paul Stevens was eighty-three years old and had served on the Court since 1975. Although appointed by a Republican (Gerald Ford), Stevens had become a solid member of the Court's more liberal block. William Rehnquist was seventy-nine years old and a leader of the conservative wing of the Court. He had been appointed as an associate justice by Richard Nixon in 1972 and elevated to chief justice by Ronald Reagan in 1986. Sandra Day O'Connor, a centrist and the first woman on the Court, was seventy-three and had been an associate justice since her 1981 appointment by Ronald Reagan. It had been more than eight years since the last Supreme Court vacancy—the longest stretch without such a vacancy since 1823.

In addition to potential Supreme Court appointments, presidents also have the opportunity to nominate lower federal judges. During the 107th Congress, Bush submitted 131 nominations to fill such vacancies on U.S. district courts and courts of appeals.[22] Because federal judges have life tenure, presidents have an opportunity to use judicial appointments to shape judicial policymaking for years to come. As such, these appointments are very important. Because they require Senate confirmation, they can also be very contentious—as we shall see in the next section. Indeed, the Senate confirmed only 100 of Bush's 131 nominations during the 107th Congress.

This chapter examines the basic relationship between the president and the federal courts. The first section analyzes the most important influence the president exerts over these courts: the power, with the consent of the Senate, to appoint their members. The chapter next explores other means by which the chief executive affects the business of the courts, and finally, it examines the reverse situation: how the federal courts, and the Supreme Court in particular, influence the actions of the president.

Presidential Appointment of Federal Judges

Perhaps the greatest impact the president can have on the courts is the selection of federal judges who share the administration's policy goals. These judges include not only the nine justices who currently sit on the U.S. Supreme Court, but also more than 800 judges who sit on lower federal courts. (States have their own independent court systems.) The Constitution established (and requires) one Supreme Court. It authorized (but did not require) Congress to create lower federal courts. Congress created lower courts almost immediately through the Judiciary Act of 1789, and that system has grown and evolved since then. All federal judges are nominated by the president, confirmed by the Senate, and once appointed serve "during good Behaviour." In other words, they have life tenure subject to impeachment or resignation. This means that once they are on the bench, federal judges can influence judicial policymaking for years to come. This is no small matter since judges rule on such controversial issues as abortion, affirmative action, school prayer, and the rights of criminal defendants.

One might think that impartial judges who objectively apply the law according to set standards of interpretation should all arrive at the same "correct" outcome in cases that come before them. In practice, however, there are very different views among judges about how to interpret legal texts. Moreover, judges are human beings who are influenced, at least in part, by their backgrounds, personal beliefs, and judicial philosophies. As a result, different judges can—and do—reach different conclusions when confronted with the same case (*Bush v. Gore* is just one of many examples). Therefore, presidents work hard to nominate judges with a similar judicial philosophy. Interest groups—well aware of the impact judges can have on policy—also take keen interest in these nominees. So, too, does the Senate, which has the power to confirm or reject nominees.

Selection of Lower Federal Court Judges

There are two basic types of lower federal courts: trial courts (called U.S. district courts) and appellate courts (called U.S. courts of appeals).[23] These are distinct from state courts. The fact that the United States has an overlapping system of state and federal courts can be confusing, especially since each state structures its court system differently than other states. As a result, we have fifty-one court systems in this country: one at the federal level and one for each of the fifty states. State courts usually hear cases involving state law, while federal courts hear cases involving federal law. Sometimes a single action can provoke cases in both state and federal law. Timothy McVeigh, for example, violated federal law when he blew up the federal building in Oklahoma City and was therefore tried in federal court. But he could also have been tried in state court for violating state law against murder. Moreover, cases involving state law that begin in state court can sometimes be appealed to federal court. This happens only when a case involves a *federal question*. A federal question exists if a state law is alleged to violate federal law, a U.S. treaty, or the U.S. Constitution. It can also exist if police or prosecutors are alleged to have violated the constitutional rights of a criminal defendant. A person convicted in state court because of evidence gathered from an unreasonable search and seizure or a coerced confession, for example, could appeal to federal court. If there is no federal question, however, the highest state court remains the court of last resort. The manner of selecting state court judges varies from state to state and is completely unrelated to federal judicial selection.

U.S. district courts are where federal criminal and civil cases originate and where trials are held. Each of these courts has jurisdiction over a geographic area called a district. Each district falls within the boundary of a single state, and by tradition, judges who come from that state staff a district's courts.[24] Every state has at least one district. Those with heavier caseloads have more than one, and Congress occasionally adds new districts to accommodate increased caseloads. Since district courts are the point of entry to the federal judicial system, they hear more cases than any other kind of federal court. There are also more of them than any other kind of federal court: currently more than 600 judges staff ninety-four district courts.

The courts of appeals are intermediate appellate courts between the district courts and the Supreme Court. Each has jurisdiction over a geographic area called a circuit, made up of several districts. There are twelve regional circuits: one for the District of Columbia and eleven numbered circuits covering the rest of the country. Unlike districts, the numbered circuits have jurisdiction over several states (the First Circuit, for example, covers Maine, Massachusetts, New Hampshire, and Rhode Island). The circuit courts hear appeals from the trial courts and decide whether the trial court made a legal error in trying the case. In other words, courts of appeals answer questions of *law* rather than questions of *fact*. Unlike proceedings in the district courts, there are no witnesses, no testimony, and no jury. Judges on the courts of appeals base their rulings on written legal arguments called briefs and on oral arguments presented by lawyers representing each side of the case. A panel of three judges usually hears appeals. A majority vote of the panel is necessary to overturn a lower court ruling, and the court of appeals issues a written opinion explaining its ruling.

Only about one-sixth of the litigants from the district courts appeal, so the caseload for the courts of appeals is significantly less than the caseload for the district courts. Despite the fact that they hear fewer cases than the district courts, the courts of appeals are very influential because of their power to set important precedents that are binding on the lower courts in their circuits. Since the U.S. Supreme Court accepts such a minuscule number of cases from the courts of appeal for review, the courts of appeals are effectively the court of last resort in more than 99 percent of the cases that come before them.[25] As such, appointments to the courts of appeals are especially important.

In theory, the appointment process for these lower federal courts is the same as for the Supreme Court: the president nominates and the Senate either confirms or rejects. In practice, presidents have traditionally had less control over the selection of these lower federal court judges than over the selection of Supreme Court justices. This is especially true at the district court level because of a practice called "senatorial courtesy." Senatorial courtesy has existed as an informal rule since the early days of George Washington's administration. It means that members of the Senate (out of courtesy) will generally refuse to confirm people to federal positions who do not have the support of the senators from the state where the vacancy exists.

Senatorial courtesy was formally institutionalized in the 1940s through the development of the so-called blue slip procedure.[26] Both senators from the state where the vacancy occurs (regardless of party affiliation) receive a letter from the chairman of the Senate Judiciary Committee asking for advice about the nominee. Enclosed is a form, printed on blue paper, where such advice can be offered. Although senators may put their support or opposition in writing and return the form, it is understood that failure to return the blue slip amounts to a veto that will prevent committee hearings on the nominee—a de facto invocation of senatorial courtesy that usually blocks the nomination.[27]

There is debate about what role should be played by those home-state senators *not* of the president's party. During certain periods, only blue slip vetoes from senators of the president's party could block a nomination.[28] During others, either home-state senator, regardless of party, could block the nomination. According to David M. O'Brien, the latter interpretation prevailed until the 1970s. It hardly mattered, though, since the overwhelming majority of nominees were confirmed (98 percent between 1951 and 1962) with only perfunctory review by the Senate.[29] Still, the threat of invoking the blue slip influenced the types of judges nominated. For example, threats by southern Democrats to block liberal nominees during the Kennedy and Johnson administrations in the 1960s led to the appointment of more conservative judges in the South than might otherwise have been the case.

Sen. Edward Kennedy, D-Mass., chairman of the Senate Judiciary Committee in 1979–1981, weakened the veto power of the blue slip—largely to help President Jimmy Carter bypass potential opposition to his more liberal nominees from fellow southern Democrats. Kennedy said that a blue slip veto would no longer preclude hearings on a nominee, but no attempt to invoke such a veto occurred during his tenure.[30] Under his tenure as chair of the Judiciary Committee, Sen. Strom Thurmond, R-S.C., continued Kennedy's practice, probably because a fellow Republican (Ronald Reagan) controlled the White House. A weakened veto power would make it more difficult for home-state Democrats to block Republican nominees.

Then, during the last six years of the Clinton administration (when a Democrat controlled the White House and Republicans controlled the Senate), Republican Senate Judiciary Committee chairman Orrin Hatch of Utah routinely allowed blue slips from home-state Republicans to prevent hearings on many Democratic nominees put forward by the president. This amounted to a strengthening of the veto power of the blue slip because it allowed home-state senators who were *not* of the same political party as President Clinton to block his nominees. Once George W. Bush became president in 2001, however, Hatch abruptly shifted gears and sought to weaken the power of the blue slip. Now that Democrats were in the same position that Republicans had been in when Clinton controlled the White House, Hatch wanted to discount the veto power of home-state Democrats, saying that support of a home-state Republican should overcome opposition of a home-state Democrat. The *New York Times* called Hatch's turnabout both ironic and audacious, since Republicans had for six years "routinely obstructed" President Clinton's judicial nominations and were now trying to remove the possibility that Democrats could do the same.[31] Not surprisingly, Senate Democrats reacted with fury to Hatch's proposal. Sen. Charles E. Schumer, D-N.Y., wrote a letter of protest signed by all nine Democrats on the Judiciary Committee and supported by all fifty Senate Democrats.[32] Before the issue could be resolved, Republican senator Jim Jeffords of Vermont defected from the Republican Party, thus throwing control of the Senate to the Democrats. Sen. Patrick Leahy, D-Vt., took over as Judiciary Committee chairman and

Republicans and Democrats have been bitterly divided over the selection of federal judges. Senate Democrats have successfully filibustered some nominations, but both parties have used tactics to stall judicial confirmations. Here, Republican senator Orrin Hatch of Utah (left), who has served as the chair of the Senate Judiciary committee since 2003, is seated next to Sen. Patrick Leahy, D-Vt., who served as chair when Democrats controlled the Senate. Whispering to Leahy is Sen. Charles Schumer, D-N.Y.

continued to enforce the blue slip rule, thus allowing home-state Democrats to block President Bush's Republican nominees.[33]

When Republicans regained control of the Senate in the 2002 midterm elections, Sen. Hatch again became chair of the Judiciary Committee. At the first meeting of the committee in January 2003, Hatch changed the blue slip procedure to prevent home-state Democrats from blocking President Bush's nominees.[34] Within four months, the rule change allowed the Judiciary Committee to hold hearings on Carolyn Kuhl, Bush's nominee to the Ninth Circuit Court of Appeals, over the objection of home-state senator Barbara Boxer, D-Calif. In a letter to Hatch, Boxer criticized his "disregard" of her prerogative as a home-state senator. "Your blue slip policy is apparently guided more by who is in the White House rather than by the powers given to us as U.S. senators," she complained.[35] After the Judiciary Committee voted in favor of Kuhl by a 109 party line vote in May 2003, Democrats—who were already filibustering the nominations of Miguel Estrada to the D.C. Circuit and Priscilla Owen to the Fifth Circuit— decided to filibuster Kuhl's nomination as well.[36] By the end of the summer of 2003, they were also filibustering a fourth nominee: William Pryor, Bush's nominee for the Eleventh Circuit.

An outgrowth of senatorial courtesy and the blue slip is that presidents have traditionally turned to home-state senators for advice about whom to nominate. Home-state senators of the same party as the president are the most influential, although some presidents have also sought at least some advice from home-state senators of the opposition party (even when they do so, presidents very rarely appoint judges of the opposing party). Especially in the early part of our history—when communication was slow and difficult, and the president was literally more isolated and removed from the various states than today—that practice made sense. It assumed that home-state senators were better able to select qualified individuals than the president because they knew more about the existing pool of candidates. Over time, however, senators came to treat district court appointments as a form of patronage. Former attorney general Robert F. Kennedy went so far as to call it "senatorial appointment with the advice and consent of the senate."[37]

G. Alan Tarr has pointed out that senatorial courtesy has influenced the type of individuals appointed to district courts. Because these appointments have long served as a form of political patronage for home-state senators of the president's political party, it is not surprising that roughly 95 percent of all district court judges appointed during the past hundred years have come from the same political party as the appointing president. Tarr also notes that "district court judges have usually 'earned' their positions by active party service in their state prior to appointment."[38]

As an attempt to ensure the quality of these judges, the American Bar Association (ABA) created its Standing Committee on Federal Judiciary in 1946 to review the qualifications of all federal judicial nominees.[39] Republicans on the Senate Judiciary Committee embraced the ABA's role—partly to block some of President Harry Truman's Democratic nominees. When Republican president Dwight D. Eisenhower entered office in 1953, he established a formal link between the White House and the ABA. The ABA would review the qualifications of all potential nominees before the president nominated anyone.

By the 1980s, however, Republicans had come to view the ABA with suspicion. Once a conservative organization, the ABA had become more liberal over time. Republicans were especially angry that four of the fifteen members of the ABA's standing committee rated Ronald Reagan's failed Supreme Court nominee Robert Bork "not qualified" in 1987. In March 2001, President George W. Bush severed the White House link with the ABA—something his father had threatened to do in 1991. In a letter to ABA president Martha W. Barnett, White House counsel Alberto R. Gonzales (who is on the list of potential Bush Supreme Court nominees) wrote: "We will continue to welcome suggestions from all sources, including the ABA. The issue at hand, however, is quite different: whether the ABA alone—out of the literally dozens of groups and many individuals who have a strong interest in the composition of the federal courts—should receive advance notice of the identities of potential nominees in order to render prenomination opinions on their fitness for judicial service."[40] When Democrats regained control of the Senate from June 2001 through the 2002 midterm elections, however, they reinstated a role for the ABA by promising not to hold hearings on Bush's judicial nominees until the Senate Judiciary Committee received their ABA ratings. Democrats insisted that the ABA ratings validate a nominee's professional qualifications and feared that Bush's attempt to bypass the ABA was part of an effort to appoint more ideologically extreme judges to the bench. They also pointed to the fact that many of the White House lawyers assigned to judicial selection in the Bush administration were affiliated with the conservative Federalist Society. The Federalist Society had long opposed the ABA's role in rating nominees.[41] Formed in 1982 in response to the perception that liberal ideology dominated law schools and the legal profession, the Federalist Society "has become a major source of conservative legal thinking, and a clearinghouse for the selection of conservative law clerks, government political appointees, judges, and other key policy-making spots in the Bush administration."[42]

In what some people see as an attempt to appoint more ideological judges, presidents in recent years have exerted greater control over the selection of lower federal court judges—especially those for the courts of appeals. The control began, ironically, as a part of President Carter's efforts to institute merit selection of federal judges. In 1977, by executive order, Carter created the Circuit Court Nominating Commission. The commission diminished the role of senators in the selection of courts of appeals judges by taking control of the screening process for nominees. Under the new system, the commission would submit a short list of qualified nominees to the president, who would then nominate someone from that list.[43] Carter also urged senators to create, voluntarily, nominating commissions to advise him on the selection of district court judges from their states. By 1979, senators from thirty-one states had created such commissions.[44] The changes were made to help ensure that the awarding of judgeships would be based on qualifications and not used merely as a form of political patronage for senators.

Despite Carter's emphasis on merit in judicial selection, his appointments remained partisan: over 90 percent of his district court appointments and just over 82 percent of his appeals court appointments were of fellow Democrats.[45] Carter also considered affirmative action to be an important criterion for judicial selection. He made a deliberate effort to place women, African Americans, and Hispanics on the federal judiciary—appointing more of each than had been placed on the bench by all previous presidents combined.[46]

Ronald Reagan transformed the selection process when he took office in 1981. He abolished Carter's commission system and seized control of the selection process as part of an effort to screen nominees to ensure that they reflected his administration's ideology. He created the President's Committee on Federal Judicial Selection, staffed by representatives of the White House and the Justice Department, to conduct the screening—which included extensive interviews of all leading candidates. Sheldon Goldman called it "the most systematic judicial philosophical screening of candidates ever seen in the nation's history."[47] Reagan attorney general Edwin Meese III bluntly said the appointments were meant to "institutionalize the Reagan revolution so it can't be set aside no matter what happens in future presidential elections."[48] By the time he left office, Reagan had set a new record for the number of lower federal judges appointed: 290 district court judges and 78 appeals court judges.[49] George Bush, who had served as Reagan's vice president before becoming president in 1989, appointed almost 200 additional federal judges during his four years as president.

Presidents Carter, Reagan, and Bush had all benefited from legislation that significantly expanded the number of federal judges. President Clinton did not. During Clinton's eight years in office, Congress created only 9 additional seats—as compared with 85 under Bush, 85 under Reagan, and 152 under Carter.[50] Clinton also faced a Senate controlled by opposition Republicans during his last six years in office. In 1997, Republican senators orchestrated an unprecedented slowdown of the confirmation process to protest what they called Clinton's "activist" (liberal) nominees. Such charges may have reflected partisan hyperbole more than fact. Studies suggest that Clinton's nominees were actually quite moderate. This was true even of those nominees confirmed before Republicans took control of the Senate.[51] Clinton's appointees also had the highest ABA ratings of the past four presidents.[52]

As a result of the Republican slowdown, one in ten seats on the federal judiciary were vacant by the end of 1997. Twenty-six seats had remained empty for more than eighteen months, and one-third of the seats in the Ninth Circuit were empty. In March 1997, House majority whip Tom DeLay, R-Texas, even suggested that congressional Republicans should begin efforts to impeach liberal federal judges.[53] Such tactics provoked outcries. Even Chief Justice William Rehnquist, a conservative appointed by Reagan, criticized the Senate for its slowdown in his annual State of the Judiciary report. "The Senate is surely under no obligation to confirm any particular nominee," Rehnquist wrote, "but after the necessary time for inquiry, it should vote him up or vote him down."[54]

In part because of Rehnquist's criticism, Senate Republicans backed away from their slowdown, and the backlog of vacancies eased in 1998. But the delay tactics returned in 1999 and continued through the rest of the Clinton presidency. By then, Republicans hoped to delay confirmation until a Republican president was elected. They were especially concerned with appeals court appointments. In 2000, the Senate confirmed only thirty-nine of eighty-one judicial nominees put forward by Clinton (an additional two nominees withdrew). Nominations of forty-two judicial candidates remained unconfirmed when Clinton left office in January 2001—thirty-eight of them had never even received a judiciary committee hearing.[55]

Despite the slowdowns and the lack of new judicial seats to fill, Clinton appointed 378 judges during his eight years in office. By the end of Clinton's second term, the number of his appointees serving on the courts narrowly surpassed the number of Reagan-Bush appointees still serving by a margin of 42.7 percent to 40.7 percent.[56] Even more than Jimmy Carter, Clinton diversified the bench through these appointments. He appointed 111 women and 62 African Americans: more of each than Ford, Carter, Reagan, and Bush combined had appointed in nineteen years (see Table 7-1).[57] Nonetheless, Republicans had the opportunity

Table 7-1   Race, Ethnicity, and Gender of all Federal Judicial Appointments, by Administration (Nixon to G. W. Bush)

President	Total appointments	Male	Female	White	African American	Hispanic	Asian	Native American	Arab American
G. W. Bush (2001–9/2003)	160	130 (81.3%)	30 (18.8%)	132 (82.5%)	12 (7.5%)	13 (8.1%)	1 (0.6%)	0	2 (1.3%)
Clinton (1993–2001)	378	267 (70.6%)	111 (29.4%)	285 (75.4%)	62 (16.4%)	24 (6.3%)	5 (1.3%)	1 (0.26%)	1 (0.26%)
G. Bush (1989–1993)	192	156 (81.2%)	36 (18.8%)	172 (89.6%)	11 (5.7%)	8 (4.2%)	1 (0.5%)	0	0
Reagan (1981–1989)	378	347 (91.8%)	31 (8.2%)	356 (94.2%)	7 (1.9%)	13 (3.4%)	2 (0.5%)	0	0
Carter (1977–1981)	258	217 (84.1%)	41 (15.9%)	202 (78.3%)	37 (14.3%)	16 (6.2%)	2 (0.8%)	1 (0.4%)	0
Ford (1974–1977)	65	64 (98.5%)	1 (1.5%)	59 (90.8%)	3 (4.6%)	1 (1.5%)	2 (3.1%)	0	0
Nixon (1969–1974)	227	226 (99.6%)	1 (0.4%)	218 (96%)	6 (2.6%)	2 (0.9%)	1 (0.4%)	0	0

Source: Alliance for Justice, "Judicial Selection Project," www.allianceforjustice.com

to make significant inroads when George W. Bush took office in 2001. By the end of his second month in office, Bush already had 94 judicial vacancies to fill (including 28 on appellate courts).[58] Bush assigned White House counsel Alberto Gonzales an active role in judicial selection. In the first two months of the Bush presidency, Gonzales interviewed some 50 potential nominees to fill those vacancies.[59] The Bush administration was eager to fill them quickly while Republicans still (with the tie-breaking vote of Vice President Cheney) held marginal control of the Senate. They especially feared that the ninety-eight-year-old Republican senator from South Carolina, Strom Thurmond, might die or resign because of ill health before the 2002 elections. If that happened, the Democratic governor of South Carolina would name a replacement. None of Bush's judicial nominees were confirmed, however, before Senator Jeffords defected from the Republican Party and threw control of the Senate to the Democrats in June 2001.

By October 2001, Bush had submitted sixty judicial nominations, but the Senate had confirmed only eight. Now Republicans accused Democrats of slowing down the confirmation process, charged that judicial vacancies would hamper the war on terrorism, and mounted a Senate filibuster against a foreign-aid spending bill as retaliation for the confirmation slowdown. Democrats denied that they had deliberately slowed down the confirmation process as Republicans had done under Clinton, pointing out that they had only controlled the Senate for four months and that the legislative agenda had been interrupted during that time by the terrorist attacks of September 11 and the ensuing anthrax scare on Capitol Hill.[60] The charges and countercharges further polarized the two sides. Democrats charged Bush with nominating ideologically extreme judges and blocked his nominations of Charles Pickering and Priscilla Owen to the Fifth Circuit Court of Appeals. President Bush, emboldened by his skyrocketing public approval after September 11, charged Democrats with obstructionism and turned the "vacancy crisis" on the federal bench into a campaign issue during the 2002 midterm elections.[61]

When Republicans regained control of the Senate as a result of those midterm elections, it appeared that Bush would now be able to gain approval of his nominees. He quickly renominated Pickering and Owen. Senate Democrats showed a willingness to vote for moderate nominees (for example, all nine Democrats on the Senate Judiciary Committee voted in favor of Edward Prado, a Bush nominee to the Fifth Circuit Court of Appeals, on April 3, 2003) but continued their vow to block "ideological extremists." They even resurrected a technique used by Republicans in 1968 to block Lyndon Johnson's nomination of Abe Fortas to the chief justice position on the Supreme Court: filibuster. Under Senate Rule 22, it takes a vote of three-fifths of the entire Senate (sixty votes) to end a filibuster. By the summer of 2003, Democrats had launched filibusters against four Bush nominees—Miguel Estrada, Carolyn Kuhl, Priscilla Owen, and William Pryor—and threatened to use the tactic against other judicial nominees. Since Republicans could not muster the sixty votes to end the filibusters, Democrats succeeded in blocking the nominations—prompting a Republican threat to change Senate rules regarding filibusters so Democrats could no longer use them against judicial nominees. Many observers believed that these skirmishes were merely a prelude to an all-out confirmation battle over a Bush nominee to the Supreme Court.

Selection of Supreme Court Justices

The president clearly dominates the process of selecting members of the Supreme Court. Despite the constitutional admonition that the Senate offer "advice and consent" on presidents' nominees, the extent to which presidents seek advice from senators on whom to nominate is minimal. A rare exception came in 1874, when President Ulysses S. Grant formally sought the advice of Senate leaders before nominating Morrison Waite to be chief justice.

While presidents have only recently come to appreciate and take full advantage of their ability to influence judicial policymaking through *lower* federal court appointments, they have long recognized the importance of Supreme Court appointments. Through its power of judicial review, the Court has the authority—when a legitimate case or controversy is brought before it—to review actions of the other branches of government and the states (as in *Bush v. Gore*), and to strike down those that violate the Constitution.

The Supreme Court's Power of Judicial Review. First used by the Court to strike down legislation in *Marbury v. Madison*, 5 U.S. 137 (1803), the Supreme

Court's unenumerated power of judicial review is an important part of our system of checks and balances. It serves as a way of policing the actions of other governmental actors and ensuring that they are acting in accordance with the Constitution. It prevents temporary legislative majorities from invading the rights of minorities and keeps strong-willed presidents from thwarting the Constitution. It is, in other words, a protection against "tyranny of the majority" and other abuses of power by government officials.

But there are also dangers associated with judicial review. After all, it is up to a simple majority of the Court to determine what the Constitution means and whether a governmental action violates it. This may seem like an easy task, but it is not. Many provisions of the Constitution are notoriously vague and ambiguous. As a result, they are susceptible to different interpretations. As we saw in chapter 1, the ambiguity of Article II has led to considerable disagreement over the scope of presidential power. Such ambiguity extends to many other important provisions of the Constitution. For example, what does "equal protection" mean? "Unreasonable searches and seizures"? "Cruel and unusual punishment"? The First Amendment says that Congress shall make no law abridging freedom of speech. But what is "speech"? Does it include libel? Campaign contributions? False advertising? Obscenity? Advocacy to overthrow the government? Flag burning? Nude dancing? These questions have all come before the Court. Reasonable people disagree about how to answer them.

The real danger of judicial review lies in the possibility that a majority of the Court might take advantage of the Constitution's ambiguities to impose its own will. Under the guise of upholding the Constitution, five unelected judges could choose to impose policies they support and nullify those they do not. Judges from both ends of the political spectrum are susceptible to that temptation. Some observers say that is what happened when a conservative majority on the Court struck down government attempts to regulate business in the early twentieth century,[62] or when a liberal majority in the 1960s and 1970s used an unenumerated "right of privacy" to strike down state laws that banned abortion and the use of contraceptives.[63]

Even when the Court is doing its best to apply the Constitution fairly and accurately, answers to many constitutional questions remain a matter of judgment. It is precisely for that reason that Supreme Court appointments are so important. Decisions reached by the Court are of vital interest to the president because they affect presidential programs, the operation of the entire political system, and the functioning of U.S. society in general. Presidents realize they can affect those decisions through their appointments to the Court. Therefore they usually take great care in the people they nominate.

Nominee Qualifications. Generally speaking, there are three broad categories of qualifications that presidents and their aides take into account when screening nominees: professional, representational, and doctrinal.[64] Surprisingly, the Constitution contains no specific qualifications for being a Supreme

Court justice. This stands in stark contrast to the very specific constitutional qualifications for the president, senators, and members of the House of Representatives.[65] Since federal law has not mandated specific qualifications either, it "is legally possible, though scarcely conceivable, that a non-citizen, a minor or a non-lawyer could be appointed to the Court."[66]

There may be no legally mandated qualifications, but there are qualifications that are important. Among them is a nominee's *professional* experience. Although President Bush severed the official relationship between the White House and the American Bar Association in 2001, the ABA ratings of nominees continue to be an important barometer for senators and the public to gauge the professional merits of a nominee. The ABA bases its ratings largely on the nominee's professional qualifications. So, too, do others who assess whether an individual is fit to serve on the Supreme Court. Thus while not required by the Constitution, every justice who has served on the Supreme Court has been a lawyer, and high professional standards have been an important criterion when selecting and confirming nominees.[67]

Representational qualifications are also an important concern when presidents screen candidates. These include the partisan affiliation of potential nominees and the geographic region they represent, as well as such factors as their race, gender, and ethnicity. With rare exceptions, presidents appoint justices from their own political party. Early in the nation's history, geographic balance was also a major consideration for presidents when deciding upon a nominee. This was especially true because Supreme Court justices then had the onerous responsibility of "riding circuit"—traveling around the country to preside over appeals in lower federal courts of a particular circuit to which they were assigned. Prior to the Civil War, presidents tried to have at least one justice from each of the circuits. By 1891, though, Congress had abolished the requirement of circuit riding, thus doing away with the most important need for geographic balance. Still, some effort is made to represent different parts of the country on the Supreme Court. Occasionally, a president tries to use a Supreme Court appointment to curry favor with a particular region of the country. Thus both Herbert Hoover and Richard Nixon tried to appoint southerners to the Supreme Court as a way to build electoral support in the South for reelection.[68]

More recently, religion, race, gender, and ethnicity have become important representational concerns. Although the Court has historically had a distinctly white, male, Protestant bias, a "Catholic seat" has existed by tradition since 1836, as has a "Jewish seat" since 1916 (although the latter remained vacant from 1969 to 1993). In 2003, there were five Protestants, two Catholics, and two Jews sitting on the Court. Since 1967, there has always been an African American on the Court, and since 1981 at least one woman (Reagan had made the appointment of a woman a campaign promise in 1980). Both Bush and Clinton gave serious consideration to appointing the first Hispanic to the Court, and many predict that George W. Bush will follow through with the idea. Such an appointment would help to build electoral support among the increasingly large Hispanic population in key electoral states such as California, Florida, and Texas.

Doctrinal qualifications refer to the perception that a nominee shares the president's political philosophy and approach to public policy issues. This is especially important given the Court's power to interpret the Constitution and exercise judicial review. As noted above, some presidents, such as Ronald Reagan, have made doctrinal considerations a central part of their screening process. Although Reagan's appointment of Sandra Day O'Connor was driven largely by representational concerns, he was careful to select a woman who fit his doctrinal qualifications. His later elevation of William Rehnquist to chief justice, his appointments of Antonin Scalia and Anthony Kennedy, and his unsuccessful nominations of Robert Bork and Douglas Ginsburg were motivated largely by doctrinal considerations. On the Court, Rehnquist and Scalia are part of a core conservative block that Kennedy and O'Connor frequently join.

In contrast, Bill Clinton was somewhat less concerned with doctrinal representation. Although applauded for their representational impact, Ruth Bader Ginsburg and Stephen Breyer actually drew some criticism from liberal Democrats who were distressed that the first Democratic president since Lyndon Johnson with the opportunity to fill vacancies on the Court (Carter made no appointments) picked candidates with moderate, mainstream—rather than activist, liberal—constitutional views. Both justices, of course, were Democrats who were more liberal than Reagan's nominees. But in the interest of avoiding a confirmation battle in the Senate, Clinton selected experienced and moderate federal appeals court judges rather than ideologues to fill his Supreme Court vacancies. Ginsburg and Breyer had strong support from both liberals and conservatives on the Senate Judiciary Committee and went on to win easy confirmation. Based on George W. Bush's lower court appointments, observers speculate that he will revert to the doctrinal approach used by Reagan in making Supreme Court nominations.

Initial Screening and Selection. As David Yalof points out, different presidents go about screening and selecting potential Supreme Court nominees in different ways. Even within a single administration, Yalof identifies a variety of factors that influence the president's initial selection process. These include (1) the timing of the vacancy, (2) the composition of the Senate, (3) the public approval of the president, (4) attributes of the outgoing justice, and (5) the realistic pool of candidates available to the president.[69] If the vacancy occurs early in their terms, presidents are usually in a stronger position politically than if the vacancy occurs at the end of their terms. On the other hand, if the vacancy occurs shortly before their reelection campaigns, or toward the end of their last terms, presidents may be more limited in the type of nominee they can send to the Senate and may feel compelled to nominate a more moderate, consensus candidate. The same is true if the opposition party controls the Senate (a common phenomenon in recent years) or if a president's approval ratings are low. Choice of a successor may also be more limited if the outgoing justice represents a particular religious or demographic group or if the president feels that a particular region of the country needs representation on the Court. And, obviously, presidents are limited by the available pool of candidates. For example, presidents may find it difficult to find a nominee who fits the precise mix of professional, doctrinal, and representational concerns that they would like.

Since 1853, the Justice Department has had formal responsibility for collecting applications and recommendations of potential nominees, who also undergo a background check by the Federal Bureau of Investigation, a unit of the Justice Department. Historically, the attorney general (the head of the Justice Department) played the primary role in this process. As Yalof notes, however, the growth and bureaucratization of both the White House and the Justice Department have led to the emergence of specialized staff units assigned to vet potential nominees.[70] The Office of White House Counsel, created as part of the president's personal staff during the Truman administration, now plays an important role—as do the chief of staff and other White House officials. In the early part of George W. Bush's administration, Alberto Gonzales led the search for all federal judges.

In some administrations, overlapping responsibilities between the White House and the Justice Department have led to internal power struggles over what type of judges to nominate. This happened during the Reagan administration. When Justice Lewis Powell resigned from the Supreme Court in 1987, Attorney General Meese and other Justice Department officials pushed for a staunchly conservative nominee: Robert Bork. On the other hand, White House counsel Arthur B. Culvahouse and Chief of Staff Howard Baker both pushed for a moderate consensus nominee. The Justice Department won, but the Senate went on to defeat the Bork nomination in one of the most contentious confirmation battles in recent history.[71]

Of course, many people have a desire to influence the nomination decision. The legal community is particularly eager to influence the selection process. This community includes professional organizations such as the ABA. Clearly the ABA's ratings can have an influence on how nominees are perceived by the public and the Senate. Other legal groups, as well as individual lawyers, also participate in the selection process. They may suggest nominees to the president or announce their evaluations of the person the president nominated. Coalitions of lawyers sometimes sign letters of support for, or of opposition to, specific nominees. Even Supreme Court justices themselves occasionally participate in the process by recommending a potential nominee to the president or even lobbying publicly for a candidate. Chief Justice William Howard Taft (1921–1930) was particularly active in that regard. More recently, Chief Justice Warren Burger suggested the nomination of Harry Blackmun in 1970 and Sandra Day O'Connor in 1981.[72]

Interest groups also lobby for and against the selection of nominees. As early as the 1880s, interest groups recognized how directly the Supreme Court could affect them and began taking an active interest in the Senate confirmation of nominees.[73] They also began to lobby presidents before nominations were announced.[74] Nowadays, they take very public stances on nominations—often before vacancies on the Supreme Court occur. Thus the National Abortion and Reproductive Rights Action League sent a letter from Kate Michelman, the group's president, to millions of households in April 2001 warning: "You and I need to be prepared to oppose George W. Bush's nominees to the Supreme Court. It could happen next week. It could happen next month." When it does, she wrote, a Bush nominee could "strangle reproductive freedom for many years to come."[75]

Senate Confirmation. Once nominated by the president, a candidate to the Supreme Court must be confirmed by the Senate. This requires a simple majority vote. Of the 149 nominations to the Supreme Court since 1789, the Senate has voted to outright reject only 12. It effectively rejected 10 others, either by voting to "postpone" consideration of the nominee or by taking no action at all. In such cases, the nomination died at the end of the Senate session. In addition, presidents have withdrawn 5 nominations in the face of certain Senate defeat. Combined, that amounts to 27 failed nominations (see Table 7-2). (Two other nominations were withdrawn on a technicality. Another nominee died after being confirmed, and 7 others declined their seats after Senate confirmation.)

The failure rate of Supreme Court nominees—18.4 percent—is the highest for any appointive post requiring Senate confirmation.[76] Five nominations have failed just since 1968. This is a reflection of the concern for the profound effect Supreme Court appointments can have on public policy.

Confirmation is also a test of presidential strength. "Weak" presidents—those who are unelected, those who face a Senate controlled by the opposition, and those in their terminal year in office—are statistically less likely to secure confirmation of their Supreme Court nominees. The unusually long period of divided government in recent years (with the White House controlled by one party and the Senate by another) has added to the contentiousness of confirmation battles. From 1969 through 2000, different parties controlled the Senate and the White House for twenty out of thirty-two years. Divided government returned again in June 2001, when Democrats regained control of the Senate. On average, confirmation rates drop from 87.9 percent when the same party controls the White House and the Senate to only 54.5 percent during periods of divided government.[77] Ongoing public policy debates over such controversial issues as race and abortion—something that journalist E. J. Dionne has called a "cultural civil war"[78]—have also contributed to intense confirmation battles. Interest groups fan the flames through their efforts for and against nominees.

Interest groups led the opposition to all the nominees rejected by the Senate or forced to withdraw in the twentieth century. John J. Parker, a southern court of appeals judge nominated by Herbert Hoover in 1930, fell victim to the com-

Table 7-2   Failed Supreme Court Nominees

Nominee and year of nomination	President and party	Composition of Senate	Action
John Rutledge, 1795	Washington (F)	19 F, 13 DR	Rejected 14–10
Alexander Wolcott, 1811	Madison (DR)	28 DR, 6 F	Rejected 24–9
John J. Crittenden, 1828	J. Q. Adams (NR)	28 J, 20 NR	Postponed 23–17
Roger B. Taney, 1835	Jackson (D)	20 D, 20 W	Postponed 24–21
John C. Spencer, 1844	Tyler (W)	28 W, 25 D	Rejected 26–21
Reuben H. Walworth, 1844[a]	Tyler (W)	28 W, 25 D	Postponed 27–20
Edward King, 1844[b]	Tyler (W)	28 W, 25 D	Postponed 29–18
Edward King, 1844	Tyler (W)	28 W, 25 D	Withdrawn
John M. Read, 1845	Tyler (W)	28 W, 25 D	No action
George W. Woodward, 1845	Polk (D)	31 D, 25 W	Rejected 20–19
Edward A. Bradford, 1852	Fillmore (W)	35 D, 24 W	No action
George E. Badger, 1853	Fillmore (W)	35 D, 24 W	Postponed 26–25
William C. Micou, 1853	Fillmore (W)	35 D, 24 W	No action
Jeremiah S. Black, 1861	Buchanan (D)	36 D, 26 R	Rejected 26–25
Henry Stanbery, 1866	A. Johnson (R)	42 U, 10 D	No action
Ebenezer R. Hoar, 1869	Grant (R)	56 R, 11 D	Rejected 33–24
George H. Williams, 1873	Grant (R)	49 R, 19 D	Withdrawn
Caleb Cushing, 1874	Grant (R)	49 R, 19 D	Withdrawn
Stanley Matthews, 1881	Hayes (R)	42 D, 33 R	No action
William Hornblower, 1893	Cleveland (D)	44 D, 38 R	Rejected 30–24
Wheeler H. Peckham, 1894	Cleveland (D)	44 D, 38 R	Rejected 41–32
John J. Parker, 1930	Hoover (R)	56 R, 39 D	Rejected 41–39
Abe Fortas, 1968	Johnson (D)	64 D, 36 R	Withdrawn
Clement Haynsworth, 1969	Nixon (R)	58 D, 42 R	Rejected 55–45
G. Harrold Carswell, 1970	Nixon (R)	58 D, 42 R	Rejected 51–45
Robert H. Bork, 1987	Reagan (R)	55 D, 45 R	Rejected 58–42
Douglas Ginsburg, 1987	Reagan (R)	55 D, 45 R	Withdrawn

Source: John Anthony Maltese, *The Selling of Supreme Court Nominees* (Baltimore: Johns Hopkins University Press, 1995), 3.

Note: F is Federalist, DR is Democratic-Republican, NR is National-Republican, D is Democrat, W is Whig, R is Republican, J is Jacksonian, and U is Unionist. Tyler, Fillmore, and Andrew Johnson were not elected.

[a]Reuben Walworth's nomination was later withdrawn.

[b]Edward King was nominated twice.

bined opposition of the American Federation of Labor and the National Association for the Advancement of Colored People (NAACP), who viewed him as antilabor and racist. Labor and the NAACP again joined forces to defeat two Nixon nominees: Clement Haynsworth, a federal court of appeals judge from South Carolina, in 1969, and G. Harrold Carswell, a federal court of appeals judge from Florida, in 1970.[79] Lyndon Johnson's nomination of Abe Fortas to be chief justice in 1968 was bitterly attacked by conservative groups because of his liberal decisions in obscenity cases and suits concerning the rights of the accused in criminal proceedings.[80] A major effort by civil rights, women's, and other liberal groups contributed to the defeat in 1987 of Reagan's nomination of Robert Bork, a controversial conservative federal appeals court judge.[81]

Sometimes other problems are involved. Some people considered Fortas's acceptance of a legal fee from a family foundation and his advising President Johnson on political matters to be unethical activities for a justice of the Supreme Court.[82] Haynsworth was criticized for ruling on cases in which he had a personal financial interest. Much of the opposition to Carswell from members of the bar, particularly law professors, stemmed from his perceived lack of professional qualifications. Sen. Roman Hruska, R.-Neb., Carswell's leading supporter in the Senate, made the situation even worse when he tried to make the nominee's mediocrity a virtue by saying on national television that mediocre people needed representation on the Supreme Court. Suddenly, Carswell was a national joke. This, coupled with some shockingly racist statements Carswell had made when running for public office ("I believe the segregation of the races is proper and the only practical and correct way of life in our states," and "I yield to no man . . . in the firm, vigorous belief in the principles of white supremacy, and I shall always be so governed") doomed Carswell's nomination.[83]

Active involvement by interest groups in every Supreme Court confirmation process dates back only to the 1960s or so. Although organized interests attempted to block Senate confirmation of a Supreme Court nominee as early as 1881, their success in blocking the confirmation of three nominees in three years (Fortas, Haynsworth, and Carswell in 1968, 1969, and 1970, respectively) marked a turning point. Since then, interest groups have taken an active stand on virtually all Supreme Court nominees, although their involvement accelerated dramatically with the Bork nomination in 1987. Starting with that nomination, interest groups moved beyond testifying at confirmation hearings and mobilizing their members to lobby their senators, to a full-fledged public relations offensive, including the use of television, radio, and print ads, coupled with mass mailings and the use of phone banks to sway public opinion. They also attempted to influence reporters and editorial writers through the use of press briefings and fact sheets they aggressively distributed.

The increased role of interest groups corresponded with the increased visibility of Senate Judiciary Committee hearings and floor votes on nominees. Prior to the twentieth century, the confirmation process was shrouded in secrecy. The Senate Judiciary Committee held hearings behind closed doors and rarely even kept records of its proceedings. As the *New York Times* wrote in 1881, the "Judiciary Committee of the Senate is the most mysterious committee in that body, and succeeds better than any other in maintaining secrecy as to its proceedings."[84]

At that time, the committee usually deliberated without hearing from any witnesses. Interest groups seldom participated in this phase of the process (none testified until 1930), and no nominee appeared before the committee until Harlan Fiske Stone in 1925. Nominees actually thought it improper to answer any questions and maintained almost complete public silence. When a reporter from the New York *Sun* asked Louis Brandeis about his nomination in 1916, Brandeis quickly replied: "I have nothing to say about anything, and that goes for all time and to all newspapers, including both the *Sun* and the moon."[85] Presidents, too, maintained almost complete public silence about their nominees. When the full Senate finally voted on a nominee, it almost always did so in closed session and often with no roll call vote. This secrecy played an important part in minimizing the role of interest groups and others who had an interest in the outcome of a nomination. So, too, did the fact that senators then were not popularly elected but chosen by state legislators. This undermined the potent threat of retaliation against senators now enjoyed by the electorate (a power on which interest groups can capitalize).

All this changed in the twentieth century. The passage of the Seventeenth Amendment to the Constitution in 1913 provided for the direct election of senators, and Senate rules changes in 1929 opened floor debate on nominations. Public opinion now mattered in a very direct way to senators—they were dependent upon it for reelection. Thus they began to use public Judiciary Committee hearings as a way of both testing and influencing public opinion. Since 1981, Judiciary Committee hearings have been broadcast live on television for the entire world to see. The emergence of the modern "public presidency" *(see chapter 3)* also led to greater involvement by presidents in promoting their nominees. As specialized staff units developed in the White House, they, too, came to be used as a way to secure support for nominees and thereby increase the likelihood of Senate confirmation. Today, the Office of Communications, the Office of Public Liaison, the Office of Political Affairs, and other staff units are all used in this manner.[86]

Even if successfully confirmed, judicial appointees may fail to vote the way the president had hoped. Ronald Reagan and his immediate successor, George Bush, appointed six justices to the Supreme Court with the avowed hope of overturning *Roe v. Wade,* 410 U.S. 113 (1973), the controversial abortion rights decision. Nonetheless, three of those appointees went on to uphold *Roe.*[87] Dwight D. Eisenhower later lamented his appointment of Earl Warren as chief justice because of his liberal voting record on the bench, and Harry Truman— never one to mince words—was furious when Tom Clark, who had been Truman's attorney general, did not vote on the Supreme Court as the president had hoped. "I don't know what got into me," Truman later fumed. "He was no damn good as Attorney General, and on the Supreme Court . . . it doesn't seem possible, but he's been even worse. He hasn't made one right decision that I can think of. . . . It's just that he's such a dumb son of a bitch."[88] Despite White House chief of staff John Sununu's prediction to President Bush that David Souter would be a "home run" for conservatives, Souter actually went on to be one of the most liberal members of the Rehnquist court. The heightened screening of judicial nominees minimizes such "mistakes," but no one can completely predict the behavior of individuals once they sit on the Court.

Other Presidential Influences on the Federal Courts

Although the appointment of federal judges is the most important method by which the president affects the courts, there are other ways to influence their activities. The first is through the solicitor general, an official Robert Scigliano calls "the lawyer for the executive branch."[89] The second is through legislation that affects the operation of the Supreme Court—a means Congress, too, has tried to use to its advantage and the president's disadvantage. The third is through the enforcement of court decisions.

Role of the Solicitor General in the Appellate Courts

The solicitor general, an official appointed by the president with the advice and consent of the Senate, plays an important role in setting the agenda of the federal appellate courts. First, the solicitor general determines which of the cases the government loses in the federal district courts will be taken to the courts of appeals. Second, of the cases the government loses in the lower courts, the solicitor general decides which to recommend that the Supreme Court hear. Unlike the courts of appeals, which must take cases properly appealed to them, the Supreme Court chooses the cases it hears.[90] The Supreme Court is more likely to take cases proposed by the solicitor general than by other parties.

Once the Supreme Court accepts a case involving the federal government, the solicitor general decides the position the government should take and argues the case before the Court. Thus "the Solicitor General not only determines whether the executive branch goes to the Supreme Court but what it will say there."[91] And what it says there usually advances the policy goals of the incumbent president.[92] Moreover, the solicitor general's influence is not restricted to cases in which the federal government itself is a party. He or she also decides whether the government will file an amicus curiae (friend of the court) brief supporting or opposing positions by other parties who have cases pending before the Court.

Amicus filings by the solicitor general increased dramatically in the twentieth century. Steven Puro, who analyzed the briefs filed from 1920 through 1973, found that 71 percent occurred in the last twenty years of that period.[93] He concluded that whether by its own initiative or as a result of an invitation from the Supreme Court, the federal government participated as amicus in almost every major domestic question presented before the Court since World War II. Particularly prominent is the government entrance into the controversial issues of civil liberties, civil rights, and the jurisdiction and procedures of the courts.

When the federal government becomes involved in a case before the Supreme Court, it is usually successful. Scigliano's analysis of Court opinions chosen at ten-year intervals beginning in 1800 shows that the United States has consistently won 62 percent or more of its litigation there. Its record as amicus is even more impressive. Puro found that in the political cases he examined, the federal government supported the winning side in almost 74 percent of its appearances. An analysis of race discrimination employment cases from 1970 to 1981 showed that the government won 70 percent of the cases in which it was a direct party and 81.6 percent of those in which it filed amicus briefs.[94]

Much has been written about why solicitors general are so successful in their appearances before the Supreme Court. Kevin T. McGuire argues that it really boils down to one thing: litigation experience.[95] They are the prototypical "repeat player." Solicitors general or members of their staff argue far more cases than any other party, including any law firm in the country.[96] Thus they develop a great deal of expertise in dealing with the Court. This expertise translates into high quality briefs and an intimate understanding of the workings of the Court. Solicitors general may also build up credit with the Court because they help the justices manage their caseload by holding down the number of government appeals. Christopher Zorn also notes that amicus filings by the solicitor general "are highest when both the administration and the Court share similar policy preferences, and drop off substantially when those preferences diverge." Zorn concludes that, like other litigants, "the solicitor general appears to explicitly take into account the probability that his position will be received favorably by the Court when formulating his litigation strategies."[97]

The Reagan administration used the solicitor general's office particularly aggressively to promote its conservative policy agenda.[98] In tandem with Reagan's appointments to both the Supreme Court and the lower federal courts, this "other campaign" led by Solicitor General Rex Lee entailed efforts to persuade the Supreme Court to change previous rulings on matters such as abortion, prayer in the public schools, busing, affirmative action, the rights of the accused in criminal cases, and federal-state relations.[99] Lincoln Caplan argued that this marked a shift away from the solicitor general's traditional posture of restraint to a posture of aggressively pushing the Court to take cases that advanced the administration's social policy agenda. The result, according to Caplan, was a temporary loss of the Supreme Court's trust in the solicitor general's presentation of facts and interpretation of the law.[100] Succeeding presidents did not continue such an aggressive use of the solicitor general's office, and Richard L. Pacelle Jr. has noted the many constraints solicitors general now face:

In trying to assist the Court as tenth justice or fifth Clerk, while fulfilling the president's agenda as "attorney general as policy maker" or pursuing the Justice Department's more neutral obligations as the "attorney general as law enforcement officer," the solicitor general has to balance a number of roles. In attempting to fulfill these roles, the solicitor general has several potentially competing constituencies to satisfy. When these factors move in the same direction, there are opportunities for the solicitor general, but that was rare in the last half-century, as divided government has been the rule.[101]

Solicitors general serve an average length of two years in their posts. They can be fired by the president, but they can also be rewarded with an even more prestigious position. Franklin Roosevelt elevated two of his solicitors general, Stanley Reed and Robert Jackson, to the Supreme Court. Likewise, Lyndon Johnson elevated Thurgood Marshall. In the first half of 2001, some observers speculated that George W. Bush might do the same with his solicitor general, Theodore Olson, who successfully argued Bush's case before the Supreme Court during the contested 2000 presidential election, although Democrats vowed to fight such a nomination. Once Democrats took control of the Senate in June 2001, the prospects of an Olson nomination diminished.

Legislation Affecting the Supreme Court

The president also can affect the actions of the Supreme Court through legislation. Presidential authority to propose bills to Congress and to work for their adoption, as well as the power to oppose measures favored by members of Congress and, if necessary, to veto them, means the president can influence legislation affecting the Court. At the same time, Congress can pass legislation concerning the Court that threatens the president's own power.

In 1937, Franklin Roosevelt became actively involved in trying to get Congress to exercise its power to expand the size of the Supreme Court. The power to establish the size of the Supreme Court is left up to Congress by the Constitution, and Congress has changed the size of the Court several times. Historically, though, Congress has done so without prompting from the president. Sometimes it has even altered the size of the Court in an effort to thwart a particular president. For example, in the latter days of the John Adams administration, the lame-duck Congress—still controlled by the Federalists—passed the Judiciary Act of 1801. That act reduced the number of justices from six to five in an attempt to prevent the incoming president, Democratic-Republican Thomas Jefferson, from appointing a replacement for ailing justice William Cushing. (Since justices have life tenure, the size of the Court would not actually decrease until a justice left the bench.) Not surprisingly, the Democratic-Republicans quickly repealed the 1801 law and restored the number of justices to six when they took control of Congress later that year. In 1807, the Democratic-Republican Congress increased the number of justices to seven to accommodate population growth in Kentucky, Tennessee, and Ohio. Thus the Federalists' attempt to thwart President Jefferson failed, and he went on to name three justices. (Ironically, Cushing recovered and lived until 1810; his successor was named by James Madison, not Jefferson.)

Congressional manipulation of the size of the Court so as to affect presidential appointments also occurred in the 1860s. The 1863 Judiciary Act expanding the Court from nine to ten members enabled Abraham Lincoln to appoint Stephen J. Field, who subsequently supported the president on war issues. Shortly thereafter, the Radical Republicans, who controlled Congress, passed legislation reducing the number of justices to prevent Lincoln's successor, Andrew Johnson, from naming justices they feared would rule against the Reconstruction program. Soon after Ulysses S. Grant was inaugurated in March 1869, the size of the Court was again expanded; this expansion, plus a retirement, enabled Grant to appoint Justices William Strong and Joseph P. Bradley. Both voted to reconsider a previous Supreme Court decision, *Hepburn v. Griswold*, that had declared unconstitutional the substitution of paper money for gold as legal tender for the payment of contracts.[102] The new decision validated the use of "greenbacks" as legal tender.[103] The three successive changes in the size of the Court within a six-year period brought the results Congress desired.

Roosevelt's 1937 "Court packing" proposal was different from these earlier examples because of his aggressive efforts to promote congressional action. Frustrated by the invalidation of much of the early New Deal legislation (between January 1935 and June 1936 the Court struck down eight separate statutes), Roosevelt proposed legislation in early 1937 that would permit him to appoint one justice, up to six in number, for each sitting member of the Court who failed to retire voluntarily at age seventy. Buoyed by his landslide electoral victory in 1936, and confident that the Democrat-controlled Congress would follow his lead, Roosevelt announced the proposal at a press conference without consulting with members of Congress. Samuel Kernell points to it as an early, failed attempt at "going public."[104] Although FDR contended that the additions were necessary to handle the Court's caseload, it was patently clear that his real purpose was to liberalize the Court. The proposal stimulated violent opposition from members of the bar, the press, and many of Roosevelt's political supporters in Congress who were angered that they had not been consulted about the plan. At this point, Justice Owen J. Roberts, a centrist who had been aligned with four conservative colleagues in striking down New Deal legislation, began to vote with the other four justices to uphold the legislation—thus giving FDR the new majority he had been seeking. The unpopularity of Roosevelt's proposal, Justice Roberts's mitigating action (which observers dubbed "the switch in time that saved nine"), and the sudden death of Majority Leader Joseph Robinson of Arkansas, who was leading the president's effort in the Senate, resulted in Congress's failure to adopt the Court-packing plan. Kernell calls it "FDR's most stunning legislative failure in his 12 years in office."[105] Yet Roosevelt won the legal battle anyway. Once Roberts switched his vote, conservative members—now in dissent—began to leave the Court. By the time he died, Roosevelt had managed to appoint all but one of the nine justices of the Supreme Court and thus secure a Court majority willing to uphold his policies.

In addition to its power to change the size of the Supreme Court, Congress can also pass legislation altering the appellate jurisdiction of the Court.[106] Presidents could conceivably propose such legislation—which could take away the power of the Supreme Court to hear appeals in specific types of cases—just as Roosevelt proposed legislation with regard to the size of the Court. As recently as the 1980s, Sen. Jesse Helms, R-N.C., proposed legislation to take away the Supreme Court's appellate jurisdiction to hear cases involving school prayer. (Helms was angered that the Court had declared state-sponsored prayer in public schools a violation of the establishment clause requirement of a separation between church and state.) Helms's effort failed, and presidents have not joined in efforts to secure passage of such jurisdiction-stripping proposals.

Presidents have been more willing to urge Congress to propose constitutional amendments to overturn Supreme Court rulings and to lobby for the passage of legislation that might undermine existing rulings. Republican presidents Reagan and George H. W. Bush sought to overturn *Roe v. Wade* by pressuring

Congress to propose a constitutional amendment outlawing abortion. Although unsuccessful in this effort, both presidents signed legislation that limited use of federal funds for abortions and made access to abortions more difficult. Bush also supported a constitutional amendment to overrule a controversial Supreme Court decision, *Texas v. Johnson*, 491 U.S. 397 (1989), that permitted flag burning as a form of protected symbolic speech. When the Supreme Court struck down the Gun Free School Zones Act in *United States v. Lopez*, 514 U.S. 549 (1995), President Clinton strongly criticized the Court and ordered Attorney General Janet Reno to come up with other ways to keep guns out of school.[107]

Enforcement of Court Decisions

Although the federal courts have the authority to hand down decisions on cases within their jurisdiction, they have no independent power to enforce their decisions. Lacking both the power of the purse and of the sword, the Supreme Court depends upon the executive branch to enforce its rulings. Thus President Eisenhower called out federal troops in 1957 to enforce court-ordered school desegregation in Little Rock, Arkansas. The order was an outgrowth of the Supreme Court's landmark *Brown v. Board of Education* ruling that overturned the "separate but equal" doctrine of *Plessy v. Ferguson*.[108]

Sometimes less forceful action by the president helps to bring about compliance with Supreme Court rulings. For instance, President Kennedy, in a June 1962 press conference, publicly supported the Supreme Court's controversial ruling in *Engel v. Vitale*, which banned state-sponsored prayer in public schools, thus setting an example for others to follow.[109] Presidents also set an example by complying with court orders aimed at them. Thus immediately after the Supreme Court held in 1952 that President Truman's seizure of the steel mills was unconstitutional, the president ordered the mills restored to private operation.[110] Likewise, President Nixon complied with the Court's 1974 ruling in *United States v. Nixon* that he turn over to a federal district court tapes of his conversations with executive aides.[111] That action produced evidence of the president's involvement in the Watergate affair, led to the House Judiciary Committee's impeachment vote against him, and ultimately resulted in Nixon's resignation.

Nonetheless, presidents have sometimes defied—or threatened to defy—the Court. The fear that President Jefferson's secretary of state, James Madison, would (with the president's blessing) defy a court order to deliver commissions that would result in the seating of Federalist judges probably influenced John Marshall's opinion in *Marbury v. Madison*. Thus Marshall gave the Jefferson administration what it wanted—it did not force delivery of the commissions—but did so by creating the power of judicial review. More blatantly, President Lincoln once ignored a federal court ruling that declared his suspension of habeas corpus unconstitutional.[112] But Lincoln's response remains an exception to the rule, for chief executives usually have enforced court decisions, even when they would have preferred not to do so.

Judicial Oversight of Presidential Action

Through its power of judicial review, the Supreme Court has the ability to invalidate presidential actions and those of other parts of the executive branch. This is a significant check on presidential power, although it is one that has been used quite infrequently. The Founders originally left open the question of who had the final power to interpret the Constitution. If, as Thomas Jefferson contended, each branch has the authority to interpret the Constitution as far as its own duties are concerned, then the president would be the judge of the constitutionality of executive actions. As a result of *Marbury v. Madison*, though, the Supreme Court has the power to make the final judgment on such matters. Although *Marbury* was decided in 1803, the Supreme Court did not declare a presidential action unconstitutional until after the Civil War.

Of the forty-two people who have served as president,[113] only a handful have been the objects of major Supreme Court decisions invalidating their actions. Even when invalidating a specific presidential action, the Court has often endorsed a broad reading of presidential power. For example, the Court, as previously noted, invalidated President Truman's seizure of steel mills during the Korean War.[114] Truman argued that government seizure to keep open the steel mills (which were involved in a labor dispute that threatened to shut them down) was essential to the war effort. But in seizing the mills, Truman ignored the provisions of the Taft-Hartley Act that permitted the president to obtain an injunction postponing for eighty days a strike that threatened the national safety and welfare. Instead, he issued an executive order seizing the steel mills, based on his authority under the Constitution and U.S. law and as commander in chief. The steel companies protested the seizure as unconstitutional, and the case went to the Supreme Court.

By a 6–3 vote, the Court invalidated the president's seizure. Although six justices voted against the specific action in question, six justices (the three dissenters plus three of the justices in the majority) explicitly recognized that presidents have a range of "inherent" power to take actions not explicitly authorized by the Constitution. The three dissenters said that power was broad enough to cover Truman's seizure of the mills. The other three justices who recognized some degree of inherent power stressed that such power is not absolute and that it was not broad enough to cover a situation such as this in which the president went against the will of Congress. Thus even though the case invalidated an action taken by a specific president, it set a precedent that actually *expanded* presidential power through the Court's recognition of inherent power.

Similarly, a unanimous Supreme Court in *United States v. Nixon* ruled against President Nixon's refusal to surrender subpoenaed White House tapes to Watergate special prosecutor Leon Jaworski.[115] In refusing to surrender the tapes, Nixon had claimed the existence of an "executive privilege" relating to private conversations between chief executives and their advisers. While the Court rejected Nixon's specific claim of privilege, it nonetheless recognized for the first time that the principle of executive privilege did have constitutional underpinnings. As with *Youngstown,* the Court ruled against a specific exercise of presidential power while at the same time expanding the general scope of presidential power.[116]

The Supreme Court has been especially deferential to presidential power in the realm of foreign affairs. In *United States v. Curtiss-Wright Export Corp.,* 299 U.S. 304 (1936), the Court recognized that presidents have a wider degree of discretion in foreign affairs than they do in domestic affairs. Justice George Sutherland went so far as to call the president "the sole organ of the federal government in the field of international relations."[117] Similarly, the Court has recognized that presidents have broad power to respond to military emergencies and wage war even in the congressional absence of war. In *The Prize Cases,* 67 U.S. 635 (1863), the Supreme Court recognized President Lincoln's power to impose a military blockade on southern ports—an act of war—even though Congress had not yet actually declared war. During World War II, the Court upheld broad executive power to impose the forced relocation of Japanese Americans and others of Japanese ancestry to federal detention centers.[118] More recently, the Court upheld the power of the president to seize Iranian assets during the Iran hostage crisis of the 1970s and use them as a bargaining chip to help free American hostages.[119] As the Bush administration continues its efforts to curtail civil liberties in order to guard against terrorist threats, courts will have opportunities to rule upon the constitutionality of those measures. *(See discussion in chapter 11.)*

In addition to establishing general parameters of presidential power, Supreme Court decisions can have significant repercussions on the fate of particular presidents. Two such decisions had a particular bearing on Bill Clinton. Had it not been for a 1988 ruling upholding (over the lone dissent of Antonin Scalia) the constitutionality of the independent counsel law, and a unanimous 1997 ruling that allowed a sexual harassment lawsuit against the president by Paula Jones to proceed while he was still in office, Clinton might have been spared the independent counsel investigation by Kenneth Starr and the impeachment trial brought about as a result of the Monica Lewinsky scandal.[120]

Conclusion

The relationship between the presidency and the judiciary is a very important one. On the one hand, the judiciary has the power to hand down rulings that have a direct effect on presidents and their policies. On the other, presidents can influence the federal courts through the power to nominate judges to serve on them. Both have long-term consequences. Supreme Court rulings are not easy to overturn. Those based on the Constitution can only be overruled by the Court itself or through the passage of a constitutional amendment. The president's power to appoint can also be far-reaching. Federal judges, unlike members of Congress and the political appointees of the executive branch, serve for life. That fact all but guarantees that the judicial nominees of George W. Bush will continue to be closely scrutinized and, in all likelihood, hotly contested.

NOTES

1. *Bush v. Gore*, 121 S. Ct. 525 (2000). Among the many accounts of the Supreme Court's role in the 2000 election, the most thorough is Howard Gillman, *The Votes That Counted: How the Court Decided the 2000 Presidential Election* (Chicago: University of Chicago Press, 2001).

2. The Florida legislature had provided for this standard by law. Florida Statute 101.5614(5): "No vote shall be declared invalid or void if there is a clear indication of the intent of the voter as determined by the canvassing board." A majority of states (including Texas) followed a similar standard (see footnote 2 of Justice Stevens's dissent in *Bush v. Gore*, 540). Ironically, the Florida Supreme Court may have failed to try to clarify that standard (by telling counties exactly how to identify the "clear intent" of the voter) because the U.S. Supreme Court had already chastised the Florida court for imposing its own interpretation of Florida law in *Bush v. Palm Beach Canvassing Board*, 121 S. Ct. 471 (2000) (see Justice Breyer's dissent in *Bush v. Gore*, 551, for a discussion of this).

3. *Bush v. Gore*, 530, 531. *Reynolds v. Sims*, 377 U.S. 533 (1964); *Gray v. Sanders*, 372 U.S. 368 (1963).

4. *Bush v. Gore*, 533 (two of the seven members who joined the per curiam opinion, Breyer and Souter, dissented on that particular point).

5. *Bush v. Gore*, Justice Souter's dissent (joined by Breyer, Stevens, and Ginsburg), 543.

6. Ibid., 546, 545.

7. Ibid., 542. They also made it clear that they thought the Court should not have reviewed *Bush v. Palm Beach County Canvassing Board*, 121 S. Ct. 471 (2000), either. In that case, the U.S. Supreme Court first reviewed the Florida Supreme Court's ruling allowing manual recounts. The U.S. Supreme Court vacated and remanded the decision in a per curiam decision, instructing the Florida Supreme Court to clarify its basis for requiring the recounts by demonstrating that its decision was based on Florida state law. The Florida Supreme Court did so and proceeded to order the recounts that were stopped in *Bush v. Gore*.

8. *Bush v. Gore*, Justice Ginsburg's dissent, 549.

9. Ibid., 550.

10. *Bush v. Gore*, Justice Breyer's dissent, 552.

11. *Bush v. Gore*, Justice Stevens's dissent, 541.

12. E. Joshua Rosenkranz, "High Court's Misuse of the Past," *National Law Journal*, January 15, 2001, A20. *Baker v. Carr*, 369 U.S. 186 (1962), though confined to jurisdictional issues, held that the Supreme Court could hear cases involving reapportionment, thus allowing court challenges to the drawing of legislative districts on the grounds that they deprived citizens of equal protection. It led to the "one person, one vote" principle articulated the next year in *Gray v. Sanders*, 372 U.S. 368 (1963).

13. *Bush v. Gore*, Justice Stevens's dissent, 541.

14. "Our consideration is limited to the present circumstances, for the problem of equal protection in election processes generally presents many complexities." *Bush v. Gore*, 532.

15. Rosenkranz, "High Court's Misuse of the Past," A20.

16. David Von Drehle et al., "In Florida, Drawing the Battle Lines," *Washington Post*, January 29, 2001, A1. See also Gillman, *The Votes That Counted*.

17. Ronald Dworkin, " 'A Badly Flawed Election': An Exchange," *New York Review of Books*, February 22, 2001, 9.

18. *Bush v. Gore*, Justice Stevens's dissent, 542.

19. Joan Biskupic, "Election Still Splits Court," *USA Today*, January 22, 2001, 1A.

20. Charles Lane, "Two Justices Defend Court's Intervention in Florida Dispute," *Washington Post*, March 30, 2001, A13.

21. Bruce Ackerman, "The Court Packs Itself," *The American Prospect,* February 13, 2001, online edition.

22. Office of Legal Policy Web site, www.usdoj.gov/olp. This site contains extensive information about judicial nominations.

23. In addition to the district courts and the courts of appeals, there are several specialized courts. These include the U.S. Court of International Trade and the U.S. Court of Federal Claims.

24. The District of Columbia and U.S. territories, such as Guam, also have district courts.

25. G. Alan Tarr, *Judicial Process and Policymaking,* 2d ed. (New York: West/Wadsworth, 1999), 40.

26. David M. O'Brien, *Judicial Roulette* (New York: Priority Press, 1988), 70.

27. Howard Ball, *Courts and Politics: The Federal Judicial System,* 2d ed. (Englewood Cliffs, N.J.: Prentice Hall, 1987), 199.

28. Ibid., 199–200.

29. Joel Grossman, *Lawyers and Judges: The ABA and the Politics of Judicial Selection* (New York: Wiley, 1965), 168, 170.

30. O'Brien, *Judicial Roulette,* 71.

31. "Doing Business in the Senate," editorial, *New York Times,* June 19, 2001, A22.

32. Thomas B. Edsall, "Democrats Press Bush for Input on Judges," *Washington Post,* April 28, 2001, A4. See also "Blocking Judicial Ideologues," editorial, *New York Times,* April 27, 2001, A24.

33. Jonathan Ringel, "Gearing Up to Vote on Court Nominees," *The Recorder,* June 18, 2001, 3.

34. Jason Hoppin, "Ninth Circuit Nominee Draws Opposition," *The Legal Intelligencer,* January 28, 2003, 4.

35. Jonathan Groner and Jason Hoppin, "Senate Democrats Grill 9th Circuit Nominee," *The Recorder,* April 2, 2003.

36. Jason Hoppin, "Bush Taps Idaho Lawyer for Ninth Circuit," *The Recorder,* May 16, 2003.

37. O'Brien, *Judicial Roulette,* 33.

38. Tarr, *Judicial Process,* 75.

39. Sheldon Goldman, *Picking Federal Judges: Lower Court Selection from Roosevelt through Reagan* (New Haven: Yale University Press, 1997), 86; see also Grossman, *Lawyers and Judges,* chap. 3.

40. Quoted in Neil A. Lewis, "White House Ends Bar Association's Role in Screening Federal Judges," *New York Times,* March 23, 2001, A13. For a recent scholarly assessment of the ABA's ratings, see Susan Brodie Haire, "Rating the Ratings of the American Bar Association Standing Committee on Federal Judiciary," *Justice System Journal* 22, no. 1 (2001): 1–17.

41. Thomas B. Edsall, "Federalist Society Becomes a Force in Washington; Conservative Group's Members Take Key Roles in Bush White House and Help Shape Policy and Judicial Appointments," *Washington Post,* April 18, 2001, A4.

42. Thomas B. Edsall, "Liberals Form Counter to Federalist Society," *Washington Post,* August 1, 2001, A5.

43. Larry C. Berkson and Susan B. Carbon, *The United States Circuit Judge Nominating Commission: Its Members, Procedures, and Candidates* (Chicago: American Judicature Society, 1980).

44. Alan Neff, *The United States District Judge Nominating Commissions: Their Members, Procedures, and Candidates* (Chicago: American Judicature Society, 1981).

45. Harry P. Stumpf, *American Judicial Politics,* 2d ed. (Upper Saddle River, N.J.: Prentice Hall, 1998), Tables 6-2 and 6-3, 180–183.

46. Goldman, *Picking Federal Judges,* 282; Stumpf, *American Judicial Politics,* 183.

47. Sheldon Goldman, "Reagan's Judicial Legacy: Completing the Puzzle and Summing Up," *Judicature* 72 (April-May 1989): 319–320.

48. Quoted in O'Brien, *Judicial Roulette*, 61–62.

49. Goldman, *Picking Federal Judges*, Tables 9.1 and 9.2. The total number of federal judicial appointments with life tenure rises to 372 if you include Reagan's four Supreme Court appointments. It rises slightly higher if you include his appointment of non–Article III judges who staff specialized courts and do not have life tenure.

50. Alliance for Justice Judicial Selection Project, "2000 Annual Report," 3. Available online, www.afj.org/jsp.

51. Ronald Stidham, Robert A. Carp, and Donald Songer, "The Voting Behavior of President Clinton's Judicial Appointees," *Judicature* 80 (July–August 1996): 16–20. See also Alliance for Justice Judicial Selection Project, "2000 Annual Report," 4–5; Sheldon Goldman and Elliot Slotnick, "Picking Judges under Fire," *Judicature* 82 (May–June 1999): 265–284; Nancy Scherer, "Are Clinton's Judges 'Old' Democrats or 'New' Democrats?" *Judicature* 84 (November–December 2000): 151–154.

52. Goldman and Slotnick, "Picking Judges under Fire," 282.

53. Michael Kelly, "Judge Dread," *New Republic*, March 31, 1997, 6.

54. John H. Cushman Jr., "Senate Imperils Judicial System, Rehnquist Says," *New York Times*, January 1, 1998, A1.

55. Alliance for Justice Judicial Selection Project, "2000 Annual Report," 5.

56. Ibid., 2.

57. Ibid., 1. For a thorough discussion of Clinton's judicial legacy, including his record on diversity, see Sheldon Goldman et al., "Clinton's Judges: Summing Up the Legacy," *Judicature* 84 (March–April 2001): 228–254.

58. "ABA a Key Player on Federal Bench," editorial, *Chicago Sun-Times*, March 27, 2001, 31.

59. Bennett Roth, "Change in Judicial Appointments Signaled by Bush; Clinton Nominees Are Pulled," *Houston Chronicle*, March 21, 2001, A1.

60. Helen Dewar, "Foreign Aid Bill Held Up by GOP; Senators Demand Action on Nominees," *Washington Post*, October 13, 2001, A3.

61. For a thorough account of this, see John Anthony Maltese, "Confirmation Gridlock: The Federal Judicial Appointments Process under Bill Clinton and George W. Bush," *The Journal of Appellate Practice and Process* 5 (spring 2003): 1–28.

62. For example, *Lochner v. New York*, 198 U.S. 45 (1905).

63. *Roe v. Wade*, 410 U.S. 113 (1973); *Griswold v. Connecticut*, 381 U.S. 479 (1965). See Robert H. Bork, *The Tempting of America* (New York: Free Press, 1990), for a criticism of both lines of cases.

64. Robert Scigliano, *The Supreme Court and the Presidency* (New York: Free Press, 1971), chap. 4.

65. For a comprehensive discussion of the Framers' debate on qualifications, see Michael Nelson, "Qualifications for President," in *Inventing the American Presidency*, ed. Thomas E. Cronin (Lawrence: University Press of Kansas, 1989).

66. Joel B. Grossman and Stephen L. Wasby, "The Senate and Supreme Court Nominations: Some Reflections," *Duke Law Journal* (August 1972): 559 n. 8.

67. Though all Supreme Court justices have been lawyers, not all have had law school degrees. Law schools as we know them did not exist in the early part of the nineteenth century, and a majority of the lawyers learned the profession through apprenticeship, rather than law schools, into the early part of the twentieth century. See David M. O'Brien, *Storm Center: The Supreme Court in American Politics*, 5th ed. (New York: Norton, 2000), 34.

68. See John Anthony Maltese, *The Selling of Supreme Court Nominees* (Baltimore: Johns Hopkins University Press, 1995), chaps. 4, 5.

69. David Alistair Yalof, *Pursuit of Justices: Presidential Politics and the Selection of Supreme Court Nominees* (Chicago: University of Chicago Press, 1999), 4–5.

70. Ibid., 7, 12–13.

71. Ethan Bronner, *Battle for Justice: How the Bork Nomination Shook America* (New York: Norton, 1989), 29–36; Mark Gitenstein, *Matters of Principle: An Insider's Account of America's Rejection of Robert Bork's Nomination to the Supreme Court* (New York: Simon and Schuster, 1992), 28–37.

72. Lawrence Baum, *The Supreme Court*, 6th ed. (Washington, D.C.: CQ Press, 1998), 31–35.

73. Scott H. Ainsworth and John Anthony Maltese, "National Grange Influence on the Supreme Court Confirmation of Stanley Matthews," *Social Science History* 20 (spring 1996): 41–62.

74. For early examples of this, see Maltese, *The Selling of Supreme Court Nominees*, 47–49, 53.

75. Quoted in Robin Toner, "Interest Groups Set for Battle on a Supreme Court Vacancy," *New York Times*, April 21, 2001, A1.

76. P. S. Ruckman Jr., "The Supreme Court, Critical Nominations, and the Senate Confirmation Process," *Journal of Politics* 55 (August 1993): 794. If you include the two nominations withdrawn on a technicality, the failure rate rises to 19.5 percent.

77. Maltese, *The Selling of Supreme Court Nominees*, 5.

78. E. J. Dionne, "A Town Hall Meeting: A Process Run Amok—Can It Be Fixed?" *ABC News Nightline*, American Broadcasting Company (ABC), October 16, 1991.

79. For extensive case studies of all three of these nominations, see Maltese, *The Selling of Supreme Court Nominees*, chaps. 1, 4, 5.

80. It should be noted that Associate Justice William Rehnquist's nomination for chief justice in 1986 was attacked by liberal groups because of his alleged insensitivity to the rights of minorities and women. He was ultimately confirmed, but the thirty-three votes against him were the most ever cast against a confirmed justice up to that point.

81. For thorough accounts of the role of interest groups in the Bork nomination, see Patrick B. McGuigan and Dawn M. Weyrich, *Ninth Justice: The Fight for Bork* (Washington, D.C.: Free Congress Foundation, 1990); and Michael Pertschuk and Wendy Schaetzel, *The People Rising: The Campaign Against the Bork Nomination* (New York: Thunder's Mouth Press, 1989).

82. Robert Shogan, *A Question of Judgment: The Fortas Case and the Struggle for the Supreme Court* (New York: Bobbs-Merrill, 1972).

83. Maltese, *The Selling of Supreme Court Nominees*, 14, 16.

84. "The Electoral Count," *New York Times*, January 30, 1881.

85. Quoted in Alpheus Thomas Mason, *Brandeis: A Free Man's Life* (New York: Viking, 1946), 467.

86. See Maltese, *The Selling of Supreme Court Nominees*, for thorough accounts of all of these developments.

87. *Planned Parenthood of Southeastern Pennsylvania v. Casey*, 505 U.S. 833 (1992).

88. Quoted in David M. O'Brien, *Storm Center: The Supreme Court in American Politics*, 5th ed. (New York: Norton, 1993), 84.

89. Scigliano, *The Supreme Court and the Presidency*, chap. 6. See also Lincoln Caplan, *The Tenth Justice: The Solicitor General and the Rule of Law* (New York: Random House, 1987); Rebecca Mae Salokar, *The Solicitor General: The Politics of Law* (Philadelphia: Temple University Press, 1992).

90. The Supreme Court's discretion has changed some over time. Since 1988, that discretion is almost absolute. Cases now come to the Supreme Court almost exclusively by way of a writ of certiorari. To grant "cert" (agree to hear a case), four

of the nine justices must vote to accept review. See Craig R. Ducat, *Constitutional Interpretation*, 7th ed. (Belmont, Calif.: West, 2000), 31.

91. Scigliano, *The Supreme Court and the Presidency*, 172.

92. Christopher Zorn, "Information, Advocacy, and the Role of the Solicitor General as Amicus Curiae" (working paper, Emory University, 1999), 1.

93. Steven Puro, "The United States as Amicus Curiae," in *Courts, Law, and Judicial Processes*, ed. S. Sidney Ulmer (New York: Free Press, 1981), 220–230.

94. Scigliano, *The Supreme Court and the Presidency*, chap. 6; Puro, "The United States as Amicus Curiae"; Karen O'Connor, "The Amicus Curiae Role of the U.S. Solicitor General in Supreme Court Litigation," *Judicature* 66 (December–January 1983): 261.

95. Kevin T. McGuire, "Explaining Executive Success in the U.S. Supreme Court," *Political Research Quarterly* 51 (June 1998): 522.

96. This situation is to be contrasted with the paucity of experience attorneys general have before the Court: traditionally, they argue only one case before their terms are over. For an interesting account of Robert Kennedy's first appearance before the Court two years after he became attorney general, see Victor Navasky, *Kennedy Justice* (New York: Athenaeum, 1980), chap. 6.

97. Zorn, "Information, Advocacy, and the Role of the Solicitor General," 9. For a discussion of similar strategy by other litigants, see Donald Songer, Charles M. Cameron, and Jeffrey A. Segal, "An Empirical Test of the Rational-Actor Theory of Litigation," *Journal of Politics* 57 (November 1995): 1119–1129.

98. Caplan, *The Tenth Justice*.

99. Elder Witt, *A Different Justice* (Washington, D.C.: Congressional Quarterly, 1986), chaps. 6, 7.

100. Caplan, *The Tenth Justice*, 79–80, 255–256.

101. Richard L. Pacelle Jr., *Between Law and Politics: The Solicitor General and the Structuring of Race, Gender, and Reproductive Rights Litigation* (College Station: Texas A&M University Press, 2003), 265.

102. *Hepburn v. Griswold (First Legal Tender Case)*, 8 Wall. 506 (1870).

103. *Knox v. Lee, Parker v. Davis (Second Legal Tender Case)*, 12 Wall. 457 (1871).

104. Samuel Kernell, *Going Public*, 2d ed. (Washington, D.C.: CQ Press, 1993), 110.

105. Ibid.

106. For a useful review of this power, see Gerald Gunther, "Congressional Power to Curtail Federal Court Jurisdiction: An Opinionated Guide to the Ongoing Debate," *Stanford Law Review* 36 (1984): 895. The most famous Supreme Court case involving this issue is *Ex Parte McCardle*, 74 U.S. 506 (1869).

107. Stumpf, *American Judicial Politics*, 429.

108. *Brown v. Board of Education*, 347 U.S. 483 (1954); *Plessy v. Ferguson*, 163 U.S. 537 (1896).

109. Stumpf, *American Judicial Politics*, 429. *Engel v. Vitale*, 370 U.S. 421 (1962).

110. *Youngstown Sheet and Tube Co. v. Sawyer*, 343 U.S. 579 (1952).

111. *United States v. Nixon*, 418 U.S. 683 (1974).

112. *Ex parte Merryman*, 17 F. Cases 144 (1861).

113. Although George W. Bush is our forty-third president, Grover Cleveland counted as both the twenty-second and the twenty-fourth president.

114. *Youngstown Sheet and Tube Co. v. Sawyer*. For a thorough history of the case, see Maeva Marcus, *Truman and the Steel Seizure Case: The Limits of Presidential Power* (Durham: Duke University Press, 1994).

115. *United States v. Nixon*, 418 U.S. 683 (1974).

116. For accounts of executive privilege, see Raoul Berger, *Executive Privilege: A Constitutional Myth* (Cambridge: Harvard University Press, 1974); Mark J. Rozell, *Exec-

utive Privilege: The Dilemma of Secrecy and Democratic Accountability (Baltimore: Johns Hopkins University Press, 1994).

117. For a discussion of this, see Lee Epstein and Thomas G. Walker, *Constitutional Law for a Changing America: Institutional Powers and Constraints*, 4th ed. (Washington, D.C.: CQ Press, 2001), 248–250.

118. *Korematsu v. United States*, 323 U.S. 214 (1944). For an account of this, see Peter Irons, *Justice at War: The Story of the Japanese-American Internment Cases* (New York: Oxford University Press, 1983).

119. *Dames & Moore v. Regan*, 453 U.S. 654 (1981).

120. *Morrison v. Olson*, 487 U.S. 654 (1988); *Clinton v. Jones*, 520 U.S. 681 (1997). For a discussion of the Lewinsky scandal, see Mark J. Rozell and Clyde Wilcox, eds., *The Clinton Scandal and the Future of American Government* (Washington, D.C.: Georgetown University Press, 2000).

SUGGESTED READINGS

Abraham, Henry. *Justices, Presidents, and Senators: A History of U.S. Supreme Court Appointments from Washington to Clinton.* 4th ed. Lanham, Md.: Rowman and Littlefield, 1999.

Baum, Lawrence. *The Supreme Court.* 7th ed. Washington, D.C.: CQ Press, 2001.

Bronner, Ethan. *Battle for Justice: How the Bork Nomination Shook America.* New York: Norton, 1989.

Caldeira, Gregory, and John Wright. "Lobbying for Justice." *American Journal of Political Science* 42 (April 1998).

Caplan, Lincoln. *The Tenth Justice: The Solicitor General and the Rule of Law.* New York: Random House, 1987.

Epstein, Lee, and Thomas G. Walker. *Constitutional Law for a Changing America: Institutional Powers and Constraints.* 4th ed. Washington, D.C.: CQ Press, 2001.

Gerhardt, Michael J. *The Federal Appointments Process: A Constitutional and Historical Analysis.* Durham: Duke University Press, 2000.

Gillman, Howard. *The Votes That Counted: How the Court Decided the 2000 Presidential Election.* Chicago: University of Chicago Press, 2001.

Goldman, Sheldon. *Picking Federal Judges: Lower Court Selection from Roosevelt through Reagan.* New Haven: Yale University Press, 1997.

Goldman, Sheldon, Elliot Slotnick, Gerard Gryski, and Gary Zuk. "Clinton's Judges: Summing Up the Legacy." *Judicature* 84 (March–April 2001).

Maltese, John Anthony. *The Selling of Supreme Court Nominees.* Baltimore: Johns Hopkins University Press, 1995.

O'Brien, David M. *Judicial Roulette.* New York: Priority Press, 1988.

Pacelle, Richard L., Jr, *Between Law and Politics: The Solicitor General and the Structuring of Race, Gender, and Reproductive Rights Litigation.* College Station: Texas A&M University Press, 2003.

Salokar, Rebecca Mae. *The Solicitor General: The Politics of Law.* Philadelphia: Temple University Press, 1992.

Yalof, David Alistair. *Pursuit of Justices: Presidential Politics and the Selection of Supreme Court Nominees.* Chicago: University of Chicago Press, 1999.

8 THE POLITICS OF DOMESTIC POLICY

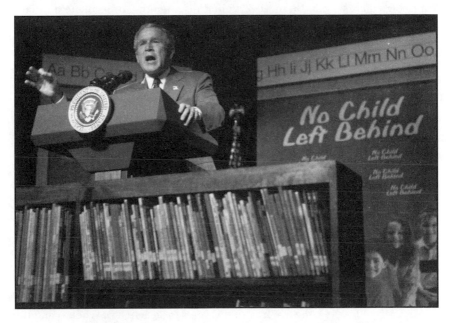

One of President Bush's domestic priorities since entering office has been education reform. Here, he is shown speaking on this topic at the C. T. Kirkpatrick Elementary School in Nashville, Tennessee.

SINCE SEPTEMBER 11, 2001, foreign affairs and national security have monopolized our attention. Before then, few observers would have predicted that George W. Bush would take such an active role in foreign policy. Like Bill Clinton before him, Bush and his Democratic opponent, Al Gore, had concentrated on domestic policy issues during the 2000 presidential campaign. However, it is worth remembering that, despite the obvious importance of domestic policy, Clinton in 1992 was the first president since FDR to win election with a campaign focused almost exclusively on domestic problems. In fact, one of Clinton's sharpest criticisms of his predecessor, President George H. W. Bush, was that he had neglected serious social and economic conditions in the United States while concentrating on foreign policy. Clinton appeared to be undaunted by the conventional wisdom, in vogue since the end of World War II, that regarded domestic policy as the black hole of presidential politics. Although Clinton became much more active in foreign policy in his second term (continuing his attempts to negotiate a Middle East peace settlement almost to the very end of his presidency), the presidential candidates in 2000 reverted to a campaign revolving around domestic issues. George W. Bush, in particular, wanted to avoid his father's mistakes. Even after the events of September 11 brought foreign policy to the forefront, Bush went to great pains to emphasize his concern not only for national security but also for economic security on the domestic front.

Whether they want to or not, presidents confront a vast array of domestic problems, issues, and demands for government action. As soon as they take office, they must consider numerous complex and costly programs competing for limited funds. Many of these programs enjoy the support of powerful interest groups and congressional leaders. Whatever the administration does (or fails to do) in response to public demands is likely to cost the president political support.

Presidents face a congested public policy agenda, the result of interrelatedness, overlapping, and layering of issues.[1] Many political scientists have classified public policy for analytical purposes, but the most widely used classification scheme, or typology, is Theodore Lowi's division of policies into distributive, regulatory, and redistributive categories.[2] He based his categories on the identity of those affected by the policies—from individuals to society as a whole—and the likelihood that the government will have to exercise coercion to implement the policy.

Distributive policies have the most diffused impact. They affect specific groups of people and provide individualized benefits. They have low visibility, produce little conflict, and are not likely to require the application of coercion. Examples of distributive policies include agricultural price supports, public works projects, and research and development programs. *Regulatory* policies affect large segments of society and involve the application of coercion. Although regulatory issues tend to be highly technical, they often are quite visible and controversial. Examples include pollution control, antitrust violations, and occupational safety and health requirements. *Redistributive* policies have the broadest impact on society. They involve the transfer of resources (wealth and income) from certain groups to others. They require coercion, are highly visible, and usually are accompanied by social or class conflict. Examples of redistributive policies include Social Security and tax reform.

Lowi argued that the type of policy determines the focus and behavior of political actors. Distributive policy politics involves limited presidential and extensive congressional participation and decision making that relies heavily on logrolling—the mutual exchange of support for legislation. Regulatory policy politics creates moderate presidential and substantial congressional interest and involvement, with frequent conflict between the president and Congress. Redistributive policy politics often is fraught with ideological disputes and presidential-congressional conflict. Presidents tend to be most involved with redistributive policy issues. This is the case whether the government is seeking to expand or to limit the scope of its activities.

Steven Shull has used Lowi's policy typology to examine presidential and congressional roles in domestic policy formation. He found that there were "some differences in presidential and congressional behavior . . . along lines anticipated by the 'theory'" and that "modest empirical distinctions" existed among the three policy categories.[3] The principal problem with Lowi's typology is the difficulty in making it operational for purposes of measurement. The problem arises because an issue may change its designation over time, starting out, for example, as a redistributive issue and becoming distributive. This is what happened to Title I of the Elementary and Secondary Education Act of 1965, a program of federal assistance to local school districts for economically disadvantaged children. As a new program, it sparked controversy because of its redistributive effects, but over time it became a routinized distribution of federal funds that was part of the established structure of school finance. In other words, Lowi's categories are not fixed in time. Shull concluded that Lowi's typology is not as useful as substantive classification based on policy content.

John Kessel has broken domestic policy into areas involving social benefits, civil liberties, natural resources, and agriculture.[4] Each area entails a specific type of politics and its own temporal pattern, both of which have implications for presidential participation. The politics of social benefits, such as housing and Social Security retirement, involves the allocation of resources. Thus it is similar to Lowi's distributive and redistributive categories. Presidents use the distribution of social benefits to build public support. As a result, they tend to pay most attention to social benefits as they approach reelection; afterward, the winners are much less concerned with these benefits. Civil rights involve a pattern of politics that is regulatory and highly sensitive because of differing conceptions of fairness. Presidents are most likely to act on civil rights issues immediately after election because these issues are highly controversial and because campaign promises must be fulfilled. The politics of natural resources, which includes environmental protection, is primarily regulatory, and agriculture mostly involves allocation. The temporal patterns in natural resource and agricultural policy politics are a function of long-range developments and entail limited presidential participation.

Whether one approaches domestic policy using Lowi's analytical typology or Kessel's substantive classifications, it is clear that as a practical matter presidents can become fully involved with only a small number of problems and issues. The

Lowi and Kessel approaches suggest that in domestic policy, presidents tend to focus on matters such as maintaining the financial integrity of the Social Security system, reforming welfare, and dealing with major civil rights proposals. They do not take up all major redistributive, social benefit, and civil rights issues, and may consciously avoid some likely to involve enormous financial or political costs. They are unlikely to become bogged down with routine distributive policies or with the technicalities of economic and social regulation. Jimmy Carter harmed himself politically when he tangled with Congress over eighteen water projects he regarded as unnecessary. Other presidents have been content to leave the distribution of "pork barrel" projects to Congress. Although George W. Bush initially vowed to slash such pork in half (from $16 billion in fiscal 2001 to $8 billion under his proposed budget), he backed off in the summer of 2001 to avoid a fight with Congress. In Bush's transportation spending bill alone, the House of Representatives had added some 900 local pork barrel projects. Proposed spending for local projects mushroomed in other areas as well. For example, Bush had proposed an allocation of $300,000 for rebuilding beaches in Brevard County, Florida, but Congress proposed $8.5 million. Budget Director Mitchell E. Daniels Jr. conceded in July 2001 that such increases were "an acceptable cost of doing business" with Congress.[5]

The range and complexity of domestic problems and issues produce a policy congestion that makes coordination the essential presidential function in this area. Coordination has been complicated, however, by the interrelatedness of domestic, economic, and national security policy. If, on the one hand, presidents attempt to coordinate specific policies through simplification—say, by proposals to balance the budget or reorganize the bureaucracy—they encounter the opposition of powerful forces mobilized around those policy issues. Ronald Reagan's 1982 proposals to move toward a balanced budget by reducing Social Security cost-of-living allowances provide an excellent example. Opposition from the "gray lobby" (senior citizens) and most members of Congress quickly stymied the idea.

If, on the other hand, presidents fail to coordinate complex policies effectively, they risk loss of popular and congressional support as well as having to deal with interest group opposition. This happened early in Clinton's first term when he lost control of his health care proposal. Lack of coordination in selling the proposal to Congress and the public allowed opponents to pick apart the plan in bits and pieces. As cracks appeared, opponents took control of the agenda, thereby dooming the president's proposal.

The Domestic Policy Process

The domestic policy process consists of actions that culminate in the development and presentation of legislative proposals to Congress, the issuance of executive orders, and the preparation and submission of annual budgets. There is a cyclical regularity to much of the policy process because annual events—such as the State of the Union, budget, and economic messages—define the broad out-lines of the president's program.[6] (Although these events occur at approximately the same time each year, the full cycles last longer than a year. The budget for the fiscal year beginning on October 1, 2003, for example, had its origins in the budget review process conducted in the spring of 2001.) Formal events for pro-posing policy, such as the president's annual submission of the budget, are sup-plemented by the emergence of policy proposals at other times during the year. Such proposals may emerge due to unexpected events or because of forces out-side the White House.

Policy Streams

The process of setting the president's domestic policy agenda can be under-stood as the convergence in the White House of three tributary streams: the first identifies *problems and issues* requiring attention; the second produces *proposed solutions* to the problems; and the third carries the *political factors* that establish the context for policymaking. According to John Kingdon, these three streams oper-ate largely, but not absolutely, independently of one another. Problems and solu-tions develop separately and may or may not be joined, and political factors may change regardless of whether policymakers have recognized a problem or whether a potential solution exists.[7]

The First Stream: Problems and Issues. Problems and issues move onto the president's domestic policy agenda either because their seriousness and high vis-ibility make it impossible to avoid them or because of presidential initiative. Examples of unavoidable problems that force the president to react include such matters as energy shortages, a failing economy, high rates of inflation and unem-ployment, the emergence of acquired immune deficiency syndrome (AIDS) as a major threat to public health, and the problems resulting from increased drug abuse. Other times, presidents act more proactively by adding items they believe are instrumental to the achievement of their goals.

Once enough important people, inside and outside the government, begin to think something should be done about a certain problem or issue, it is likely that the president will react by adding the item to the administration's domestic agenda.[8] This pressure may occur as a consequence of changes in economic and social indicators, such as rates of inflation, unemployment, energy costs, infant mortality, and students' scores on various standardized tests. Influential decision makers in the presidency, the bureaucracy, Congress, the private sector, and state and local governments routinely monitor changes in a large array of indicators. Whether these changes add up to a problem is a matter of interpretation. That interpretation takes place in the context of the symbolic significance of the mat-ter, the personal experiences of the president and the other decision makers with it, and the relationship of the subject to other problems and issues.

The president and other decision makers may be moved to recognize a con-dition as a compelling problem because of a "focusing event," such as a disaster or a crisis. For example, the near meltdown of a reactor at the Three Mile Island power plant in western Pennsylvania in March 1979 thrust nuclear safety to the forefront of the domestic agenda; prior to this event, safety proponents had struggled for years with little success to gain recognition for this issue. More recently, the terrorist attacks of September 11, 2001, forced the issue of domestic security onto the agenda and led to quick passage of the U.S.A. Patriot Act, while the massive power outage that affected eight U.S. states in August 2003 drew attention to the vulnerability of the nation's aging electrical grid and brought debate over a proposed energy bill to the forefront.

On occasion, presidents have no choice but to deal with a problem, even though they may prefer not to do so. The 1992 riots in Los Angeles forced a reluctant George Bush to propose legislation to aid the damaged city, while events in Somalia, Haiti, and Bosnia forced Bill Clinton to devote more attention than he wished to foreign policy. Similarly, the collision of a U.S. Navy surveillance aircraft with a Chinese F-8 interceptor over the South China Sea in April 2001 and the subsequent detention of the U.S. flight crew by the Chinese government forced George W. Bush to focus attention on the diplomatic standoff.

Some problems and issues remain on the agenda through successive presidential administrations. Feasible solutions may not have been found, solutions may have been tried unsuccessfully, or the problem may have been "solved" only to reemerge in a different form. Health care exemplifies such an issue. Harry S. Truman proposed a comprehensive national health insurance program in 1945 as an additional Social Security benefit.[9] The American Medical Association and major business associations successfully attacked the proposal as "socialized medicine." Both John F. Kennedy and Lyndon B. Johnson advanced proposals for national health insurance, and in 1965, Congress responded partially with Medicare, a health insurance plan for Social Security retirees age sixty-five and over. Since then, pressures have continued for a plan that would provide universal coverage. In the 1970s, universal coverage received support from Richard M. Nixon and Jimmy Carter, as opinion polls showed that a majority of the population favored some kind of national health insurance program. During the recession in the early 1990s, health care reform became a salient issue as millions of workers either lost or feared losing health insurance along with their jobs. In 1991, Harris Wofford, an unknown Pennsylvania Democrat, defeated a popular Republican ex-governor and former U.S. attorney general, Richard Thornburg, in a special Senate election by advocating health care reform. Bill Clinton made the need for health care reform one of the central issues in his 1992 presidential campaign, and it became one of the principal goals of the domestic policy agenda in his first two years, although it failed to pass Congress. Contenders for the 2004 Democratic presidential nomination, including Howard Dean, John Kerry, and Richard Gephardt, made health care reform a priority. With health costs skyrocketing and an increase in the number of uninsured Americans, the issue again became a salient one. When a Roper Center Poll asked, "If you had to choose, would you rather have the federal government take some action to provide health care for uninsured people, or cut the federal taxes that you pay?" 63 percent of respondents said "provide health care for uninsured" and only 25 percent said "cut federal taxes."[10] Even George W. Bush proposed an expensive prescription drug benefit for Medicare.

Sometimes presidents have broader discretion to determine which problems and issues to emphasize. In such cases, three goals affect the selection of problems and issues to address: reelection (for a first-term president), historical achievement, and a desire to shape public policy.[11] Presidents vary in the emphasis they place on these goals. Nixon's willingness to propose innovative policies for welfare reform and revenue sharing, even at the expense of alienating some of his conservative supporters, reflected his concern with historical achievement.[12] As he approached his reelection campaign, Carter shifted from making agenda decisions on the basis of his beliefs to making them on the basis of politics. Reagan consistently defined domestic policy in terms of his conservative ideology, even at the risk of electoral disadvantage.

The Second Stream: Solutions. Once a problem or an issue has been recognized, the availability of a solution becomes an important determinant of whether it will rise to a high position on the president's agenda.[13] Solutions take several forms, ranging from *direct actions,* such as legislative proposals or executive orders, to *symbolic actions,* such as appointment of a study commission or a task force, to *no action.* Problems can have several solutions, and a single solution can be applied to more than one problem. Some solutions come attached to a problem; others will be consciously selected from among competing alternatives. Most solutions that are coupled with problems on the president's agenda come from ideas generated outside the presidency. This is due, in part, to time constraints facing executive advisers and the relatively small size of the institution of the presidency in relation to the policy-making environment as a whole. Aside from the presidency, the principal policy idea sources are Congress, the bureaucracy, interest groups, universities, think tanks (research institutes), and state and local governments. Within the presidency, the president's campaign promises (such as George W. Bush's pledge to cut taxes) are a source of policy proposals and a benchmark for evaluating externally generated ideas.[14] In addition, the president's domestic policy staff may develop new ideas once the president is in office.

Many of the ideas that emerge as proposed solutions to problems on the president's agenda have been circulating among members of "issue networks." Issue networks are simply groups of individuals and organizations supporting certain policy positions. Such networks might consist of members of Congress and their legislative aides, bureaucrats, interest groups, the media, scholars and other experts in research organizations, and representatives of state and local government. Together they promote specific ideas and proposals, such as campaign finance reform, energy policy, and a patients' bill of rights. Issue networks are motivated by their participants' desire to advance personal and organizational interests and to influence public policy in accordance with the groups' values. Network participants study, analyze, and discuss problems and solutions among themselves, and they attempt to inform and influence the major decision makers in government, the most important of whom is the president.

The process by which policy ideas develop, advance, and either succeed or fail is often lengthy and generally diffuse. John Kingdon describes it as a "policy primeval soup" in which ideas are continually bumping into one another and surviving, dying, combining, or emerging into new forms.[15] Those ideas that do manage to become incorporated into a president's specific policy proposal are evaluated according to three criteria: economic, political, and technical feasibility.

The *economic feasibility,* or cost, of a potential solution is especially important, as demands for federal expenditures far outweigh the government's capacity to supply the necessary funds. Few proposals for major new spending programs survive in an era of resource constraints. Proposals to restrain or reduce spending are more attractive to a president struggling to control the budget deficit. A proposal's *political feasibility* is determined initially by its compatibility with the values and interests of other important decision makers, particularly those in Congress. Ultimately, a proposal must gain the acquiescence, if not the acceptance, of the public. The *technical feasibility* of a proposal—the question of its workability—does not receive as much attention as its economic and political costs. Some ideas—such as proposals for welfare reform that maintain reasonably high payments, reduce inequities between recipients in different states and between recipients and the working poor, and do not increase the cost to the government—are economically and politically very attractive but unworkable in practice. Presidents Nixon and Carter made this discovery, much to their dismay, after the failure of their major efforts to achieve welfare reform.[16]

Similar problems plagued the Clinton administration and the Republican leaders of the 104th Congress as they sought to develop a mutually acceptable welfare reform bill in 1995. Both sides wanted legislation that would reduce welfare dependency with no increase in the budget. Not only were such goals incompatible, but Clinton and the Republicans disagreed fundamentally over the means to achieve them.[17] Twice, in December 1995 and January 1996, Clinton vetoed Republican bills that would have ended welfare as a federal entitlement by turning it over to the states. Then in August 1996 he signed a compromise bill.[18] Such conflict among the three criteria always exists. Budget costs may rule out a proposal that is politically and technically feasible, such as rapid cleanup of toxic waste sites. Political costs may prevent acceptance of a workable proposal that is compatible with a tight budget, such as freezing Social Security cost-of-living increases. Eventually, a short list of presidential proposals emerges from a multitude of potential solutions.

The Third Stream: Political Factors. The last of Kingdon's three policy-making streams is the one carrying political factors.[19] Such factors affect the setting and implementation of the president's agenda and include the national mood, the balance of political forces, and events within the government.

The *national mood* is a somewhat amorphous phenomenon, difficult to define. It is not identical to public opinion, nor can it be ascertained through survey research. National mood is perhaps best described as the perception among important decision makers that a consensus exists, or is building, among various attentive publics and political activists for specific government policies. Politicians sense this mood in suggestions, requests, and other communications from interest groups, state and local government officials, corporate executives, and politically active citizens; in news media coverage of events; and in editorial commentary. The national mood also reflects the influence of social movements such as civil rights, environmentalism, and family values. Without a favorable national mood, major new policies—such as health care reform during the Clinton administration or George W. Bush's proposal to drill for oil in the Arctic National Wildlife Refuge as part of a broader energy independence plan—are not likely to be adopted. In short, the national mood is a reflection of the politically relevant climate or temper of the times.

Considerably more concrete than the national mood is the extent of consensus and conflict that determines the *balance of political forces*. The prospects for adoption of a proposed policy change depend on the balance of organized interests and other forces, but assessing the balance on any issue is largely a matter of informed guesswork. The complex pattern of pluralistic political forces and the fragmentation of government authority combine to provide a strong advantage to the *opponents* of policy change. Often, heavy political costs are associated with even raising an issue for consideration, let alone obtaining adoption of a proposal. This is particularly the case with existing government programs, most of which have powerful clientele groups ready to defend them. Clientele interests, in triangular alliances with agencies that administer the programs and congressional subcommittees with jurisdiction, engage in bargaining and logrolling to maintain and enhance the programs. To overcome government's natural inertia, a strong constituency for political change must be mobilized; without it, a proposal will encounter much difficulty. For example, the Carter administration's efforts to enact a national energy policy were unsuccessful despite widespread shortages of fuels until compromises made the proposal acceptable to the oil industry and consumer interests. More recently, Clinton's proposal for health care reform failed due to strong opposition from a variety of special interests that tipped the balance of political forces against the proposed change.

Events within government are the third major political factor shaping the president's policy agenda. Election outcomes can produce fundamental changes in the agenda. The 1980 election, which brought Ronald Reagan to the presidency and gave the Republicans control of the Senate for the first time in a quarter of a century, was such an event. An ideologically defined, conservative agenda replaced the liberal agenda in effect since the New Deal. Similarly, the 1994 election, in which the Republicans captured control of both houses of Congress for the first time in forty years, profoundly reshaped President Clinton's domestic agenda. Much of the revised agenda consisted of defensive reactions to Republican proposals to curtail affirmative action and regulatory policies affecting the environment, occupational health and safety, and business and financial practices, and to achieve major cost savings in Medicare. Moreover, this new agenda did not include health care reform, and the welfare reform proposal was conservatively fashioned to compete with Republican plans. "Divided government"— one political party controlling the White House and another controlling at least one house of Congress—has also made implementing policy more difficult. From 1969 through 2003, the same political party controlled the White House and both houses of Congress for only seven out of thirty-five years.[20]

Jurisdictional matters are another intragovernmental development that may affect agenda setting. Disputes over bureaucratic and committee turf often delay or prevent action, although jurisdictional competition occasionally accelerates consideration of a popular issue. In addition, a proposal may be structured so it will be handled by a committee or an agency favorably disposed to it.

In sum, the most significant domestic policy action is likely to occur when the national mood and election outcomes combine to overcome the normal inertia produced by the balance of political forces and the fragmentation of governmental authority among numerous bureaucratic and congressional fiefdoms. Once items begin to rise on the agenda, however, organized political forces attempt to shape policy proposals to their advantage or to defeat the proposals outright.

Resources and Opportunities

Successful policy leadership results from advancing appropriate solutions to specific problems under favorable political circumstances. Not all policy proposals can receive presidential attention and consideration. Some are not compatible with an administration's overall objectives and ideology, but many otherwise acceptable proposals never become part of the president's agenda because limited resources cannot be wasted on them. Quite simply, presidents must establish priorities.[21] This is accomplished through what political scientist Paul Light calls a "filtering process," which maintains an orderly flow of problems and solutions to the president and merges them to produce policy proposals. The objectives of the process are to control the flow of items so important problems, issues, and alternatives receive attention without overloading the president and to ensure that policy proposals have been formulated with due regard to relevant political factors. There are two filters through which problems and solutions pass as they are melded into presidential decisions: resources and opportunities.

Resources: Political Capital. One of the president's most important resources is political capital, the reservoir of popular and congressional support with which presidents begin their terms. As they make controversial decisions, they "spend" some of this capital, a precious resource they can seldom replenish. Presidents

Rivals for the 2004 Democratic presidential nomination, such as retired general Wesley Clark and former Vermont governor Howard Dean, were sharply critical of President Bush's domestic policies.

must decide which proposals merit the expenditure of political capital and in what amounts. Reagan, for example, was willing to spend his capital heavily on reducing the role of the federal government, cutting taxes, and reforming the income tax code, but not on antiabortion or school prayer amendments to the Constitution. Material resources determine which proposals for new programs can be advanced and the emphasis to be placed on existing programs.

Bill Clinton did not have enough initial political capital to enact his ambitious agenda.[22] Although he won a clear electoral college victory and had a 6 percent vote margin over incumbent president George Bush, he received only 43 percent of the popular vote because of Ross Perot's third-party candidacy. Immediately after the election, the Republican Senate leader, Bob Dole, pointedly claimed to speak for the 57 percent of the electorate who had opposed Clinton. Furthermore, while Clinton's victory temporarily ended twelve years of divided government, the potential for ending presidential-congressional stalemate over domestic policy was diminished with the simultaneous Republican gain of ten House seats. Congressional Republicans, no longer constrained by loyalty to their own president, were free to oppose Clinton. Moreover, the centrist New Democrat stance Clinton adopted to win election was not shared by a majority of congressional Democrats, who were considerably more liberal. Finally, the damage to Clinton's image done in the campaign by allegations of sexual misconduct and avoidance of military service in Vietnam reduced the public's trust and support.

These factors limited the capital Clinton had to spend on advocating potentially controversial domestic policies.

George W. Bush also entered office with limited political capital. In the 2000 presidential election, he lost the popular vote to Al Gore and took power only after a protracted dispute over which candidate had won Florida's electoral votes. In addition, he faced the highest disapproval rating of any incoming president since polling began (25 percent according to the Gallup Poll).[23] In May 2001, he lost the marginal control of the Senate Republicans had enjoyed since January after Sen. James Jeffords (R-Vt.) defected and became an independent. The return to divided government, which lasted until the 2002 midterm elections, made the passage of Bush's initiatives more difficult. Interestingly, Bush did not act as though he had only limited political capital when he entered office. Instead, he proceeded confidently, as if he had a mandate for his conservative agenda. "I know the value of political capital," Bush said just before his inauguration, "how to earn it and how to spend it."[24] He attempted to earn additional capital by proceeding swiftly with a few key proposals that seemed to enjoy broad support, such as his tax cut and education reform. After the September 11, 2001, terrorist attacks, Bush sought—with mixed success—to parlay his high public approval ratings into support for his domestic policy initiatives.

Opportunities. In addition to resources, Light argues, presidents need opportunities to formulate the agenda. These opportunities are often described metaphorically as windows: they open for a while and then close. They may be scheduled or unscheduled. Scheduled opportunities to shape the agenda occur in conjunction with the annual cycle of presidential messages to Congress (State of the Union, budget, and economic report), the congressional calendar, and action-forcing deadlines, such as renewals of program authorizations. An administration's greatest opportunity to set the agenda occurs during January and February, when Congress begins a new session and presidents deliver their messages, and in August and September, when Congress returns from recess and earlier proposals can be replaced or modified.[25] Unscheduled opportunities come about as the result of focusing events or changes in political conditions. Both scheduled and unscheduled windows of opportunity eventually close, some sooner than others. An opportunity is more likely to be seized and an issue given a high place on the president's agenda when problems, solutions, and political factors come together.[26] Without a viable solution and in the absence of favorable political conditions, a problem has a limited chance of moving up on the agenda. For instance, popular support for biomedical research is substantial, but the slow pace of development of treatments and cures for diseases such as cancer limits presidential attention to the issue.

Opportunities also fluctuate as a presidential term progresses. In a president's first year in office, Congress and the public have high expectations of policy change based on campaign promises and the election mandate. Opportunities tend to be at their peak during a new administration's so-called honeymoon period. In the second and fourth years of a president's term, concern focuses increasingly on the forthcoming election campaigns, and policy opportunities decline. The third year frequently is regarded as crucial, for the administration is by then experienced, mature, removed from immediate electoral pressures, and anxious to make its mark.[27] Opportunities are most likely to be exploited effectively then and in the first year of a president's second term—assuming there is one. Because a second term is also a final term, the president's "lame-duck" status tends to restrict further policy opportunities. The effects of lame-duck status on presidential initiatives are especially notable following the midterm congressional election in a president's second term.

There are conflicting patterns in the progression of opportunities as presidents move through their terms. On the one hand, as they acquire experience and expertise, they become more effective and thus increase their policy opportunities. On the other hand, as their congressional and popular support declines through the term, they lose opportunities. Light describes these as cycles of increasing effectiveness and declining influence.[28] It is ironic that as presidents become more skilled at finding opportunities, they become less able to utilize them.

The Domestic Policy Environment

The most outstanding characteristic of the domestic policy environment is its complexity. Myriad actors—individuals, groups, and other government institutions and agencies—all pursue a seemingly incalculable range of objectives and protect countless interests. Although presidential power is limited, the president is better situated than anyone else to give direction and bring some degree of coordination to the federal government's domestic policies.

The fragmentation of political power and influence that is the hallmark of the U.S. political system is the product of a heterogeneous and pluralistic society and of constitutional arrangements designed to produce deliberate, rather than expeditious, government decision making. Nowhere is the fragmentation of power more apparent and more profound than in the domestic policy environment.

Interest Groups

Outside the government, thousands of interest groups constantly seek to influence policy. They range from organizations concerned with all of the government's activities, such as Americans for Democratic Action, to those focused on a single issue, such as the National Rifle Association (NRA), dedicated to preventing the adoption of strict gun control legislation. Interest groups are concerned not only with virtually every government program that distributes benefits to individuals and organizations and regulates their conduct but also with possibilities for new programs. Simply stated, the objectives of interest groups are to secure the adoption of policies beneficial to their members and to prevent the adoption of policies they view as harmful to them. Interest groups operate in all sectors of domestic policy—agriculture, civil rights, social welfare, and natural resources. They include organizations that represent business; labor; the professions; consumers; state and local governments and their subdivisions; public officials; social groupings based on age, sex, race, religion, and shared attitudes and experiences; and groups presenting themselves as protectors of the unorganized public interest. In sum, interest groups represent every aspect of society and help convey our myriad interests to policymakers.[29] Within the national government, interest groups attempt to exert influence directly on Congress, the bureaucracy, the courts, and the presidency. As we saw in chapter 3, presidents have responded to the increasingly important role of interest groups by assigning individual White House aides as liaisons to groups in such policy areas as civil rights, education, and health. This eventually led to Nixon's establishment of the Office of Public Liaison. Interest groups have also attempted to exert influence indirectly, principally by endorsing and making campaign contributions to presidential and congressional candidates and by urging their members to bring pressure to bear on the White House and on their representatives in Congress.

It is difficult to measure the effectiveness of interest group influence on public policy because there are multiple points of access to government decision makers; numerous groups usually seek to influence a particular policy or set of related policies; and other powerful forces also are at work. Nonetheless, there is widespread belief that the growth in interest group activity since 1965 has contributed substantially to the rise in federal spending on domestic programs and the expansion of federal regulation into noneconomic areas, such as consumer protection, product safety, and occupational safety and health.[30] The demands of interest groups, often asserted as a matter of "right" and defended on grounds of fairness or improvement of quality of life, have strained the federal government's fiscal capacity and created societal conflicts.

Mancur Olson, an economist, has argued that societies with large numbers of powerful "distributional coalitions" (his term for interest groups) have experienced insupportably high public spending and little or no economic growth as a consequence of those groups' political influence. The groups press for public benefits for their members even though the result may be disadvantageous to the community as a whole. According to Olson, unless an interest group encompasses most of the population, there is "no constraint on the social cost such an organization will find it expedient to impose on the society in the cause of obtaining a larger share of the social output for itself."[31] Thus, to a substantial extent, domestic policy politics has become the pursuit of narrow group interests, even at the expense of the general public interest, which is usually unorganized, unarticulated, and difficult to identify or define. The president is better situated, in terms of political resources, than anyone else to define, enhance, and defend the public interest. That is the president's principal challenge in the domestic policy area. Harry Truman was fond of saying his job was to act as a lobbyist for the American people, most of whom are unrepresented by lobbyists.

Separation of Powers and Federalism

The pattern of interest group activity traditionally has been described as "policy subgovernments," mutually beneficial triangular relationships among interest groups, administrative agencies, and congressional subcommittees. Subgovernments, and the more open and amorphous issue networks that cut across and intersect with them, contribute to the fragmentation of power and influence in the domestic policy environment. That fragmentation is enhanced by constitutional arrangements dividing power among the government branches and between the national and state governments and also by the internal structures of Congress and the federal bureaucracy. The constitutional design—which established a system of "separated sharing powers"—was created to prevent the abuse of power.[32]

The Framers invented federalism as a means of resolving the seemingly insoluble conflict between advocates of a consolidated system of government and the proponents of state sovereignty. Their ingenious compromise, which artfully avoided establishing a precise boundary between national and state powers, has been adapted to the needs of the times by successive generations of political leaders. The current system of federalism still leaves primary responsibility for most basic government services in the hands of the states and their local subdivisions. These services include public education, public health, public safety, and construction and maintenance of streets, roads, and highways. The federal government has programs that help finance state and local activities in these and other areas, and it exerts a substantial degree of influence on them by virtue of its grant and regulatory programs. Still, most of the federal government's domestic policy activity does not entail direct federal administration.

Presidential leadership in domestic policy requires the president to work with Congress, federal administrators, and state and local officials. In these relationships, the president has limited power to command and must rely instead on personal skills as a political leader—principally persuasion and bargaining—to achieve goals.

The structure of authority in Congress has varied over time, with a prevailing tendency toward fragmentation. The reforms of the early 1970s, while strengthening somewhat the majority party leadership in the House, provided individual members with extensive opportunities for influencing policy.[33] Consequently, Congress often found it difficult in the following decades to give direction to public policy, and presidents encountered problems in their relations with Congress. Unlike their predecessors in the late 1950s and 1960s, presidents from the mid-1970s to the early 1990s could not easily negotiate agreements with top party leaders and one or two influential chairs in each house and be confident those agreements would prevail in floor voting. Rather, the presidents had to deal separately, in each chamber, with several committee chairs, subcommittee chairs, and party leaders. Agreements reached at one stage in the legislative process often came undone later.

The congressional environment changed dramatically following the Republican takeover in 1994. In the House, the new majority leadership under Speaker

Newt Gingrich, R-Ga., imposed tight discipline on Republican members and committee chairs, all eager to implement a conservative policy revolution.[34] Party government not seen since the first decade of the twentieth century seemed to have returned. Although the new Senate was predictably less disciplined, its Republican majority demonstrated considerable unity given the disruptiveness of the presidential candidacies of Majority Leader Bob Dole and Phil Gramm of Texas. Though the conservative revolution did not occur during the Clinton administration, the right was heartened by the election of George W. Bush in 2000 and the 2002 midterm elections, in which Republicans regained control of the Senate. The effects of extensive congressional fragmentation on the president's involvement in domestic policy have been mixed. Congress has been unable to counterbalance the presidency by providing alternative policy leadership, but at the same time, presidents have found it increasingly difficult to lead Congress. Congressional influence has been extensive, if only in a negative sense, because of its inertia and its ability to resist presidential direction. Whether this condition will change with increased centralization of authority and purpose on the part of the congressional majority remains to be seen.

Fragmentation of a different sort characterizes the federal bureaucracy. As noted in chapter 6, an independent power exists in the bureaucracy that is based in career civil servants, who constitute a permanent government. The members of the permanent government have professional and agency loyalties and close ties to the interest groups that constitute their clientele and to the congressional subcommittees with jurisdiction over their appropriations and the legislation that authorizes their programs. Subgovernments and issue networks comprise members of the permanent government and complicate presidential control of policy development and implementation in or by the bureaucracy. In addition, the fragmentation resulting from the size and complexity of the federal bureaucracy creates enormous problems of management and policy coordination for the president.

The Domestic Policy Apparatus

The need for presidential coordination in domestic policy has been recognized for some time. The principal effort to enable presidents to provide the necessary coordination was development of a domestic policy staff apparatus in the Executive Office of the President. The domestic policy staff evolved slowly, in conjunction with the development of the president's legislative role. (*See chapter 5.*) This evolutionary process relied initially on the Bureau of the Budget (BOB); eventually it saw the establishment of a separate staff to formulate and implement domestic policy.

BOB: Central Clearance and Legislative Program Planning

From the early nineteenth century until the creation of the Bureau of the Budget in 1921, the president's role in domestic policy formulation was ad hoc and unorganized.[35] In its first year of operation, the BOB established the requirement that all agency legislative proposals for the expenditure of federal funds had to be submitted to it before being sent to Congress. Any proposal the bureau determined not in accord with the president's financial program would not be sent forward to Congress. Moreover, agencies were to inform Congress if any pending legislation had been found not in accord. This procedure, known as "central clearance," was expanded during Franklin Roosevelt's administration to cover the substantive content of proposed legislation. Early on, central clearance was used to ensure that legislative proposals of various departments and agencies were compatible with the president's overall program goals.[36] Over time, however, it acquired additional functions, among them supervising and coordinating executive branch legislative initiatives, providing a clear indication to congressional committees of the president's position on proposed legislation, and making various administrative units aware of one another's goals and activities.

Beginning in 1947, the BOB's domestic policy role expanded to include participation in the development of the president's legislative program.[37] The bureau's Legislative Reference Division worked directly with Truman's White House staff in reviewing agency recommendations and integrating them into a comprehensive legislative program. The addition of responsibilities to formulate policy involved BOB personnel in the pursuit of the president's political goals. Dwight D. Eisenhower delegated even more power to the BOB. When he first took office in 1953, Ike was unprepared to send a legislative program to Congress. He was also less interested in domestic policy than Truman had been. Therefore, he relied heavily on the BOB to formulate a domestic program. The centralized clearance and planning processes lodged in the bureau were compatible with Eisenhower's penchant for systematic staff operations, so he continued to employ it as a clearinghouse for policy throughout his presidency. By 1960, annual submissions to the BOB of legislative proposals by departments and agencies were commonplace. The result was a highly routinized process nearly impervious to new ideas. This system suited Eisenhower and his limited interest in domestic policy initiatives. It did not suit John F. Kennedy or Lyndon B. Johnson, both of whom placed a much higher priority on domestic policy than Ike had. To overcome the rigidities and bureaucratic domination of the BOB-based program planning process, JFK and LBJ sought ideas and suggestions from nongovernment sources.[38]

Task Forces and Study Commissions

The mechanism used by Kennedy and Johnson for gathering policy advice was the task force, a group consisting of experts from inside and outside the government. Before his inauguration, Kennedy appointed several such groups to advise him on the major issues and problems the new administration would be facing. The reports of these task forces, and of a number of others appointed after he took office, provided the basis for much of Kennedy's New Frontier program.[39]

Although Kennedy remained eager for new ideas and suggestions, he did not rely heavily on outside sources of advice after the initial round of task forces. Instead, he turned primarily to his cabinet for suggestions. In the spring of 1964, Johnson appointed task forces with the specific mission of developing a distinctive program for his administration. They were made up of outsiders and operated in secret. Johnson was so pleased with their reports, which furnished much of the form and substance of his Great Society program, that he made task forces a regular part of his program development process. The White House staff coordinated task force operations, and the BOB integrated the proposals into the annual legislative program. Johnson favored the task force process because it largely avoided the ordeal of bargaining with departments and agencies and because it was not adulterated by bureaucratic, congressional, and interest group pressures.[40] He used the device so extensively, however—in 1967 alone at least fifty task forces were preparing reports—that it became routinized, losing the informality and flexibility that had made it so valuable for developing new proposals.

The presidents who followed Johnson made little use of task forces. (Nixon appointed fourteen during his campaign, but their suggestions did not figure prominently in his initial legislative proposals.) Instead, they relied on more formal advisory bodies, such as commissions and White House conferences, to study issues and problems and to gather outside recommendations. Presidential commissions are broadly representative bodies often appointed to defuse highly sensitive issues. In September 1981, for example, President Reagan appointed the National Commission on Social Security Reform to develop a solution to a Social Security funding crisis. Although the commission did not solve the problem, it provided "cover" under which the principals, Reagan and House Speaker Thomas P. O'Neill, D-Mass., could work out a compromise.[41] As one of his first official actions, President Clinton appointed the Task Force on National Health Care Reform to develop the administration's proposed legislation within a hundred days.[42] Headed by the first lady, Hillary Rodham Clinton, and the senior adviser for policy development, Ira Magaziner, the task force consisted of 500 experts from inside and outside government, who divided themselves into thirty-four groups and operated secretly. The unprecedented size, the cumbersome secret process, and Hillary Clinton's role made the task force a target for criticism well before it had finished its work. Five months after the deadline, the unwieldy body produced a 1,350-page proposal for a Health Care Security Act. The delay in developing the proposal postponed congressional consideration of it until 1994, when it got caught up in election year politics. The proposal's "complexity, high cost, and obtrusive bureaucracy made it an easy target for Republicans" and contributed to the failure of Congress to enact it.[43]

Because of the representative character of presidential commissions, their reports often blur critical issues. This occurs as a consequence of their efforts to obtain consensus. Commissions may also make findings and suggestions that embarrass the president, as did the 1970 Scranton Commission report, which blamed campus unrest on President Nixon.

White House conferences bring together groups of experts and distinguished citizens for public forums held under presidential auspices. Their principal function is to build support among experts, political leaders, and relevant interests for presidential leadership to deal with the problems at issue. Neither White House conferences nor presidential commissions have served as the basis for major legislative proposals, but they have given legitimacy to certain presidential undertakings.

Domestic Policy Staffs

Since Johnson, presidents have used domestic policy staffs in the Executive Office of the President and a politicized Office of Management and Budget (OMB) to develop legislative programs. Nixon established the Domestic Council in 1970 as part of a reorganization of the presidency, in which the Bureau of the Budget was renamed the Office of Management and Budget. The Domestic Council comprised the president, the vice president, the attorney general, and the secretaries of agriculture, commerce, housing and urban development, interior, labor, transportation, treasury, and health, education and welfare, as well as the director and deputy director of OMB. The council was to be a top-level forum for discussion, debate, and determination of policy analogous to the National Security Council (NSC). (See chapter 10.) Like the NSC, the Domestic Council had a staff of professionals and support personnel. Headed by John Ehrlichman, the presidential assistant for domestic policy, the staff dominated Nixon's domestic policy-making process during the last two years of his first term (1971–1972).[44]

The council conducted its activity through work groups headed by one of six assistant directors. These groups prepared working papers for the president, evaluated departmental proposals for legislation, and participated in drafting presidential messages to Congress and preparing supportive materials for specific legislative proposals. In addition to assisting the president in formulating policy proposals, the Domestic Council advocated, monitored, and evaluated policy.[45] This arrangement, in effect, made Ehrlichman the president's general agent for domestic policy. Under him, the council centralized control over domestic policy in the White House. The president's interests, as defined and expressed by Ehrlichman, took precedence over the interests of departments and agencies, as conveyed by cabinet members and agency heads.

The council's domination of domestic policy did not survive Ehrlichman's departure from the White House in April 1973.[46] The influence of the staff was clearly a function of Ehrlichman's status with the president. Under Ehrlichman's successor, Kenneth Cole, the Domestic Council became more of a service unit, and OMB resumed many of the functions of planning legislative programs.

In addition to the development of a presidential staff for domestic policy, Nixon effected a major transformation in OMB by using it for political purposes. The OMB director became indistinguishable from other high-level presidential assistants, and a layer of political appointees, called "program assistant directors," was placed above OMB's career staff. Nixon's politicization of OMB reduced its ability to serve the institutional needs of the presidency as an impartial professional staff agency.[47]

President Ford used OMB to facilitate the unusual transfer of power from Nixon to himself after Nixon's resignation, and Ford relied on it to help plan and coordinate programs in a more traditional and less partisan manner than Nixon had. Initially, Ford intended to give the Domestic Council a major planning role by making Vice President Nelson Rockefeller its chair. However, Rockefeller never became Ford's general agent for domestic policy. The long delay in congressional confirmation of Rockefeller's appointment and his conflict with White House chief of staff Donald Rumsfeld appear to have prevented such a development.[48] The council's staff director, James Cannon, a Rockefeller appointee, never gained influence with Ford, who sought advice from a wide range of sources, including OMB, several cabinet members, and the Economic Policy Board, established in 1974 as a result of Ford's concern with economic policy problems. (*See chapter 9.*) That emphasis partly explains why Ford seldom used the Domestic Council for policy planning. Indeed, by fall 1976, the council no longer participated in legislative programming, and the staff was engaged in such diverse activities as answering presidential mail, preparing policy option memoranda, drafting presidential statements on legislation, and helping to explain the president's program to Congress.[49]

President Carter abolished the council shortly after taking office, but he retained a domestic policy staff headed by one of his top aides, Stuart Eizenstat. In some respects, Eizenstat and his staff acquired a policy-making role resembling that of Ehrlichman and the Domestic Council in the Nixon administration. However, Eizenstat and his staff members did not dominate the domestic policy process, and they functioned more in the roles of "effective administrator and of contributing advisor."[50]

Ronald Reagan, who came to office with a set, ideologically defined policy agenda and a strong commitment to cabinet government, created a new policy apparatus. The principal units were OMB, the Office of Policy Development (OPD), and seven cabinet councils. OMB's domestic policy involvement was especially crucial during Reagan's first year in office (1981), when the prime objective of drastically reducing the role of the federal government was linked to a budget reduction strategy implemented through use of the congressional budget process. (*See chapter 9.*) OMB director David Stockman was the principal architect of the first substantial rollback of the government's domestic programs since the New Deal.

The OPD was the Reagan administration's equivalent of Carter's domestic policy staff. Headed by a presidential assistant for policy development, the OPD worked through cabinet councils, which had jurisdiction over economic affairs, commerce and trade, human resources, natural resources and environment, food and agriculture, legal policy, and management and administration.[51] The councils' members included appropriate cabinet and subcabinet officers and OMB personnel and the White House staff. Each council had a secretariat composed of department and agency representatives and used working groups to provide expertise and analyze issues.

The OPD–cabinet council system did not, however, become the directing force for domestic policy. Other factors, particularly the president's long-range objectives and budget pressures, determined the agenda from the administration's beginning. Reagan's domestic policy apparatus worked out "details secondary to the president's fixed view of government."[52] In other words, it performed an administrative, rather than an advisory, role.

Developments in the first year of Reagan's second term resulted in further diminution of the OPD–cabinet council system. The newly appointed White House chief of staff, former secretary of the treasury Donald Regan, moved quickly to bring the three major policy areas—economics, national security, and domestic policy—under his control. The number of cabinet councils was reduced from seven to two: Economic Affairs and Domestic Policy. (The National Security Council, a statutory body, remained as it was.) Secretary of the Treasury James Baker and Attorney General Edwin Meese III chaired the economic and domestic policy councils, respectively. The OPD was reduced in size, and its director reported to Regan. In addition to simplifying and reducing the size of the OPD–cabinet council system, Regan centralized authority over domestic policy in his office. However, the two remaining cabinet council chairs, Meese and Baker, enjoyed substantial autonomy to pursue their own policy projects. By early 1986, Regan had gained control of all access to the president with respect to domestic policy not under the purview of the two cabinet councils.

The diminished domestic policy apparatus of Reagan's second term reflected a shift in the administration's orientation from changing policies to defending them. Having accomplished most of his initial domestic agenda, principally curtailment of the growth of federal agencies and a reduction in spending on them, Reagan concentrated his energies on national security and economic policy objectives. The domestic policy apparatus under Reagan was at least partially deinstitutionalized.

The same condition continued under Reagan's vice president and successor, George Bush.[53] The assistant to the president for economic and domestic affairs, Roger Porter, a former Harvard professor, directed the Office of Policy Development. The OPD and the White House Office of Cabinet Affairs provided staff support for the Domestic Policy Council and the Economic Policy Council. However, major issues usually bypassed the cabinet council system and were resolved by Chief of Staff John Sununu or the budget director, Richard Darman. Sununu's self-defined role was to protect the conservative integrity of the administration against those who urged the president to pursue more politically pragmatic options, while Darman functioned as a nonideological guardian of the budget and advocate of economic growth. Both intervened frequently on low-level issues. However, some cabinet members, such as Secretary of Housing and Urban Development Jack Kemp and Secretary of Transportation Samuel Skinner, took the lead in developing major domestic legislative proposals and pushing them in Congress.[54]

The domestic policy process during the first two years of the Clinton administration was frequently frenetic and uncoordinated.[55] The Domestic Policy Council did not meet regularly. Development of health care reform, the principal initiative, was the responsibility of the large task force headed by Hillary Clinton and Ira Magaziner. Cabinet members, such as Health and Human Services Secretary Donna Shalala, did not play major roles in developing initiatives.

Although formally lodged in a Domestic Policy Council chaired by a high-level presidential assistant, the policy process was operationally centered in the president himself. Clinton, with his deep interest in domestic policy, presided over numerous wide-ranging and intensive meetings with his advisers that shifted back and forth between various policy alternatives. There was no single individual, such as the chief of staff, or group comparable to Reagan's Legislative Strategy Group responsible for resolving disputes, imparting coherence and practicality to the many proposals, and moving them to Congress in a timely manner. Clinton resisted delegating such authority, and despite his intellectual brilliance and energy, he was unable to "ringmaster" the domestic policy process effectively on his own.[56]

The situation changed dramatically after the Republicans won control of both congressional houses in the 1994 midterm elections. (Although Republicans had controlled the Senate as recently as 1986, they had not controlled the House of Representatives since 1954.) The new Republican majority largely controlled policymaking through most of 1995, and for a time the "Republican revolution" seemed to live up to its name.[57] Then came the notorious budget battle of 1995–1996, when Republicans pushed for sharp cuts in entitlement programs. President Clinton reasserted himself, exercised his first veto in response to the proposed cuts, and rallied opposition to the Republican plan. House Speaker Newt Gingrich refused to compromise, and the stalemate led to government shutdowns, which the public blamed on the Republicans. In the end, Clinton won the political battle.

Paul J. Quirk and William Cunion have noted that the government shutdowns led to a new phase of Clinton's domestic presidency. It began in January 1996 and ran through the eruption of the Monica Lewinsky scandal in early 1998. It was marked by an unusual degree of cooperation between Clinton and the Republican majority in Congress, leading to a "notable amount of significant legislation," including a major overhaul of the welfare system.[58] With the help of political strategist Dick Morris, Clinton followed a centrist strategy of "triangulation." He finally seemed to master the art of domestic policymaking. But cooperation and policy output came to halt in 1998 and 1999 with the Lewinsky scandal and the ensuing impeachment of the president.

In contrast to Clinton's frenetic style, George W. Bush's domestic policy process was highly structured. Bush, unlike any of his predecessors, came to office with a master's degree in business administration (from Harvard's Business School). He surrounded himself with high-level advisers who had experience not only in government but also as chief executive officers of major businesses.

The strength of this business model was its efficiency; Bush insisted on a highly disciplined staff. He was comfortable surrounding himself with a strong team of advisers, and he proved willing to delegate decision making. Yet he was also willing to exert control. As Bill Keller wrote in the *New York Times Magazine:*

Bush is undoubtedly Reagan's superior in the executive management of a divided, competitive staff. Reagan delegated all but the biggest decisions. He recoiled from internal conflict and could not bear to fire anyone. . . . The Reagan years were marked by angry resignations, endless wars of leaks and back-stabbing. Bush, perhaps by virtue of his business education and experience—and his years as, in effect, a junior White House staff member to his father—is more personally engaged in sorting out the issues, maintaining the discipline and culling the misfits. By comparison with that of Reagan's day, the tension between the diplomats and the moralists, between the tax eliminators and the deficit hawks, between the idealists and the realists, has been contained and synthesized into a common cause. A result is that Bush is less likely than Reagan to be constrained by contention in his own ranks.[59]

Conclusion

Presidents approach the task of making domestic policy with varying amounts of resources and differing policy opportunities. Their domestic policy leadership depends to a large extent on their effectiveness in using the available resources to exploit existing opportunities and create new ones. They are most apt to do this effectively when the three components of the policy stream—problems, solutions, and politics—converge. A president's ability to bring these three tributary streams together is one indication of effective policy leadership.

Successful policy leadership requires presidents to spend their resources carefully and exploit opportunities skillfully. To do so they must pay particular attention to four strategic factors: goals, priorities, timing, and costs and benefits.

Modest, flexible *goals* usually are easier to achieve than those that are extensive and ideologically derived. So, too, are goals that enjoy substantial support among the public and policy-making elites. In establishing their goals, presidents take such considerations into account along with their own values and beliefs. A primarily pragmatic set of objectives tends to be easier to accomplish than one ideologically derived. Such objectives are less likely, however, to have an impact on society than more visionary and comprehensive ones. In some circumstances, ideological goals may be highly appropriate. For example, Ronald Reagan initially struck a responsive note in Congress and the public with his unabashedly conservative domestic program. Presidents are free to be as pragmatic or as ideological as they wish in establishing their goals. However they decide, the mix they choose affects their policy leadership.

Closely related to goals, *priorities* also affect policy leadership. Presidents who clearly define their priorities generally have been more successful than those who have not done so because the policy process can handle only a few major issues at a time, even though many contend for attention. If a president does not indicate preferences, other participants will pursue their own objectives, possibly to the detriment of the president's. Nor is it realistic for presidents to expect that all of their goals will receive consideration to the exclusion of those of other participants. In this respect a comparison between Carter and Reagan is instructive. Carter developed a lengthy domestic agenda and insisted that all of his goals were vitally important to the nation and deserving of enactment. Congress responded by taking its time in dealing with Carter's program and by pursuing many of its own objectives. Some of Carter's goals, such as welfare reform and national health insurance, were never adopted; others, such as a national energy policy, were passed in greatly modified form after extensive delay and bargaining. Many congressional Democrats complained that Carter failed to provide them with direction and guidance for his domestic proposals. In contrast, Reagan made his priorities clear from the beginning and continued to do so. Congress had little doubt about which goals Reagan considered vital—and on which he would spend political capital—and which goals were less important to him. Cutting domestic spending, strengthening national defense, and reducing and reforming taxes took precedence over balancing the federal budget, ending legalized abortion, and restoring school prayer.

Timing, the third strategic consideration in successful policy leadership, is crucial to effective exploitation of opportunities. If opportunities are missed, they may be lost indefinitely. Good timing also involves taking advantage of the regular policy and electoral cycles. Proposals submitted at appropriate times in those cycles have greater likelihood of adoption. Proposals also can be withheld until conditions are ripe for their submission. A proposal with limited support can be moved to the top of the agenda and pushed successfully as the result of a disaster, a crisis, or some other focusing event. Presidents able to time the presentation of proposals to coincide with favorable events and conditions are more likely to be effective policy leaders than those lacking such a sense of timing. Two presidents whose timing of domestic proposals was effective were Franklin Roosevelt, during the first hundred days of the New Deal, when the Great Depression provided the rationale for a comprehensive set of economic recovery and reform laws, and Lyndon Johnson, who in early 1964 used the shock of the Kennedy assassination to secure passage of the Civil Rights Act. In contrast, Bill Clinton's poor timing of his health care reform and welfare reform proposals contributed to their failure.

Finally, successful policy leadership requires presidents to be attentive to the *costs and benefits* of raising problems for consideration and posing solutions. As presidents decide which problems and issues to emphasize, they focus on political benefits. They select agenda items according to the prospective electoral, historical, and programmatic benefits of the times.[60] When presidents select solutions for problems they are addressing, their emphasis is on costs.[61] Political costs, assessed in terms of congressional, electoral, bureaucratic, and interest group support, enter presidential calculations at each stage of the process. Increasingly, presidents and other actors have tended to view political costs in terms of avoiding blame and claiming credit for the outcomes.[62]

Economic costs have sharply limited the alternatives in recent years as budget pressures have mounted. These pressures force presidents to make hard choices, such as whether to support new programs and which existing programs to emphasize, maintain, or reduce. Technical costs and questions of workability also enter the selection of policy alternatives.

No prescription or formula can guarantee that a president will provide successful domestic policy leadership, in part because some problems, such as the high unemployment rate among African American men, are very difficult to solve—or solutions do not exist. Another reason for the absence of a workable formula is that conditions constantly change. Some problems may be solved only to reemerge in a new form; others may decline in importance. Solutions viable today may not be a few years hence, or solutions may have unanticipated consequences that become problems in their own right. Political conditions, such as the popular mood or control of Congress, are in flux, so strategies may have to be modified frequently. Because many of the requirements of successful policy leadership are not fixed, what worked well for one president may be only partially useful to those who come later.

Even presidents who take office committed to concentrating their energies on domestic policy encounter extensive frustrations. They may enjoy some initial successes, as did Reagan; but the difficulties of accomplishing additional objectives eventually increase, and the sharing of power with Congress, the bureaucracy, and organized interests becomes ever more burdensome. The natural tendency is for presidents to turn their attention to national security or economic policy. In these areas, the challenges are more immediately threatening to the general welfare; the constraints on a president's ability to act, although very real, are not as frustrating; and successful policy leadership appears less elusive.

NOTES

1. The concept of "issue congestion" was developed by Hugh Heclo, "One Executive Branch or Many?" in *Both Ends of the Avenue,* ed. Anthony King (Washington, D.C.: American Enterprise Institute, 1983), 26–58.

2. Theodore J. Lowi, "American Business, Public Policy, Case Studies, and Political Theory," *World Politics* (July 1964): 677–715.

3. Steven A. Shull, *Domestic Policy Formation: Presidential-Congressional Partnership?* (Westport, Conn.: Greenwood Press, 1983), 155; Shull, "Change in Presidential Policy Initiatives," *Western Political Quarterly* (September 1983): 497.

4. John H. Kessel, *Presidential Parties* (Homewood, Ill.: Dorsey, 1984), 112–115.

5. Jonathan Weisman, "Bush to Accept Budget 'Pork,'" *USA Today,* July 10, 2001, A1.

6. Kessel, *Presidential Parties,* 68–69.

7. The policy-stream metaphor borrows from Paul Light, "The Presidential Policy Stream," in *The Presidency and the Political System,* ed. Michael Nelson (Washington, D.C.: CQ Press, 1984), 423–448; and John W. Kingdon, *Agendas, Alternatives, and Public Policies,* 2d ed. (New York: HarperCollins, 1995), 85–86.

8. This discussion follows Kingdon, *Agendas,* chap. 5.

9. This discussion of the development of the health care issue follows B. Guy Peters, *American Public Policy: Promise and Performance*, 3d ed. (Chatham, N.J.: Chatham House, 1993), 230–235.

10. John Schmid, "Democrats Think Big on Health Care Reform," *Milwaukee Journal Sentinel*, July 27, 2003, 1A.

11. Paul Light, *The President's Agenda: Domestic Policy Choice from Kennedy to Reagan*, 3d ed. (Baltimore: Johns Hopkins University Press, 1991), chap. 3; and Light, "Presidential Policy Stream," 427–428.

12. Ironically, Nixon's preoccupation with the judgment of history helped cut short his presidency. He consistently explained the installation of the secret taping system in the Oval Office as motivated by his desire to have a complete and accurate record for use by historians. That taped record provided the "smoking gun" that led to the House Judiciary Committee vote impeachment charges, which prompted his resignation in August 1974.

13. Kingdon, *Agendas*, 142–143.

14. Jeff Fishel, *Presidents and Promises: From Campaign Pledge to Presidential Performance* (Washington, D.C.: CQ Press, 1984).

15. Kingdon, *Agendas*, 131.

16. Vincent J. Burke and Vee Burke, *Nixon's Good Deed: Welfare Reform* (New York: Columbia University Press, 1974); Laurence E. Lynn Jr. and David deF. Whitman, *The President as Policymaker: Jimmy Carter and Welfare Reform* (Philadelphia: Temple University Press, 1981).

17. Jack W. Germond and Jules Witcover, "On Welfare, It's Politics as Usual," *National Journal*, August 5, 1995, 2021.

18. "Social Policy," *Congressional Quarterly Weekly Report*, November 2, 1996, 3148–3149.

19. This discussion is based on Kingdon, *Agendas*, chap. 7.

20. Democrats maintained united government from 1977 through 1980 and again from 1993 through 1994. Republicans have maintained united government since the 2002 midterm elections.

21. This discussion follows Light, "The Presidential Policy Stream," 440–446.

22. Paul J. Quirk and Joseph Hinchcliffe, "Domestic Policy: The Trials of a Centrist Democrat," in *The Clinton Presidency: First Appraisals*, ed. Colin Campbell and Bert A. Rockman (Chatham, N.J.: Chatham House, 1995), 264–267.

23. David W. Moore, "Initial Job Approval for Bush at 57 percent, but Highest Disapproval of any President since Polling Began," Gallup Poll release, February 6, 2001, www.gallup.com.

24. Quoted in Ron Fournier, "Bush's Test: To Unite the Great Divide," *Pittsburgh Post-Gazette*, January 21, 2001, A9.

25. Light, "The Presidential Policy Stream," 444–445.

26. Kingdon, *Agendas*, 194–195.

27. Kessel, *Presidential Parties*, 60.

28. Light, *The President's Agenda*, 36–38.

29. For an excellent account of interest groups, see Scott H. Ainsworth, *Analyzing Interest Groups: Group Influence on People and Policies* (New York: W. W. Norton, 2002).

30. Harold Wolman and Fred Tietlebaum, "Interest Groups and the Reagan Presidency," in *The Reagan Presidency and the Governing of America*, ed. Lester M. Salamon and Michael S. Lund (Washington, D.C.: Urban Institute Press, 1985), 299–301.

31. Mancur Olson, *The Rise and Decline of Nations* (New Haven: Yale University Press, 1982), 44.

32. Richard E. Neustadt, *Presidential Power and the Modern Presidents: The Politics of Leadership from Roosevelt to Reagan* (New York: Free Press, 1990), 29.

33. Leroy Rieselbach, *Congressional Reform: The Changing Modern Congress* (Washington, D.C.: CQ Press, 1994); Roger H. Davidson, ed., *The Postreform Congress* (New York: St. Martin's Press, 1992).

34. Donna Cassata, "Republicans Bask in Success of Rousing Performance," *Congressional Quarterly Weekly Report*, April 8, 1995, 986, 988, 990; Jennifer Babson, "Armey Stood Guard over Contract," *Congressional Quarterly Weekly Report*, April 8, 1995, 987; and Adam Clymer, "House Party: With Political Discipline It Works Like Parliament," *New York Times*, August 6, 1995, E6.

35. Lester M. Salamon, "The Presidency and Domestic Policy Formulation," in *The Illusion of Presidential Government*, ed. Hugh Heclo and Lester M. Salamon (Boulder: Westview Press, 1981), 179.

36. Richard E. Neustadt, "The Presidency and Legislation: The Growth of Central Clearance," *American Political Science Review* (September 1954): 641–670; Robert S. Gilmour, "Central Clearance: A Revised Perspective," *Public Administration Review* (March–April 1971): 150–158.

37. Richard E. Neustadt, "The Presidency and Legislation: Planning the President's Program," *American Political Science Review* (December 1955): 980–1018; Larry Berman, *The Office of Management and Budget and the Presidency* (Princeton: Princeton University Press, 1979), 42–43; Stephen J. Wayne, *The Legislative Presidency* (New York: Harper and Row, 1978), 103–105.

38. Norman C. Thomas and Harold L. Wolman, "The Presidency and Policy Formation: The Task Force Device," *Public Administration Review* (September-October 1969): 459–471.

39. Text of the reports were published in *New Frontiers of the Kennedy Administration* (Washington, D.C.: Public Affairs Press, 1961).

40. Lyndon B. Johnson, *The Vantage Point* (New York: Holt, Rinehart and Winston, 1971), 326.

41. Paul Light, *Artful Work: The Politics of Social Security Reform* (New York: Random House, 1985), 232.

42. Quirk and Hinchcliffe, "Domestic Policy," 274–275.

43. Ibid., 275.

44. Raymond J. Waldman, "The Domestic Council: Innovation in Presidential Government," *Public Administration Review* (May–June 1976): 260–268.

45. Margaret Jane Wyszomirski, "The Roles of a Presidential Office for Domestic Policy: Three Models and Four Cases," in *The Presidency and Policy Making*, ed. George C. Edwards III, Steven A. Shull, and Norman C. Thomas (Pittsburgh: University of Pittsburgh Press, 1985), 134.

46. John Helmer and Louis Maisel, "Analytical Problems in the Study of Presidential Advice: The Domestic Council Staff in Flux," *Presidential Studies Quarterly* (winter 1978): 52–53.

47. A sharp debate rages over politicization of OMB and the institutionalized presidency generally. Berman, in *The Office of Management and Budget*, argues that politicization has damaged, if not destroyed, the capacity of OMB to serve the institutional needs of the presidency in a professional manner. In contrast, Terry Moe, in a seminal essay, views politicization as a logical (indeed necessary) institutional development resulting from the extensive and steady growth of "expectations surrounding presidential performance." See "The Politicized Presidency," in *The New Direction in American Politics*, ed. John E. Chubb and Paul E. Peterson (Washington, D.C.: Brookings, 1985), 269.

48. Wyszomirski, "The Roles of a Presidential Office," 136–137.

49. Wayne, *The Legislative Presidency*, 123.

50. Wyszomirski, "The Roles of a Presidential Office," 140.

51. For an extended description of the OPD–cabinet council system, see Chester A. Newland, "Executive Office Policy Apparatus: Enforcing the Reagan Agenda," in *The Reagan Presidency*, 153–159. Martin Anderson, who was Reagan's first director of the OPD, provides a participant's perspective on the cabinet councils in *Revolution* (New York: Harcourt Brace Jovanovich, 1988), chap. 19.

52. Ibid., 160.

53. This discussion follows Colin Campbell, "The White House and the Presidency under the 'Let's Deal' President," in *The Bush Presidency: First Appraisals*, ed. Colin Campbell and Bert A. Rockman (Chatham, N.J.: Chatham House, 1991), 210–212.

54. Julie Rovner, "On Policy Front, Home Is Not Where Bush's Heart Is," *Congressional Quarterly Weekly Report*, February 2, 1991, 292.

55. This discussion follows Colin Campbell, "Management in a Sandbox," in *The Clinton Presidency*, 77–80.

56. Ibid., 79.

57. Paul J. Quirk and William Cunion, "Clinton's Domestic Policy: The Lessons of a 'New Democrat,'" in *The Clinton Legacy*, ed. Colin Campbell and Bert A. Rockman (New York: Chatham House, 2000), 208.

58. Ibid., 210–211.

59. Bill Keller, "The Radical Presidency of George W. Bush," *New York Times Magazine*, January 26, 2003, 26.

60. Light, *The President's Agenda*, 71.

61. Ibid., 134–136.

62. R. Kent Weaver, *Automatic Government: The Politics of Indexation* (Washington, D.C.: Brookings, 1988), chap. 2.

SUGGESTED READINGS

Ainsworth, Scott H. *Analyzing Interest Groups: Group Influence on People and Policies.* New York: W. W. Norton, 2002.

Baumgartner, Frank R., and Byron D. Jones. *Agendas and Instability in American Politics.* Chicago: University of Chicago Press, 1993.

Kessel, John H. *Presidents, the Presidency, and the Political Environment.* Washington, D.C.: CQ Press, 2001.

Kingdon, John W. *Agendas, Alternatives, and Public Policies.* 2d ed. New York: Longman, 2003.

Lammers, William W., and Michael A. Genovese. *The Presidency and Domestic Policy: Comparing Leadership Styles, FDR to Clinton.* Washington, D.C.: CQ Press, 2000.

Light, Paul C. *The President's Agenda: Domestic Policy Choice from Kennedy to Clinton.* 3d ed. Baltimore: Johns Hopkins University Press, 1999.

Quirk, Paul J., and William Cunion. "Clinton's Domestic Policy: The Lessons of a 'New Democrat.'" In *The Clinton Legacy*, ed. Colin Campbell and Bert A. Rockman. New York: Chatham House, 2000.

Rudalevige, Andrew. *Managing the President's Program: Presidential Leadership and Legislative Policy Formulation.* Princeton: Princeton University Press, 2002.

Shull, Steven A. *American Civil Rights Policy from Truman to Clinton: The Role of Presidential Leadership.* Armonk, N.Y.: M. E. Sharpe, 1999.

Warshaw, Shirley Anne. *The Domestic Presidency: Policy Making in the White House.* Boston: Allyn and Bacon, 1996.

9 THE POLITICS OF
ECONOMIC POLICY

During the Great Depression, Franklin Roosevelt used radio broadcasts from the White House, known as "fireside chats," to persuade the public to support his unprecedented economic policies.

ECONOMIC ISSUES DOMINATED THE 1992 presidential election campaign and most of the following decade. Polls indicated that the public blamed President George H. W. Bush and his administration for the 1991–1992 recession. Bush insisted the economy was fundamentally sound and recovery from the recession had begun. The Democratic candidate, Bill Clinton, charged that Bush had indeed neglected the economy and focused his campaign on economic issues. A sign stating, "It's the Economy, Stupid," hung on the wall of his national campaign headquarters.[1] Clinton promised to end the recession, ensure long-running prosperity through investments in human capital and physical infrastructure, and reduce the substantial federal budget deficit. That year's independent candidate, Ross Perot, stressed the importance of ending the deficit and reducing the expanding national debt. The electorate responded by choosing Clinton while giving Perot 19 percent of the vote. Not surprisingly, the deficit and other economic issues dominated Clinton's first two years in office. Quite surprisingly, however, Clinton got only modest credit for presiding during a period of record economic growth with low inflation that coincided with a near-miraculous transformation in the annual budget from a $290 billion deficit in 1992 to a $69.2 billion surplus in 1998. Although Clinton enthusiasts hailed this turnaround as a great achievement, many analysts saw it as the product of luck and the efforts of Alan Greenspan, chairman of the Federal Reserve Board. As one pair of analysts concluded, "[T]he bounty of the 1990s resulted less from Clinton's personal stewardship of prosperity than from his willingness to follow the learned advice of others and, more fundamentally, from economic forces beyond his control."[2]

A radically different story has unfolded for George W. Bush. Entering office as an economic slowdown was beginning, Bush largely escaped blame for rising unemployment, dramatically lower stock prices, a resurgence in budget deficits to all-time highs, and declining public confidence in corporate America. The terrorist attack of September 11, 2001, partly explains the public's forbearance as the nation's economy reeled from damage to its financial infrastructure and severely reduced air transportation. Two military actions overseas, assistance to New York, airline bailouts, and expanded spending for defense and homeland security increased federal spending at the same time revenues declined as a result of tax cuts and a sputtering economy. It remained to be seen whether this economic record would make a difference at the ballot box in 2004.

Clinton's and Bush's attentiveness to economic matters was not new. Presidents have been concerned about the condition of the economy since the early years of the Republic. Some who confronted serious economic adversity, such as Martin Van Buren in 1837, Ulysses S. Grant in 1873, Grover Cleveland in 1893, Theodore Roosevelt in 1907, and Warren G. Harding in 1921, did little more than ride out the storm. The electorate, however, reacted by denying reelection to Van Buren and by inflicting sizable losses on the president's party in the midterm congressional elections of 1838, 1874, and 1894. In fact, the existence of a relationship between business cycles and election results was known long before Edward Tufte's precise empirical analysis of the phenomenon.[3] Only since the 1930s, however, have presidents attempted to control business cycles through public policy, and the public has come to expect them to do so.

This chapter examines the president's economic policy responsibilities and activities. It begins by distinguishing between actions designed to manage the entire economy (macroeconomic policy) and those meant to control specific aspects of the economy (microeconomic policy). The primary focus of the chapter is on macroeconomic policy. The chapter reviews presidential efforts to manage the economy from 1933 to 2003 and then describes the politics of macroeconomic policymaking. Next we analyze how the president makes economic policy and the ways in which presidents since Dwight D. Eisenhower have handled the problem of coordinating economic policy. The chapter concludes with an assessment of the congressional role in macroeconomic policymaking.

Macroeconomic Policy

Management of the entire economy by the government is known as *macroeconomic policy,* and the government has two principal tools to use: fiscal policy and monetary policy. Using fiscal policy, the government tries to regulate the level of the nation's economic activity by varying taxes and public expenditures. A policy of increasing spending and reducing taxes aims to expand the economy; one of decreasing spending and increasing taxes aims to contract it. A budget deficit (when spending exceeds tax revenues) stimulates economic activity, whereas a budget surplus (when tax revenues exceed spending) slows the economy. The president and Congress jointly make fiscal policy. They determine expenditures through budgeting and appropriations, and they establish taxes through legislation. Monetary policy refers to a government's efforts, through its central bank (in the United States, the Federal Reserve System), to regulate economic activity by controlling the supply of money—currency and credit. An independent agency, the Board of Governors of the Federal Reserve System, makes monetary policy. Although fiscal policy and monetary policy constitute distinct realms of policymaking, administrations seek to coordinate them.

Since the Great Depression of the 1930s, the goals of macroeconomic policy have remained constant: to hold down the rate of inflation, to establish and maintain full employment, and to achieve a steady rate of economic growth. However, policymakers have pursued these goals through alternative theories: classical conservative economics, Keynesianism, monetarism, and supply-side economics.

Conservative economic theory lost credibility during the Great Depression when the administrations of Herbert Hoover and Franklin D. Roosevelt (at the outset) stressed balancing the budget and failed to restore confidence in the economy and produce the desired upturn. FDR quickly discovered that emergency spending and loan programs provided relief and produced a measure of recovery. The ideas of John Maynard Keynes, a British economist Roosevelt met in 1934, offered an explanation for why fiscal stimulus is effective and eventually provided a rationale for deficit spending. Keynes argued that an economic decline is caused by a drop in private demand for goods and services. Government could stimulate demand by increasing its own expenditures or increasing those of consumers by reducing taxes. The temporary deficits created by fiscal stimulation would be financed by government borrowing and repaid during periods of hyperactivity in the economy. Eventually the economy's recovery following mobilization during World War II, which was supported by government spending, provided most economists with empirical validation of Keynes's basic theories. Conservative economics, however, retained its hold on many political leaders, such as Eisenhower, who made balanced budgets their goals and regarded fiscal stimulation of lagging demand as an emergency measure.

While Keynesianism was establishing itself as the new orthodoxy, another theory emerged to challenge it. The monetarists, under the leadership of economist Milton Friedman, held that the key to maintaining economic stability lay not in stimulating demand but in limiting the growth rate of the money supply to no more than the growth rate of the economy. Inflation occurs, monetarists claim, when the money supply expands too rapidly. The only remedy for inflation is a painful contraction in the money supply. Monetarists hold that fiscal policy and the size of budget deficits are subordinate to monetary policy and the growth rate of the money supply, which for them constitute the basic means of managing the economy.

Monetarism gained adherents as the limitations of Keynesianism became apparent during the 1970s. Keynesian theory has an inflationary bias—its primary defect as a macroeconomic theory. Decisions on taxing and spending are made by the president and members of Congress—politicians concerned with reelection—and not by professional economists. Consequently, it has proved easier in practice to increase spending and cut taxes, the Keynesian prescription for expansion, than to cut spending and increase taxes, the theory's remedy for inflation. In the 1970s, when inflation became the nation's leading economic problem, political decision makers were unwilling to impose the Keynesian solution. Although the inflationary bias of Keynesianism is a political defect rather than a weakness in the theory itself, this bias nevertheless has made it less attractive than other theories as a guide to policy.

Monetarism, whatever its theoretical merits and limitations, offered a politically palatable way to control inflation through the autonomous Federal Reserve Board, known as the Fed, which reduces inflation by contracting the money supply. Political officeholders can blame the consequences of monetary contractions, such as high interest rates and rising unemployment, on the Fed and its amorphous supporters: "Wall Street" investing interests and the banks. But monetarism also became politically unattractive when efforts to control inflation proved painful during the late 1970s. By the early 1980s a new theoretical approach, supply-side economics, had emerged and been embraced by President Ronald Reagan.

Essentially, supply-side economics is an amalgam of Keynesianism and monetarism.[4] Supply-siders endorse strict monetary restraint as the means of controlling inflation, but they also believe, unlike pure monetarists, that fiscal policy can be used to achieve macroeconomic policy objectives. The supply-siders assert, however, that the Keynesians misdirect government efforts. Instead of stimulating demand through higher spending and tax cuts for consumers, the supply-siders seek to stimulate supply through tax cuts that provide incentives to encourage investments and productivity, which in turn increase the supply of goods and services. The additional jobs created ultimately fuel consumer buying, though the focus of the policy is producers, not consumers. Supply-siders are not disturbed by budget deficits resulting from tax-cut incentives. They believe an expanded economy will not be inflationary and eventually will generate enough revenues at lower rates of taxation to balance the budget.

Supply-side economics draws sharp criticism from both liberals and conservatives who doubt the validity of assumptions on which the theory rests. Liberals charge that it is another version of the discredited "trickle down" approach to economic policy, under which tax advantages for the affluent are justified on the grounds that they eventually lead to prosperity for all. Conservatives fear that supply-side tolerance of budget deficits will lead to excessive rates of inflation and will erode confidence in the monetary system. Critics, who would like supply-side policies to work, do not believe they can. Experience since 1981 with a massive cut in federal income taxes, phased in over several years and based on supply-side reasoning, supports their pessimism. The economy steadily expanded during the 1980s and 1990s, but a balanced budget was not achieved until 1998, when there was a modest surplus. The Democrats, whose willingness to raise taxes in 1993 helped increase government revenues, claimed credit for this accomplishment. But when signs of an economic slowdown emerged in late 2000, the issue of tax cuts reemerged during the presidential campaign, and after a new administration was in place, Republicans passed two dramatic tax reductions at the urging of President Bush. These new efforts provided another opportunity to observe how the federal budget will be affected by supply-side policies in the long run.

For nearly two decades, federal policymakers were forced to rely more heavily on monetary policy than on fiscal policy to manage the economy. In the face of large and persistent deficits, there was little room for increasing spending or reducing taxes, actions that would have further expanded the deficit. Moreover, Republicans and Democrats disagreed vehemently over the level and purposes of government spending and the structure of taxes—who pays how much. In this intractable setting, monetary policy instruments became the only viable alternative for macroeconomic management.[5] Although the appearance of budget surpluses seemed to breathe new life into fiscal policy, this revival would prove short-lived if the Bush tax cuts adopted in 2001 and 2003 were so large that the federal government once again began to run a deficit.

Microeconomic Policy

Microeconomic policy is a term used to describe government regulation of specific economic activities; it also encompasses antitrust policy, which is designed to prevent business monopolies and stimulate competition. Microeconomic policies focus on specific industries or on economic practices in several industries. They are designed to affect directly the infrastructure of the economy and only indirectly its overall performance. Modern presidents generally have paid less attention to microeconomic than to macroeconomic policy, largely because the former's impact is more narrowly focused. Most presidents, however, have on occasion endorsed specific microeconomic policies or used microeconomic policy tools to achieve macroeconomic or other policy goals, such as Reagan's pursuit of deregulation.

Before the Great Depression, presidents were involved exclusively with microeconomic policy and did not regard overall management of the economy as a primary policy responsibility. To preserve competition in the market, Theodore Roosevelt and William Howard Taft vigorously enforced the Sherman Anti-Trust Act of 1890—Roosevelt with great fanfare and Taft with quiet effectiveness. Woodrow Wilson persuaded Congress to establish an independent regulatory agency, the Federal Trade Commission, with extensive authority to regulate anticompetitive and unfair business practices. Roosevelt, Taft, and Wilson believed the federal government should act to correct imperfections in the operations of the free market economy.

During the New Deal, Franklin Roosevelt endorsed legislation that established or strengthened independent regulatory agencies: the Securities and Exchange Commission, the Federal Power Commission, the Federal Communications Commission, the Civil Aeronautics Board (CAB), and the National Labor Relations Board. These agencies received broad grants of authority to regulate the interstate aspects of specific industries, such as trade in stocks and bonds, electric power and natural gas, broadcasting and wire communications, and air transportation, as well as economywide activities such as labor-management relations. FDR experimented with government intervention, hoping to improve the operation of certain economic sectors or the overall health of the economy.

FDR's successors varied in their use of microeconomic policies. Presidents Harry S. Truman, Eisenhower, John F. Kennedy, and Lyndon B. Johnson accepted the legitimacy of government regulation of economic activity that had been established by 1940, including antitrust policy. They differed mainly in the intensity with which they enforced regulations and in their willingness to use certain microeconomic policy tools.

Beginning in the late 1960s and continuing into the 1970s, Congress passed a new set of statutes expanding federal regulation of economic activity as a way to achieve noneconomic goals, such as a cleaner physical environment, safer automobiles and other consumer products, and a higher degree of safety and health in the workplace. Presidents initially approved the new regulatory activities, but as their economic costs became apparent, Richard Nixon and Gerald R. Ford raised questions about the appropriateness of federal regulation in general. A deregulatory movement gained support, endorsed by Ford and Jimmy Carter. Ford assigned overall responsibility for deregulation to a member of the Council of Economic Advisers (CEA) and issued an order requiring agencies to analyze the impact of their actions on inflation. Carter established the Regulatory Analysis Review Group, chaired by a CEA member, which was responsible for reviewing new rules and regulations with potential economic costs of $100 million or more. There is little evidence, however, that these actions reduced the volume of new regulations or the economic impact of regulation on industry.[6] Carter also supported legislation that deregulated the airline and trucking industries. (The CAB ceased to function at the end of 1984, but the Interstate Commerce Commission continued to regulate railroads.)

Reagan promised in his 1980 election campaign to reduce substantially the amount of federal regulation; he argued that regulation was a primary cause of the decline of productivity in the economy. Reagan established the Task Force on Regulatory Relief, headed by Vice President George Bush, to analyze the economic effects of existing and proposed regulations. This task force prepared the way for the establishment, in the Office of Management and Budget (OMB), of the Office of Information and Regulatory Affairs to review proposed agency regulations, a unit that continued into the twenty-first century. Reagan also mandated by executive order that all major regulations be subjected to cost-benefit analysis, authorizing the OMB director to delay the implementation of regulations and requiring each agency annually to prepare a regulatory program that specified all regulatory actions in progress and those planned for the future. The Reagan administration used OMB procedures to kill or slow regulations, enforced regulations less intensely, and pursued cooperative, rather than confrontational, means to achieve compliance.[7]

President George H. W. Bush did not change the regulatory review process established under Reagan. Like Reagan, Bush involved his vice president, Dan Quayle, in an antiregulation effort, naming him chair of the Council on Competitiveness, which had broad authority to intervene in drafting federal regulations. However, Bush's regulatory policy differed markedly from that of his predecessor. Whereas Reagan implemented a regulatory reform agenda based on his conservative ideology, Bush had no holistic vision for regulatory reform, nor did he continue Reagan's opposition to social regulation—especially occupational safety and environmental protection. Bush gave stronger support to economic regulatory policy, and he appointed moderates to regulatory positions, actions in sharp contrast to Reagan's practice of naming conservative appointees, who were philosophically opposed to regulations.[8]

The Clinton administration abolished the Council on Competitiveness and left most responsibility for regulatory review in OMB, with enhanced guidelines for public access and a shift in substantive emphasis. Whereas Reagan and Bush had required that the benefits of regulations outweigh costs, Clinton "required only that benefits justify costs."[9] Regulatory policy initially was not a major concern of the Clinton administration; it grew in importance as part of the Reinventing Government Initiative headed by Vice President Al Gore. Regulation also became a political issue. Following their takeover of Congress in 1995, the Republicans introduced legislation designed to provide relief from environmental regulation to businesses and individuals.[10] The bills restricted the authority of federal agencies to issue regulations by returning to the Reagan-era justification of proposed rules. The proposals also made it easier for parties likely to be subject to regulations to challenge them before they were issued.[11] Clinton responded by threatening to veto any legislation that greatly relaxed environmental regulation, and he adopted a strong defensive posture regarding efforts to weaken and relax federal regulation generally.

During the early months of his administration, George W. Bush triggered fears among environmentalists, organized labor, and consumer advocacy groups that he would seek to overturn regulations deemed harmful by business. The administration declared a sixty-day delay while it reviewed new rules approved by the departing president during his final days in office. These included rules to lower the level of arsenic in drinking water, ban road construction and limit logging on 60 million acres of federal forests, require higher efficiency for air conditioners, reduce diesel exhaust in the air, and reduce repetitive-motion injuries in the workplace.[12] Some rules were reversed, grabbing the headlines and allowing critics to suggest Bush would favor business interests, but the administration's actions were initially mixed. OMB's regulatory review applied stringent cost-benefit criteria to proposed regulations, but OMB was forced to act with greater moderation and in a less probusiness manner than it had first assumed.[13] But there can be little doubt about the administration's agenda of reduced regulation. OMB has annually solicited suggestions about federal regulations that should be revised or rescinded, receiving seventy-one suggestions in 2001 and nearly four times as many in 2002.[14]

In all modern presidential administrations, microeconomic policies have been secondary to macroeconomic policy. Microeconomic policies, such as vigorous antitrust enforcement or support for deregulation, can be used to achieve macroeconomic policy goals and to highlight the theoretical rationale for administration policy. But microeconomic policies cannot replace fiscal and monetary policies as the primary means by which presidents discharge their responsibilities for the health of the nation's economy.

Presidents and the Economy: 1933–2003

The president's role as manager of the economy dates from FDR's New Deal, with its commitment to use the federal government's power to bring about recovery from the Great Depression. Keynesian economics and its prescription of increased government spending to compensate for inadequate private spending for investment and consumption provided a theoretical justification for government intervention. Ultimately, it was not the New Deal reforms or recovery programs that ended the depression but the huge increase in government spending during World War II. All of the nation's unused productive capacity—capital facilities and human resources—were mobilized to achieve victory, and government borrowing financed much of that mobilization.

After the war Congress passed the Employment Act of 1946, committing the government to the maintenance of "maximum employment, production, and purchasing power." This act translated into law the widespread expectation, developed during the Roosevelt administration, that the government would guarantee to the fullest extent possible a prosperous economy. It also made the president primarily responsible for providing economic policy leadership, although it failed to furnish him with many new tools for the task. The Employment Act created the CEA and an accompanying staff to provide professional analysis and advice, and it required the president to report annually to Congress on the condition of the economy and to offer proposals for improving or maintaining its health. Ultimate power over the president's economic proposals, however, remained with Congress.

From the end of World War II until the late 1960s, presidents and Congress fought each other over economic policy. Truman struggled unsuccessfully with Congress over its desire to reduce wartime taxes, but he was somewhat more effective in controlling the inflation that resulted from spending for the Korean War. Eisenhower's conservative policies tended to prevail over the plans of a Democratic Congress to increase domestic spending. The Eisenhower administration was marked by two recessions, in 1954 and 1958, with a period of economic expansion between them. The Kennedy-Johnson administration fully embraced Keynesian theory, and a 1964 income tax cut had the desired effect of expanding the economy and increasing revenues. It was thought that economic forecasting and management of the economy had developed to the point where fine-tuning of unemployment and the inflation rate was possible.[15]

In 1966, however, economic conditions began to change. Vietnam War expenditures rose rapidly, the deficit increased, and President Johnson shifted his focus from economic expansion to economic restraint. Congress resisted Johnson's requests for higher excise taxes, and for political reasons he refrained from asking for income tax increases, fearing that Congress would raise embarrassing questions about the war and its cost on the eve of midterm elections. By the time Johnson had requested additional income taxes and Congress had approved a temporary 10 percent income surtax, the economy had begun a prolonged inflationary period that drastically changed conditions that had been relatively stable since 1946. (The first twenty-five years of the post–World War II period had been characterized by an inflation rate of approximately 3 percent a year, an unemployment variance between 4 percent and 8 percent, and sustained growth in the gross domestic product.)

Presidents since Johnson have had to contend with a changing and frequently intractable economy. Inflation rates crept upward into double digits in the late 1970s and early 1980s before declining; unemployment remained high by postwar standards into the mid-1990s; and the federal budget ran a deficit every year between 1970 and 1997 (see Table 9-1). Underlying these developments have been systemic factors beyond the control of the government: the increased dependence of the economy on foreign sources of raw materials, especially oil; the growing

Table 9-1   Inflation, Unemployment, and Federal Budget Deficits/Surpluses, 1970–2003

	Inflation[a]	Unemployment[b]	Deficit/surplus[c]
1970	5.7%	4.9%	$–2.84
1971	4.4	5.9	–23.03
1972	3.2	5.6	–23.37
1973	6.2	4.9	–14.91
1974	11.0	5.6	–6.14
1975	9.1	8.5	–53.24
1976	5.6	7.7	–73.73
1977	6.5	7.0	–53.66
1978	7.6	6.6	–59.19
1979	11.3	5.8	–40.73
1980	13.5	7.1	–73.84
1981	10.3	7.6	–78.98
1982	6.2	9.7	–127.99
1983	3.2	9.6	–207.82
1984	4.3	7.5	–185.39
1985	3.6	7.2	–212.33
1986	1.9	7.0	–221.25
1987	3.6	6.2	–149.77
1988	4.1	5.5	–155.19
1989	4.8	5.3	–152.48
1990	5.4	5.6	–221.23
1991	4.2	6.8	–269.36
1992	3.0	7.5	–290.40
1993	3.0	6.9	–255.11
1994	2.6	6.1	–203.28
1995	2.8	5.6	–164.01
1996	3.0	5.4	–107.51
1997	2.3	4.9	–21.99
1998	1.6	4.5	+69.19
1999	2.2	4.2	+125.6
2000	3.4	4.0	+236.4
2001	2.8	4.7	+127.3
2002	1.6	5.8	–157.8
2003	2.1[d]	6.1[d]	–401[e]

[a] Percent increase in the consumer price index.

[b] Percent of the civilian noninstitutional population sixteen years of age or over.

[c] In billions of dollars.

[d] Mid-year rates.

[e] Estimated, August 2003.

Sources: For budget deficits: Congressional Budget Office Historical Budget Data, Table 1 (www.cbo. gov/). For data on inflation and unemployment: Department of Labor, Bureau of Labor Statistics, Household Data, Table 1, and History of CPI-U U.S. (www.stats.bls.gov/home.htm).

interdependence of the U.S. economy with those of other industrial democracies; the declining productivity of the U.S. economy in relation to foreign competition; the growth and maturation of domestic social welfare programs based on statutory entitlements; and a commitment to improve the quality of the physical environment even at substantial cost to economic growth and productivity.

Richard Nixon responded to this changing economic environment by consistently pursuing the classical conservative course of reducing federal spending to balance the budget. In addition, he took the extraordinary step, for a conservative Republican, of freezing prices and wages in August 1971. Wage and price controls were imposed by Roosevelt and Truman during World War II and the Korean War, but Nixon has been the only president to adopt them when the nation was not fully mobilized for war. He acted under authority Congress delegated to the president in the Economic Stabilization Act of 1970, which it passed over his strong objections. The wage and price freeze experience during 1971–1973 suggests that peacetime wage and price controls are at best a temporary means of curbing inflation and that they can quickly become a political liability unless their impact is moderated—Nixon did not suffer the political consequences in 1972, but congressional Republicans did.

Upon taking office in August 1974, President Ford assumed that the principal economic problem confronting the United States was inflation, and he pushed to cut federal spending. Instead, economic conditions changed, and Ford spent his last year as president combating a recession that contributed to his electoral defeat in 1976. Ford's successor, Jimmy Carter, fared little better. Carter initiated an antirecession program of increased federal spending and tax cuts to stimulate business investment. The economy responded almost too quickly, and he was confronted with surging inflation rates that reached double digits during his last two years in office.

Perhaps Carter's most important decision affecting the economy was his naming of Paul Volcker as chairman of the Federal Reserve Board in 1979. Volcker's appointment reflected Carter's frustration with Keynesian theory's inability to provide solutions to the problem of stagflation, a combination of a stagnant economy and rising prices. Essentially a monetarist, Volcker moved quickly to curb inflation by restraining the growth of the money supply, the first time monetarism had a prominent role in macroeconomic policymaking.

The rate of inflation did not respond quickly to Volcker's efforts to tighten the money supply, but interest rates on consumer loans rose sharply, undoubtedly contributing to Carter's defeat by Ronald Reagan in the 1980 election. One of Reagan's campaign pledges had been to restore vitality to the economy through a revolutionary program of major reductions in taxes and spending. Congress responded positively to Reagan's initiatives in 1981 by enacting the largest income tax cut in U.S. history and by reducing domestic spending in nonentitlement programs. Congress also supported Reagan's proposals for a major defense buildup, projected over five years, from 1981 through 1986.

The results of the Reagan administration's macroeconomic policies were mixed. The Fed can claim credit for curtailing inflation, which fluctuated between annual rates of 1.9 and 4.3 percent from 1983 through 1988. The economy also began a sustained period of growth that lasted from 1983 through 1990. Before that growth spurt, however, the United States experienced the most severe recession since World War II, with unemployment rising to 10.75 percent in the fourth quarter of 1982. In spite of the prosperity achieved after 1982, unemployment did not drop below 5 percent until fifteen years later.

On the negative side, the Reagan administration's macroeconomic policies produced massive federal budget deficits. The deficits grew rapidly through a conjunction of forces: the recession of 1982 caused revenues to fall and triggered automatic countercyclical spending (such as unemployment compensation); the tax cuts and increased defense spending authorized in 1981 became effective, reducing revenues and increasing some expenditures. The result was a large structural, or permanent, deficit as the increases in federal revenues promised by supply-side advocates failed to materialize and Congress refused to provide sizable additional cuts in nondefense spending. Finally, interest payments rose quickly to pay for government borrowing needed to close the gap between spending and revenues. From $990 billion in 1980, the debt rose to $3.1 trillion ten years later.[16]

Although the deficits proved embarrassing to President Reagan because they violated traditional conservative values of fiscal restraint, they also brought political advantage to the administration. The unprecedented deficit spending put money in the pockets of American consumers, creating additional demand that in turn stimulated the economy and served as the basis for the sustained recovery from the 1981–1982 recession. That recovery was crucial to Reagan's 1984 reelection victory, for voters concluded that his economic policies had worked quite well. The deficits also provided Reagan with an effective argument for restraining the growth of nondefense spending.

George H. W. Bush's victory in the 1988 presidential election was an endorsement of the status quo. The country was prosperous and not at war. The only economic policy mandate Bush received derived from his pledge that there would be "no new taxes." He kept this promise until October 1990, when he faced the prospect of an enormous deficit that would trigger automatic budget cuts. His administration negotiated a budget deal with Congress that would balance the budget by 1996, a goal overwhelmed by unanticipated expenditures for the Persian Gulf War and the costs of bailing out failed savings and loan institutions insured by the federal government.[17] The deficits for fiscal 1991 ($269.36 billion) and 1992 ($290.40 billion) were the highest to that point in U.S. history. The recession that began in late 1990 and continued into 1992 meant Congress could not cut spending or raise taxes, thus impeding administration and congressional efforts to curb the deficit.

The 1992 election gave a clear indication of voter dissatisfaction with the condition of the economy, but it produced no general agreement on economic policies. Bill Clinton lacked a clear electoral mandate—he received only 43.3 percent of the vote—and he had failed to provide concrete proposals for deficit reduction out of fear of antagonizing the voters. "While concerned about ending deficits, the voters [were] even more concerned with preventing the spending cuts and tax increases necessary to accomplish that goal."[18] During the campaign, Clinton promised an economic stimulus package and a middle-class tax cut; deficit reduction was a distant concern. This plan began to change on December 3, 1992, during his first meeting with Fed chair Alan Greenspan, who argued that the key to prosperity was convincing Wall Street that the new administration was committed to reducing the budget deficit.[19]

President Clinton moved quickly to address economic problems. His economic program, unveiled on February 17, 1993, contained three parts: deficit reduction; long-term investments in research, education and training, and physical infrastructure; and short-term spending to stimulate the economy. By a single vote in each chamber, Congress passed legislation (called a reconciliation bill) that reduced the deficit by $496 billion over five years, mainly through tax increases on the wealthy. However, the investment spending proposals were severely reduced or deferred, and a Senate filibuster mounted by Republicans killed the stimulus package. Economic conditions improved quickly under Clinton but not fast enough to avoid devastating losses in the 1994 congressional midterm elections. Unemployment dropped, inflation was moderate, and the economy grew at a healthy annual rate.[20] As a result of the 1993 deficit reduction package and a stronger than anticipated economic performance, the budget deficit fell from nearly $300 billion in 1992 to just over $108 billion by 1996[21] and turned the corner with a modest surplus in 1998. This goal was reached in just one year, five years earlier than anticipated in the 1997 budget agreement between Clinton and congressional Republicans.[22]

Evaluated in terms of conventional indicators, Clinton's economic policies succeeded, but he received delayed political rewards. In the 1994 congressional elections, regarded as a referendum on Clinton's overall performance, the voters handed the Democratic Party a stunning defeat as the Republicans gained control over Congress for the first time in forty years. No Republican legislator had voted for the economic package, and the Democrats were branded as the party of high taxes. During the 1996 election and by the end of Clinton's term, however, his contributions to national prosperity seemed to underlay his reelection and the strong public support he received even in the midst of the impeachment controversy. (See chapter 5.)

Ultimately, "Clinton's fiscal policy served as a laboratory for a change in economic thought." Rather than relying on government deficits to stimulate economic activity, Clinton sought "balanced budgets—or better yet, surpluses— [which] are believed to hold down interest rates, free capital for the private sector and reassure investors about long-term economic stability."[23] Thus the conventional Keynesian strategy for pursuing an expansionary fiscal policy was turned on its head. Ironically, this challenge to traditional economic thinking may have laid the groundwork for George W. Bush's initial legislative victories on economic policy.

Approval of a massive tax cut at the outset of the Bush administration reversed a key feature of the Clinton legacy—budget surpluses large enough to pay off the accumulated national debt and maintain solvency for the big-ticket programs of Social Security and Medicare. Clinton had been almost too successful. When estimates of future surpluses grew to $5.6 trillion over ten years, Democrats' arguments against "giving the people their money back" (Bush's central argument) were undermined.[24] This debate occurred before 9/11, when new pressures arose to increase spending for defense and homeland security. As the economy lagged in the face of economic dislocation and consumer uncertainty, government revenues fell even further and the deficit mounted. From a surplus of $127 billion in FY01, the federal budget returned to deficits in FY02 at $158 billion and a projected $455 billion in FY03, an all-time record that will exceed the previous high of $290 billion registered in 1992 under Bush's father. Nor are projections for the future any rosier; in July 2003, the White House projected a deficit in FY04 of $475 billion, without including the costs of occupying Iraq, and deficits were expected to remain above $200 billion through FY08.[25]

What caused this erosion in federal finances, and what were its implications? Bush's OMB director, Joshua Bolten, "attributed 53 percent to the economic downturn, 24 percent to war, homeland security and other new programs, and 23 percent to the three successive tax cuts enacted since 2001."[26] Bolten also argued that the tax cuts, by spurring economic growth, would help solve the deficit problem. Not surprisingly, others, including Democrats, disagreed, stressing the short-sightedness of massive tax cuts that produced lost revenue and growing interest payments. The Center on Budget and Policy Priorities projected substantially higher deficits than the administration, saw them extending well into the future, and primarily attributed them to Bush policies. They argued that when one assesses policies enacted since 2001, "tax cuts will account for the majority of the deterioration in the budget caused by actions taken by policymakers."[27] Others questioned whether the real purpose of the 2003 tax cuts was to stimulate the economy. If so, why would Bush have waited so long to launch a stimulus program, and why were the cuts not designed to provide maximum stimulus? Instead of proposing rebates for lower-income persons, who tend to spend the extra money, benefits went primarily to more affluent taxpayers, who tend to save it.[28]

Just as controversial are the likely consequences of structural budget deficits. Those concerned with rising national debt point to the sudden reversal. "It took the federal government 28 years (1970–98) to produce a surplus, but only 4 years to return to deficit."[29] "A policy of endlessly rising deficits . . . constitutes an explicit decision by today's adults to collectively shift the current cost of government from themselves to their children and grandchildren."[30] The national debt ceiling—the limit to which the Treasury is authorized to borrow—was quietly raised on the day after approval of the 2003 tax cuts to $7.384 trillion to accommodate deficit spending accumulating at the rate of more than $1.5 billion a day.[31] Other critics point to the Bush administration's failure to address the looming costs of financing Social Security and Medicare expenses for the baby boom generation, the first of whom will be eligible for early retirement and partial benefits in 2008 and full-benefits with Medicare in 2011. As one study concludes, "[A] significant opportunity to pre-fund future retirement and health benefits was missed."[32]

These arguments echo those heard in Washington from 1986 through 1996, when Congress and successive presidents struggled to bring runaway deficits under control. Has the Bush administration merely miscalculated and been beset by bad luck, or is this a premeditated strategy to reverse the growth of government? Allen Schick argues for the second interpretation.

This is a president whose eyes are wide open to the short and long-term fiscal and policy implications of the revenue losses he has imposed on the federal government. . . . He sees revenue privation as the only or best weapon to change the course of budgetary history. . . . Bush firmly believes that only a vastly larger, perhaps unmanageable deficit can curb the relentless expansion of government.[33]

When government becomes depleted of resources, Congress will realize that spending must be curbed and programs cut.

Without ascribing such dire motives to the president, it is easy to predict that economic and budget policy will prove to be enormously controversial in the near future. Bush's commitment to tax reduction is much like Reagan's; unlike Reagan, Bush has a Congress whose majority is unified in support. Even a Republican Congress, however, is less likely to support the spending cuts and radical program redesigns required to restore a balanced budget. Thus it is likely that Bush will have to contend with these issues throughout his term in office, whether four or eight years, and will leave a legacy to his successor much like that bequeathed to Reagan's.

The Politics of Macroeconomic Policymaking

Presidents do not make macroeconomic policy in a vacuum solely according to economic theories. Their decisions in this crucial area are intensely political and are affected by consideration of other policy goals (including microeconomic policy), electoral politics, interest group politics, and bureaucratic politics among institutional participants in the policy-making process. In a very real sense, the United States has a political economy, and the nation is an economic polity. The president is the focal point of the relationships involved in both entities.

Policy Politics

The achievement of macroeconomic policy goals is affected by, and has an effect on, other policy goals. National security policy objectives, for example, often have a profound impact on economic policy. In the 1980s, substantial increases in defense spending beginning in fiscal year 1982 reflected the consensus that U.S. military strength had declined compared with that of the Soviet Union. These increases, however, hindered efforts to balance the budget. The end of the cold war between the United States and the Soviet Union, in late 1991, precipitated a budget struggle over the disposition of the "peace dividend" congressional Democrats believed should result from the reduction of tensions. In the October 1990 budget agreement between President Bush and Congress, any reductions in either defense or discretionary domestic spending were to be devoted to reducing the deficit.

Over the same period, budget-balancing efforts in domestic programs conflicted with commitments made to Social Security beneficiaries, welfare recipients, retired federal employees, and numerous other groups served by federal programs. In addition, the macroeconomic goals of economic growth, increased productivity, and full employment often appeared to be at odds with regulatory policies designed to improve environmental quality, enhance occupational safety and health, increase the safety of automobiles and other consumer products, and protect consumers against a variety of unfair business practices. Fiscal policy frequently served as the arena for resolving such trade-offs.

Electoral Politics

Macroeconomic policy has important implications for electoral politics. It has long been recognized that presidential administrations and congressional majorities manipulate fiscal policy to produce short-term improvements in economic conditions to enhance their party's election prospects. They may adjust the timing and location of benefits to achieve this end, making policies that amount to marginal adjustments rather than fundamental restructuring of the economic system.

Presidents do not automatically avoid hard political choices and cave in to election pressures from party and special constituencies.[34] Ronald Reagan remained firm throughout his presidency in his commitment to the 1981 income tax cut based on supply-side theory, even though it meant proposing and defending record peacetime budget deficits (of around $200 billion) that were anathema to his conservative supporters. Reagan's immediate successor, George Bush, reluctantly agreed to tax increases of $146 billion as part of a five-year, $496 billion deficit reduction package. (Opponents attacked him for breaking that pledge in the 1992 election campaign, and he expressed regret at having done so.) In response to congressional pressures from Republicans and conservative Democrats and to advice from his economic advisers, Bill Clinton abandoned his campaign promise of a tax cut for the middle class and settled for half of the major investments in human resources and infrastructure that were key elements in his proposed 1993 economic program. His final package included deficit reduction achieved through $240 billion in tax increases and $246 billion in spending cuts, both of which had significant political implications.[35] During his first two-and-a-half years in office, George W. Bush saw 2.5 million jobs disappear during a sluggish recovery. To counter charges that he had ignored problems at home to address those abroad, the president accepted a tax cut in 2003 that was less than half his original proposal and failed to include several important policy changes (such as eliminating double taxation of dividends), calculating that it was the best he could achieve.[36]

Interest Group Politics

In making economic policy, presidents and Congress also are subjected to pressures from several important interest groups, including business, labor, agriculture, the financial community, state and local governments, and foreign governments. The effect of these interests on policy varies according to the issues and the current economic conditions at home and abroad.

Business and labor interests are the most organized and thoroughly entrenched. Businesses use umbrella organizations, such as the Chamber of Commerce of the United States and the National Association of Manufacturers, to exert influence, as well as industry-based trade associations such as the Automobile Manufacturers Association and the American Gas Association. Individual companies, especially large corporations, also try to shape policy. Businesses usually concentrate their lobbying on microeconomic policies that specifically affect their operations but may also be concerned about inflation, tax burdens, and interest rates, areas of macroeconomic policy. Organized labor encompasses the giant AFL-CIO (American Federation of Labor and Congress of Industrial Organizations) and a host of independent unions. Its position on macroeconomic policy issues usually contrasts sharply with that of business. Labor, much more worried about unemployment than inflation, supports fiscal stimulation of the economy in periods of recession and opposes the use of monetary restraints to curb inflation. Like business, labor takes great interest in microeconomic policy directly affecting its interests, including regulation of labor-management relations and regulations in behalf of occupational safety and health.

Agricultural interest groups, though shrinking in membership, remain quite diverse. The American Farm Bureau Federation and the National Grange support conservative policies, while the National Farmers Union and the National Farmers Organization take much more liberal stances. Regardless of their ideologies, farm organizations tend to oppose monetary policies that result in high interest rates because the use of credit is an essential feature of farm management.

The financial community consists of two principal components, the securities exchanges, or Wall Street, and banks and other financial institutions. (Wall Street and financial institutions buy and sell "paper"—government and private financial obligations—and bonds, the longer-term securities.) Wall Street registers its reactions to monetary and fiscal policies—investor confidence—through the prices of corporate stocks traded on the major stock exchanges. Bond prices move upward or downward inversely with interest rates and thus reflect monetary policy shifts; interest paid on short-term government and commercial paper also fluctuates as monetary policy changes. Administrations seek to have their policies favorably received by Wall Street and by major banks and other leading financial institutions. A vote of "no confidence" by the financial community in the government's economic policies makes the administration vulnerable to criticism by political opponents and weakens its popular support. As in the broader business world, members of the financial community tend to support conservative fiscal policies and monetary restraint to control inflation. They fear large deficits, whether due to high spending levels or sizable tax cuts.

With the advent of the Great Society domestic programs in the mid-1960s, state and local governments became vitally interested in macroeconomic policy. The federal government is a source of funding for a wide range of state and local programs in areas such as education, welfare and social services, housing and urban development, transportation, and health care. Consequently, many state and local governments, collectively—through national associations, such as the U.S. Conference of Mayors—and individually—through the efforts of members of Congress—have exerted pressure to maintain the flow of federal funds, even though this goal could be accomplished only at the expense of larger and potentially inflationary budget deficits.

Presidents Reagan and Bush sought a major reordering of federal fiscal responsibilities, hoping to reduce state and local dependence on federal funding. This effort failed to accomplish its most revolutionary goals, but it triggered a rethinking of federal aid and its implications for macroeconomic policy.[37] In the face of mounting budget deficits in 1993 and 1994, Republicans and conservative Democrats opposed Clinton's infrastructure spending, which they viewed as more appropriate for state and local governments to fund. Conservatives also demanded that financial responsibility for major redistributive programs be shifted to the states. In 1995 the Republican majority in Congress proposed ending entitlement status for welfare (Aid to Families with Dependent Children) and Medicaid by converting federally funded programs—accompanied by extensive federal rules and regulations—to programs giving block grants to states. States would be freed from most federal controls, but funding would be fixed and would not increase as demands for services expanded. Initially, Clinton opposed these changes by vetoing two Republican versions, but in 1996 he compromised with the Republicans. Much to the dismay of many Democrats, welfare (but not Medicaid) lost its entitlement status and became a block grant program.[38] President George W. Bush has proposed changes in Medicaid that would largely accomplish the Republicans' 1995 goal.

Presidents and their administrations are constrained to some degree by the effect of economic policy decisions on the economies of other countries. Foreign governments have an intense interest in U.S. macroeconomic policy. Friendly governments—the European Community, Japan, and Saudi Arabia—favor a dollar that is neither overvalued nor undervalued and a healthy U.S. economy with full employment and a low inflation rate. If the dollar is weak, the value of much of their international currency reserves declines, and their goods are less competitive in U.S. markets, a problem that arose during 2002–2003. If the dollar is too strong, their investment capital migrates to the United States, and the high competitiveness of their products in U.S. markets threatens to provoke trade restrictions. When unemployment in the United States rises, the major market for their goods contracts. When interest rates are higher in the United States than in Europe or Japan, investment capital moves to the United States. Consequently, foreign governments press U.S. administrations to keep the exchange value of the dollar from fluctuating widely and to hold down interest rates.

Presidents do not respond to all interest group constituencies, and the constituencies whose support they do seek vary in importance to them. In no case, however, do presidents make macroeconomic policy decisions without regard to some interest groups, which are major features in the politics of economic policymaking.

The Economic Subpresidency

In discharging the role of economic manager, chief executives seek to meet popular and elite expectations that their actions will result in a prosperous economy. Presidents must develop and implement policies and build support for them in the public and in the Washington community. To accomplish these complex and demanding tasks, presidents need information, advice, and administrative assistance to focus energy on major issues, integrate the policies of their administrations, take account of all-important interests, and maintain the administration's cohesion. This advice and assistance is provided by a set of specialized organizations located in the presidency and in the executive branch, organizations that have been called "the economic subpresidency." All those engaged in making, defining, communicating, and implementing economic policy decisions, "whether they act personally or as part of an institution," are part of this policy-making system.[39] How presidents use the economic subpresidency varies across administrations and with economic conditions, but this system is central to policymaking and presidential management of the economy. Staff members serve in one of four major administrative units—the CEA, OMB, the Treasury Department, or the Fed—or on various intragovernmental committees and councils. Leading members of these units over the past five decades are listed in Tables 9-2 through 9-5.

The Council of Economic Advisers

The Council of Economic Advisers has three members, appointed by the president and subject to Senate confirmation, plus a small staff of approximately thirty-five, divided evenly between professional economists and support personnel. Traditionally, most CEA members and professional staffers have had extensive experience in business or government. The CEA's chair (see Table 9-2) is responsible for administering the council, hiring staff, representing the CEA on other government councils and committees, and reporting to the president. He or she establishes the council's orientation according to the president's overall objectives. The chair's relationship with the president largely determines the CEA's influence in shaping economic policy.

The CEA has no operational responsibility but serves entirely in a staff capacity. It gathers information, makes economic forecasts, analyzes economic issues, and prepares the annual *Economic Report of the President,* presented to Congress. It provides the president with expert economic advice, and members occasionally act as public spokespersons for the president. The council usually has not brokered agreements among conflicting parties or coordinated policymaking within the administration, although its members tend to reflect the theories and policy

Table 9-2   Chairs of the Council of Economic
Advisers, 1953–2003

President	Chair	Years
Eisenhower	Arthur F. Burns	1953–1956
	Raymond T. Saulnier	1956–1961
Kennedy	Walter W. Heller	1961–1963
Johnson	Walter W. Heller	1963–1964
	Gardner H. Ackley	1964–1968
	Arthur M. Okun	1968–1969
Nixon	Paul W. McCracken	1969–1971
	Herbert Stein	1972–1974
Ford	Herbert Stein	1974
	Alan Greenspan	1974–1977
Carter	Charles L. Schultze	1977–1981
Reagan	Murray L. Weidenbaum	1981–1982
	Martin Feldstein	1982–1984
	Beryl Sprinkel	1985–1989
G. Bush	Michael J. Boskin	1989–1993
Clinton	Laura D. Tyson	1993–1994
	Joseph E. Stiglitz	1995–1997
	Janet L. Yellen	1997–1999
	Martin Baily	1999–2001
G. W. Bush	R. Glenn Hubbard	2001–2003
	N. Gregory Mankiw	2003–

Source: www.whitehouse.gov/cea.

views of the president. In general, Democratic presidents have had Keynesian CEA members, and Republicans have selected classical conservative and monetarist economists. Reagan, for example, appointed a conservative economist to chair the CEA at the start of his presidency and added a monetarist and a supply-sider. All three were committed to free trade, reduced government spending, a balanced federal budget, and limited federal intervention in the economy.

If presidents believe they need economic expertise and share basic interests and values with CEA members, the council may play an important role in economic policymaking. The council's expertise enhances presidential policies, and its analyses and forecasts acquire political significance through association with the presidency. However, the council can do only what the president asks and allows it to do.

Under the first President Bush, the CEA played a more significant role with respect to the deficit than it had under Reagan. Its chair, the monetarist economist Michael J. Boskin (1989–1993), enjoyed the president's confidence and often acted as a spokesperson for the administration. President Clinton appointed Laura D'Andrea Tyson (1993–1994) of Stanford University, who was an expert on trade policy and not a professional macroeconomist, to chair his CEA. When Tyson became chair of another White House coordinating unit—the National Economic Council—in 1995, three others succeeded her as CEA chair: Joseph E. Stiglitz (1995–1997), Janet L. Yellen (1997–1999), and Martin Baily

(1999–2001). The rapid turnover is one indicator that the CEA may not have played an important role in Clinton policymaking.

The council's forecasts help set the boundaries of the president's legislative program and budget proposals. It is to the president's advantage for the council to approach its advisory task deductively, fitting program pieces together within the framework of his overall objectives. The council's contribution to policymaking is primarily conceptual and not in the realm of implementation or coordination. This is the reality that confronted George W. Bush's first CEA chair, R. Glenn Hubbard (2001–2003), a professor of economics and business at Columbia University, who had served in the Treasury Department under President Bush's father and was a major architect of the administration's 2003 tax cut proposals.[40] He was succeeded by N. Gregory Mankiw, a Harvard economist who had worked with the council for a brief time during the Reagan administration and was expected to keep a low profile.[41]

The Office of Management and Budget

Presidents receive economic advice of a different sort from the roughly five hundred employees in the Office of Management and Budget. Whereas the CEA's primary concern is controlling the business cycle and achieving sustained economic growth, OMB's major focus is allocating resources to federal administrative agencies and their programs through the annual preparation of the president's budget. Its institutional bias is toward holding down spending. It is the principal instrument through which the president fashions the expenditure component of fiscal policy. In addition, OMB provides economic forecasts to the president and acts as a "legislative and regulatory gatekeeper" by conducting detailed policy analysis of proposed bills and agency rules.[42]

The Office of Management and Budget was originally a presidential staff agency (known as the Bureau of the Budget) comprising an elite group of government careerists devoted to serving the presidency, whoever the particular president might be. Since Nixon reorganized it in 1970, OMB has been more actively involved in serving the president's political needs. Beginning in the Nixon administration, OMB directors (see Table 9-3) have participated in developing presidential policies and building support for them. The budget has become as much a political weapon as a managerial tool or an instrument of fiscal policy.

The politicization of OMB and the political use of the budget were never more apparent than during the Reagan administration and David Stockman's tenure as budget director (1981–1986). Stockman dominated federal budgeting in a manner previously unknown. He centralized the executive budget process in OMB and involved himself extensively in the congressional budget proceedings through direct negotiations and bargaining with congressional committees.

Under Stockman's successor, the economist James C. Miller III (1986–1988), OMB continued to serve Reagan's political interests but much less visibly. During the first Bush presidency, OMB was a major player in the economic subpresidency.

Table 9-3   Directors of the Budget Bureau/Office of
Management and Budget, 1953–2003

President	Director	Years
Eisenhower	Joseph M. Dodge	1953–1954
	Rowland R. Hughes	1954–1956
	Percival F. Brundage	1956–1958
	Maurice Stans	1958–1961
Kennedy	David E. Bell	1961–1962
	Kermit Gordon	1962–1963
Johnson	Kermit Gordon	1963–1965
	Charles E. Schultze	1965–1968
	Charles J. Zwick	1968–1969
Nixon	Robert P. Mayo	1969–1970
	George P. Shultz	1971–1972
	Casper Weinberger	1972–1973
	Roy L. Ash	1973–1974
Ford	Roy L. Ash	1974–1975
	James P. Lynn	1975–1976
Carter	Bert Lance	1977
	James T. McIntyre	1978–1981
Reagan	David Stockman	1981–1986
	James C. Miller III	1986–1988
G. Bush	Richard G. Darman	1989–1993
Clinton	Leon E. Panetta	1993–1994
	Alice Rivlin	1994–1996
	Franklin D. Raines	1996–1998
	Jacob J. Lew	1998–2001
G. W. Bush	Mitchell E. Daniels Jr.	2001–2003
	Joshua B. Bolten	2003–

Sources: John H. Kessel, *Presidents, the Presidency, and the
Political Environment* (Washington, D.C.: CQ Press, 2001), chap.5;
"The Decision Makers," *National Journal*, June 23, 2001; and www.
whitehouse.gov/omb

Its director, Richard G. Darman (1989–1993), and the White House chief of staff,
John Sununu, were the principal negotiators with Congress concerning fiscal
policy. (Darman dealt primarily with spending, and Sununu with taxes.) OMB
also became the dominant agency for economic forecasting.

The budget remained the main instrument for achieving the president's policy goals during the Clinton administration. Clinton named Leon E. Panetta
(1993–1994), chair of the House Budget Committee, as his first OMB director.
Panetta was a "deficit hawk" (a strong advocate for deficit reduction) and a
Democratic loyalist who possessed parliamentary acumen and budgetary expertise.[43] He played an important role in shaping Clinton's 1993 economic plan and
selling it to Congress. When Panetta became Clinton's chief of staff in June 1994,
the economist Alice Rivlin (1994–1996) became OMB's director. Rivlin had
served previously as director of the Congressional Budget Office and was even
more hawkish on the deficit than Panetta. Their presence "ensured that deficit
reduction would command considerable attention" as the administration shaped
economic policy.[44] Rivlin was succeeded by Franklin D. Raines (1996–1998) and

Jacob J. Lew (1998–2001). George W. Bush chose as OMB director Mitchell E. Daniels Jr. (2001–2003), a lawyer with political experience on Capitol Hill and in the Reagan White House but not in budget-related positions.[45] Joshua B. Bolten, a lawyer and investment banker, was named as Daniels's successor in May 2003. He brought to the position Capitol Hill and previous White House experience in the first Bush administration. He impressed the president as policy director for the Bush-Cheney campaign in 2000 and as White House deputy chief of staff for policy during Bush's first two years in office.[46]

The Treasury Department

The third institutional participant in the economic subpresidency is the Treasury Department, which is responsible for collecting taxes, managing the national debt, controlling the currency, collecting customs, and handling international monetary affairs, including management of the balance of payments and the value of the dollar in relation to other currencies. With more than 115,000 employees, it is the primary government source of information on revenues, the tax system, and financial markets. It also takes the lead in developing tax bills and steering them through Congress.[47]

Traditionally, the Treasury Department has been concerned about the adequacy of revenues, the soundness of the dollar, and the cost of financing the debt. To finance the debt, the department has advocated either low interest rates or a balanced budget. Before the Reagan administration, a situation in which high interest rates accompanied a large deficit was anathema to the institutional interests of the Treasury. Its position altered substantially under President Reagan and Donald T. Regan (1981–1985), secretary of the Treasury during Reagan's first term (see Table 9-4). An avowed believer in supply-side economics, Regan argued that temporary deficits resulting from tax-cut incentives would lead ultimately to economic growth, expanded revenues, and balanced budgets. He opposed efforts to reduce the deficit by raising taxes. He was much more concerned with the supply of money in the domestic economy than with the exchange value of the dollar. Regan's successor as secretary, James A. Baker III (1985–1988), concentrated heavily on exchange rate problems.

Secretary of the Treasury Nicholas F. Brady played a marginal role in the economic subpresidency under President George H. W. Bush. One veteran White House observer and analyst suggests that the "patrician" Brady was no match for the "pit bull approach of his two economic policy colleagues," Darman and Sununu.[48]

President Clinton's first two secretaries of the Treasury, Lloyd M. Bentsen (1993–1994) and Robert E. Rubin (1995–1999), were central participants in the economic subpresidency. By appointing Bentsen, a moderate Democrat with business experience who chaired the Senate Finance Committee, Clinton sought to reassure the business community.[49] The appointment of Rubin, a Wall Street investment banker who had served in the Clinton administration as chair of the National Economic Council (see discussion later in the chapter), accomplished a

Table 9-4   Secretaries of the Treasury, 1953–2003

President	Secretary	Years
Eisenhower	George M. Humphrey	1953–1957
	Robert Anderson	1957–1961
Kennedy	C. Douglas Dillon	1961–1963
Johnson	C. Douglas Dillon	1964–1965
	Henry H. Fowler	1965–1968
	Joseph W. Barr	1968–1969
Nixon	David M. Kennedy	1969–1971
	John B. Connally	1971–1972
	George P. Shultz	1972–1974
	William E. Simon	1974
Ford	William E. Simon	1974–1977
Carter	W. Michael Blumenthal	1977–1979
	G. William Miller	1979–1981
Reagan	Donald T. Regan	1981–1985
	James A. Baker III	1985–1988
	Nicholas F. Brady	1988–1989
G. Bush	Nicholas F. Brady	1989–1993
Clinton	Lloyd M. Bentsen	1993–1994
	Robert E. Rubin	1995–1999
	Lawrence H. Summers	1999–2001
G. W. Bush	Paul H. O'Neill	2001–2002
	John W. Snow	2003–

Sources: John H. Kessel, *Presidents, the Presidency, and the Political Environment* (Washington, D.C.: CQ Press, 2001), chap. 5; "The Decision Makers," *National Journal*, June 23, 2001; and www.ustreas.gov.

similar purpose. Both men were deeply involved in shaping the 1993 economic program.[50] Lawrence H. Summers, a Rubin protégé as deputy secretary, served as secretary from 1999 to 2001. George W. Bush selected Paul H. O'Neill (2001–2002) as Treasury secretary, a ten-year veteran of OMB who later worked for International Paper before becoming CEO of Alcoa Aluminum.[51] But O'Neill proved to be an outspoken cabinet secretary whose comments sometimes questioned the administration's tax-cutting policies (he was not a supply-sider), frequently irked influential members of Congress, failed to calm investors in 2002 during the corporate scandals, and even upset international currency markets.[52] In short, he proved ineffective in the job and was the first member of the Bush cabinet to leave his position, replaced in January 2003 by John W. Snow. Snow had been CEO of CSX Corporation, a railroad freight company, and chairman of the Business Roundtable, an elite corporate lobbying group. Snow accumulated Washington experience in the Nixon and Ford administrations, holds a Ph.D. in economics as well as a law degree, and has had extensive exposure to public policy matters.[53]

Organizationally, the Treasury Department is divided between large units with major line responsibilities, such as the Internal Revenue Service, and policy-related units, such as the office of the undersecretary for monetary affairs. The policy-related units, located in the office of the secretary, never have provided coordination of economic policy for an administration, although the potential exists for them to do so.[54] About 20 percent of the department's workforce, including Secret Service, the Customs Service, and much of the Bureau of Alcohol, Tobacco, and Firearms, was shifted to the new Department of Homeland Security.

The Federal Reserve Board

The Federal Reserve Board is an independent agency charged with responsibility for regulating the money supply and the banking system. Its seven members are appointed by the president to fourteen-year terms with the consent of the Senate. The president designates one member of the board to act as its chair for a four-year term, but the chair, an important source of institutional influence, often serves beyond that limit, as shown in Table 9-5. The Fed has three ways of controlling the money supply: the discount rate, reserve requirements, and open-market operations, the buying and selling of government securities that set the federal funds rate.

The discount rate is the interest rate charged commercial banks to borrow from the Federal Reserve. An increase in the discount rate tightens the availability of credit because it forces banks to charge more to their borrowers. Reserves are liquid assets banks hold to meet demands for ready cash from their depositors. The Federal Reserve requires commercial banks belonging to it to maintain a certain percentage (usually ranging from 10 to 20 percent) of their deposit liabilities in the form of cash in their vaults or on account with the regional reserve bank for this purpose. A reduction in the reserve requirement increases the amount of money banks may loan to their borrowers, whereas an increase in the reserve requirement decreases the availability of bank credit.

Most recently, attention has centered on the thirteen consecutive reductions in the federal funds rate enacted by the Federal Open Market Committee (FOMC) since January 2001. From a level of 6.5 percent, on January 1, 2001, the rate was progressively reduced to 1 percent, on June 25, 2003, producing the lowest consumer interest rates since 1958. These policy decisions were designed to encourage economic expansion. Unemployment had risen from an annual average of 4.0 percent in 2000 to 4.7 percent in 2001 and 5.8 percent in 2002; it then hit 6.4 percent in June 2003. In 1995, the FOMC began releasing explicit statements of its short-term policy objectives[55] and now issues a statement after each of its meetings, not just those in which a rate change has been approved. Since March 2002 it has also reported the positions of its twelve voting members, the seven members of the Federal Reserve Board and five of the twelve Federal Reserve Bank presidents.

Although neither the president nor Congress can tell the Fed how to conduct monetary policy, the board traditionally has been the target of political pressures, especially during adverse economic conditions. Depending on circumstances, the inflation resulting from expansionary monetary policy or the stagnation and unemployment caused by restrictive policy can draw fire. During the Clinton

Table 9-5   Chairs of the Federal Reserve Board,
1951–2003

President	Chair	Years
Eisenhower	William McC. Martin	1951–1961
Kennedy	William McC. Martin	1961–1963
Johnson	William McC. Martin	1963–1969
Nixon	William McC. Martin	1969–1970
Nixon	Arthur F. Burns	1970–1974
Ford	Arthur F. Burns	1974–1977
Carter	Arthur F. Burns	1977–1978
Carter	G. William Miller	1978–1979
	Paul A. Volcker	1979–1981
Reagan	Paul A. Volcker	1981–1987
Reagan	Alan Greenspan	1987–1989
G. Bush	Alan Greenspan	1989–1993
Clinton	Alan Greenspan	1993–2001
G. W. Bush	Alan Greenspan	2001–

Sources: John H. Kessel, *Presidents, the Presidency, and the Political Environment* (Washington, D.C.: CQ Press, 2001), chap. 5; and "The Decision Makers," *National Journal*, June 23, 2001.

administration, members of Congress and Wall Street frequently criticized the Fed for raising interest rates at the first sign of inflation and reducing them too slowly, but relations between the president and the Fed chair, Alan Greenspan,[56] were generally cordial. Clinton twice reappointed Greenspan (1996 and 2000) to the post he first assumed in 1987 under Ronald Reagan, and George W. Bush has announced publicly that he expects to reappoint Greenspan when his current term expires on June 20, 2004. Greenspan has been heartily praised. "No aspect of U.S. policy in the 1990s is more widely hailed as a success than monetary policy. Fed Chairman Alan Greenspan is often viewed as a miracle worker."[57]

The strongest clash between the Clinton administration and the Fed occurred in 1994, when Greenspan, with help from the banking industry, torpedoed a Treasury Department proposal to create a Federal Banking Commission that would have consolidated bank regulation in a single agency.[58] The proposal would have combined the responsibilities shared by the Fed, the Treasury Department's Office of the Comptroller of the Currency and its Office of Thrift Supervision, and the independent Federal Deposit Insurance Corporation. Greenspan's relations with George W. Bush have also sometimes been rocky. In February and July 2003, he warned Congress about the impact of ballooning deficits projected to flow from President Bush's latest tax cut proposals. (The Fed chairman had endorsed the 2001 tax cuts.) By stressing the need for budget discipline, he weakened the case for even larger proposed tax cuts.

Presidents and Economic Policy Coordination

The independence of the Fed, the operational needs and organizational interests of the Treasury Department, and the institutional perspectives of other

First appointed Chairman of the Federal Reserve Board by President Reagan in 1987, Alan Greenspan has worked with one Democratic and three Republican presidents, thereby continuing the tradition of long-serving chairs.

departments and agencies have led presidents to seek various ways to coordinate economic policy. For reasons explained in chapter 6, the cabinet has not been a satisfactory vehicle for collective leadership. Instead, presidents have developed a variety of intragovernmental councils and committees designed to provide a cohesive macroeconomic policy and integrate it with other policy objectives. Most of these entities failed to survive the administrations of their creators, for subsequent presidents sought mechanisms more compatible with their own operating styles. However, a brief review of these undertakings reveals common patterns in their approaches and indicates the essential requirements for a minimal amount of coordination.

Probably the most significant development for macroeconomic policymaking occurred under President Kennedy with the creation of the "troika," an informal committee consisting of the chair of the CEA, the secretary of the Treasury, and the director of the budget. The troika's original purpose was to coordinate economic forecasting, but it quickly became a mechanism for developing cooperation within the economic subpresidency in formulating fiscal policy. This arrangement contrasted with President Eisenhower's sharply focused groups, which, although they met often, were too numerous to bring about effective coordination. When joined by the chair of the Fed to coordinate monetary policy, the group has been known as the "quadriad." These participants have a "mutual interest in cooperation, not in their legal independence from each other. For an administration's economic policy to succeed, the Fed should pursue a parallel monetary policy," and vice versa.[59]

Working with staff support from the CEA, the Treasury Department, OMB, and occasionally the Fed, the troika/quadriad has helped many presidents formulate macroeconomic policy in a rapid, adaptive manner with some measure of protection from political and bureaucratic pressures. Not all presidents have made extensive use of the troika, but it is a natural institutional grouping that continues to operate, with the Treasury Department assuming responsibility for revenue estimates, OMB generating estimates of federal expenditures, the CEA forecasting economic trends, and the Fed (when involved) projecting money supply requirements.

Under Lyndon Johnson, the troika operation became regularized, and it emerged as the principal mechanism for the development of fiscal policy advice and alternatives.[60] President Nixon was uncomfortable with attempts to make policy by cabinet-level committees and designated Secretary of the Treasury John B. Connally (1971–1972) in early 1971 as his economic "czar," with responsibility for making major decisions. Connally dominated the troika, but his successor as Treasury secretary, George P. Shultz (1972–1974), operated in a more collegial manner. At the start of his second term, in January 1973, Nixon made Shultz assistant to the president for economic affairs and named him to chair a new cabinet-level coordinating body, the Council on Economic Policy. Shultz, working through interdepartmental committees, became the dominant figure in making and expounding economic policy for the Nixon administration.

Shultz's more inclusive machinery ushered in a series of presidential experiments with coordinating councils, a series of "troika plus" groups. Gerald Ford used the Economic Policy Board (EPB), which operated in a formal and structured way to coordinate domestic and foreign economic policies. The secretary of the Treasury chaired the EPB, which also included the secretaries of labor, commerce, and state, the chair of the CEA, the director of OMB, and the assistant to the president for economic affairs. The latter official also directed the small EPB staff, housed in the Executive Office of the President. Departments and agencies provided information, analysis, and expertise.[61] President Carter replaced the EPB with the Economic Policy Group (EPG), cochaired by the secretary of the Treasury and the chair of the CEA. The EPG was a large, unwieldy body. It had no staff, was accessible to a wide range of interested officials, and was not organized as a formal advisory body to the president. Its operations remained so unstructured that it was unable to coordinate even minor policy initiatives.[62]

President Reagan replaced the Economic Policy Group with the Cabinet Council on Economic Affairs (CCEA). Like its predecessor in the Nixon administration, the CCEA was a forum for discussion of issues and alternatives. Roger Porter, veteran of the Ford EPB, was its secretary and informally coordinated its operations. In addition to the council, the troika met regularly to coordinate economic forecasting. But coordination efforts did not ensure that struggles for influence would disappear. The major participants in these battles were Treasury Secretary Donald Regan, OMB Director David Stockman, and White House assistants James Baker and Edwin Meese. The administration had clearly defined macroeconomic policy goals: to reduce the role of the federal government in the U.S. economy, thus reducing taxes and spending; and to increase productivity, savings, and investment, thus ensuring vigorous and sustained economic growth and full employment. There was, however, sharp disagreement over the means to that end. That conflict reflected competition among classical conservative, monetarist, and supply-side theories and focused on the significance of federal budget deficits. The winners in the conflict were Regan and Meese—the supply-side advocates. Stockman was the principal loser.[63]

Reagan's immediate successor, George Bush, continued the advisory group, renaming it the Economic Policy Council. Porter once again managed its activities, with the help of his staff in the Office of Policy Development, and served as assistant to the president for economic and domestic affairs.[64] However, the council met irregularly and did not establish an effective roundtable process for preparing issues for presidential decisions. Nor did the troika, which fell into disuse during Reagan's second term, reacquire its importance. No single individual or group had responsibility for defining for the economic subpresidency how policies were to be integrated.

Given the high priority President Clinton placed on economic issues during the 1992 campaign, it is not surprising that he was deeply involved in making economic policy. One of his first acts was to establish a National Economic Council (NEC) to coordinate domestic and international economic policies in a way similar to the National Security Council's coordination of foreign and military policymaking.[65] Operating with a professional staff of about twenty, the NEC's first chair, Robert Rubin, established an open, collegial, and nonhierarchical process that incorporated a wide and balanced range of economic considerations into the issue recommendations sent to the president.[66] The NEC's effectiveness became apparent during the 1993 budget battles: cabinet members worked through the budget and refrained from the infighting and leaks that had plagued previous administrations.[67] All was not well, however, because Clinton's economic advisers frequently clashed with his political advisers, who had managed his campaign. These conflicts concerned the primary focus of the administration's economic program and were fought both within the presidency and publicly.[68] The economic advisers stressed the importance of deficit reduction and the impact of policy on financial markets. The political advisers wanted to emphasize the populist issues that had helped to elect Clinton.[69] Rubin emerged as the dominant economic adviser and continued in that role after becoming secretary of the Treasury. His successor at the NEC, Laura Tyson, was unable to parlay coordination into influence; Gene Sperling, the next director, proved more successful.[70]

President George W. Bush's initial director of the NEC, Lawrence Lindsey, brought an especially rich foundation of personal experience to the position. A former member of the Federal Reserve System's Board of Governors, Lindsey served on the CEA's staff under Reagan and became a staunch defender of supply-side tax cuts; he also was a special White House assistant in the administration of George H. W. Bush. As the younger Bush's economic adviser during the 2000 presidential election and the architect of his tax-cut plan, Lindsey entered the White House amid widespread expectations that he would enjoy the president's confidence, though this became an issue during his two years of service.[71] Lindsey resigned his post in December 2002 at the same time Secretary of the Treasury O'Neill did his, a major shakeup in the administration's economic team that attracted much media attention.[72] Lindsey was succeeded in the White House by Stephen Friedman, a longtime partner in the Wall Street investment firm of Goldman Sachs, with extensive experience in public service.[73]

As in other areas of policy, the nation is heavily dependent on presidents' attitudes, values, and operating styles for economic leadership. Congressionally established advisory mechanisms, such as the CEA, are helpful, and presidents can take other measures to assist them in identifying issues and achieving policy coordination; but advisory staffs and coordinating mechanisms provide no guarantee that the president will adopt effective policies or achieve his objectives. There is also an important check on presidential economic policymaking—Congress's power over taxing, spending, and the monetary system.

The Congressional Role in Macroeconomic Policy

Most of the executive branch agencies and processes involving macroeconomic policy and the president's economic role were established by statute: the Federal Reserve Act of 1914, the Budget and Accounting Act of 1921, and the Employment Act of 1946. Traditionally, Congress has dealt with economic policy through separate consideration of tax legislation and annual appropriations. Tax bills have entailed redistributive issues—that is, questions of who bears the burdens and which special interests will secure favorable provisions, or "loopholes." The congressional tax-writing committees (House Ways and Means and Senate Finance) have jealously guarded their powers and have been unwilling to propose new tax legislation that does not accommodate special interests. Appropriations decision making, centered in the House and Senate Appropriations Committees, traditionally focuses on incremental changes in department and agency budget requests. The politics of the budget process is a highly stylized game in which the institutional participants play specific roles. The primary consideration in Congress is the amount of increase or decrease in each agency's base, which is the previous year's appropriation. The total level of expenditures is the sum of the thirteen major appropriations bills passed annually.[74]

Congress does not attempt consciously to shape fiscal policy through its tax-ing or spending legislation. Rather, its money decisions are the product of its fragmented authority structure, as reflected in the multiplicity of powerful com-mittees and subcommittees, the weakness of party organizations, and the strong constituency orientation of members because of their constant concern with reelection.

Although the Budget and Accounting Act of 1921 required the president to prepare an annual budget and a comprehensive plan for spending, and although the Employment Act of 1946 required an annual economic report projecting revenues and expenditures in light of economic forecasts, Congress imposed no such requirements on itself. Fiscal policy was whatever remained of the presi-dent's program after it emerged from "a piecemeal and haphazard legislative process."[75] The inability of Congress to participate rationally on an equal basis with the presidency in shaping fiscal policy led to conflict during the Nixon administration, when federal spending became a politically significant issue. Spending grew rapidly in response to previously enacted statutory "entitle-ments" that could not be disregarded without revising the original authorizing legislation. Entitlements include Social Security benefits; federal retirement, farm price support, and welfare payments; and food stamps. Most entitlement payments to individuals increase automatically with the cost of living.[76] The problem was compounded by "off-budget" spending through loan guarantees and tax credits. This was the beginning of runaway budget deficits, which bur-geoned from 1971 to 1997 as spending on entitlements and other mandatory programs grew four times faster than did spending in discretionary areas.[77]

Nixon challenged Congress to curb spending; when it did not do so, he fre-quently vetoed spending bills and made extensive use of impoundment. The primary response of Congress to this controversy with Nixon and to frustration over its inability to shape policy was the Budget and Impoundment Control Act of 1974, which created a procedure for handling impoundments. More impor-tant, that statute established a congressional budget process, created House and Senate Budget Committees, and provided Congress with independent staff sup-port for macroeconomic forecasting and budget analysis in the form of the Con-gressional Budget Office.

Central to the congressional budget process in its present form are the budget resolution and the reconciliation legislation.[78] The budget resolution must be approved by both House and Senate but does not require the president's signa-ture. As such it does not have the force of law, but it serves as the vehicle for changes in budget policy, allocates available money to congressional appropria-tions committees, and may activate reconciliation legislation. The extent to which the budget resolution changes budget policy, as opposed to reflecting existing policies, determines its importance. Usually the budget resolution is merely the means by which Congress organizes its action, but it has also set in motion major changes in fiscal policy. Presidents Reagan (in 1981) and Clinton (in 1993), each with sharply different objectives, used the congressional budget process to change taxing and spending policy. In 1995 Republican congressional leaders used the budget process to impose far-reaching policy changes Clinton strongly opposed.

Each budget resolution contains totals for revenues, expenditures, the deficit or surplus, and the national debt for the next fiscal year. Congress must adhere to these totals as it makes taxing and spending decisions. The budget resolution also contains target totals for the next four fiscal years and allocations of new budget authority for the next year to the major areas of federal spending—for example, defense, agriculture, and interest on the national debt.[79] It may also include reconciliation instructions.

Reconciliation is the process Congress uses "to bring revenue and spending under existing law into conformity with the levels set in the budget resolution."[80] It proceeds in two stages. First, Congress incorporates in the budget resolution binding instructions to specific committees—those that have jurisdiction over revenues and mandatory spending programs—to recommend statutory changes that will achieve the spending and revenue levels set in the resolution. Next, the House and Senate enact the committees' recommendations in a reconciliation bill. Reconciliation is an optional process that has tended to be used when either the president or Congress seeks a multiyear deficit reduction agreement. Reconciliation legislation has become the major means of reducing the deficit. The 1995 reconciliation bill stalled in January 1996 after a protracted battle between President Clinton and Congress over how to achieve a balanced budget by 2002. Although not far apart on the amount of savings needed, they disagreed fundamentally over spending priorities and the congressional insistence on removing entitlement status from Medicaid and welfare.

Some observers, however, see a more dire development in the evolution of the congressional budget process.

Fiscal 2003 is the year when it became clear that the federal budget process is nothing more than a completely empty shell. Congressional budget resolutions are now enacted only so that the reconciliation procedures can be used to avoid a filibuster in the Senate with legislation that increases the deficit. Budget resolutions generally include appropriations levels that virtually everyone knows are artificially low and cannot be met unless gimmicks are used. The budget committees, which for most of the past three decades had assumed the responsibility for at least keeping their House and Senate colleagues informed about the budget consequences of their actions, have gone silent.[81]

The creation of the congressional budget process did not substantially change "the established process in Congress for raising and spending money."[82] Nor did it make Congress more fiscally responsible. What the congressional budget process did produce was a change in executive-legislative budget relationships.[83]

For a while, the increased centralization of budgetary decision making in Congress enhanced the legislative branch's ability to influence presidential budget policies while providing the president with greater leverage over congressional budget decisions. Congress and the president became, as Allen Schick put it, "more interdependent: each [was] more vulnerable than before to having its budget preferences blocked or modified by the other."[84]

From 1981 onward, Congress was locked in protracted conflict with Presidents Reagan, George H. W. Bush, and Clinton over fiscal policy and the deficit. After a brief respite, the same has held true with George W. Bush. Reagan and the older Bush attempted to control the deficit through spending cuts and resisted tax increases, while Congress fought to protect pork barrel projects benefiting its constituencies and entitlements and other programs that enjoyed wide popular or strong interest group support. Clinton won congressional support for his five-year deficit reduction package in 1993 but then waged intense budget battles with a Republican-controlled Congress during his final six years in office. Although George W. Bush won congressional support for massive tax cuts during his first months in office, subsequent battles have focused on the timed phase-in of those cuts and the administration's spending priorities. It is still not clear how budget issues will play with the public. Cutting the budget deficit proved not to be a winning election issue in recent years, as George H. W. Bush found out in 1992, Clinton in 1994, and Gore in 2000. Perhaps cutting taxes and expanding the deficit will prove more successful for George W. Bush in 2004.

Conclusion

Can the president bring order and cohesion to macroeconomic policy? Can the presidency serve as the instrument for effective management of the economy? Such questions have become increasingly important since 1970 as the U.S. economy has matured, interdependence with other economies has increased, and the ability to raise productivity, sustain economic growth, and keep inflation and unemployment at acceptably low levels has faltered from time to time. Clearly, the challenge macroeconomic policy poses to presidents is of continuing importance. Presidents face formidable obstacles and problems as they respond to that challenge.

Three major obstacles confront presidents in the performance of their economic policy-making roles: expectations are inordinately and unrealistically high, they have only limited authority to meet those expectations, and the base of knowledge on which they act is often limited and unreliable. The problem of unrealistic expectations is not peculiar to macroeconomic policy. To be elected, modern presidents have tended to make sweeping promises, and the American people have developed a deep faith that a strong, capable president can provide solutions to their most pressing problems.

As presidents try to develop policies that will meet popular expectations, they encounter problems. The first President Bush discovered as the recession of 1991 dragged into 1992 that the public is impatient for tangible results and the pressure for actions that can provide a "quick fix" is great. Approaching elections heighten the search for measures that will produce immediate results. Nor is it easy to sort through conflicting goals. Curbing inflation, for example, may lead to unwelcome consequences, such as increased unemployment and high interest rates. The popular bias against inaction runs deep; yet sometimes inaction may be the most prudent course to follow. In short, exaggerated popular expectations that the president will manage the economy effectively may limit his capacity to do so. Even an ostensibly healthy economy may not ease the apprehensions of the public, as Clinton discovered in 1994 when many voters, "driven by perceptions of job insecurity and sluggish wage growth," were concerned about the future of the economy and their family finances in the midterm elections.[85]

Presidents quickly discover that their authority to act is limited. In the area of macroeconomic policy three factors restrict the ability to act: congressional prerogatives, the independence of the Federal Reserve Board, and the absence of coordinating power within the executive branch. Presidents must collaborate with Congress in making fiscal policy. Their ability to increase or reduce taxes or spending depends on congressional responsiveness to their leadership, to their effectiveness as communicators and as persuaders.

Monetary policy is equally confining because of the independence of the Fed. The only resources the president has available to influence the Fed are persuasion and the periodic opportunity to appoint new members to the board and to designate its chair. Although presidents have regularly exerted pressure on the Fed, there is no assurance that monetary policy will be compatible with fiscal policy or that it will not impede the achievement of other policy objectives. As John Kessel concludes, "[P]residents are in the position of having only partial control (shared power in fiscal policy, only power to persuade in monetary policy) over blunt instruments that only sometimes lead to the desired economic results."[86]

Economics provides a shaky foundation for recommending policies directly affecting the operation of the entire economy. Economic forecasting is an inexact science subject to large margins of error. The validity of the projections of the Council of Economic Advisers, the Office of Management and Budget, the Treasury Department, and the Federal Reserve Board depends on the assumptions that underlie them and on the quality and quantity of information available. The assumptions vary with the institutional orientation of the agency making the forecast, the theories of the economists on the agency's staff, and political pressures affecting the agency. The Fed's assumptions, for example, reflect the influence of monetarism; OMB's, a traditional concern with budget balancing. As Stockman's account of his tenure as OMB director indicates, there is pressure on forecasters to resolve budget problems by adopting best-case, or "rosy," scenarios of economic performance.[87] If the assumptions underlying a forecast prove wrong, then policies based on the forecast may lead to unanticipated outcomes. For example, the record deficits incurred during his administration initially caught President Reagan by surprise because he enthusiastically accepted OMB's rosy scenario.

The nation has moved from a conservative consensus on economic policy in the 1920s and early 1930s to a Keynesian consensus in the 1950s and 1960s to a lack of consensus in the 1980s, 1990s, and beyond. Policies have shifted from Nixon's imposition of wage and price controls to Reagan's embrace of supply-side theory, the older Bush's pragmatism, Clinton's emphasis on long-term growth and investment in human capital, and the younger Bush's embrace of supply-side prescriptions for growth. Despite all these changes, presidents still lack the capacity to control the economy even though rapidly changing economic conditions, in the United States and elsewhere, would seem to require a maximum amount of adaptiveness. The president's ability to respond to new situations, such as a sudden, large increase in the price of oil, is limited. Institutional arrangements, both statutory and constitutional, restrict presidents' actions and dictate that they rely primarily on persuasion to accomplish their objectives. Moreover, experience with different processes for economic policymaking and coordination suggests that the internal structure of the presidency has little effect on policy outcomes in this area. Beyond economic conditions, over which the president has little control, the factors that appear to affect economic policymaking and outcomes most substantially are a president's ideology and leadership.

NOTES

1. John P. Frendreis and Raymond Tatalovich, *The Modern Presidency and Economic Policy* (Itasca, Ill.: Peacock, 1994), 300.

2. Raymond Tatalovich and John Frendreis, "Clinton, Class, and Economic Policy," in *The Postmodern Presidency: Bill Clinton's Legacy in U.S. Politics*, ed. Steven E. Schier (Pittsburgh: University of Pittsburgh Press, 2000), 41–42. Also see the review of Clinton's accomplishments by Paul J. Quirk and William Cunion, "Clinton's Domestic Policy: The Lessons of a 'New Democrat,'" in *The Clinton Legacy*, ed. Colin Campbell and Bert A. Rockman (Chatham, N.J.: Chatham House, 2001), 214–216.

3. Edward R. Tufte, *Political Control of the Economy* (Princeton: Princeton University Press, 1978).

4. A. James Reichley, "A Change in Direction," in *Setting National Priorities: The 1982 Budget*, ed. Joseph A. Pechman (Washington, D.C.: Brookings, 1981), 236–240.

5. John H. Kessel, *Presidents, the Presidency, and the Political Environment* (Washington, D.C.: CQ Press, 2001), 150–151.

6. Alan Stone, *Regulation and Its Alternatives* (Washington, D.C.: CQ Press, 1982), 262.

7. Lester M. Salamon and Alan J. Abramson, "Governance: The Politics of Retrenchment," in *The Reagan Record*, ed. John L. Palmer and Isabel V. Sawhill (Washington, D.C.: Urban Institute Press, 1984), 47.

8. Marshall R. Goodman, "A Kinder and Gentler Regulatory Reform: The Bush Regulatory Strategy and Its Impact" (paper presented at the annual meeting of the Midwest Political Science Association, Chicago, April 1991).

9. Robert W. Hahn and Robert N. Stavins, "National Environmental Policy during the Clinton Years," in *American Economic Policy in the 1990s*, ed. Jeffrey Frankel and Peter Orszag (Cambridge: MIT Press, 2002), 587.

10. David S. Cloud, "Industry, Politics Intertwined in Dole's Regulatory Bill," *Congressional Quarterly Weekly Report*, May 6, 1995, 1219–1224; and Bob Benenson, "GOP

Sets the 104th Congress on New Regulatory Course," *Congressional Quarterly Weekly Report,* June 17, 1995, 1693–1697.

11. David S. Cloud, "Dole's Bill: An 'Aggressive' Position," *Congressional Quarterly Weekly Report,* May 6, 1995, 1221.

12. James A. Barnes, "Is Bush Poisoning His Well?" *National Journal,* April 14, 2001, 1120–1121; and Eric Pianin, "Administration Revisits Forest Lands Rules; Paper Industry, Western Governors Want Protective Regulation Scaled Back," *Washington Post,* July 7, 2001, A2.

13. Eric Pianin and Mike Allen, "Clinton Forest Rules to Stand," *Washington Post,* May 4, 2001, A1; Cindy Skrzycki, "OMB to Revisit Costs, Benefits of Rules," *Washington Post,* May 29, 2001, E1; Amy Goldstein, " 'Last-Minute' Spin on Regulatory Rite: Bush Review of Clinton Initiatives Is Bid to Reshape Rules," *Washington Post,* June 9, 2001, A1; Marilyn Geewax, "Bush Proving to be No Radical When It Comes to Regulation," Cox News Service, June 13, 2001; and Juliet Eilperin, "GOP Won't Try to Halt Last Rules by Clinton: Hill Power Shift Forces Retreat on Spring Plans," *Washington Post,* July 30, 2001, A1.

14. Shawn Zeller, "Free Market Crusaders," *National Journal,* January 11, 2003, nationaljournal.com/cgi-bin/ifetch4?ENG+NJMAG+7-njindex+1092762-REVERSE +0+1+41+F+4+4+1+Shawn+AND+Zeller+AND+PD%2f01%2f10%2f2003%2d%3e 01%2f26%2f2003.

15. Walter W. Heller, *New Dimensions in Political Economy* (New York: Norton, 1966).

16. Jackie Calmes, "The Voracious National Debt," *Congressional Quarterly Weekly Report,* March 24, 1990, 896.

17. George Hager, "Deficit Shows No Gain from Pain of Spending Rules," *Congressional Quarterly Weekly Report,* July 20, 1991, 1963. Bush also encountered shortfalls in revenues arising from "technical reestimates" and higher projected spending for Medicaid.

18. Frendreis and Tatalovich, *The Modern Presidency,* 314.

19. Richard W. Stevenson, "The Wisdom to Let the Good Times Roll," *New York Times,* December 25, 2000, A1.

20. Clinton's term averages can be found in Tatalovich and Frendreis, "Clinton, Class, and Economic Policy," Table 1, 44. Unemployment data can be found in Harold W. Stanley and Richard G. Niemi, *Vital Statistics on American Politics 1999–2000* (Washington, D.C.: CQ Press, 2000), Table 11-10.

21. George Hager, "Time Is Ripe for Agreement but Gridlock Dies Hard," *Congressional Quarterly Weekly Report,* November 16, 1996, 3280–3281.

22. Daniel J. Palazzolo, *Done Deal? The Politics of the 1997 Budget Agreement* (Chatham, N.J.: Chatham House, 1999). Palazzolo contends that the process of moving toward a balanced budget was fifteen years in the making, stretching back to 1982.

23. Stevenson, "The Wisdom to Let the Good Times Roll," A12.

24. Glenn Kessler, "Bush Tax Cut Pares Government's Role," *Washington Post,* May 21, 2001, A1.

25. Jonathan Weisman, "White House Foresees 5-year Debt Increase of $1.9 Trillion," *Washington Post,* July 16, 2003, A1.

26. Ibid.

27. Richard Kogan and Robert Greenstein, "Sanitizing the Grim News: The Administration's Efforts to Make Harmful Deficits Appear Benign," July 18, 2003, Center on Budget and Policy Priorities, www.cbpp.org/7-18-03bud.htm.

28. Allen Schick, "Bush's Budget Problem" (paper presented at the conference on The George W. Bush Presidency: An Early Assessment, Princeton University, April 25–26, 2003), 20, 23.

29. Ibid., 4.

30. Testimony of Peter G. Peterson, president, The Concord Coalition, before the House Financial Services Committee, April 30, 2003, 3, www.concordcoalition.org/federal_budget/030430petersontestimonyexecsummary.htm. At the time of his testimony, Peterson was chairman of the Federal Reserve Bank of New York and had served as secretary of commerce in the Nixon administration.

31. See www.brillig.com/debt_clock.

32. Douglas W. Elmendorf, Jeffrey B. Liebman, and David W. Wilcox, "Fiscal Policy and Social Security Policy during the 1990s," in *American Economic Policy in the 1990s*, 117.

33. Allen Schick, "Bush's Budget Problem," 3–4, 5.

34. Paul E. Peterson and Mark Rom argue that presidents have little incentive to "manipulate the economy for either electoral or partisan reasons." In Peterson and Rom's view presidents can best achieve their diverse objectives through economic policies that maintain a balance between inflation and steady economic growth with minimal rates of unemployment. See Peterson and Rom, "Macroeconomic Policymaking: Who Is in Control?" in *Can the Government Govern?* ed. John E. Chubb and Paul E. Peterson (Washington, D.C.: Brookings, 1989), 149.

35. George Hager and David S. Cloud, "Democrats Tie Their Fate to Clinton's Budget Bill," *Congressional Quarterly Weekly Report*, August 7, 1993, 2122–2129.

36. Richard W. Stevenson, "Bush Signs Tax Cut Bill, Dismissing All Criticism," *New York Times*, May 29, 2003, www.nytimes.com/2003/05/29/politics/29TAX.html.

37. David R. Beam, "New Federalism, Old Realities: The Reagan Administration and Intergovernmental Reform," in *The Reagan Presidency and the Governing of America*, ed. Lester M. Salamon and Michael S. Lund (Washington, D.C.: Urban Institute, 1984), 440; and Paul E. Peterson, *The Price of Federation* (Washington, D.C.: Brookings, 1995), 69.

38. Peri Arnold, "Clinton and the Institutionalized Presidency," in *The Postmodern Presidency*, 26–28.

39. James E. Anderson and Jared E. Hazleton, *Managing Macroeconomic Policy: The Johnson Presidency* (Austin: University of Texas Press, 1986), 14.

40. For a brief profile, see "The Decision Makers," *National Journal*, June 23, 2001, 1896.

41. Jonathan Weisman, "Bush Tax-Cut Adviser Resigns," *Washington Post*, February 27, 2003, A9.

42. Joseph A. Davis, "Policy and Regulatory Review: Growth in Legislative Role Sparks Concern in Congress," *Congressional Quarterly Weekly Report*, September 14, 1985, 1809.

43. M. Stephen Weatherford and Lorraine M. McDonnell, "Clinton and the Economy: The Paradox of Policy Success and Political Mishap" (paper presented at the annual meeting of the American Political Science Association, Chicago, August 31–September 3, 1995), 21.

44. Ibid., 28.

45. For a brief profile, see "The Decision Makers," 1905.

46. Ibid.

47. Anderson and Hazleton, *Managing Macroeconomic Policy*, 27.

48. Colin Campbell, "The White House and the Cabinet under the 'Let's Deal' President," in *The Bush Presidency: First Appraisals*, ed. Colin Campbell and Bert A. Rockman (Chatham, N.J.: Chatham House, 1991), 211.

49. Frendreis and Tatalovich, *The Modern Presidency*, 56.

50. Weatherford and McDonnell, "Clinton and the Economy," 20–21.

51. For a brief profile, see "The Decision Makers," 1987.

52. "Treasury: Blunt? Yes. Politically Savvy? No," *National Journal*, January 24, 2003, nationaljournal.com/members/news/2003/01/0124nj_oneill.htm.

53. See Snow's biography at www.ustreas.gov/organization/bios/snow-e.html.

54. Colin Campbell, *Managing the Presidency: Carter, Reagan, and the Search for Executive Harmony* (Pittsburgh: University of Pittsburgh Press, 1986), 123–135. Also see Kessel, *Presidents, the Presidency, and the Political Environment,* 127–129.

55. Cheryl L. Edwards, "Open Market Operations in the 1990s," *Federal Reserve Bulletin,* November 1997, 862, www.federalreserve.gov/pubs/bulletin/1997/199711lead. pdf.

56. For a brief bio of Dr. Greenspan, see www.federalreserve.gov/bios/Greenspan. htm.

57. N. Gregory Mankiw, "U.S. Monetary Policy during the 1990s," in *American Economic Policy in the 1990s,* 19.

58. Paul Starobin, "One-Two Punch," *National Journal,* April 2, 1994, 768–883.

59. Kessel, *Presidents, the Presidency, and the Political Environment,* 138.

60. Anderson and Hazleton, *Managing Macroeconomic Policy,* 83.

61. Roger B. Porter, *Presidential Decision Making: The Economic Policy Board* (New York: Cambridge University Press, 1980).

62. Campbell, *Managing the Presidency,* 138.

63. David A. Stockman, *The Triumph of Politics: Why the Reagan Revolution Failed* (New York: Harper and Row), 1986.

64. Campbell, "The White House and the Cabinet under the 'Let's Deal' President," 210.

65. Frendreis and Tatalovich, *The Modern Presidency,* 70.

66. Paul Starobin, "The Broker," *National Journal,* April 16, 1994, 878–883.

67. Weatherford and McDonnell, "Clinton and the Economy," 21.

68. Bob Woodward, *The Agenda: Inside the Clinton White House* (New York: Simon and Schuster, 1994).

69. Weatherford and McDonnell, "Clinton and the Economy," 39.

70. Kessel, *Presidents, the Presidency, and the Political Environment,* 143; Tatalovich and Frendreis, "Clinton, Class, and Economic Policy," 47; and Stevenson, "The Wisdom to Let the Good Times Roll," A13. For an overall evaluation of the Clinton economic policy-making system, see Jonathan M. Orszag, Peter R. Orszag, and Laura D. Tyson, "The Process of Economic Policy-Making during the Clinton Administration," in *American Economic Policy in the 1990s,* 983–1027.

71. For a brief profile, see "The Decision Makers," 1894–1895.

72. Still another major figure, Harvey Pitt, chairman of the Securities and Exchange Commission, had resigned a month earlier amid controversy over his role in selecting members to serve on a corporate accounting watchdog board.

73. See www.whitehouse.gov/news/releases/2002/12/20021212-9.html.

74. The appropriations do not include entitlement programs, such as Social Security, Medicare, and Medicaid, or interest on the national debt.

75. James L. Sundquist, *The Decline and Resurgence of Congress* (Washington, D.C.: Brookings, 1981), 199.

76. R. Kent Weaver, *Automatic Government: The Politics of Indexation* (Washington, D.C.: Brookings, 1988).

77. Palazzolo, *Done Deal?* 20.

78. This discussion follows Allen Schick, *The Federal Budget: Politics, Policy, Process* (Washington, D.C.: Brookings, 1995), chap. 5.

79. Schick defines budget authority as "legislation that enables an agency to incur obligations. Obligations occur when agencies take any action . . . that commits the government to the payment of funds." Ibid., 19.

80. Ibid., 82.

81. Stan Collender, "Happy New Year?" *National Journal,* July 1, 2003, national journal.com/members/buzz/2003/budget/070103.htm.

82. Allen Schick, "The Evolution of Congressional Budgeting," in *Crisis in the Budget Process: Exercising Political Choice,* ed. Allen Schick (Washington, D.C.: American Enterprise Institute, 1986), 8.

83. Ibid., 15.

84. Ibid.

85. Alfred J. Tuchfarber, Stephen E. Bennett, Andrew E. Smith, and Eric W. Rademacher, "The Republican Tidal Wave of 1994: Testing Hypotheses About Realignment, Restructuring, and Rebellion (paper presented at the annual meeting of the American Political Science Association, Chicago, August 31–September 3, 1995), 20–21.

86. Kessel, *Presidents, the Presidency, and the Political Environment,* 151.

87. Stockman, *The Triumph of Politics,* 97–98, 329–332.

SUGGESTED READINGS

Anderson, James E., and Jared E. Hazleton. *Managing Macroeconomic Policy: The Johnson Presidency.* Austin: University of Texas Press, 1986.

Collender, Stanley E. *The Guide to the Federal Budget: Fiscal 2000.* Washington, D.C.: Brookings, 1999. Published annually.

Fisher, Louis. *Presidential Spending Power.* Princeton: Princeton University Press, 1975.

Frankel, Jeffrey, and Peter Orszag. *American Economic Policy in the 1990s.* Cambridge: MIT Press, 2002.

Frendreis, John P., and Raymond Tatalovich. *The Modern Presidency and Economic Policy.* Itasca, Ill.: Peacock, 1994.

Kessel, John H. *Presidents, the Presidency, and the Political Environment.* Washington, D.C.: CQ Press, 2001.

Kettl, Donald F. *Leadership at the Fed.* New Haven: Yale University Press, 1986.

Mills, Gregory B., and John L. Palmer, eds. *Federal Budget Policy in the 1980s.* Washington, D.C.: Urban Institute Press, 1984.

Niskanen, William A. *Reaganomics.* New York: Oxford University Press, 1988.

Palazzolo, Daniel J. *Done Deal? The Politics of the 1997 Budget Agreement.* Chatham, N.J.: Chatham House, 1999.

Porter, Roger B. *Presidential Decision Making: The Economic Policy Board.* New York: Cambridge University Press, 1980.

Schick, Allen. *The Federal Budget: Politics, Policy, Process.* Rev. ed. Washington, D.C.: Brookings, 2000.

Stein, Herbert. *Presidential Economics: The Making of Economic Policy from Roosevelt to Reagan and Beyond.* 3d rev. ed. Washington, D.C.: AEI Press, 1994.

Stockman, David A. *The Triumph of Politics: Why the Reagan Revolution Failed.* New York: Harper and Row, 1986.

Tufte, Edward R. *Political Control of the Economy.* Princeton: Princeton University Press, 1980.

Wildavsky, Aaron, Naomi Caiden, and Aaron B. Wildavsky. *The New Politics of the Budgetary Process.* 4th ed. New York: Addison-Wesley, 2000.

10 THE POLITICS OF NATIONAL SECURITY POLICY

Throughout the military actions in Afghanistan and Iraq, British Prime Minister Tony Blair stood firm as George Bush's staunchest international ally, symbolized by their joint media appearances following several war summits conducted during March and April 2003.

NATIONAL SECURITY POLICY USUALLY REFLECTS long-term geopolitical conditions in the world. Examples are the longstanding alliance of the United States with the United Kingdom; the conflict between the United States and the Soviet Union following World War II; the intractability of religious and cultural differences in the Balkans, the Middle East, and Northern Ireland; and the vital role played by oil-producing states in the global economy. Seldom do single events serve as dramatic turning points that reshape the direction of policy, but millions of people were convinced their lives and U.S. foreign policy were permanently altered by the events of September 11, 2001, when a series of terrorist attacks fully or partially destroyed two symbols of American power in the world: the twin towers of the World Trade Center in New York City and the Pentagon, headquarters of the U.S. military, just across the Potomac River from Washington, D.C.

In a coordinated attack, three airliners carrying large fuel supplies were hijacked by small groups of men, who then sacrificed their own lives and those of the passengers by flying the planes directly into the targets. A fourth aircraft, presumably headed for Washington, D.C., crashed before reaching its goal, the attack foiled by passengers aboard the plane. Millions witnessed the second attack on the World Trade Center on live television, the fireball and crumbling towers becoming searing images in their collective memory. For days the nation's normal life seemed suspended as attention focused on stories of emergency evacuations, reports of heroic rescue efforts, the search for missing loved ones, and the expanding investigation. About 3,000 persons died in the two incidents. In the aftermath, the economy was seriously disrupted with the stock exchanges closed for four days and the nation's air transportation system first shut down, and then resuming operation at severely reduced levels. The airlines entered a prolonged tailspin.

Only the surprise Japanese attack on Pearl Harbor, in December 1941, which led to American involvement in World War II, had a similar galvanizing effect on the nation. Before the week was over, President George W. Bush secured congressional approval of an emergency appropriation of $40 billion for disaster relief and increased preparedness. Congress also approved, by near unanimous votes (98–0 in the Senate; 420–1 in the House), a resolution authorizing the president to use "all necessary and appropriate force against those nations, organizations, or persons he determines planned, authorized, committed or aided the terrorist attacks ... or harbored such organizations or persons."[1] National unity and patriotic fervor prevailed on Capitol Hill, where partisan conflict and recrimination had been building in the expected battle over budget priorities. In a vast outpouring of solidarity, people throughout the nation attended religious services and nondenominational ceremonies, gave blood, donated money, and flew the American flag out of remembrance and support for those who had died or suffered losses. The nation's citizens almost seemed reluctant to return to their daily routines as the government prepared a response, an unspoken acknowledgment, perhaps, that life in the United States had been irrevocably changed.

The administration clearly recognized how dramatically these events had altered its direction and focus. President Bush, in a news conference held two days after the attacks, acknowledged that "this is now the focus of my administration. We will be very much engaged in domestic policy, of course. I look forward to working with Congress on a variety of issues. But now that war has been declared on us, we will lead the world to victory."[2]

Mobilizing public support for a war effort and fashioning an international response became the principal concerns of an administration that had been forced to scramble on the day of the attacks. On September 11, President Bush had been in Florida at an event designed to build public support for his education program when he learned of the attacks. He returned to Washington by way of military installations in Louisiana and Nebraska only after the situation had stabilized and the danger of attempts on the White House and *Air Force One*, his plane, had been resolved. In his prime-time address to the nation that evening, Bush quietly reassured the American people that everything was being done to help the injured, continue the federal government's operations without interruption, and find those responsible for the attacks. In the following days his rhetoric escalated to a virtual declaration of war against the enemies of civilization. The United States was about to launch a sustained assault against a very different kind of enemy in hopes of eradicating terrorism.

This effort began in Afghanistan with forces from the United States and other nations targeting the al-Qaeda terrorist organization of Osama Bin Laden and the fundamentalist Taliban regime that had provided it with sanctuary. Coordinated international efforts against other known terrorist organizations grew in the following months. But global unity diminished in 2002 when the United States expanded its focus to include the "rogue state" of Iraq, whose alleged ties to terrorism proved difficult to document.

The new war on terrorism was a far cry from the national security challenges that had dominated most of the last half of the twentieth century, which stemmed from the U.S.-Soviet rivalry. The dominant countries in world affairs following World War II, the United States and the Soviet Union led two armed camps of nations—one democratically governed, the other ruled by Communist Party dictatorships. The industrial democracies and the communist bloc coexisted in an uneasy peace, maintained in part by the threat of mutual nuclear annihilation. At the same time, each power grouping actively courted the support of the "uncommitted" developing countries, nations of the so-called third world. These countries, most facing enormous economic and social problems, varied in their orientations toward Washington and Moscow. Superimposed on the basic pattern of U.S.-Soviet competition was the twentieth-century technological revolution in communications, transportation, and weaponry, which had the effect of shrinking the world and making the risks of military confrontation greater than ever. In addition, the United States grew more economically interdependent with other countries, especially suppliers of basic raw materials, such as oil.

In an environment characterized by military precariousness and economic interdependence, no chief executive could focus primarily and indefinitely on domestic policy. Modern presidents from Franklin D. Roosevelt to Bill Clinton—and now George W. Bush—have been drawn almost irresistibly to concentrate instead on national security policy (foreign affairs and military policy). The reasons for this predictable emphasis across administrations are at least twofold:

first, the crucial importance of the United States in the international community; and second, the political advantages presidents normally derive from devoting much of their energy to national security.[3]

Ronald Reagan came into office in 1981 committed to bringing about a conservative revolution in domestic and economic policy but found himself drawn toward national security policy issues. His successor, George Bush, was preoccupied with foreign and military policy from the start of his administration and only reluctantly turned his attention homeward when the economy faltered and his reelection campaign approached. In that campaign, Bill Clinton successfully attacked Bush for neglecting the health of the economy and serious domestic problems and promised that, if elected, he would concentrate on them. Much to his dismay, Clinton discovered upon taking office that the end of the cold war brought new conflicts and still greater uncertainty to international affairs. Clinton eventually involved himself extensively with foreign policy; in the last few months of his presidency, he seemed to become consumed by the desire to produce a long-evasive Middle East peace settlement.

During his initial hundred days in office, George W. Bush dealt primarily with domestic policy. An unexpected crisis arose with China when a U.S. plane collided with a Chinese fighter and was forced to land on Chinese territory, a reminder that foreign policy frequently intrudes unexpectedly on the national agenda. Since the terrorist attacks of September 2001, the war on terrorism and the overthrow of Saddam Hussein's regime in Iraq have become the defining features of Bush's presidency, projects that will determine whether he wins a second term in office.

This chapter examines the president's role in making and directing national security policy. It reviews the major concepts and issues that have dominated that policy area since World War II. It then defines the essential national security policy-making problem as one in which the president is both the solution and the problem. Finally, the discussion turns to the relationship between the president and Congress with respect to national security and the problem of organizing an effective policy-making system for national security.

Issues in National Security Policy: Search for a New Consensus

For more than two decades, from the end of World War II until March 1968, America's principal national interest was clear-cut: military containment of communism. But when the North Vietnamese Tet offensive precipitated Lyndon Johnson's decision to end the escalation of American involvement in the Vietnam War, the broad consensus undergirding U.S. national security policy began to disintegrate, a process that continued until communist power collapsed in Eastern Europe in 1991. Until Tet, a succession of presidents from both political parties had consistently pursued the doctrine of *containment*. Bipartisan support for the consensus in Congress gave presidents a free hand in formulating and implementing foreign and military policies. The only effective constraints imposed on presidential actions were the boundaries of the consensus, which began to break up in 1968, when it became apparent that containment could be preserved only through an indefinite, limited war in Vietnam or greatly expanded U.S. involvement that carried risks of conflict with the Soviet Union.

Even after the United States failed to "contain" communism in Vietnam, presidents continued to employ single, overarching concepts to build domestic political support for their national security policies. They found that "selling programs to Congress and the American people in the postwar era was always made easier if they could be clothed in one garment."[4] Détente, human rights, the "evil empire," a "new world order," engagement, and enlargement have emerged as successors to containment, but none has proved to be the core of an enduring national consensus. It remains to be seen whether the Bush administration's response to the threats of terrorism, tyrants, and weapons of mass destruction will provide the sustained political support missing for so long. A recent study from the Council on Foreign Relations eloquently made the case for the importance of having such a consensus:

From the fall of the Berlin Wall in 1989 to the fall of the Twin Towers in 2001, and even now after the Iraq War of 2003, the United States has not had a consistent national security strategy that enjoyed the support of the American people and our allies. This situation is markedly different from the Cold War era, when our nation had a clear, coherent, widely supported strategy that focused on containing and deterring Soviet communist expansion. The tragic events of September 11, the increase in terrorism, and threats from countries such as North Korea and, until recently, Iraq create an imperative once again to fashion and implement a coherent national security strategy that will safeguard our national interests.[5]

Efforts to Rebuild Consensus, Nixon through Clinton

In 1972 and 1973, President Nixon told the American people that a policy of *détente* would ease, if not end, the precarious Soviet-American tensions of the cold war. The government would implement détente through actions such as cultural exchanges, increased trade between the two countries, and negotiations to limit strategic nuclear weapons. Established attitudes and behavior patterns are not easy to change, however, and Nixon and his successor, Gerald Ford, found it convenient to seek support for their policies by citing threatening Soviet actions in various parts of the world, such as Africa, Latin America, and the Middle East.

Jimmy Carter effectively campaigned on the pledge, which he reaffirmed at the outset of his administration, that morality, manifested in universal commitment to the defense of *human rights*, would be the cornerstone of U.S. foreign policy. But the United States found it easier to protest and threaten to take action against human rights violations in countries not vital to its interests, such as the Soviet Union and its allies, than in those that were vital, such as South Korea and South Africa. Indeed, misguided application of the human rights doctrine hastened the downfall of the shah's friendly but authoritarian government in Iran and contributed to the establishment of the equally oppressive, but virulently anti-American, Islamic republic of Ayatollah Ruhollah Khomeini. Furthermore, the United States did not have the capacity to enforce the doctrine against powerful violators.

Reagan took office proclaiming belligerently that his administration's framework for national security policy was continued opposition to, and competition with, the Soviet Union, which he once called "the evil empire."[6] In practice, however, his anti-Soviet stance was less than doctrinaire—strong rhetoric was combined with restrained conduct. For example, Reagan's administration, intent on limiting nuclear weapons and curtailing the arms race, achieved the first arms reduction agreement of the cold war, the Intermediate Range Nuclear Forces Treaty. It was a singular accomplishment—one realized, however, not through belligerent opposition but through painstaking, lengthy give-and-take negotiations.

Reagan's ability to construct a new consensus with a strategic vision based on superpower conflict was further undercut by the Iran-contra affair.[7] Journalists and political critics had posed persistent questions about explanations of the administration's actions and the president's knowledge of international events. Was it the president who set American foreign policy or his aides in the State Department, the Central Intelligence Agency (CIA), and the National Security Council (NSC)? These questions seemed fully justified when the administration acknowledged in November 1986 that it had sent a small number of obsolete weapons to Iran as a means of contacting and encouraging moderate political elements. Reagan vigorously denied that there had been any explicit exchange of arms for hostages, although each hostage's release had been preceded by an arms shipment. In late November 1986, the president acknowledged that profits from the arms sales ($10 million–$30 million) had been diverted to the Nicaraguan contras through a numbered Swiss bank account. This was a direct violation of the Boland amendment, adopted by Congress in 1984, which prohibited use of government funds to support covert operations against the government of Nicaragua. Reagan claimed he had not been fully informed about the matter.

Selling arms to Iran in apparent exchange for American hostages called into question the commitment of the United States to resisting terrorism and isolating countries, such as Iran, that support terrorism. The action also undermined the U.S. position of neutrality in the seven-year war between Iran and Iraq and damaged its relations with moderate Arab states such as Saudi Arabia. Rather than establishing a new consensus, Reagan's methods provided lessons in how not to manage foreign policy. His detached administrative style, which entailed extensive delegation and a disdain for factual details, allowed him to address "the big picture" but also left many critical decisions to his subordinates. The operation of the foreign policy process, especially the independent role played by the NSC staff, contributed a great deal to Reagan's political difficulties and did little to protect him from foreign policy mistakes.

In contrast to Reagan, his successor, George Bush, was a hands-on president deeply engaged in the formulation and implementation of national security policy. He concerned himself with its details and participated actively in negotiations with foreign leaders. In addition, he approached foreign policy with a pragmatic, rather than ideological, orientation. Critics complained, however, that his administration's foreign policy was purely tactical and lacked a strategic design.[8] The "new world order" Bush announced following the collapse of communism in Russia and throughout Eastern Europe was unable to sustain a national consensus, in part because its meaning remained unclear.

Bush continued the policies of the late Reagan years but with greater flexibility and adaptiveness.[9] He provided "a kind of competent Reaganism" and "restore[d] professionalism to the conduct of foreign policy."[10] In the Persian Gulf War, in 1991, for example, Bush skillfully mobilized domestic and world opinion behind the most effective international coalition since World War II. He demonstrated the ability of the United States to project its power far from its home base. However, by not removing Iraqi president Saddam Hussein from power and bringing peace and stability to the Middle East, the United States failed to realize fully the fruits of victory and created problems for both of Bush's successors.

Despite its success, the Bush foreign policy was essentially reactive. Its major initiatives—the invasion of Panama and the Gulf War—were responses to crises. The absence of a strategic framework led to an emphasis on individual problems and to policies that lacked cohesion. While Bush spoke grandly of a new world order, he gave little indication of its shape and dimensions. His administration was unable to develop a strategic design for the post–cold war world or a replacement for the Soviet threat as the unifying force linking the United States with the NATO countries and Japan. Moreover, the absence of a strategic focus for national security left the Bush administration with little sense of how to counter calls for isolationism or to cope with the increasing impact of international factors on the domestic economy.

From the outset, Bill Clinton's administration expressed a wide array of high-minded goals, including the expansion of democracy and human rights; the alleviation of disease, hunger, and poverty; growing globalization as free markets proliferated within states and free trade grew between them; and control of weapons of mass destruction.[11] Frequently, however, the administration encountered difficulty in translating these goals into workable policies in specific instances, such as the failed effort at nation building in Somalia, the intervention to restore democracy in Haiti, the early uncertainty about policy in Bosnia, and inaction in the face of genocide in Rwanda. Nor did the administration ever clearly resolve the question of when military power could appropriately be employed, despite having reported to Congress more frequently than any of its five predecessors (in compliance with the War Powers Resolution, discussed in "The Assertion of Congressional Powers" below), after using force in Bosnia, Haiti, Somalia, Iraq, Afghanistan, Sudan, and Kosovo. (See Table 10-1.) Clinton's

Table 10-1 Presidential Use of Force Reported in Compliance with the War Powers Resolution, 1969–2003

President/term	Times complied with War Powers Resolution
Nixon (1969–1974)	0
Ford (1974–1977)	4
Carter (1977–1981)	1
Reagan (1981–1989)	14
G. Bush (1989–1993)	7
Clinton (1993–2001)	60
G. W. Bush (2001–)	20[a]

Sources: Richard F. Grimmet, "War Powers Resolution: Presidential Compliance," original release March 2001 and updated version June 9, 2003, *CRS Issue Brief for Congress,* Congressional Research Service, Library of Congress, March 21, 2001 and June 6, 2003. www.house.gov/markgreen/crs.htm. Also see CRS Report RL31185 "The War Powers Resolution: After Twenty-eight Years."

[a]Through June 9, 2003.

administration also vacillated between multilateralism and unilateralism as means to achieve its ends, sometimes acting alone and at other times refusing to act unless allies joined in the effort.

The first extensive statement of the administration's strategy appeared in July 1994 and identified three central themes: domestic renewal, engagement abroad to enlarge market democracies, and multilateralism as a primary mode of operation.[12] Market democracies would be extended ("enlargement") and threats contained ("engagement") to achieve renewal at home.[13] Two of Clinton's biggest foreign policy successes—enactment of legislation implementing the North American Free Trade Agreement (NAFTA) and renewing and expanding the General Agreement on Tariffs and Trade (GATT)—were justified as improving the American economy. By 1998, however, there had been important shifts in the Clinton administration's official statements. Defending the nation from terrorism, drug trafficking, and crime, as well as from weapons of mass destruction, became more prominent goals than advancing market economies. There was also recognition that managing the international financial markets was a critical task, an appropriate goal given the widespread impacts of financial crises in Mexico and Asia.[14] But the new statement of goals still lacked a unifying statement of purpose. Although Clinton was active on many fronts and willing to employ military force, his inability to articulate a clear strategy ultimately worked to the administration's disadvantage.

G. W. Bush's National Security Strategy

On September 17, 2002, the Bush administration released the long-awaited statement on National Security Strategy, the first since 1999. Although the 1986

Goldwater-Nichols Department of Defense Reorganization Act had mandated that such a report be issued within a president's first five months in office and annually thereafter, the Clinton administration had failed to issue one during its final year, and Bush's first report emerged twenty months late. In fact, Bush had ordered a wide-ranging strategic review in 2001 that was interrupted by the September terrorist attacks. Glimmers of the new strategy appeared in his 2002 State of the Union message and in two speeches delivered in June at West Point and Fort Drum. Two other, internal documents, partially released in December 2002, had developed the administration's thinking.[15] Together, these three documents and three speeches constituted a reformulation of American strategy praised by some observers as the boldest, most sweeping statement of grand strategy since the Marshall Plan was introduced in 1947[16] and reviled by others as an attempt to create an "arrogant empire."[17]

Even before 9/11, the Bush administration had signaled its intention to adopt a different approach to the world by withdrawing from five international treaties, discontinuing major peace initiatives launched by the Clinton administration toward North Korea and the Middle East, and adopting an assertive tone that suggested a unilateral, rather than multilateral, mode of action. In the wake of the terrorist attacks, these trends were heightened. "It [9-11] produced a mobilization of American power and yet a narrowing of American interests. Suddenly, Washington was more powerful and determined to act. But it would act only for its own core security and even preemptively when it needed to."[18]

In his State of the Union message of January 2002, President Bush had warned three states to halt their pursuit of weapons of mass destruction and their sponsorship of terrorism. Iraq, Iran, and North Korea constituted what the president termed an "axis of evil."[19] In confronting the dangers posed by terrorist and rogue states, the interests of other states and their leaders were of secondary concern. Pakistan, for instance, was pressured to support American efforts in Afghanistan, and Turkey to support those in Iraq. Pakistan complied, but Turkey resisted. France, Germany, and Russia defied American pressure in the United Nations and opposed action against Iraq, signaling a political division that seemed to threaten the foundations of NATO, cornerstone of American foreign policy for a half-century.

Beyond the issue of alliance relations lay a more fundamental question: How should the United States wield its dominant, hegemonic power in the world? The administration's answer centered on three threats to American interests: terrorists, who use "premeditated, politically motivated violence" against innocents;[20] rogue states led by tyrants who sometimes support terrorists and aggressively seek weapons of mass destruction to further their own goals; and failing states, "countries in which the central government does not exert effective control over . . . significant parts of its own territory" and are therefore susceptible to terrorist intimidation or become sources of regional instability.[21] Notably, Russia and China, great power competitors of the past and future, are identified as undergoing internal changes that produce common values and opportunities for peaceful competition. In his letter of submission that accompanied the strategy, Bush summarized how America would relate to these international forces:

We will defend the peace by fighting terrorists and tyrants. We will preserve the peace by building good relations among the great powers. We will extend the peace by encouraging free and open societies on every continent.[22]

The new strategy stimulated enormous discussion and provoked enormous controversy.[23] Promoting democracy, free markets, and free trade throughout the world, particularly in Muslim nations, could be a means to enhance self-determination and human rights or a means to extend America's global control. Some observers doubted the administration's sincerity in endorsing institutions such as the United Nations, the World Trade Organization, and NATO, and suspected a real preference for "coalitions of the willing"—temporary assemblages of supportive allies. How would the administration resolve the contradiction between promoting democracy and using undemocratic regimes to combat terrorism? Probably causing the most public discussion were two controversial military strategies: "preemption—striking an enemy as it prepares an attack . . . [and] prevention—striking an enemy even in the absence of specific evidence of a coming attack."[24] In the wake of 9/11, the administration argued that action must be taken before the nation suffers a catastrophic attack. Unlike the leaders of major nations such as Russia and China, terrorists and tyrants are unlikely to be deterred from launching attacks by threats of retaliation since their behavior is irrational. Thus the United States and its allies must use intelligence to discover capabilities and then act appropriately even if an attack may not be imminent. This logic underlay the U.S. action against Iraq, whose leader, Saddam Hussein, resisted international inspection of his chemical, biological, and nuclear weapons programs, and thereby provided a justification for preventive action.

The Council on Foreign Relations argues that the new Bush strategy has not yet created a new consensus. Three groups offer contending perspectives on the new global realities.[25] Neoconservatives, mostly in the Republican Party and including several notable figures in the Bush administration,[26] stress the importance of maintaining U.S. military dominance and being willing to use force preemptively and alone, if necessary. Moderates in both the Republican and Democratic Parties identify the same three international threats but believe that alliance-based containment and deterrence, policy instruments of the past, can continue to provide national security. Finally, liberals (mostly Democrats) stress the need for diplomatic and economic cooperation as the best way to address global poverty, weapons proliferation, and international resentment of U.S. power, the long-term dangers to American security. Thus rather than articulating a new national strategy, the Bush administration has delivered the opening salvo on a major foreign policy debate likely to continue for some time.

A Frustrating Search

Perhaps we should not be surprised that successive administrations have found it difficult to develop public support for a strategic consensus. Articulating a new foreign policy requires taking positions on scores, if not hundreds, of difficult issues, something politicians are reluctant to do.[27] Moreover, from an American perspective, the international environment is full of contradictory pressures and has become more and more unmanageable. With the disappearance in 1991 of the Soviet Union as one of the world's two superpowers, the number of regional and communal (ethnic, religious, tribal) conflicts has proliferated. China aspires to become a great power and other nations, such as Iran, hope to become regional powers. There are also history-laden animosities that have now come to the surface, particularly between India and Pakistan and in the Balkans, where the United States and its NATO allies intervened in Bosnia and Kosovo.

"Security" has also taken on new meanings with threats arising from uncontrolled immigration, international drug dealers, and most dramatically, international terrorists. In the view of the Bush administration, these threats have become just as pressing as those from ambitious nation-states. In marked contrast to the cold war era, the new international agenda is heavily—some argue predominantly—economic, raising issues that intermingle with domestic social and macroeconomic policy matters and triggering lobbying efforts by a new range of interest groups. Recent presidents have not enjoyed the discretion or broad support in foreign and military policy accorded their predecessors at the height of the cold war. It remains to be seen whether the new Bush strategy will win such support.

The National Security Policy-Making Problem

Exercising effective international leadership is difficult for the United States; the governmental structure established in the Constitution—separate institutions sharing power—creates continuing tension between the president and Congress over the control of national security policy. Edward S. Corwin observed that the Constitution "is an invitation to struggle" between the two branches "for the privilege of directing American foreign policy."[28] Although the struggle continues, and power over foreign policy is divided, the president has played the dominant role in shaping national security policy through most of the country's history. Presidential advantages of unity, secrecy, and dispatch are especially compelling during periods of crisis and potential conflict.

Dependence on presidential leadership carries risks, however. The idiosyncrasies of individual presidents' operating styles and personalities (see discussion in chapter 4) can be sources of uncertainty and noncohesiveness in policy and can exacerbate the institutional tensions between Congress and the president. (To some extent this happened during the Iran-contra affair.) The United States needs in its national security policy "institutions that provide continuity" and "structures and processes that promote coherence."[29] The problem is that if institutions, structures, and procedures respond to the short-term needs and whims of individual presidents, discontinuity in policy is likely to multiply. National security policymaking presents the United States with a circular and seemingly inescapable problem: the country depends on the president for central policy leadership, born of constitutional arrangements and operational imperatives, but this produces discontinuity in policy and a lack of cohesiveness that result from a policy-making system geared to presidential domination. The remainder of this chapter explores this paradox.

The President, Congress, and National Security

The powers of the federal government in international affairs are "inherent, plenary, and exclusive."[30] They are not granted expressly by the Constitution; rather they derive from the nation's existence as a sovereign entity in the international community and cannot be exercised by the states or anyone else. The Constitution, however, is ambiguous in its assignment of the power to control foreign relations. Both the president and Congress have formal constitutional powers in this area, indicating that the Founders intended control to be shared. In a 1793 debate with James Madison in the *Gazette of the United States,* Alexander Hamilton argued that direction of the nation's foreign policy is inherently an executive function.[31] Madison's position—that since the power to declare war is vested in Congress, presidential powers in this regard are merely instrumental—has not been borne out by subsequent events. Longstanding practice and necessity have combined to make the president *the sole organ* of the United States in the conduct of its external affairs. Presidents have monopolized negotiations and communications with other governments from the early years of the Republic.

Congress, however, has retained the ability to influence the substantive content of the foreign and defense policies the president implements. Major policies developed by the president cannot remain viable for long without congressional support in the form of implementing legislation and appropriations. Nevertheless, throughout most of U.S. history the president has been, and is today, the "most important single factor in the determination of American foreign policy."[32]

The Powers of the President

In addition to the inherent powers derived from the country's involvement in the international community, the president has formal and delegated powers over national security. These stem, respectively, from specific constitutional provisions and Congress. The constitutional foundation is relatively modest: the power to receive ambassadors and ministers, the power to negotiate treaties, designation as commander in chief of the armed forces, the general grant of executive power, and the clause enjoining the president to "take care that the laws be faithfully executed." Operationally, these provisions result in four major areas of presidential authority—recognition and nonrecognition of other governments;

making, implementing, and terminating international agreements; the appointment of personnel to conduct foreign and military policy; and the use of military force as a means of achieving policy goals.

Recognition and Nonrecognition of Foreign Governments. Article II, Section 3, of the Constitution grants the president power to "receive Ambassadors and other public Ministers"—in essence, authority to recognize foreign governments. Because foreign diplomats are accredited to the president, the decision about whether to receive them and thus recognize their governments is exclusively the president's. By implication, the chief executive can also refuse to grant that recognition or withdraw it.

Traditionally, under international law, governments grant recognition to other governments provided the latter are stable, have effectively established their authority, and are meeting their international obligations. Recognition allows the American government to express its approval or disapproval of foreign regimes, an effective weapon when exercised by a nation as powerful and influential as the United States. Other nations may alter their conduct at the prospect of U.S. recognition or the threat of its withdrawal. Once recognition is granted or relations are broken this leverage is lost.

There are some well-known instances in American diplomatic history concerning the use of this power. After the Russian Revolution in 1917–1918, the United States refused to recognize the communist government of the Soviet Union on the grounds that it had obtained power illegally, expropriated foreign-owned property without compensation, and oppressed its citizens. Yet in 1933 FDR established diplomatic relations with the Soviet Union when practical considerations made recognition advantageous to the United States. President Harry Truman, overcoming strong opposition in the State Department, granted recognition to the new state of Israel in 1948, making the United States the first nation to do so. U.S. support has been vital to the survival of Israel ever since.

When a communist regime took power in China in 1949 after a revolutionary struggle, the United States refused to recognize it, instead regarding the nationalist government on the island of Taiwan as the legitimate government of China. Not until 1979 did the United States establish diplomatic relations with the People's Republic of China (PRC) and withdraw recognition from Taiwan. At the same time, however, the United States did not recognize PRC sovereignty over Taiwan. Despite challenges in Congress, the Carter administration's policies toward the two Chinas were upheld. Similarly, reestablishing normal relations with Vietnam in July 1995 encountered opposition from those who viewed President Clinton's action as self-serving—he had avoided military service in the war (1965–1973). In its defense, the administration argued that it sought to achieve economic gain for both countries and an end to the internal debate that had divided America for thirty years.

Although presidents are legally free to exercise the recognition power on their own, political prudence dictates that they take congressional views and public opinion into consideration, effectively limiting the range of presidential discretion.

International Agreements. The Constitution also provides the president with authority to conduct negotiations with other nations that result in treaties or binding executive agreements. The constitutional basis for the treaty-making power is found in Article II, Section 2, which declares that the president "shall have power, by and with the Advice and Consent of the Senate, to make treaties, provided two thirds of the Senators present concur." The authority to make executive agreements is not mentioned explicitly, but its constitutionality is "universally conceded,"[33] perceived as arising from the president's role as the nation's official organ for the conduct of foreign relations and as a means for exercising powers in the Commander-in-Chief and "Take Care" Clauses of the Constitution.[34] In addition, executive agreements may be concluded pursuant to provisions of valid treaties and of existing legislation.

Treaties require Senate approval, but executive agreements do not. The Senate's own members limited its role in the treaty-making process in 1789, when they set a precedent by refusing to advise George Washington on provisions of a treaty under negotiation. The Senate may, however, amend or attach reservations to treaties submitted for its approval. Amendments change the content of a treaty and thus require additional negotiations with the foreign nation; reservations merely clarify the Senate's understanding of the treaty's provisions. The requirement of a two-thirds vote for approval gives the Senate substantial leverage over the executive in the treaty-making process, something presidents can sidestep by using executive agreements instead.[35]

The dramatic change in the relative importance of executive agreements and treaties can be seen in Table 10-2. By the late nineteenth century, agreements concluded in the previous fifty years slightly outnumbered treaties. That ratio widened over the next fifty-year period (1889–1939), then exploded during the period 1939–1989, when 11,698 new executive agreements were concluded as opposed to only 702 treaties. Congress repeatedly has expressed its disapproval of the use of executive agreements in lieu of treaties, but the only limitation it has imposed, in the Case-Zablocki Act of 1972, is to require that the legislature be notified of all such agreements. Although Congress is free to take action against executive agreements to which it objects, it has been unable to impose effective limits on the president's power to make them.[36] As Table 10-3 shows, the ratio of executive agreements to treaties changed markedly under Clinton compared with that of his immediate predecessors, mainly because of the unusually large number of trade treaties concluded during his administration. It would be premature to see this as altering the longer term trend. The agreement/treaty ratio under George W. Bush moved closer to the recent historical pattern but was marked by a striking decline in overall activity during the administration's first two years, probably reflecting both the emphasis on counterterrorism and the shift away from multilateralism.

Table 10-2   Treaties and Executive Agreements Concluded by the United States, 1789–1989

Period	Treaties	Executive agreements
1789–1839	60	27
1839–1889	215	238
1889–1939	524	917
1939–1989	702	11,698
Total	1,501	12,880

Source: *Treaties and Other International Agreements: The Role of the U.S. Senate,* Congressional Research Service, Library of Congress, January 2001, Table II-1. Report submitted to the Committee on Foreign Relations, U.S. Senate, 106:2, Senate print 106-71.

Why use treaties at all? Presidents are compelled by domestic political considerations to submit international agreements for Senate approval as treaties. Approval by the Senate gives an international agreement a degree of legitimacy that otherwise would be lacking. For instance, President Carter submitted the agreement providing for gradual termination of U.S. control of the Panama Canal to the Senate as a treaty. He apparently calculated that such action would be difficult to defend publicly in any case and avoidance of Senate approval could impose unacceptable political costs on his administration. For similar reasons, Carter submitted the second Strategic Arms Limitation Talks (SALT) agreement to the Senate as a treaty even though approval was unlikely.

On several occasions, however, modern presidents have taken important action through executive agreements, knowing that Congress was unlikely to support a treaty. In 1940, Franklin Roosevelt exchanged fifty "overage" destroyers for ninety-nine-year leases on bases in British possessions in the Western Hemisphere; in 1973, the United States and North Vietnam ended hostilities and exchanged prisoners of war through an executive agreement; and in 1981, the United States and Israel negotiated an agreement for strategic cooperation in the Middle East.

The decision to designate an international agreement as a treaty is the president's, based on political, rather than legal, grounds.[37] But few agreements are self-executing, forcing presidents to take note of congressional views since the administration will require legislation or an appropriation for implementation. During the Clinton administration, two important agreements, NAFTA and GATT, required legislation to become effective, allowing Congress to conduct an extensive debate over the merits and demerits of the agreements. Clinton needed the support of congressional Republicans because a majority of Democrats—fearing negative consequences for U.S. jobs—opposed both bills.

Although the president's power to negotiate international agreements is subject to political and constitutional limitations, the power to terminate such agreements is not. The Supreme Court ruled in 1979 that the president could

Table 10-3   International Agreements, 1969–2002

President/Term	Executive agreements	Treaties	Ratio
Nixon (1969–1974)	1,116	180	14.2:1
Ford (1974–1977)	677	99	25.6:1
Carter (1977–1981)	1,169	148	17.9:1
Reagan (1981–1989)	2,840	125	22.7:1
Bush (1989–1993)	1,350	67	20.2:1
Clinton (1993–2001)	2,058	209	9.9:1
Bush (2001–)a	262	21	12.5:1

Sources: *Treaties and Other International Agreements: The Role of the U.S. Senate,* Congressional Research Service, Library of Congress, January 2001. Data from Table II-2. Report submitted to the Committee on Foreign Relations, U.S. Senate, 106:2, Senate print 106-71. Data for 2000–2002 from Office of Treaty Affairs, U.S. Department of State.

aThrough 2002.

unilaterally abrogate a defense treaty with Taiwan that was part of the agreements establishing diplomatic relations between the United States and the People's Republic of China.[38] Reinterpretation also gives presidents expanded power in the treaty area. The Reagan administration provides the best example: in 1985, it broadened the terms of the 1972 Anti-Ballistic Missile (ABM) Treaty, over the objections of the Senate and the Soviet Union, to accommodate development of the strategic defense initiative.[39] President George W. Bush announced in May 2001 that he would proceed with development and deployment of an antimissile defense system and hoped to establish a "new framework" with Russia that was likely to take the form of an executive agreement rather than a new or amended ABM treaty.[40] It remains to be seen how Congress, U.S. allies, and Russia will respond to this fundamental change in longstanding strategic policy.

Appointments. As noted in chapter 6, the power to appoint subordinates is an important part of presidential control over policy but a power shared with the Senate. The most important appointments affecting national security are the positions of secretary of state, secretary of defense, director of central intelligence, and the president's assistant for national security affairs. With these appointments, presidents indicate the direction and orientation of the foreign and military policy of their administrations.

The choice of a well-known figure with definite policy views to serve as secretary of state—such as the selection of Gen. George C. Marshall by President Truman, John Foster Dulles by President Dwight D. Eisenhower, and Gen. Alexander Haig by President Reagan—reflects the intention to rely heavily on the secretary for advice and guidance. If presidents choose a relatively unknown individual—Kennedy's designation of Dean Rusk and Nixon's of William P. Rogers—it indicates that the executive intends to play the dominant role in foreign policy formulation and to relegate to the secretary management of the foreign affairs bureaucracy. President Clinton selected Warren M. Christopher, a soft-spoken lawyer with a reputation as a shrewd negotiator, as a way to remain consistent with his campaign focus on domestic, rather than foreign, policy. Clinton signaled the reversal of policy emphasis at the beginning of his second term when he named Madeleine K. Albright, known for her strong policy views, to replace Christopher. George W. Bush's selection of Gen. Colin L. Powell, broadly implied throughout the 2000 election campaign, communicated the president's intention to assemble an experienced and respected group of foreign policy advisers.

Similarly, the choice for the secretary of defense indicates the president's plans for that department. Kennedy's choice, Robert S. McNamara, president of the Ford Motor Company, signified the president's determination to make the armed forces more efficient through application of modern management techniques. Clinton reinforced the idea that he intended to leave most national security matters to subordinates when he named a highly regarded defense intellectual, Rep. Les Aspin, D-Wis., as secretary of defense. In 2001, George W. Bush's selection of Donald Rumsfeld, a senior Republican with extensive Washington experience and a reputation for being a hard-driving manager, made it clear that Bush would assemble a star-studded team of national security advisers.

The position of director of central intelligence involves managing the CIA and coordinating the activities of the intelligence community.[41] This was often a politically controversial position during the cold war because the CIA and other intelligence agencies had engaged in covert activities designed to assassinate foreign political leaders and overthrow foreign governments. Critics also charged the CIA with ineffective intelligence work, such as the failure to anticipate the Iranian revolution of 1978–1979 and Iraq's invasion of Kuwait in 1990. CIA directors have tended to be either intelligence professionals, such as William Colby and Robert Gates, or experienced politicians, such as George H. W. Bush and William Casey. The latter, Reagan's first CIA director, apparently played a major role in the Iran-contra affair, but he died before the congressional investigation into the affair.[42] Reagan appointed FBI director William Webster, a former federal judge, as Casey's successor to remove the aura of illegality and scandal associated with the agency. Robert Gates, President George H. W. Bush's first nominee to head the CIA, was confirmed only after lengthy hearings and floor debate.[43] R. James Woolsey, Clinton's replacement for Gates, attracted little notice until 1994, when the nation was shocked to learn that a sensitive CIA operative, Aldrich Ames, had been a Soviet mole for nine years, a revelation that eventually forced Woolsey's resignation.[44] George W. Bush retained Clinton's final CIA director, George J. Tenet, a move designed to enhance continuity much as John F. Kennedy had by retaining Allen Dulles as director of the CIA and Richard Nixon did by keeping Richard Helms. In the aftermath of the World Trade Center and Pentagon attacks of September 2001, some members of Congress questioned whether Tenet should be retained as director, but the administration gave him a strong vote of confidence.

One of the most important national security appointments, that of the national security assistant, is not subject to Senate approval. Over the years McGeorge Bundy, Henry Kissinger, Zbigniew Brzezinski, and Colin L. Powell have held this post, whose occupants have frequently come to dominate foreign policy decision making. In 2001 George W. Bush named Condoleeza Rice to the position. She played an important role in coordinating administration deliberations and mediating the reportedly strongly opposing views of Secretaries Rumsfeld and Powell on policy in Afghanistan and Iraq.[45] The president also designates personal representatives to conduct negotiations or perform specific missions without the requirement of confirmation. Distinguished career diplomats Ellsworth Bunker and Sol Linowitz were used by Carter in this way, just as several earlier presidents called upon prominent Democratic statesman W. Averell Harriman.

The appointment power helps presidents control both the conduct and the content of foreign and defense policy. Presidents enjoy wide latitude in exercising the power, but they must be sensitive to the limits imposed by international and domestic politics reflected in the Senate.

The Use of Military Force. The Constitution states, "The President shall be Commander in Chief of the Army and Navy of the United States" and of the state militia when it is called into federal service (Article II, Section 2). It does not, however, define the nature of the president's powers and duties as commander in chief. In fact, extensive powers pertaining to the use of military force are found in Article I, the legislative article. Most important, Congress is empowered to declare war. Constitutionally, then, the power to use military force is shared between Congress and the president. Historical practice, however, has resulted in a vast expansion of presidential authority to use force at the expense of the powers of Congress. The dominance of the president in this regard has been almost total in wartime; in times of peace, Congress has partially reclaimed the ground it lost. The result has been the continual aggrandizement of presidential power.[46]

Presidents have sweeping war powers based upon the Constitution, statutory delegations of authority by Congress, and judicial interpretations. The constitutional foundation of the president's war powers was established early in the Civil War when Abraham Lincoln married the Commander-in-Chief Clause to the "Take Care" Clause.[47] As discussed in chapter 1, Lincoln used the resulting war powers to justify a wide range of actions to suppress the rebellion: activation of state militias, expenditure of appropriated funds for unauthorized purposes, suspension of the writ of habeas corpus in militarily insecure areas, and the imposition of a naval blockade of Confederate ports. The Supreme Court upheld the legality of the blockade in the *Prize Cases*, in which it declared that the president had a duty to defend the nation by appropriate means, including military action.[48] The refusal of the Court to overturn any of Lincoln's actions until after the war set a precedent of judicial deference followed in later wars.

Lincoln's actions demonstrated that the president's war powers extend far beyond mere military command. During World War II, the president's powers as commander in chief expanded exponentially under FDR. Among other things, Roosevelt ordered the internment of all persons of Japanese ancestry, including both naturalized and native-born U.S. citizens, who were residing in the Pacific Coast states. The Supreme Court acquiesced in this deprivation of basic civil liberties.[49] Roosevelt created emergency agencies with sweeping regulatory powers and succeeded in his demand that Congress repeal certain sections of the Emergency Price Control Act that constrained his powers during the national emergency.

Delegations by statute have further contributed to the development of the president's war powers. As discussed in chapter 1, during World War I, Congress enacted laws that authorized the president to regulate, requisition, and purchase a wide range of materials and products, to prohibit exports, to license trade, to censor international communications, to regulate enemy aliens in the United States, and to seize and operate the railroads. These powers were expanded during World War II, and many delegations were open-ended, neither revised nor withdrawn until passage of the National Emergencies Act of 1976.

In short, once war is declared, presidential powers are vast. To ensure national survival, presidential directives are followed without regard to constitutional considerations and with the acquiescence, if not full approval, of the Supreme Court and Congress. Some leading constitutional scholars have charged that the Constitution is suspended in wartime and the president becomes a de facto dictator.[50]

The president's power to use military force in peacetime, or even in periods of undeclared war, is less clear-cut. Although the Supreme Court has been reluctant to resolve questions in this area, Congress has been more assertive of its prerogatives. However, the president still has substantial responsibilities and concomitant powers to protect American lives and property abroad, discharge international obligations, and preserve national security. Constitutional language is vague, and statutory enactments are an incomplete guide to the exercise of this authority.

Following World War II, although Congress and the president were united in the commitment to contain communism, the authority of the president to commit U.S. troops to fight abroad was a sensitive issue. On several occasions between 1945 and 1965, presidents sent U.S. forces into combat or placed them in situations that could easily lead to combat.[51] These included the Korean War, the dispatch of four divisions to Western Europe as a permanent commitment to NATO, Eisenhower's responses to Chinese pressures on Taiwan and to increased tensions in the Middle East, the 1965 intervention in the Dominican Republic, and the Vietnam War.

Vietnam produced the most extensive and controversial instances of presidential war making in the post–World War II era, partly because it was America's longest conflict of the twentieth century (see Table 10-4). Beginning with

Table 10-4   Duration of U.S. Wars Since 1900

War	Date War Began	Length
World War I	April 6, 1917	1 year, 7 months, 5 days
World War II	Dec. 8, 1941	3 years, 8 months, 6 days
Korea	June 27, 1950	3 years, 1 month
Vietnam	Feb. 14, 1962	10 years, 11 months, 13 days
Persian Gulf	Jan. 17, 1991	1 month, 10 days
Kosovo	March 24, 1999	2 months, 27 days
Afghanistan	Oct. 7, 2001	2 months
Iraq	March 19, 2003	1 month, 14 days

Source: *USA Today*, March 26, 2003, Reported on History News Network www.hnn.us/articles/1689.html.

Truman, presidents made commitments of military aid and provided military advisers to the government of South Vietnam. By the end of 1963, more than 16,000 military advisers were in that country, many of them actively participating in combat although not formally authorized to do so. In August 1964, the Johnson administration reported a confrontation in the Gulf of Tonkin between a North Vietnamese gunboat and a U.S. destroyer. At Johnson's request, Congress passed the Gulf of Tonkin Resolution, which authorized the president to "take all necessary steps including use of armed force" to assist nations belonging to the Southeast Asia Treaty Organization (to which the United States was a signatory) in defense of their freedom. On the authority of the Constitution, the Southeast Asia Treaty, and the Gulf of Tonkin Resolution, Johnson ordered a vast increase in the strength of U.S. forces in Vietnam; by late 1967, they exceeded 500,000. He also authorized military commanders to conduct air raids against military targets in North Vietnam.[52] President Nixon extended the scope of military operations even while trying to negotiate an end to U.S. involvement in the war. In 1970, he ordered a covert invasion of Cambodia and the bombing of Laos to destroy enemy supply and staging areas, and in December 1972, he authorized the bombing of the North Vietnamese capital city of Hanoi and the major port city of Haiphong. These actions were taken without consulting Congress.

Initially, Congress backed administration efforts to contain communism in Southeast Asia through the use of military force. As the war dragged on, however, popular support began to wane, a widespread domestic protest movement began to take shape, and opposition to U.S. policy rose abroad from the country's allies and from developing nations. Many members of Congress questioned the wisdom and the legality of placing the decision to use military force entirely in the president's hands. As long as presidential use of force appeared to be successful, congressional opposition was minimal. When the use of force appeared to be failing, or the risks increased and the costs in popular support became too great, Congress reasserted its constitutional authority to participate as an equal partner with the president in determining where and under what conditions the United States would wage war.

Although Americans remain sensitive to the experience with war powers during the Vietnam years, events can overtake caution. As noted at the outset of this chapter, Congress overwhelmingly endorsed President Bush's request for authority to wage war on terrorism in September 2001, issuing a blank check to take whatever action he deemed necessary.[53] In October 2002, caution reemerged. Congress did not approve the administration's version of a resolution for the use of force in Iraq that was described as "the broadest request for military authority by any White House since President Lyndon B. Johnson won approval of the Gulf of Tonkin resolution in 1964."[54] Instead, Congress approved a version negotiated by the House International Relations Committee that placed modest restrictions on the president's actions.[55]

The Assertion of Congressional Powers

Congress has substantial constitutional powers enabling it to claim parity with the president in shaping national security policy: the Senate's role in the treaty approval and appointment confirmation process; authorizations and appropriations needed to implement presidential decisions that are not self-executing; and the power to declare war. However, operational realities and a bipartisan foreign policy consensus led to presidential domination of national security policy during the cold war.

The failure of the Vietnam War—labeled by critics as a "presidential war"—ended, at least temporarily, Congress's deference to White House domination of national security policy. During the 1970s, Congress limited presidents' ability to wage undeclared war, reduced unrestrained use of executive agreements, restored the treaty as the principal means of making international agreements, reassessed its sweeping delegations of authority to presidents in past wars and emergencies, and curbed secrecy and covert activities in the conduct of foreign and military affairs.

The most important congressional attempt to reclaim powers lost or given to the executive was the War Powers Resolution of 1973. Passed over Nixon's veto, House Joint Resolution 542 provided that the president might commit the armed forces to combat only in the event of a declaration of war, specific statutory authorization, or a national emergency created by an attack on the United States or its armed forces. The resolution urged the president to consult with Congress in "every possible instance" before committing forces to combat abroad, and it required consultation after such commitment. Specifically, it required a written report to Congress within forty-eight hours of a commitment and required ending the commitment within sixty days unless authorized by Congress. The commitment could be extended for thirty additional days if the president certified to Congress that military conditions required continued use of the forces to ensure their safety. Finally, it stated that, through use of a concurrent resolution that would not be subject to presidential veto, Congress might order the disengagement of U.S. forces before the end of the first sixty days. (A Supreme Court decision in an unrelated case would force

Congress to substitute a joint resolution for the concurrent one, but the former is subject to the veto.)[56]

The effectiveness of the War Powers Resolution as a congressional means of controlling presidentially initiated military action is unclear. Through June 9, 2003, presidents had submitted 106 reports under the resolution (see Table 10-1), though most of these involved routine updates of ongoing force commitments.[57] In only one instance, the rescue of the *Mayaguez*, a merchant ship seized by Cambodian gunboats in 1975, did the president trigger the sixty-day clock. President Ford submitted 4 reports, Carter 1, Reagan 14, George H. W. Bush 7, Clinton 60, and George W. Bush 20 through June 3, 2003. Since its passage, all presidents have regarded the War Powers Resolution as an unconstitutional encroachment on their powers, and their reports have carefully avoided any acknowledgment of its constitutionality. In addition, they have been able to circumvent the intent of the resolution by not activating the sixty-day clock and by stating that merely informing Congress meets the resolution's requirement of consultation. The position of the executive has been consistent across administrations, while Congress has been unable to formulate a corresponding "unitary position or statement of institutional interest."[58] Nor has Congress challenged the president by starting the sixty-day clock on its own. Congress considered triggering the clock in 1983, in legislation involving the multinational force in Lebanon, but ultimately authorized U.S. participation in the force for eighteen months. This was done after an agreement was reached with the White House.[59]

President Bush's actions during the Persian Gulf War of 1990–1991 are typical of how presidents deal with the War Powers Resolution.[60] Before sending U.S. armed forces to the gulf in response to Iraq's August 2, 1990, invasion of Kuwait, Bush notified congressional leaders of the planned deployment on August 8. The next day, he sent the Speaker and the president pro tem a letter in which he stated that the report was "consistent with" the War Powers Resolution. During the next six months, there was a massive buildup of U.S. forces in the gulf area, the United States and Iraq exchanged bellicose threats, and the United Nations adopted a resolution imposing a deadline for Iraq to withdraw from Kuwait. At no point, however, did either the president or Congress begin the sixty-day countdown. As he had from the beginning, the president continued to argue that he had the authority to force Iraq to leave Kuwait without congressional approval. Nevertheless, on January 8, 1991, one week before the UN deadline, Bush asked Congress to approve a joint resolution authorizing the use of force. Congress did so four days later by votes of 52–47 in the Senate and 250–183 in the House.[61] When Bush signed the resolution, he reasserted his position that the War Powers Resolution was unconstitutional. The resolution approved on January 12, 1991, has been recognized as the functional equivalent of a declaration of war. Whether Bush weakened his position—that he already had the authority to initiate hostilities—is an unanswered question.

The effect of the War Powers Resolution on the constitutional roles of the president and Congress in making decisions about war and peace is unclear. At the very least, the legislation was a symbolic victory for Congress, serving notice that sustained military commitments outside the country could no longer be made by presidential fiat but required congressional approval and, by implication, popular support. However, there is "growing consensus" that the resolution "has not worked as Congress envisioned."[62] Presidents have neither consulted Congress in "any meaningful manner" nor have they sought to make the law work by invoking its provisions.[63] Instead, they have sought to circumvent it. For its part, Congress has been unwilling to challenge presidential nonresponsiveness to the War Powers Resolution, and the courts have been unwilling to intercede until it does so.[64] Michael Glennon summarized the effectiveness of the resolution: "Whatever congressional intent underlay the War Powers Resolution, any expectation that its procedures would actually lead to collective legislative-executive judgment in the war-making process was mistaken."[65] Presidential evasion, congressional acquiescence, and judicial deference have combined to bring about this result.[66]

Despite its failings, the resolution persists because it suits congressional purposes. It "allows Congress the luxury of being politically comfortable with its decisions regarding a military action while providing a convenient forum for criticizing the President."[67] Congress can use the War Powers Resolution to force the president to end an unpopular military operation, or it can criticize presidential failure to comply with the procedural requirements of the resolution when public opinion is supportive or divided. Either way, Congress cannot lose.[68] The resolution reminds presidents that, under the Constitution, they share with Congress the crucial decision to lead the nation into war. Thus far presidents have been no more willing than Congress to ask the Supreme Court to resolve the lingering ambiguities—an unwillingness that may stem on both sides from uncertainty about the outcome.[69]

Despite the desire to share in making national security policy as well as increased institutional knowledge and competence, Congress has not assumed added responsibility.[70] Even the traditional "power of the purse" that rests on congressional appropriation of funds has been eroded, with presidents supporting international projects by spending money from lump sum accounts and reprogramming funds from one purpose to another, effectively exercising "presidential spending power in national security."[71] Structurally, Congress has difficulty asserting its prerogatives, and reforms during the 1970s, especially in the House, fragmented power even further, making it still more difficult for Congress to speak authoritatively. The proliferation of subcommittees and the growing interdependence of domestic and foreign policy issues added to the number of congressional participants in national security policy matters. These developments, along with additional pressures from interest groups and other domestic constituencies, made interbranch consensus more elusive. Although Republican majorities moved to consolidate legislative power in the 1990s *(see chapter 5),* the structural problems remain.

The constitutional "invitation to struggle" is still present. Four paths are possible for Congress: reversion to the pattern of acquiescence in presidential domination that prevailed from World War II until 1973; directing policy on its own because of popular pressures or distrust of the president's policies and capabilities; collaboration tempered by a sense of constitutional and political responsibility to be constructively critical; and all-out conflict, a pattern that nearly erupted during the impeachment of President Clinton in December 1998. On the eve of the scheduled House vote on articles of impeachment, Clinton ordered an air attack on Iraq for failure to cooperate with UN weapons inspectors responsible for overseeing that country's disarmament after the Persian Gulf War. The impeachment vote was delayed for several days. Congressional members questioned the president's motives in launching an attack that had been delayed numerous times in the past, including a month earlier. Republican leaders publicly spoke out against the action and expressed doubts about the president's credibility. Editorials wondered whether he was "risking lives to cling to power."[72] Thus impeachment imposed enormous strains on the delicate institutional relationships essential for effective foreign policy.

Organizing and Managing National Security

Beyond dealing with the constitutional issues and political considerations involved in national security policy, the president also confronts a formidable administrative task: organizing the presidency and the executive branch to formulate and implement policy. This requires establishing and changing structures and processes that enhance decision making and interagency coordination. As the Iran-contra investigation revealed, a lax approach to these tasks can be costly, but it is also possible to overemphasize them. One has to remember that "good organization does not insure successful policy, nor does poor organization preclude it."[73] Designing an effective system accomplishes three primary functions: it "creates capabilities" for performing tasks beyond the reach of individuals; it "vests and weighs particular interests and perspectives" by increasing or reducing the probability of their inclusion in decision making; and it "legitimates decisions" by ensuring that relevant parties are consulted and that decisions are made by proper authorities.[74]

Although there is no specific model to which national security organization must conform, the policy-making system that is established must be capable of adapting to changing events and conditions, and it must be able to accommodate the operating style of the presidents, whose constitutional roles make them the focal point of the policy-making process. Congress has enacted legislation—the National Security Act of 1947 was the most far-reaching—establishing organizational units to aid presidents in the conduct of national security policy. The principal units are the National Security Council and its staff, the Departments of State and Defense, the Joint Chiefs of Staff, and the Central Intelligence Agency. Though Congress has established these staffing units, it cannot prescribe how presidents will employ them. How they choose to work through staff, cabinet, and independent agencies is a matter totally at their discretion.

The National Security Council is the basic structure for the management of national security affairs. Since the council's creation in 1947, presidents have used it in various ways. Congress established the council in response to the pressures of the cold war and in reaction, at least in part, to the administrative confusion that often characterized Franklin Roosevelt's freewheeling approach to management. Chief executives, upon taking office, must define their roles in the national security policy-making system before they can design and manage the roles and relationships of other major participants in it.[75] According to conventional wisdom, the basic choice every president must make is whether to manage the system through the secretary of state and the State Department, as Truman did, or to centralize it in the White House, as Nixon did, with the national security assistant playing the major role. Failure to decide on a consistent approach is likely to result in confusion over policy goals and lack of cohesion in policy implementation, as was the case with Clinton.[76] Neither his national security assistant and the NSC staff (which nearly doubled in size to an all-time high of a hundred professionals),[77] nor Clinton's secretary of state and the State Department were clearly in charge. The result was a series of ad hoc reactions to crises, problems, and domestic pressures.

Cecil Crabb and Kevin Mulcahy have developed a typology for analyzing presidential management of national security that is based on responsibility for policymaking and policy implementation.[78] They have identified four presidential management styles—department-centered, formalized, collegial, and palace guard—with accompanying roles for the national security assistant—administrator, coordinator, counselor, and agent (see Figure 10-1). Presidents such as Truman, with limited interest in the formation and implementation of foreign policy, deputize the secretary of state to act and speak for them and rely primarily on the State Department for analysis and implementation. In this *department-centered* style, the national security assistant plays the corresponding role of administrator (Adm. Sidney Souers) and acts primarily as a high-level staff aide who supervises the advisory process and facilitates the presentation of views to the president but does not act independently or function as a primary policy adviser.

Dwight Eisenhower looked to the national security bureaucracy—the Departments of State and Defense and the intelligence community—for policy recommendations, carefully examined a wide range of proposals and plans, and retained control over policymaking and implementation, exemplifying the *formalized* management style. His national security assistant, Robert Cutler, functioned as a coordinator, whose principal task was to facilitate the decision making of the president and secretary of state by defining options and managing the flow of ideas and information. Although no subsequent president has fully followed Eisenhower's management example, some academics still praise its advantages while others criticize its lack of flexibility.[79]

The *collegial* management style, typified by Kennedy and Johnson, involves an informal national security process in which the president deals with ad hoc

Figure 10-1   Presidential Management Styles and National Security Assistant's Roles

Implementation Responsibility

	Low	High
Low *Policymaking Responsibility*	Department-centered administrator	Formalized coordinator
High	Collegial counselor	Palace guard agent

Source: Cecil V. Crabb Jr. and Kevin V. Mulcahy, *American National Security: A Presidential Perspective* (Pacific Grove, Calif.: Brooks/Cole, 1991), 189.

working groups. This system centralizes decision making in the White House, with the NSC staff performing independent analysis and policy review functions. National security assistants serve as counselors, major policy advisers safeguarding the president's interests, a role exemplified by McGeorge Bundy under Kennedy and Walt Rostow in the Johnson administration. Brent Scowcroft played such a role in the first Bush administration,[80] and Clinton's management of national security policy evolved to approximate the collegial style, with Sandy Berger serving as a counselor.[81] The *palace guard* management style, associated with Richard Nixon, centralizes policymaking in the White House and maintains a tight rein on implementation.[82] Nixon's national security assistant, Henry Kissinger, acted as the president's agent, directing the policy-making process, serving as the president's closest policy adviser, and on occasion actively implementing policy by conducting negotiations with foreign governments.

Experience since 1947 suggests the administrator role is likely to be ineffective unless the president and the secretary of state are capable, hands-on decision makers. The agent role carries the risk that national security assistants may go into business for themselves, acting without presidential knowledge or approval as Reagan claimed was the case with Adm. John Poindexter and his assistant, Lt. Col. Oliver North, in the Iran-contra affair. Whether presidents choose the coordinator or counselor role for a national security assistant should be determined by their management style. In either case, the national security assistant's personality must be compatible with the designated role.[83] Carter's system suffered because Zbigniew Brzezinski was an ambitious, assertive individual more suited to the role of agent than administrator, which Carter apparently wished him to play.

Reagan vacillated in establishing a preferred management style and had six individuals serve as national security assistant. This instability became most evident during Reagan's second term, when turmoil prevailed in the relationship between Secretary of State George Shultz and the NSC staff. One national security assistant, Robert McFarlane, acted as a policy advocate rather than as an honest broker and carried out special missions for the president.[84] An unanswered question lingers: Could any conceivable system for managing foreign policy have overcome Reagan's deliberate disengagement from policymaking and his lack of interest in and concern with policy implementation?

National Security Organization and Management under George W. Bush

President George W. Bush's challenge has been to harmonize many powerful voices. Given the presence of several high-visibility, assertive personalities in cabinet positions and a highly experienced vice president, observers wondered what kind of role would be played by the national security assistant, Dr. Condoleeza Rice. The president gave Rice a vote of confidence at the outset of the administration when she, and not the vice president, was designated, in the absence of the president, to chair meetings of the principals committee. The committee is "the senior interagency forum for consideration of policy issues affecting national security"[85] and includes the secretaries of defense, state, and treasury as well as the White House chief of staff, the director of the CIA, and the chairman of the Joint Chiefs of Staff.[86] Other members of the administration attend such meetings when matters touch their areas of responsibility; the vice president is free to attend all meetings and his chief of staff and national security adviser attend as well. Dr. Rice was a steadying force during the period following September 11, 2001, when the administration fashioned a response to terrorism and launched the military action in Afghanistan. Clashes between Secretaries Rumsfeld and Powell, veterans of many bureaucratic battles, were just as bitter as observers had predicted. Rice helped to manage the policy-making system and ensure that the president's options were preserved.[87] She also emerged as a forceful defender of the administration's policies on television talk shows and through newspaper interviews. Early estimates suggest that Rice, a veteran of the NSC system operated by Scowcroft, fills a counselor's role.[88]

The size of the NSC staff was initially reduced by 30 percent, to about seventy, but had crept upward again to eighty to eighty-five members by mid-2003.[89] Interagency cooperation is achieved through a set of NSC Policy Coordination Committees, seventeen of which were created at the administration's outset.[90] Each was staffed by a professional from the NSC; some were under the direction of the secretary of state and others under the national security assistant. Thus the administration created a variation of the formalized system established by Eisenhower that accommodates strong cabinet secretaries within a White House–centered staff system. This system is also consistent with the president's preference of reserving final judgment for himself. As in all other administrations, the product is a combination of the president's personal style, the qualities of the principal advisers assembled to help him, and the president's confidence in their advice.

The Bush team functioned smoothly during its first real test, the terrorist attacks on the World Trade Center and the Pentagon. Both President Bush and Secretary of State Powell were out of town at the time of the attack, but they returned to Washington to become central figures in fashioning the national response. Vice President Cheney and National Security Adviser Rice coordinated initial responses from the Presidential Emergency Operations Center, a nuclear attack shelter in the basement of the White House. This twenty-first century attack was met with twenty-first century government organization: the president remained in contact with the White House team throughout the crisis by secure telephone and even convened a teleconference meeting of the National Security Council. Upon his return to Washington, the president met regularly with the NSC and coordinated action with the FBI and the Transportation Department, as well. In short, the system worked smoothly, producing several critical decisions about both tactics and strategy and projecting an image of calm determination after a jittery first day.[91]

Far more controversial was the administration's performance prior to and following the March 2003 invasion of Iraq. Although conclusions must await an authoritative history, it appears that a powerful alliance of Vice President Cheney, Secretary Rumsfeld, and his principal deputy, Paul Wolfowitz, pressed aggressively for action against the regime of Saddam Hussein, survivor of the Persian Gulf War. The administration was convinced that Hussein was actively developing weapons of mass destruction and was a threat to use them, something he had already done against both Kurd nationalists within his own country and during the war with Iran. A debate ensued over whether the United States should take unilateral action against this "outlaw regime" or work through the United Nations. In the short run, Secretary Powell won the internal policy battle. In a dramatic speech delivered at the UN on September 12, 2002, the president challenged that organization to enforce its sixteen previous resolutions on Iraq. He agreed to delay action until UN inspectors were once again dispatched to Iraq, supported by a unanimous November vote in the Security Council. However, reports from the inspectors made it clear that Hussein's regime was refusing to disclose and destroy its weapons, and the United States prepared for military action by assembling its forces in the region. President Bush issued several warnings of his intent to act and sought to build both national and international support behind such action. For a time it appeared that only British prime minister Tony Blair would join the effort as both traditional (France, Germany) and new (China, Russia) allies on the Security Council opposed military action. Ultimately, Spain, Italy, Poland, Australia, Japan, and forty-four less significant nations joined the truncated "coalition of the willing," placing into question U.S. relations with reluctant NATO partners and the other great powers.[92]

Launched on March 19, 2003, the military action in Iraq proved remarkably successful. Following a massive air assault, American and British ground forces made rapid progress from the invasion launch point in Kuwait. Audiences around the world were able to experience the rapid advance and intense fire

The entry of U.S. troops into Baghdad triggered demonstrations by Iraqi citizens against the regime of Saddam Hussein, whose statues were toppled and defaced; but support waned and resistance grew as the occupation of Iraq continued.

fights with the help of "embedded journalists" traveling with the attacking forces. Despite being badly outgunned, the Iraqi forces used neither biological nor chemical weapons against the invaders; coalition forces were also unable to find evidence that such weapons existed, the prime justification for the war. After the president announced the end of combat operations in a triumphal speech aboard the USS *Abraham Lincoln* on May 1, criticism mounted in both Britain and the United States that the administrations had used misleading intelligence to sell the military action to skeptical publics. American media particularly focused on the following sentence from the 2003 State of the Union message:

The British government has learned that Saddam Hussein recently sought significant quantities of uranium from Africa.[93]

In early July 2003, the White House acknowledged that this charge represented faulty intelligence, a report CIA and State Department intelligence officials had questioned for months. In fact, the same claim was not repeated in Secretary Powell's case for using military force presented to the United Nations eight days later.[94] Several statements had been made during fall 2002 that Iraq had reestablished a nuclear weapons program, but each had been rebutted either within the government or by UN specialists.[95] Nonetheless, the president used the nuclear threat as part of his justification for war. Without evidence of an imminent threat—a questionable nuclear argument and no evidence of chemical and biological weapons—the president's motivation, war rationale, and credibility were called into question.[96] In the following three weeks, a succession of administration figures stepped up to shoulder the blame for the speech error: CIA Director Tenet, Deputy National Security Advisor Stephen Hadley, Director of Presidential Speechwriting Michael Gerson, and National Security Advisor Rice. Finally, hoping to bring the media furor to a halt, the president stated in late July that he took full responsibility for the statement.

The postwar peace went far less smoothly than the war. The much-respected British newsweekly *The Economist* asked, "Did the Bush administration spend too much time thinking about how to secure military victory, and too little working out what to do with the country once Saddam Hussein had been removed?"[97] As many critics had predicted, nation building, led by the Christian, western, pro-Israeli United States, proved enormously difficult in a confused political setting with warring religious and ethnic factions. Without definitive evidence that Saddam Hussein and his sons had died in the assault on Baghdad, the specter of his return haunted American efforts. Two factors began to erode public support: isolated but steady attacks on American forces that produced continued casualties and the cost of maintaining American military forces in Iraq, about $4 billion a month.[98] As the 2004 elections loomed, Democrats sought to make faulty intelligence about weapons of mass destruction into a campaign issue.[99] Although the second President Bush had sought to complete the effort launched in 1991 by the first President Bush, it remained unclear whether the son would succeed where the father had partially prevailed.

Conclusion

National security is the president's most important policy responsibility, presenting complex problems of leadership and management. For the nation, preserving and protecting its sovereignty and independence is of paramount interest. To a great extent, success depends on every president's personal performance. Presidents must interpret and exercise their powers within constitutional and statutory limits. To succeed, they must have congressional cooperation, which requires consultation. Yet operational realities require that presidents be accorded ample latitude to act independently and often secretly. Tensions inevitably arise between Congress and the president over national security policy,[100] but the tasks involved are primarily executive in nature, and executive control of foreign and military policy persists in spite of Congress's major constitutional role.[101] The Constitution and political prudence require "shared power and balanced institutional participation" as norms in national security decision making.[102]

Perhaps the most important lesson in this regard is that since 1945 most of the nation's successful foreign policies—the Truman Doctrine, the Marshall Plan, NATO, the Panama Canal treaty, arms control, and the Persian Gulf War—"have been adopted by Congress and the people after meaningful debate."[103] For the most part, the major failures—FDR's Yalta agreements with Stalin, the Bay of Pigs invasion, the Vietnam War, and the Iran-contra affair—have been initiated and implemented unilaterally by presidents. In the case of the Iraq War, Congress approved action, but it remains unclear whether Bush will be saddled with the blame for a failed adventure.

In the emerging international system, the United States remains the world's dominant power both militarily and economically. Yet that does not mean America can always assert its will unilaterally. Finding the means to exercise power responsibly remains both the nation's and the president's major challenge.

NOTES

1. "Authorization for Use of Military Force," joint resolution adopted September 14, 2001, *Washington Post,* September 15, 2001, A4.

2. Remarks of George W. Bush in a news conference on September 13, 2001, as reported by eMediaMillWorks, www.washingtonpost.com.

3. The "two presidencies" thesis holds that presidents enjoy relatively greater success with Congress in foreign policy than in domestic policy. According to Terry Sullivan, modern Republican and Democratic presidents have had approximately equal success with foreign policy proposals, but Democratic administrations have done better with domestic policy because of their party's longtime domination of Congress. See Sullivan, "A Matter of Fact: The 'Two Presidencies' Thesis Revitalized," in *The Two Presidencies: A Quarter Century Assessment,* ed. Steven A. Shull (Chicago: Nelson Hall, 1991), 143–157. On the rise of partisan and ideological bickering over foreign policy issues in Congress during the 1990s, see James M. McCormick, Eugene R. Wittkopf, and David M. Dana, "Politics and Bipartisanship at the Water's Edge: A Note on Bush and Clinton," *Polity* 30 (fall 1997): 133–149.

4. James Chace, "Is a Foreign Policy Consensus Possible?" *Foreign Affairs* 57 (fall 1978): 30.

5. Lawrence J. Korb, *A New National Security Strategy in an Age of Terrorists, Tyrants, and Weapons of Mass Destruction* (New York: Council on Foreign Relations, 2003), 1.

6. Strobe Talbot, *The Russians and Reagan* (New York: Vintage Books, 1984).

7. The most comprehensive and informative account of the Iran-contra affair is by Theodore Draper, *A Very Thin Line: The Iran-Contra Affairs* (New York: Hill and

Wang, 1991). For the perspective of two participants in the congressional hearings, see William S. Cohen and George J. Mitchell, *Men of Zeal* (New York: Viking, 1988). The role of the CIA and its director William Casey receive careful attention from Bob Woodward in *Veil: The Secret Wars of the CIA, 1981–1987* (New York: Simon and Schuster, 1987). Also essential to a full understanding of Iran-contra is the report of the Tower Commission (John Tower, Edmund Muskie, and Brent Scowcroft). President's Special Review Board, *Report of the President's Special Review Board* (Washington, D.C.: Government Printing Office, 1987).

8. Terry L. Deibel, "Bush's Foreign Policy: Mastery and Inaction," *Foreign Policy* 84 (fall 1991): 20–22; Steven V. Roberts, "The Second Sin of George Bush," *New Leader*, March 11–15, 1991, 3.

9. Daniel P. Franklin and Robert Shepard, "Analyzing the Bush Foreign Policy" (paper presented at the annual meeting of the American Political Science Association, Washington, D.C., August 29–September 1, 1991), 2–3.

10. Deibel, "Bush's Foreign Policy," 3–4.

11. David C. Hendrickson, "The Recovery of Internationalism," *Foreign Affairs* 73 (September–October 1994): 26–43. For similar criticisms, see Richard N. Haas, "Paradigm Lost," *Foreign Affairs* 74 (January–February 1995): 43–58; and Larry Berman and Emily O. Goldman, "Clinton's Foreign Policy at Midterm," in *The Clinton Presidency: First Appraisals*, ed. Colin Campbell and Bert A. Rockman (Chatham, N.J.: Chatham House, 1995), 290–324.

12. William J. Clinton, *A National Security Strategy of Engagement and Enlargement* (Washington, D.C.: Government Printing Office, 1994).

13. Berman and Goldman, "Clinton's Foreign Policy," 302–303.

14. William J. Clinton, *A National Security Strategy for a New Century* (Washington, D.C.: The White House, October 1998). For commentary, see Emily O. Goldman and Larry Berman, "Engaging the World: First Impressions of the Clinton Foreign Policy Legacy," in *The Clinton Legacy*, ed. Colin Campbell and Bert A. Rockman (New York: Chatham House, 2000); and James M. McCormick, "Clinton and Foreign Policy: Some Legacies for a New Century," in *The Postmodern Presidency: Bill Clinton's Legacy in U.S. Politics*, ed. Steven E. Schier (Pittsburgh: University of Pittsburgh Press, 2000).

15. These documents were National Security Policy Directive 17 and Homeland Security Policy Directive 4, released on December 12, 2002. See Korb, *A New National Security Strategy*, Appendix B.

16. John Lewis Gaddis, "A Grand Strategy of Transformation," *Foreign Policy* (November–December 2002), www.foreignpolicy.com/issue_novdec_2002/gaddis.html.

17. Fareed Zacaria, "The Arrogant Empire," *Newsweek*, March 24, 2003, 18ff.

18. Ibid.

19. George W. Bush, State of the Union message, January 29, 2002, www.whitehouse.gov/news/releases/2002/01/20020129–11.html.

20. Korb *A New National Security Strategy*, Appendix B, 107.

21. Susan E. Rice, "The New National Security Strategy: Focus on Failed States," Brookings Policy Brief #116-2003, 1, www.brookings.org/comm/policybriefs/pb116.htm.

22. Letter of submission from George W. Bush, September 17, 2002, published in Korb, *A New National Security Strategy*, Appendix B, 99.

23. See, for example, three Brookings Institution policy briefs: Ivo Daalder, James M. Lindsay, and James B. Steinberg, "The Bush National Security Strategy: An Evaluation," Policy Brief #109-2002, www.brookings.org/comm/policybriefs/pb109.htm; Michael E. O'Hanlon, Susan E. Rice, and James B. Steinberg, "The New National Security Strategy and Preemption," Policy Brief #113-2003, www.brookings.org/comm/policybriefs/pb113.htm; and Rice, "The New National Security Strategy."

24. O'Hanlon, Rice, and Steinberg, "The New National Security Strategy and Preemption," 2.

25. These three options are discussed in depth and presented as alternative drafts of presidential speeches in Korb, *A New National Security Strategy*, 1–96.

26. Prominently mentioned in many accounts are Vice President Cheney, Secretary of Defense Donald Rumsfeld, and Deputy Secretary of Defense Paul Wolfowitz.

27. See the comments of Lee Hamilton, former member of the House, D-Ind., as reported by Charlie Cook, "China Crisis Halts Slide of Bush's Poll Ratings," *National Journal*, April 21, 2001, 1186.

28. Edward S. Corwin, *The President: Office and Powers*, 4th ed. (New York: New York University Press, 1957), 171.

29. Ibid.

30. Joseph E. Kallenbach, *The American Chief Executive* (New York: Harper and Row, 1966), 485.

31. Corwin, *The President*, 179.

32. Ibid., 185.

33. Ibid., 213.

34. Ibid.; Kallenbach, *The American Chief Executive*, 502.

35. The treaty-making process entails three distinct stages: negotiation, Senate approval, and ratification by the president. Contrary to popular understanding, the Senate does not ratify a treaty—it approves the treaty negotiated by the president. The president may refuse to sign, that is, to ratify, a treaty approved by the Senate, either because of amendments or reservations or because it was negotiated by a previous administration.

36. Cecil V. Crabb Jr. and Pat M. Holt, *Invitation to Struggle: Congress, the President, and Foreign Policy*, 4th ed. (Washington, D.C.: CQ Press, 1992), 6.

37. Harold Hongju Koh argues, however, that Congress should create by statute its own procedures for determining when international agreements should be submitted to the Senate for approval. See Koh, *The National Security Constitution: Sharing Power after the Iran-Contra Affair* (New Haven: Yale University Press, 1990), 195.

38. *Goldwater v. Carter*, 444 U.S. 996 (1979). Although the Court based its decision on the recognition of foreign governments, the case has been interpreted as authorizing unilateral presidential breaking of treaties in accordance with their terms.

39. Koh, *The National Security Constitution*, 43.

40. David E. Sanger and Steven Lee Myers, "Bush Seeks Missile Shield Along with Nuclear Cuts; Calls '72 Treaty Outdated," *New York Times*, May 2, 2001, A1. It was later revealed that the Bush administration was considering a radical departure from the past—abandoning all strategic weapons treaties to maximize flexibility in making nuclear force decisions. Michael R. Gordon, "U.S. Weighing Future of Strategic Arms Pacts," *New York Times*, May 9, 2001, A1

41. The intelligence community consists of the Central Intelligence Agency; the National Security Agency; the Bureau of Intelligence and Research in the Department of State; the Defense Intelligence Agency; the intelligence offices of the army, navy, air force, and marine corps; and the intelligence offices in the Departments of Energy and Treasury. Crabb and Holt, *Invitation to Struggle*, 25.

42. Woodward, *Veil*, chap. 25.

43. Pamela Fessler, "Gates Confirmed to Lead CIA into Post-Soviet Era," *Congressional Quarterly Weekly Report*, November 9, 1991, 3291–3292.

44. Aldrich Ames was the Soviet branch chief of the CIA's counterintelligence group. From 1985 through 1993, he sold sensitive information, including the names of the entire network of spies that the United States had established in the Soviet Union during the cold war, to the KGB. Most of those agents were executed. For accounts of the Ames case, see Tim Weiner, David Johnson, and Neil A. Lewis,

Betrayal (New York: Random House, 1995); and David Wise, *Nightmover* (New York: HarperCollins, 1995). Also see Donna Cassata, "Congress Jumps to CIA's Aid in Its Quest for Identity," *Congressional Quarterly Weekly Report,* January 7, 1995, 41–42.

45. Bob Woodward, *Bush at War* (New York: Simon and Schuster, 2002).

46. Corwin, *The President,* chap. 6; Arthur M. Schlesinger Jr., *The Imperial Presidency* (Boston: Houghton Mifflin, 1989), chaps. 1–7.

47. Corwin, *The President,* 229.

48. *Prize Cases,* 67 U.S. (2 Black) 635 (1863).

49. *Korematsu v. United States,* 323 U.S. 214 (1944).

50. Clinton Rossiter, *Constitutional Dictatorship: Crisis Government in Modern Democracies* (New York: Harcourt, Brace, 1963).

51. Such actions have numerous precedents, including Jefferson's dispatch of the navy to stop the Barbary pirates from seizing U.S. merchant ships and holding their crews for ransom, and Theodore Roosevelt's contribution of U.S. Marines to the international expeditionary force that put down the Boxer Rebellion in China in 1904.

52. Larry Berman, *Planning a Tragedy: The Americanization of the War in Vietnam* (New York: Norton, 1982). For a comparative analysis of how Eisenhower and Johnson dealt with pressures to intervene militarily in Vietnam, see John P. Burke and Fred I. Greenstein, *How Presidents Test Reality: Decisions on Vietnam, 1954 and 1965* (New York: Russell Sage Foundation, 1989).

53. Ivo H. Daalder and James M. Lindsay, "The Bush Revolution: The Remaking of America's Foreign Policy" (paper delivered at the conference on The George W. Bush Presidency: An Early Assessment, Princeton University, April 25–26, 2003), 28.

54. Mike Allen and Charles Lane, "Resolution Likened to '64 Vietnam Measure," *Washington Post,* September 20, 2002, A20.

55. The House vote was 296–133, with all but 6 Republicans approving and Democrats dividing 81 yes and 126 no. The Senate vote was 77–23, with all but 1 Republican approving and Democrats dividing with 21 voting no; the independent also voted no.

56. The Supreme Court's decision in *Immigration and Naturalization Service v. Chadha,* 462 U.S. 919 (1983), which held that the legislative veto was unconstitutional, made this provision inoperative.

57. Richard F. Grimmett, "War Powers Resolution: Presidential Compliance," *CRS Issue Brief for Congress,* Congressional Research Service, Library of Congress, Washington, D.C., March 21, 2001, updated June 9, 2003.

58. Robert A. Katzman, "War Powers: Toward a New Accommodation," in *A Question of Balance: The President, Congress, and Foreign Policy,* ed. Thomas E. Mann (Washington, D.C.: Brookings, 1990), 55.

59. Ibid., 66.

60. Joshua Lee Prober, "Congress, the War Powers Resolution, and the Secret Political Life of 'a Dead Letter,' " *Journal of Law and Politics* 7 (1990): 177–229.

61. Carroll J. Doherty, "Bush Is Given Authorization to Use Force Against Iraq," *Congressional Quarterly Weekly Report,* January 12, 1991, 65–70.

62. Katzman, "War Powers," 35; Thomas M. Franck, "Rethinking War Powers: By Law or by 'Thaumaturgic Invocation'?" *American Journal of International Law* 83 (1989): 768.

63. John M. Hillebrecht, "Ensuring Affirmative Congressional Control over the Use of Force: Two Proposals for Collective Decision Making," *Stanford Journal of International Law* 26 (1990): 511.

64. See *Lowry v. Reagan,* 676 F. Supp. 333 (D.D.C. 1987); and *Dellums v. Bush,* 752 F. Supp. 1141 (D.D.C. 1990). In *Lowry,* the district court rejected the request of 110 members of Congress that it issue a declaration that President Reagan was required to file reports under the War Powers Resolution concerning two incidents in the

Persian Gulf. The court held that it could not act because Congress had not acted on the issue. In *Dellums*, the court rejected the request of 45 Democratic members of Congress that it enjoin President George Bush from conducting military operations in the Persian Gulf without a declaration of war by Congress. The court held that the issue was not ripe for decision because a majority of Congress had not sought relief and the executive had not committed itself to a course of action that made war imminent.

65. Michael J. Glennon, *Constitutional Diplomacy* (Princeton: Princeton University Press, 1990), 102–103.

66. Koh, *The National Security Constitution*.

67. Prober, "Congress, the War Powers Resolution," 229.

68. Ibid., 223–226, 229.

69. Citing as precedent the history of presidential war making, the Court could sustain the resolution. Or the Court might choose to overturn it, noting that since the resolution was forced on the presidency at a time of institutional weakness, it "undercuts the legitimacy of the executive branch." I. M. Destler, "The Constitution and Foreign Affairs," *News for Teachers of Political Science* (spring 1985): 15.

70. James L. Sundquist, *The Decline and Resurgence of Congress* (Washington, D.C.: Brookings, 1981), 270.

71. William C. Banks and Jeffrey D. Straussman, "A New Imperial Presidency? Insights from U.S. Involvement in Bosnia," *Political Science Quarterly* 114 (summer 1999): 200.

72. William Safire, "On Impeachment Eve," *New York Times*, December 17, 1998, A31. On the comments of Senate majority leader Trent Lott and House whip Tom Delay, see R. W. Apple Jr., "No Reservoir of Credibility," *New York Times*, December 17, 1998, A1, A15. On the air attacks more generally, see Francis X. Clines and Steven Lee Myers, "Biggest Attack Since '91 War—Britain Gives Support," *New York Times*, December 17, 1998, A1, A15.

73. *Report of the U. S. Commission on the Organization of the Government for the Conduct of Foreign Policy* (Washington, D.C.: Government Printing Office, 1975), 1. Also see Burke and Greenstein, *How Presidents Test Reality*, esp. chap. 13.

74. Graham T. Allison and Peter Szanton, "Organizing for the Decade Ahead," in *Setting National Priorities: The Next Ten Years*, ed. Henry Owen and Charles Schultze (Washington, D.C.: Brookings, 1976), 232–233.

75. Alexander L. George, *Presidential Decisionmaking in Foreign Policy: The Effective Use of Information and Advice* (Boulder: Westview, 1980), 146.

76. Burt Solomon, "When It Comes to Geopolitics . . . Who's Painting the Big Picture?" *National Journal*, March 5, 1995, 550–551.

77. Ivo H. Daalder and I. M. Destler, "A New NSC for a New Administration," Policy Brief #68-2000, The Brookings Institution, www.brookings.org/comm/policy-briefs/pb68.htm.

78. Cecil V. Crabb Jr. and Kevin V. Mulcahy, *American National Security: A Presidential Perspective* (Pacific Grove, Calif.: Brooks-Cole, 1991), chap. 9. The discussion relies on Crabb and Mulcahy.

79. See most recently the following minidebate: Fred I. Greenstein and Richard H. Immerman, "Effective National Security Advising: Recovering the Eisenhower Legacy," and Arthur Schlesinger Jr., "Effective National Security Advising: A Most Dubious Precedent," *Political Science Quarterly* 115 (fall 2000): 335–351.

80. Larry Berman and Bruce W. Jentelson, "Bush and the Post–Cold War World: New Challenges for American Leadership," in *The Bush Presidency: First Appraisals*, ed. Colin Campbell and Bert A. Rockman (Chatham, N.J.: Chatham House, 1991), 99–103. Also see Burt Solomon, "Making Foreign Policy in Secret May Be Easy, but It Carries Risks," *National Journal*, January 12, 1991, 90–91.

81. Anthony Lake, who held the position before Berger, is best thought of as a coordinator according to a written communication from Professor Kevin Mulcahy.

82. Crabb and Mulcahy, *American National Security*, 189–190.

83. Ibid.

84. Kevin V. Mulcahy, "The Secretary of State: Foreign Policymaking in the Carter and Reagan Administrations," *Presidential Studies Quarterly* (spring 1986): 296.

85. To view the text of the National Security Presidential Directive that established the Bush system, see www.fas.org/irp/offdocs/nspd/nspd-1.htm.

86. Jane Perlez, "Directive Says Rice, Bush Aide, Won't Be Upstaged by Cheney," *New York Times*, February 16, 2001, www.nytimes.com/2001/02/16/politics/16SECU.html.

87. For a fascinating account, see Woodward, *Bush at War.*

88. Written communication from Professor Kevin Mulcahy.

89. Ivo Daalder and I.M. Destler, "How Operational and Visible an NSC?" The Brookings Institution, February 23, 2001, www.brookings.org/views/op-ed/daalder/20010223.htm.

90. The original NSC Coordination Committees were in the following areas: a) regional committees for Europe and Eurasia, Western Hemisphere, East Asia, South Asia, Near East and North Africa, Africa; and b) functional committees for Democracy, Human Rights, and International Operations; International Development and Humanitarian Assistance; Global Environment; International Finance; Transnational Economic Issues; Counter-Terrorism and National Preparedness; Defense Strategy, Force Structure, and Planning; Arms Control; Proliferation, Counterproliferation, and Homeland Defense; Intelligence and Counterintelligence; Records Access and Information Security; Trade Policy Review Group. National Security Presidential Directive 1, www.fas.org/irp/offdocs/nspd/nspd-1.htm.

91. David E. Sanger and Don Van Natta Jr., "In Four Days, a National Crisis Changes Bush's Presidency," *New York Times*, September 16, 2001, A1.

92. An official list of the coalition members can be found at www.whitehouse.gov/infocus/iraq/news/20030327-10.html.

93. Full text of the speech is available at www.whitehouse.gov/news/releases/2003/01/iraq/20030128-19.html.

94. Walter Pincus, "White House Backs Off Claim on Iraqi Buy," *Washington Post*, July 8, 2003, A1; Walter Pincus, "CIA Asked Britain to Drop Iraq Claim; Advice on Alleged Uranium Buy Was Refused," *Washington Post*, July 11, 2003, A1.

95. Walter Pincus, "Bush Faced Dwindling Data on Iraq Nuclear Bid," *Washington Post*, July 16, 2003, A1.

96. Dana Milbank, "Bush Remarks Confirm Shift in Justifying War; Standard of Proof for Weapons Drops," *Washington Post*, June 1, 2003, A18.

97. "Problems, Problems," *The Economist*, June 30, 2003, www.economist.com/agenda/PrinterFriendly.cfm?Story_ID=1889007.

98. Richard Morin and Claudia Deane, "Support for Bush Declines as Casualties Mount in Iraq," *Washington Post*, July 12, 2003, A1.

99. Jim VandeHei and Helen Dewar, "Democrats Sharpen Attack on Bush over Iraq," *Washington Post*, July 16, 2003, A17.

100. Barbara Hinckley suggests that the conflict between presidents and Congress is largely symbolic, staged to convince the public that both institutions are alert and active and that policymaking is democratic. Hinckley, *Less than Meets the Eye: Foreign policymaking and the Myth of the Assertive Congress* (Chicago: University of Chicago Press, 1994), 175, 193.

101. Paul E. Peterson, "The International System and Foreign Policy," in *The President, the Congress, and the Making of Foreign Policy*, ed. Paul E. Peterson (Norman: University of Oklahoma Press, 1994), 12–14.

102. Koh, *The National Security Constitution*, 207.

103. Stephen E. Ambrose, "The Presidency and Foreign Policy," *Foreign Affairs* (winter 1991–1992): 136.

SUGGESTED READINGS

Berman, Larry. *Planning a Tragedy: The Americanization of the War in Vietnam.* New York: Norton, 1983.

Burke, John P., and Fred I. Greenstein. *How Presidents Test Reality: Decisions on Vietnam, 1954 and 1965.* New York: Russell Sage Foundation, 1991.

Crabb, Cecil V., Jr., and Kevin V. Mulcahy. *American National Security: A Presidential Perspective.* Pacific Grove, Calif.: Brooks-Cole, 1991.

Draper, Theodore. *A Very Thin Line: The Iran-Contra Affairs.* New York: Hill and Wang, 1991.

Fisher, Louis. *Congressional Abdication on War and Spending.* College Station: Texas A&M University Press, 2000.

———. *Presidential War Power.* Lawrence: University Press of Kansas, 1995.

George, Alexander L. *Presidential Decisionmaking in Foreign Policy: The Effective Use of Information and Advice.* Boulder: Westview, 1980.

Glennon, Michael J., and J. William Fulbright. *Constitutional Diplomacy.* Princeton: Princeton University Press, 1990.

Henderson, Philip G. *Managing the Presidency: The Eisenhower Legacy—From Kennedy to Reagan.* Boulder: Westview, 1988.

Henkin, Louis. *Constitutionalism, Democracy, and Foreign Affairs.* New York: Columbia University Press, 1992.

———. *Foreign Affairs and the United States Constitution.* 2d ed. Oxford: Oxford University Press, 1997.

Hinckley, Barbara. *Less than Meets the Eye: Foreign Policymaking and the Myth of the Assertive Congress.* Chicago: University of Chicago Press, 1994.

Johnson, Loch K. *Bombs, Bugs, Drugs, and Thugs: Intelligence and America's Quest for Security.* New York: New York University Press, 2000.

Koh, Harold Hongju. *The National Security Constitution: Sharing Power after the Iran-Contra Affair.* New Haven: Yale University Press, 1990.

Korb, Lawrence J. *A New National Security Strategy in an Age of Terrorists, Tyrants, and Weapons of Mass Destruction.* New York: Council on Foreign Relations, 2003.

Mann, Thomas E., ed. *A Question of Balance: The President, the Congress, and Foreign Policy.* Washington, D.C.: Brookings, 1990.

Peterson, Paul E., ed. *The President, the Congress, and the Making of Foreign Policy.* Norman: University of Oklahoma Press, 1994.

President's Special Review Board (Tower Commission). *Report of the President's Special Review Board.* Washington, D.C.: Government Printing Office, 1987.

Schlesinger, Arthur M., Jr. *The Imperial Presidency.* Rev. ed. Boston: Houghton Mifflin, 1989.

Spanier, John, and Steven W. Hook. *American Foreign Policy Since World War II.* 15th ed. Washington, D.C.: CQ Press, 2000.

Woodward, Bob. *Bush at War.* New York: Simon and Schuster, 2002.

11 GEORGE W. BUSH: CHALLENGES OF A WARTIME PRESIDENT

George W. Bush delivered extemporaneous remarks to relief workers during a September 14, 2001, visit to "Ground Zero" at the site of New York's World Trade Center, noting that their courageous efforts had served as an example for the entire nation.

IN PROSECUTING THE WAR AGAINST TERRORISM, the administration of George W. Bush found a mission, a sense of purpose that had eluded its operations for most of its first year. Having taken office after the bitterly contested 2000 presidential election, Bush faced substantial obstacles during his first months in office, with widespread doubts about his legitimacy and competence. As we have seen, he not only lost the popular vote to his Democratic opponent, Al Gore, but also launched the administration with the highest disapproval rating recorded for any incoming president since polling began (25 percent).[1] Despite Republican control of the House and (through Vice President Dick Cheney's tie-breaking vote) nominal control of the evenly divided Senate, Bush could not secure congressional passage of any of his major proposals during his first hundred days in office. He then lost control of the Senate when—at least partly due to treatment by the White House and the Republican leadership—Sen. James Jeffords of Vermont left the Republican Party to become an independent. Programs such as "Saturday Night Live" lampooned Bush as inept and unprepared to be president, and even serious political observers speculated that Cheney was the power behind the throne. Former Reagan chief of staff Ken Duberstein, for example, said it was "the first time in our history we've had a president and a prime minister"—a pointed suggestion that Bush was the titular head, Cheney the real power.[2] Bush also proved an especially polarizing figure, with Democrats slow to forget the 2000 election outcome. As discussed in chapter 3, an analysis of the twenty-eight Gallup and CBS News/*New York Times* presidential approval polls taken before September 11, 2001, found that "Bush's approval ratings averaged 88 percent among self-identified Republicans but only 31 percent among Democrats. This 57-point differential marked Bush as an even more polarizing figure than the former record holder, Bill Clinton (with an average partisan difference in approval of 52 points for the comparable period of his administration)."[3]

Prior to September 11, 2001, the administration had cautiously sought its footing. Like most other administrations, its early identity was defined largely in terms of that of its predecessor—in this case, "un-Clinton."[4] This self-conscious attitude spanned items small and large; from establishing new norms for White House dress and decorum to discontinuing international negotiations, the new administration asserted its distinctiveness and independence from the immediate past.

Bush went to great lengths to undo a number of Clinton's actions. Last-minute regulations proposed by the outgoing administration, covering a wide range of environmental and occupational safety matters, were put on hold and reviewed; the president ultimately rejected a substantial number. Similarly, Bush adopted a strikingly lower public profile, a seemingly calculated move. He was more reluctant than his predecessor to monopolize the public sphere, speaking more softly and far less frequently, even passing up opportunities to enhance his public image. Well before it had articulated a new national strategy in foreign policy, the administration had moved away from Clinton-era commitments and modes of conducting international relations. The United States withdrew from several proposed treaties, including the Kyoto Protocol on climate change, disengaged from Middle East peace talks, and abruptly discontinued discussions with North Korea. In economics, the contrast could not have been sharper. Clinton had started his first year with a substantial tax increase that ultimately helped produce budget surpluses; Bush reversed direction with tax cuts approved in the first half-year that helped produce a return to budget deficits.

The moment that changed the Bush presidency: On the morning of September 11, 2001, White House chief of staff Andrew H. Card, Jr., informs the president that a second plane has struck the World Trade Center in New York.

Moreover, the designs of the tax changes were polar opposites: Clinton increased and then Bush reduced the tax bite on the same group—high-income taxpayers.

Bush experienced two major shocks during the first year: losing Republican control of the Senate and the terrorist attacks on New York City and Washington, D.C. The former seemed to disorient the administration, producing a period of drift and uncertainty. Moderate Republicans sounded the alarm. Sen. Olympia J. Snow of Maine said Jeffords's defection "should be a wake-up call for our party's leaders that the voices of moderate Republicans must be welcomed and respected."[5] Sen. John McCain—Bush's rival for the 2000 Republican nomination—was even more pointed: "Tolerance of dissent is the hallmark of a mature party, and it is well past time for the Republican Party to wake up."[6] The Republican faithful began publicly to express concern about the administration.[7] In late June 2001, Vice President Cheney had another in a series of health scares, and doctors implanted a sophisticated defibrillator that could administer an electric shock to the heart if it went into a chaotic rhythm. It was Cheney's third major heart-related procedure since the November election.[8] The health of the economy also faltered. In less than five months, the projected budget surplus of $281 billion shrunk by more than $120 billion, and pundits began to predict a return to budget deficits. Bush's approval rating fell to its lowest point: 51 percent according to a Gallup poll conducted September 7–10, 2001. Media commentators questioned whether Bush could find a defining moment to legitimize his leadership and rally support for his policies.

Then came September 11, and the biggest terrorist attack in U.S. history. Suddenly, Bush became a wartime president. Soon thereafter, standing on the rubble of the World Trade Center, he picked up a megaphone and—in one of his first unscripted moments before television cameras as president—spoke from the heart to the firefighters. As R. W. Apple Jr. wrote in the *New York Times*, Bush's response to the national crisis helped assuage lingering doubts about the legitimacy of his election and his capacity to govern: "You could almost see him growing into the clothes of the presidency."[9] Virtually overnight, Bush's approval rating jumped from 51 to 86 percent. Gallup called the 35-point jump "the highest rally effect for any president in the past half century."[10] By September 22, 2001, Bush's approval rating had reached 90 percent: the highest recorded by the Gallup organization for a president.[11] The shock of the attack energized the Bush administration and gave it a sense of purpose. Many observers saw the event and its aftermath as a new start for the administration.

A Wartime Presidency

The events of a single morning transformed Bush into a "wartime president," a term widely used post-9/11 by journalists and pundits, who frequently drew comparisons to such disparate figures as Franklin D. Roosevelt, Lyndon B. Johnson, and Bush's own father, George H. W. Bush. What exactly does it mean to be a wartime president, and what are the consequences of being one? In the short run, the rally effects that followed the terrorist attacks, the swiftly won war in Afghanistan, and what appeared at first to be an easy victory in Iraq lent Bush an air of invincibility. Some observers, however, have predicted dire consequences for the long run. For example, the *Los Angeles Times,* in its July 4, 2003, edition, carried a long discussion on the "curse of wartime presidents."

Every president who has led this country into full-scale war has paid a heavy price politically and personally. Most chose not to run for reelection and, upon leaving office, saw their vision for America rejected by the voters, their party defeated and their rivals elected. Some left office with shattered reputations, fading into a marginalized obscurity and irrelevance. And the few who survived the grueling reelection campaigns were swiftly cut down by illness or assassination.[12]

On its face, this discussion is accurate. War presidents such as James Madison, James Polk, Woodrow Wilson, Harry Truman, and LBJ did not seek reelection. Three who did seek reelection and won (Abraham Lincoln, William McKinley, and FDR) died soon thereafter. Arguably, however, this reading of history is strained. Other factors played a role in decisions about seeking reelection, and the only president who chose to run and suffered defeat (George H. W. Bush) almost certainly lost for reasons other than his involvement in a war. Polk,

Wilson, FDR, and LBJ faced serious health problems, which, though probably exacerbated by the pressures of conflict, were not likely a direct result of their wartime experiences. Others (such as Madison, Truman, and Bush) survived long after leaving office. Furthermore, while the reputations of some presidents have suffered because of their wartime leadership, those of several others have not. Polk, Lincoln, Wilson, FDR, Truman, and even Johnson have been listed as either "great" or "near-great" presidents in various rankings by historians and political scientists.[13] (See Table 4-1.)

Despite this wide variation in experience, there are likely to be unique challenges associated with serving as a wartime president, challenges that have a direct bearing on presidential performance. We posit five and discuss how George W. Bush and his administration have dealt with them.

Challenge 1: A Dramatic Reshuffling of Agendas

Wartime forces a dramatic reshuffling of the national agenda and alters the administration's standard operating procedures.

The disruptive effects of a suddenly mounted military campaign posed a particularly salient personal challenge for Bush. His style of leadership (a corporate CEO style translated into politics), established in two gubernatorial elections and repeated in the presidential election of 2000, was clearly defined: run on a limited number of policy issues that are translated into clear goals steadfastly pursued once in office.[14] Maintaining focus and forward momentum is critical to achievement, and disruptive factors are challenges to be overcome. Did Bush and his administration demonstrate alacrity in adjusting to the new situation?

Although issue lists for the 2000 election vary, it is clear that tax cuts, education reform, Social Security and Medicare reform, faith-based initiatives, and modernization of the military were central themes and priorities. Policy choices made prior to 9/11 now vied with a host of new issues thrust on the administration by the terrorist attacks and the prospect of war. These included homeland security and antiterrorist measures many people regarded as threats to civil liberties. The attack forced Bush (who, prior to 9/11, had seemed determined to focus on domestic problems) to make foreign policy a major component of his agenda.[15] In the immediate aftermath, the new demands and their attendant politics crowded out existing priorities. Ultimately, however, the administration held fast to its original list of goals and applied its general strategy—a clear goal steadfastly pursued—to its "war on terrorism," which the president portrayed in rather simplistic terms as a clear-cut battle against "evil." Although it was initially unclear just whom the United States could fight in this war on terrorism (al-Qaeda and the terrorist threat, after all, spanned borders and proved to be amorphous foes), war against Afghanistan and Iraq became tangible ways to prosecute the struggle.

Homeland security became the dominant political issue heading into the 2002 midterm elections. The president turned the tables on the Democrats by appropriating their idea of establishing a Department of Homeland Security, making it his own. The Democrats' proposal implied that Bush's original response had been inadequate—creating a White House position for Tom Ridge to serve as coordinator of government-wide security efforts centered on a Homeland Security Council. But when Bush pushed for unprecedented flexibility in managing this new giant department, Senate Democrats balked, opening them up to charges of defending special interests at the cost of the national interest. Thus the administration replaced one strategy for enhancing homeland security that proved ineffective—department and agency heads were recalcitrant when Ridge sought more modest reorganization[16]—with another that their political opponents had originally suggested but later proved hesitant to implement. Not only was the administration nimble politically, but it also demonstrated a surprising willingness to experiment in its administrative thinking.

The administration's ways of doing business did not escape the effects of 9/11 though there was an effort to assure the public that the president's hand on the tiller remained steady and changes in the way of doing business were modest. Change, however, was inevitable. White House staff, almost across the board, assumed new, emergency-related responsibilities. For example, Josh Bolten, later to become director of OMB, headed a new coordinating group, the Domestic Consequences Principals Committee, charged with assessing the full extent of how the attacks would ripple through the nation.[17] Andrew Card, White House chief of staff, made it clear that the president's time had to be even more carefully controlled than usual to accommodate the up to three hours of daily war-related meetings and intelligence briefings.[18] In addition, Bush's travel schedule, in and out of Washington, was curtailed.[19] The National Security Council and the council's Principals Committee met far more frequently, as one would expect. Because the changes occurred before the president's first year in office had been completed, the administration was probably better able to adjust its standard operating procedures. Relatively new schedules and practices are more malleable than ones deeply embedded by time.

Part of reshuffling the national agenda during wartime involves an increased concern with national security that often induces government to curtail civil liberties. Lincoln suspended habeas corpus during the Civil War (an action later endorsed by Congress). Congress enacted legislation during World War I that made it a felony to "utter, print, or publish disloyal, profane, scurrilous, or abusive language about the form of government, the Constitution, soldiers and sailors, flag, or uniform of the armed services, or by word or act support or favor the cause of the German Empire or its allies in the present war, or by word or act oppose the cause of the United States."[20] FDR authorized the internment of Japanese Americans in "relocation centers" during World War II. The Korean War and fear concerning the spread of communism helped fuel heavy-handed government investigations of U.S. citizens during the McCarthy era. Nixon authorized a range of domestic covert actions, including wiretaps and break-ins, against opponents of the Vietnam War.

It is not surprising, then, that 9/11 forced the Bush administration to rethink the existing balance between liberty and the need for national security. Congress overwhelmingly passed the Patriot Act in October 2001, which, among other things, increased the FBI's authority to spy on U.S. citizens without having to show any evidence of a crime, gave the Justice Department power to detain people secretly and indefinitely—again without showing any evidence of a crime—if the government suspects the detainees have critical information about terrorism, allowed immigration hearings to be closed from public scrutiny, and allowed government monitoring and tracing of e-mails without probable cause. The next month, Bush signed an executive order authorizing military commissions, instead of civilian courts, to try terrorists. He also classified Taliban and al-Qaeda prisoners captured by the United States during the war in Afghanistan as "unlawful combatants" rather than "prisoners of war." This distinction meant that the prisoners were not entitled to protections accorded by the Geneva Conventions. The administration argued that as suspected terrorists, they were members of a criminal organization, not the military. Nearly 700 of these "unlawful combatants" have been held for almost two years at a U.S. naval base in Guantanamo Bay, Cuba, where they are outside the jurisdiction of U.S. courts and normal constitutional protections.[21] Such actions have provoked criticism from the International Committee of the Red Cross (ICRC), the UN High Commissioner for Human Rights, the American Civil Liberties Union, and others, and have led to legal challenges. Al Gore, in a strongly critical speech delivered at New York University on August 7, 2003, accused the Bush administration of "gross civil rights abuses."[22] Attorney General Ashcroft responded to the public criticisms with a nationwide tour that often resembled a campaign rally more than a public policy debate.[23] The debate over the administration's curtailment of civil liberties is likely to become a campaign issue in 2004. It is also an issue that may color how historians treat the Bush administration's handling of the war.

Aside from the issue of civil liberties, how did the Bush administration handle the more general disruptions to its agenda caused by 9/11? Did it ultimately maintain its long-term focus after adjusting for short-term imperatives? Certainly, some liberals believe the administration to be no less committed to its overall domestic program. William Greider, who makes the case that Bush is a manifestation of a conservative political movement with a coherent agenda designed to roll back much of the twentieth century's progressive legislation, says the administration's goals are clear and have remained consistent despite the war on terrorism:

- Eliminate federal taxation of private capital
- Gradually phase out the pension-fund retirement system as we know it
- Withdraw the federal government from a direct role in housing, healthcare, assistance to the poor, and many other long-established social priorities
- Restore churches, families, and private education to more influential roles in the nation's cultural life

• Strengthen the hand of business enterprise against burdensome regulatory obligations, especially environmental protection
• Smash organized labor.[24]

Although Greider's own ideological fervor no doubt colors his enumeration of the Bush administration's goals, the perspective is instructive. In many ways, following the midterm elections of 2002, the administration pushed its agenda even more aggressively than it had before 9/11. It attempted (with mixed success) to parlay the president's boost in public approval into legislative success for his pre-9/11 priorities. The administration even claimed that delaying confirmation of Bush's conservative judicial nominees would hinder the nation's war on terrorism.[25] "By all accounts, the subtext for the current President Bush's ambitious plans is the failure of the first President Bush to put forth a bold agenda after his Gulf War triumph. This president's advisers are seeing to it that the public perceives the son differently."[26] The administration has successfully balanced a crisis response with its preexisting domestic program.

Challenge 2: Economic Strains and Dislocations

Wartime produces economic strains and dislocations likely to exacerbate existing economic problems and provoke new ones.

Historically, wartime conditions have triggered extreme economic conditions and the most dramatic departures from usual government practices: the introduction of wage and price controls designed to curb inflation, creation of new regulatory agencies, and efforts at central coordination designed to maximize the utilization of scarce resources and enhance national mobilization. For Lyndon Johnson, inflation was triggered by the desire to avoid a full-scale public debate with Congress over the true cost of the war and its potential impact on his domestic initiatives; when a tax surcharge was introduced, it was too little and too late to prevent a surge in inflation whose effects continued through the next decade. Under Bush, this wartime challenge took on different features in the immediate aftermath of 9/11 and in the aftermath of the invasion of Iraq. In each instance, the Bush administration can be fairly criticized for failing to place the nation on a wartime footing.

The terrorist attack on New York City, in particular, triggered major economic dislocations that reverberated through the country for months. The immediate impact on the nation's air traffic system was enormous, necessitating public action to prevent the airlines from going bankrupt. Federal assistance for New York City and its residents was immediately approved, though delayed in delivery. In the face of such a disaster, Congress did not hesitate to open the federal coffers, which meant, after having reduced federal revenues substantially with the earlier tax cut, opening the lockbox that politicians from both parties had promised for Social Security.

The attacks also came in the midst of what has now been recognized as a brief recession, officially concluded in November 2001, but which seemed to linger without meeting the strict economic definition. In fact, 2002 ended as a major economic disappointment. As discussed in chapter 9, consumer confidence was shaken by the terrorist attacks themselves and the ongoing scares over possible chemical and biological attacks, heightened by the isolated but frightening incidents of anthrax delivered through the postal system. Stocks continued to decline, particularly in the wake of accounting scandals associated with Enron and other formerly high-flying corporations. With lower revenues triggered by tax cuts and faltering individual and corporate income, FY2002 ended with a substantial budget deficit, the first after four consecutive years of budget surpluses. Furthermore, the deficit for FY2003 was projected to grow as the administration expanded the war on terrorism—the creation of the Department of Homeland Security and military action in Iraq would require substantial new expenditures.

In this case, the Bush administration faced an atypical problem: conducting a war in the face of recession, not inflation. The traditional pump-priming effect of increased government expenditures was nowhere to be found. The Federal Reserve continued its policy of lowering interest rates, but there was little evidence that the expansionary monetary and fiscal policies were having much effect. Unemployment continued to grow (up nearly 50 percent in two years, from 4 to 5.8 percent by the end of 2002) as jobs disappeared.

The president's actions revealed his disappointment and concern. By the end of 2002, Bush had replaced three of the six principal members of his economic team (chair of the Securities and Exchange Commission, secretary of the treasury, chair of the National Economic Council), and two more were replaced early in 2003 (chair of Council of Economic Advisers, director of OMB), leaving only the secretary of commerce in place. In looking toward the administration's budget proposal for FY2004, Bush proposed to accelerate the phase-in of tax cuts approved in 2001. Some observers saw an underlying illogic to the plan, which had been sold as a jobs and growth package. How could the United States be fighting a war while lowering government revenues? As many commentators noted, this would be the first time in national history that taxes declined in wartime, a step that prevented citizens from enlisting behind the war effort. Was such a move wisdom or folly? Was it being driven by political (2004 electoral calculations), rather than policy (prosecution of the war), necessity? Was Bush repeating the Johnson mistake of understating the cost of war and (in the case of Iraq) the occupation-reconstruction and running the risk of long-term economic costs?

These important questions gained even greater prominence on the night of September 7, 2003, when President Bush announced in a televised address to the nation that he would ask Congress for $87 billion to support the U.S. efforts in Afghanistan and Iraq during FY2004. If approved by Congress, this appropriation would make total expenditures for the action in Iraq about $150 billion and would increase the deficit to an estimated $562 billion. In contrast, the Persian Gulf War cost $82.5 billion, with only $9 billion paid by the United States.[27]

Such a major financial commitment ensured attention during the 2004 election campaign. In light of these uncertainties, fully assessing Bush's performance in this critical area now would be premature.

Challenge 3: Public Support Threatened

Wartime threatens public support for the administration.

Wartime presidents must rally public support for the extraordinary effort and personal losses that will surely follow. The public needs clarity and nobility of purpose, as well as knowledge of the demands they are likely to face. FDR is often praised as a model in this regard, forging an "extraordinary bond with the American people."[28] According to historian David Kennedy, "He very clearly and consistently communicated . . . what was at stake and why it was important for the U.S. to take part in this struggle."[29] Using rhetoric is one of four ways wartime presidents may work to sustain public support.

The Rhetorical Test

Using FDR's performance as a standard, explaining American action in Afghanistan was an easier task for Bush than explaining (some would say selling) action in Iraq. According to John Keegan, in the surge of patriotism that followed the attacks of 9/11, "any President who proclaimed American values and expressed the determination to punish enemies of the U.S. would enjoy" high levels of support.[30] Bush's speeches at the National Cathedral and on two occasions before joint sessions of Congress seemed to meet that challenge.

The president was less successful on Iraq. For Afghanistan, Bush "was forced by circumstance to lead the country into war," but Iraq was "a war of his own choosing," undertaken in the face of determined international opposition and domestic doubts.[31] During fall 2002, when the president and administration figures began to establish the justification for action against Iraq, imprecision and exaggeration underlay their assertions about Iraq's nuclear program, the capability of a fleet of unmanned Iraqi aircraft, and Iraqi links with al-Qaeda.[32] These factual misrepresentations threatened to create a major "credibility gap" (a term previously used to describe the public's distrust of Lyndon Johnson during Vietnam) for the Bush administration in the summer of 2003. At that time, the media, seizing upon admissions that the president's State of the Union portrayal of Saddam Hussein as actively pursuing uranium for a nuclear weapons program had not been the case, asked whether the administration had intentionally sought to mislead the American public. Credibility was further strained by the fact that coalition forces could not find the stockpiles of chemical and biological weapons the administration had predicted to be in Iraq.[33] It began to appear that, at best, the administration had oversold the threat posed by Iraq, excluding the qualifiers intelligence agencies usually apply to such information, presenting a worst case analysis instead.[34] A PIPA poll issued on July 23, 2003, found that 48 percent of respondents felt Bush had mishandled the evidence used to justify going to war with Iraq. Sixty-one percent said their confidence in the president had been shaken at least a little by the way he had used the evidence (21 percent said their confidence had been shaken "a little," 19 percent said it had been shaken "some," and 21 percent said it had been shaken "a lot").[35] If it is the case that wartime presidents can choose to engage the public through "persuasion or manipulation,"[36] modern presidents must take care that the former neither *becomes* nor is *perceived* to be the latter. Administration defenders accused the "liberal media" of misrepresenting the administration's misleading statements, but their arguments were unconvincing.[37]

Objective realities also soured. American casualties mounted in the postwar period; by Labor Day 2003, the number of military personnel killed and wounded since May 1 exceeded the number killed and wounded during the six-week combat phase.[38] Relations between Palestinians and Israel disintegrated despite the president's personal efforts to design a "roadmap" to Mid-East peace. "Every week events from Baghdad to Jerusalem seem[ed] to be spinning out of the control of a Bush team that, during the president's trip to the region in late May, seemed intent on demonstrating that it now had the power to transform the region."[39] Iraq was very far from being the thriving democracy the administration had promised.[40] Commentators and editorial cartoonists began using the Q-word: two major bombings in August, sustained resistance, and rising costs made Iraq resemble the *quagmire* of Vietnam. Even outspoken supporters of using force in Iraq—such as former Senate Foreign Relations Committee chair Joseph R. Biden, D-Del.—argued that Bush had failed to articulate fully "what his policy is in general and, specifically, that securing Iraq will cost billions of dollars, require tens of thousands of American troops for a considerable amount of time, and that it's worth it . . . [and] in our national interest to stay the course."[41] In other words, Biden denied that Bush had met the FDR standard of clarifying purpose and articulating costs.

In the face of growing public and elite doubts, Bush went on the offensive. He addressed the nation on September 7, 2003, one year before the general election phase of his reelection campaign would begin and four days before the second anniversary of the terrorist attacks on the United States. (He had not requested time for a major national speech since his announcement on May 1, 2003, that the war's combat phase had ended.) Once again, Bush justified the action in Iraq as the next phase in the war on terrorism, though he sidestepped all the details of linking Saddam Hussein to al-Qaeda and ignored the issues surrounding unfound weapons of mass destruction. As he argued, "[T]he surest way to avoid attacks on our own people is to engage the enemy where he lives and plans. We are fighting that enemy in Iraq and Afghanistan today so that we do not meet him again on our own streets, in our own cities."[42] In response to calls for greater clarity about the drain on American resources, he announced the budget request for FY2004 and made it clear that the administration, through the United Nations, would seek both financial and military assistance from other countries, action many critics had been demanding. Ultimately, however, he could not provide an end date or final cost, stating that the war against terrorism "will take time and require sacrifice." In his peroration, he sought to rally support for a larger purpose:

Fellow citizens: We have been tested these past 24 months, and the dangers have not passed. Yet Americans are responding with courage and confidence. We accept the duties of our generation. We are active and resolute in our own defense. We are serving in freedom's cause, and that is the cause of all mankind.[43]

Modern presidents, however, no longer rely exclusively on rhetoric to generate public support; they also use stagecraft, a task that requires many conscious, carefully calculated efforts.

Stagecraft

Bush's swift (and in retrospect, premature) declaration of the end of the combat phase of the war in Iraq on May 1, 2003—a tacit declaration of victory—was a carefully staged photo opportunity. His "tail-hook" landing in an S-3B Viking Navy jet on the USS *Abraham Lincoln* was designed to convey the image of a strong, courageous leader in control. Presidents have long relied on visual stagecraft to reinforce their rhetoric. White House aide Michael Deaver perfected the technique during the presidency of Ronald Reagan. Donald Regan, who served as treasury secretary and White House chief of staff during the Reagan administration, later wrote that Deaver "saw—designed—each presidential action as a one-minute or two-minute spot on the evening network news, or picture on page one of the *Washington Post* or the *New York Times*, and conceived every presidential appearance in terms of camera angles. . . . Every moment of every appearance was scheduled, every word was scripted, and every place where Reagan was expected to stand was chalked with toe marks."[44] In short, Deaver knew how to pick a backdrop that would symbolize the point Reagan was trying to convey, and he concentrated on the most minute details—down to what lighting and camera angles would most flatter the president.

Some have argued that Bush's stagecraft rivals—perhaps even surpasses—Reagan's.[45] Deaver himself says the Bush administration understands the visual "as well as anybody ever has."[46] The tail-hook landing on the *Abraham Lincoln* was just one of many examples. When Bush spoke at Mount Rushmore in 2002, Elisabeth Bumiller of the *New York Times* noted that his aides "positioned the best platform for television crews off to one side, not head on as other White Houses have done, so that the cameras caught Mr. Bush in profile, his face perfectly aligned with the four presidents carved in stone."[47] When Bush spoke to thousands of marines and their families at the Marine Corps Air Station Miramar in California in August 2003, Air Force One landed next to two rows of fighter jets lining the tarmac. As the *Los Angeles Times* reported: "From Air Force One, Bush strode between the AV-8B Harrier IIs and F/A-18 Hornets, wearing a lightweight, military jacket despite the warm temperatures."[48] Once again, the image was picture perfect.

Such stagecraft is not immune to criticism. For example, Sen. Robert C. Byrd, D-W.Va., explicitly contrasted Bush's performance on the USS *Abraham Lincoln* with that of the ship's namesake:

As I watched the President's fighter jet swoop down onto the deck of the aircraft carrier *Abraham Lincoln*, I could not help but contrast the reported simple dignity of President Lincoln at Gettysburg with the flamboyant showmanship of President Bush aboard the USS *Abraham Lincoln*. President Bush's address to the American people announcing combat victory in Iraq deserved to be marked with solemnity, not extravagance; with gratitude to God, not self-congratulatory gestures. American blood has been shed on foreign soil in defense of the President's policies. This is not some made-for-TV backdrop for a campaign commercial. This is real life, and real lives have been lost. To me, it is an affront to the Americans killed or injured in Iraq for the President to exploit the trappings of war for the momentary spectacle of a speech.[49]

Nonetheless, the White House knew that most Americans would respond to and remember positive visual images, and it carefully designed stagecraft to help maintain the high approval ratings Bush had enjoyed since 9/11.

High ratings were important, not only for pursuing the war on terrorism but also for implementing a domestic agenda. Prior to the terrorist attacks, the president could claim no mandate for sweeping policy changes; it was much easier to do so after his approval ratings skyrocketed to the highest ever recorded for a president and Republicans regained control of the Senate in the 2002 midterm elections. Maintaining high approval ratings, however, has proved difficult. Though they stayed relatively high for a long period of time, the ratings began a consistent drop after reaching 90 percent on September 22, 2001. They remained over 80 percent for six months and above 70 for another four. Bush's approval ratings did not dip below 60 percent until the end of 2002. By early March 2003, however, they had dropped to 57 percent.

With plummeting economic confidence and "State of the Country" ratings, Bush feared he might suffer the same fate as his father, who went from an approval rating of 89 percent during the Persian Gulf War to losing his reelection bid the next year when faced with an economic recession and criticism of his domestic agenda. The second Bush administration hoped to capitalize on the boost in his approval ratings after the start of the Iraq war (up to 69 percent in a March 24–25, 2003, Gallup poll), especially since it initially appeared that the war had ended so successfully. The stagecraft at the USS *Abraham Lincoln* was part of that effort. But continued American casualties and allegations that Bush had misled the public about the threat posed by Iraq eroded that support. His approval rating dwindled to 50 percent in a Gallup poll conducted September 19–21, 2003 (seven points lower than his approval rating when he entered office in January 2001), and his disapproval rating almost doubled from 25 percent in January 2001 to 47 percent in September 2003. Moreover, a PIPA poll released July 23, 2003, found that only 49 percent felt Bush had managed the situation in Iraq well. Economic confidence was also low: Gallup found that only 24 percent felt the economy was "excellent" or "good"; 76 percent said it was "only fair" or "poor."[50] PIPA also found that swing voters were considerably more critical of Bush's handling of Iraq than the general population—a potential concern for the president's 2004 reelection bid. Only 38 percent of swing voters approved of Bush's handling of Iraq (as compared with 49 percent of the general public). Fifty-two percent of swing voters felt Bush had misled the public when presenting the evidence to justify war with Iraq (as opposed to only 36 percent of the general population). While the swing voters polled divided evenly when asked whether they voted for Bush or Gore in 2000, a majority said that they were more likely to vote for a Democrat in the next presidential election.[51] Thus despite its conscious efforts to buttress public support, the administration had reasons to be concerned in the aftermath of the military action in Iraq.

Communications Structures

Following the September 11 terrorist attacks, Bush established new communications structures in the White House, such as the Coalition Information Center (CIC), an around-the-clock White House communications operation designed to build public support abroad for the war on terrorism (especially among Muslims in the Middle East). The new operation coordinated daily press briefings at CIC offices around the world (including London, Islamabad, and Kabul) and booked interviews of U.S. officials and other supporters of U.S. policy on international media (ranging from the BBC to Al Jazeera, the Arabic language satellite television network). The administration recognized that the never-ending news cycle created by globalization required a twenty-four-hour operation at the White House. At the same time, the CIC reached out to Muslims in the United States as well as those abroad in an effort to highlight the administration's sensitivity to Islamic tradition. Shortly after 9/11, for example, it arranged a meeting at the White House between the president and ambassadors from fifty-three Muslim countries, held in honor of the holy month of Ramadan. During the meeting, guests knelt and touched their foreheads to the floor in prayer. The president then hosted an Iftar dinner (which breaks the dawn-to-dusk fast observed daily by Muslims during Ramadan). The CIC also arranged for a Muslim, Yahya Hendi, to give the opening prayer at the U.S. House of Representatives.[52] As discussed in chapter 3, the White House expanded the CIC and turned it into a permanent Office of Global Communications in January 2003.

The Office of Global Communications and existing White House communications structures such as the Office of Communications (see chapter 3) have sought to build and maintain public support for presidential initiatives. They have coordinated the administration's "line-of-the-day" and helped to formulate long-range communications plans (including strategies for using "going public" and stagecraft to reinforce the message and build public support). Much of the work of the CIC and the Office of Global Communications has been aimed at a worldwide audience—especially people in the Middle East. In April 2003, the Office of Global Communications arranged for conciliatory greetings from President Bush and

British prime minister Tony Blair to be broadcast on Iraqi state television.[53] At the same time, the office arranged for Arabic-speaking U.S. foreign service officers to give briefings in Qatar and to highlight U.S. humanitarian efforts in Iraq.[54] In July 2003, the office began producing and selling a glossy magazine called *Hi* throughout the Middle East. The first issue contained features on sandboarding, Arab students at U.S. universities, the study of Arabic poetry in the United States, and jazz musician Norah Jones. Aimed at young people, it was designed to highlight a positive image of the United States. The office also floated plans in July to spend $62 million to develop an Arabic language television network that would portray the United States in a positive light.[55] In addition, the CIC and the Office of Global Communications tried to influence U.S. opinion. In August 2003, for example, the office issued a report titled "Results in Iraq: 100 Days toward Security and Freedom," which touted how the U.S.-led occupation of Iraq had increased global security and improved the lives of Iraqis. The White House coupled the release of the report with remarks to reporters by President Bush, who used the opportunity to dismiss criticism of his handling of Iraq as "pure politics."[56]

Using Elections to Win Validation and Build Political Capital

Not all presidents choose to campaign actively in midterm elections, particularly during wartime, but Bush did so, and the effort paid off. With the exception of 2002, the president's party since World War I has consistently lost seats in midterm elections when the nation has been on a war footing. On average, the loss had been twenty-eight seats in the House and four in the Senate.[57] Even after Pearl Harbor, the midterm elections in 1942 produced a fifty-seat loss in the House and nine-seat loss in the Senate. FDR largely sat out of that election; his extensive travel prior to election day was designed to advance the war effort rather than help party candidates. James Barnes suggests that Roosevelt had probably learned from Woodrow Wilson's experience in 1918, when the president had overtly campaigned for Democrats in October only to suffer what was portrayed as repudiation of Wilson himself at the ballot box: nineteen seats lost in the House and six in the Senate, with the losses turning both chambers over to the Republicans. In 1950, Truman, like FDR, campaigned little; the Democrats lost twenty-nine seats in the House and six in the Senate. A similar fate befell LBJ in 1966. Following Johnson's landslide victory over Goldwater in 1964 and the enormous Democratic congressional majorities that came into office with him, Democrats lost forty-seven seats in the House and three in the Senate. Johnson had planned and scheduled extensive campaign appearances but canceled them at the last minute, possibly because the polling showed that losses were imminent and he hoped to avoid the appearance of personal repudiation. Nixon broke the cycle in 1970 by campaigning "furiously" near election day; losses were held to twelve in the House—and his party gained two seats in the Senate. Finally, Republicans under George H. W. Bush in 1990 lost a modest number of seats, eight in the House and one in the Senate. Bush had campaigned hard but seldom struck a partisan, anti-Democratic tone.

In view of this historical record, George W. Bush did remarkably well in 2002. He exceeded Wilson and Nixon as an active campaigner, putting his high public approval scores on the line, openly endorsing and campaigning aggressively for Republican candidates, especially in the Senate. The results were heartening: gains of six House seats and two Senate seats, which meant his party retained control of the House and regained control of the Senate, even if only narrowly. Although the Republicans enjoyed favorable conditions going into this election— fewer vulnerable seats to defend and redistricting outcomes that favored their candidates—and evidence accumulates that the longstanding pattern of midterm losses by the president's party is weakening (Clinton also bucked the trend in 2000), the departure from past experience is still notable. Furthermore, Bush derived benefits from his midterm efforts beyond maintaining working majorities in both chambers.

Bush showed himself to be willing to put his presidency on the line when he campaigned aggressively for a Republican Senate and House in the 2002 elections. If he had failed, it would have been interpreted as a repudiation by the American people, and seriously weakened him in both foreign and domestic policy. The fact that he succeeded, however, added significantly to his political capital. . . . Bush's risk-taking in the 2002 elections impressed the political class in Washington and enhanced his credibility.[58]

As with midterm elections, not all wartime presidents choose to pursue active campaigns for their own reelections. For example, Johnson in 1964 and Nixon in 1972 chose to be seen as presidential rather than political. Although Bush delayed the official announcement of his reelection campaign until May 2003, it was launched with a fund-raising effort that dwarfed those of his potential Democratic opponents, raising more money in the April–June period than all his opponents combined, $34.4 million to $31 million.[59] There were signs of underlying problems, however, despite Bush's relatively strong (though declining) public approval rating: the highest number of Americans on unemployment relief since 1982, increasing doubts about the justification for war with Iraq, and casualties that continued to mount in spite of the announcement of victory.[60] Reelection was far from a certainty. Indeed, several polls taken at the end of the summer of 2003 must have given Bush pause. A Zogby poll conducted September 22–24, asked: "Do you think President Bush deserves to be reelected or do you think it is time for someone new?" Forty-three percent said Bush deserved reelection, while 49 percent said it was time for someone new (8 percent were not sure). A CNN/*Time* poll conducted July 16–17, 2003, found only 50 percent either "very likely" (33 percent) or "somewhat likely" (17 percent) to vote for Bush for reelection, while 46 percent were either "very unlikely" (36 percent) or "somewhat unlikely" (10 percent) to vote for him.[61]

It is tempting to argue that presidents who lead the country into war should not expect reelection, but the reality is more complex and the historical record mixed. Most recently, this proposition might seem to be borne out by the experiences of Harry Truman and Lyndon Johnson, who withdrew from consideration for their party's nomination in the face of eroding public support during the Korean and Vietnam Wars. Nearly 34,000 Americans died in Korea and 58,000 in Vietnam, with hundreds of thousands more suffering injuries. In both cases, controversy surrounded the onset of conflict and the conduct of the war. But there were extenuating circumstances. Both Truman and Johnson had entered the presidency as a result of their predecessors' deaths and therefore had served longer than a single term. Truman had already been elected once on his own in 1948, so that by the June 1950 onset of military conflict in Korea, he had been in office for more than five years. Johnson, whose escalation of American forces in 1965 made the war his own, served nearly a year of Kennedy's unexpired term.

The electoral fates of four other twentieth-century presidents seem not to have been affected by war. Woodrow Wilson led the nation into war the year following his reelection in 1916. Ill health and respect for the two-term tradition precluded his pursuit of a third term. Although controversy still rages about whether Franklin D. Roosevelt maneuvered a reluctant nation into war, final action was propelled by the attack on Pearl Harbor, a full year after FDR had violated the two-term tradition. Furthermore, he was reelected to a fourth term in 1944. Richard Nixon survived Vietnam despite the widespread escalation pursued during his first term in office and went on to a landslide victory in 1972 before peace talks had been concluded. It might be argued that Watergate, which led to Nixon's downfall, was war related; the president justified the illegal actions of the White House Plumbers Unit on the grounds of national security. But the war did not figure into an electoral defeat. George H. W. Bush, of course, led the United States to rapid success and received nationwide acclaim for his wartime leadership only to lose his reelection campaign twenty months later largely due to widespread concern about the economy. Only insofar as the war and its aftermath distracted the administration or added to the perception of inattention could it be argued that the war factored into his defeat.

Nonetheless, it is difficult to imagine presidents not recognizing the potential electoral impact of a decision to launch military action. In the short run, we know presidents can expect a rally effect associated with conflict; as wars drag on and casualties mount, however, an erosion of support is to be expected.[62] Pursuing an active campaign holds potential dangers. If the president is seen as playing politics with the war—using 9/11 for fund-raising[63] or the aircraft carrier landing for campaign ads—it is not clear how the public will react.

As this review indicates, the Bush administration met reasonable success on several fronts in its efforts to maintain public support under wartime conditions. Rhetorical flourishes met expectations in the wake of 9/11, communication strategies were modified, the midterm elections were vigorously pursued to a successful conclusion, and the reelection campaign was launched. Several of the administration's bold efforts paid off handsomely. But there was lingering uncertainty about the administration's overall honesty with the American people and the danger that using wartime conditions for campaign advantage could backfire.

Challenge 4: Doubts about the President's Performance

Wartime triggers doubts about the president's oversight of the military, conduct of the war, and maintenance of alliance relations.

Like wartime presidents before him, Bush confronted questions about strategy, tactics, and purpose. These arose in connection with both Afghanistan and Iraq and were fairly typical. How many American military personnel were required to perform the mission? Would air power suffice, or was there a need for "boots on the ground"? Were the commanders being given adequate support in personnel, material, and battlefield flexibility? Was military progress too slow or too rapid? Were American casualties unnecessary, the result of sloppy procedures or friendly fire? Were American forces imposing unnecessary civilian casualties?

Bush experienced less second-guessing about military operations than might have been expected. Small military coalitions reduced the number of issues surrounding the military chain of command and coordination with allies. Unlike in Bosnia and Kosovo, the American military assumed unquestioned leadership in Afghanistan and Iraq. Similarly, the system of embedded journalists in Iraq provided the media with unprecedented opportunities to report on the war in real time—only the few seconds required for satellite transmissions separated reporters from audiences. This system created its own problems, particularly the difficulty of grasping the full picture as opposed to the small slices being viewed in isolation, but it significantly reduced many of the complaints about access that journalists typically voice during wartime.[64]

Nonetheless, questions arose about the conduct of the war in both Afghanistan and Iraq, particularly when progress appeared slow or inconsistent with prewar planning. In Afghanistan, the Northern Alliance seemed excruciatingly deliberate in launching its ground offensive, a delay that triggered strategic reconsideration within the administration on whether to change the plan or persist.[65] In Iraq, the "shock and awe" air offensive seemed overhyped when life in Baghdad largely went on as normal; the original decision to bypass two southern Iraqi cities in which the populations were expected to rebel appeared to be a miscalculation when American forces had to return to protect the supply lines;[66] fanatical, suicidal attacks by Iraqi irregulars contradicted the expectation of mass surrenders; military officials openly questioned whether there were sufficient forces to finish the job, particularly if there was extensive street fighting in Baghdad. The war ran longer than the 100-hour, one-sided engagement called the Persian Gulf War and thereby invited greater controversy.

Questions about strategic issues were also much in evidence. Afghanistan presented an unusually complex array of internal political factions and regional "allies" whose assistance the administration solicited. The Northern Alliance was a misnomer for a collection of ethnically based, armed bands that interacted more as competing warlords than as a coherent rebel force. Pakistan and an assemblage of former Soviet republics largely unfamiliar to nonspecialists in the area (Turkmenistan, Uzbekistan, Tajikistan, Kyrgyzstan, and Kazakhstan) were suddenly thrust into the role of important supporting actors. The twists and turns of the multiple plots proved dizzying. The Taliban suddenly collapsed in early December after heavy U.S.-British air attacks that began on October 7, 2001, ground offensives conducted by the Northern Alliance with help from American special forces, and a marine incursion in the southern part of the country. American forces played a larger role in the aftermath of the collapse, seeking to roust out remnants of the Taliban and al-Qaeda, find Osama Bin Laden, and provide support for the transitional government of Hamid Karzai.

Iraq raised a host of different strategic issues, many of which emerged in the UN maneuvering that preceded combat. How would the neighboring Arab states react to an American invasion? The administration claimed there were numerous Arab states that needed to remain quiet allies, but when Saudi Arabia denied the United States use of its airfields, it appeared that only Jordan fell into this camp. Would the United States receive the kind of local military assistance it needed? After painful weeks of negotiations, Turkey, a staunch NATO ally, ultimately refused access to its territory, severely hampering the opening of a second front in northern Iraq. Jordan apparently provided clandestine assistance. Would fundamentalist Muslim states intervene? Neighboring Iran, another state on Bush's "axis of evil" list, was a long-time enemy of Hussein but saw itself as a defender of Iraqi Muslims and had a record of supporting terrorism. Both Iran and Syria (also guilty of aiding terrorists) had to be reasonably concerned about U.S. forces being targeted against their regimes.

In many respects, the postcombat phases of both wars have been more controversial than the military operations. In each instance, questions arose about whether the Bush administration had adequately prepared for the postwar challenges of nation building and had fully appreciated the problems arising from creating a political power vacuum. Removal of the Taliban and Baathist regimes invited lawlessness, looting, and the collapse of critical public services, particularly in Iraq's largely urban society. A continued American presence—aided in Afghanistan but not in Iraq by the United Nations—ensured on-going casualties and months of additional active service, something that friends and family had a difficult time accepting.

How was this maelstrom of issues managed? In this most disciplined of White Houses, there was a fairly standard message about the president's role during the war with Iraq: aides portrayed a wartime leader who preferred to make big decisions, then let them be implemented by the experts with little presidential meddling.[67] Thus it was made known that Bush approved the first night's attack by "bunker buster" bombs dropped from Stealth fighters and sea-launched tomahawk missiles in an effort to kill Saddam Hussein and his sons, but the American commander on the ground, General Tommy Franks, redirected resources to capture the southern oilfields in Iraq.[68] The picture that emerged was of a "hands-off commander in chief . . . [who] does not weigh in on troop movements, timing of any advances, or targeting of the air campaign."[69] The role did not come naturally to Bush, who during the action in Afghanistan had learned to be a coach, not a quarterback.[70] But there was a second side to the White House portrait.

For weeks before he gave the order to attack [in Iraq], Bush demanded detailed briefings on war plans and quizzed military advisers about weaponry, troop movements and the positioning of warships. Aides say he is immersed in the details of war planning but will leave battlefield decisions to military commanders.[71]

But the president's immersion in detail was not limited to the planning stages as he was reportedly an avid consumer of war information during the conflict as well.[72]

There are two schools of thought about presidents' wartime management: we want presidents to be as knowledgeable as the military and clearly in charge (*hands-on model*), but we do not want them to meddle unnecessarily (*hands-off model*). The White House made sure the public saw Bush in both roles.[73]

How effective was Bush's performance as commander in chief, and what should the evaluative criteria be? Assessments would be premature at this point, especially about Iraq. There are too many unanswered questions about who set the military strategy (for example, Bush's role in approving the rolling start to the war before all troops were in place) and the nature of the interaction among key administration figures and military leaders. The grounds for evaluation have also recently been reassessed. Eliot Cohen, author of a book on four wartime leaders reportedly read by George W. Bush during the summer of 2002, proposes a different evaluative framework.[74] Rather than adopting the conventional answer—that success requires political leaders who resist the temptation to meddle in military questions (the hands-off image)—Cohen suggests the need for political leaders to be uncivil in their conduct of civil-military relations.[75] Only by prodding the military and posing questions based on a thorough understanding of details (the hands-on image) can political leaders hope to produce the outcomes war is designed to achieve. When asked about the Bush administration's performance, Cohen responded cautiously that he thinks it successfully engaged in the kind of "unequal dialogue" with the military required for success:

[I]f I can believe what I see in the media, and I take it all with a grain of salt, it appears that Rumsfeld is a very active secretary of defense, rather along the lines essential for a good civil-military dialogue: pushing, probing, querying. But not, I think, dictating in detail what the military should do.

The Bush administration was engaged in what was a very intensive dialogue with senior military leadership, and I think that was right. You certainly get the strong sense that some key decisions were political and that Bush made them—the decision, for example, to begin the war with that aerial attack on Saddam's bunker.[76]

Only further research will help determine which portrait—the engaged, detail-mastering president or the delegating CEO—is more accurate. Even before those studies are completed, however, it seems clear that the administration's experience with Afghanistan was a stage rehearsal for Iraq, where the stakes were considerably higher. Bob Woodward's detailed account of how the administration fashioned an antiterrorism strategy and implemented it in Afghanistan provides some of the answers needed for an evaluation of Bush's performance. The president learned to master his natural impulsiveness and impatience; discovered ways to provoke people, force decisions, and insist on his own policy priorities; and developed a feel for his unique role in public relations—progressing from sometimes costly impulsiveness to delivering a steadier message.[77] The early reviews are favorable, but as always, evaluation depends heavily on the long-term success of the policies put into place.

Challenge 5: Balancing Foreign Policy with Political Necessity

Wartime raises questions about how presidents balance the conduct of foreign policy with self-serving motives and political necessity.

"You want to win this election, you better change the subject. You wanna change this subject, you better have a war," explains Robert DeNiro's political operative in "Wag the Dog." "It's show business."[78]

In the 1997 movie *Wag the Dog*, a fictional administration hypes the threat posed by a foreign power, linking it to Islamic fundamentalism and nuclear weapons. An imaginary war sweeps everything else from the public's mind, including potentially disastrous administration scandals. Would a modern president stoop to such depths? Has the Bush administration done so? Is the Bush administration pursuing Middle East policies designed to favor the petroleum industry with which both Bush and Vice President Cheney have deep ties?[79]

The most disturbing thing about these questions is that they can be posed. Since the onset of World War II, administration critics have regularly questioned the real motives lying behind presidents' foreign policies and frequently seen deception rather than honesty. (We hasten to point out that this is not exclusively a twentieth-century phenomenon as the widespread questions surrounding James K. Polk's maneuvers prior to the Mexican-American War of 1846 will attest.)[80] Lyndon Johnson's credibility gap, the perception of frequent and systematic lying about the onset of war and its progress, became a firmly engrained feature of American politics after Watergate. Nixon's dirty campaign tricks, stonewalling of congressional investigations, penchant for conducting secret diplomacy, and unauthorized bombing of Cambodia contributed to the perception of rampant White House lying. Even Dwight D. Eisenhower, a figure of moral rectitude, was caught in a lie in 1960 when he initially claimed the U-2 spy plane shot down by the Soviets was a weather plane. Jimmy Carter successfully won the presidency with the promise "I'll never lie to you," further evidence of how widespread the belief had become that modern presidents consistently misrepresent the truth.

For some highly critical observers, "misleading the public has been a consistent strategy for the Bush team on issues ranging from tax policy and Social

Security reform to energy and the environment. So why should we give the administration the benefit of the doubt on foreign policy?"[81] Al Gore also made that charge in his August 7, 2003, speech at New York University: "The president's mishandling of and selective use of the best evidence available on the threat posed by Iraq is pretty much the same as the way he intentionally distorted the best available evidence on climate change, and rejected the best available evidence on the threat posed to America's economy by his tax and budget proposals."[82] In the media tumult surrounding how intelligence may have been used or misused to justify the war in Iraq, charges were leveled that Vice President Cheney and his chief of staff intimidated CIA analysts by meeting with them directly about possible links between Iraq and al-Qaeda as well as weapons of mass destruction, pressuring them to provide the right story in their estimates.[83] Nor is the intelligence arena the only one that has excited comment. This administration has been described as having "an unhealthy, Nixonian obsession with secrecy,"[84] demonstrated most recently by the Domestic Security Enhancement Act of 2003, also known as Patriot II, an extension of the legislation adopted in 2001 in the wake of 9/11. As one public watchdog group asked:

Was the Bush Administration waiting for the bombs bursting in Baghdad to spring this latest, urgent, national security legislation on the American people and Congress, another drive-by mooting of our customary democratic discourse and deliberative processes?[85]

For many, the persistent penchant for secrecy and the aggressive assertion of presidential prerogative to withhold information is eerily reminiscent of the Nixon administration's self-serving modus operandi.[86] Doubts about motives naturally follow.

Vietnam and Watergate are lenses through which journalists, pundits, analysts, political scientists, and members of the public view contemporary events. For members of the baby boom generation and those who are older, it is impossible to escape these generational experiences, corrosive and distasteful as they may be. What remains surprising, however, is how oblivious the Bush administration is toward the potential problems posed by the lingering effects of these outlooks on politics. Both the president and vice president appear committed to reversing what they regard as erosions of presidential power over the past three decades. Repeated confrontations with Congress, civil libertarians, and the media, however, trigger fears and responses that could be self-defeating, prompting observers to adopt the worst case interpretation of administration actions. Rather than moving the nation beyond the effects of Vietnam and Watergate, the administration's actions may well be renewing the resistance to what are perceived as new encroachments on American democracy.

It is unlikely that Bush's wars in Afghanistan and Iraq are examples of reality imitating the movies. The terrorist attacks were real, and the need to respond was unavoidable. Pressures to mobilize an effective homeland defense arose from all quarters, and the administration proposed a controversial strategy to prevent and preempt attacks before terrorists could exact another round of unacceptable losses.[87] Leaders who believe they are engaged in a war for survival are susceptible to believing the ends justify the means, but given the unique experiences of the past three decades, Americans are especially sensitive about presidential actions that sacrifice one for the other. Balancing democracy with the demands of war was a constant issue during the cold war, and the Bush administration has fallen into the practiced roles of their predecessors. Much as we have slipped back into budget deficits, the nation may have unwittingly returned to longstanding debates and practices consistent with the pressures of conflict with an unknown and only partially understood enemy. Perhaps expecting the Bush administration to show more sensitivity to these widespread fears is expecting too much. If the administration's performance does not improve, however, the United States will be condemned to repeating history rather than learning from it.

Conclusion

War confronts presidents with a set of distinctive challenges. Particularly in the case of mounting a sudden response to an unexpected assault, administrations run the risk of severe disruption and dislocation. We have drawn on the presidency literature and journalistic discussions to identify five challenges for wartime presidents and evaluated how effectively the administration of George W. Bush has contended with them. Although the record is mixed, the administration's performance has generally been positive.

It took the Bush administration most of a year to develop an effective response to the new agenda issues of homeland security and the prosecution of terrorists, though its policies remain both unproven and controversial. Rather than allowing these new issues to completely displace its pre-9/11 programmatic agenda, the administration found ways to direct attention and energy back to these priorities even while preparing for a second stage in the war on terrorism—regime change in Iraq. Thus short-term response was successfully blended with long-term focus even though the responses to new problems remain controversial.[88]

It is difficult to disentangle the administration's economic strategy in the wake of 9/11 from its larger economic program of massive tax reductions. That is precisely the point: the administration did not retreat from its earlier policies even in the face of mounting budget deficits exacerbated by military action in Afghanistan and Iraq. The economic recovery has proceeded slowly despite monetary and fiscal policies of historic stimulative proportions. In short, this remains an enormous policy gamble consciously chosen by the Bush administration when a retreat would have been politically possible. As we learned from the Vietnam War experience, short- and long-term effects of wartime economic action and inaction can be quite different.

Politically, the administration has established a relatively successful record in maintaining public approval, although not without missteps and potential landmines for the future. Presidential approval has eroded from the historic highs registered in the immediate aftermath of 9/11 as the public reacts to continued military casualties, questions about the credibility of administration justifications for military action, and an American occupation of uncertain duration. Nonetheless,' the president met the expectations for inspirational rhetoric in the weeks following 9/11, pursued a bold strategy to buttress the administration's position in Congress during the 2002 midterm elections, and successfully launched the reelection campaign. When public doubts mounted in summer 2003, Bush launched a renewed effort to buttress support, accompanied by potentially major changes in policy. Like other wartime presidents, he confronted the challenge of balancing partisan messages with unifying, above-politics rhetoric. It remained unclear how images from Bush's role as commander in chief will play when used for political purposes in 2004.

Bush's performance as commander in chief remains a White House image construct, largely emphasizing the conventional hands-off model but also suggestive of the revisionist hands-on model. Not enough detail has emerged to give us grounds for a confident assessment, though the early readings have been favorable. Even at this point, it is tempting to give the president relatively high marks for learning techniques during the action in Afghanistan that strengthened the president's own and his administration's performance in Iraq. Although strains in traditional alliances have not yet fully healed and may prove to be most costly in the long run, the administration's greatest misstep seems to have been in overselling the imminent threat posed by Saddam Hussein. This is likely to mean that Congress will have less confidence in future assessments of international dangers from this president and his successors.

Inattention to historical context and implications may help explain why the Bush administration's aggressive pursuit of the war on terrorism has at times taken on the appearance of the Nixon administration's worst traits: excessive secrecy, lying, open-ended assertion of presidential prerogative, and the abandonment of democratic principles. In its urgency to combat imminent dangers and prevent a recurrence of 9/11, the administration has been remarkably insensitive to how its actions might be perceived as self-serving rather than noble. To be fair, the problem may lie less in reality than in the eyes of the beholders—a generation sensitized to these dangers given the nation's collective experiences of three decades ago. Understanding how previous administrations attempted to meet the challenges of a wartime presidency—the missteps and successes of predecessors—may be the best way to enhance current presidential performance.

NOTES

1. David W. Moore, "Initial Job Approval for Bush at 57 Percent, But Highest Disapproval of Any President Since Polling Began," Gallup Poll release, February 6, 2001, www.gallup.com.
2. Quoted in Martin Kettle, "Hidden Powerhouse in the U.S. Presidency: While George Bush Takes the Public Eye, Vice-President Cheney Pulls the Washington Strings," *The Guardian* (London), April 28, 2001, 19.

3. Gary C. Jacobson, "The Bush Presidency and the American Electorate" (paper prepared for delivery at the conference "The George W. Bush Presidency: An Early Assessment," Woodrow Wilson School, Princeton University, April 25–26, 2003), 4. Published as chapter 8 in Fred I. Greenstein, ed., *The George W. Bush Presidency* (Baltimore: Johns Hopkins University Press, 2003), 199.

4. David Frum, *The Right Man: The Surprise Presidency of George W. Bush* (New York: Random House, 2003), 12–30.

5. Quoted in Richard L. Berke, "A Question of Governing from the Right," *New York Times*, May 25, 2001, A1.

6. Ibid., A21.

7. Richard L. Berke and Frank Bruni, "Crew of Listing Bush Ship Draws Republican Scowls," *New York Times*, July 2, 2001, A11.

8. David E. Sanger, "Cheney's Doctors Expect to Implant Device for Heart," *New York Times*, June 30, 2001, A1.

9. R. W. Apple Jr., "President Seems to Gain Legitimacy," *New York Times*, September 16, 2001, A6.

10. David W. Moore, "Confidence in Leaders: Americans Rally around Government Leaders in Wake of Terrorist Attacks," Gallup poll release, September 14, 2001, www.gallup.com.

11. Jeffrey M. Jones, "Bush Approval Ratings One Year after the Peak," Gallup poll release, October 1, 2002, www.gallup.com. Gallup began its presidential approval polls in 1938, when Franklin Roosevelt was president.

12. Ed Stockly, "War's Curse on the White House," *Los Angeles Times*, July 4, 2003, part 5, 29.

13. A survey of major polls of presidential ranking since 1948 (Schlesinger poll, 1948; Schlesinger poll, 1962; Marandell-Dodder poll, 1968; *Chicago Tribune* poll, 1982; Murray-Blessing poll, 1982; C-SPAN poll, 2000) shows Lincoln, FDR, and Wilson in the top ten in all of them; Polk made the top ten in the first four polls and twelfth place in the last two; Truman made the top ten in every poll since 1982; and LBJ made the top ten in three of the four polls since 1982. See also Frank P. King, *America's Nine Greatest Presidents* (Jefferson, N.C.: McFarland, 1997), which ranks Polk, Lincoln, FDR, and Truman among the top nine; and Charles F. Faber and Richard B. Faber, *The American Presidents Ranked by Performance* (Jefferson, N.C.: McFarland, 2000).

14. John C. Fortier and Norman J. Ornstein, "Congress and the Bush Presidency" (paper prepared for delivery at the conference "The George W. Bush Presidency: An Early Assessment," Woodrow Wilson School, Princeton University, April 25–26, 2003), 3–10. Published as chapter 6, "President Bush: Legislative Strategist," in Greenstein, *George W. Bush Presidency*, 138–145.

15. William Drozdiak, "Crisis Forces Shift in Policy as Bush Assembles Coalition," *Washington Post*, September 17, 2001, A9.

16. David Von Drehle and Mike Allen, "Bush Plan's Underground Architects," *Washington Post*, June 9, 2002, A1.

17. Dana Milbank, "White House Staff Switches Gear," *Washington Post*, September 17, 2001, A25; Walter Pincus and Karen DeYoung, "U.S. Says New Tape Points to Bin Laden," *Washington Post*, December 9, 2001, A1.

18. Elisabeth Bumiller, "President Keeps the Battlefield Close at Hand," *New York Times*, March 30, 2003, www.nytimes.com/2003/03/30/international/worldspecial/30BUSH.html.

19. Jennifer Loven, "Despite Pressures of Wartime Presidency, Bush's Routine Changes Little," *Associated Press*, March 22, 2003, www.augustachronicle.com/stories/032303/ira_124-3927.shtml.

20. Espionage Act of 1917, as amended in 1918, quoted in James C. Foster and Susan M. Leeson, *Constitutional Law: Cases in Context*, vol. 2, *Civil Rights and Civil Liberties* (Upper Saddle River, N.J.: Prentice Hall, 1998), 168.

21. Associated Press, "U.S. Warned About Harming Detainees," August 2, 2003, www.findlaw.com.

22. Randal C. Archibold, "Back in Fray, Gore Urges Voters to Fire Bush," *New York Times,* August 8, 2003, A15. For a defense of the Bush administration's actions, see Robert H. Bork, "Civil Liberties after 9/11," *Commentary* (July–August 2003): 29–35.

23. Eric Lichtblau, "Ashcroft's Tour Rallies Supporters and Detractors," *New York Times,* September 8, 2003, A14.

24. William Greider, "Rolling Back the 20th Century," *The Nation,* May 12, 2003, www.thenation.com/doc.mhtml?i=20030512&s=greider.

25. Helen Dewar, "Foreign Aid Bill Held Up by GOP; Senators Demand Action on Nominees," *Washington Post,* October 13, 2001, A3.

26. Linda Feldman, "How Does Bush Compare with Other War Presidents?" *Christian Science Monitor,* March 5, 2003, posted on the History News Network, hnn.us/articles/1046.html#potus3-6-03.

27. Dana Milbank and Mike Allen, "Bush to Double Iraq Spending: President Seeks $87 Billion More for Postwar Effort," *Washington Post,* September 8, 2003, A1.

28. Michael Beschloss, Doris Kearns Goodwin, David Kennedy, David McCullough, John Keegan, and Edward Luttwak, "How Bush Rates: Does He Measure Up to Other Wartime Presidents," *Time,* December 31, 2001, www.time.com/time/poy2001/nprez.html.

29. Ibid., www.time.com/time/poy2001/nprez.html.

30. Ibid., www.time.com/time/poy2001/nprez.html.

31. Dan Balz, "President Faces Different Test this September," *Washington Post,* September 12, 2002, A1.

32. Dana Milbank, "For Bush, Facts Are Malleable: Presidential Tradition of Embroidering Key Assertions Continues," *Washington Post,* October 22, 2002, A1.

33. David Wise, "If Bush Is Lying, He's Not the First," *Washington Post,* June 15, 2003, B1.

34. Warren P. Strobel and Jonathan S. Landay, "After a Year, Iraq Case Failing," *Philadelphia Inquirer,* July 20, 2003, A16.

35. Program on International Policy Attitudes (PIPA), a joint program of the Center on Policy Attitudes and the Center for International Security Studies at Maryland, School of Public Affairs, University of Maryland, news release, July 23, 2003.

36. James R. Arnold, *Presidents under Fire: Commanders in Chief in Victory and Defeat* (New York: Orion Books, 1994), 290.

37. See, for example, Byron York, "The Truth About Bush's 'Lies': An Attack from the Left Misfires," *National Review,* June 16, 2003, www.nationalreview.com/york/york060303.asp.

38. Vernon Loeb, "Number of Wounded in Action on Rise," *Washington Post,* September 2, 2003, A1.

39. David E. Sanger, "Some Grim News About Iraq: Bush Warns of a Heavy Burden," *New York Times,* September 8, 2003, A11.

40. Dana Milbank, "In Game of Expectations, Bush Usually Wins," *Washington Post,* June 8, 2003, A5.

41. Joseph R. Biden Jr., "The National Dialogue on Iraq + One Year," Brookings Institution Leadership Forum, July 31, 2003, www.brookings.org/comm/events/20030731.htm.

42. See www.whitehouse.gov/news/releases/2003/09/20030907-1.html; and speech transcript in *Washington Post,* September 8, 2003, A16.

43. Ibid.

44. Donald T. Regan, *For the Record* (New York : Harcourt Brace Jovanovich, 1988), 248.

45. Elisabeth Bumiller, "Keepers of Bush Image Lift Stagecraft to New Heights," *New York Times,* May 16, 2003, A1.

46. Quoted in ibid.

47. Ibid.

48. Edwin Chen, "President Rallies Marines but Warns of Risks in Iraq," *Los Angeles Times*, August 15, 2003, 18.

49. Remarks by Sen. Robert C. Byrd, U.S. Senate Chamber, May 6, 2003, appeared as "A Troubling Speech" on www.commondreams.org/views03/0506-01.htm.

50. Gallup poll, July 7–9, 2003, www.gallup.com.

51. PIPA news release, July 29, 2003.

52. Mike Allen, "Fighting the Image War to Gain Muslim Support; Information Center Plans Prayer, Traditional Dinner," *Washinton Post*, November 15, 2001, A32.

53. Mike Allen, "U.S. Uses Iraqi TV to Send Its Message," *Washington Post*, April 11, 2003, A1.

54. Mike Allen, "Bush Concerned by Iraq Looting, but Confident in Plan; Administration Seeks to Bolster Campaign's Image in Arab World," *Washington Post*, April 13, 2003, A37.

55. Andrew Buncombe, "Bush Launches Magazine to Teach Young Arabs to Love America," *The Independent* (London), July 18, 2003, 12.

56. Elisabeth Bumiller, "After the War; Bush Sees 'Good Progress' in Iraq but With Work to Do," *New York Times*, August 9, 2003, A6.

57. James A. Barnes, "Wartime Presidents, Midterm Losses," *National Journal*, October 13, 2001, 3198–3199.

58. Peter J. Wallison, "Is George W. Bush Following the Reagan Model?" (lecture at the Ronald Reagan Library, March 19, 2003), www.aei.org/news/newsID.16713, filter./news_detail.asp.

59. Dan Balz and Thomas B. Edsall, "Bush Raises More Money than All Nine Challengers," *Washington Post*, July 16, 2003, A1.

60. David S. Broder, "Black Thursday for Bush," *Washington Post*, July 15, 2003, A19. On declining poll numbers, see Richard Morin and Claudia Deane, "Support for Bush Declines as Casualties Mount in Iraq," *Washington Post*, July 12, 2003, A1.

61. For these and more up-to-date polls, go to www.pollingreport.com.

62. John E. Mueller, *War, Presidents, and Public Opinion* (New York: Wiley, 1973).

63. Maureen Dowd, "Photo Op-portunism," *New York Times*, May 15, 2002, on the three commemorative photos marketed to Republican contributors for $150, including one of the president on Air Force One on September 11, 2001.

64. There was pronounced criticism about lack of access during the Persian Gulf War (1991). At that time, the Department of Defense "allowed reporters to travel in the war zone, but coverage was strictly limited. Only small, closely supervised, Pentagon-approved pools of correspondents could cover the actual fighting. Pool reporters were constantly accompanied by Defense Department public affairs officers who controlled where they could go and whom they could interview. All copy was then subject to censorship by the military. The Pentagon was especially concerned about what visual images would be seen by the American people. By keeping television crews away from the fighting and releasing their own visually hypnotic films of high-tech bombing raids ('military Nintendo,' as the *Nation* put it), the Pentagon sanitized the war. Indeed, much of the coverage of the war consisted of official Allied briefings for reporters." John Anthony Maltese, *Spin Control: The White House Office of Communications and the Management of Presidential News*, 2nd ed., rev. (Chapel Hill: University of North Carolina Press, 1994), 220.

65. See the discussion in Bob Woodward, *Bush at War* (New York: Simon and Schuster, 2002), 260 ff.

66. R. W. Apple Jr., "Bush's Peril: Shifting Sand and Fickle Opinion," *New York Times*, March 30, 2003, www.nytimes.com/2003/03/30/international/worldspecial/29CND-ASSE.html.

67. Loven, "Despite Pressures of WartimePresidency."

68. Ron Fournier, "Bush's Wartime Performance under Scrutiny," *Associated Press,* Cincinnati Enquirer/Post, March 28, 2003, customwire.ap.org/dynamic/stories/W/ WAR_BUSH_AS_COMMANDER?SITE=OHCIN&SECTION=HOME.

69. Terry Moran, "Bush No Micro-Manager," *ABC News,* March 26, 2003, abc-news.go.com/sections/wnt/Politics/Iraq_commanderinchief030326.html.

70. Bob Woodward, *Bush at War,* 176, 246.

71. Judy Keen and Lawrence McQuillan, "Bush Dives into Details of Iraq Conflict," *USA Today,* March 21, 2003, 6A.

72. Elisabeth Bumiller, "President Keeps the Battlefield Close at Hand."

73. Dick Polman, "Bush Spin Doctors Flip between Hands-On and Hands-Off Image," *Philadelphia Inquirer,* April 6, 2003, A11.

74. Eliot A. Cohen, *Supreme Command: Soldiers, Statesmen, and Leadership in Wartime* (New York: Free Press, 2002).

75. Lawrence D. Freedman, "Calling the Shots: Should Politicians or Generals Run Our Wars?" (review of *Supreme Command*), *Foreign Affairs* (September–October 2002), www.foreignaffairs.org/20020901fareviewessay9741/lawrence-d-freedman/calling-the-shots-should-politicians-or-generals-run-our-wars.html.

76. Eliot Cohen interview, conducted by Stephen Goode, "The Character of Wartime Statesmen," *Insight,* May 26, 2003, 42 ff.

77. Bob Woodward, *Bush at War,* 130–131, 144, 158. Bush committed some costly verbal gaffes at the outset—using the word "crusade" and targeting Osama Bin Laden "dead or alive" (94, 100–101). Comparable errors were scarce in the war on Iraq.

78. Paul Krugman, "Waggy Dog Stories," *New York Times,* May 30, 2003, www.nytimes.com/2003/05/30/opinion/30KRUG.html.

79. Michael Dobbs, "Halliburton's Deals Greater than Thought," *Washington Post,* August 28, 2003 A1.

80. Arnold, *Presidents Under Fire,* chap. 5.

81. Paul Krugman, "Standard Operating Procedure," *New York Times,* June 3, 2003, A31.

82. Quoted in Archibold, "Back in the Fray," A15.

83. Walter Pincus and Dana Priest, "Some Iraq Analysts Felt Pressure from Cheney Visits," *Washington Post,* June 5, 2003, A1.

84. Charles Lewis, "Even in Wartime, Stealth and Democracy Do Not Mix," *Center for Public Integrity,* February 12, 2003, www.public-i.org/dtaweb/report.asp?ReportID =506&L1=10&L2=10&L3=0&L4=0&L5=0.

85. Ibid.

86. Mike Allen, "Counsel to Assertive Presidency," *Washington Post,* May 19, 2003, A17.

87. Michael E. O'Hanlon, Susan E. Rice, and James B. Steinberg, "The New National Security Strategy and Preemption," Policy Brief #113-2003, www.brookings.org/comm/policybriefs/pb113.htm.

88. John Mintz, "Government's Hobbled Giant: Homeland Security Is Struggling," *Washington Post,* September 7, 2003, A1.

SUGGESTED READINGS

Campbell, Colin, and Bert A. Rockman, eds. *The George W. Bush Presidency: First Appraisals.* Chatham, N.J.: Chatham House, 2003.

Cohen, Eliot A. *Supreme Command: Soldiers, Statesmen, and Leadership in Wartime.* New York: Free Press, 2002.

Frum, David. *The Right Man: The Surprise Presidency of George W. Bush*. New York: Random House, 2003.

Greenstein, Fred I., ed. *The George W. Bush Presidency*. Baltimore: Johns Hopkins University Press, 2003.

Gregg, Gary L., II, and Mark J. Rozell, eds. *Considering the Bush Presidency*. New York: Oxford University Press, 2003.

Woodward, Bob. *Bush at War*. New York: Simon and Schuster, 2002.

RESULTS OF PRESIDENTIAL

CONTESTS, 1912–2000

Year	Republican nominee (in *italics*) and other major candidates	Democratic nominee (in *italics*) and other major candidates	Election winner	Division of popular vote[a] (percent)	Division of electoral vote[b]
1912	*William Howard Taft* (incumbent president)	*Woodrow Wilson* (governor of New Jersey)	Wilson (D)	42–23	435–8
	Theodore Roosevelt[c] (former president)	James Champ Clark (representative from Missouri and Speaker of the House)			
1916	*Charles Evans Hughes* (justice, U.S. Supreme Court)	*Woodrow Wilson* (incumbent president)	Wilson (D)	49–46	277–254
	Elihu Root (former secretary of state)	None			
1920	*Warren G. Harding* (senator from Ohio)	*James Cox* (governor of Ohio)	Harding (R)	60–34	404–127
	Leonard Wood (general)	William McAdoo (former secretary of the Treasury)			
	Frank Lowden (governor of Illinois)	A. Mitchell Palmer (attorney general)			
	Hiram Johnson (senator from California)				
1924	*Calvin Coolidge* (incumbent president)	*John W. Davis* (former solicitor general)	Coolidge (R)	54–29	382–136
	Hiram Johnson (senator from California)	Alfred Smith (governor of New York)			
		William McAdoo (former secretary of the Treasury)			
1928	*Herbert Hoover* (former secretary of commerce)	*Alfred Smith* (governor of New York)	Hoover (R)	58–41	444–87
	Frank Lowden (governor of Illinois)	James Reed (senator from Missouri)			
		Cordell Hull (representative from Tennessee)			
1932	*Herbert Hoover* (incumbent president)	*Franklin D. Roosevelt* (governor of New York)	Roosevelt (D)	57–40	472–59
	Joseph France (former senator from Maryland)	Alfred Smith (former governor of New York)			
		John Garner (representative from Texas and Speaker of the House)			

Results of Presidential Contests, 1912–2000 *(Continued)*

Year	Republican nominee (in *italics*) and other major candidates	Democratic nominee (in *italics*) and other major candidates	Election winner	Division of popular vote[a] (percent)	Division of electoral vote[b]
1936	*Alfred Landon* (governor of Kansas) William Borah (senator from Idaho)	*Franklin D. Roosevelt* (incumbent president) None	Roosevelt (D)	61–37	523–8
1940	*Wendell Willkie* (Indiana lawyer and public utility executive) Thomas E. Dewey (U.S. district attorney for New York) Robert Taft (senator from Ohio)	*Franklin D. Roosevelt* (incumbent president) None	Roosevelt (D)	55–45	449–82
1944	*Thomas E. Dewey* (governor of New York) Wendell Willkie (previous Republican presidential nominee)	*Franklin D. Roosevelt* (incumbent president) Harry Byrd (senator from Virginia)	Roosevelt (D)	53–46	432–99
1948	*Thomas E. Dewey* (governor of New York) Harold Stassen (former governor of Minnesota) Robert Taft (senator from Ohio)	*Harry S. Truman* (incumbent president) Richard Russell (senator from Georgia)	Truman (D)	50–45	303–189
1952	*Dwight D. Eisenhower* (general) Robert Taft (senator from Ohio)	*Adlai Stevenson* (governor of Illinois) Estes Kefauver (senator from Tennessee) Richard Russell (senator from Georgia)	Eisenhower (R)	55–44	442–89
1956	*Dwight D. Eisenhower* (incumbent president) None	*Adlai Stevenson* (previous Democratic presidential nominee) Averell Harriman (governor of New York)	Eisenhower (R)	57–42	457–73
1960	*Richard Nixon* (vice president) None	*John F. Kennedy* (senator from Massachusetts) Hubert Humphrey (senator from Minnesota) Lyndon B. Johnson (senator from Texas)	Kennedy (D)	49.7–49.5	303–219
1964	*Barry Goldwater* (senator from Arizona) Nelson Rockefeller (governor of New York)	*Lyndon B. Johnson* (incumbent president) None	Johnson (D)	61–39	586–52

Results of Presidential Contests, 1912–2000 (Continued)

Year	Republican nominee (in *italics*) and other major candidates	Democratic nominee (in *italics*) and other major candidates	Election winner	Division of popular vote[a] (percent)	Division of electoral vote[b]
1968	*Richard Nixon* (former Republican presidential nominee) Ronald Reagan (governor of California)	*Hubert Humphrey* (incumbent vice president) Robert F. Kennedy (senator from New York) Eugene McCarthy (senator from Minnesota)	Nixon (R)	43.4–42.7	301–191
1972	*Richard Nixon* (incumbent president) None	*George McGovern* (senator from South Dakota) Hubert Humphrey (senator from Minnesota) George Wallace (governor of Alabama)	Nixon (R)	61–38	520–17
1976	*Gerald R. Ford* (incumbent president) Ronald Reagan (former governor of California)	*Jimmy Carter* (former governor of Georgia) Edmund Brown, Jr. (governor of California) George Wallace (governor of Alabama)	Carter (D)	50–48	297–240
1980	*Ronald Reagan* (former governor of California) George Bush (former director of Central Intelligence Agency) John Anderson (representative from Illinois)	*Jimmy Carter* (incumbent president) Edward M. Kennedy (senator from Massachusetts)	Reagan (R)	51–41	489–49
1984	*Ronald Reagan* (incumbent president) None	*Walter F. Mondale* (former vice president) Gary Hart (senator from Colorado)	Reagan (R)	59–41	525–13
1988	*George Bush* (vice president) Robert Dole (senator from Kansas)	*Michael Dukakis* (governor of Massachusetts) Jesse Jackson (civil rights activist)	Bush (R)	53–46	426–111
1992	*George Bush* (incumbent president) Patrick Buchanan (journalist)	*William Clinton* (governor of Arkansas) Paul Tsongas (former senator)	Clinton (D)	43–37	357–168
1996	*Robert Dole* (senator from Kansas) Patrick Buchanan (journalist)	*William Clinton* (incumbent president) None	Clinton (D)	49–41	379–159
2000	*George W. Bush* (governor of Texas) John McCain (senator from Arizona)	*Al Gore* (incumbent vice president) Bill Bradley (former senator)	Bush (R)	47.9–48.4	271–267

Note: The table begins with the year 1912 because presidential primaries were first held that year.

[a] Division of popular vote is between the Republican and Democratic nominees.

[b] Division of electoral vote is between the Republican and Democratic nominees.

[c] When the Republican convention failed to choose him as its nominee (selecting instead the incumbent president, William Howard Taft), former president Theodore Roosevelt withdrew from the party and created the Progressive Party. As the Progressive Party nominee, Roosevelt received 27 percent of the popular vote and 88 electoral votes.

APPENDIX B

PERSONAL BACKGROUNDS OF U.S. PRESIDENTS

President	Age at first political office	First political office / Last political office[a]	Age at becoming president	State of residence[b]	Father s occupation	Higher education[c]	Occupation
1. Washington (1789—1797)	17	County surveyor / Commander in chief	57	Va.	Farmer	None	Farmer, surveyor
2. Adams, J. (1797—1801)	39	Surveyor of highways / Vice president	61	Mass.	Farmer	Harvard	Farmer, lawyer
3. Jefferson (1801—1809)	26	State legislator / Vice president	58	Va.	Farmer	William and Mary	Farmer, lawyer
4. Madison (1809—1817)	25	State legislator / Secretary of state	58	Va.	Farmer	Princeton	Farmer
5. Monroe (1817—1825)	24	State legislator / Secretary of state	59	Va.	Farmer	William and Mary	Lawyer, farmer
6. Adams, J. Q. (1825—1829)	27	Minister to Netherlands / Secretary of state	58	Mass.	Farmer, lawyer	Harvard	Lawyer
7. Jackson (1829—1837)	21	Prosecuting attorney / U.S. Senate	62	Tenn.	Farmer	None	Lawyer
8. Van Buren (1837—1841)	30	Surrogate of county / Vice president	55	N.Y.	Tavern keeper	None	Lawyer
9. Harrison, W. H. (1841)	26	Territorial delegate to Congress / Minister to Colombia	68	Ind.	Farmer	Hampden-Sydney	Military
10. Tyler (1841—1845)	21	State legislator / Vice president	51	Va.	Planter, lawyer	William and Mary	Lawyer
11. Polk (1845—1849)	28	State legislator / Governor	50	Tenn.	Surveyor	U. of North Carolina	Lawyer
12. Taylor (1849—1850)	None	None / a	65	Ky.	Collector of internal revenue	None	Military
13. Fillmore (1850—1853)	28	Stale legislator / Vice president	50	N.Y.	Farmer	None	Lawyer
14. Pierce (1853—1857)	25	State legislator / U.S. district attorney	48	N.H.	General	Bowdoin	Lawyer
15. Buchanan (1857—1861)	22	Assistant county prosecutor / Minister to Great Britain	65	Pa.	Farmer	Dickinson	Lawyer

Personal Backgrounds of U.S. Presidents *(Continued)*

President	Age at first political office	First political office / Last political office[a]	Age at becoming president	State of residence[b]	Father's occupation	Higher education[c]	Occupation
16. Lincoln (1861–1865)	25	State legislator / U.S. House of Representatives	52	Ill.	Farmer, carpenter	None	Lawyer
17. Johnson, A. (1865–1869)	20	City alderman / Vice president	57	Tenn.	Janitor-porter	None	Tailor
18. Grant (1869–1877)	None	None / a	47	Ohio	Tanner	West Point	Military
19. Hayes (1877–1881)	36	City solicitor / Governor	55	Ohio	Farmer	Kenyon	Lawyer
20. Garfield (1881)	28	State legislator / U.S. Senate	50	Ohio	Canal worker	Williams	Educator, lawyer
21. Arthur (1881–1885)	31	State engineer / Vice president	51	N.Y.	Minister	Union	Lawyer
22. Cleveland (1885–1889) 24. (1893–1897)	26	Assistant district attorney / Governor	48	N.Y.	Minister	None	Lawyer
23. Harrison, B. (1889–1893)	24	City attorney / U.S. Senate	56	Ind.	Military	Miami of Ohio	Lawyer
25. McKinley (1897–1901)	26	Prosecuting attorney / Governor	54	Ohio	Ironmonger	Allegheny	Lawyer
26. Roosevelt, T. (1901–1909)	24	State legislator / Vice president	43	N.Y.	Business-man	Harvard	Lawyer, author
27. Taft (1909–1913)	24	Assistant prosecuting attorney / Secretary of war	52	Ohio	Lawyer	Yale	Lawyer
28. Wilson (1913–1921)	54	Governor / Governor	56	N.J.	Minister	Princeton	Educator
29. Harding (1921–1923)	35	State legislator / U.S. Senate	56	Ohio	Physician, editor	Ohio Central	Newspaper editor
30. Coolidge (1923–1929)	26	City councilman / Vice president	51	Mass.	Storekeeper	Amherst	Lawyer
31. Hoover (1929–1933)	43	Relief and food administrator / Secretary of commerce	55	Calif.	Blacksmith	Stanford	Mining engineer
32. Roosevelt, F. (1933–1945)	28	State legislator / Governor	49	N.Y.	Business-man, landowner	Harvard	Lawyer
33. Truman (1945–1953)	38	County judge (commissioner) / Vice president	61	Mo.	Farmer, livestock	None	Clerk, store owner
34. Eisenhower (1953–1961)	—	None / a	63	Kan.	Mechanic	West Point	Military

431

President	Age at first political office	First political office / Last political office[a]	Age at becoming president	State of residence[b]	Father's occupation	Higher education[c]	Occupation
35. Kennedy (1961–1963)	29	U.S. House of Representatives / U.S. Senate	43	Mass.	Business-man	Harvard	Newspaper reporter
36. Johnson, L. (1963–1969)	28	U.S. House of Representatives / Vice president	55	Texas	Farmer, real estate	Southwest Texas State Teacher's College	Educator
37. Nixon (1969–1974)	34	U.S. House of Representatives / Vice president	56	Calif.	Streetcar conductor	Whittier	Lawyer
38. Ford (1974–1977)	36	U.S. House of Representatives / Vice president	61	Mich.	Business-man	U. of Michigan	Lawyer
39. Carter (1977–1981)	38	County Board of Education / Governor	52	Ga.	Farmer, business-man	U.S. Naval Academy	Farmer, business-man
40. Reagan (1981–1989)	55	Governor / Governor	69	Calif.	Shoe salesman	Eureka	Entertainer
41. Bush (1989–1993)	42	U.S. House of Representatives / Vice president	64	Texas	Business-man, U.S. senator	Yale	Business-man
42. Clinton (1993–2001)	30	State attorney general / Governor	46	Ark.	Car dealer	Georgetown	Lawyer
43. Bush, G. W. (2001–)	48	Governor / Governor	54	Texas	U.S. President	Yale	Business-man

[a] This category refers to the last civilian office held before the presidency. Taylor, Grant, and Eisenhower had served as generals before becoming president.
[b] The state is where the president spent his important adult years, not necessarily where he was born.
[c] Refers to undergraduate education.

APPENDIX C

THE CONSTITUTION
ON THE PRESIDENCY

ARTICLE I

Section 3. . . . The Vice President of the United States shall be President of the Senate, but shall have no Vote, unless they be equally divided.

The Senate shall chuse their other officers, and also a President pro tempore, in the Absence of the Vice President, or when he shall exercise the Office of President of the United States.

The Senate shall have the sole Power to try all Impeachments. When sitting for that Purpose, they shall be on Oath or Affirmation. When the President of the United States is tried the Chief Justice shall preside: And no Person shall be convicted without the Concurrence of two thirds of the Members present.

Judgment in Cases of Impeachment shall not extend further than to removal from Office, and disqualification to hold and enjoy any Office of honor, Trust or Profit under the United States: but the Party convicted shall nevertheless be liable and subject to Indictment, Trial, Judgment and Punishment, according to Law.

Section 7. . . . Every Bill which shall have passed the House of Representatives and the Senate, shall, before it become a Law, be presented to the President of the United States; If he approve he shall sign it, but if not he shall return it, with his Objections to that House in which it shall have originated, who shall enter the Objections at large on their Journal, and proceed to reconsider it. If after such Reconsideration two thirds of that House shall agree to pass the Bill, it shall be sent, together with the Objections, to the other House, by which it shall likewise be reconsidered, and if approved by two thirds of that House, it shall become a Law. But in all such Cases the Votes of both Houses shall be determined by yeas and Nays, and the Names of the Persons voting for and against the Bill shall be entered on the Journal of each House respectively. If any Bill shall not be returned by the President within ten Days (Sundays excepted) after it shall have been presented to him, the Same shall be a Law, in like Manner as if he had signed it, unless the Congress by their Adjournment prevent its Return, in which Case it shall not be a Law.

Every Order, Resolution, or Vote to which the Concurrence of the Senate and House of Representatives may be necessary (except on a question of Adjournment) shall be presented to the President of the United States; and before the Same shall take Effect, shall be approved by him, or being disapproved by him, shall be repassed by two thirds of the Senate and House of Representatives, according to the Rules and Limitations prescribed in the Case of a Bill.

ARTICLE II

Section 1. The executive Power shall be vested in a President of the United States of America. He shall hold his Office during the Term of four Years, and, together with the Vice President, chosen for the same Term, be elected, as follows. Each State shall appoint, in such Manner as the Legislature thereof may direct, a Number of Electors, equal to the whole Number of Senators and Representatives to which the State may be entitled in the Congress: but no Senator or Representative, or Person holding an Office of Trust or Profit under the United States, shall be appointed an Elector.

[The Electors shall meet in their respective States, and vote by Ballot for two Persons, of whom one at least shall not be an Inhabitant of the same State with themselves. And they shall make a List of all the Persons voted for, and of the Number of Votes for each; which List they shall sign and certify, and transmit sealed to the Seat of the Government of the United States, directed to the President of the Senate. The President of the Senate shall, in the Presence of the Senate and House of Representatives, open all the Certificates, and the Votes shall then be counted. The Person having the greatest Number of Votes shall be the President, if such Number be a Majority of the whole Number of Electors appointed; and if there be more than one who have such Majority, and have an equal Number of Votes, then the House of Representatives shall immediately chuse by Ballot one of them for President; and if no Person have a Majority, then from the five highest on the list the said House shall in like Manner chuse the President. But in chusing the President, the Votes shall be taken by States, the Representation from each State having one Vote; a quorum for this Purpose shall consist of a Member or Members from two thirds of the States, and a Majority of all the States shall be necessary to a Choice. In every Case, after the Choice of the President, the Person having the greatest Number of Votes of the Electors shall be the Vice President. But if there should remain two or more who have equal Votes, the Senate shall chuse from them by Ballot the Vice President.] [1]

The Congress may determine the Time of chusing the Electors, and the Day on which they shall give their Votes; which Day shall be the same throughout the United States.

No Person except a natural born Citizen, or a Citizen of the United States, at the time of the Adoption of this Constitution, shall be eligible to the Office of

President; neither shall any Person be eligible to that Office who shall not have attained to the Age of thirty five Years, and been fourteen Years a Resident within the United States.

In Case of the Removal of the President from office, or of his Death, Resignation, or Inability to discharge the Powers and Duties of the said Office,[2] the Same shall devolve on the Vice President, and the Congress may by Law provide for the Case of Removal, Death, Resignation or Inability, both of the President and Vice President, declaring what officer shall then act as President, and such Officer shall act accordingly, until the Disability be removed, or a President shall be elected.

The President shall, at stated Times, receive for his Services, a Compensation, which shall neither be increased nor diminished during the Period for which he shall have been elected, and he shall not receive within that Period any other Emolument from the United States, or any of them.

Before he enter on the Execution of his Office, he shall take the following Oath or Affirmation: — "I do solemnly swear (or affirm) that I will faithfully execute the Office of President of the United States, and will to the best of my Ability, preserve, protect and defend the Constitution of the United States."

Section 2. The President shall be Commander in Chief of the Army and Navy of the United States, and of the Militia of the several States, when called into the actual Service of the United States; he may require the Opinion, in writing, of the principal Officer in each of the executive Departments, upon any Subject relating to the Duties of their respective Offices, and he shall have Power to grant Reprieves and Pardons for Offenses against the United States, except in Cases of Impeachment.

He shall have Power, by and with the Advice and Consent of the Senate, to make Treaties, provided two thirds of the Senators present concur; and he shall nominate, and by and with the Advice and Consent of the Senate, shall appoint Ambassadors, other public Ministers and Consuls, Judges of the supreme Court, and all other officers of the United States, whose Appointments are not herein otherwise provided for, and which shall be established by Law: but the Congress may by Law vest the Appointment of such inferior Officers, as they think proper, in the President alone, in the Courts of Law, or in the Heads of Departments.

The President shall have Power to fill up all Vacancies that may happen during the Recess of the Senate, by granting Commissions which shall expire at the End of their next Session.

Section 3. He shall from time to time give to the Congress Information of the State of the Union, and recommend to their Consideration such Measures as he shall judge necessary and expedient; he may, on extraordinary Occasions, convene both Houses, or either of them, and in Case of Disagreement between them, with Respect to the Time of Adjournment, he may adjourn them to such Time as he shall think proper; he shall receive Ambassadors and other public

Ministers; he shall take Care that the Laws be faithfully executed, and shall Commission all the officers of the United States.

Section 4. The President, Vice President and all Civil Officers of the United States, shall be removed from office on Impeachment for, and Conviction of, Treason, Bribery, or other high Crimes and Misdemeanors.

ARTICLE VI

. . . This Constitution, and the Laws of the United States which shall be made in Pursuance thereof, and all Treaties made, or which shall be made, under the Authority of the United States, shall be the supreme Law of the Land; and the Judges in every State shall be bound thereby, any Thing in the Constitution or Laws of any State to the Contrary notwithstanding.

The Senators and Representatives before mentioned, and the Members of the several State Legislatures, and all executive and judicial Officers, both of the United States and of the several States, shall be bound by Oath or Affirmation, to support this Constitution; but no religious Test shall ever be required as a Qualification to any Office or public Trust under the United States.

AMENDMENT XII *(Ratified June 15, 1804)*

The Electors shall meet in their respective states and vote by ballot for President and Vice-President, one of whom, at least, shall not be an inhabitant of the same state with themselves; they shall name in their ballots the person voted for as President, and in distinct ballots the person voted for as Vice-President, and they shall make distinct lists of all persons voted for as President, and of all persons voted for as Vice-President, and of the number of votes for each, which lists they shall sign and certify, and transmit sealed to the seat of the government of the United States, directed to the President of the Senate; — The President of the Senate shall, in the presence of the Senate and House of Representatives, open all the certificates and the votes shall then be counted; — The person having the greatest number of votes for President, shall be the President, if such number be a majority of the whole number of Electors appointed; and if no person have such majority, then from the persons having the highest numbers not exceeding three on the list of those voted for as President, the House of Representatives shall choose immediately, by ballot, the President. But in choosing the President, the votes shall be taken by states, the representation from each state having one vote; a quorum for this purpose shall consist of a member or members from two-thirds of the states, and a majority of all the states shall be necessary to a choice. [And if the House of Representatives shall not choose a President whenever the right of choice shall devolve upon them, before the fourth day of March next following, then the Vice-President shall act as President, as in the case of the death or other constitutional disability of the President—][3] The person having the greatest number of votes as Vice-President, shall be the Vice-President, if such number be a majority of the whole number of Electors appointed, and if no person have a majority, then from the two highest numbers on the list, the Senate shall choose the Vice-President; a quorum for the purpose shall consist of two-thirds of the whole number of Senators, and a majority of the whole number shall be necessary to a choice. But no person constitutionally ineligible to the office of President shall be eligible to that of Vice-President of the United States.

AMENDMENT XX *(Ratified Jan. 23, 1933)*

Section 1. The terms of the President and Vice President shall end at noon on the 20th day of January, and the terms of Senators and Representatives at noon on the 3d day of January, of the years in which such terms would have ended if this article had not been ratified; and the terms of their successors shall then begin.

Section 2. The Congress shall assemble at least once in every year, and such meeting shall begin at noon on the 3d day of January, unless they shall by law appoint a different day.

Section 3.[4] If, at the time fixed for the beginning of the term of the President, the President elect shall have died, the Vice President elect shall become President. If a President shall not have been chosen before the time fixed for the beginning of his term, or if the President elect shall have failed to qualify, then the Vice President elect shall act as President until a President shall have qualified; and the Congress may by law provide for the case wherein neither a President elect nor a Vice President elect shall have qualified, declaring who shall then act as President, or the manner in which one who is to act shall be selected, and such person shall act accordingly until a President or Vice President shall have qualified.

Section 4. The Congress may by law provide for the case of the death of any of the persons from whom the House of Representatives may choose a President whenever the right of choice shall have devolved upon them, and for the case of the death of any of the persons from whom the Senate may choose a Vice President whenever the right of choice shall have devolved upon them.

Section 5. Sections 1 and 2 shall take effect on the 15th day of October following the ratification of this article.

Section 6. This article shall be inoperative unless it shall have been ratified as an amendment to the Constitution by the legislatures of three-fourths of the several States within seven years from the date of its submission.

AMENDMENT XXII *(Ratified Feb. 27, 1951)*

Section 1. No person shall be elected to the office of the President more than twice, and no person who has held the office of President, or acted as President, for more than two years of a term to which some other person was elected President shall be elected to the office of the President more than once. But this Article shall not apply to any person holding the office of President when this Article was proposed by the Congress, and shall not prevent any person who may be holding the office of President, or acting as President, during the term within which this Article become operative from holding the office of President or acting as President during the remainder of such term.

Section 2. This Article shall be inoperative unless it shall have been ratified as an amendment to the Constitution by the legislatures of three-fourths of the several States within seven years from the date of its submission to the States by the Congress.

AMENDMENT XXIII *(Ratified March 29, 1961)*

Section 1. The District constituting the seat of Government of the United States shall appoint in such manner as the Congress may direct:

A number of electors of President and Vice President equal to the whole number of Senators and Representatives in Congress to which the District would be entitled if it were a State, but in no event more than the least populous State; they shall be in addition to those appointed by the States, but they shall be considered, for the purposes of the election of President and Vice President, to be electors appointed by a State; and they shall meet in the District and perform such duties as provided by the twelfth article of amendment.

Section 2. The Congress shall have power to enforce this article by appropriate legislation.

AMENDMENT XXV *(Ratified Feb. 10, 1967)*

Section 1. In case of the removal of the President from office or of his death or resignation, the Vice President shall become President.

Section 2. Whenever there is a vacancy in the office of the Vice President, the President shall nominate a Vice President who shall take office upon confirmation by a majority vote of both Houses of Congress.

Section 3. Whenever the President transmits to the President pro tempore of the Senate and the Speaker of the House of Representatives his written declaration that he is unable to discharge the powers and duties of his office, and until he transmits to them a written declaration to the contrary, such powers and duties shall be discharged by the Vice President as Acting President.

Section 4. Whenever the Vice President and a majority of either the principal officers of the executive departments or of such other body as Congress may by law provide, transmit to the President pro tempore of the Senate and the Speaker of the House of Representatives their written declaration that the President is unable to discharge the powers and duties of his office, the Vice President shall immediately assume the powers and duties of the office as Acting President.

Thereafter, when the President transmits to the President pro tempore of the Senate and the Speaker of the House of Representatives his written declaration that no inability exists, he shall resume the powers and duties of his office unless the Vice President and a majority of either the principal officers of the executive department or of such other body as Congress may by law provide, transmit within four days to the President pro tempore of the Senate and the Speaker of the House of Representatives their written declaration that the President is unable to discharge the powers and duties of his office. Thereupon Congress shall decide the issue, assembling within forty-eight hours for that purpose if not in session. If the Congress, within twenty-one days after receipt of the latter written declaration, or, if Congress is not in session, within twenty-one days after Congress is required to assemble, determines by two-thirds vote of both houses that the President is unable to discharge the powers and duties of his office, the Vice President shall continue to discharge the same as Acting President; otherwise, the President shall resume the powers and duties of his office.

NOTES

1. The material in brackets has been superseded by the Twelfth Amendment.
2. This provision has been affected by the Twenty-fifth Amendment.
3. The part in brackets has been superseded by Section 3 of the Twentieth Amendment.
4. See the Twenty-fifth Amendment.

INDEX

441

CREDITS

12 Joseph E. Kallenbach, *The American Chief Executive: The Presidency and the Governorship* (New York: Harper and Row, 1966), chap. 2. **58** Data drawn from National Election Studies, Center for Political Studies at the University of Michigan's Institute for Social Research; Table 2a.1, http://www.umich.edu/~nes/nesguide/toptable/tab2a_1.htm. Responses to Question: "Generally speaking, do you usually think of yourself as a Republican, a Democrat, an Independent, or what?" **60** Excerpted from *Gallup Report*, November 1988, 6, 7; *The Gallup Poll Monthly*, November 1992, 9. Used by permission. 1996 data provided by Gallup Organization from poll conducted November 3 to November 4, 1996; 2000 data released Nov. 6, 2000, and posted on Web site, www. gallup.com. **90** Michael Nelson, ed., *The Guide to the Presidency*, 2d ed., pp. 1698–1703. © 1996 by CQ Press. Reprinted by permission of the publisher. January 1996 to present from Gallup Web site www.gallup.com. **95 and 96** Samuel Kernell and Gary C. Jacobson, *The Logic of American Politics*, pp. 241 and 243. © 2000 by CQ Press. Reprinted by permission of the publisher. **103** Harold W. Stanley and Richard G. Niemi, *Vital Statistics on American Politics, 2003–2004* © 2003 by CQ Press. Reprinted by permission of the publisher. **132** Reprinted by permission of Greenwood Publishing Group, Inc. Westport, Conn., from *The Leadership Question* by Bert A. Rockman. © 1984 by Praeger Publishers; Fred I. Greenstein, *Personality and Politics*, p. 27. ©1975 by W. W. Norton. Used by permission of the author. **133** Harold W. Stanley and Richard G. Niemi, *Vital Statistics on American Politics 1999–2000*, Table 6-2, 244–245. © 2000 by CQ Press. Reprinted by permission of the publisher. **136** Edward Pessen, *The Log Cabin Myth: The Social Backgrounds of the Presidents*, p. 68. © 1984 by Yale University Press, New Haven, Conn. Used by permission of the publisher. **145** James David Barber, *The Presidential Character: Predicting Performance in the White House*, 4th ed. (Englewood Cliffs, N.J.: Prentice Hall, 1992). **146** James David Barber, *The Presidential Character: Predicting Performance in the White House*, 4th ed. (Englewood Cliffs, N.J.: Prentice Hall, 1992). For Barber's views on Clinton, see the *News & Observer* (Raleigh, N.C.), January 17, 1993. **193** Adapted from Barbara Sinclair, "Hostile Partners: The President, Congress, and Lawmaking in the Partisan 1990s," in *Polarized Politics: Congress and the President in a Partisan Era*, Jon R. Bond and Richard Fleisher, eds. (Washington, D.C.: CQ Press, 2000), 145. **230** MaryAnne Borrelli, *The President's Cabinet: Gender, Power and Representation* (Boulder: Lynne Rienner Publishers, 2002), chap. 2. **270** Alliance for Justice, "Judicial Selection Project: Annual Report 2000," http://www.afj.org/jsp/report2000. **277** John Anthony Maltese, *The Selling of Supreme Court Nominees* (Baltimore: Johns Hopkins University Press, 1995), 3. Table 1. © 1995. Reprinted by permission of the Johns Hopkins University Press. **342, 344, and 346** John H. Kessel, *Presidents, the Presidency, and the Political Environment*, chap. 5. © 2001 by CQ Press. Reprinted by permission of the publisher. **367** Richard F. Grimmet, "War Powers Resolution: Presidential Compliance."*CRS*

PHOTOGRAPHS